21.00 cc
01

DISCARD

THE
MANIFESTO

BY JOHN DUNLAVY.

AMS PRESS
NEW YORK

INDIANA
UNIVERSITY
LIBRARY

NORTHWEST

THE
MANIFESTO,

OR A

DECLARATION OF THE DOCTRINES AND PRACTICE

OF THE

CHURCH OF CHRIST.

BY JOHN DUNLAVY.

Then shall ye return, and discern between the righteous and the wicked; between him that serveth God and him that serveth him not.
We are made as the filth of the world—the off-scouring of all things unto this day.

והיא כתובה פנים ואחור ונכתוב אליה קינים והגה והי: Ezek. 2. 10.

PLEASANT HILL, KY.
P. BERTRAND, PRINTER.
::::::::::::
1818.

Reprinted from the edition of 1818, Pleasant Hill
First AMS edition published in 1972
Manufactured in the United States of America

International Standard Book Number:0-404-08460-5

Library of Congress Catalog Card Number:74-134416

AMS PRESS INC.
NEW YORK, N.Y. 10003

PREFACE.

OF making many books there is no end, and much study is a weariness of the flesh. The writing of so many books on various religious subjects, may appear irksome to some and lead them to conclude that nothing will be gained by reading any more, for matters never come to such a concluding point as to remove uncertainty and promote union and common agreement among professors. And among the various sentiments industriously propagated how shall the inquirer know with whom to cast his lot? But admitting that little is yet effected to the satisfaction of the multitude, this is no reason that men should cease to search after the hid treasure; for every one who believes there is truth, must acknowledge that it is attainable. And what if considerable labor be expended in acquiring it?

The first chapter, containing a very concise essay on the Being of God, was not occasioned by the expectation that sentimental atheism is generally or extensively prevalent; although it is known to have its advocates in places, who are not backward in attempting to infuse the poison into others. It was therefore considered not improper to state a few particulars for the relief and strength of honest people, who might be beset with its corruptions. Unbelief of the holy scriptures, or infidelity towards an orderly revelation and the correctness of the christian faith, is more prevalent; yet neither was the second chapter, which relates to the truth of the scriptures, designed as an attempt to convince mankind by the dint of argument in the letter; but rather, together with the former, as a prelude to the following work, that it may give, at least, an honest exhibition, or rather declaration, of the basis on which the practical work of the gospel, to which it relates, is built; and in the mean time, that a few useful reflections might be presented to the thinking part of mankind.

The following sheets have been written in great plainness and familiarity; as usefulness and information have been more studied than elegance of style or even systematic order. I have made a free use of the original languages, particularly the Greek, frequently using an appeal to the learned for the correctness of the amendments of the common reading. Few, if any, amendments are offered to the translation from the Hebrew scriptures, without the support of Hebrew critics in one view or another: and I have built no doctrine on a criticism drawn from the original text, but used it only for elucidation. For it has not been my object to provoke to a contention of letters, but to minister truth to those who desire it. And when we have opened the faith of the gospel; and shown wherein we and others have been in error, it is not done for contention or to provoke others to resist. And should any be inclined to do so; they may consider; that we feel very little inclination to contend with dry systematics, but to inform those who seek salvation. If we should ever make a reply of any considerable labor or extent, we shall first look to see something of more weight and reason than those things which have been written heretofore; as the malicious slanders of James Smith; the puerile superficials of a John Baily; the chimerical reveries of a Christopher Clarke; the fabricated aspersions of a FALLEN LORENZO Dow; or even the disingenuous attracks of a B. W. Stone, who would likely never have been noticed in public, only for his peculiar standing.

By treating a variety of subjects nearly connected, and yet not closely enough to be discussed together, sundry repetitions occur, which have unavoidably swelled the volume to a greater size. But considering that many, not to say most readers, would feel the force of evidence better, by having it laid open freely on one subject at once, than by being referred from one to another, I have used freedom in that respect, the increased size of the book, and censure of speculating critics, notwithstanding. One subject is generally enough to digest at a time; and a man who buys a book, is no more obliged to read it through and digest it all at once, or on a sudden, than he who kills a beef, is obliged to eat it in a day.

To have found the everlasting gospel, the perfect work of God, is one thing, and to be perfected in the knowledge and experience of the same is another. Of the first we speak confidently, having no remaining doubt. But as to the second, our proficiency is only according to our time and travel. The everlasting gospel is only in its increase on the earth, as yet far short of its meridian; and my experience only in minority. If therefore a much clearer elucidation of many subjects in the following work, should hereafter appear, it will be no disgrace to the gospel, in the one faith, one cross, one self-denial, and one Christ. And my junior age and short experience in the gospel is a sufficient apology for the imperfection which in time may appear in the following work; or rather which appears already; for were the whole work to be reprinted immediately, I can see many places which could be stated in much greater perfection. And it is our privilege to grow in the knowledge of God. Or should any calculation of time which depends on the letter, and not clearly expresssed, hereafter be more correctly and satisfactorily opened as the light increases, it will not be inconsistent with our present faith. Had the work been inspected by those who are farthest traveled in the faith, it would no doubt have been much more perfect: but they were at too great a distance.

Some errors have escaped inspection until too late to be corrected in the press, mainly in orthography; but it is presumed there are none but such as the intelligent reader can easily discover.

INDEX.

	Page.
ON the Being of God,	1
Of the Truth of Revelation,	18
Of God, in a Compendious View of his Attributes,	26
Of the nature of God's Decrees; or what a Decree is,	33
Of man as the offspring of God, and of responsibility,	35
Of the gospel offers, and man's capability of complying; and whether God's decrees at all intercept its free operation,	46
Of justification by faith and obedience: and of imputation,	66
The subject continued, by inquiring into the nature and design of the death of Christ, and whether it is imputed to us for justification,	82
The subject continued; in relation to the legal sacrifices and other matters,	104
Objections against the foregoing doctrines, stated and obviated,	126
The Doctrine of Election, and the Foreknowledge of God,	168
The subject continued,	183
Of the Times and Seasons, or accepted time and day of salvation,	209
The appointed and correct Order of God for the Confession and Forgiveness of Sins,	217
The subject continued, as it respects the work of God in the Gospel,	229
Evidences relating to the Church of Christ, mainly Negative,	251
More Negatives. The absence of Christ. Christians do not commit Sin,	260
Some objections against the sinless life of a christian answered and the point confirmed,	270
Inimitable Love and Union obtain in the Church of Christ, and are manifested in a Joint Inheritance in things temporal as well as spiritual,	284
Without the cross of Christ no power over sin. The Abomination that maketh desolate, or Man of sin,	296
The order and works of the Generation do not appertain to Christ or his church,	303
Marriage a civil right and carnal relation of the world, therefore doth not belong to the Church of Christ,	317
Christ's people not of this world,	325
Of the Resurrection; more particularly as it relates to the person of Jesus Christ,	349
The subject continued; with some attention to prophetic scriptures,	358
The Resurrection, with more immediate relation to the Saints,	365

Of some scriptures incapable of a proper acceptation on the principle of their relating to the resurrection of the animal body, - - - - - - - - - 376

The resurrection the same as regeneration; and a progressive work, - - - - - - - - - 379

Of the last judgment; by way of Appendix to the foregoing chapters, - - - - - - - - - 401

A LETTER.

Of Freedom in religious conversation, - - - - 439

Free and friendly observations on the sentiments and practice of the Superscribed, and the subjects of the revival, - 448

The subject continued, with farther remarks on the writings of the Superscribed, - - - : - - - 475

Further observations and corrections; together with sundry matters pertaining to the revelation of Christ in his everlasting kingdom, - - - - - - - - 487

THE MANIFESTO,

OR

A DECLARATION

OF THE

DOCTRINES & PRACTICE

OF THE

CHURCH OF CHRIST.

PART I.
ON THE DECREES OF GOD.

CHAPTER I.
On the Being of God.

THE *belief* of the existence of God, of his character, and the relation which subsists between God and men, is the foundation and spring of all religion. The existence of God is proved in the first place, by the consent of all nations; and the argument is corroborated by that consent increasing and becoming more confirmed, as any people become more enlightened in general and consistent knowledge; so that it may be fairly concluded, that none, in any enlightened land, deny the Being of God from real belief; but that those who do, only use such denial as a pretext for giving latitude to their own desires, and not being subject to the will of God, whose nature and ways they do not love, being lovers of pleasure more than lovers of God.

But that the belief of the Being of God obtains among the nations of the earth, is an indisputed fact. Now this belief was either taught by nature or revelation, these being the only two methods of gaining such belief. If the first; that belief is either true, or nature is a false guide, and therefore no more to be trusted; accordingly the necessity of revelation becomes unavoidable, or man must be forever in uncertainty, and existing truth forever unknown, which is absurd. But if nature is true, teaching that God is, the point is proved, and nature is an helper to revelation. But if the belief of the Being of God be said to be through revelation from God, that saying acknowledges that God IS.

And that God doth exist, is farther proved by the existence of the things which are seen. For the existence of that which is seen and otherwise directly meets the senses, is not denied, being self-evident.

But that which really exists, is either a necessary existence or produced by another. For it cannot be both; because a created, or produced, necessary existence would be an absurdity, an impossibility; for a necessary existence includes the idea, or the attribute of independence, and therefore also of self-existence and self-government. But no material or visible being possesses these attributes. Again; a necessary existence is necessarily what it is, there being no previous or separate being, power or agency, to cause it to be this or that. It is therefore necessarily unchangeable. But no visible being possesses this attribute. A necessary existence is necessarily from everlasting and without any beginning, or initiation into existence; for, to suppose a time when there was no existence, is to deny existence altogether, contrary to self-evident and conscious fact; for no cause can produce an effect equal to itself, much less superior, and nonentity, or no cause, could never produce an effect to be the cause of all other things. A necessary being is necessarily perfect and infinite, there being no supposable objection to the necessary or self-existence of an infinitely perfect being which will not equally militate against all necessary existence of the most limited character or attributes; and there is no superior or previous power to set bounds to a primary and necessary existence. But existences are extant and evident to our senses, none of which, thus in the reach of our senses or subject to our immediate contemplation, exhibit or possess the attributes of a necessary self-existent being; they are therefore all dependent on God, a necessary, self-existent, infinitely perfect Being, whose wisdom, power and other attributes are displayed in his works of creation, providence and grace. On this principle the existence of God is clearly proved to a demonstration. But further:

What is here stated is not intended to contradict this truth, that revelation and the light of nature agree to support the belief of God's existence. For as the belief, or knowledge of God's existence, was received by man in his first creation, he has never been able, through all the windings of his disobedience, to erase the impression from his heart; however he may have corrupted or transformed it into vain notions; while in the mean time, the revelation of God has not been altogether wanting, which has still renewed the impression, and the light of nature and reason have borne witness to the fact, arguing from the works of God in his creation and providence. " Because " that which may be known of God, is manifest in them: for God " hath shewed it to them. For the invisible things of Him from the " creation of the world, are clearly seen, being understood [contem-" plated] by the things which are made, even his eternal power and " God-head, that is, Deity."

It is vanity to plead that the belief of God's existence may be the fruit or workings of the imagination. For the imagination is the imagery, or power of forming on the mind the imagery of things which do exist; and though this imagery may be transformed into a thousand corrupt and inconsistent shapes, it always proves the existence of the original, and the imagination can never extend so far as to a nonentity or annihilation, there being no prototype. And if the mind infers the existence of God from the contemplation of things which are seen to exist, that is a correct testimony of nature that God is. Thus false notions of God among mankind, though formed according to their corrupt inclinations, who have departed from the true God, prove the existence of the true God; and a false worship, or worship offered to idols, proves the propriety of worship offered to the true God according to his own appointment, which has been the original instigation of that impious worship of idols, through the subversion and ignorance of the human mind. Thus the Israelites, being taught of the true God to offer burnt offerings and sacrifices to him, and to praise him in the dance, as at the red sea, when they turned to their idol, offered the same worship. But this iniquitous conduct was so far from condemning sacrifices and dancing in the worship of God, that it really supported them both, and both alike.

In like manner, before the true Christ did actually appear, the imagination could receive no impression of his character and works, for the want of an original, although much had been said in prophetic language by that Spirit who knew him, which is all made plain enough in the event of its accomplishment, and stands as an abiding monument of the existence of that Spirit, whom we call God. But after Christ appeared there could be false christs in plenty; for the imagination had then found an original. Thus all the incoherent and contradictory, corrupt and insufficient schemes and professions of christianity, conclusively argue the propriety of christian worship and the truth of primitive christianity. And the outcry of many to find the true and perfect way, argues the propriety and originality of that faith which views christianity as the true and perfect way of God, saving the people who have it from all sin and criminal imperfection.

The common argument that nature produces all her works without the acknowledgment of any pre-existing cause or being besides, is very lame; too much so for any man who is compos mentis to depend on it, unless for the sake of warding off conviction and living after his own corrupt will. For in the first place, it lacks acknowledged data. There are no first principles to be stated which command the approbation of common sense. And without these no argument can be supported; for it is vanity to undertake to convince a man of sense, unless the argument be grounded on principles which he either acknowledges, or cannot deny without violating common sense and sacrificing his character as a reasonable man. But there are no such principles from which to argue that nature, abstractedly from God, produces all the beings and works which we see, and with which we are daily conversant. It remains to be proved that God doth not exist before the above argument can be valid.

On the contrary; it is abundantly evident that material nature can of herself produce nothing which has the appearance of actual operation or power. She is endued with a certain order of production, in each part, according to its own line or species; but turn her out of that particular line, and her operations become abortive, or ineffectual, which proves that all her operations proceed from a superior power. For there is no effect without a cause, the atheist himself being judge, and no effect can exceed the cause, or even equal it. All the works of nature therefore depend on a power superior to man, her pre-eminent boast for intelligence, wisdom and art. For no living child of nature, not even man in his utmost degree of wisdom, who by the acknowledgment of the atheist himself, possesses intelligence above all others, can, by his own contrivance, or wisdom, produce his own likeness, or even the smallest particle of animal life in the best formed matter: nature, therefore, independently of a superior cause, cannot create living beings. If men are capable of propagating their own species, this depends on a law which none of them have been able to develope, which proves that the capability is the product of superior power and wisdom. For, were this power within the compass of the wisdom of men, they could explain the principles to satisfaction; as well as the artist can those of a watch. But man in this law has no superiority over other animals, each after its kind being endued with a like capability. And were this law within the compass of man's wisdom, or intelligence, it would not account for his origin; for the cause is always prior to the effect: and so of all the other parts of creation. The argument is therefore good, that all the laws and operations of nature necessarily depend on another cause, which is prior to nature and also superior, even incomprehensible. For in strict propriety no effect can be produced, unless by a superior cause. To talk, therefore, of the absurdity of believing in an incomprehensible Being, called God, as the atheist disputes, only shews his own ignorance and impiety.

Doctor Benjamin Rush, after his labored and faithful *inquiry into the cause of animal life*, very pertinently proceeds: "Should it be "asked, what is that peculiar organization of matter, which enables "it to emit life, I answer, I do not know. It is true, the votaries of "chymistry have lately attempted to imitate it; but no arrangements "of matter by their hands have ever produced a single living fibre, "nor have any of their compounds produced a substance endowed "with the properties of dead animal matter. Lavoisser labored in "vain to produce that simple animal substance we call bile. That "the human body is composed of certain matters which belong to "the objects of chymistry, there can be no doubt; but their propor- "tions and manner of aggregation, are unknown to us."

"The great Creator has kindly established a witness of his un- "searchable wisdom in every part of his works, in order to prevent "our forgetting him, in the successful exercises of our reason."

That there are existences, some active and some inactive, is not to be denied: but these existences argue as much in favor of the existence of God as a pre-existing cause, as of nature producing her own works independently of him; not to say much more, when we look at the order and harmony which exist among the works of creation, adapting every part, as far as we are able to comprehend the whole.

to the end for which it is created: and christians can see and comprehend these subjects as truly and as perfectly as the sons of independent nature. Here are an order and harmony, the cause of which none of these sons of independent nature can describe, or even discriminately nominate, without having recourse, directly or indirectly, to that being whom we call God. Moreover, the undeniable facts of the fleeting state of all earthly existences, both animate and inanimate, and not only of the fleeting and transient state, but also their uncertainty and subjection to a thousand incidental causes of destruction, none of the animal part being able to retain their present state of existence according to their own choice, and none having in themselves the power of continuance independently of choice, render the notion of self-existence, or necessary existence, or independence in them, too absurd and preposterous to obtain a place among men. For a necessary, self-existent being, not perfectly master of self-government and self-preservation, is as great an absurdity as an intelligent being not conscious of his own existence. Neither is there any such being as is called nature independent of the creatures or productions, or seperate from them, to which these sons of nature can point, or show any traces, to prove its existence to men of reason. But their *adorable nature* is dependent for her existence on the fruit of her own womb; (if any such being be supposed;) which, therefore, must necessarily exist previously to her existence, and be the creators of their own creator.

Besides; those sons of nature can assign no approved or good reason for the existence of those transient beings, particularly of the rational part, whose mental powers indicate in their very constitutional existence, and earnestly reach after an endless duration; I say no good reason for their existence, seeing they have to resign it again in so short a period and be no more, which is the inevitable consequence of the notion of no God, and is also acknowledged by the atheist. *That nature* must be cruel indeed to her sons. But the belief of the being of God, and particularly as it embraces christianity, ministers full relief on that subject, by bringing life and immortality to light by the gospel.

The atheist scoffs at the argument drawn from the order and harmony which appear in creation, to prove that God is, and that he is intelligent, wise and good. But all his scoffing and misrepresentations will never take away from the eyes of thinking beholders, the visible effects of wisdom and goodness in the order and harmony which appear in creation, all parts being adapted to their proper purposes, not excluding the convenience and comfort of the inhabitants for the time being. Without extending our thoughts to the various parts of the planetary system, which receive the enlivening rays of the sun, placed in the midst of the whole, we may contemplate with ease the earth on which we live, which is in the view of our senses, and the subject of our daily experience, and there see every thing adapted to the support and comfort of animal life, from man the most intelligent, and therefore the most important, down to the meanest animal within our survey.

But the atheist obstinately insists on a principle not granted, not proved, not possible, that if God be immutably good, his creatures cannot suffer any thing evil, or at all disagreeable; hence he objects to the active employments in which men are necessarily engaged to procure their support. This principle supposes man incapable of transgression, which is neither granted, proved, nor possible, unless he could be equal to his Creator, which is impossible, because the effect can in no case equal the cause in actual production. This is true in nature, and on the principles of natural reason and experience; without troubling the atheist with revealed mysteries which he so much abhors: nature cannot produce an instance. It also supposes that no benefit can be obtained by a painful experience, which is equally false, as all people of sober reflection can witness.

The atheist also scoffs at the indication of endless existence constitutionally in man, as though the argument stood on this principle, that every man will obtain what he desires. But he changes the ground of argument; the inextinguishable indication of endless existence as really exists in the constitution of man as the desire of happiness, and no power can eradicate it, even in the imagination. It has been argued that this as properly proves the endless future existence of beasts as of men, for that they as really look for it and desire it. Truth is not to be rejected for any of its necessary consequences; if the endless future existence of the beasts be thus proved, let them have it; that will not prevent the endless life of men. But that there is any real prospect or contemplation of a future existence in that part of the creation called brutal, is not proved. They all appear to have a dread of present sufferings, and cautiously to avoid death; but that will not prove the prospect of futurity.

The atheist contests the being of God, and man's being his creature, because man was created subject to many miseries, or capable of becoming subject; making no account of an acknowledged and irresistible truth, that happiness is the more consummate, and that men appreciate it the better, when preceded by the contrary, or contrasted with misery. It is therefore in no wise inconsistent with infinite wisdom, power and goodness in God, that man was created capable of subjecting himself to miseries of his own procuring, that he may learn the better to appreciate his own happiness when he is delivered. And those distressing miseries which the atheist objects against the being of God, as Creator and Governor, to which man is subjected above other animals, only argue his greater worth and the greater degrees of enjoyment to which his constitution points in the event: for the capability of great sufferings indicates the capability of great happiness. And christians are witnesses for themselves, (and they are the best judges, having experienced both conditions,) and can show the fruits, which are sufficient evidence to reasonable men, that they have more real happiness, in the present tense, than those who reject the faith of Christ. In vain does the atheist object that the greater part of men are appointed to irrecoverable and endlesss misery. Christianity doth not teach so; but on the contrary, that none will fail of final and eternal happiness who do not lose it by their own voluntary choice, while it is yet in their reach and they know the way.

The atheist ungenerously ranks all religions on one scale; not considering like a man of reason, as he professes to be, *exclusively forsooth*, that all false religions, (all which contrast with the christian,) argue in confirmation of the true; not only because false religions, or counterfeits, are an evidence of the existence and truth of the genuine, but also because christianity hath long since prophesied that such would be. But no religion will stand but that which comports with sound reason.

But after all the objections of the atheist against the being of God as man's Creator and Governor, they are easily retorted on himself; for these visible evils, of which he complains, obtain in the world, and the proof cannot be destroyed. " *The world*," says he, " *is a necessary agent.*" If so, it is either intellectual and provident, or it is not; if not, and it is the cause of all things, (according to his doctrine,) it has communicated to man, and in some sort to other animals, that which it doth not itself possess, neither any thing equivalent: which is impossible; for the effect is always inferior to the cause. But if the material world be intelligent, or nature, or the universe, whichever is the necessary agent and cause of all things, the producer of man, it must be cruel indeed to have brought man into being to be perplexed and tormented as he is, during his existence, without the least prospect or intimation of a reparation in a better state; but though, as the atheist says, *the worst of men are commonly the arbiters of the world, and those whom fortune loads with her favors*, and consequently the best of men the most exposed to common evils, yet there is no hope of having matters adjusted in another life. This is inexpressibly more unreasonable, cruel and unrighteous, than the belief of God and his works, who will bring all things to order, and give the upright man a life of endless felicity. In vain therefore may the atheist cavil against the sufferings of Jesus Christ, whom God gave to be a leader and a guide to his people, (I do not say suffering to appease an angry God or satisfy offended justice; this doctrine doth not belong to the gospel,) or of the sufferings of his apostles and other ministers, who were leaders of those whose sufferings are to eventuate in a greater good and better appreciated. If God suffers these things to be, they are not in vain. *They work for us a far more exceeding and eternal weight of glory.* Christianity therefore is the most consistent and righteous, and atheism the most unreasonable and unjust.

" *The world*," says the atheist, " *is a necessary agent.*" And again: " *The universe is a cause, it is not an effect;—The world has always been; its existence is necessary; it is its own cause.*" The necessary existence of a first cause is unavoidably acknowledged by all; for, to suppose the first cause to be created or produced, would be to place a cause prior to the first, which is absurd. The necessary existence of any first cause or agent, being admitted, includes, with the same facility of mind and reason, the existence of infinite power, wisdom, and every other perfection. For no reason can be given why a Being of infinite power, wisdom and every other perfection, should not necessarily exist, which would not equally, (not to say more so,) militate against the necessary existence of a being imperfect. The necessary existence therefore of God, infinitely perfect, is admitted with as much facility and simple reason as the necessary existence of the universe supposing it to be a self-existing agent. There is nothing therefore unreasonable in the belief *that God is, and that he is the rewarder of them that diligently seek him.* But there is something very unreasonable in atheism, that nature, (for nature, the world, the universe and matter are all confounded and considered as one by the atheist;) I say, that nature should be the necessarily existent parent of men, independent and self-existent; and should introduce them into existence in the midst of unavoidable sufferings in body and mind, (for men have intelligent, provident and reflecting minds, and we are obliged to believe it, although we can neither see nor comprehend them,) and cannot supply them with a portion to make them comfortable, either in this life or the life to come—For they desire, they intensely reach after an endless life, and no reasoning can prevent them : it is incorporated with their existence. Whence these dreadful and shocking disappointments and miseries to the human race ? Doth intelligent and just nature (and nature must be intelligent, or not the parent of intelligent man,) bring men into existence to suffer all these things for nought, and then cease to be forever ? For, according to atheism, there can be no sin, no transgression in man—he necessarily doeth whatever he doeth—he hath no choice in his conduct. A reasonable man need not be told that atheism is unreasonable—is unjust. So false is the futile and ungenerous cavil of the atheist, that religion excludes and rejects reason, and *that faith*, in religion, *is consent without evidence.*

But it is proved that, according to reason, a necessary agent is necessarily perfect; but nature is imperfect in all her works, and unable to make out the road to perfection, even to make her children perfect according to their kind, but man, the noblest part of her productions, must be left more exquisitely wretched than all the rest; ever in pursuit of something permanently to fill his mind and can never find it, and she can point out no practicable method to cure him. We are therefore compelled by reason to admit of the Being of God, *and our faith is not consent without evidence.* I will not deny that God and his works are greatly illustrated by revelation from that God who is superior to all our reason, and from whom ours is only an emanation of his own; but revelation is so congenial with reason in man, that the honest are readily gained to the faith, where revelation is fairly and justly exhibited to view in those who have it.

The atheist objects to the Being of God because he is said to punish a rebellious people or nation. But do not the most kind and affectionate parents punish refractory children by way of chastisement? And is it not acknowledged, by the atheist himself, that the best of governments punish rebellious subjects, even to cutting them off, for the good of the community, when they become such a nuisance as to require such severity? Yea, he says they do it of necessity. If therefore it be related of God, that he hath cut off some, or even many, for the good of the whole, it argues nothing against his existence or his goodness, for it is all done for the procuring and securing of a greater benefit. And even those who have been cut off, or afflicted with the greatest punishments known by man, if they have not made a full and final rejection of the everlasting gospel, are not out of the reach of eternal life and peace. I know this is not acknowledged by those who confine the work of God in the gospel, to the narrow limits of this life; but it accords with the gospel of Christ, as shown in its place.

As for the monstrous affair relating to the sin of David, king of Israel, and the seventy thousand slain by the pestilence, the objector hath surely never impartially considered the subject in its connection. David sinned indeed; and was chastised by the destruction of the people, his subjects; but they had sinned also as a people; for the anger of the Lord was kindled against Israel before David numbered the people, not by caprice, as the atheist speaks, but on account of their iniquities, against which his displeasure is as necessary as his existence.

I know the atheist objects that it is incompatible with the existence of God, possessing the perfections which are attributed to him, that man should be capable of transgression at all, and accordingly he ascribes every evil, or improper action in man, to the immediate agency of God, who necessarily imposes it on every man to do this and that: (for he denies the possibility of a choice, or freedom, in God or in man, whether man be the son of God or of nature.) But such arguing is weak in the man who is *exclusively* a reasoner; for that man does transgress and is liable to go astray, and therefore needs restraint, is a fact undeniable, and acknowledged by the atheist himself. And this stubborn fact is utterly inconsistent with his doctrine of man, who, according to him, is moved in a certain line of conduct without any choice, and acts by imperious necessity, whether he be the son of nature or of God. Besides; as before stated, it is impossible that man should be equal to his Maker; for a created uncreated being is impossible, contradictory and absurd; and no effect can equal the cause; it is therefore impossible that men should possess the perfection of Deity. Consequently it is impossible that man, who is a rational being, should not be subject to trial, whether he would obey his superior or not. And where there is no possibility of falling, or of transgressing, there can be no trial; it was therefore impossible that man could have been created impeccable, or out of the reach of transgression.

Why then, says the atheist, did God create man? For his own good pleasure in the display of his own glory and perfections, and for the good pleasure, that is, the happiness of man. God being infinitely good, it is reasonable that he should exercise infinite delight in the works of his power, and in communicating happiness to his creatures as they become fit to receive and use it. God's wisdom is much more displayed by creating man a reasonable and responsible being, than it could have been by creating him in an unavoidable line of conduct: a machine can make no active offering of praise to its former. And much greater foundation is laid for the glory, honor, immortality and eternal life of man, by his being made capable of choosing good or evil, and putting him in a situation to bring him to the trial, than could have been by a contrary procedure.

Man was not required to transgress, by any imperious or insurmountable necessity, he was only required by the temptation, and he yielded to his disgrace. Had he remained stedfast in his obedience with integrity, it had been much more to his honor, than to have been prevented from falling by irresistible power or necessity. And God's foreknowing that he would fall, is no good reason why he should not be put to the trial, seeing that man in the nature of things, as shown above, could never arrive to the summit of that happiness of which he is capable, without such trial. Neither is God's foreknowledge of the event of man's trial any evidence against the most consummate goodness in God, or his good will to his creatures, especially considering that he stood ready, at the time appointed, or when it would be the most expedient, all things considered, to introduce Christ the Redeemer, and by him to reinstate man into a superior state of happiness, better confirmed and better appreciated, after experiencing the contrary. All these things are included in christianity.

This view of the subject shows the unreasonableness of the man of boasted reason, who objects, *If God could not make man impeccable, why did he make him at all? and then punish him for not being impeccable?* It is not so; man is not punished for not being impeccable; but for unnecessary transgression. And he is subject to chastisement to bring him to a sense of his duty, and to punishment for transgressions committed against better information, according to their nature and the degree of unrighteousness.

But the atheist, impatient of restraint, or the least subjection to God, insists that God, if he exists at all, is required to clear the way for man to be happy at once, and to prevent by absolute power every degree of pain or distress; thus implicitly, not to say explicitly, demanding that God ought to be subject to the will of his creatures in every punctilio; as if that would be *reasonable ;* or as if parents ought to be subject to the desires of children or minors, and use no more chastisement than the minors would love. Would they ever know the benefits of dutiful obedience? But men will all learn in the event, that God is more wise, as well as more patient than they.

But let the atheist tell, why his *good, necessary* and *self-existing nature, the parent of men,* hath produced men, and still propagates them, exposed to such miseries, when she has no power nor wisdom to consummate their happiness. For if he insist that light will sometime break in on the people; her cruelty is inexcusable towards those who have heretofore perished out of existence without any fault in them, and those who now exist in the same condition: and for all these there is no hope. For it is poor consolation for my distress that sometime, perhaps a thousand or two years hence, some people will see better times, for a few days, and then sink into an unconscious chaos with all the rest. But the only possible apology for this conduct of the all-producing nature is, that she is absolutely incapable of the sensation of good or evil, happiness or misery, being unconscious, unintelligent and improvident; she is therefore not the parent, or producer, of man, who is intelligent, conscious and provident, having the sensation of good and evil, happiness and misery, both in himself and others, and therefore far superior to his boasted cause, *nature*. Thus the necessary existence of *nature*, as excluding the Being called God, is reasoned out of existence.

The atheist combats the notion of the existence of God, because he is called a Spirit, insisting that the existence of a Spirit, or any being distinct from matter, is impossible. " The idea of *spirituality*," says he, " is an idea without model." Without material form no doubt he means. But whence comes this idea? All ideas are either real or imaginary; and the imagination cannot form an idea of any thing which has no existence, or strictly no model; for it is only the imagery of realities, though often variously formed and mingled together. And as no known assemblage, modification, organization or combination of material existences can produce a result which is spiritual, it follows of course, that spirit does exist, and is made known to our senses by sufficient evidence, else the imagination had never formed the idea. " *But wherein*," says the atheist, " *is modern theology superior to that of the savages? The savages acknowledge a great spirit for the master of the world*" And why do they acknowledge such a master? First; very rationally; Because they see that done which no material being can be descried or discovered to do. And secondly; Because all nations have acknowledged the existence of God from time immemorial, before men had time to contrive or the imagination to paint, *without a model*, such an idea. It is therefore, commensurate with man's existence, and was communicated to him in his creation. But as men, through ignorance and other causes, differ in opinion on various subjects, while the existence of the things is indisputable so in relation to God and his worship, there are various opinions and practices, all which argue the existence of the original facts, as counterfeits argue the existence and utility of the genuine, without which there could be no motive for the counterfeit.

The similitude by which the atheist attempts to redicule and confront the existence of God is not only imperfect but contemptible. " *The savages, like all ignorant people, attribute to spirits all the effects, of which their inexperience cannot discover the true cause. Ask a savage what moves your watch. He will tell you*, it is a spirit. *Ask your divines what moves the universe. They answer* it is a spirit." But the artist can point out, even to the savage the spring of motion in the watch, and its author; yet the greatest artist, the master of reason, even the atheist, *exclusively eminent*, cannot point out to the most enlightened nation or man, the spring of motion in the universe, much less the author of it, one side of that necessary existence called God. As to the superiority of modern theology, (that is christianity; for nothing in contrast with that is of sufficient utility;) above that of the savages, it will appear in its consistency, reasonableness and other superior and appropriate fruits. By christianity I do not mean every thing called by that name. Nothing is worthy of that name, except that which is consistent in its principles, reasonable in its requisitions, intelligible to the human mind, peaceable in its measures, and happifying to its subjects, imposing no arbitrary measures on its friends or enemies.

But the atheist combats the existence of God from the consideration that he is said to be incomprehensible. " *We are told,*" says he, " *that divine qualities are not of a nature to be comprehended by* " *finite minds. The natural consequence must be,* that divine quali- " ties are not made to occupy *finite minds.*" If God be not a proper subject of contemplation for man, to occupy his mind, because he is incomprehensible, it follows as a natural consequence, that man is not made to occupy the mind of man, for man is incomprehensible to man. The life of man is an inexplicable mystery to man; and his intellectual part, which we call by the name of spirit, and whose existence is undeniable, according to the irresistible evidence of sense, and according to whose volitions the material system is moved to different actions, is utterly inexplicable to man in his present state of existence, not to say, ever will be : its mode of existence and method of operation are unknown, whether it be accounted for by the creating power of God or by the assemblage of material essences. But its existence is irresistibly confirmed.

Let us instance a case by which it will appear evident that the spirit is an agent entirely distinct from the material body or any of its properties. It is known in ten thousand instances, to men of sober reflection, that fleshly propensities, or passions, invite to the enjoyment of certain objects, which by a co-operation with the bodily organs create more or less pleasure, when the intellectual power informs the man that such an object is improper and attended with so much evil, as to overbalance the pleasure, and in many cases, even convert it into pain. In other instances, when the object is justifiable and properly adapted to the regular appetites of the body in due subordination, the delight also which it gives, innocent, the intellect approves the invitation. Now what are these passions, but sensations arising from the intimate connection of the affections with the material body, in the constitution of animal life ? And what is the intellectual power, but the more noble and superior faculty, which in its proper order soars above those inferior objects ? If it be said that the intellect and the affections are only different faculties of the same being, and if the latter be only a property of the body so is the former. The answer is, that neither the one nor the other is of the

BEING OF GOD.

body but of the spirit; which is proved by the resistance which is offered to the inclinations of the body and the subjection required; for no active principle can resist itself. These passions run precipitately, being excited by bodily sensation; but the intellect, as though more distantly connected with the body than the affections, or by some cause less exposed to its influence, is able to govern the whole, in direct opposition to these passions. And though in the first introduction of the most important truths, we get access to men only by the senses and then to the affections, the intellect is calculated in its proper office, to govern the whole into such regulation, that these fleshly passions have nothing to do in the case; and will always do so in important matters, substantiated by proper evidence, where it is not violently wrested from its seat. This agency of the spirit shows that it is distinct from the body, and not of it, by any assemblage or organization whatever, and that it is capable of an existence and agency when disengaged from it. And though it is unknown to us how that can be, its present order of existence and agency shows that it is capable of both, by the power of the same agent that created it. Yet its mode of existence and method of operation are beyond the science of man in his present stage of action. And it is not a necessary, or self-existing agent, else it would understand and comprehend itself—its mode of existence and manner of operation—man could comprehend himself and analyze his own existence. But all nature cannot do this; nature therefore, or matter, cannot be man's author; for every correct author, or artist, can analyze his own work. The existence therefore of this intellectual faculty, or spirit, irresistibly proves, by the evidence of sense, the existence of a necessary, self-existent agent, superior to all nature; that agent is called God.

Again, the atheist argues; "*If God be an infinite being, there cannot be, either in the present or future world, any relative proportion, between man and his God. The idea of God can never enter the human mind.*" And again; "*Thus in saying God is infinite, you annihilate religion for man, who is a finite being.*" These are all self-evidently false positions. The mind of man unfailingly discovers a relative proportion between two existences although the one be infinitely superior to the other: this needs no proof. And the idea of God, both as to his existence and character, although he is infinite and incomprehensible, hath entered the human mind, and it retains it, and all the reasoning of unbelievers can never get it away. It is easily understood, that the idea and proof of the existence of any being, and correct (as far as it goes) knowledge of its character, are very different matters from a perfect comprehension.

The atheist aims to demolish, as at one stroke, the evidence of miracles in favor of the existence of God and the truth of religion, thus. "*Is a miracle capable of annihilating the evidence of a demonstrated truth? Although a man should have the secret of healing all the sick, of making all the lame to walk, of raising all the dead of a city, of ascending into the air, of stopping the course of the sun*

" and moon, can he thereby convince me, that two and two do not
" make four, that one makes three and that three make only one?"
Query; Why could not *this shrewd reasoner* have informed himself
that christianity calls for no miracles to prove such contradictions;
but, when they are used at all, to confirm those things which are according to men's reason, though often out of the reach of it to discover until taught by superior wisdom? But he continues to ask if these
miracles can convince him, " That a *God*, whose immensity fills the
universe, could be contained in the body of a Jew; that the *Eternal*
could die like a man?" Let these wise men once more be taught
that christianity teaches no such doctrines. The *Eternal* cannot die,
but a man could die. Christianity saith not that the God of immensity was contained in the body of a Jew, or of any man. *Heaven,
and the heaven of heavens cannot contain him.* The body of that
worthy Jew, to whom the atheist alludes, could not contain his appropriate rational spirit which was in connection with it, which was occupied in contemplations and engagements far superior.

But this is not to contradict, that the fulness of Deity dwelt in that
man—that of all the character and perfections of Deity he was a partaker, having the proper benefit and aid of the power, wisdom and
other perfections of that God with whom he stood in union. But why
could not God dwell in that man, and by him be revealed to the
world? God is love. Is there any reason why love could not be in
that man, and be shown out in his life and actions? and so of the rest.

But he continues to inquire if the above miracles can convince
him, " *That a God, who is said to be immutable, provident and sen-*
" *sible, could have changed his mind upon his religion and reformed*
" *his own work by a new revelation?*" If these be the reasonings
of the sole proprietor of reason, (for he saith that, *every man who
reasons soon becomes an unbeliever*) it is time to displace reason
from the precedency. Doth not every man of reason know that even
short sighted men, (those of the most provident cast,) might see far
enough forward to know, that in many cases, temporary laws might
be advantageously enacted, which it would be proper by and by to rescind and supersede by a more effectual and permanent code? Did
it indicate an improvident and mutable being to find him continually
intimating that a great change would come at an after period, and to
find it such when it came, as to show that it was signified by all that
went before? These are the works of a permanently provident and
immutable God.

Such palpably erroneous and distorted statements as those in the
above paragraphs, show the disingeneous man and the weakness of
his cause.

But as I have no intention to pursue the atheist throughout his
haunt, it begins to be time to leave him for the present, lest I should
incur the censure of wasting time by making serious replies to unworthy cavilings. For some, not to say many, of his assertions are
too preposterous not to make his intelligent abettors blush. I shall
however take notice of one or two particulars more.

BEING OF GOD.

He asserts that "*The idea of infinity is to us an idea without mo-*
"*del, without archetype, without object.*" How so? Because created beings are not infinite? But if the idea of infinity be without model, archetype or object, whence comes the idea? For people have the impression that the thing is, and all our ideas are by sensation and reflection on the things which the senses perceive. But the idea of infinity is as constitutional and congenial to man as his thoughts. Did any man of mature reflection ever extend his thoughts so far as not to conceive that he left an infinity beyond? Not one. And with relation to God, or any first cause, the thought of a necessary, self-existing agent, not infinite, not perfectly acquainted with himself and all his works, or not possessed of every perfection, is as absurd as to deny existence altogether. But this is not nature, according to the atheist himself, who acknowledges that the world is evidently not governed by an intelligent being—and yet this unintelligent being is, according to him, the parent of intelligent man: an effect superior to the cause, which is absurd. Whence then is man? He is the offspring of God as christianity saith. Why then can he not comprehend his Maker? Because it is contrary to the reason and nature of things for the inferior to comprehend the superior, as well as for the effect to equal the cause. A superior power, or degree of wisdom or skill, may accommodate itself to the making of an inferior work, but an inferior cannot produce a superior. Man therefore is not the offspring of nature, or matter, who evidently possesses more intelligence than all animate or inanimate matter besides.

Again; If man be the offspring of nature, and possess no other medium of information; and if nature cannot be in disorder, from what source is the notion of the infinite, wise and powerful God? Is it the orderly work of nature to teach falsehoods? Is ignorance in man so powerful a contriver that all wisdom cannot contradict its productions? Or are there extant certain invisible, inimical agents, unconnected with nature, that infuse corruption into the human mind? Whether is it most rational to believe in the necessary existence of such demons, or to acknowledge in full faith the existence of a powerful, wise and perfect God, who after men have, in his wisdom, been suffered to try their utmost according to nature, without effecting happiness, will lead them in a way which by their own wisdom they knew not, to level their pride and display his own wisdom and forbearance, love and goodness, in their more consummate and confirmed happiness, according to the christian faith?

But the atheist objects to christianity as being unreasonable, because contrary to nature, and confronts the idea of God's confounding the wisdom of men, thus; "You tell us, theologians, that *what*
"*is folly in the eyes of men is wisdom before God, who delights to*
"*confound the wisdom of the wise.* But do you not say that human
"wisdom is a gift of heaven?—Is it not strange that one can be the
"friend of your God, only by declaring himself the enemy of reason
"and good sense?" Thus he always misrepresents the christian religion, which hath shown what kind of wisdom God sees fit to con-

found—the wisdom of those who are wise to do evil, wise in corruption—that wisdom which is *earthly, sensual, develish*—not reason and good sense. But let the atheist object as he may, it is an undeniable fact that the ways of mankind are corrupt, and that their wisdom needs an overturning; they need a work to counteract their natures. Such a work as nature with all her laws and wisdom independently of God, can never accomplish. For this corrupt nature, or the corruption and depravity of man, the atheist can assign no consistent reason; for according to him there is no God, men therefore could not have become wicked by departing from his laws; neither could they have been corrupted by deviating from the laws of nature, for her laws are irresistible, and men are inevitably obedient to them. Christianity alone can solve the mysteries of human depravity, and reveal man to himself.

It is not intended to object to the propriety of speaking of the laws or works of nature. But these laws and works can be interrupted and subverted; which conclusively bespeaks their dependence on another cause and their subjection to another power, and that these laws are nothing more than certain qualities and capacities with which the whole creation hath been endued, every part in its own order, adapting each to its proper intention, by the power and wisdom of the Creator. For the confusion, jaring principles and contrary operations, which are found among the different parts of creation, are so far from weakening the evidence of a creating and governing power, that they rather confirm it, because without such a power the whole would be reduced to a perfect chaos.

The greatest pitch of power, wisdom, intelligence and the like, to which atheists can point, is in men, the most noble of nature's sons; neither can they show an evidence or a trace of her existence, power, wisdom, or any thing of the kind, beyond men; she has given them no communicable or ostensible laws or rules, by which to regulate their conduct, or to indicate her being possessed of such power and wisdom as they ascribe to her. And it is inconsistent with reason, to suppose any one can communicate to others that which he or she doth not possess. One may in some cases communicate through another as a medium, that which he who is the medium doth not originally possess; but the communicator must be equal to the thing communicated by actual possession, as it is granted that no effect can exceed the cause, neither can it equal it.

How preposterous therefore to suppose that nature without life, can communicate life to her children, even as far as to a toad or a fly! Or that without mental powers, she can communicate wisdom and intelligence to men! Or that without forethought or plan, she could create men or other beings capable of wisely laying out their pursuits, being provident of futurity! Or that without eyes or sight or any equivalent power, she could minister to men and other animals, that organ of the most delicate and exquisite structure, and of incontrovertable and definite discernment! In these few examples we may see the absurdity of such notions; as well as in ten thousand more of the minute and exquisitely wise and useful operations in the formation of man.

Once more. It is much more consistent with reason and common sense to believe in God, a Being, independent, necessarily existing, as he is, and therefore unchangeable, self-existent, and possessing power and wisdom adequate to the works of creation and providence, and to a happy result in the end, and who hath also made known his will to this intent, as the great first cause on whom all are dependent, than to believe in the necessary existence, or independence of nature and all creation, or its dependence on its own laws which cannot be pointed out by itself or its children, which is also dependent on its own productions for its existence. But a pre-existing cause is necessary to every effect, and the faith of it irresistible. And these advocates for nature cannot point out any such independent, all-sufficient Being, distinct from that God whom christians worship.

As for the all-sufficient laws of nature of which they talk, it is easily proved on the principles already stated, that no such laws can possibly exist; because no laws can exist without a legislator, or an agent capable of containing them; or in other words, no principle of agency can exist without a subject capable of containing those principles and putting them into operation. But the existence of the laws of nature to which are attributed all effects and operations, depends on the pre-existence of nature's works, (for nature's laws exist only in her works, or are the gift of another, even God,) which places the effect before the cause, or the product prior to the principle, which is absurd.

This part of the subject is to meet the reasonings, or reveries of those who contemplate the existence of nature some how abstractedly from material existences. That matter cannot be the pre-existing, independent, cause, is proved before. He therefore, who denies the existence of God, to be consistent, must deny all existence, all agency, all language and even all thought, for it will not be denied that he who is capable of thought must also have an existence, and that existence, not being necessary, or self-sufficient, must have a previous cause, which is none but God, the only self-sufficient Being, as already proved.

These things are written, not because there is any deficiency of evidence in the revelation of God, relative to his existence, character and works in the gospel, but to show the unbeliever a few of his weaknesses, and some of his dishonesty, on his own ground. For notwithstanding that many professed christians, kings, princes and priests, with their followers, have been, and still are, extravagantly wicked, (but these have neither part nor lot in christianity,) and have truly given much occasion to unbelievers, the latter have been very superficial and uncandid in their investigations of the subject of christianity.

CHAPTER II.

Of the Truth of Revelation.

AFTER the Being of God, it seems necessary to the existence of true religion, in the spirit of unity, without which there can be no perfect human happiness, to believe in revelation, or to believe that God hath made known his mind and will to men; by such infallible proofs as to satisfy the understanding, the heart and conscience, and be a firm and unsuspected foundation whereon to build for everlasting. This will naturally have respect in the first place to the truth of the scriptures, which relate to the making-known of his will at sundry times and in divers manners, by the prophets; by his Son Jesus Christ, and in connection with him, by his apostles and other followers. Abundance hath been written on this subject with great energy of thought and reason; but still the desired end is not effected, which yet must be.

The holy scriptures, no doubt, carry an evidence of their truth and divine original, in the very face of them, beyond common writings.

The subject matter of them, in great part, is beyond the possible knowledge of men, on any other principle than that of their origin being divine—The sublimity and worth of their communications, being of a spiritual and eternal nature, carry forcible evidence that they never sprung from an earthly minded creature without divine influence —The honesty with which the writers have recorded their own crimes and those of one another argues with great propriety that they were not governed by that ruling and selfish passion of mankind, ever partial to themselves and to their peculiar party, but by that spirit of truth, which would not build on a foundation of deceit, and will let God be true but every man a liar, giving to God the supremacy, as the only fountain of worth, and acknowledging men to have no good in them except what they receive from HIM—The universally attributing of the glory and praise of all good things and of all excellence to God alone, evinceth that they were not dictated by that self-pleasing self-exalting spirit of man who ever loves the pre-eminence.

The miracles which were wrought by the ministers of God; by Moses and some of the prophets; by Jesus Christ and his followers, are, in their own nature and place, incontestible proof of their divine original; but not direct, especially to those who have not seen them and do not credit the record. For should a man deny the truth of the record, there is no direct proof of the existence of those miracles, the existence of which must be confirmed before they can have their influence in confirming the divinity of the scriptures. But indirectly, the record of those miracles is a weighty and serious proof. For it is not reasonable to suppose that such a record of facts could have been forged, and they attested to have been done in so public a manner as they were, and the forgery not have been detected at the time and the scheme overthrown. Neither is it probable, or possible in the face of the inquiring and aspiring temper which prevails in some at all times, that such a forgery could have been made and guarded until palmed on the people for truth, by dating the facts out of the remembrance of those who were then living; for they would have immediately inquired why these things were never known before, and especially as they are said to have been done, at least most of them, in the presence of a learned and enlightened people, such a people too as were enemies to the performance of many of these miracles, and would rather they could have been denied. But added to all this, their enemies have confessed many of the facts, as many writers have shown.

But the history of the facts in that open and public manner in which they are related, in a long succession of time, with the undoubted existence of the people among whom they were wrought, and as nothing can be produced really to overturn the evidence, is no contemptible proof of their truth. For the history without unequivocal evidence to the contrary, hath at least a right to the same weight with other history. And as to the things which are narrated being out of the ordinary knowledge and experience of man, and therefore considered by some as matters of doubtfulness, the real truth is the contrary in the circumstances with which those things are connected; inasmuch as they are not alledged in favor of any of the vanities or temporal pursuits of men, but that everlasting substance which could never have entered into the heart of man without the existence and influence of superior wisdom; a substance which is not according to the selfish and inferior pursuits and propensities of men, but beyond and contrary to them all, and therefore exposed to be denied had it been possible to conceal them. For the very existence of the profession of christianity, as before observed, to the extent to which it obtains; notwithstanding all the variety of forms and contradictions of sentiments, is a strong argument of its truth, as being originally divine. And so are the false religions which obtain in the world, not excepting mahometanism, an argument in favor of the true; because, however men may vary and new model, mix and divide, every one of these forms must have had something from which to take its rise, as much as counterfeit money, for the contrivance of which there could have been no motive without the existence and worth of the true.

Now the existence of christianity is either by the doctrine of nature, or by revelation, and is either true or false. If by the doctrine of nature and false, nature is no longer to be trusted, and it is time for men who regard truth to cease pleading the authority of nature; but if true, nature confirms the authority of revelation and hath her instructions from the same source. But if christianity, or revelation, hath its existence by the work and revelation of God, as the scriptures say, those scriptures which give an account of its origin from first to last, are of divine original: christianity and they stand or fall together.

It is utterly uncandid and ineffectual to object against the truth of revelation, as some do, certain things contained in the scriptures of the old testament, which are so full of metaphors and parables, and customs now unknown, as the account of *the man who had his shoe loosed in Israel*, as containing absurdity, because they cannot understand the reason of such things. All men cannot equally understand all matters which obtain in the present tense, even those things in which they agree as far as the mind of each one is capable of apprehending them. And how shall they who have not made practical religion their business, understand all the customs and their reasons, which obtained in ages of which they have no accurate knowledge? But whatever is to become of such matters as those, they are not set forth as the evidence by which the truth of the scriptures is to be evinced, and the judgment of men concerning such matters cannot destroy that evidence for which men cannot account on any other principle than that of divine authority.

The truth of revelation, or the reality of the work of which the scriptures speak and out of the spirit of which they sprang, together with the credibility of the scriptures, in their own place and proper use, by no means depends on the logical accuracy of the language or narative, neither on the rigidly accurate consistency of all the parts in matters of less consequence, especially when we consider the exposedness of the scriptures to errors through translations and transcriptions. Translations read differently in some instances. As for example, the difference of twenty years in two accounts of the age of Ahaziah when he began to reign, is removed in the Greek translation called the Septuagint: it is twenty-two in each place. (See 2 Kings 8. 26. 2 Chron. 22. 2.) But to be able to reconcile punctiliously and literally all naratives in matters of less consequence or of a parabolical nature, is no more necessary to support the credibility of the scriptures, or the faith of that work of salvation to which they relate, either immediately or more remotely, or to be in possession of that salvation, than an accurate reconciliation of all historical facts relating to any country, or people, is necessary to the belief of the existence of that people. The truth of the scriptures, or of revealed religion, is not materially affected by these things. There are not difficulties enough, or of a sufficiently serious and irreconcilable nature, to effect much with honest minds, while these same scriptures carry in their face, evidences which may almost be called intuitive, and which could come from no other source than that to which they are ascribed.

For in the next place; the things which are taught by the scriptures, as the duty and life of a christian, are of such a nature and have such a tendency to counteract the current, or rather torrent, of man's nature and propensities, that it is impossible that they should ever have originated from that source. For it is a principle in nature as well as revelation, that as is the fountain such is the stream, and that no effect can exceed or be contrary to the cause.

Now should men have contrived a scheme of religion, it would have been adapted to their own inclinations; and whatever mortifications they might have counted necessary to obtain the end, that end, or acquisition, would have been accommodated to the natural feelings of the predominant principle; as it is said the mahomedans are led through much mortification. (To which they have been instigated likely by the knowledge of the self-denial and mortifications of the flesh practised by christians.) with the prospect of a paradise of sensual delights; so that the whole plan is accommodated to the predominant sensual appetites of men. And this principle is proved in fact by the immensely superior number of those who profess christianity on the express principle of its being founded on the revelation of God, who accommodate the faith and rules of Christ to their own taste, until there is no discoverable difference, farther than the profession, between them and the non-professors.

But there is no principle in man ever to have produced that practical cross-bearing and self-denial which, according to the scripture account, Jesus Christ taught his followers by word and by works. That cross on which is crucified the flesh with its affections as well as its lusts. *For they that are Christ's have crucified the flesh with the affections and lusts.* That cross therefore which everlastingly buries, without hope of restoration, all that lust of concupiscence which is the life of the world, so that it is said, *He that will seek to save his life shall lose it*, and which gives the promise of an everlasting reward in the enjoyment of that, for which natural men have no relish and of which they can have no real knowledge, is the cross of Christ, which is enjoined on the people who profess his name, to bear every day. This is that cross and this the self-denial taught in the scriptures, which men naturally abhor, and which therefore there is nothing in them to have contrived.

I am not unaware that the earthly reasoning of men will make this cross an objection to the truth of genuine christianity, saying it is unreasonable because unnatural. But if unnatural whence came it? Surely not from nature; not from the spirit of iniquity, or principle of evil, which christians call the devil, who ruleth in men, and who inclineth men to foster their natural lusts; for it is a principle of reason, as well as revelation, that nature is not divided against itself, and that satan is not divided against satan.

But we need not marvel if such reasoning be found in those who professedly disbelieve revelation and allow themselves to be ruled by nature, when, preposterous as it is, those who acknowledge the truth of revelation, and that nature, as it now exists in men, is contrary to God and to all good, argue in the same way, and reject the gospel which inculcates the same practical cross and self-denial, on that same account. These things show, as before stated, that if men had contrived a scheme of religion they would not have had such a cross in it, there being no source in them ever to conceive of such a thing, as being necessary or proper. These things also show that the professed christians and those whom they call infidels, have religion nearly allied together: all being of the earth, they savor alike the things of the earth.

But it is time to advertise the reader that the truth of the scriptures, or of revelation, stands on an entirely different footing since the establishment of the faith of Christ's second appearing from what it has done for ages before. Men have been contending about names and sentiments, abetting the scriptures in the letter while they had not the fruits of christianity to show in its defence. But the profession of christianity was reproached and *the name of God blasphemed among the Gentiles*, by the unhallowed lives of professors. The divisions, the animosities, the wars and bloodsheddings, the cruel and inhuman barbarities exercised in many places against each other, the avarice of the major part of its ministers, as fast as they obtained power to support their avaricious temper, with many such iniquities, have furnished the enemies of revelation with good reasons against its truth, and do yet where these evils are practised.

For while the professors taught that the scriptures were the foundation on which the church was built, and that church was such a poor, mangled, divided, corrupt and incoherent thing, its members violating the precepts and example of him whom they professed to serve, and of the scriptures by which they professed to be governed, more especially in modern ages, they had poor arguments to offer in their defence; mainly those which were far-fetched by abstruse reasonings on history and other topics, or those which were only internal and therefore incapable of being used to good advantage for the want of concomitant works as a confirmation. But it is a poor method to prove the truth of the scriptures or of the profession of christianity, to talk of an inward treasure, the proper and convincing fruits of which cannot be seen. Not disputing but many arguments used by many in those times and to this day, in defence of revelation, are proper and irrefragable in their own nature and place, but often inefficacious for the want of their proper concomitants—true gospel fruits. For the profession of christianity connected with the life of a man of the world is a flagrant inconsistency.

Now it is very exceptionable for those who believe the scriptures, to teach that the church is built on the scriptures; for according to the scriptures, the house of God, or church of the living God, is the ground and pillar [base, or foundation and style] of the truth, and the law goeth forth of Zion and the word of the Lord from Jerusalem, and not Zion from the law, or Jerusalem from the scriptures; neither are the scriptures ever said to be the foundation on which the church is built. The saying of the apostle to the Ephesians, (2. 20.) "And " are built on the foundation of the apostles and prophets, Jesus Christ " himself being the chief corner-stone," hath been alledged as a proof that the church is built on the scriptures. But the argument is foreign and inconclusive; for the foundation of the apostles and prophets is evidently that foundation on which they were built, or to which they bore witness, which could not be the scriptures; for they were built before the scriptures were written, and stood firm while they were writing them, each one according to his day; and the foundation to which they bore witness was Christ. *To him gave all the prophets witness*, as well as the apostles, saying, *Other foundation can no man lay than that is laid, which is Christ*. Or the foundation of the apostles and prophets is the revelation of the truth of God, which centres altogether in Christ, who is the chief corner-stone. Some professors may object, that this is popish doctrine. And what then? It is the truth of God; and is any truth objectionable because a people accounted corrupt believe it? The revelation of God is in the true church of Christ, in every place where that church is, and is its foundation and support, as well as its cement and Spirit of union.

There are serious disadvantages attending the opinion that the scriptures are the foundation of the church, which show themselves in the fruits of those churches or societies who believe so, none of them being able to exhibit the genuine fruits of the gospel, the unity of the Spirit in the bond of peace, love, which is the bond of perfectness, and the like. And it is natural that this should be the case; for it is undeniable that the scriptures have suffered by the hand of time, through transcribings and translations, and have lost, especially to the English reader, and others who have them by translation only, much of that perfection which they at first had, consequently the building which is built on them, or even squared by them alone, must be proportionably imperfect and uncertain. But this is not all; The scriptures in no case represent themselves as the foundation of the church, but the revelation of God, or Christ himself; it is therefore subverting the scriptures, and as they are true, subverting the truth, to make them the foundation. " For other foundation can no man lay than that " is laid, which is Christ."*

But in the progress of the work of God and in the increase of the church in the second appearing of Christ, matters will have a different train, and the truth of the scriptures be confirmed, while they serve their own proper use in the hands of the people of God. " All " (holy) scripture is given by inspiration of God, and is profitable for " doctrine, for reproof, for correction, for instruction in righteous-" ness; that the man of God may be perfect, thoroughly furnished " to all good works."† In the true church of Christ the genuine fruits of the gospel may be found in such a manner as eventually to confound all scruples as to the truth of revelation; for in its progress, which hath already begun to appear, may be found—peace, for its members do not go to war against men's lives, or property, or rights—safety, for its members shed no human blood—union, or the unity of the Spirit in the bond of peace, for there is one body and one Spirit, one faith, one baptism, being all baptized by one Spirit into one body: one Lord Jesus Christ, one God and Father of all, who is above all and through all in them all. No place is found for selfishness, covetousness, or partiality; *for they have all things common and no man calleth any thing which he posseth his own.* No room is left for even a plausible suspicion of worldly or sinister views in their possessions:

1 *Cor.* 3. 11. † 2 *Tim.* 3. 16.

for they gain their living by their own industry, and their preachers receive not a cent of pay in money or other value of earthly goods as a compensation for preaching. And the testimony which they bear against sin in nature and works, including the visible and manifest order of their lives, cuts off all room for sensual indulgences.

No doubt the suspicious will surmise that worldly motives are the object; but as the most judicious cannot point out the room for such surmisings, they will have no weight with the candid. And believers being able to live thus together, supported only by that faith and revelation which they profess, to live without any external bond, in closer communion than any who have such bonds, to live in freedom from destructive wars, and wasting contentions among themselves, stand as a lasting monument of the truth of the faith of Christ which they profess, and of their being built on the true foundation, as well as a silencing proof of the truth of revelation, and of those scriptures which bear witness of such a church, because experience proves that no faith one side of that which is grounded on revelation, yea, none one side of the faith of Christ in his second appearing, is able to produce such fruits.

The church thus built upon the foundation which God hath laid in Zion, and instructed by that guide whom Christ promised, of which promise a record is made in the scriptures to stand as a lasting witness showing who is the guide of his people; I say, the church built on that foundation and instructed by that guide, is not subject to the fluctuation and inconstancy to which they are subject who undertake to build on the scriptures as their foundation and director. Most of them indeed undertake to modify that foundation to their own understanding, forming systems, as they say, according to the scriptures; but none of these plans are able to keep the people together on that principle, during a revival of the light and power of God to any great extent, however they may answer for a form in times of deep insensibility or profound darkness.

But the church of God, built on the true foundation, and taught by the Holy Spirit according to promise, is able to understand the scriptures and apply them to their right use, and the youngest of its members possess a sufficiency of understanding and find enough of the Spirit to keep on the foundation in union. And the unfaithful cannot abide; *for the foundation is a stone of stumbling and a rock of offence to them who stumble at the cross being disobedient.* The church on this foundation will, in its progress, wipe off all reproach from the name of christianity and confirm the truth of revelation.

But we have no intention of treating largely on this subject, or of entering minutely into the arguments and obviating the objections of naturalists against the existence of God or the truth of revelation, as that work of God has begun on the earth, which in its progress will obliterate every trace of infidelity or doubt respecting the Being of God, the certainty of his revelations to men or the truth of christianity. In the mean time, what is here stated may subserve the promotion of that work of God, by ministering at least some instructions to honest minds, who may be beset with the flattering baits of infidelity But the publication is mainly intended for those who believe in the Being of God and acknowledge the propriety of worshiping him.

CHAPTER III.

Of God, in a Compendious View of his Attributes.

I COME in the next place to speak of God in his relation to his creatures. God is the author of all other beings, the fountain-head, of whom and for whom all his creatures were made, and by whom they live

The first thing to be considered in the character of God as related to his creatures, particularly to men with whom we have mainly to do, is his POWER. His eternal power is clearly seen in his works, which is so intimately connected with his Deity, or existence as God, that *it* is seen also. (Ro. 1. 20.) Power is indispensible in the works of God, in his creation and providence. It was necessary that God should have power in himself, adequate to the execution and management of the works which he intended, and that he should have in himself the knowledge that he did actually possess that power, independently of all other beings. He is at no loss for power. These things will not be controverted by many.

The next particular to be noticed in contemplating the divine character, in his relation to his creatures, is his WISDOM. It was necessary that God should possess wisdom to plan his works in the best manner to effect the proposed end; so that his true character might appear in his works, in the best manner possible, his own glory be declared, and the happiness of his creatures secured on the most fair and elegible terms, or if lost, that the character of God should remain unblemished and finally unimpeached and the unhappy sinner be left inexcusable, to confess and deplore his own folly and guilt. " Lo this " only have I found, that God hath made man upright; but they have " sought out many inventions." (Eccl. 7. 29.) " Come now, and let us reason together, saith the LORD." " Say ye to the righteous that " it shall be well with him; for they shall eat the fruit of their doings. " Woe to the wicked : it shall be ill with him ; for the reward of his " hands shall be given him." (Isa. 1. 18. and 3. 10.) God's wisdom appears in his works, and is more and more conspicuous as men become acquainted with his ways. But his wisdom is like himself, incomprehensible by the finite mind. " O the depth of the riches both of " the wisdom and knowledge of God ! how unsearchable are his judg-" ments, and his ways past finding out !" (Ro. 11. 33.) The wisdom of God is the fountain-head of all the little portions of wisdom in men, which he bestows as they have need. Thus God gave wisdom to Solomon; and saith James, " If any of you lack wisdom, let him ask " of God, who giveth to all men liberally and upbraideth not ; and it "shall be given him. But let him ask in faith." (Ja. 1. 5. 6.) But that God doth inherit in himself an inexhaustible fountain of wisdom will be readily acknowledged.

His KNOWLEDGE is intimately connected with his wisdom in the order of his attributes. Thus the apostle speaketh of the depth of the riches both of the *wisdom* and *knowledge* of God. His knowledge may be considered as the offspring or emanation of wisdom, and viewed as having a special relation towards the objects on which it fixes, or the works of God, and those of his creatures, which are the objects of his notice and attention. That God's knowledge is equal to all demands, or that there is no lack of knowledge in God, and that it is unlimited in and of himself, its source being inexhaustible, will be readily granted. " Known to God are all his works from the beginning of the world." " In whom are hid all the treasures of wisdom " and knowledge." (Act. 15. 18. Col. 2. 3.) But the knowledge of God will come into consideration hereafter.

God's RIGHTEOUSNESS and JUSTICE come next in order, being essentially one; but the first of which, if any distinction be made, may be considered as the inherent and necessary attribute of God, from which the second issues forth and is inseparable from all his works and ways, which are all righteous, just and equal. " Shall not the judge " of all the earth do right?" And again, " The LORD is righteous." And again, " The LORD our God is righteous in all his works which " he doeth." The righteousness and justice of God, in connection with his power, wisdom, and the like, are the defence of all truth and righteousness in men, as well as the source from which spring the protection and confidence of all just men, by which a happy event is secured to them. " For the rod of the wicked shall not rest upon the " lot of the righteous." " For the righteous LORD loveth righteousness." " Say ye to the righteous, That it shall be well with him; " for they shall eat the fruit of their doings." (Psm. 125. 5. and 11. 7. Isa. 3. 10.) So that no man need be afraid to practise righteousness, because of the present sufferings and reproach, while God is righteous who stands engaged for the issue. All acknqwledge God's righteousness in words, though many maintain such sentiments concerning God as greatly tarnish his character, not to say they would utterly supplant all righteousness and justice in him and his works. But we will take a more familiar and free contemplation on this subject in the sequel.

" GOD IS LOVE." It would be in vain to attempt to point out in words the whole character of God in its true colors: The only design of what is here stated is to take a compendious view of the attributes of God as he stands related to men, amongst which that of *love* is by no means to be omitted, being that which he hath set forth in the gospel, as the uniting cord between God and men; " God is " love; and he that dwelleth in love dwelleth in God, and God in him." " For God so loved the world, that he gave his only begotten " Son, that whosoever believeth in him should not perish, but have " everlasting life.." (1 Ino. 4. 16. and Ino. 3. 16.) And abundantly

ATTRIBUTES.

more to the same puport. But I must not in this place give a loose rein to feelings on this subject, as I should be carried too far from the present design.

The GOODNESS of God may be considered as the handmaid and the offspring of love. Goodness, as well as love and all the rest, is properly an attribute or quality, and not a foundation or primary existence. And without love there can be no goodness, and without righteousness and justice there can be no true love or goodness, and without power and wisdom and knowledge, there could be no righteousness, or justice, or love, or goodness in God. God is perfect, and no part of his character can be lacking or rejected without rejecting God. The goodness of God is made known to men in the works of nature and grace, or in the accommodations for the support and comfort of the body, in return for which all are called to be exercised with gratitude, and in the provision which he has made in Christ for the salvation of the soul by the gospel, in return for which, and influenced by a just respect to the recompence of reward, all honest men devote themselves and their all to God in the gospel of Christ. " For " the love of Christ constraineth us." (2 Cor. 5. 14.)

The MERCY of God may be viewed as comprehended in his love and goodness. This though properly an attribute of God, the principle of which is necessarily included in his character, hath no place to exercise itself without having respect to creatures in distress, or some state of wretchedness, want or dependence, as it hath particular relation to misery, that is something to move *mercy* or *pity*, and especially so, as it is exercised toward the fallen race. And out of this state of things the term *mercy* seems to have arisen. Nevertheless, that original attribute or perfection of Deity, as it exists essentially in Him, and by which he is moved to relieve the distressed, is essentially and unchangeably the same, and could have been exercised towards his dependent creatures, who would always have stood in need of his aid, had they never known sin or guilt or any of the wages of sin. No doubt the impression of this essential attribute in Deity, produced from the heart and tongue of Zacharias, that rich expression, " Through the tender mercies of our God ;" in the Greek, *Through the compassionate bowels of the mercy of our God.* The Hebrew word also, [חסד] so often translated *mercy*, is considered as denoting the deepest immotions and strongest affections of the heart, as those between parents and children; which the Greeks expressed by [ςοργη,*] *innate love*, or that which is natural to the order of beings towards their own offspring, relatives, and finally to all.

---

* *This is that natural affection of which the apostle represents some of the heathen as being destitute,* αςοργους, *without natural affection, or having no desire for the happiness of others. (Ro. 2. 31.) This is the natural affection or compassionate disposition common to the human family, and which to violate is iniquity. This is it which is so often construed into the lusts of the flesh, or sexual propensities by modern devotees to a carnal life, who object to living a life of*

GOD'S HOLINESS is so universally acknowledged and ascribed to him by all, that nothing need be said to gain the consent of mankind, that it is an essential attribute. Without that infinite contrariety to sin, and opposition to every thing wicked or impure, called *holiness*, there could be no God—without holiness, no mercy, no goodness, no love, no justice, no righteousness, no wisdom, no power in an original subject, no light, no truth. Accordingly in all the ascriptions of praise to God, holiness has a leading place. Thus in Isaiah's vision of the Lord, he heard one crying to another and saying, " Holy, " holy, holy is the Lord of hosts; the whole earth is full of his glo-" ry." (Isa. 6. 3.) And in the vision which John had of the church of God, the four living creatures, each of whom had six wings as the seraphim seen by Isaiah, and who were full of eyes within, " Rest " not day and night, saying, Holy, holy, holy, Lord God Almighty, " who wast and art and art to come." (Rev. 4. 8)

But the holiness of God is particularly proper and necessary to be remembered on account of its practical use. For as God is essentially and necessarily holy, it cannot be expected that he can possibly acknowledge an unholy being in that intimate and near relation to him, which accompanies salvation. The necessity of holiness in the people of God was early taught. " Ye shall be holy: for I the Lord " your God am holy." (Lev. 19. 2.) And when Christ appeared who first revealed the perfect way, in which alone men could become holy, the exhortation was not forgotten; " But as he who hath called " you is holy, so be ye holy in all manner of conversation, Because " it is written, Be ye holy ; for I am holy." Accordingly the people of God are habitually represented as a holy people ; and although under the law they could be no more than ceremonially holy, it is not so in the gospel; " For the law made nothing perfect, but the bring-" ing in of a better hope doth; by the which we draw nigh to God." (Heb. 7. 19.) This doctrine of holiness utterly supplants and finally overthrows the notion of any man or people being christians unless they have found that which takes away all sin and saves them from all unholiness. Those therefore who pretend to be christians while they commit sin, or acknowledge they do, are to be judged out of their own mouth ; and those also who profess, and yet teach that christians are all subject to commit sin, are to be esteemed mockers of the work of Christ. " He who despised Moses' law died without " mercy, under two or three witnesses ; of how much sorer punish-" ment, suppose ye, shall he be thought worthy, who hath trodden " under foot the Son of God, and hath counted the blood of the cove-" nant, wherewith he was sanctified, an unholy thing, and hath done " despite to the Spirit of grace. ?" (Heb. 10. 28. 29.)

crucifixion to the flesh with the affections and lusts, after the example of Christ, lest by renouncing the fleshly works of the first Adam they should fall under the apostolic reprobation and lose their relation to Christ the quickening spirit.

ATTRIBUTES.

GOD IS TRUTH. Nothing can with more propriety be attributed to God than *truth*. His Spirit is *truth*; his word is *truth*; Jesus the Son of God, the Word who was made flesh, is *truth*, and dwelt amongst us full of grace and truth. Without *truth* there could be no holiness, no righteousness, no justice, nor any thing else truely valuable or excellent. To lack truth is inconsistent with the respectable and good character of a man, and how much more must such an insinuation reflect dishonor on the character of the righteous Judge of all the earth, the God who cannot lie. Yet many seem to hope, as the great source of their comfort, that God will not fulfil his word in all things against sin, laying judgment to the line and righteousness to the plummet. They hope that the soul that sinneth shall not *surely* die, believing the devil, the father of lies more than God who cannot lie, and that they shall have peace though they add drunkenness to thirst, or at least are sinful and not holy. But these know not that relation to the God of truth which accompanies salvation.

After this cursory view of the character and attributes of God, which comprehends those most commonly spoken of, I thought to have desisted from this part and to have proceeded to the main body of the work, as it relates more immediately to those things which are influential on the practice. But while I look into the writings of the apostles, I see another character or attribute ascribed to God, which seems to pervade and comprehend the whole, and is of so much consequence to living christianity, that I cannot feel my mind relieved without noticing it. The following words communicate the subject matter of this attribute.

GOD IS LIGHT, and in him is no darkness at all." (1 Ino. 1. 5.) When we speak of light as pertaining to the character of God, or of God as being light, it is not to be understood that this light is limited to God as peculiarly belonging to him, and making manifest to him his own character, purposes and works, together with the character and works of his creatures; but also that every one who cometh to the knowledge of God is a partaker of that perfect light which is the true God, according to the degree of his acquaintance with God; so that no man can with any propriety be called a christian, or be said to know God as he is revealed in Christ, unless he also walk in that light which is God, as Christ also walked. For any one therefore to walk in darkness, or not to enjoy that perfect light and knowledge of the truth, by which he is delivered from all uncertainty or doubt about the true way of God and eternal life, and about his own character and standing before God, is incompatible with being a christian, or true follower of Christ. " This then is the message which
" we have heard of him, and declare to you, that God is light and in
" him is no darkness at all. If we say that we have fellowship with
" him, and walk in darkness, we lie, and do not the truth: but if we
" walk in the light, *as he is in the light*, we have fellowship one with
" another, and the blood of Jesus Christ his Son cleanseth us from all
" sin." (1 Ino. 1. 5.) The inference is clearly to the point, that because God is light, therefore his people walk in the light as he is in

the light, for he walketh in them, as it is written again, " I will dwell
" in them and walk in them, and I will be their God and they shall be
" my people." (2 Cor. 6. 16.) Equally clear is the doctrine of
Christ from his own mouth, showing that because he is light the people who follow him are freed from wandering in uncertainty or walking in darkness ;—" I am the light of the world ; he that followeth me
" shall not walk in darkness, but shall have the light of life." (Ino.
8. 12.) This is true gospel language. Much darkness was consistent with being an honest Jew, under the law, which was at best but
a shadow ; but we speak not of Jews but of christians ; and we never
read in the holy scriptures of an uncertain or a doubting christian;
they know in whom they have believed, and they know that they are
of God by the Spirit which he hath given them, and the Spirit is
truth.

The pernicious sentiment, so very prevalent among professors, that
men may be christians and yet remain in great doubt and uncertainty
whether they are christians or not, is such a destructive heresy, and
such a powerful engine to retain people asleep in sin, that it ought
to be pierced with the sword of the Spirit wherever it is accessible ;
and for this cause, nowithstanding that the subject is more extensively treated in another place, I have been particular to notice it here,
as being counteracted by this doctrine, *that God is light, and that
they who are of God dwell in the light*, that the reader may have the
impression of the truth of God fixed in his heart, as it were from the
beginning, and know that they who are christians indeed walk in the
light of God, being partakers of divine nature.

I have been the more careful to make some practical remarks on
the character and attributes of God, that readers may be impressed
with some influential sense of what a man must be, when he becomes
a son of God in Christ; that he must be like God in all the graces
of the spirit; for as Jesus Christ, who was the first true tabernacle
of God among men, which the LORD pitched, and who is the head
of the body, the church, had the fulness of the Deity dwelling in him
bodily, so each and all of the members who, in union with the head,
constitute the true body or church, which is Christ, are partakers of
the same Spirit and same divine nature, that God may be all and in
all. " And of his fulness have all we received, and grace according
" to grace." And the glory," said Jesus to the Father. " which thou
" gavest me, I have given them ; that they may be one, even as we
" are one." " Now if any man have not the Spirit of Christ he is
" none of his." (Ino. 1. 16. and 17. 22. Rom. 8. 9.)

I have not in this small tract been careful to follow the order of
systematics, in their distributions and arrangements of the attributes
of God ; neither have I proposedly taken into view all which they
enumerate, as his infinity, eternity, unchangeableness, omniscience,
and the like. Neither have I attended to the usual distribution of
communicable and incommunicable, or the famous distinction of the
justice of God into distributive, remunerative and vindictive, with
many other distinctions which one or another has named, who knew

not what he said or whereof he affirmed. But my leading object in stating what I have done in this place is to open the way for what is yet to be said.

Nevertheless, let it be remembered, with respect to the attributes of God, that no one of them, neither all of them together, comprehend God so as to enable us to know definitively what God is. He is incomprehensible. We cannot know God except as he reveals himself in his character, his attributes and his works. We cannot have any just conceptions of God as lacking any one attribute belonging to the perfection of his character, and yet when we view all these to the extent of our sphere, there is yet that behind of his Essence and Being, of which we are ignorant. All these attribues, or perfections, are qualities none of which can exist abstractedly or alone. Thus if we speak of his holiness; holiness is a quality which implies a being, as it were, previously extant, to be holy, or a being capable of containing holiness. If we speak of love; love is a quality or attribute of some being presupposed by the very naming of this attribute. If we speak of goodness; goodness is also an attribute or perfection of some being or existence presupposed or at least included in the thought, and so of the rest. Yet so intimately and essentially do these perfections belong to the very essence of his nature and being, that we may say in truth and with safety, that *God is truth, God is light, God is love, God is holiness;* for there is nothing in God but what is *truth*, there is nothing in God but what is *light*, there is nothing in God but what is *love*, there is nothing in God but what is *holiness*, and so of the rest. On the whole, no one can have any just conception of God otherwise than as his character is revealed in his word and works; neither can any have a just and correct knowledge of God, even by revelation, any farther than as they grow into an acquaintance with him by travelling into the same nature in the work of redemption and holiness, by the gospel.

Nevertheless, according to the privilege given to us in the revelations which he makes of himself, to teach us our duty and our relation to him, we may talk freely of his character and his works, in the things which pertain to our salvation and redemption. For God hath revealed himself in Christ, that in our sphere we may know him with certainty, in all his character, and speak of him with safety. So that while on the one hand, we are unable fully to comprehend all or any one of the perfections of Deity, God being incomparably superior to man, on the other hand, there is nothing in God which, in our sphere, and to the extent thereof, we may not know with certainty and safety, as fast as we overcome evil. For although no man hath seen God abstractedly at any time, yet the only begotton Son who is in the bosom of the Father hath revealed him—*hath revealed God, whole God*, in himself who is the *brightness* of his glory and the *character* of his person, or *subsistence*. And nothing short of the correct and perfect knowledge of God in his whole character can ever complete the happiness of man, who was created in the image of God. And for this cause he hath sent his Son into the world, in whom dwelt all the fulness of the Godhead bodily, to be our example and to reveal God to us, that we might find salvation in being conformed to the image of his Son, and so to God himself, and in no other way. Thus God's people live as knowing the unknowable and seeing him who is invisible.

" GOD is a SPIRIT ;" or more properly and emphatically, " GOD is SPIRIT. This is perfectly consistent with the Greek text, and conveys a much more noble sentiment of God and fixes on the mind a more noble impression, than to say, he is *a Spirit*, as though he were a circumscribed or limited being. There are many spirits all limited and dependent beings, but there is one God, independent, and in all his character and perfections unlimited. But God is SPIRIT; and is therefore the proper fountain from whom all created spirits proceed. Moreover God is Spirit; it is therefore no marvel that he is not satisfied with fleshly or material worship; " God is Spirit; and they that worship him, must worship him in spirit and in truth." (Ino. 4. 24.) And no marvel that God will increase the work of the Spirit in his people until they are finally redeemed in the Spirit and the flesh made void. And what if we should say that *God is Spirit*, comes nearer to pointing out what God is, in his real Being or Essence, than any other name, character or attribute, ascribed to him by the Spirit of revelation, not even excepting the name by which he was made known to Moses, I AM THAT I AM, or I WILL BE WHAT I WILL BE, expressing his unchangeableness and independence ? We can have some understanding, according to our sphere, of the existence of a Being who is Spirit in the abstract, as a primary Being or foundation existence, independent of any distinct being, attribute or quality, and yet as it were the proper basis for all good qualities, and without all and every one of which we cannot conceive of that Spirit, that Existence, whom we call God. Spirit is a real existence ; a proper agent; a subject of power, of righteousness, holiness, love, and the like. A Being who is Spirit is also the proper subject of volition and free agency. But if we speak of love it is not an independent idea; it presupposes some subject or agent to inherit and exercise that love. If we speak of justice; it presupposes a Being who is just, distinct from the idea of justice, as its possessor seat, or the place of its habitation. If we speak of light ; though by some supposed to be a real body, it seems nearest the truth to say, that it presupposes some being capable of illumination and reflection, and that where there is no body to contain light there can be no light. If we speak of power or wisdom, it is a dependent idea, presupposing a Being powerful or wise, and so of the rest.

But when we say that *God is Spirit*, we express the idea of an existence, not material, yet real, capable of volition and agency ; I say we conceive and express the idea of the Being of God, according to our sphere, for beyond that he is incomprehensible to us, we know nothing ; and the circle of our knowledge is small in the infinite I AM. Yet when we say God is Spirit, we can conceive that that Spirit is capable of volition and agency ; and is also capable of possessing in himself as his essential qualities, attributes or perfections, *power*, *wisdom*, *righteousness and justice*, *holiness*, *truth*, *goodness*, *love*, *mercy*, *light*, *independence*, *self-existence*, and the like. Accordingly, when we speak or read of the Spirit of God, it is God the Spirit; if of the Spirit of truth, we have respect to God the Spirit, who is Truth; that Spirit who could not exist or ever have existed without truth; if of the Spirit of holiness, it is God the Spirit, who is holy, essentially holy in his very nature; if of the love of God, or Spirit of love, it is no other than God the Spirit who is love, " For God is love, " and whosoever dwelleth in love dwelleth in God and God in him;" if of the Spirit of unity in the bond of peace, it is none else but that Spirit who is God, and is one, in himself and all who know him, being in them and to them, the uniting bond in abiding peace towards God and one another. Thus when a man receives the Spirit of Christ, he receives God who is Spirit; and when the Spirit of Christ abideth in any man, he hath abiding in him that God who is Spirit; and he hath both the Father and the Son. "At that day ye shall know "that I am in my Father, and ye in me, and I in you " " If a man " love me, he will keep my words: and my Father will love him, and "we will come unto him, and make our abode with him."(Jno.14. 20.)

CHAPTER IV.

Of the nature of God's Decrees; or what a Decree is.

IT HATH been already intimated that God works according to plan; and that in that plan of things, wisdom is profitable to direct. " The " LORD possessed me," saith Wisdom, " in the beginning of his way, " before his works of old"(Pro. 8. 22.) And that God's plans are most free, according to his own understanding and wisdom, and without his being influenced by the desires or wishes of any other being, or any exterior cause whatever, will likely not be denied by any who have the knowledge of " Him who worketh all things according to " the counsel of his own will." Neither can it well be denied that God's plans are consistent with each perfection of his nature. As there is no jar in the perfections or attributes of Deity, it is impossible that God should lay any plan, or fix any decree, by which mercy would be sacrificed to justice or justice to mercy, righteousness justice or truth, be sacrificed to power, wisdom, independence, self-sufficiency, his own glory, or any thing whatever. For although the glory of God is the ultimate end of all his works, as well as the greatest happiness and highest perfection of his creatures, whatever is planned or executed for the praise of his glory, is all done in perfect union with righteousness, truth, equity and every other perfection in God. So that, speaking after the manner of men, we may say he consults all these in the plans which he lays out, or the decrees which he makes; and that all is done according to the understanding and reason with which man is endued by the Creator, insomuch that each one will see and be satisfied of the propriety of each plan or decree, in the event of his acceptance and salvation, or convinced in the event of his rejection and damnation. For neither is it possible, that God should lay any plan or make any decree, which would contradict or thwart the intelligence, reason or free agency with which man is endued by his Creator, as being his offspring. Because, take away man's reason and free agency, or require that which is contrary thereto and out of man's reach, and he is no more amenable for his actions, or subject to praise or blame. But of this hereafter.

The decrees of God may be divided into two general classes. The first class comprehends all the purposes of God, concerning what he intends to do immediately as at the beginning, or by the agency of his creatures at any time after they had an existence in their proper order. The fixed determination of God to effectuate such works as he sees are necessary and proper, may be properly called a decree. The second class comprehends those things which creatures are required to do as acts of obedience to God's will, and on the doing of which their own acceptance depends, as *If ye be willing and obedient ye shall eat the good of the land.* Or any established law or rule for the people, may be called a decree, as the sentence passed by the apostles and elders at Jerusalem concerning circumcission. So a determinate rule of court is called a decree of the court, and the courtiers are required to observe it, and in case of violation are punishable.

The decrees of God are to be known and understood by the revelation of his true character, the declaration of his will by the word revealed, and by the works of creation and providence, or by the works of nature and grace. Beyond these sources we have no occasion to inquire after the decrees of God; these are sufficient; for God doth not work inconsiderately; what he doeth he purposed to do, and that which he requireth his creatures to do, is also according to counsel. Neither is it to be forgotten that in all God's decrees and works, he hath consulted the good of his creatures as really as his own glory; for notwithstanding that his own glory is his ultimate end, the happiness and final glorification of his creatures, each in his proper sphere and lot, are so connected with his glory, that the one serves to promote the other. And it is not possible it should be otherwise; because, for God to create beings capable of everlasting happiness and not have respect thereto, in all his purposes and works, would tarnish his glory and be incompatible with his goodness, love, mercy and other attributes; and it is also impossible that creatures, as men are, created in the image of God and after his likeness, should be happy and not glorify God. True happiness therefore in the proper sphere and order which belong to men, as the offspring and accountable creatures of God, is a justifiable motive to duty, and not contrary to the purposes of God; a motive which God uniformly proposes to induce men to obedience, and without which no motive can reach them to profit, in a state of nature, fallen as it is. And whereas God promotes his own glory by his creatures, through their agency and the good which he doeth for them, according to the counsel and wisdom of his own will, although it remains true, that a man cannot be profitable to God as he that is wise may be profitable to himself, yet in filling up the purposes of obedience, and the works which God hath appointed him to do, a man may, in his own sphere, be profitable to God in the promotion of his glory.

But we are particularly interested in the decrees of God, and the execution of them, as they relate to men. And here let it be remembered according to what has been already stated, that it is impossible God should decree any thing to be done by himself or otherwise, unless it is his will it should be done. This is a natural inference from the nature and character of God as he is revealed to men: he is not a capricious, uncertain being like them; "He is of one mind." It would indeed be inconsistent with the voluntary and free agency of a man, acting without constraint, to decree any thing to the contrary of his own will, and how much more so in the infinitely free and perfect Being who is of one mind and none can turn him, and to whom all his works are known from the foundation of the world. This is a first principle, a dictate of common sense, and needs no farther proof.

CHAPTER V.

Of man as the offspring of God, and of responsibility.

THAT God created man according to his purpose or decree, needs not be denied if we attend to the counsel or reasoning which he held at his creation. " And God said, Let us make man in our im-
" age, after our likeness, and let them have dominion over the fish
" of the sea, and over the fowl of the air, and over the cattle, and over
" all the earth, and over every creeping thing that creepeth upon the
" earth. So God created man in his own image; in the image of
" God created he him; male and female created he them. And God
" blessed them: and God said to them, Be fruitful and multiply, and
" replenish the earth, and subdue it; and have dominion over the fish
" of the sea, and over the fowl of the air and over every living thing
" that moveth upon the earth." Thus man came forth from God, as his real offspring, as said Paul, " Forasmuch then as we are the offspring of God;" in the image of God, as it were God in miniature, the image and glory of God; God in his sphere, having dominion over all; yet a dependent creature of God; endued by him in the creation, with the capability of propagating his own species, the offspring of himself in his own likeness. This capability of propagation was found in the cooperation of the organs of the material body in the male and female; which material body stood in so intimate a relation to the spirit which came directly from God, that the two constituted in each one distinct person, one man and one woman; so that by the

cooperation of the procreative powers in the male and the female a race of beings were propagated and continued, who are not merely material bodies, but men like their original in all their physical powers and properties. Thus mankind are the offspring of God, the image and glory of God to this day. We shall consider their fall and corruption by sin hereafter.

This material body was made of the earth, earthy, adapted to serve as a habitation of the spirit, and to answer every necessary purpose for the time being. So that the first man is said to be of the earth, earthy; and not only the first man, but all his posterity, for *as is the earthy such are they also that are earthy.* Adam's sons are like himself. But the spirit came immediately from God, and is that by which man is properly the offspring of God, and that in which the man properly and finally consists, and without which man would not be man in his proper order. " And the LORD God formed man of the " dust of the ground, and breathed into his nostrils the breath of life; " and man became a living soul." In this soul, or spirit, man is capable of rising again to God, notwihstanding all which he hath suffered by the fall, and of being manifestly the image and glory of God, in the redemption which is in Christ Jesus the Lord; for, *He who is joined to the Lord is one Spirit;* and again; *The second man is the Lord from heaven; and as is the heavenly such are they also that are heavenly.*

Thus God in the execution of his purpose and decree, created man to be the true representation of himself, and to stand as the image and glory of God forever, and so to declare his power and set forth his glory, more perfectly than all the material heavens and earth could do besides.

But man transgressed the law of God, violated the will of God made known to him, and so fell from his proper lot and place in which he was created. It appears needless to consume time and labor in this place to prove this point, which is so abundantly acknowledged, and on which so much hath already been written. All man's works from his infancy declare, that they spring from a source which cannot pertain to God, being utterly subversive of all good. All men in their natural state evince by their works, the truth of the scriptures, " That " God hath made man upright, but they have sought out many inven- " tions." (Eccl. 7.29.) And again; "There is none righteous, no not " one; there is none that understandeth, there is none that seeketh " after God; they are all gone out of the way, they are together be- " come unprofitable; there is none that doeth good, no, not one: de- " struction and misery are in their ways; and the way of peace have " they not known: there is no fear of God before their eyes."

The inquiry at present is, Did God decree that man should act as he did, and so fall from his primeval state of rectitude and happiness? To this we are obliged, by the force of truth, to answer in the negative; That God did not decree that man should commit such a deed, neither was it the genuine fruit nor necessary consequence of any of God's appointments. *God made man upright, but they have sought* out *many inventions* for themselves· For as before stated, it is impossible that God should appoint or decree any thing contrary to his own will or any of his perfections: and for his creatures to do his will, or to act according to his will or appointment is no transgression but obedience; and no fall or evil consequence could be the result of such doing, but on the contrary life and peace; "Not every one that saith unto "me, Lord, Lord, shall enter into the kingdom of heaven; but he that "doeth the will of my Father who is in heaven." "But the mercy "of the LORD is from everlasting to everlasting upon them that fear "him, and his righteousness to children's children; to such as keep "his covenant, and to those that remember his commandments to do "them."(Matt. 7. 21. Psa. 103. 17, 18.) It cannot be transgression in men to act as they are called to act by God's appointment; and to say that it was necessary that man should sin according to the order of his creation, or by God's appointment, is to say that God is the proper and primary author of sin, or rather that there is no such thing as sinning against God.

It was no doubt necessary that man should be tried and learn by experience to resist temptation; and admitting that God knew that his fall would be the result of his trials, that was not to prevent God from placing him in those circumstances which were necessary to that experience without which he could never have been a tried and safe subject of obedience, or a safe keeper of his own peace and happiness; especially considering that God gave him warning of his danger, and foretold him the consequence of disobedience: "In the "day that thou eatest thereof thou shalt surely die." But it was, and still is impossible, that God should place man in circumstances where he would unavoidably be unnecessarily tempted.

But if God did not decree that man should fall, it may be asked, Did he decree or appoint that he should not? To this we answer in the affirmative, that God did pass a decree that man should not sin or fall: for without sinning he could not have fallen. This decree was the law of God which man broke, and by the violation of which he fell. For without such a decree, he could not have sinned; because, "Where there is no law there is no transgression; for sin is the transgression of the law." And without such a decree, neither could man ever have proved his obedience nor have been ever confirmed in happiness, for he would have remained untried. And so necessary is trial in the servants of God, that he would not finally crown his own Son, or place him as the foundation on which to build his church, until he was perfectly tried even to death, *a tried stone*, and was made perfect through sufferings. Neither will any of his saints ever be finally crowned with the crown of righteousness and eternal life, until they pass through the perfect fiery trial, and experience that trial of their faith which is more precious and more refining than that of gold, and learn by the things which they suffer—until they know how to keep themselves in the love of God. It was, therefore, as correct and necessary that the first Adam and his posterity should be tempted and tried as that the second and his seed should.

From what is here said, it will naturally be understood, that God did not decree in that order of decrees which was first described, that man should not sin or fall, that is, he did not decree absolutely that he should not sin, *nolens volens*, or that he would interpose an arbitrary or forbidding power to prevent him in the face of motive and man's free agency. Such a decree or preventing act would have annulled all accountableness in man and made his withstanding of the temptation a necessary act, destitute of either praise or blame, justification or condemnation. So that there existed no possible way for man to arrive at the perfection of his order, or that summit of blessedness of which he was capable by creation, and which was his ultimate destination in the spirit, the glory of God and the enjoyment of him, only to let him be tried by temptation, and the result be attended to as occasion required.

God did decree absolutely and without reserve to provide a remedy for man, to recover him from the fall and its consequences. Not indeed to restore Adam and his posterity into his first order in the flesh, or mend up that order, but to reinstate them into the favor of God, and in the line of their duty and happiness, in Christ the second Adam, so much farther on their way—as many as will yield obedience to that plan. This decree is executed in Christ, in his first and second appearing, after it had been set forth by many shadows and various forms in the law of Moses. And as we desire to make as short work on this subject as will consist with duty and perspicuity, we are now ready to enter on the ground where the things immediately relating to salvation concentrate, and where we may inquire with freedom into the decrees of God as they respect men in their present standing. We are still his offspring.

But God is a free, moral agent, *who worketh all things according to the counsel of his own will*, or in other words, who doeth all things as he seeth and judgeth it best to do them, all things considered. As the offspring of God, therefore, man is also a free, moral agent, influenced in his actions by his own mind and judgment.

But as we have now to treat of man in his fallen, corrupt state, it becomes necessary to inquire, whether by the fall his moral agency was destroyed, or is become at all different from what it was. To this proposition the reply is negative. It is not destroyed; it is not different from what it was in the creation; for let that be taken away and a man is no more amenable for his conduct. This will become evident by inquiring wherein moral agency consists, or on what it depends. Whether on the man's holiness and the rectitude of his actions, or on the physical powers of the mind. And it is evident it cannot depend on the first; because in that case, having once become corrupt or unholy, he could no more be a moral agent, consequently no longer responsible; but it is granted that man has not lost his responsibility to God and to his fellow creatures. Besides; in that case he could no more be influenced by reason, or by motives presented to the intellect. But man is still influenced by motive, and gained by reason; and God always addresses himself to man according to these principles. "Come now, and let us reason together saith the LORD." Moral agency, therefore, depends on the other source; The physical powers of the mind; those powers without which man would not be man, or the offspring of God in his own image. Now these powers were not taken away by the fall, for the change produced by sin was not physical but moral. It left the man physically what he was, constituted of body and mind, or rational spirit, with the animal life. The result then of this inquiry is, that man is found to be a moral agent, that his actions have respect to good and evil, sin duty, obedience and disobedience, since the fall as really as before; and that his moral agency depends on the physical powers, or faculties of the mind, or rational spirit.

I have not continued to use the double epithet, *free, moral agent*, from the consideration that the single phrase is sufficient, as I know no difference between a moral agent, and a free, moral agent; for the action which is not free, or the effect of choice, is not a moral action, and neither praise nor blame, justification nor condemnation can attach to an action of that kind. Moral actions are those only which come within the limits of volition or choice; and all such actions are criminal or justifiable, in proportion to the agent's acquaintance with the nature of the case; except where they are of so little weight as to be indifferent. An involuntary or unavoidable action, if such may be called agency at all, cannot be criminal; neither are such counted criminal by the laws of God or men: the knowledge and intention of actions or the motives, leading to them, constitute their criminality or righteousness. Should a man, in an unexpected hour, be taken up into the air by a whirlwind or hurricane, and thrown on another man with such violence as to kill him, and the first escape with his life, would either God or man account him guilty? I trow not. But, should he stand on an eminence where there would be no necessity of falling, and designedly throw himself on the other and kill him, he would be guilty.

It may be objected, that the being irresistibly taken up and thrown down again, would be no agency at all, but a being acted upon; but to act knowingly and unwillingly, (as some say they sin, but not willingly,) while moved onward by the unavoidable influence of a necessarily governing principle or the secret ordination of heaven, is quite another matter. But it is easy, as well as just, to reply, that the necessary and unavoidable influence of an irresistible, governing principle, is as compulsory as irresistible impulse on the body. Who can withstand that which is necessary and irresistible? Or who can be blamed for doing that which he is invincibly necessitated to do? or for not doing that which he is invincibly and necessarily unable to do? Not one. And let men talk as they may about sinning reluctantly, and against their will, it is all a hypocritical, deceptious affair, for self justification; for when the matter comes into the light, it is found that no necessarily governing principle or power, known or unknown, leads or prompts any man to sin, without his own choice or consent. And this makes him criminal, according to the knowledge which he has of what is sin or what is duty; for it is not the man's choice to sin for the sake of sinning in the abstract, but to do certain actions to which sin is attached, either necessarily or by consequence of their relation to other matters. I will not deny, that they who are ignorant of the gospel, which is the only mean of obtaining power over sin, are under the government of a principle which is invincible by them in their present situation, by which they are led into sin and cannot avoid it; but this principle, invincible in that situation, is their own nature, or their own inclination and choice to do those things which are iniquitous; and their criminality is only in proportion to their light and power, and the opposition to these, which they practise in their actions: but they have not salvation.

But it is argued that as every man acts by the influence of motive, in all his moral actions, and there are opposite and contradictory motives, some to do good and some to do evil, every motive must influence according to its present weight on the mind, or its real estimation, consequently the man must be influenced and governed by the superior motive, or that which is of the first importance. The question then is, can a man commit sin, or can he not, his actions being unavoidable, the necessary product of irresistibly superior motive?

In the process of this discussion, it may be necessary for the satisfaction of some to premise a few things respecting the faculties of the mind or rational spirit, and their order. The common enumeration and arrangement have been, The *judgment, will* and *affections*, or according to others, the *judgment*, the *affections* and the *will*. The enumeration of the faculties has also been carried to a much greater extent, and the arrangement made very different from either of the foregoing; and this may be done with propriety, because it is beyond a doubt that the spirit in man is capable of operations, of various classes which are not definitively expressed in any of these. It is not my intention to be minute, or extensively particular in this place; but to prepare the way for the free use of the terms as they may be needed in the following pages, I will make a general enumeration.

The first operation of the mind is the reception of ideas, or the impressions of certain objects presented to it. That power or faculty of the mind by which this operation is performed may be called the RECEPTACLE of those ideas or impressions. The INTELLECT may be noticed next, that faculty by which the rational spirit understands those ideas. COMPARISON, or the comparing of ideas together, by which the mind observes the likeness and unlikeness of things presented to it. The JUDGMENT, or the power of deciding on the propriety and impropriety, superiority and inferiority, goodness and evil of actions or things according to evidence. CONSCIENCE, or the MORAL FACULTY, by which the mind determines in favor of the good and against the evil according to evidence; and accuses and condemns if disobeyed, but approves and justifies the obedient. DETERMINATOR, or that power of the mind by which it determines which of two different or contrary objects to prefer. The CHOICE, or power of choosing after the determination is closed. The MEMORY, which is simply the power of retaining and reflecting upon ideas or impressions received before. The IMAGINATION, or the power of forming the imagery of things in the mind, the ideas or impressions of which have been received before. The AFFECTIONS, which environ and embrace the object of the choice, or that which obtains the ascendency in the mind; as love, approbation, complacency. The PASSIONS; as in the first place, those by which an object is repelled, or rejected from the mind, as hatred, reprobation, aversion, abhorrence. But these are more properly the counterpart of the affections; for if we love one object, we necessarily hate the contrary; if we approbate one, we necessarily reprobate the contrary. On this principle it is stated in the holy scriptures, that, No man can serve two masters; for he will hate the one, and love the other; or else he will hold to the one and despise the other (Math. 6. 24.) These are prone to move with violence and impetuosity, and need to be regulated and governed by the judgment and consideration. But the PASSIONS most prominent in the human life, are those animal sensations, or fleshly appetites and propensities, arising from the connection of the spirit of man with the material body, in the constitution of animal life. These move inconsiderately, and impetuously; and seize with avidity the coveted object. By these mankind are, precipitately hurried, often into extravagant evils, and the whole spirit, or mind, is as it were, absorbed, in the pursuit of animal and fleshly pleasures and indulgences. By these mankind are governed in all their pursuits, untill they are arrested by something of greater importance presented to the intellect and apprehended by it. All these may, in common language, be comprehended in the general term, AFFECTIONS; but the above distinctions are not without their use. And to the last class pertain the affections and lusts of the flesh which all christians crucify. And the gospel alone, when received and obeyed, is calculated to furnish any of the human family with power to regulate the affections, subdue the passions and crucify the lusts. To these might be added the *will* by which the inclination and determination are conclusively fixed; also *reason*, *consideration* and the like, but being comprehended in the foregoing, and so commonly understood, I shall at present leave any further distinctions to those whose province it more immediately is to make them.

It may however be proper here to add, that when we speak of the different faculties of the mind or spirit, we do not intend that these are really different powers or parts distinct from each other, of which the spirit is composed, like the body, of its different members; but as the spirit is the immediate offspring of God, it is one, and these different faculties are the different modes, capacities or lines of operation in the same spirit. Thus when we speak of the intellect, we mean the spirit capable of understanding; when of the judgment, we mean the spirit capable of giving judgment; and when of the conscience, we mean the same spirit approving the good and condemning the evil. Thus also we say, the spirit, and sometimes the soul, the mind, the rational spirit, and the like, to denote one and the same thing. Now to return to the subject in hand. It is contended that every man follows that motive which bears with the greatest weight on his mind, at the instant when he acts or when he concludes which of two different actions to do, because to choose that action, or that course of actions, or manners, which bears with the least weight, and consequently hath the least influence, would be irrational, and contrary to being influenced by motive, and make void the use of argument, by proposing reason and evidence to induce to action: it would be like the heaviest weight in the scale being elevated by the preponderance of the lightest. I shall not contest this reasoning; I see no method to overturn it. For although many men do many things which they would much rather not do; they make choice of these rather than their alternatives, which to them appear still worse, and of two evils they choose the least; which is a good rule, as it relates to natural things. It is true many actions of men are done so inadvertently and inconsiderately, that they afford no opportunity for inquiring into the spring of them, and many so trivial, that they are not worth an investigation; but subjects of this kind are most properly elucidated by those examples which are evident and capable of clear investigation; and by these it is easily proved that men have leading, and to them superior motives, which they follow in all their actions.

But if every man be necessarily led by the first or superior motive, how can any man be guilty of sin, or in any sense criminal, being necessarily led to every action by an exterior cause? For motive is not in the man; in him is only the receptacle of that which cometh from without, the subject on which the motive may fasten itself. Men are not born with motives in them; all these are received through the medium of the natural senses, as hearing and seeing. But in men is found a spirit or mind capable of receiving the impressions of all things which are presented to it through their senses, and of surveying and comprehending them as far as they are represented or laid open, and all real facts thus opened are congenial with the physical powers of the mind. Thus a man hath in him no motive to worship God, until he is taught that God is, whether he learn God's Being from his works, or by revelation. But the impression of the being of God is so congenial with the physical make or constitution of the spirit which came from God, his proper image that it can never be erased, and the propriety of worshiping him is quite easy—a reasonable duty. "I beseech you therefore breathren, "by the mercies of God, that ye present your bodies a living sacri- "fice holy and acceptable to God, which is your reasonable service." (Ro. 12. 1.) A man hath no motive to repent of his sins, until he learns that he is a sinner, and something of the nature and consequense of sin. But when these things are known, repentance readily appears proper. And no man hath any motive to obey the gospel until he is taught something of the necessity and benefit of it. But when these things are known, nothing can be presented with motives really superior, or equal.

But if men are necessarily influenced to follow the superior mogives in all their actions, and if these motives are not innate or physically in men, but must come from some other source, the question again returns, Can any man commit sin or be at all criminal? Is not every man completely under the power of some other being, or source of influence either good or bad, so that if his actions be of the wicked class they are not criminal in him, for how can he help them, the first motives irresistibly prevail, and if they be of the good class in the matter of them, what recommendation are they to him? Or what do they make in his favor? They may indeed be negatively innocent as having in them neither good nor evil to him; for how can he avoid them? and who thanks him for his good deeds?

But it being granted that men follow the first motives to them, or those which feel most engaging for the time present, will not prove that they always follow and obey the really and intrinsically superior motives. For men do not always acknowledge the full weight of such motives, or they do not admit the most worthy motives into the account. But for this also they must have a motive, which is to escape the influence of the superior motive which would influence them contrary to the pursuit of some inferior object which they have in view: herein is dishonesty. But it will be said that this inferior object is the superior motive with them at that time, else they would not follow it. Granted; but how comes it to be superior to them? Because it is so in itself? Not so; for that is contrary to our proposition and to matter of fact. Is it superior because they who follow it believe it to be superior? Not so; for they believe the contrary, else they would not be afraid or unwilling to admit that which is really superior, to its full estimation. For example; the drunkard believes that sobriety is better than drunkenness in every respect; for his own health, for the wealth of him and his family, and for the comfort, peace and good morals of them all; and often looks at it, and considers how much better it would be to be sober and temperate; but the gratification of a carnal thirst for spirituous liquors, the love of such company as suits his disposition, the desire to drown perplexing thoughts, and often those very thoughts and convictions which relate to superior objects and motives, some or all of these inferior motives prevail, he chooses and practises on the inferior making them the superior to him by his own act; I say making them the superior to him by giving them the first place.

The question now is are these motives irresistible? If so the drunkard is as innocent and as respectable as the sober and temperate man. Or when a man is tempted to defile his neighbours wife, and he commits the atrocious deed, if the temptations are irresistible he is just as innocent as he who respects lawful wedlock, or becomes an eunuch for the kingdom of heavens sake. And the man who is offended by his neighbour and avenges himself, by taking his neighbours life, is just as innocent as he who was taken up in a hurricane and irresistibly and without intention or design thrown on the other so as to kill him. It will be said in this last case, the force was mechanical and therefore not a proper similitude of the influence of moral motive, which is only mental and therefore not irresistible in the same manner. But an irresistible is irresistible, and can any man show or discover the difference in the effects of irresistibles? Every man unfailingly follows the intrinsically superior motive known to him according to his best judgment or he does not: if he does not, which both fact and acknowledgement prove to be the case, then moral motive is not irresistible; because were it irresistible the superior motive known must always have the irresistibility, as certainly as the heaviest piece of metal will have the preponderancy in an equal scale, and every man would necessarily follow it. Thus it is evident by the scriptures that moral motive is not irresistible; *Ye do always resist the Holy Ghost.* Now no motives could be named of more intrinsical estimation than those proffered by the Holy Spirit, yet they resisted them with success; and they could not resist those motives which were not in their reach.

But moral motives not being irresistible will not prove that men do not follow those motives which they esteem the greatest; and that motive which is esteemed the greatest, is the greatest at the time, for motives are superior or inferior according to their estimation; for whatever inclines or finally induces the mind to certain actions in preference to others, is the pre-eminent motive in that mind. But moral motives not being necessarily irresistible, leaves room for man's accountableness, because he is on that principle at liberty to choose or refuse; whereas to be carried irresistibly by any power mechanical or mental, excludes all choice, and without choice no man can be commended or blamed, he is in nothing superior to a machine.

But the question remains: How are these things reconcilable? Men are invariably governed by that motives which is to them the superior one; yet have the power of choosing their ways, when different ways are presented with their attending motives. Just on this principle the matter is all plain, that motives are non of them irresistible; and that men have in themselves that faculty or power by which they are able, most deliberately and freely, to choose the way to go and the actions to do according to the best of their judgment, and according to evidence received, which power I have denominated the DETERMINATOR. Without this there could be no free agency. By this power it is the province, and privilege of every man to determine what motives to set in highest place, the really inferior which are most agreeable to his corrupt inclinations or those which are superior by intrinsic worth.

By this I do not mean that every man, or any one, can give himself information, without the aid of some other means, what is the superior motive. But when different objects are presented to the mind to invite the man to this or that, and the reasons and evidences are also brought into view, why this or that is superior and the other inferior, it is the prerogative and province of every man to be as free as God in determining, according to his best judgment, which to choose—which motive to set on the throne, giving it the first place

OFFSPRING. 45

a his mind, choice and affections, whether that which is intrinsically inferior but most agreeable to the man's inclinations and passions, or that which is intrinsically superior, in real worth, and therefore justly claims the pre-eminence in the judgment. For when the whole matter is developed, this is the point where all the real contrast between motives centres. Because when men come to be governed by their judgment, their whole care and labor is to have the judgment properly informed of different matters, which are the best, and if both cannot be obtained or pursued, the most valuable is chosen as soon as the judgment decides which that is. In case therefore of necessary errors of judgment for the want of light, or information, there is no criminality : the man has done the best he knew. But when the judgment is informed and the man doth not live up to its instructions, it is a selfevident principle, as well as scriptural, that he is guilty. It has been already proved that he can be under no necessary or irresistible influence to do what he knows is wrong. But when a man is governed by the passions, motives may be presented to the choice through the intellect and judgment, of quite superior quality to those which the passions present, and the superior be rejected and the inferior prefered, in the face of judgment and conscience, by the choice being determined in favor of the passions. And on this pivot turns man's accountableness; he is here called upon, to exercise his prerogative and determine the choice in favor of the superior motive, or his best judgment, and to put that choice into practice, or if he neglect, to do it at the expense of his justification.

This is the unhappy condition of the whole human race, to be governed by the passions, and ever will until the passions are taken captive and put under arrest, at least so far as to give every man a fair trial whether he will determine his choice in favor of the passions or the judgment. When man fell from God he fell into himself, from the government of the spirit to that of the flesh, from the government of the judgment to that of the passions, and there he remains until arrested by the gospel. But in that situation he calls in the aid of the judgment and other faculties, to subserve the work of the passions: and by the passions and affections, is the way to arrest man's attention and gain him to give the judgment the lead; when this is done matters are on a fair train to be all *put right*. I have spoken of the province and the prerogative of every man to determine the choice in favor of the superior motive according to his best judgment. This implies that there must be light in the understanding, and the judgment be formed before any thing decisive can be done. It also agrees with the doctrine of all motive being exterior, or out of the man. And every true motive to good deeds is from God, the Father of lights, from whom cometh every good and perfect gift. But where the light and information are but partial the decision of the judgment will be weak ; yet when men follow their best judgment, and yield to the best light and information in their reach, unbiassed by selfish and inferior motives, they are released from condemnation and in the fair way to become perfectly right. And this is free agency, unhampered and without a blemish, for a man to determine his choice according to the best of his judgment, and not to be necessarily carried by inferior motives which are congenial to his inclinations and passions, in violation of his better judgment. And this is man's province, *Lord of his proper sphere*, of which none can spoil him—*this is his prerogative*, of which none can rob him: and no man or God can do his duty for him. Without this province and this prerogative, man could not be man, he could not, be the offspring and the image of God.

CHAPTER. VI.

Of the gospel offers, and man's capability of complying; and whether God's decrees at all intercept its free operation.

Notwithstanding that man remains to be man, through the fall and all its consequences, he is a lost creature, ruined by sin, sunk into darkness and death; the powers of his mind are set on wrong objects and their true order subverted, so that the passions rule, and the intellectual powers, which according to their true order ought to rule and be primarily subservient to God alone, are become subservient to the passions and the flesh; until those noble powers, in the possession of which, man continues to be physically the image and offspring of God, are degraded to the inferior purposes of corruption and misery, and although the mind and conscience remain, both the mind and conscience are defiled.(Tit. 1. 15.) The gospel is the only mean of recovery from all this ruin; and it is sent to the human race on the most liberal terms, excluding none who are willing, or who will be prevailed upon to receive salvation on God's terms. We are now to inquire what are these terms; and whether they are adapted to man's condition, or whether it is in the power of man to comply with the proposals made to him in the gospel. The gospel is commonly called the ordinary, not to say, as it really is, the only, mean of salvation. But if the proposals, or provision in the gospel, be out of man's reach, in his present, fallen state, it is no mean of salvation to him; for that which is not adequate to the effect, is no mean of any matter whatever; and if man hath not power to comply with the proposals of the gospel, there must be some other mean of salvation, for him or he must go without.

But as we are treating of the decrees of God and the things relating thereto, and have just been treating of man's free agency, we shall make some examination, whether there be any contrast between the decrees of God and man's free agency, or whether these do in any respect infringe on this, so as to prevent its unrestrained operation. And here let it be considered, that if any irresistible decree or decrees of God, that certain things shall unfailingly come to pass, should coun-

OF THE GOSPEL.

teract the free agency of man, or prevent him from choosing according to his best judgment, such a decree would carry him irresistibly and take away his accountableness, for the same reason as irresistible motive or mechanical force: and that would be contrary to the call and doctrines of the gospel, which are most liberal and unreserved. " Come unto me, all ye that labor and are heavy laden, and I will give " you rest." " Whosoever will let him take the water of life freely." And again; " He that believeth on him is not condemned; but he that believeth not is condemned already, *because he hath not believed* on "the name of the only begotten Son of God:" not because any decree of God stood in the way to prevent him.(Mat. 11. 28. Rev. 22 17. jno., 3. 18.) Now to suppose any decree of God, absolute or permissive to interpose, or at all to be the most remote acting cause, why any man doth not believe, that decree preventing him, or rendering the gospel invitations abortive, would be to charge God with duplicity in the gospel offer, and tarnish the immaculate glory of his character. And those decrees of God, which propose to men their duty and require obedience, are the ground work with the necessary, attending motives, to induce men to use their free agency and make a wise choice. There is, therefore, no contrast between the decrees of God and man's free agency.

The gospel of Christ is the mean appointed of God for man's recovery and final redemption. It is the power of God to salvation, to every one that believeth, and by it life and immortality are brought to light. By the gospel is made known, who is the salvation of God to the ends of the earth; " Neither is there salvation in any other: for " there is none other name under heaven given among men whereby " we must be saved," except the name of Jesus Christ. " For I de-" termined" saith the apostle, " not to know any thing among you, " save Jesus Christ and him crucified. "(Act. 4. 12. 1. Cor. 2. 2.) The Spirit of God also, (that is Christ, for the Lord is that Spirit. 2. Cor. 3·17.) is made known by the gospel; and the ministers of the gospel are the ministers of Christ, to preach Christ to the people, to minister Christ, and to minister the Spirit to the people; ,, For we " preach not ourselves, but Christ Jesus the Lord; and ourselves " your servants for Jesus' sake,—But we have this treasure in earthen " vessels, that the excellency of the power may be of God and not of " us." " And again; " Not that we are sufficient of ourselves to " think any thing as of ourselves; but our sufficiency is of God; who " also hath made us able ministers of the new testament; not of the " letter, but of the Spirit·" " And again; " He therefore, that mini-" stereth to you the Spirit, and worketh miracles among you,(doeth " he these things)by the works of the law, or by the hearing of faith? (2. Cor. 4. 5, 7. and 3. 5, 6. Gal. 3. 5.) Thus it appears, by these and a multitude of other scriptures, that in the gospel is all necessary provision for man's salvation, being indeed the power of God to salvation, because Christ the power of God and the salvation of God is therein ministered to men.

Now the question is to be discussed; is this gospel of God sufficiently adapted to the recovery of men from their present fallen condition, or is some additional mean or help, requisite to their recovery and final salvation? If the gospel is sufficiently adapted to their recovery, it is so completely accommodated to their present circumstances that they are able without additional aid to receive it and to comply with its terms. And on that principle they can be chargeable with their own ruin who perish under the gospel sound and on no other; this being the only way of salvation or hope. Or it amounts to the same to say, if Christ is a Savior, sufficiently adapted to the salvation of men, his terms and proposals must be and are so exquisitely accommodated to their present circumstances, sin, guilt, death and all other things considered, that they are able to comply with all that which he proposes, and to do what he requires, without farther aid than his offers include. For no man can be criminal in not doing what he is required, unless the requirement be fair and equal; and no requisition can be fair and equal which requires more duty or obedience than the man is able to yield, unless when he has previously and willingly spent his ability. (Mark this.) Accordingly God deals with man on reasonable terms; "Come now, let us reason together, saith the Lord." (Isa. 1. 19.) And all the proposals of the gospel, the calls and invitations, the warnings and threatenings are made in the open acknowledgement, that man stands on equal ground with his Maker and Redeemer, nothing being required of God, but what is in the reach of man to perform. " Look unto me, and be ye " saved, all the ends of the earth; for I am God, and there is none " else." "Ho, every one that thirsteth, come ye to the waters, and " he that hath no money; come ye, buy and eat; yea, come; buy " wine and milk, without money, and without price." "Jesus stood " and cried, saying, If any man thirst, let him come unto me and " drink." "And he said unto them, Go ye into all the world and " preach the gospel to every creature. He that believeth and is bap-" tized shall be saved; but he that believeth not shall be damned." " And the Spirit and the Bride say, Come. And let him that heareth " say, Come. And let him that is athirst come. And whosoever " will, let him take the water of life freely." (Isa. 45. 22. and 55. 1. Jno. 7. 37. Mar. 16. 15 and 16. Rev. 22. 17.) Thus fairly, equitably and unreservedly are the proposals of the gospel universally made.

It is vain to plead, that all these proposals are insufficient without the help of God to enable mankind to do their duty; for if the provisions of the gospel are not equal to the necessities of those to whom it is sent, it is an imperfect thing, a mere blank and a reproach to its author. For to propose salvation to any man on such a plan as is not equal to its accomplishment without additional aid, and that additional aid cannot be had unless on such terms as the man is not able to comply with, is only to mock the man's misery and cruelly to aggrevate his distress. And it is granted on all hands, that he who rejects the gospel is the most miserable of all beings, unspeakably more guilty and wretched than they who never heard it. But with what propriety, if the gospel comes with such proposals that he cannot comply with them without further aid and that aid is never given? "This is the condemnation, that light is come into the world, and " men loved darkness rather than light, because their deeds were " evil." But whence this condemnation, or judgment, if they were not capable of coming to the light and submitting to its requisitions. But the gospel is furnished with every necessary supply; and the commission of Christ and his ministers includes every supply which the believing and obedient need. "He that believeth is not con-" demned." "And being made perfect (through sufferings) he be-" came the author of eternal salvation to all them that obey him." (Heb. 5. 6.) "He came to his own, and his own received him not. " But to as many as received him, to them gave he power to become " the sons of God, even to them who believed on his name. And of " his fulness have all we received and grace for grace [or according " to grace]" (Jno. 1. 11, 12, 16.) "The spirit of the Lord is upon " me, because he hath anointed me to preach the gospel to the poor; " he hath sent me to heal the broken hearted, to preach deliverance to "the captives, and the recovering of sight to the blind, to set at liberty " them that are bruised, to preach the acceptable year of the Lord, " (Luke 4. 18, 19.") But it is unnecessary to multiply scriptures on this point. It is granted that the gospel opens a sufficient door and treasure of salvation to those who receive and obey it; or in other words who believe, which always implies obedience, for faith without works is dead, being alone. It is also granted that all may receive who will ; but it is argued that none are, or can be willing, until their will is renewed, by the work of God's spirit, in some operation distinct from the preaching of the word, or beyond it. Thus that gospel of Christ, which is the only mean of salvation which God hath ever made known to men, and which is the power of God to salvation to every one who believeth, is set aside as being inefficacious to salvation until men are first saved, or regenerated, by a necessarily previous work of God, which work there is no evidence, way or method of obtaining, unless God see fit to do it, acting according to his sovereign appointment or decree, according to some, and yet the man must perish for not receiving and obeying Christ, when it is impossible for him to comply. This is indeed an absurdity and a wicked accusation of God, and such it will appear to those who consider what has been proved; that it is every man's prerogative, and that pivot on which his fate has finally to turn, to determine his own choice, and to choose whom he will obey, and that in this light God always treats with men. "Choose ye whom ye will serve."

Besides; it is a wild notion amongst men, that to will the thing which is good, is a spiritual act, or the act of some new spiritual power, whereas the will is entirely a physical power, among the rest of those which belong to the physical man, and to will the thing which is good is no more a spiritual act, than to will the thing which is evil: but the will is fixed on a better object. But the act is as much spiritual in the one case as in the other, each being the act of the intellectual and rational spirit. Man is constitutionally as spiritual in his powers of mind before he believes and obeys Christ as after; as much so as he has any occasion to be; being possessed of that rational spirit with which God indued him as the image of himself, including all these intellectual powers in their proper order, which are capable of contemplating and being exercised, filled and made happy in divine and spiritual things. These are the powers, as before stated, which capacitate man for moral, and I may add, for spiritual agency; these are they which make man superior to the irrational animals. Were it not for these, the irrational animals could contemplate, understand and enjoy God, in the spirit in as superior a stile as man. But the work of the gospel is to gain men to the contemplation and enjoyment of their proper element in obedience to God, and when this work is effected they are not only physical but spiritual. Accordingly a natural man, carnal and sold under sin, who has not yet found Christ in the gospel, may have a will to do good, but lack the power; "To will is present with me, but how to perform that which "is good I find not; (Ro. 7. 10.) but he finds how to perform by the gospel, which shows him what his power and duty are.

When people pray to God, that he would give them wills to believe the gospel, or to believe in Christ, or to keep his commandments, or whatever is necessary or desirable, do they understand themselves? *Ye ask ye know not what.* Do such people expect that God will give them other wills besides those which they have? Or when they look to God, or to heaven, as they speak, for wills, what do they mean? Do they expect that God will create other and better wills, and send to them? If the WILL be a physical power of the mind, or spirit, it is certain that every man is furnished with that faculty; but if the WILL be not a physical faculty or power of the mind, a man can, in his best condition, will nothing, either good or evil: What then do they mean when they pray for wills to be given to them? Every man hath his will, or faculty so called from its appropriate functions. The grand desideratum, or requisite, is the gaining of the will to the right object and there fixing it. To accomplish this all important purpose, the gospel is furnished with ample means. Instead, therefore, of praying to God to do the work, true wisdom directs all who hear the gospel, to attend to its counsels, and hearken to God, praying and beseeching them to give him their hearts and wills, and be reconciled to him; or, which is the same, to his ministers who minister in the behalf of God and of his Son. "Now then, we are embassadors for [on the behalf, "or instead of] Christ; as though God did beseech you *by us; we "pray you, in Christ's stead,*[or on the behalf of Christ,] *be ye recon- "ciled to God,"* If we desire God to hear us, let us hear him and instead of asking him to give us wills, hearts and dispositions; let all men submit to God's requests to them, give their hearts and their wills to him, be disposed to his service, be ready at his call, (all which is their reasonable service and his reasonable request,) and all will be well. And the gospel is the repository of all these privileges, to be received and occupied by faith.—Thus men become renewed *in the*

OF THE GOSPEL.

spirit of their minds—*Thus God giveth the new heart and printeth his laws in their inward parts.* But to return to the point in hand.

It is also granted, that faith is the first thing requisite, and the beginning of all the receiving and obeying of Christ in the gospel; that which lays the foundation of justification and salvation in every one, and through which all are made partakers of Christ. It will hardly be disputed, that faith in the work of salvation is always accompanied and made perfect by works of obedience. " For in Jesus " Christ neither circumcission availeth any thing, nor uncircumcissi- " on; but faith which worketh by love." " Circumcission is nothing, " and uncircumcission is nothing, but the keeping of the command- " ments of God·" " Seest thou how faith wrought with his works, " and by works was faith made perfect?" (Gal.5. 6. 1. Cor. 7. 19. Ja. 2. 22.) And these are the fair and equal terms on which salvation by the gospel is offered, these are the proposals with which men are called and required to comply—believing and obeying. This is the unalterable decree of God, that *He that believeth and is baptized shall be saved*; and that, *He that believeth not shall be damned*: faith worketh by love; and as many as are baptized into Christ have put on Christ; they are baptized into his death, and are dead with him, and alive with him to God. But the question is, are men capable of believing the gospel on its own authority, without any additional aid or separate and previous work of the spirit preparatory to their believing? Or is the testimony of God in the gospel which his ministers preach to men sufficient to beget or produce faith in those who hear, without such previous, preparatory work?

To give satisfaction on this subject let it be considered, that if men are not capable of believing the gospel on its own authority, or by the testimony of God in it, without such previous work, the gospel can be of no service to men in the state of nature, to open their eyes, and to turn them from darkness to light, and from the power of satan to God, the work for which his ministers are sent. (Acts 26. 18.) It is therefore no more the power of God to salvation; because instead of being saved by the gospel and through faith, they are saved previously to the knowledge or influence of either. Or if it be argued that this previous work of the spirit is not saving, but only preparatory to believing, rendering men capable of believing, it still renders the gospel ineffectual until that work is done, consequently, the preaching of the gospel or word of God, is no longer the mean of faith ; but faith cometh by hearing, and hearing by the word of God ; if men are incapable of believing without said previous work, they are no longer guilty by not believing; for, as already proved, no man can be justly required to do that which is invincibly out of his reach, unless in the case of wilfully spending his power by some wrong conduct, which could not be the case here, because a man cannot disbelieve the gospel until he hear it and have an opportunity of believing, and there is no promise of God to do in every man such preparatory work, or to enable every man to believe : and if that work be necessary, and yet be not done, in every man, those who never receive it and therefore never believe or obey, are clear. Neither can their possibly be any method for men to take, to get that work done in them, for the first thing is to believe, and whatsoever is not of faith is sin. On this plan therefore of a necessarily previous work of the spirit, before believing, how uncandid and disingenuous is that saying of Christ, "He that believeth not is condemned already ; *because he "hath not believed* in the only begotten Son of God." But let God be true ; but every man a liar ; and so remain, until he come to the acknowledgment of the truth of God.

I speak of God as the God of truth who cannot lie, and of the gospel and its proposals, and of the testimony of God in it, as being all the most liberal and fair, without any deception. The proposals then are plain and intelligible, addressed to men's understanding and reason, leaving them in the unmolested right and prerogative, to act freely, and setling them, in that respect, on just and equal footing with God, because he giveth to all a fair opportunity to plead their cause. And we have seen clearly enough, that there is no other plan on which God can be just, and condemn the unbeliever.

I know it is sometimes argued that God can do with men what he will, and that he hath a right to do what he will with them. But in such a case as this it is foolish talking. We know that God hath a right to do what he will with his creatures ; but we know also, that it is impossible that God should will to do that which is unjust, unfair, or unreasonable. It is impossible that he should propose to men a plan for their salvation, in their own language, in plain intelligible terms, consistent with the understanding and reason of men, and yet the pivot on which their salvation is to turn be kept out of their sight or reach, and then condemn them on the principle of not complying. God hath therefore no right to do that which is unjust with his creatures ; or to propose to them salvation on terms apparently fair and equal, and adapted in all things to their condition, when radically, and by some unknown prerequisite, and unattainable by them, they are out of their reach: God who cannot lie, neither can he do unjustly, "God is not a man that he should lie ; neither the son "of man that he should repent: hath he said and shall he not do it? or ᐣ hath he spoken, and shall he not make it good."(Num. 23. 19.)

It is probably time to remove another shelter of the enemy in souls who are bound under sin—agrievous difficulty. Man is fallen and corrupted, his mind and conscience defiled, hence it is argued that his reason is unsafe, and it is dangerous to appeal to it in the things pertaining to the work of God, or his dealings with men for their salvation. And so far is this carried by some, that when they are completely run aground in argument, they will ward off conviction by pleading that men's reason is unsafe, and we may be mistaken. Now let it be considered to what this kind of reasoning would lead. (For such count it good reasoning.) If man's reason is so subverted and unsafe that he cannot reason safely, what is the use of offering him such an argument, for how shall he know whether it is right or wrong, just or unjust ? the argument overthrows itself. If man cannot reason safely, what is the use of offering him any argument or of using means for his conviction? And wherein is the propriety of God's addressing the reason and conscience of men in all his dealings with them? If there be in man, no certain receptacle of evidence, no criterion of truth, no intellectual powers capable of examining and deciding on genuine faith in God or any other truth; for faith is conviction, the fruit of evidence. On that plan all endeavors to convince men of the truth, are void; and all the pungent arguments of the apostles and ministers of Christ are a blank, a mere affectation. How do men come to believe that God is? or that Christ is? or that there is such a town in China as Pekin, who never saw that place? They all believe it by evidence, and there is no uncertainty or doubt in the case. But God, before whose eyes all things are naked and bare and who knows men in every part, by his dealings with them proves to full evidence, that reason in man is the very same as in himself; and, that man is capable of being informed and convinced of what is right and what is wrong, by the same reasons which appear just to him. Witness Abraham; *Wilt thou also destroy the righteous with the wicked? Shall not the Judge of all the earth do right?* (Gen. 20. 11, &c.) and God agreed to his reasoning. And so it is found in every case, that good reason to men is good reason to God, provided the intellectual and reasoning powers of men are devested of prejudice and left to their proper operations. Thus the reason of man tells him that it is wrong to punish a just man; that it is duty to relieve the distressed; to render to man his due, and to worship God. In all which, and a multitude of other cases, the sameness of reason, as it exists in God and in man, is evident.

All this however is not intended to argue that the understanding, knowledge and reasoning powers of man are equal to those of God. Man is limited to his own sphere; but as far as man's reason is informed of the nature of things, its decisions accord with the mind of God. And it cannot otherwise be, because the reasoning powers in man came from God, as his offspring, and are the patterns of his own. Hence it is that a man feels guilty for doing those things which God hath forbidden, because he is convinced in his heart that God's requisitions are fair and his prohibitions just; for until this is his conviction, he feels himself under no burden of guilt. And many things are required by God, and many disapproved, of which man has no knowledge until informed; but when informed, and the reasons shown him, his reason acknowledges their propriety on the one hand and their impropriety on the other. It is also according to reason in God and in man, that man should submit to what God requires in those things which he cannot wholly comprehend, because he believes God is the greatest, best and wisest judge. On the whole, it is evidently safe to address the reason of men for their information and conviction in the things partaining to God and salvation, and improper to reject reason in maintaining any sentiment or practice.

But the ground on which men's reasonings are unsafe and preposterous, is their reasoning from their feelings and passions, according to fallen nature in its corrupt state, being governed by these themselves, and requiring God's works and judgments to be subject to the same, that their own will may be done instead of the will of God. But to submit to right reason, as it obtains in the true order of man's mind, addressed by the revelation of God, is no other than to submit to the will of God.

Many indeed speak scornfully of appealing to the rationality of men, and especially in the unregenerate and unbelieving, for the consistency and propriety of the gospel testimony. But it might be asked, with what propriety would the gospel be preached to the world of unbelievers, if that opinion were patronised by its advocates, that it is inconsistent with reason? Could that which is unreasonable be recommended to mankind for their acceptance? Although the gospel could not have been contrived by the reason of men, but by the revelation of God, and is not to be taught in the wisdom of men, nor in the words of their wisdom, but in the wisdom and words of the Holy Spirit, yet when taught, it is congenial with the reason of men, and calculated to gain their consent to its truth. And this agreement of the gospel testimony with the rationality in man, shows the source of that rationality, and that it is the same in men as in God, consequently, that men are not deceived in receiving that for the true gospel which is according to right reason. It also shows that we are not wrong in appealing to the rationality of man in conjunction with the revelation of God for the trial of sentiments, and expecting to demonstrate the true judgment of God in so doing. God doth not require men to worship him in uncertainty, or without reason, but with the spirit and with the understanding. (Cor. 14. 15.)

Now to pursue the inquiry, *Whether men are capable of believing the gospel on its own authority, or the authority of the testimony of God therein,* without additional aid, or any previous internal and direct operation of the spirit, preparatory to believing, the position may be renewed, *That if they are not, they cannot be guilty for not believing.* For the only foundation of guilt in man is his transgressing against knowledge and power. The man who has done wrong and knows he ought and could have done better, is subject to guilt, and none else. Who feels guilty in doing the best he knows and has power to do? And who can violate knowledge and power, and feel innocent?

I will not deny, that people may feel in great distress on account of failing in their duty, when they know not how to perform it, neither believe they are able, through the teaching of false guides. The opinion may also be palmed upon them, that they are guilty; but the conscientious feeling of guilt is out of the question, any father than the mind is convinced of the propriety of the duty, and of its practicability. Thus many public preachers urge the necessity and duty of believing in Christ for salvation, as the *sine qua non,* or one thing needful, of every man's acceptance; and at the same time maintain that no man can believe as the gospel requireth, until God lend his aid and do that work in him which none else can do; and, preposterously enough to be sure, presume to charge the guilty culprit with the enormous crime of rejecting Christ, crucifying the Son of God, trampling him under his feet, counting the blood of the covenant, wherewith he was sanctified an unholy thing, and doing despite to the Spirit of grace. And all this atrocious criminality is for not complying with an impossibility; for God hath not yet wrought in them the indispensible, preparatory work. Thus have multitudes been beaten and ground, as it were, between two milstones, surrounded with the terrors of death and the forebodings of eternal vengeanc, by those who pretend to be preachers of the true gospel, sent of God, to turn sinners from darknss to light, and none of them could tell one soul the way, so that he could surely find it. Blind guides leading the blind.

But such will object, that this statement is ungenerous; that they do not teach that men are criminated or condemned for not complying with an impossibility, but for not complying with their obvious duty; which, is in the first place, to believe in Jesus Christ as he is offered in the gospel, and then God would set them on safe ground, and supply them with every needful aid to perform all the rest. But even after men are convinced of the truth of the gospel and the propriety and duty of believing in Christ, can they comply with this duty, until God do that additional, previous work? No matter what that work is called. Some call it *regeneration*, some *illumination*, and some, *the giving of a new principle of spiritual life*. But is it possible for them to comply without it, or before it is wrought? The answer is negative. How then are they guilty, if they would call on him and submit to his hand? " For whosoever shall call on the name of the Lord shall " be saved. But how shall they call on him in whom they have not " believed?" or how shall they submit to him in whom they have no faith? " And without faith it is impossible to please him, for he that " cometh to God must believe that he is, and that he is the rewarder "of them that diligently seek him." (Heb. 11. 6.)So that faith, according to the scriptures, and according to the acknowledgement of those preachers, is the first point to be gained towards acceptance; for whatsoever is not of faith is sin, and if faith is out of man's reach, before such additional, or previous work, men are left where they were, to be condemned for not complying with an impossibility. It is vanity to plead, it is not an impossibility, because the things which are not possible with men are possible with God; and that although men cannot believe of themselves, (as they term it,) that therefore believing is not their reasonable duty, for there is possibility and power in God for them to believe, and they ought to come to God, and he would afford them help: he hath given full authority. But he that cometh to God must believe. The good and gracious physician has infallible medecine in plenty, and he will give it to the sick man, if he will only just *get well, take it, and use it!!*. "But he that believeth not is con- " demned already; because he hath not believed in the name of the " Son of God." Why condemned for not beleving? Because it is his privilege to believe; not of himself, as the blind object, who can-

OF THE OFFERS

not discern the difference between a man's believing of himself, or on his own authority, and his believing on the authority of God, proclaimed in the gospel.

But if the testimony of God, promulgated in the gospel, be not sufficient authority for men to believe, or if they cannot believe, without some additional authority or power, how are they condemned for not believing? Would it not be unjust in God, to make such proposals of eternal life to men, so encouraging and unreserved, on the reasonable terms of believing and obeying, if these terms are out of the reach of those to whom these offers are made? Are not all these offers a specious parade, unworthy of the character of the Creator and Judge of all men? Would it not be cruel and unjust in a physician to offer a sick man relief, and hold out the most flattering encouragements of life, but have the matter covertly depending on such conditions that a compliance would be impracticable? Would not every one cry out against him, as being ungenerous and wicked? How ungenerously then, must such a representation of God's dealings with men, tarnish the glory of his character? What? is God more unjust than man? Or shall that be fabricated on God, with impunity, which would ruin the character of a man? But God, say they, hath a right to do what he will with his creatures, and to treat them as seemeth good to him. I have already proved that notion to be falsely applied in such matters as these: it is an evasion of the devil, to injure the souls of men. God hath no right, neither doth he claim any, to make specious proposals of mercy to his creatures, under the mask of their being true, and then not verify his sayings: " Hath he spoken, and shall he not make it good?

Yea, but say some, God is just and his character unstained, the fair offers of the gospel and man's inability to believe, notwithstanding; because, although they have now no power to believe, or at all to comply with the terms of the gospel, they once had power when God first created them, which power they have now lost by the fall and the consequent sins; it is, therefore, just in God, to offer them salvation on such terms as are out of their reach, and require them to comply, with the awful sanction of more aggravated guilt than if they had never heard, and so leave them without excuse, because they have wasted the power which they had. He is therefore at full liberty to select whom he will as the election of his grace, and minister to them, as the special objects of his favor, all needed aid, and leave the rest without that aid, to perish in their unbelief, adding to all their other sins the sin of rejecting and despising Christ. Many are the subterfuges of the carnal mind, to escape the force of truth, and many the ungenerous charges which are palmed on the character of the righteous God, but none more heinous than this. It is common for those who love their own ease and disobedience, to roll over their own sin and that of others, on God. The subject however is worthy of a fair examination.

And in the first place, let it be enquired to whom is the gospel sent? To man, it will be granted; *Go teach all nations.* In what

OF THE GOSPEL.

state? as being sinners or as being holy as they were before the fall? Not as holy, but sinners who were ruined by the fall before the gospel was sent. *"They that are whole need not a physician; but they that are sick. I came not to call the righteous, but sinners, to repen-*"*tance."* (Luk. 5. 31, 32.) "For the love of Christ constraineth us, "because we thus judge, that if one died for all, then were all dead." (2. Cor. 5. 14.) "But God hath commended his love towards us, in " that while we were yet sinners, Christ died for us." The gospel therefore in its first proposals, its first mission into the world, in the whole commission of Christ and his ministers, hath respect to men in their fallen state, to open their eyes, and to turn them from darkness to light, and from the power of satan to God, that they may receive forgiveness of sins, and inheritance among them that are sanctified by faith towards God. The gospel then is professedly for the purpose of recovering and saving men to whom it is sent, from all the effects of the fall. As said the angel, " And thou shalt call his name JESUS, " for he shall save his people from their sins." (Matt. 1. 21.) and John the baptist, "Behold the Lamb of God which taketh away " the sin of the world." Jno. 1. 20.) "For when we were yet with- " out strength in due time Christ died for the *ungodly*. For scarcely " for a righteous man will one die ; yet peradventure for a good man " some would even dare to die. But God commendeth his love to- " ward us, in that *while we were yet sinners Christ died for us."* (Ro. 5. 6. &c.) But it is needless to multiply scriptures ; it is sufficiently plain that the gospel is sent on purpose for the recovery and salvation of those who have suffered the effects of the fall, and it comes to them with most unreserved and flattering proposals, that *whosoever will may be saved*. It is therefore impossible in the nature of things, that any man can have lost any power or capability of believing and obeying the gospel, or any qualification for being saved by it, which he had when it was sent to him, until he hath heard it and proved its influence on him. And as long as the gospel is in his offer with the same proposals, it will remain in the same unreserved liberality, and his access to its salvation be as free as to the streams of water, unless he waste his own power and day of his visitation by disobedience : he will then be self-condemned and know for what.

But to suppose or plead that the truth and justice of God are vindicated, in proposing such equitable and apparently practicable terms in the gospel, while secretly depending on a power out of man's reach or disposal, by urging or intimating that man lost his power to believe and obey, or forfeited his right to divine aid by the fall, and that therefore God hath a *right* to deliver whom he will and to leave the rest to perish, chargeable with the sin of unbelief and disobedience, is so far from exculpating the character of God, that it accuses and criminates him before the bar of reason and common sense, which he himself hath created in every man's breast. As if a physician should come to a sick man, who had gone into the water after being warned against it, and brought on himself an attack of the pleurisy, and propose on very flattering terms to cure him of his discase, by which he had been seized through his intemperance; terms apparently easy to be complied with, but on account of something covered under an occult reserve in his mind, or withheld in time of need, the man is unable to receive the cure, but rendered more miserable by hearing the news, while doing the best he can. The physician then replies, in person or by his abettors, *that it is just he should die of his disease, because he destroyed his health by going into the water;* and yet the doctor knew all this before, and proposedly undertook to recover him from the effects of his transgression. Would this argument exculpate the doctor in the judgment of charity, reason or common sense? Would not rather every man condemn him as a traitor, unwilling or unable to cure the man, but taking pleasure in his misery? Thus God is unjustly charged with mocking the miseries of men, by offering them salvation on equal terms, suited to their condition, and then withholding the necessary aid to complete the plan, after having declared it already sufficient.

There seems to have been a proverb in Israel, that *The fathers have eaten sour grapes and the children's teeth are set on edge,* indicating their belief, that the children were suffering for their fathers' deeds. But this was an unjust proverb, and the LORD reproved it saying; "What mean ye that ye use this proverb concerning the land " of Israel? Behold, all souls are mine; as the soul of the father, so " also the soul of the son is mine: the soul that sinneth it shall die." And it was ordained by the law of Moses; "The fathers shall not be " put to death for the children, neither shall the children be put to " death for the fathers: every man shall be put to death for his own " sin." (Ezek. 18. 2. &c. Deut. 24. 16.) And if under the law, surely no less under the gospel, the soul that sinneth shall die, each one for his own sin, and not the sin of his father; and the just shall live by his faith and in his obedience. We need not deny that by one man sin entered into the world and death by sin; and so death passed upon all men, for that all have sinned. But I am no more personally guilty by Adam's transgression, without my own acts, than by his being created innocent. If death has passed upon all men, it is plain enough how it came so to do; *because all have sinned.* Neither is it any more positive sin in me to have been born in a corrupt and fallen nature, and thereby in a state of the deepest depravity, than to have been born in a state of purity. My sin, and the sin of every other man and woman, is yielding to temptation.

Mankind, it is true, are by the fall corrupted as coming from a corrupt source, and therefore more easily inclined to evil than to good; the current of their nature is evil; so manifestly do the effects of the fall appear in them according to what is written, that "*By one* " *man sin entered into the world* and death by sin and so death passed " upon all men, for that all have sinned," and that "*By one man's diso-* " *bedience many were made sinners.*" For "*Who can bring a clean* " *thing out of an unclean?* Behold, I was shapen in iniquity; *and in* " *sin did my mother conceive me,*" [in lust of coition. Heb. by a work in which God is not known, and in which he hath no place or

OF THE GOSPEL.

part, having been excluded from the begining. Ro. 5. 12, 19. Job. 14. 4. Psms. 51. 5.] But all these things prove no actual or positive sin without the actions which are the fruits of this fallen nature, "Then "when lust hath conceived, it bringeth forth sin, and sin, when it is "finished bringeth forth death." (Ja. 1. 15.) A man therefore dies for his own sins. Every man has to give an account of himself, but none of his father; it is therefore impossible that God should charge a man with the sin of his father Adam, so as to withhold from him the benefits of the gospel or any thing belonging thereto, or to distinguish one from another without respect to their works.

The very popular argument of long standing, that Adam was the head and representative of the human race, whether it be said natural, legal or federal, and that by his representation or headship, they became criminated, is too absurd and preposterous to obtain in the mind of any reflecting and consistent man. As well might the citizens of America be criminated with the legislative acts of their representatives who guaranty the practice of negro slavery. But every man who from a real principle of equity towards God and his fellow men, keeps his hands clean from the execrated practice, and his heart and tongue free, by holding no fellowship with it, but rather reproving it, is personally innocent from the criminality of those iniquitous acts. Notwithstanding; being a member of the community he may for a time be subjected, though guiltless, to many of the inconveniencies and distresses which result from those laws. And many who are by nature, or from infancy, as it were imbued in the principles and spirit of slavery, naturally run into the same unrighteous practice, and so, especially after being taught better things, become more or less guilty of the deeds of their fathers or representatives, by doing the same things. So Adam, being the natural head of his posterity, by ordinary generation, hath imbued and initiated them all into the nature of iniquity, and they by doing the same deeds and others of the same nature, and so taking part with their father's iniquity, and especially after being informed that these things are wrong, became guilty with him ; *And so death passed upon all men for that all have sinned. Truly ye bear witness that ye allow the deeds of your fathers.* But as they who keep themselves clear of the practice and positive iniquity of slavery, being of the community where the evil obtains, may suffer many temporary evils which result from it, so the posterity of Adam who never committed actual sin, and are therefore not guilty, suffer some of the evil effects of his sin. "For until the law sin was in the world : but sin is not impu- "ted where there is no law. *Nevertheless, death reigned from Adam* "*to Moses, even over them that had not sinned after the similitude of* "*Adam's transgression.*" (Ro. 5. 13, 14.)

But this is not to prevent them from salvation by the gospel, for it is sent to save from the sin of Adam and all its branches, all those who believe and obey. "For as by one man's disobedience many "were made sinners, (disobeying in his nature and after his example ; *for that all have sinned.*) so by the obedience of one shall many

" be made righteous." (Even all those who obey as he did after his example and in his spirit; *For if any man have not the spirit of Christ he is none of his ; and He that doeth righteousness is righteous even as he is righteous :* on the very same principle.).

As for the more modern argument that as Levi paid tithes in Abraham, so Adam's posterity sinned in him, it utterly disannulls all charge of guilt against Adam's posterity ; (otherwise than as stated above ;) neither does it even prove or exemplify the nature of sin communicated from Adam to his posterity, much less any personal or real guilt. For it is evident that Levi did not actually or really pay tithes in Abraham, neither did Abraham's paying of tithes communicate any disposition to Levi to do the same, as Adam's transgression did, by giving iniquity the prevalence in nature, to his children. The apostle in showing the superiority of the priesthood of Christ, who was made priest after the order of Melchizedec, over that of Livi of the seed of Abraham, hath this language, which is evidently metaphorical. " And, *as I may so say*, Levi also who receiveth tithes, paid " tithes in Abraham. For he was yet in the loins of his father when " Melchizedec met him." (Heb. 7. 9, 10.) If therefore it be asked, " Must I believe that Levi paid tithes in the loins of Abraham, and " yet deny, that mankind rendered disobedience unto God in Adam " when he violated the law of God ?" It is easy to reply, Thou art not obliged to believe either the one or the other, because revelation hath taught neither ; unless by mankind be meant the first parents only, or by disobedience be meant the receiving of a sinful disposition in nature, as stated above.

It is nevertheless true, that as certainly as Adam's seed, had he kept covenant with God, as their proper father and head, would have inherited the blessing as their legal and proper inheritance, legally descending to them by their keeping the covenant of God with him, (for if the heirs violate the law or covenant of their father they forfeit their right of inheritance,) so certainly and equitably, when he broke the covenant, they lost the whole, together with him. For when the father, or representative in covenant, forfeits the right of inheritance, or barters it away, in his lifetime, the heirs are disinherited of course. Yet they are not guilty of their fathers deeds, unless they make them theirs by approving or doing the same. And when Adam fell, his posterity, in that character and standing, were put past recovery. No hope remained of their ever coming to the tree of life, unless by becoming the heirs of another covenant head, the children of another parentage. This parentage with the right of inheritance is found in good order and safe standing in Christ ; to whom lost men become united by faith, and keep covenant together with him, and by his grace, who hath kept it safely on their behalf. For as he hath kept the covenant without a flaw, the inheritance is secured to those who by faith enter into the same perfect law of liberty and continue therein ; and they become joint heirs with him, who are not of those who draw back to perdition, but of those who believe to the saving of the soul. For the just shall live by faith ; but if he

OF THE GOSPEL.

draw back my soul, saith God, shall have no pleasure in him. The gospel therefore remains in its full authority according to its proposals; which are to recover man from the ruin and evils of the fall; and these proposals are sanctioned by the authority of God, with full privilege for every one to believe and obey.

If then this privilege is sanctioned by the authority of God and the calls and invitations are given to every one, why may not, or why cannot any one believe? Can any good reason be given why any man shall not, or cannot, believe the testimony of the God of truth? Men can believe a man, if he come to them with a reasonable report, and why not believe God? Or rather how shall they disbelieve, who have already the persuasion, or faith, that God is a God of truth, and that the scriptures are true? No doubt, one principal source of difficulty on this subject, is the notion that faith is a direct and special gift or operation of God, whereby the soul is renovated and moulded into the divine nature, previously to the workings of faith or the man's obedience. Thus men look for the fruits of faith or the gospel, before they put it into operation by living according to Christ the true example, author and finisher of faith. Whereas it is the duty of every one who receives the knowledge of the truth, or testimony of God in the gospel, to put it into practice, according to the measure of his faith, and then expect the fruits with an increase of faith. But faith without obedience can neither sanctify nor justify, as shown in its place. "If we receive the witness [or Greek, testimony] of men "the testimony of God is greater: for this is the testimony of God "which he hath testified concerning his Son. He who believeth "hath the testimony in himself;(it hath entered into him by the report of the gospel, and he hath laid it up and put it to its proper use.) "he who believeth not God hath made him a liar, because he hath "not believed the testimony which God hath testified concerning his "Son." And very justly should he be charged with this sin who will not believe on the authority of God. "And this is the testimony (of God concerning his Son, to be believed and which whosoever doth not believe maketh God a liar,) that God hath given to us "eternal life: and this life is in his Son." (1. John 5. 9. &c) Thus fully is the authority of God declared for the faith and acceptance of every man, that he who disbelieveth it maketh God a liar. No good reason therefore can be given, why men may not believe, and believing walk in obedience and receive eternal life, wherever the gospel is to bear out this testimony.

But the stumbling blocks are to be removed. Another of which is, that to believe is a spiritual act, and therefore, men cannot believe to acceptance until they become in some measure spiritual. But if we attend to the apostle's language, and the place which faith fills in the work of salvation, this argument will be found to be improper. "Now faith is the substance [or confidence,] of things hoped for, the "evidence [or Greek, conviction, that is, the fruit of the evidence] things not seen. For by it the elders obtained a good report. "Through faith we understand that the worlds were framed by the "word of God; so that things which are seen were not made of things which do appear. By faith Abel offered to God a more excellent sacrafice than Cain; by which he obtained witness that he was righteous, God testifying of his gifts: and by it he, being dead, yet speaketh. [Greek, λεγεται, is spoken of."Heb. 11. 1—4-]Now it is observable, that it is the same faith by which we believe that God created the worlds by his word, and by which Abel offered to God an acceptable sacrafice, and obtained witness that he was righteous. And the same is to be said of all the rest of the champions of mighty and righteous works, whom the apostle enumerates: it was the same faith he first described, *the confidence of things hoped for, the conviction of things not seen*. Now, if that act of the mind by which we believe, that the worlds were framed by the word of God, can be the act of the natural man's mind, or if he can believe that God created the worlds by the word of his power, and yet be in a state of nature, it is then proved, that a natural man is capable of that faith which has Christ and his salvation as its object. Or if a natural man can believe that Abel offered a more excellent sacrafice than Cain, and obtained the testimony of God in his favor, so that he is spoken of after he is dead, (for by the faith of those who speak of him he is spoken of and not by his own faith only,) then also a natural man can believe, that is, be convinced, of the truth, that *God is and is the rewarder of them that diligently seek him*, and that God is revealed in Christ, and Christ in the gospel, for every man who will receive him. Faith, therefore, is no more a spiritual act than any other act of the mind; but is properly a physical act, or rather the effect of evidence on the mind, and hath nothing spiritual in it, farther than as its objects are spiritual; and the evidence of the truth of such spiritual objects is rational, adapted to the rational powers of the physical man, in his unrenewed state. Unless this statement be admitted, it is folly in the extreme, to preach the gospel to the world of mankind, who are wholly lying in the wicked one, and in nature, and require them to believe, and then charge with the sin of unbelief and of making God a lyar, those who do not believe; for the poor wretches have no other authority on which to believe, having nothing in them which is spiritual, nor ever can have until they actually believe and obey: they may then begin to know the truth and be made free. (Jno. 8. 30.

But the principle is abundantly justified in the scriptures; that the evidence of the gospel is adapted to the mind and capacity of the physical man to beget or produce faith in him, and therefore, that the unregenerate man is capable of believing in order to his justification and the receiving of the Spirit of Christ. " That he might be just and the justifier of him that believeth in Jesus." Here is faith before justification. " But to him that worketh not, but believeth on him that justifieth the ungodly, his faith is counted for righteousness." Here the ungodly is justified through faith; the ungodly, therefore, can and may believe, and thus be saved from his ungodliness. "There-" fore, being justified by faith, we have peace with God through " Lord Jesus Christ; by whom also we have access by faith into the

OF THE GOSPEL.

"grace wherein we stand." (Ro. 3. 26. 4. 5. and 5. 1, 2.) Thus faith every where precedes justification, and also our access to the grace of God wherein we stand; "For he that cometh to God must (first) "believe that he is." Again; "He that believeth on me, as the scripture hath said, out of his belly shall flow rivers of living water. (But "this spake he of the Spirit which they that believed on him should "receive.") "In whom ye also trusted, *after that ye heard the word* "*of truth*, the gospel of your salvation: in whom also, *after that ye* "*believed*, ye were sealed with that Holy Spirit of promise." (Jno. 7. 38. 39. Eph- 1. 13.) Thus faith is explicitly placed before receiving the Spirit of promise, or that Spirit which is promised in Christ to his people, and is the medium through which that Spirit is received; "That we might receive the promise of the Spirit through faith." (Gal. 3. 14.) Faith therefore, or believing, is no spiritual act; neither is there any thing in it which requires a man to be spiritual before he can believe: but it is the unquestionable privilege of all men who hear the gospel to believe and obey, that they may be saved.

People often object to the notion of men's believing of themselves; when they please, and the like. But such objections only show the ignorance and wilfulness of those who make them. We are not pleading for men to believe *of themselves*, though it be true that each one must believe *for himself*: another cannot believe for him. Neither are we pleading for any to believe out of due time; we only insist on the propriety, and necessity of their believing the gospel on the authority of God, when they hear it. I have before stated that motive comes to the man from without him, and I now state that evidence and authority for a man to believe the gospel are not of himself, they are from God, and sent to him by that gospel which is of God, that he may believe and be saved. "So then, faith "cometh by hearing, and hearing by the word of God," (Ro. 10. 17.) "And this is the word which by the gospel is preached to you," [1 Pet. 1. 25.] Thus men are required to believe, not on their own authority, but on the authority of the word of God, or the preaching of the gospel to them for their salvation. "For after that in the "wisdom of God the world by wisdom knew not God, it pleased God "by the foolishness of preaching to save them that believe." [1.Cor. 1. 21.]

Men cannot believe without evidence; those therefore who have not heard the gospel, neither had any opportunity of hearing it, are not expected to believe it: people are only required to observe and do the duties in the compass of their knowledge and power. "For to "whom much is given, of the same shall much be required; and to "whom little is given, of him shall little be required."[Luke 12. 28] And if the servant who knew not his Lord's will and did not perform, was beaten, it was only with few stripes, for his correction, that he might be stirred up to know his duty and to do it; for nothing short of knowing the will of God and doing it can ever amount to salvation. But where the gospel is preached men have no such excuse to plead, as not hearing; they may all hear, for the sound has gone forth; and it comes with such evidence as can be resisted by perverseness or inattention only, and such authority as authorises all and every one to know and believe. But amidst the clearest ministrations people may remain in a criminal degree of unbelief, as was the case with the Jews. They did not believe and yet were guilty in rejecting Christ, *Whom with wicked hands they crucified and slew.* They resisted the evidence which was spread before their senses; for it came accompanied by a doctrine in many things different from their law; and especially contrary to their traditions; but most of all contrary to their carnal nature, their pride and their lusts; this doctrine was of the necessity of denying self and bearing the cross, at which they stumbled. And their prejudices and perverse will ran so high, that they would not give the subject a fair trial. When Jesus had raised Lazarus, they perversely rolled the evidence away, saying, "What do we? for this " man doeth many miracles. If we let him thus alone all men will " believe on him"—" Then from that day forth they took counsel " together to put him to death." [John 11. 47. &c.] And soon after, " They consulted that they might put Lazarus also to death; because " that by reason of him many of the Jews went away and believed." [Jno. 12. 10,11.] And after Peter with John had healed the lame man at the temple gate, and the Jews had seen the effects of the faith of Christ in that instant, so clearly that they had no method to conceal it, they wilfully took methods to prevent the knowledge of it among the people, for, "They conferred among themselves, say- " ing, What shall we do to these men? for that indeed a notable " miracle hath been done by them is manifest to all them that " dwell in Jerusalem; and we cannot deny it. But, that it spread " no further among the people, let us straitly threaten them, that they " speak henceforth to no man in this name. And they called them, " and commanded them not to speak at all, nor teach in the name of " Jesus." [Act. 4. 15. &c.] By such ungenerous methods do men violate their own judgment, and evade the force of evidence. Many when they hear the gospel, are eagle-eyed enough to perceive the cross very soon, and keep out of the way, or ward off the conviction, or violate their own faith, just because the gospel leads to a life of self-denial and obedience to God, and affect to be uncertain whether it is the true gospel or not, when the real difficulty is their own unwillingness to bear the cross of Christ, against their own wills.

The gospel carries its own evidence with it; its terms and exhibitions being so open and manifest, the tidings are generous and fair, with sufficient authority for every man's faith. When I say, the gospel, I do not mean any thing and every thing which is called gospel among men. Nothing is worthy of that name except that which is evidently built on the revelation of God in Christ, who is the chief corner-stone—secures the unshaken confidence of eternal life to all without exception, who keep their union to it—and manifests in them all, the cross of Christ and his righteousness, visibly, to all men, so that all men can know them to be his disciples. That which presents

OF THE GOSPEL.

no cross against the carnal nature, leaving men to pursue their sensual appetites, without being plagued with the self-denying life of Jesus Christ, can readily be received as the gospel of Christ, with liberal faith, although it affords its subjects no additional certainty of eternal life. "I am come in my Father's name, and ye receive me "not: if another shall come in his own name, him ye will receive." (Jno. 5. 43.)

No doubt the term faith or believing is frequently used in the scriptures in a more extensive sense than here stated, as meaning the whole dispensation of the gospel, some special miraculous gift, (1 Cor. 12. 9.) the christian temper and power, or even the whole of the christian life. (1. Jno. 5. 1.) Faith also is a law, the law and rule of a christian's life. (Ro. 3. 27. and Cor. 9. 21.) And most of these senses and perhaps more, are included in that faith by which a man is finally justified, of which we will take some notice hereafter. But at present I have been speaking particularly of faith, as that operation by which a man first consents to the truth of the gospel, and closes in with the proposals on the authority of God. This may be weak at first and somewhat wavering; but still sufficient, though like a grain of mustard seed, to unite the man to the work of God and to his people, that he may increase and grow up into all things in Christ. *Him that is weak in the faith receive ye.*

This is faith in the strict and peculiar sense of the term. Conviction; or the consent of the mind to the truth of the gospel on proper evidence. This is that faith which embraces the calls and offers of God, to men for their salvation, by the gospel of Jesus Christ, and thereby opens the way for them to enter on the path of obedience and begin to receive all the graces of the spirit. This is that faith of which every man is capable who hears the testimony of the gospel opened, and will surely receive unless he neglect or repel the evidence. For every man hath power to believe, that is, he is capable of being convinced of the truth of the gospel, and of the method of salvation in Christ, on the testimony of God, contained in the gospel. But it will be objected that simply this consent of the mind to gospel truth is not sufficient for justification and salvation, for many are established in this truth in their mind who know nothing of justification, regeneration or salvation. True enough; neither any are justified, regenerated or saved simply by faith; obedience or a continuance in the word of God which they have heard and believed, are necessary. "Blessed are they who hear the word of God and "keep it." (Luk. 11. 28.) "Then said Jesus to those Jews who "believed on him, If ye continue in my word then are ye my disci- "ples indeed; and ye shall know the truth, and the truth shall make "you free." (Jno. 8. 31, 32.) They were not yet free, although they believed on him; neither did he intimate any need to receive any other kind of faith, or to hear any other word, all they needed was to continue in the use of what they had received, and they should know the truth by experimental acquaintance, and be made free.

CHAPTER VII.

Of justification by faith and obedience : and of imputation.

AS we are advancing into the discussion of the doctrine of justification ; it is expedient to advertise the reader, of the order and leading principles which are stated and supported ; that he may have his mind prepared for the reception of what is written, and may understand it with more ease. Justification is a subject of the utmost consequence in the life of a christian, and ought to be correctly understood. Justification is found in Christ alone ; the author [or first leader] and finisher [or perfecter] of faith ; who first introduced the faith of the gospel, first put it into practice, and first received the end of faith ; the crown of righteousness. The foundation work of justification is from God alone, in the gift of his Son. This is a work of the grace of God, absolutely free, an emination of his own eminently free love ; unmoved by any goodness or worthiness, any request or desire in mankind towards God, or any thing exterior to himself, only that he fixed it on the fallen race who were in need. Accordingly as God freely gave his Son to be our Redeemer, and the foundation of our justification, he also gave with him, the gospel of salvation, to be preached to all nations for their faith and obedience. " *By whom we have received grace and apostleship, for the obedience of faith, among all nations, in the behalf of his name.*" " He that " spared not his own Son, but delivered him up for us all, how shall " he not with him also freely give us all things?" (Ro. 1. 5. Greek. and 8. 32.)

The first and radical ground, therefore, is Jesus Christ the crucified man, as he is exhibited in the gospel : He is the foundation which God hath laid in Zion. " Wherefore also it is contained in " the scripture, Behold, I lay in Zion a chief corner-stone, elect, pre- " cious ; and he that believeth on him shall not be confounded." " For I determined not to know any thing among you, save Jesus " Christ and him crucified," as the proper foundation of their faith, who were to be crucified with him. And again ; " Who hath bewitched you, that ye should not obey the truth, before whose eyes Jesus Christ hath been evidently set forth crucified among you?" (1 Pet. 2. 6. 1. Cor. 2. 2 Gal. 4. 1.) The second or mediate ground of justification is faith in Christ, or in God and in his Son. " Being there- " fore justified by faith, we have peace with God, through our Lord " Jesus Christ." " But without faith it is impossible to please him ; " for he that cometh to God must believe that he is, and that he is the " rewarder of them that diligently seek him." Therefore thirdly. The proximate and finishing ground, or cause, of justification, as the fruit of the two former, in perfection, is obedience. Obedience is the crowning point in justification, and in the whole of salvation. And the faith of Christians is that which worketh by love, and by works

is made perfect. "*Who hath bewitched you, that ye should not obey
" the truth ?" And the intention of the gospel, from first to last, is
to bring mankind to obedience, *even the obedience of faith ;* as will be
opened in the sequel. Thus the work of the gospel for our salvation is built in the free
grace of God which runs through the whole plan from first to last,
and is the grand foundation, and support of the whole building.
Had he not given his son, we could never have believed on him, and
had we not believed we could never have obeyed. Accordingly, the
ground of our justification is threefold. First ; Christ the gift of
God ; secondly ; our own faith, or believing in him ; and thirdly ;
our own correct obedience to that faith. For notwithstanding all
that God hath done for our salvation, our benefit depends finally on
the reception we give the Saviour whom he hath provided and the
obedience which we yield to him. To the obedient and none else ;
to them who by patient continuance in well-doing, seek for glory
and honor and immortality, God will render eternal life. Therefore,
" Let us lay aside every weight, and the sin which doth so easily be-
" set us, and let us run with patience the race that is set before us,
" looking to Jesus [τον της πιςεως αρχηγον και τελειωτην] the first
" leader and perfecter of faith ;" both his and ours.

THAT JUSTIFICATION and final salvation are attained by the
faith of the gospel of Christ, is acknowledged by those who bear the
name of Christ. Accordingly we read of being justified by faith and
through faith. " Seeing it is one God who shall justify the circum-
" cission by faith, and the uncircumcission through faith." (Ro. 3.
30.) But it is also as certain that justification and salvation are not
attained simply by believing, or by faith only. For although faith is
a *sine qua non* in the terms of our acceptance with God, for " With-
" out faith it is impossible to please him ;" yet it is certain that without obedience also, it is impossible to please him, accordingly we
may see the grounds of our justification in the words of inspiration
from God. " Who will render to every man according to his deeds ;
" to them who by patient continuing in well-doing, seek for glory and
" honor and immortality, eternal life ; but to them that are conten-
" tious, and do not obey the truth but obey unrighteousness, indig-
" nation and wrath, tribulation and anguish, upon every soul of man
" that doeth evil ; of the Jew first, and also of the Gentile : but glory,
" honor and peace to every man that worketh good ; to the Jew first
" and also to the Gentile : for there is no respect of persons with
" God." [Ro. 2. 6, 11.] "But to do good and to communicate for-
" get not ; for with such sacrifices God is well pleased." [Heb. 13.16.]
" Not every one who saith unto me, Lord, Lord shall enter into the
" kingdom of heaven ; but he that doeth the will of my Father who
" is in heaven." [Matt. 7. 21.] " And being made perfect, he be-
" came the author of eternal salvation to all them that obey him."
[Heb. 5. 9.] " If ye know these things happy are ye if ye do them."
" If ye keep my commandments ye shall abide in my love ; even as
" I have kept my Father's commandments and abide in his love."

OF JUSTIFICATION

[Jno. 13. 17. and 15. 10.] " And whatsoever we ask we receive of " him, because we keep his commandments, and do those things " which are pleasing in his sight." [1. Jno. 3. 22.] " Blessed are " they that do his commandments, that they may have right to the " tree of life, and may enter in through the gates into the city." [Rev. 22. 14.]

These are a few out of many passages of scriptures which show in plain terms that our acceptance with God depends as much on obedience as faith, not to say much more, because there may be faith without obedience, but not obedience without faith. Therefore all who have obedience are justified; but not any who have faith without obedience. And after all which the apostle hath written of the necessity of faith, and of being justified by faith, it is remarkable that he hath never said, *By faith alone.* But the apostle James hath brought the matter out in'plain terms ; that justification *by faith without works* is altogether a false notion, and counts *faith without works* no more towards justification than the body without the spirit towards a living man. As therefore the spirit is the substance and source of life to the man, so is obedience, or works, the true source and ground of justification. The apostle's words are so clear and argumentative that they appear sufficient to satisfy and convince any unbiased mind. " What doth it profit, my brethren, though a man say he hath faith, " and have not works ? can faith save him ? If a brother or sister be " naked and destitute of daily food, and one of you say unto them, " Depart in peace, be ye warmed and filled ; notwithstanding ye give " them not those things which are needful to the body, what doth it " profit ? Even so faith, if it hath not works, is dead, being alone. " Yea a man may say, Thou hast faith and I have works : show me " thy faith *without thy works,*" If thou canst ; or as the generality of Greek copies read. " Show me thy faith *by thy works,*" if thou hast any, for no evidence short of this will do, " and I will show thee " my faith *by my works.* Thou believest that there is one God; thou " doest well: the devils also believe and tremble. But wilt thou know, " O vain man ! that faith (if thou hast it,) without works is dead? " Was not Abraham our father *justified by works,* when he had of- " fered Isaac his son upon the altar ? Seest thou how *faith wrought* " *with his works, and by works was faith made perfect ?* And the " scripture was fulfilled, which saith, Abraham believed God, and it " was imputed to him for righteousness : and he was called the " friend of God. Ye see then how that by works a man is justified, " and not by faith only. Likewise also ; was not Rahab the harlot " justified by works, when she had received the messengers, and had " sent them out another way ? For as the body without the spirit *is* " *dead, so faith without works is dead also.*"

It has been argued that the justification of which James speaks, is only the evidence, or justification of a man's faith. But the Spirit by the apostle saith, it is the man who is justified ; and that is more to those who are governed by revelation, than the sayings of a thousand to the contrary. And however true, which is not to be disputed,

AND IMPUTATION.

that Abraham was justified by faith; it is so far from being by faith alone, that all things pertaining to the whole matter, as well as the apostle's testimony, show, that without obedience he had not received a particle of justification. Touching the offering of his son Isaac, it is plain enough, that his justification before God, and his securing the blessing to himself and his posterity, rested in his obedience; as it is written; " For now I know that thou fearest God, seeing thou " hast not withheld thy son, thine only son, from me." " By myself " have I sworn, saith the Lord, that because thou hast done this thing " and hast not withheld thy son, thine only son; that in blessing I " will bless thee, and in multiplying I will multiply thy seed as the " stars of heaven, and as the sand which is upon the sea shore ; and " thy seed shall possess the gate of his enemies : and in thy seed " shall all the nations of the earth be blessed; *because thou hast* " *obeyed my voice.*" (Gen. 22. 12, &c.) And in this act of obedience according to the words of James as quoted above, " The scrip- " ture was fulfilled which saith, *Abraham believed God and it was* " *imputed to him for righteousness*, and he was called the friend of " God." But all this will not disannul or pervert the doctrine that Abraham was justified by faith, for his faith was the source and spring of his obedience, and without believing he had not obeyed. As it is again written ; " By faith Abraham, when he was tried, of- " fered up Isaac ; and he that had received the promises offered up " his only begotten son, of whom it was said, That in Isaac shall thy " seed be called : accounting that God was able to raise him up, " even from the dead." (Heb. 11. 17, &c.) But Abraham was not justified *by faith without obedience* ; for he was justified by works, while his faith wrought by works, and by works was faith made perfect. Obedience therefore, even the obedience of faith, is the proximate, finishing and perfecting cause of every man's justification.

And with respect to the promise of a seed by Sarah, of which it is said, " Abraham believed God and it was counted to him for right- " eousness," (Ro. 4. 3.) it is to be observed he did all that was for him to do in the case, and when he was told to do more he obeyed. He in the first instance offered a variety of animals in sacrifice, as God bade him, and afterwards when the promise was renewed, at the commandment of God, he circumcised himself and all the males in his house. And that was the time of which the apostle speaks with so much energy of Abraham's faith, that " Being not weak in " faith, he considered not his own body now dead, when he was about " an hundred years old, [for at the time of the first promise he was " not of that age] neither yet the deadness of Sara's womb: he stag- " gered not at the promise of God, through unbelief; but was strong " in the faith, giving glory to God ; and being fully persuaded that " what he had promised he was able also to perform. And there- " fore it was imputed to him for righteousness." [v. 19. 22.] This was that faith which was accompanied with such manifest fruits of obedience as stated above. To believe God is to do well, and unquestionably a righteous matter, and justly imputed for righteousness, when the spirit of obedience is included, as shown in its place, but without obedience justification can never be perfected in any one. The known truth is that Abraham was a righteous man in his day and time, before any of these things were said of him. He believed God and obeyed him from the time that God called him saying, " Get thee out of thy country, and from thy kindred, and from " thy father's house ; for by faith Abraham, when he was called to go " out into a place which he should after receive for an inheritance, " *obeyed ;* and he went out not knowing whether he went," [Gen. 12. 1. Heb. 11. 8.] Thus Abraham obeyed and forsook his father's house, for the promise of God which was far off : a work which few in our days are willing to do for the substance when it has actually come. No wonder then that such a man's faith was imputed to him for righteousness, when it was so firm and always accompanied with obedience. It was therefore imputed to him for righteousness, to serve the purpose in his day, until the day of perfect righteousness should come.

" But if Abraham were justified by works he hath whereof to glo-" ry, but not before God." And though he hath not whereof to glory before God, that is not to prevent him from having the justification and approbation of his own conscience, and that too, on such terms as God acknowledges and approves. For if our heart condemn us not, then have we confidence towards God ; even though we have no cause of boasting before him, we may be justified and accepted. Or will God reject a man and condemn him for doing his duty ? "Now to him that worketh is the reward not reckoned of grace, "but of debt." This is the common order of works and rewards among men. Besides ; no work of men, either professed or performed, engaged God to shew mercy to the fallen race of men, either to Abraham as the father of the faithful, or to any of his children. All this is of his free grace, according to his own nature of love. " Not by " works of righteousness which we have done, but according to his " mercy he saved us, by the washing of regeneration, and renewing " of the Holy Ghost." [Tit. 3. 5.] But query ; Is the apostle to be understood that the Jews and others before them, who did the works which God commanded them, earned a reward of debt, or that God owed them any thing for their services ? Or did they not, under the whole dispensation of the law, receive every blessing by promise ? For if God gave the inheritance to Abraham by promise, as the apostle asserts, [Gal. 3. 18.] his family must have received it by the same, as far as they had it at all. Accordingly they pleaded from time to time, the promise of God made to their father Abraham. " But to " him that worketh not, but believeth on him that justifieth the un-" godly, his faith is counted for righteousness." To him that worketh not. Query : Is it to him who yields not obedience to the truths which he believes, that his faith is counted for righteousness ? or to him who has the faith of his father Abraham and walks in the steps of that faith, which always led him to the most punctual obedience ? or in other words, as it now pertains to the gospel, who has the faith of Jesus Christ, who always did the things which pleased the Father? For " It was not written for his sake alone, that it was imputed to " him; but for us also, to whom it shall be imputed, if we believe " on him that raised up Jesus our Lord from the dead."

What works then were these which are excluded from justification? The ceremonial works of the Mosaic law, and all such; which are dead works, beggarly elements, and have no tendency to justify the spirit or to purify the conscience. " For it is not possible that " the blood of bulls and of goats should take away sins."(Heb. 10.4.) But when David also describeth the blessedness of the man to whom the Lord will not impute sin, he includes the real character of the man, saying, " Blessed is the man to whom the Lord imputeth not " iniquity, and in whose spirit there is no guile." (Psa. 32. 2.) It is therefore evident that David knew nothing of justification without obedience, as all his writings show; and it is also certain that Paul was too well acquainted with the spirit of David to apprehend that he expected any such matter; but when he would cut off the Jewish christians at Rome, and elsewhere, from their rooted attachment to their legal works, he wisely omitted the honesty of the man's spirit, or his obedient character, which in David's day was founded in ceremonial observations, and only mentions his sins being covered and not imputed. " Even as David also discribeth the blessedness of the " man to whom God imputeth righteousness without works, saying, " Blessed are they whose iniquities are forgiven, and whose sins are " covered. Blessed is the man to whom the Lord will not impute " sin." Now David had not named works as a part of the character which he discribed, but the integrity of the spirit. The man then to whom iniquity is not imputed, when viewed in his whole character, is he who has none; the sins which he has heretofore committed being forgiven when covered according to the order of the dispensation in which he lives; which was done under the law by confessing and making a sin-offering in the appointed order, and in the gospel by confessing, forsaking and presenting the whole man a living sacrifice to God, being baptized into the death of Christ, to die to sin and live to God after his example.

And whenever the apostle excludes works from any part in justification, or the works of the law, as expressly named in different places, it is sufficiently clear that he has respect to those ceremonial observances, and not to any moral duty, or any act of obedience required in the gopel dispensation; for as before shown, these have their full weight in our acceptance with God. But there is no principle on which the spirit and practice of obedience to the law of God, can be excluded from our justification, without overturning the doctrine of Christ and his apostles. For Christ came not to distroy the law or the prophets, but to fulfil; and the true righteousness of every christian, is the righteousness of the law fulfilled in him, in obedience to the faith, or law of Christ. So that, although, as Christ Jesus fulfilled the ceremonial observances of the law, he disannulled them, as that which is old and ready to vanish away, he kept the law in the spirit and substance, in a manner which could not have been effected by the old dispensation, and thus became, in truth, the end of the law for righteousness to those who believe in him. " There " is therefore now no condemnation to them who are in Christ Jesus, " who walk not after the flesh but after the Spirit. For the law of " the Spirit of life in Christ Jesus hath made me free from the law " of sin and death : for God; sending his own Son in the likeness of " sinful flesh, and on account of sin [to do it away, or as a sin-offering, if any prefer that reading ; for in that also he was our example, and so condemned sin in the flesh? that which was impossible for the " law [to do,] in that it was weak through the flesh, *that the right-* " *eousness of the law might be fulfilled in us who walk not after the* " *flesh but after the spirit.*" (Ro. 8. 1, 5.) Notwithstanding therefore, that the external form of the administration of the law may be changed, as divine wisdom hath seen it best, the true spirit of the law and its fulfilment remain for christians as much as for any people, and never were truly kept by any until Christ came. " Do we " then make void the law through faith ? God forbid : yea, we es-" tablish the law." (Ro. 3. 31.) And how is the law established, but by maintaining and doing the things contained in it, with unshaken faith in them and obedience to them ? or by finding and keeping that substance of which the old law was a shadow ?

" Thou shalt love the Lord thy God with all thy heart, and with " all thy soul, and with all thy mind. This is the first and great " commandment. And the second is like unto it, Thou shalt love " thy neighbour as thy self. On these two commandments hang all " the law and the prophets." [Matt. 22. 37, 40.] " For he that lov-" eth another hath fulfilled the law. For this, Thou shalt not com-" mit adultery, Thou shalt not kill, Thou shalt not steal, Thou shalt " not bear false witness, Thou shalt not covet ; and if there be any " other commandment it is briefly comprehended in this saying, " namely, Thou shalt love thy neighbour as thy self. Love worketh " no ill to his neighbour : therefore love is the fulfilling of the law." [Ro. 13. 8. &c.] " For all the law is fulfilled in one word, even in " this, Thou shalt love thy neighbour as thy self." [Gal. 5. 15.] Now " the end of the commandment is charity, out of a pure heart, and of " a good conscience, and of faith unfeigned," [Tim. 1. 5.] " And " whatsoever we ask we receive of him, because we keep his com-" mandments, and do those things which are pleasing in his sight. " And this is his commandment, That we should believe on the name " of his Son Jesus Christ, and love one another as he gave us com-" mandments." [1. Jno. 3. 22, 23.] These scriptures are sufficient to show that the true spirit and obedience of the law remain unalterable, and that when the apostle excluded the law and the works of the law from any part in our justification and salvation ; he intends the external, or ceremonial law, of meats and drinks and divers washings and carnal ordinances [or justifications of the flesh.] " Therefore by " the deeds of the law there shall no flesh be justified in his sight ; " for by the law is the knowledge of sin," and again, " Therefore we

AND IMPUTATION.

"conclude that a man is justified by faith without the deeds of the "law." And, as if to show that he intended precisely that law which was a separating wall between the Jews and Gentiles, he adds; " Is " he the God of the Jews only? is he not also of the Gentiles? Yes, " of the Gentiles also: seeing it is one God who shall justify the cir- " cumcission by faith and the uncircumcission through faith. Do " we then make void the law through faith? God forbid: Yea, we " establish the law." Those ceremonies indeed could not take away sin, " Which were a shadow of things to come; but the body [or " substance,] is of Christ." (see Ro. 3. 20, 28, to 31. Col. 2. 17.) But after all the great change which was made, which was indeed great, from the shadow to the substance, christians are not left without law, even the same eternal law of love; " Being not without law " to God but under the law to Christ. (1. Cor. 9. 21.) " Now where " no law is there is no transgression; for sin is the transgression of the " law;" if therefore, the law doth not remain in full force, after the abolishing of the Jewish ritual, no sin could be committed. But it is true of those who have received the christian faith as well as others that, " Whosoever committeth sin transgresseth also the law; for " sin is the transgression of the law." (Jno. 3. 4.) But the necessity of a change from the shadow to the substance was indispensable; for as it then was in the hands of the Levitical priesthood, it made nothing perfect, there was by it no salvation, and the best they could do was to look forward to something to come, depending on the promises. For had not this been the case there had been no need for Christ to have come in another order of priesthood; as saith the apostle, " If therefore perfection were by the Levitical priesthood (for " under it the people received the law,) what further need was there " that another priest should arise after the order of Melchisedec, and " not be called after the order of Aaron? For the priesthood being " changed [μετατιθεμενης, transposed] there is made of necessity a " change [μετατιθησις, transposition] also in [of] the law." (Heb. 7. 11, 12.) Thus the law was transfered from Aaron to Jesus Christ; and in him the substance appears, the law is perfectly kept and the promises are fulfilled, and they who were excluded from salvation and the inheritance of the promise for the time being, may come forward and receive the promise. For the law gave no inheritance; although it bore witness to the promise which was made long before, and the righteousness of God for justification, and served as a shadow of good things until the substance should come, even Christ in whom the promise is fulfilled to all who believe in him with obedience, who walk not after the flesh but after the Spirit. " For if the " inheritance be of the law, it is no more of promise: but God gave " it to Abraham by promise. Wherefore then serveth the law? it " was added because of transgressions, till the seed should come to " whom the promise was made; and it was ordained by angels in the " hand of a Mediator. Now a Mediator is not a Mediator of one; " but God is one. Is the law then against the promises of God. " God forbid: for if there had been a law given which could have " given life, verily righteousness should have been by the law. But

"the scripture hath concluded all under sin, that the promise by faith
"of Jesus Christ might be given to them that believed. But before
"faith came we were kept under the law, shut up to the faith which
"should afterwards be revealed. Wherefore the law was our school-
"master pointing to Christ, that we might be justified by faith.
"But after that faith is come we are no longer under a school-mas-
"ter. For ye are all the children of God by faith in Christ Jesus."
"But now without the law, the righteousness of God is manifested,
"being witnessed by the law and the prophets; even the righteousness
"of God through the faith of Jesus Christ, unto all and upon all
"them that believe." (Gal. 3. 18, 26. Ro. 3. 21, 22.)

If therefore we find the apostle speaking of " Knowing that a man
"is not justified by the works of the law, but by [or Greek, except
"through] the faith of Jesus Christ;" (Gal. 2. 16.) we may readily
understand what those rejected works are, and what is that faith of
Christ through which a man is justified; that which acknowledges
Christ Jesus as an example and a leader, and follows him, yielding
punctual obedience to him in all things, and finds justification to the
soul in so doing; not in yielding obedience to a law of ceremonial
and carnal commandments which have no part in Christ, but the law
of faith, the law of the spirit of life in Christ Jesus, and in walking
not after the flesh, but after the spirit.

From this view of matters we may learn what is to become of the
doctrine of imputation, or the justification of one by the righteousness of another. It is indeed remarkable that such a multitude of
people should so strenuously adhere to such a doctrine as that of the
righteousness of Christ being imputed to them for their justification,
when no such fact is proved, or even once named, in the scriptures
which they claim as the rule of their faith and practice. And though
it is never once named, in the revelation of God, they maintain that
the only ground of any man's justification and acceptance with God,
is the righteousness of Christ imputed to him. But they say it is a
fair and necessary consequence of what the scriptures plainly teach.
Although the phrase, *righteousness of Christ*, is not found at all in
the scriptures, I have no objection against the phrase, provided it be
understood and used according to the law of the faith of Christ. But
it must appear very remarkable that God should build, or rather
be said to build so great a work as the justification of all his people,
on a ground which he hath never once explicitly taught, or even
named.

But it is said the righteousness of God is named, that Christ is
God, and that which is imputed to those who believe, for their justification, is *the righteousness of God by faith in Jesus Christ*. I have
no objection to offer against the righteousness of God being the
righteousness of Christ, and also being the righteousness of his people, by which they are justified. But unhappily for that cause, the
righteousness of God is never in revelation, said to be imputed to any
man or any order of people, for their justification, or for any thing
else. And on what principle can any man be benefited by the right-

eousness of Christ, unless he possess it in reality and not by imputation, and then the character will appear in proper colors according to the teaching of the beloved apostle John, (1. Epist. 3.7.) " He " that doeth righteousness is righteous, even as he is righteous :" on the very same principle. And when Paul speaks of the righteousness of God without the law, being manifested, which was witnessed by the law and the prophets, even the righteousness of God by faith in Jesus Christ, it is to, and upon all them that believe; (Ro. 3. 21, 22.) it is shown or manifested to them and seen upon them. Now what righteousness can be seen or manifested upon believers? the imputed righteousness of Christ, or their own obedience? Some may say it is their own obedience as a proof of the imputed righteousness of Christ. But how is this to be proved? the apostle saith it is the righteousness of God, through the faith of Jesus Christ, the very same righteousness manifested to them and upon them all. The natural construction is, that having received the faith of Christ they obeyed as he did. And what is the righteousness which was witnessed by the law and the prophets? It is said to be by faith; and no doubt; as one of the prophets hath it, that "The just shall live " by faith," and he is truly a just man who hath a good faith and obeyeth it. He shall live. But the righteousness witnessed by the law and the prophets was also by obedience, and abundantly more so, as those may see who consult them.

For the solitary text to be found in the prophets so emphatically used by the apostle, cannot support the doctrine of life or justification by faith without obedience, or by the righteousness of Christ imputed. It is the just man who lives by his faith; not the unjust, he disobeys and makes shipwreck. But the just man lives by his faith, not holding it as an occult principle, but as the moving spring to his obedience, as the farmer or mechanic lives by his art, by occupying it. He is faithful, stable and true. This is all contained in the Hebrew word [אמונתו] used by the prophet and not excluded from that of the apostle, and is all of the nature of the christian faith.

But the doctrine of justification by the righteousness of Christ imputed to believers is maintained, on principles which are counted sufficient to support it. Such as, That he is our surety to God. That in that character he paid to God for us the debt which we owed—satisfied divine justice for our offences—suffered the penalty of the law which we had incurred, in his own person and in our room, and the like.

This subject has been so abundantly treated on for ages, in its different branches, that it would not comport with the design or limits of the present work to notice the half of what hath been said, or of the arguments used on each side of the question. I intend to pay some attention to the principal grounds on which the doctrine is supported, to show in as plain language as possible that they will not stand. That Christ sustains the glorious character of Redeemer and Mediator between God and man is not to be disputed, and that he is the true and only medium of access to the Father is also true. But that he was our surety to God, to pay in our room that debt in which we had failed, so as to release us from the payment, is quite another matter, unsupported in the scriptures. Jesus is once called the surety of a better testament (Heb. 7. 22.) and this he was in the character of Mediator. Now let us inquire, in a covenant, testament or any instrument of promise or obligation, wherein a surety is advisable: Who gives the surety and for whose satisfaction and safety is he given? Doth the obligor give the surety to the obligee, for his safety and satisfaction? or doth the obligee to the obligor? Not the obligee to the obligor, but the obligor to the obligee, or the testator to the legatee. Thus a man who executes a bond furnishes security that he will perform the obligation, or contents of that bond. Now the question is, Who is the author of that better testament, or covenant? God or man? If man be the author and Jesus the Mediator or security, between the two, no doubt but he is man's surety to God, a sponsor to God on man's behalf, that man will perform what he hath therein promised. But the new and better covenant did not originate in man, God is the author, of his own free grace; not of works lest any man should boast. If then God is the author of that better covenant or testament; and he hath therein made promise to do certain things for man, God is the obligor; consequently he gave the security, and Jesus in the character of Mediator, is God's surety to man, that God will perform what he hath promised. And to this agree the words of the apostle,(Ro. 15. 8.) "Now I say, that Jesus Christ was a minister of the circumcission for the truth of God, to confirm the promises made to the fathers." And in every other character which he sustains, pertaining to the office of Mediator, he is given of God to the people. Thus " Behold, I have given him a witness to the people, a leader and a " commander to the people." (49. 8.) " Whom God hath set forth " a mercy seat, through faith in his blood, to declare his righteous-"ness." (Ro. 3. 25.) Thus by this plain and familiar statement, it is evident, that Jesus Christ hath not at all done what is so often ascribed to him in the character of surety of the better testament. And if we consider Christ as the advocate with the Father; whether we use the word ADVOCATE, from the latin word *advoco*, to call to, or retain the greek word PARACLETE, from παραχαλεω [paracaleo] to exhort, or comfort, it amounts to the same thing, he is given of God to the people to exhort, call and encourage them to come to God, in full confidence of his being as good as he hath promised. Thus he is a mediator between God and man, an advocate with the Father, calling them to come to God, and an exhorter and comforter with the people, encouraging them to come, and showing them that the way is open, and making intercession for them. " Now the Lord is that " spirit; and where the spirit of the Lord is there is, liberty." " Like- " wise the spirit also helpeth our infirmities; for we know not what " we should pray for as we ought; but the spirit itself maketh inter- " cession for us with groanings which cannot be uttered. And he " that searcheth the hearts knoweth what is the mind of the spirit,

AND IMPUTATION.

" because he maketh intercession for the saints according to God," (2Cor. 3. 17. Ro. 8 25, 27.) and answerable to the order of his work. For Christ to have paid to God in our room the debt which we owed to him, or to his law, so as to release us from paying the same, would have been a poor business for us, as well as a poor errand into the world, for him. To have released us from the obligation and duty, and consequently to have deprived us of the privilege of loving God and serving him. For we have before proved that love is the fulfilling of the whole law.

As for satisfying divine justice for our offences and paying the penalty of the divine law, we read of no such matters in the holy scriptures, we are therefore under no obligation from that quarter to believe them. We read of satisfaction in one part of those scriptures which speak of Christ and his sufferings and works; but it is not relating to any satisfaction made by him to God in our room, but to the satisfaction which he would take in seeing the fruit of his own labors. " He shall see of the travail of his soul and shall be satisfied." (Isa. 53. 10.) What Jesus Christ did for us, on our behalf, and for our salvation, he did on quite another principle than to pay our debt, or to suffer the penalty of divine law, or to satisfy divine justice in our room, or to appease an angry God or offended justice, or the like, (for these all mean one thing,) to release us from any obligation, by vicarious sufferings or proxy payment.

For what purpose then did Christ come into the world, and do and suffer all that he did? This is an important question, and worthy of a sober reply. It comprehends the whole of that relation which Christ bears to God and to men as Mediator between them both. The following particulars are proposed to give satisfactory information on this subject

He came to reveal the Father to men. " No man hath seen God " at any time; the only begotten Son, who is in the bosom of the " Father, he hath revealed him." (Jno. 1. 18.) " He that hath seen me hath seen the Father." (14. 9.) The true knowledge of God was not with men, but he is revealed in Christ, Who is *the brightness of his glory and the character* [the express image] *of his existence.* (Heb. 1. 2.) By this revelation, men are taught what God is, and how far they are fallen from their original rectitude; for as man was created in the image of God and to be the glory of God, and had fallen by sin, God sent another, a second or a new man, in his own image *more deeply expressed*, to be the beginning of a new creation, in whom to recover man from his fall and restore him to favor and fellowship in a more happy condition than at the first.

He came to open *the new and living* way; a way before unknown, and containing in it true and eternal life, being infinitely preferable to the ministration of death and condemnation which was before. " But if the ministration of death, written and engraven in " stones, was glorious, so that the children of Israel could not sted- " fastly behold the face of Moses for the glory of his countenance; " which glory was to be done away; how shall not the ministration "of the Spirit be rather glorious? for if the ministration of condemnation be glory, much more doth the ministration of righteousness exceed in glory." (2 Cor. 3, 7, 8, 9.) "Having therefore, brethren, boldness to enter into the holiest by the blood of Jesus, *by a new and living way*, which he hath consecrated for us through the vail, that is to say, his flesh, and having an high priest over the house of God, let us draw near with a true heart, in full assurance of faith." (Heb. 10. 19, &c.)

And as he came to open the new and living way, he also came to be our example, that we should walk in his steps. "But if, when ye do well, and suffer for it, ye take it patiently, this is acceptable with God. For even hereunto were ye called? because Christ also suffered for us, leaving us an example that ye should follow his steps." (1 Pet. 2, 20, 21.) "If any man will come after me, let him deny himself, and take up his cross daily, and follow me." "And he that doth not take up his cross and follow after me, is not worthy of me." (Luk. 9. 23. Matt. 10. 38.) Thus he is our forerunner, the author and finisher of our faith, the first who introduced it into the world, and the first who perfected it by obedience. For as the faith of Abraham was made perfect by works, so is also the faith of Jesus Christ made perfect in obedience; as well as that of all christians, who are called to "Lay aside every weight, and the sin which doth so easily beset us, and run with patience the race which is set before us, looking to Jesus the author and finisher of faith; who for the joy that was set before him, endured the cross, despising the shame, and is set down at the right hand of the throne of God." (Heb. 12. 12.) Thus for our benefit he came to set us the example of denying self and doing the will of God. "Him that cometh to me I will in no wise cast out. For I came down from heaven, not to do mine own will, but the will of him that sent me." (Jno. 6. 37, 38.)

He came into the world that men might be saved and have eternal life through him. "For the Son of man is come to seek and to save that which is lost." "For God so loved the world, that he gave his only begotten Son, that whosoever believeth in him should not perish, but have everlasting life. For God sent not his Son into the world to condemn the world; but that the world through him might be saved." (Luk. 19. 10. Jno. 3. 16, 17.)

He came to reconcile the world to God, by revealing God to men and showing them the terms of reconciliation, to wit, "That God was in Christ reconciling the world to himself, not imputing their trespasses unto them." (2 Cor. 5. 19.) This is the subject in relation to which there has been so much darkness in the world of professors, so much error, and much contention, supposing that God in Christ, or through him, was reconciled to the world, contrary to the language of the scripture, instead of the world being reconciled to him; which would mean, if any thing, either that God had through Christ become an approver of man's ways, corrupt and sinful as they are, or else, that God had been so angry at sin and sinners as to put him cut of his proper element, and make him unwilling to receive the returning sinner until he had spent his vengeance on the sinner or his substitute; which having done on Jesus Christ, he becomes calm and can be approached by a returning penitent, whom he now receives with the utmost complacency. But these things are incompatible with the perfections of God, and not worthy to be imputed to him. The scripture is plain enough that men through Christ are reconciled to God, and are then at peace with him; and that establishes peace between the God of peace and men of peace.

The same is true of the word *atonement*, which has commonly been understood as applied to God, the effect of a pacifying satisfaction, to appease his anger, when the scripture so expressly declares that *we have received it*, and also shows that atonement is the same as reconciliation. " For if, when we were enemies, we were recon-
" ciled to God by the death of his Son; much more, being *reconciled*,
" we shall be saved by his life. And not only so, but we also joy in
" God through our Lord Jesus Christ, by whom *we have now re-*
" *ceived the atonement* or *reconciliation*." (Ro. 5. 10, 11.) This connection is a testimony for the English reader, that *the atonement* here said to be received is the same as *reconciliation*, that is, the effect or fruit of the death of Christ, or being reconciled to God, as mentioned in the former clauses. The Greek word also here rendered *atonement* is properly rendered by *reconciliation*. (Ro. 5. 10, 11.) And by whichever word it be rendered, it is evidently that which must take place in the creature, for God is unchangeably the same. And that change, or reconciliation, must also be in reality; not by imputing the righteousness of another; the scriptures make no mention of any such thing in the case. (See B. W. Stone's Letters on Atonement.)

He came to be the end of the law for righteousness to those who believe in him. That is, to put an end to the Mosaic law, by fulfilling it in himself and showing the people how to be righteous without it, by believing in him, confessing him, and doing the will of God as he did, and thus becoming their sacrifice and their righteousness, as it is written, " And this is the name whereby he shall be called The
" Lord our righteousness." (Jer. 23. 6.) " For Christ is the
" end of the law for righteousness to every one that believeth. For
" Moses describeth the righteousness which is of the law, that the
" man who doeth those things shall live by them. But the righteous-
" ness which is of faith speaketh on this wise—That if thou shalt con-
" fess with thy mouth the Lord Jesus, and shalt believe in thine heart
" that God hath raised him from the dead, thou shalt be saved." (Ro. 10. 4. 5, 9.) Thus Christ is the end of the law for righteousness to those who believe in him and confess him. " But now without the law
" (according to the order of the Greek text,) the righteousness of
" God is manifested, being witnessed [or more properly testified] by
" the law and the prophets; even the righteousness of God by the
" faith of Jesus Christ, unto all and upon all them that believe." (Ro 3. 21, 22.) And that he is the end of the law for righteousness to

those who believe, not merely by offering himself a sacrifice, or sin-offering to God in their room, but by doing the will of God as it ought to be done and so becoming an example and establishing that which should supersede the law, is evident from very pointed language of the apostle, where he speaks particularly on that subject, and quotes the words of David in the fortieth psalm, with literal application to Christ as doing the thing here contended for. " For " it is not possible that the blood of bulls and of goats should take " away sins. Wherefore, when he cometh into the world he saith, " Sacrifice and offering thou wouldest not, but a body hast thou pre-" pared me : in burnt offerings and sacrifices for sin thou hast had " no pleasure : then said I, Lo, I come (in the volume of the book " it is written of me) to do thy will, O God. Above, when he said, " Sacrifice, and offering and burnt offerings, and offering for sin, thou " wouldest not, neither hadst pleasure therein ; (which are offered by " the law ;) then said he, Lo, I come to do thy will, O God. He " taketh away the first, that he may establish the second. By the " which will we are sanctified, through the offering of the body of " Jesus Christ once." (Heb. 10. 4, to 10.) Thus expressly it is stated what he established as the second, to succeed the law of sacrifices which was first, that is, doing the will of God. And then the whole plan is according to the words of Christ before. (Matt. 7. 21.) " Not every one that saith unto me, Lord, Lord, shall enter into the " kingdom of heaven; but *he that doeth the will of my Father* who " is in heaven." If then Jesus and his apostle preached the true gospel, if they understood what it is, and are safe guides to eternal life, this is the way—To do the will of God after his example, and influenced by the faith that is in him, the first, as well as principal leader and perfecter of faith. And though it is also said that he offered a sacrifice for sins, the connection and effect show, that this is not contrary to what is here contended for, but that he offered himself as a sin-offering to the people, and to God as their example and leader, and thus the effect was produced in the people, while he, as their forerunner, gave himself an offering and a sacrifice of a sweet smelling savor to God. " And every priest standeth daily minister-" ing, and offering oftentimes the same sacrifices, which can never " take away sins ; but this man, after he had offered one sacrifice for " sins, forever sat down on the right hand of God; from henceforth " expecting till his enemies be made his footstool. For by one offer-" ing he hath perfected forever them that are sanctified." (v. 11 to 14.) Instead of the various and repeated offerings of the levitical priesthood, one offering, in the true head and leader of his people, was sufficient, for the perfecting of himself and of all those who are finally sanctified, who are all those who perseveringly walk in the same narrow, new and living way which he hath consecrated. Hence the apostle exhorts ; " Having therefore, brethren, boldness to enter " into the holiest by the blood of Jesus, by a new and living way, " which he hath consecrated for us through the vail, that is to say, " his flesh ; and having an high priest over the house of God, let us

AND IMPUTATION.

" draw near with a true heart, in full assurance of faith, having our " hearts sprinkled from an evil conscience, and our bodies washed " with pure water." Then after some awful admonitions and warnings to those who had believed, not to violate their faith, but to maintain their confidence with perseverance, he concludes; " Now the " just shall live by faith: (not the unjust, or sinful;) *but if he* [the " just; for the words *any man*, are not in the Greek text; if he] *draw* " *back*, my soul shall have no pleasure in him. But we," he continueth, " are not of those who draw back to perdition; But of them " that believe to the saving of the soul." Why so ? because we have any exclusive gift of faith, or peculiar privilege? By no means; but because we persevere in faith and the righteous use of it, continuing to be just men, having gained that power by the gospel, as we also exhort others to do. Let these things suffice at present, to show how Christ is the end of the law to believers; not by offering up himself a sacrifice as our surety or substitute, but by consecrating *for us*, through his flesh, and by his own example, a new and living way, *to do the will of God* as the *second, the substance*, to supersede the first, the unprofitable shadows of the law. " For such an high " priest became us, who is holy, harmless, undefiled, separate from " sinners, and made higher than the heavens; who needeth not daily, " as those high priests, to offer up sacrifice, first for his own sins, and " then for the people's; for this he did once, when he offered up " himself." [Heb. 7. 26, 27.] In this the pre-eminence and perfection of his sacrifice are clearly manifest, because one offering was sufficient, instead of the continual offerings of other priests.

Jesus Christ came into the world to give his life a ransom for many, even for all who will receive and obey him, as it is written; " Even " as the Son of man came not to be ministered unto, but to minister, " and to give his life a ransom for many." " Who gave himself a " ransom for all, to be testified in due season." " That he by the " grace of God should taste death for every man." [Matt. 20. 28. 1 Tim. 2. 6. Heb. 2. 9.]

He came into the world, lived and died, to be the leader and captain of salvation to his people, to lead them through the warfare against sin, to final victory. " Behold, I have given thee for a witness " to the people, for a leader and commander to the people." " But " we see Jesus who was made a little lower than the angels for the " suffering of death, crowned with glory and honor; that he by the " grace of God should taste death for every man. For it became " him, for whom are all things, and by whom are all things, in bring-" ing many sons to glory, to make the captain of their salvation per-" fect through sufferings. For both he that sanctifieth, and they who " are sanctified are all of one: for which cause he is not ashamed " to call them brethren; saying, I will declare thy name among my " brethren; in the midst of the church will I sing praise unto thee. " And again I will put my trust in him." [Isa. 55. 4. Heb. 2. 9. &c.]

A leader, worthy to be trusted; because he would never lead in any wrong or forbidden path, and would never give ground to his enemies, but endured all things for the sake of those who would follow him. "For Christ also hath once suffered for sins, the just for [or "by] the unjust that he might lead us to God [so in the Greek,] be-"ing put to death in the flesh, but quickened in the spirit." [1 Pet. 3. 18.] In perfect agreement also with his character as a leader of the people, and given to them of God, for that purpose, to lead them to him, he is the Mediator of the new testament, the surety of a better testament on God's behalf, and for the benefit and satisfaction of the people, as already shown. Thus he came to be in all things the salvation of God to the ends of the earth, a light to lighten the Gentiles and the glory of his people Israel.

Other particulars might be named, as his taking away, or bearing the sin of the world, but all these are either included in those already stated, or will be in those subjects yet to be considered in connection with this. But in all these things, which comprehend the purposes of his coming into the world, there is not a word of his righteousness, or what he has done and suffered, being imputed to believers for their justification. Neither is there any prospect of any man's being a partaker with Christ in his salvation and his glory, unless he first partake with him in his sufferings and death, unless he embrace the same faith of Christ, to do the will of God, walking as he walked. "For in that he died, he died unto sin once ; but in that "he liveth, he liveth unto God. Likewise reckon ye also yourselves "to be dead indeed to sin, but alive to God through Jesus Christ "our Lord." "For if we be dead with him, we shall also live with "him : If we suffer we shall also reign with him : if we deny him, "he also will deny us." [Ro. 6. 10, 11. 2 Tim. 2. 11, 12.]

CHAPTER VIII.

The subject continued, by inquiring into the nature and design of the death of Christ, and whether it is imputed to us for justification.

BUT it will be alledged that if we inquire directly into the purposes and effects of his death, we will find the doctrine of justification by the imputed righteousness of Christ, well supported. We shall therefore inquire into his death in relation to those points, or why it was necessary for him to die. And seeing he became man, and was subject to the ordinary infirmities of humanity, it was necessary in the order of things that he should experience the dissolution of the animal life, by putting off the earthly man, and should pass into glory as the proper forerunner of his people, and that his victory and triumph should be proclaimed for the encouragement of others to come forth in his name to the same reward. "Ought not Christ "to have suffered these things and to enter into his glory ?" "Thus "it is written, and thus it behoved Christ to suffer, and to rise from "the dead the third day ; and that repentance and remission of sins

AND IMPUTATION.

"should be preached in his name among all nations." (Luke 24. 26, 46, 47.)

It was necessary he should die to confirm the new covenant, that is, the testament or will, and secure the inheritance, according to order, to the heirs of the promise. Thus it was necessary, not only that he should live a minister of the circumcission to confirm the promises made to the fathers, but also, as no testament or will is confirmed until after the death of the legator, and as it was impossible for God to die, but possible for his surety of the better testament, who was made a little lower than the angels for the suffering of death, it was necessary that he should die, that by his death he might confirm the legatees in the possession of the inheritance; having faithfully kept the covenant himself, and never forfeited the right of inheritance to his seed. "And for this cause he is the medi-
" ator of the new testament, that by means of death, for the redemp-
" tion of the transgressions under the first testament, they who are
" called might receive the promise of eternal inheritance. For
" where a testament is, there must of necessity be the death of the
" testator. For a testament is of force after men are dead: other-
" wise it is of no strength at all while the testator liveth. Where-
" upon neither the first testament was dedicated without blood."
(Heb. 9. 15, to 18.) But this was only a shadow or sign for the time then present. For the first testament was imperfect, so that the transgressions which were under it could not be redeemed, that is, done away, and the people redeemed from them. For in that testament there was no real death of the testator, all things being in shadows; no real testator had ever appeared, capable of the suffering of death; neither had any been found to condemn sin in the true seat of it, the flesh, and set the example of dying to sin and living to God, as Jesus did, putting his people on the true line, according to the law of the spirit of life, to come into the possession of the promised inheritance. But when Christ thus appeared as the mediator of the new and better testament, he consecrated the new and living way through the vail, that is to say, his flesh, and put the heirs on the safe way to the inheritance, redeeming them from all their transgressions, and then confirmed the whole by his death.

It was necessary that he should die, and visit the dark abodes of departed spirits, and return again amongst the living, that his triumphant victory over death and sin might be made known to all, his salvation proclaimed, and his government established as head over all things to the church. "For to this end Christ both died, and rose,
" and revived, that he might be Lord both of the dead and living."
" For, for this cause was the gospel preached to the dead also, that
" they might be judged according to men in the flesh, but live ac-
" cording to [the purpose and work of] God in the Spirit;" accordingly the quick and the dead shall all be judged by one judge and on the same principles.

The learned Macknight, of Scotland, seems to have been compelled, by the irresistible force of literal truth, to translate νεκρούς, [necrois] correctly, *the dead*, which, as it would seem, to avoid giving support to the Roman catholic doctrine of purgatory, or any other prospect of the gospel's being a remedy for souls out of the earthly tabernacle, (which last idea the simple and natural translation confirms,) he has given a very unnatural and forced translation, or rather construction of the whole together, to compel the phrase, *the dead*, to mean *in sin*, notwithstanding the evident contrast stated by the words of the apostle, between the dead and those in the flesh, which by such a construction is lost. For it is remarkable that the apostle in the whole of this discourse hath used the term *flesh*, in one uniform sense, meaning the animal body. And as though he proposedly avoided the confusion of ideas which would arise by using the same words in different meanings, he hath used these two phrases, *lusts of men*, and *will of the Gentiles*, to express the evils commonly ascribed to the flesh.

But the words of the apostle Paul are not to be omitted, which serve as a farther elucidation of this subject. For concerning Christ he saith ; " And, being found in fashion as a man, he humbled him-" self, and became obedient unto death, even the death of the cross : " wherefore God also hath highly exalted him, and given him a name " which is above every name ; that in the name of Jesus Christ eve-" ry knee should bow, of those in heaven and those on earth and those " under the earth ; and every tongue confess that Jesus Christ is " Lord, to the glory of God the Father." (Phil. 2. 8 to 11.) The Greek word translated things, in our English Bibles, is so translated without reason ; which may easily be perceived by the common reader, because inanimate and unconscious beings are not expected to bow the knee in the name of Jesus. This is only expected of those who are capable subjects of his salvation, or of the contemplation of his character and works. This text therefore, irresistibly relates to the worship paid to him and to God in his name by the inhabitants of heaven and of earth and of those under the earth, that is, of those who have departed from the material body, which they have left in the earth, but have not ascended to heaven, having not yet been saved.

He died to set forth and recommend the love of God to a dying world of men for their salvation, and to engage them to follow him and live to him who died for them. " But God hath commended " his love towards us, in that while we were yet sinners, Christ " died for us. Much more then, being now justified by his blood, " we shall be saved from wrath through him. For, if when we were " enemies, we were reconciled to God by the death of his Son ; " much more being reconciled we shall be saved by his life ;" *if we make it our own by living as he lived*. " For the love of Christ " constraineth us ; because we thus judge, that if one died for all, " then were all dead ; and that he died for all, that they who live " should not henceforth live to themselves, but to him who died for " them and rose again." (Ro. 5. 8, 9. 2. Cor. 5. 14, 15.)

These things comprehend the purposes and effects of the death of Christ in general terms. They might be stated in a number of dif-

AND IMPUTATION.

ferent manners according to the variety of language used in the scriptures, to express by various phrases, one and the same thing. But to notice all these expressions distinctly would be unnecessary. My purpose is to satisfy and convince those who are in reach of the truth, that there is no such doctrine, as that of justification by the imputed righteousness of Christ, contained or supported in the scripture account of the purposes and effects of his coming into the world and dying. But it may be alledged that although the point cannot be proved by considering the subject in general terms, it can, by descending to particulars, and that there are a number of concise and well expressed arguments contained in plain scriptures, which have not been introduced, by which it can be confirmed. We shall now have recourse to these, after once more reminding the reader of the unaccountableness, not to say the injustice of the notion, that God should fix the justification or final salvation of men, on that ground, which is not once named in all the revelations which he hath made on those subjects : that is, justification by the imputed righteousness, of Christ as their surety, to pay their debt to law and justice in their room. We have seen that no such character belongs to Christ, consequently the fabric which is built on it must fall. But let us proceed;

" Christ died for the ungodly," and " While we were yet sinners Christ died for us." (Ro. 5. 6, 8.) " Christ hath suffered for us in the flesh." (1 Pet. 4. 1.) Hence it is concluded, that he died as a surety or substitute in our room and stead. And it is farther argued, that the preposition " for" [υπερ] signifies " in the room and stead of." If that be true, then Christ died [υπερ] in the room and stead of our " sins that they might not die but be saved ; for it is written, " That Christ died for [υπερ] our sins." (1 Cor. 15. 3.) But this consequence is not only false, but too absurd to be admitted. The argument therefore, from which it is fairly drawn, that is, that " for," [υπερ] necessarily signifies " in the room and stead of," is false. But the apostle hath stated the nature and design of Christ's suffering for us, for our sakes, on our account, or in our cause, that we might follow his example ; " For even hereunto were ye called : because " Christ also suffered for us, leaving us an example, that ye should " follow his steps." (1 Pet. 2. 21.) Thus while believers are engaged in the cause of Christ as he suffered for them, they also suffer for him. " For to you it is given in the behalf of Christ, [υπερ Χριςʋ] " not only to believe on him, but also to suffer for his sake. [υπερ " αυτʋ] Phil. 1. 29.) So in another place, the apostle, speaking of the gospel, saith, " Whereof I, Paul, am made a minister, who now " rejoice in my sufferings for [υπερ] you, and fill up that which is " behind of the afflictions of Christ in my flesh for his body's sake, " [υπερ τʋ σωματος αυτʋ] which is the church." (Col. 1. 24.) And John ; " In him we have known love, because he laid down his life " for [υπερ] us : and we ought to lay down our lives for [υπερ] the " brethren." (Jno. 3. 16.) These authorities are sufficient to show us and all candid men, that the doctrine of Christ's dying for us and for our sins, contains in it no foundation for that of his dying in our room and stead, or of vicarious obedience or sufferings, proxy payment, or surety righteousness, or the righteousness of Christ in any other character imputed to believers, on any account unless by doing as he did and being righteous on the same principle with him. " He that doeth righteousness is righteous even as he is righteous."

But another argument for justification by the imputed righteousness of Christ, is that righteousness is imputed to them that believe. Hence it is concluded, that this righteousness which is imputed must be the surety righteousness of Christ. But we have before seen that whatever righteousness is imputed, or whatever was imputed for righteousness, was that which existed in the man, his own faith accompanied by obedience to the extent of what was required in every case. Although faith alone will never save any man, or establish any man in an abiding state of justification, it may introduce him into the path. For he who believes the truth on sufficient evidence and agrees to it in his heart, with determination to obey, has done all he can do until something farther offers, he is therefore justified. Thus Abraham's faith was counted, reckoned, or imputed to him for righteousness. But in what spirit or practice was it imputed to him? of obedience or disobedience? Not of disobedience but of obedience. For when God commanded him to circumcise all the males in his house, had he refused, or had he not from the time of believing stood in the spirit of obedience to God as far as his duty was made known, his justification had been null, and that which was imputed to him for righteousness would not have been thus imputed. And on the same principle of obedience was righteousness to be imputed to Abraham's family, whether Gentiles or Jews. " For in Jesus Christ " neither circumcision availeth any thing, nor uncircumcision; but " faith which worketh by love." And again; " Circumcision is " nothing, and uncircumcision is nothing, but the keeping of the " commandments of God." (Gal. 5. 6. 1 Cor. 7. 8.) " For we say " that faith was reckoned to Abraham for righteousness, and he re- " ceived the sign of circumcision, a seal of the righteousness of the " faith which he had, being yet uncircumcised; that he might be the " father of all them that believe, though they be not circumcised; " that righteousness might be imputed to them also; and the father " of the circumcision, to them who are not of the circumcision only, " but who also walk in the steps of that faith of our father Abraham " which he had yet being uncircumcised." (Ro. 4. 9, 11, &c.) And what were the steps of that faith of Abraham? Obedience; which appears in every case, *and by works was faith made perfect.* Deny it if ye can. But " He staggered not at the promise of God through " unbelief; but was strong in faith, giving glory to God. And being " fully persuaded, that what he had promised he was able to perform. " And therefore it was imputed to him for righteousness. Now it " was not written for his sake alone, that it was imputed to him; but " for us also, to whom it shall be imputed, if we believe on him that " raised up Jesus our Lord from the dead; who was delivered for "our offences and raised again for our justification." (Ro. 4, 9, &c.) But in all this, where is there a word or a hint of any righteousness of Christ imputed to any christian, of the Jews or Gentiles, to Abraham or to us, or any thing else except the faith of each one, including his obedience? For who will venture to separate them? Or if obedience be denied to have any connection or availableness in the point of justification, after the apostle Paul hath said so pointedly that the faith which availeth in Jesus Christ, is that which worketh by love, and James, that by works a man is justified and not by faith only, there is still nothing said of the righteousness of Christ being imputed to any; the nighest the whole account comes to it is, each one's own faith, and not the faith, the obedience or righteousness, of another. Now my faith is not the obedience or righteousness of Jesus Christ, as my substitute or surety, neither was Abraham's.

But for what purpose, and on what principle, was he delivered for our offences, and raised again for our justification? Not on the principle of imputation, by transferring our offences to him! or his righteousness to us? for the revelation of God speaks of no such matter, either here or any where else. But he was delivered for our offences to remove them and prevent or put a stop to them, by bringing in everlasting righteousness, and making an end of sin; and he was raised again for our justification, that he might be our confidence and our support in God, " *I will put my trust in him*;" that our faith and hope in God, and the execution of our redemption in Christ, might not fail, but have an inexhaustible treasure of evidence and support; " I foresaw the Lord always before my face; " for he is on my right hand that I should not be moved: therefore " did my heart rejoice, and my tongue was glad: moreover also my " flesh shall rest in hope, because thou wilt not leave my soul in hell, " neither wilt thou suffer thine holy One to see corruption." And all these things take effect on the principle, and according to the plan of God's free grace, as stated by the apostle Paul. " But now, " without the law, the righteousness of God is manifested (not im-" puted,) being witnessed [or testified] by the law and the prophets; " even the righteousness of God through the faith of Jesus Christ, " unto all and upon all them that believe: for there is no difference; " for all have sinned, and come short of the glory of God; being " justified freely by his grace, through the redemption that is in Christ " Jesus; whom God hath set forth a propitiation [or mercy seat, Greek, the place in which God appeared to show his glory and to commune with the people] through faith in his blood, to declare (not to work out and impute,) his (that is God's) righteousness for " the remission of sins, that are past; through the forbearance of " God; (not through the imputed righteousness of Christ;) to de-" clare, I say, at this time his righteousness, that he might (have an opportunity to) be just and the justifier of him that believeth " in Jesus," [or, as in the Greek, " of him that is of the faith of " Jesus, having the same faith with him." See Heb. 2. 13. Acts 2; 25, 27 Ro. 3. 21, 26.] Thus he was raised for our justification;

even him; "Who verily was fore-ordained before the foundation of "the world, but was manifest in these last times for you, who by him "do believe in God that raised him up from the dead, and gave him "glory; that your faith and hope might be in God." (1 Pet. 1. 20, 21.) And if we by him believe in God, it will be accounted to us for righteousness, provided we do not make shipwreck of our faith by putting away a good conscience or neglecting obedience. Now a good conscience depends on living honestly in all things; which those who put away, make shipwreck concerning the faith, and of course lose their justification. (1 Tim. 1. 19. Heb. 13. 18.)

But faith without obedience cannot justify any man. A man may believe the truth of God, the doctrine of the gospel, the only way of salvation, and be firmly persuaded of it, but have no intention of obeying: such an one hath neither part nor lot in justification; his faith will be imputed to him for the greater condemnation; such, in some measure, were those rulers of the Jews, who believed on him but did not confess him, because they loved the praise of men more than the praise of God. (Jno. 12. 52, 52.) Simon the sorcerer believed, but was not justified. Devils also believe. It may be objected that the faith of devils is not a proper ground of argument, to prove that men may believe and not be justified, because of the gospel's being offered only to men. But as the apostle hath used it I consider myself safe, and the argument proper. James hath proved that a man cannot be justified without works; and Paul, after all he hath said of the necessity of the faith of Christ, and of its excluding the works of the law, it is remarkable, hath never once excluded obedience to the gospel; nay, so far from it, that he uses believing and obeying as synonymous terms, in one of his most particular descriptions of faith. "But they have not all obeyed the gospel; for "Esaias saith, Lord who hath believed our report?" And this is not all, in the conclusion of this same epistle, he hath finally concentrated the whole work and design of the gospel in obedience, not indeed to the outward ceremonies of the law, but to God in the faith of Christ—the obedience of faith. "According to my gospel "and the preaching of Jesus Christ, according to the revelation of the "mystery which was kept secret since the world began, but now is "manifest and by the scriptures of the prophets, according to the "commandment of the everlasting God, made known to all nations "for the obedience of faith." (See Ro. 1. 16. & 16. 25, 26.) And in his epistle to the Galatians, in which he so firmly maintains the faith of Christ in contrast with the works of the law, obedience is introduced as the grand substance, without which their faith and standing would all go to ruin. "O foolish Galatians who hath be-"witched you, that ye should not obey the truth, before whose eyes "Jesus Christ hath been evidently set forth crucified among you." Jesus Christ was set forth to them, as the object of faith, and the apostle looked for obedience. They had believed with extraordinary zeal and great blessedness; but their turning away from the obedience of faith to that of the law, was making havoc of their faith.

AND IMPUTATION.

"Are ye so foolish? having begun in the Spirit, are ye now made perfect by the flesh?" In like manner also Peter considers faith and obedience as occupying the same place in union, putting the *disobedient* in contrast with *believers*; "He that believeth on him shall not be confounded." "Unto you, therefore, who *believe* he is precious; but unto them who are *disobedient*, the stone which the builders disallowed, the same is made the head of the corner, and a stone of stumbling, and a rock of offence, even to them who stumble at the cross, being *disobedient*." (Gal. 1. 3. 1 Pet. 2. 6, 7.)

Another argument in defence of justification by the imputed righteousness of Christ, is grounded on such scriptures as these. "Surely he hath borne our griefs, and carried our sorrows: yet we did esteem him, [paid attention to him,] stricken, smitten of God, and afflicted. But he was wounded for our transgressions, he was bruised for our iniquities: the chastisement of our peace was upon him; and with his stripes [bruise, Heb.] we are healed. All we like sheep have gone astray; we have turned every one to his own way; and the Lord hath laid on him the iniquity of us all—for the transgression of my people, was he stricken—Yet it pleased the Lord to bruise him; he hath put him to grief: when thou shalt make his soul an offering for sin; he shall see his seed; he shall prolong his days, and the pleasure of the Lord shall prosper in his hand. He shall see of the travail of his soul, and shall be satisfied; by his knowledge shall my righteous servant justify many; for he shall bear their iniquities—Because he hath poured out his soul unto death; and he was numbered with the transgressors; and he bare the sin of many, and made intercession for the transgressors." "Who his own self bare our sins, in his own body on the tree, that we being dead to sin should live unto righteousness; by whose stripes [bruise, Greek,] ye were healed." (Isa. 53. 4, 5. &c. 1 Pet. 2. 24.) These scriptures contain the substance of the arguments drawn from that class; and from them we may infer the following propositions. That Jesus bore our sins—That he suffered for, or by our sins—That he is the Mediator or Intercessor through whom we obtain deliverance.

That Jesus bore our sins therefore is granted on all hands. And he could not otherwise have been a suitable leader and Captain to his people; he could not otherwise have been a competent forerunner and example to his people, whose steps we are to follow. He could not, without bearing our sins, have been properly qualified to commiserate our wretchedness, and minister suitable relief. "For it became him, for whom are all things, and by whom are all things, in bringing many sons to glory, to make the Captain of their salvation perfect through sufferings—Wherefore in all things it behoved him to be made like unto his brethren; that he might be a merciful and faithful high priest in things pertaining to God, to make intercession for the sins of the people—For we have not an high priest who cannot be touched with the feeling of our infirmities; but was in all points tempted like as we are, yet without

"sin." He therefore had no sin of his own; but it behoved him to bear ours, that a suitable fellow feeling and brotherhood might be consummated between us; "For both he that sanctifieth and they who are sanctified, are all of one; for which cause he is not ashamed to call them brethren." (Heb. 2. 10, 11. and 4. 15.) But we shall enquire more particularly how he came to bear our sins, and in what respect he bore them. It was the doing of the Lord, "The Lord hath laid on him the iniquity of us all." Or as the Hebrew text is, JEHOVAH *hath caused the iniquity of us all to meet in him,* (See margin of Bibles,) that is, to intercept him. But say the people, He imputed them to him as our substitute or surety, and his sufferings and obedience will be imputed to us for justification. This however is man's doctrine. The scriptures have not stated any such matters. For the elucidation of this point, I will give a concise descant on the above texts from the fifty-third of Isaiah, and illustrate them by other scriptures. The prophet saith, "*He is despised and rejected of men; a man of sorrows, and ac-*
"*quainted with grief; and we hid as it were our faces from him; he*
"*was despised and we esteemed him not,*" [paid no attention to him.] Such is the natural enmity of this world against God, that he who will serve God must be despised by this world, and he also that will be the friend of the world is the enemy of God. (Jas. 4. 4.) But the prophet viewing, in the gift of prophecy, this man, as a man of sorrows and acquainted with grief, as his abiding condition of life and not as a matter of an hour or a day—sorrows and grief, such as were incident to the human race, only infinitely greater than in any other man *(For his visage was marred more than any man, and his form than the sons of men,)* breaks out into this reflection; "Surely he
"*hath borne our griefs, he hath carried our sorrows;* (those death-
"ly burdens which belong to us sinners—he seems like one of us;)
"*yet we did esteem him,* [paid attention to him] *stricken,* (or *touched,*
"with our distresses) *smitten of God* (who sent him on this errand
"and in whose cause he suffered these things) *and afflicted.* (Little
"as we regarded him for his peculiar excellence.) *But he was wound-*
"*ed for (through Heb.) our transgressions, he was bruised for*
"*(Heb. through) our iniquities : the chastisement of our peace was*
"*upon him;* (the very chastisement through the enduring of which
"we may find peace;) *by his stripes, (Heb. bruise) we are healed,*
"(as fast as we suffer the same bruising for, or on account of sin
"which he hath suffered for, or through our sins; "Because Christ
"also suffered for us, leaving us an example that ye should follow
"his steps," "For he that hath suffered in the flesh hath ceased
"from sin." 1 Pet. 2. 21. and 4. 1.) *All we like sheep have gone astray, we have turned every one to his own way; and* JEHOVAH *hath caused the iniquity of us all to meet in him,* [to intercept or head him; that he may experience the depth of our miseries.] *He was oppressed* [or as it hath been understood and the Hebrew text will well bear, *It was exacted* of him, that is, all the obedience, subjection, humiliation and sufferings which God requireth of us, he

AND IMPUTATION.

also exacted of him ; and very properly, as he undertook to be a perfect example and faithful leader. Accordingly] *he was afflicted, yet he opened not his mouth : he is brought as a lamb to the slaughter, and as a sheep before her shearers is dumb, so he opened not his mouth,* (but endured all these things in the most perfect innocence, and goodness. For he must necessarily come to death under the burdens which befel him in opening and consecrating for us the new and living way in which alone the honor of God could be secured in our salvation ; I say he must necessarily suffer death, under all the ignominy and envious persecutions which they were to expect, whose example he had undertaken to be, else his example had not been consummately complete, as shown in its place. And he came to death under all the burden of our sins, which he had borne through his life, as saith the apostle; " Who his own self bare our " sins in his own body on the tree, that we being dead to sin (as he was) " might live unto righteousness ; by whose stripes [or bruise,] ye " were healed. Being bruised as he was, and after his example." (1 Pet. 2. 21, 24.) *He was taken from prison and from judgment.* This is the same Hebrew particle here rendered *from* prison and *from* judgment, which in a foregoing verse is rendered *for* our transgressions and *for* our iniquities, which I have rendered *through* or *by* as being most correspondent to its common use, and as most clearly expressing the import of that scripture. The same particle is also rendered *by* in the margin of the verse now before us, thus, " He was taken away *by* distress and *by* judgment." The same also is used in this member of the sentence, " *For he was cut off out of the land of the living ;*" and in this also, *For* [by] *the transgression of my people was he stricken*; [the stroke was upon him.] (See margin.) By the transgressions [or iniquities] of my people he was led to death is the Greek version. *And he made his grave with the wicked, and with the rich in his death ; because he had done no violence, neither was any deceit in his mouth."* The wicked, such as Pilate, gave him honor, and the rich, as Joseph of Arimathea ; such was the innocence of his life, that many respected him and gave him an honorable burying, according to the manner of the Jews. Yet JEHOVAH *was pleased to bruise him ; he hath put him to grief.* He put him into that very lot which he knew he could not fill without being bruised and put to grief ; and especially because God dwelt in him ; for that was the cause of the maltreatment which he received from men. They hated him without cause ; and the reproaches of them that reproached God fell on him. Yet this lot it behoved him to fill to the last extremity, or fail of consecrating the new and living way for his followers.

" *When thou shalt make his soul an offering for sin, he shall see* " *his seed, he shall prolong his days, and the pleasure of JEHOVAH* " *shall prosper in his hand.*" Who shall make his soul an offering for sin ? God the Father ? And to whom shall he offer him ? To himself, to spend his fury upon him ? Nay but to the people ; for in them the atonement is to be made ; in them reconciliation is to be wrought; in them justification must be begun and consummated. "In this was manifested the love of God towards us, because that God "sent his only begotten Son into the world that we might live through "him. Herein is love, not that we loved God, but that he loved us, "and sent his Son to be the propitiation for our sins." "And ye know "that he was manifested to take away our sins—He that committeth "sin is of the devil: for the devil sinneth from the beginning. For "this purpose the Son of God was manifested, that he might destroy "[or dissolve] the works of the devil." (1 Jno. 4. 9, 10, and 3. 5, 8.) Thus God put him among the people to be their captain, and to make war against the devil, to resist him, to destroy him, and dissolve his works, (as the summer distroys the winter cold, and dissolves the frost and snow,) and lead them to the victory; thus he gave him to the people to destroy satan and deliver them, although he knew it would, and necessarily must, cost him his life, as well as all the other sufferings which his soul endured; thus it pleased JEHOVAH to bruise him, and thus he made his soul an offering for sin; thus we are justified by his blood and reconciled by his death; and thus our consciences are by his blood purged from dead works to serve the living and true God. (Ro 5. 9, 10. Heb. 2. 14, 15. and 9. 14.) *By his knowledge shall my righteous servant justify many;* (not by his righteousness imputed to them;) *for he shall bear their iniquities;* (and they, believing in him that he hath overcome, will unite themselves to him, in the same faith with him, and overcome as he overcame;) *And he was numbered with the transgressors;* (he was counted a malefactor because he did the work of God which he was sent to do;) *and he bare the sin of many and made intercession for the transgressors.* [In the Hebrew, *He headed* or *intercepted the transgressors.*] He stood between them and God to turn them from their rebellion and lead them to God in obedience and subjection to his will.

From these few remarks, which I have made the more numerous because of the great confidence of many in this chapter for the support of justification by the righteousness of Christ imputed, or transferred to them; from these reflections, I say, it may readily be seen that it will all bear a very rational and consistent acceptation without yielding any support to such a scheme; Yea farther, that it actually militates against that doctrine, in some parts directly in its most natural and literal construction, and the whole of it indirectly, because where so much is said of Christ and his sufferings, not an explicit word is said of imputing our sins to him or his righteousness to us. But this is the unhappy ground of that doctrine all through; no scripture names it, nay, so far from it, that the phrase, "*Righteousness of Christ,*" is not once found in the old or new testament, much less with this predication, *Imputed to us,* or to any. Yet, as before observed, I have no objection to the phrase, provided an evangelical use be made of it; for it is no more than *the righteousness of God,* which phrase is used, or *the righteousness of one,* who, no doubt, is Christ, that very righteousness by which the faithful are all justified,

AND IMPUTATION. 93

and are *righteous even as he is righteous*, but not by imputing his righteousness to them: that predication is always absent in that connection. But farther;

The Lord caused the iniquity of us all to meet in him, so that he bore them, by preparing him a body, and sending him into the world as a man, a servant, and subject to death in that body, which consisted of flesh and blood as ours do, and contained the same appetites, passions and propensities, and by the intimate union of which with his soul, he was exposed to every temptation to which we are exposed: for it was necessary for him to be made like those whom he came to save. " But we see Jesus, who was made a little lower than
" the angels for the suffering of death, crowned with glory and honor;
" that he, by the grace of God, should taste death for every man.
" For it became him, for whom are all things, and by whom are all
" things, in bringing many sons to glory, to make the Captain of
" their salvation perfect through sufferings. For both he that sanc-
" tifieth and they who are sanctified are all of one: for which cause
" he is not ashamed to call them brethren. For as much then as the
" children are partakers of flesh and blood, he also himself likewise
" took part of the same; that through death he might destroy him
" that had the power of death; that is the devil, and deliver them
" who through fear of death were all their lifetime subject to bond-
" age. For verily he took not on him the nature of angels, but he
" took on him the seed of Abraham. Wherefore in all things it be-
" hoved him to be made like unto his brethren; that he might be a
" merciful and faithful high priest in things pertaining to God, to
" make reconciliation for the sins of the people. For in that he him-
" self hath suffered, being tempted, he is able to succour them that
" are tempted." (Heb. 2. 9, &c.)

This scripture shows how he bore our sins in the primary sense of it—by taking on him the same nature, not of angels but of the seed of Abraham, that wicked race, and being made in all things like his brethren, and so being exposed to sin in every point by temptation, but never yielding. And these things will agree to the testimony of John the baptist, " Behold the lamb of God who taketh away the sin of the world."

Now sin is not a substance, but a quality, with respect to its nature, and is manifested and supported by actions. When, therefore, these actions are not committed, and the nature which produces them is resisted and overcome, sin is taken away, or it ceases to be. As Jesus Christ therefore was sent into the world to be the captain of our salvation, and that the world, through him, might be saved, and as his doctrine is, " If any man will come after me, let him deny himself and take up his cross, and follow me," and as he is the forerunner to whom we are to look, standing in the same place with those whom he came to save, and having a fellow feeling of their infirmities, (Heb. 4. 15.) being beset on every hand with the same temptations, but resisting with such success that he did no sin, bearing a daily cross against all the nature of evil, until he at last became triumphant, thus setting us an example that we should follow his steps, and at the same time giving all those who receive him power to become the sons of God by doing as he did, he takes away the sin of the world and destroys the workings of the devil in men; for he was manifested that he might destroy the works of the devil. And again; " Ye know that he was manifested to take away our sins; and in him " is no sin. Whosoever abideth in him sinneth not: whosoever sin- " neth hath not seen him, neither known him." (1 Jno. 3. 5, 6.) He also bore our sins by feeling the keen and malignant opposition of sin and sinners against God and against himself as the true minister and defender of God's cause in the world, while in the mean time, he devoted his whole heart and life to the accomplishment of that work which he came to do, not once yielding to the resentment or malice of the wicked. As it is written, " For the zeal of thine " house hath eaten me up; and the reproaches of them that re- " proached thee, are fallen upon me." (Psm. 69. 9. Ro. 15. 3.) Thus he bore the reproaches, the opposition and persecution of wicked men and devils, which all proceeded from the opposition of sin to God, which led men to hate God, through all his life, until he triumphantly finished his course on the cross, and in his resurrection and ascension. *He endured the cross despising the shame and is set down at the right hand of the throne of God.* In thus bearing our sins, he had to contend against the carnal mind, or the enmity in himself, that is, in his flesh; for that body which he inhabited consisting of the same flesh and blood with ours, was no less inclined to its own ways, and no more disposed to obey God, than ours. Accordingly he was tempted in all points like as we are; (Heb. 4. 15.) and such temptations could not have existed without the same nature to be tempted and that by the same things. For it is folly in the extreme to suppose that any man or being can be tempted when there is no room or place in him to receive the temptation, nothing in him to love the bait. It may indeed, be objected, as it has already, that when Christ is said to be tempted, it does not mean that he was affected or made to suffer by the temptation, but only that he was reproached and persecuted to provoke and overcome him, and in that way he suffered being tempted, or that the temptation was offered to him, as God is sometimes said to be tempted, but cannot really, so as to be effected by it. I grant that such language is admissible, and the objection plausible; but it can be obviated; not only because his being tempted in all points like as we are, will not admit an explication of that kind, but also because the apostle in stating that he suffered being tempted, makes it a qualifying of him for succouring them that are tempted, as being experienced in the same temptations; " For in that he himself hath suffered being tempted, he is able to succour them that are tempted," (Heb. 2. 18.) which unequivocally proves that the temptation is the same in him and in them.

On the same principle, Jesus is spoken of as " Having abolished the enmity in his flesh," (Eph. 2. 15.) for that could not be abolished in his flesh, which was not there. But it will likely be argued that the enmity is explained by the apostle in the same sentence, to be *The law of commandments contained in ordinances*, which stood as a separating wall between the Jews and the Gentiles. But this law of commandments was not the enmity, although it was the middle wall of partition supporting the enmity between the Jews and Gentiles; and was, by the appointment of God himself, kept by the Jews, as a shadow to represent in a figure the destruction of sin in the flesh, or the carnal mind, which is the absolute and real enmity. This real enmity could never be destroyed or abolished, but rather kept alive, by the law of commandments, " Which stood only in " meats and drinks and divers washings and carnal ordinances, [justi-" fications of the flesh, Greek,] imposed on them (who lived after " the flesh,) until the time of reformation." (Heb. 9. 10.) But this abolishing of the real enmity remained for Jesus to effectuate in his flesh, who could do that which none could ever do before him, by condemning sin in the flesh where it hath its seat. " For God, send-" ing his own Son in the likeness of sinful flesh, and on account of " sin, (because it ought to be removed) condemned sin in the flesh, " that which the law could not do, because it was weak through the " flesh; that the righteousness of the law might be fulfilled in us " who walk not after the flesh, but after the Spirit." " Wherefore " then serveth the law? It was added because of transgressions till " the seed should come to whom the promise was made, and it was " ordained by angels in the hand of a mediator." This then is the seed who, Having abolished the enmity in his flesh, took away the exhibition of the enmity, the law of commandments in ordinances. For when the real enmity was once destroyed there was no longer any need of keeping up its destruction, in effigy, as if it yet held its place " And that he might reconcile both (Jews and Gentiles) to God in " one body, by the cross, (which he bore all his life) having slain the " enmity thereby, he came and preached peace to them that were far " off and to them that were nigh." (Eph. 2. 16, 17.) For Jesus having once slain or abolished the enmity in himself; that is, in his flesh, was a proper leader and forerunner of his people to whom they may all look, in one body, whether Jews or Gentiles; because there is now no partition except the cross of Christ, at which indeed the unbelieving Jews stumble, and which the Gentiles count foolishness, but to those who are saved, whether Greeks or Jews, it is the power of God and the wisdom of God, and by which the world is crucified to them and they to the world. But thus he bore our sins. And to these things agree also the words of the prophet Isaiah when speaking of Christ as entering on the work of salvation. (59. 16, and 63. 5.) " And he saw that there was no man and wondered that there was " no intercessor; therefore his arm brought salvation unto him and " his righteousness it sustained him." And again; " And I looked " and there was none to help; and I wondered that there was none " to uphold; therefore mine own arm brought salvation unto me; " and my fury it upheld me." Thus he began the salvation in himself, and was made perfect through sufferings, as the apostle states.

For he trode the wine press alone (not, was trodden in it,) and of the people there was none with him. Thus he bore our sins. And in the contest between his faith of obedience to God, supported by the spirit of God in him, [for the fulness of the godhead dwelt in him bodily,] and the enmity or nature of the flesh supported by the malice of wicked men and devils let loose on him, he suffered what he did in the garden, when he said, "My soul is exceeding sor-
" rowful even unto death, and fell on his face and prayed, saying, O
" my Father, if it be possible, let this cup pass from me: neverthe-
" less not as I will, but as thou wilt. And there appeared an angel
" unto him from heaven, strengthening him. And being in an ago-
" ny he prayed more earnestly, and his sweat was as it were great
" drops of blood falling down to the ground." (Matt. 26. 38, 39. Luke 22. 43, 44.) And thus the malice of earth and hell pursued him while the zeal for his Father's house consumed him, until on the cross he appeared to be forsaken of God, to put the matter to a fair and last trial, that he might prove out his faith in God, and his sonship. " Now from the sixth hour there was darkness over all the
" land unto the ninth hour. And about the ninth hour Jesus cried
" with a loud voice, saying, Eli, Eli, lama sabachthani? that is to say,
" My God, my God, why hast thou forsaken me? and when he had
" cried again with a loud voice, he yielded up the ghost." [Matt. 27. 45, 46, 50.] Thus he gave his life a ransom for many. And thus he escaped from the hands of his enemies. He spent his life but saved his soul to life eternal. Thus he bore our sins through the contest, and in his own body on the tree, resisting to blood, striving against sin, until he came off victorious, having never yielded to sin, and now ministers the same spirit to all who follow him; " For
" if any man have not the spirit of Christ he is none of his."
" Let this mind be in you which was also in Christ Jesus; who being
" in the form of God, thought it not robbery to be equal with, or as*
" God; but made himself of no reputation and took upon him the
" form of a servant, and was made in the likeness of men; and, be-
" ing found in fashion as a man, he humbled himself and became
" obedient unto death, even the death of the cross. Wherefore
" God hath highly exalted him, and given him a name which is above
" every name." (Phil. 2. 5, to 9.)

For a farther elucidation of his bearing our sins, we may remark, that he bore with the weaknesses and infirmities of his people to help them on their way, and encourages them to do the same towards one another. "We then that are strong ought to bear the
" infirmities of the weak, and not to please ourselves. Let every
" one of us please his neighbor for his good to edification. For even
" Christ pleased not himself: but, as it is written, " The reproaches
" of them that reproached thee fell on me." " Now the God of
" patience and consolation grant you to be like-minded toward one
" another, according to Christ Jesus." " Bear ye one another's

---

* *For the translation, as God. See Doddridge's note on this text.*

" burdens and so fulfil the law of Christ." " And be ye kind one to another ; tender-hearted, forgiving one another, even as God in Christ* hath forgiven you." (Ro. 15. 1, &c. Gal. 6. 9. Eph. 4. 32.) This language of the prophet Isaiah, " Surely he hath borne our griefs, and carried our sorrows," though by the words which follow, " Yet we did esteem him stricken, smitten of God, and afflicted," it would naturally be understood to relate to the proper and true sense of his bearing our iniquities, is by the evangelist Matthew, applied to the deliverances which he wrought for the people, while residing among them. " When the even was come, they brought unto him many that were possessed with devils : and he cast out the spirits with his word, and healed all that were sick ; that it might be fulfilled which was spoken by Esaias the prophet saying, Himself took our infirmities, and bare our sicknesses." [Mat. 8. 16, 17.] This was no doubt therefore included in his bearing our sins in the more emphatical and radical sense, being a fruit of it, and helps to show how he bears our sins and iniquities—that he bears them away as the scape goat under the law bore away the sins of Israel never to be seen again. But he also suffered for our sins. This part is greatly elucidated by what has just been said ; for his bearing our sins, and suffering for them, or for us, are too intimately connected to be treated of altogether distinctly ; while he bore, he suffered, and thus he became " A man of sorrows and acquainted with grief; for he was despised and rejected of men." But this has been already expounded.

But the apostle to the Hebrews as quoted above, shows particularly what made it necessary for him to suffer—That he might be made perfect, a perfect captain and leader of his people well acquainted by experience with all their sufferings and trials, an approved leader who could not be foiled with temptation so as to commit sin, in whom the people might safely trust. " For it became " him, for whom are all things, and by whom are all things, in " bringing many sons to glory, to make the captain of their salva- " tion perfect through sufferings." " For in that he himself hath " suffered, being tempted, he is able to succour them that are tempt- " ed." " For we have not an high priest who cannot be touched " with the feeling of our infirmities ; but was tempted in all points " like as we are, yet without sin. Let us therefore come boldly to " the throne of his grace, that we may obtain mercy, and find grace " to help in time of need." Thus also Jesus Christ is a sure corner-

---

* Εν Χριϛω, *the phrase here used by the apostle, is so correctly and universally translated* in Christ, *that I know not how our translators thought of rendering it* for Christ's sake, *unless to compel the scriptures to sanction a preconcerted scheme, of which they were in full possession, but had no scripture to support it: perhaps they thought it right so to do. Dr. Doddridge and Scott have rendered the phrase* in Christ; *but as though predetermined to support the ingrafted and popular scheme by this text, have added,* and for his sake.

"stone, well tried, whereon the church is built, a spiritual house, as "it is written;" "Behold, I lay in Zion, for a foundation stone, a tried "stone, a precious corner-stone, a sure foundation: he that believeth "shall not make haste." Or as the apostle Peter hath it, by an exact quotation of the Septuagint Greek, and by no means contrary to the Hebrew; " And he that believeth on him shall not be confounded." He will trust to his foundation, or leader, and not go before him. (See Heb. 2. 10, 18. and 4. 15, 16. Isa. 28. 16. 1 Pet. 2. 6.)

But the above scriptures state that Jesus is the intercessor, through whom we obtain deliverance, that he made intercession for the transgressors, that he made reconciliation for the sins of the people. Intercessor, is only another word to mean, mediator, and we have seen how he maketh intercession, or mediation for the transgressors, by bearing or taking away the sins of the world, and the sins of those who follow him, as the Lord's servant, as again written, " Behold " my servant whom I uphold; mine elect, in whom my soul delight- " eth; I have put my spirit upon him: he shall bring forth judg- " ment to the gentiles. He shall not cry, nor lift up, nor cause his " voice to be heard in the street. A bruised reed shall he not " break, and the smoking flax shall he not quench: he shall bring " forth judgment to truth. He shall not fail nor be discouraged, till " he have set judgment in the earth: and the isles [or nations] shall " wait for his law." " And in his name shall the Gentiles trust." [Isa. 42. 1, 4. Matt. 12. 21.] Again when the cause of enmity, is removed, the result will be reconciliation. Sin therefore, which is the cause of enmity and hindrance to reconciliation, being taken away by Jesus Christ, the way is opened through him, *the new and living way which he hath consecrated through the vail, that is to say, his flesh*, for reconciliation to take place, according to the scripture which saith, " That God was in Christ reconciling the world to himself; not imputing their trespasses to them." [2 Cor. 5. 19.] It is therefore the privilege of every one to be reconciled to God, by believing in Christ, and taking up his cross, and following him, as he gave the example. For in this way, and this alone, God was at all in Christ reconciling the world to himself, and not imputing their trespasses to them: because he is sure to impute sin or righteousness wherever the one or the other is found; for it is gospel doctrine, that, " We must all appear before the judgment seat of Christ; " that every one may receive the things done in his body, according " to that he hath done, whether it be good or bad;" [2 Cor. 5. 10.] not according to what he hath believed or had imputed to him, as being done by another. As therefore sin, the true cause of enmity, is found in men, there the change must take place. " Now " then, we are ambassadors for Christ, as though God did beseech " you by us: we pay you, in Christ's stead, [or on the behalf of " Christ] be ye reconciled to God." [2 Cor. 5. 20.]

There is therefore no support to the doctrine of justification by the imputed righteousness of Christ, in the above train of argumentation, from those scriptures which are alledged; because, excepting that he is peculiarly the forerunner, the leader and the head, having in all things the foreway and the pre-eminence, what he hath done, he hath done to leave us an example that we should follow his steps, instead of doing it to be imputed to us, to release us from doing the same. Did he suffer for us? We are called to suffer for him; "For " unto you it is given in the behalf of Christ, not only to believe on " him, but also to suffer for his sake." [Phil. 1. 29.] Did he suffer for sins? or rather on account of sin, and for doing well. We are called to do the same. " For it is better, if the will of God be so, " that ye suffer for well-doing than for evil-doing. For Christ also " hath suffered for sins, the just for the unjust, [or, on account of sin " the just on account of, or by the unjust, as the connection also shows,] " that he might bring [Greek lead] us to God." " For as much " then as Christ hath suffered for us in the flesh, *arm yourselves* " *likewise with the same mind*, for he that hath suffered in the flesh " hath ceased from sin." (1 Pet. 3. 17, 18, and 4. 1.) Was he dispised and rejected of men? So are his people. " Being defamed " we entreat : we are made as the filth of the world, the off-scour-" ing of all things unto this day." " And ye shall be hated of all " men for my name's sake." " If the world hate you, ye know " that it hated me before it hated you. If ye were of the world, " the world would love his own : but because ye are not of the world, " but I have chosen you out of the world, therefore the world " hateth you." (1 Cor. 4. 13. Luke 21. 17. Jno. 15. 18, 19.) Was he persecuted by the wicked, for the work of God in which he was engaged? So are his people. " Remember the word that I said " unto you ; The servant is not greater than his Lord. If they " have *persecuted me*, they will also *persecute you ;* if they have " kept my saying, they will keep yours also. But all these things " will they do unto you for my name's sake, because they know not " him that sent me." " Persecuted but not forsaken." " I now " rejoice," saith Paul, " in my sufferings for you, and fill up that " which is behind of the afflictions of Christ in my flesh for his bo-" dy's sake, which is the church." (V. 20, 21. 2 Cor. 4. 9. Col. 1. 24.) Thus he and his people suffer together in the same cause. Was he a man of sorrow and acquainted with grief? So are his people ; " Verily, verily, I say unto you, That ye shall weep and " lament, but the world shall rejoice : and ye shall be sorrowful, but " your sorrow shall be turned into joy," (Jno. 16. 20.) Thus he also *shall see of the travail of his soul, and shall be satisfied, who for the joy that was set before him endured the cross, despising the shame, and hath set down on the right hand of the throne of God.* Had he the iniquities and sins of all laid on him? So do his people bear the sins of the world and suffer under them. Ezekiel, in vision, bore the iniquity of the house of Israel and Judah, and the Lord laid on him the iniquity of that nation. (Chap. 4. 4.) The prophet Daniel bore the sins of his people before the Lord and confessed them : (Dan. 9. 20.) and so of other prophets. And Aaron bore the sins and the judgment of the people of Israel in the office of high priest; but not the punishment of their sins.

But as these examples pertain to a former dispensation, and will be considered as types only, we shall attend to some of the apostle's language and exercise, in addition to what hath been shown a little above, " Now while Paul waited for them (Silas and Timotheus) at " Athens, his spirit was stirred in him, when he saw the city wholly " given to idolatry." Why was his spirit stirred? Because he felt the burden of their idolatry; as he also felt the unbelief of the Jews at Corinth; " And when Silas and Timotheus were come from " Macedonia, Paul was pressed in spirit, and testified to the Jews " that Jesus was Christ." (Acts 17. 16. and 18. 5.) But not only in these particular instances did he bear the burden of the sin of mankind, and suffer on account of their sins, that he might lead them to God, but this was the spirit and the work of his ministry. " Know- " ing therefore the terror of the Lord, we persuade men: but we " are made manifest to God; and I trust also are made manifest " in your consciences." " For the love of Christ constraineth us; " because we thus judge that if one died for all then were all dead." " My little children of whom I travail in birth again until Christ be " formed in you." (2 Cor. 5. 11, 14. Gal. 5. 19.) But we need not presume to instance all the cases. All the apostles' labors and sufferings, and all the zealous endeavors which they spent for the salvation of men, prove them to have been possessed of the spirit of Jesus, whom zeal for his Father's house consumed, and who spent his life for the salvation of men. For did Jesus lay down his life for us? We are called also to lay down our lives for him and for one another. " For whosoever will save his life shall lose it; and " whosoever will lose his life for my sake shall find it." " For thy " sake we are killed all the day long; we are accounted as sheep " for the slaughter." " In him we have known love; [in the Greek] " because he laid down his life for us; and we ought to lay down " our lives for the brethren." " Ye shall indeed drink of my cup " and be baptized with the baptism that I am baptized with." (Matt. 16. 25. Ro. 8. 36. Jno. 3. 16. Matt. 20. 28.)

Christ Jesus therefore is our forerunner, our leader and our example, instead of doing what he did as our surety, to cover our sins, or to justify us by imputing to us any of his doings or sufferings. So far from dying to impute his dying to us, that we might not die, he died to set us the example, and to introduce us into the same death, that we may have fellowship with him in his sufferings and in his reward. " Know ye not, that so many of us as were bap- " tized into Jesus Christ were baptized into his death? Therefore " we are buried with him by baptism into death; that like as Christ " was raised up from the dead by the glory of the Father, even so " we should walk in newness of life—For in that he died, he died " unto sin once; but in that he liveth he liveth unto God. Likewise " reckon ye also yourselves to be dead indeed unto sin, but alive " unto God through Jesus Christ our Lord." This is the true result of the whole matter with all true believers, as well as with those to whom the apostle wrote. (Ro. 6. 3. &c.)

But it may be argued by some, that God himself punished his own Son, and that by that punishment he suffered death in the most proper and material point of view. And that God would not afflict him in any other character than that of a surety, or a substitute, for he *did no sin, neither was guile found in his mouth*. Yet thus it is written; " We did esteem him, [pay some attention to him] " stricken, smitten of God, and afflicted—Yet it pleased the Lord to " bruise him; he hath put him to grief: when thou shalt make his " soul an offering for sin, he shall see his seed." " Awake, O sword, " against my shepherd, and against the man that is my fellow, saith " the Lord of hosts : Smite the Shepherd, and the sheep shall be " scattered." " For it is written, I will smite the Shepherd, and the " sheep of the flock shall be scattered." (Isa. 53. 4, 10. Luke 13. 7. Matt. 26. 31.) These things God is said to have done; hence it is argued that Christ did live and suffer as our surety, that his righteousness of obedience and suffering might be imputed to us for our justification.

To obviate these arguments it is insisted that God is sometimes said to do that which he doth not interpose to prevent, because in some cases God is said to do that which is afterward ascribed to another very opposite cause. Thus it is said that *God hardened Pharaoh's heart*, and again, that Pharaoh hardened his own heart. Again, It is said that God moved David to number Israel, " And the anger " of the Lord was kindled against Israel, and he moved David against " them to say, Go number Israel and Judah." But in another place it is said that satan did it; " And satan stood up against Israel and provoked David to number Israel." (2 Saml. 24. 1. 1 Chron. 21. 1.) In this manner it is insisted that God is said to smite, or bruise his Son, and to smite the Shepherd, when in reality the devil and wicked men did it all, but God did not interpose by any absolute or coercive power to prevent it. And this reasoning cannot well be overturned; for we cannot believe that God and the devil join issue in the same mind, so that the devil should aim to do the will of God; *for what concord hath Christ with belial ?* And that the devil and his agents did this deed is not to be denied. *For satan put it into the heart of Judas to betray him ;* and *Him ye have taken*, said the apostle, *and by wicked hands have crucified and slain.*

But this is not all which ought to be advanced for the elucidation of this subject. The sufferings which he endured by the hands of the wicked, from first to last, were laid on him because of his attachment to the Father; *The zeal of thine house hath eaten me up;* and although the Father was not unaware of the consequence, he did not in the least remit the requisition of obedience and a full performance of what he had undertaken. For it was not only expedient, but indispensably necessary, that Jesus, having undertaken to reveal the Father, and to set an example of self-denial and obedience for men, should not fail. *He shall not fail nor be discouraged till he have set*

judgment in the earth. And it was entirely proper and equal in the Father, to require of him all that punctuality and rigid adherence to the truth and character of God which were necessary to perfectly glorify God, manifest the contrast between the way of God and that of fallen man, and secure the salvation of the human race. *Thus he was stricken, smitten of God, and afflicted;* and *thus JEHOVAH was pleased to bruise him;* he hath put him to grief; and *thus he made his soul a sacrifice for sin,* by sending him into the world to execute that purpose and to accomplish that work in the fulness of the Spirit, which could not fail to excite the indignation of those lost beings whom he came to save, until they took his life. Thus the Shepherd was smitten of God; and the work was so strange and the trial so great that the sheep of the flock were scattered. God therefore did not bruise his Son absolutely or directly, but indirectly and by consequence—he did not take vengeance on him for the crimes of others. And an attention to the connection of the words of Zechariah will show that if he took vengeance on the shepherd, he also did on the people; " Smite the Shepherd and the sheep shall be scattered; and I will turn my hand upon the little ones;" and give them a portion of the same smiting. And so it came to pass; for as Jesus was persecuted to death so were his people in the same cause and by the same sword; as it is written, " For thy sake we are killed all the day long; we are accounted as sheep for the slaughter." (Ro. 8. 36.)
" Awake, O sword, against my Shepherd, and against the man my " fellow, [Heb. *the man next to me,* or my neighbor, who takes part " with me and not with the world,] saith the Lord of hosts." It hath long been taught that this was *the sword of justice,* or justice itself spending its fury on the meek Lamb of God, for crimes not his own. But to say he was slain by the sword of justice, or by justice considered as a sword, is to detach all criminality from his murder: for what justice doeth must be at least innocent. But something very different from justice is the sword of the Lord. " De- " liver my soul from the wicked who are thy sword : from men who " are thy hand." (Psm. 17, 13, 14.) Never was there a more unjust sword than that which slew the innocent Saviour. His most inveterate enemies could not convict him of sin, nor lay any just accusation against him; neither did they suppose any such thing in him as suretiship or imputed guilt; but slew him merely in the rage of their malice against God, and in the ignorance of his true character, which indeed they refused to know. *They hated him without cause.* Well therefore did the apostles, on every occasion, charge his death on the wickedness of the Jews, saying, " Ye denied the holy and the just " One, and killed the prince of life ; of whom ye have been now the " betrayers and murderers." " Him, being delivered by the deter- " minate counsel and foreknowledge of God, ye have taken, and by " wicked hands have crucified and slain." (Act. 2. 23.)
But these last words will no doubt be claimed by the abettors of the decrees of God, as appointing and ordaining every thing to come to pass just as it does, and of justification by imputed righteousness,

AND IMPUTATION.

as proving those points. *Him, being delivered by the determinate counsel and foreknowledge of God*, they understand as teaching that he was delivered up to death by the determinate counsel of God. But such a construction only shows the traditionary bias of their minds, and their unacquaintance with divine truth in its connection. It was not to death that he was delivered by the determinate counsel and foreknowledge of God, but to be a leader and example to the people to lead them to God, and so redeem them from all iniquity, while they should follow him, laying aside every weight, and the sin which doth so easily beset, and run with patience the race set before them, looking to Jesus the author and finisher [Greek, *the chief leader and perfecter*] of faith, being the first who lived up to the true faith, and first obtained its end. This is the decree of which I spoke before; That God did decree in direct and absolute terms, not to be reversed, to send a deliverer to redeem mankind from their fall. But when he came in this lovely character, they hated him without cause; for the sake of God who dwelt in him, and whose holiness burnt against their evil nature, so that the reproaches of them that reproached God fell on him; therefore they took him and with wicked hands crucified and slew him.

The foreknowledge of God no doubt comprehended what would be the result of his being thus set forth; but that was no reason why God should not do that which was necessary to be done for man's recovery and God's good pleasure and glory, seeing the Son of God was also willing to come, saying; " Lo, I come, in the volume of " the book it is written of me, I delight to do thy will, O my God; " yea, thy law is written in my heart. I have preached righteousness " in the great congregation: lo, I have not refrained my lips, O Lord " thou knowest it." (Psm. 40. 17, 18, 19.) Thus he was delivered, or set forth to view, according to the Greek text, and thus evilly was he entreated when he came.

This subject is farther illustrated by the parable of the householder, who planted a vineyard and let it out to husbandmen, and sent his servants in vain, who at two different times were some of them killed, and the rest stoned or beaten; " But last of all he sent unto " them his son, saying, They will reverence my son. But when the " husbandmen saw the son they said among themselves, This is the " heir; Come, let us kill him, and let us seize on his inheritance. " And they caught him and cast him out and slew him." (Matt. 21. 33, &c.) This parable Jesus applied to the Jews, concerning himself as the stone which the builders rejected, and yet it is made the head of the corner.

The following words also will no doubt be considered as favoring the doctrine of justification by the imputed righteousness of Christ, where the people are said to be gathered against Christ: " For to " do whatsoever thy hand and thy counsel determined before to be " done." (Acts 4. 28.) The argument is, that God determined that he should suffer these things as our substitute or surety; for there was no cause in him to expose him to such sufferings, being *holy and harmless.* But as no mention is made of any imputation of our sins to him, or of his righteousness to us, it would be forced and unnatural to infer the one or the other from these words. Not denying that God saw it necessary that Christ should die; as it is written; *" Ought not Christ to have suffered these things, and to enter into his glory ?"* according to what we have before spoken of the necessity of his death. The force of this text appears to be, that the things had come to pass according to what the Spirit of God by the prophet had foretold; his counsel had seen and his hand had described by the hand writing of the prophet in whom his counsel was. And this is the primary sense of the word προοριζω [pro-orizo] the Greek word here used, according to its explanation by Prius definio, *to define* or *determine before hand*. " Who by the mouth of thy servant " David hast said, Why did the heathen rage and the people ima- " gine vain things ? The kings of the earth stood up, and the rulers " were gathered together against the Lord and against his Christ. " For of a truth, against thy holy child Jesus, whom thou hast " anointed, both Herod and Pontius Pilate, with the Gentiles, and the " people of Israel were gathered together, for to do whatsoever thy " hand and thy counsel (by the said David) determined before to be " done." And precisely in this manner the apostle Peter hath expounded the same event, on a former occasion. " But those things, " which God before had shewed by the mouth of all his prophets, " that Christ should suffer, he hath so fulfilled." (Acts 3. 18.)

CHAPTER IX.

The subject continued; in relation to the legal sacrifices and other matters.

BUT other arguments are used in defence of being justified by the imputed righteousness of Christ. One is, That the sacrifices under the law were typical of Christ; and hence it is concluded, that Christ is our substitute, and that our sins were imputed to him. But this argument is founded in error, common as it is, and long as it has been sanctioned by tradition. Where do we read in the holy scriptures, that those sacrifices typified Jesus Christ, any more than other men ? Or what was to be seen in that service peculiarly applicable to him ?

That the law was typical, as having a shadow of good things to come, is taught clearly enough. And that the high priest was typical of Christ, is not to be doubted; " For the law maketh men high " priests who have infirmities; but the word of the oath, which was " since the law, maketh the Son, who is consecrated for ever more." (Heb. 7. 28, and other places.) Also that the most holy place, into which the high priest went once every year, not without blood, was typical of the kingdom of heaven where Christ reigns, will be grant-

AND IMPUTATION.

ed; "For Christ is not entered into the holy places made with "hands, which are the figures of the true; but into heaven itself, "now to appear in the presence of God for us." (Heb. 9. 24.) In many other respects the law was typical of things in the gospel kingdom. But all these will not prove that the sacrifices were typical of Christ, or represented him. As Aaron the high priest was typical of Christ, it may not be improper to conclude that the sacrifice which he offered was typical of Christ, in a secondary view, when " He gave himself for us an offering and a sacrifice to God for " a sweet smelling savor," and when " Through the eternal Spirit he " offered himself without spot to God." [Eph. 5. 2. Heb. 9. 14.] What I mean by this sacrifice being typical of Christ in a secondary view is, that it was immediately the offering of the priest as the leader of the people, as Christ offered himself once, as the leader of his people. For the law made no provision for the priests, more than for others, to offer themselves to God, holy and living sacrifices: it remained for Jesus Christ to consecrate the new and living way. And it is worthy of notice that he is never said to have offered himself to God, as a sacrifice for sin, or a sin offering, but an offering and a sacrifice for a sweet smelling savor, a living sacrifice in obedience to God's will, as our example and forerunner. Thus, " When he said, sacrifice, and offering, and burnt offerings, " and offering for sin, thou wouldest not, neither hadest pleasure " therein; (which are offered by the law;) then said he, Lo, I come " (for what? to be made a sin offering to God? Nay; but) to do " thy will, O God. He taketh away the first, (the sacrifices and of-" ferings of the law,) that he might establish the second. (The doing " of the will of God and walking in it after Christ, to God's accept-" ance.) By the which will we [who belong to the true body of " Christ,] are sanctified, [in doing as he did,] through the offering of " the body of Christ once." [Heb. 10. 8, 9, 10.]

The translators have here added the words, *for all*, which are not in the Greek text, and are an unnecessary supplement; for though he offered himself *for all* as the head and forerunner of the body, *the offering of the body of Christ* includes the offering of all the members, who have all to offer themselves to God once for everlasting. " I beseech you, therefore, brethren, by the mercies of God, " that ye present your bodies a living sacrifice, holy, acceptable to " God, which is your reasonable service." [Ro. 12. 1.] But if the phrase *once for all* be understood as relating to the sufficiency of the one offering instead of the many offerings under the law, that acceptation is correct, and the meaning of the text remains unimpaired. For in this we see the perfection and pre-eminence of his offering above those under the law, that whereas they were continued because incapable of effecting salvation; his one offering was sufficient. " For such an high priest became us who is holy, harmless, undefiled, " separate from sinners, and made higher than the heavens; who " needeth not daily as those high priests, to offer up sacrifice, first "for his own sins, and then for the people's: for this he did once, "when he offered up himself." [Heb. 7. 26, 27.]

These scriptures, but especially that including the quotation from the fortieth psalm, proves pointedly what Christ established, as the ground of our acceptance with God, first and last—*Doing the will of God.* "*He that doeth the will of my Father who is in heaven, shall enter into the kingdom.* The sacrifices therefore under the law did not typify Christ as a sin offering to God as being our substitute, but rather the sacrifices of service in obedience to God, which the people have to offer to God in the gospel church, that spiritual house to offer up spiritual sacrifices, acceptable to God through Jesus Christ: no imputation of our sins or guilt to him, neither of his righteousness to us. Now the phrase, *to God,* in the above quotation from the epistle to the Hebrews, (9. 15.) hath not respect to the giving of the offering, as being *offered to God,* but to the quality or character of the person or thing offered. Not, he offered himself *to God,* without spot; but, he offered himself *without spot to God,* that is, *without spot before God,* or in his sight. The phrase is in the same construction in the Greek text as that by which Stephen described Moses, which the translators have rendered, *exceeding fair;* in the Greek *fair to God.* (Acts 7. 20.) These things are plain to the candid among the learned.

Now let us enquire how the sacrifices under the law would apply to Christ, as representing him. "Here is a transgressor; he "brings a lamb to the altar; he lays his hand upon its head and con-"fesses his sins; he must then with his own hands slay it and have "it burnt on the altar before his eyes. (Levit. 1. 4, 5. and 5. 5, &c. See also B. W. Stone's Letters on Atonement, Pag. 30.) Observe; the transgressor had to lay his hand on the head of the beast in the presence of the ministering priest, (not immediately the high priest,) and there confess his sins, and then with his own hand kill the sacrifice, flay it and cut it in pieces, ready to be laid on the altar and burnt. This was the common and regular order of that ritual. If then this sacrifice represented or typified Christ, when a sinner believes in him, he is to lay his hand on his head, confess his sins, kill and crucify him, before the priest. (Who the priest is I need not say.) Now who will suppose that this is the work of a returning penitent, *to crucify the Son of God afresh?* But we have pursued the subject far enough to see that these things will not apply.

Let us now enquire how these sacrifices will apply to those which men have to offer when they believe the gospel. In the presence of the gospel priest, or minister of Christ, he lays his hand on the head of the beast to be sacrificed, which is his own carnal nature, and there confesses his sins, kills the beast that it may be burnt on the altar of God; that is, having confessed his sins, he sets himself, soul and body, to resist the practice and nature of evil, and thus to crucify the carnal mind that it may die forever. "And they that are "Christ's have crucified the flesh with its affections and lusts." Thus denying himself and taking up his cross, he follows Christ.

not doing his own will, but the will of his Father in heaven. Thus the man gives himself up wholly a living sacrifice for the destruction of the flesh, that the spirit may be saved. There must be a whole surrender, without reserve or dishonesty, as the sacrifices under the law must be whole and without blemish. And as under the law, Aaron offered the first offering himself, and afterwards the people offered through him; so Christ made the first offering; and whereas he had no sins to confess, and none of which to repent, after having entered into the way, by the door of confession and repentance which was opened for the people, the baptism of John, saying, *Thus it becometh us to fulfil all righteousness*, he publicly offered himself a sacrifice and an offering to God, for a sweet smelling savor, for the destruction of the nature of the flesh which he had assumed. " And though he was a Son, yet learned he obe-
" dience by the things which he suffered; and being made perfect,
" he became the author of eternal salvation to all them that obey
" him." " For every high priest is ordained to offer gifts and sa-
" crifices; wherefore it is of necessity that this man have somewhat
" also to offer." [Heb. 5. 8, 9, and 8. 3.] Every man had also to find his own sacrifice and not the high priest in his stead, nor God, by any special gift, either to the man or in qualifying and commissioning the high priest, but every man had to furnish an offering for himself out of his lawful substance, and bring it to the high priest and there offer it to God through him.

These sacrifices then were not types of Christ bearing the iniquities of the people by imputation, but rather types or symbols of the people dying each one for his own sin, or each one giving himself in sacrifice to God for the destruction of the flesh, or fleshly nature, [which is the life of the natural man] that the spirit may be saved. And seeing the man could not both die and live, according to that carnal dispensation, the beast died in his room, and his life was spared; so in the gospel, the beast, which is the carnal mind, or nature, is put to death, and the spirit is saved.

It is not improbable that some who have no correct understanding of the gospel, may not feel reconciled with this exposition of the nature of the sacrifices; but let such prove the matter and see if they can discover any application of them to the gospel, [as they were confessedly shadows of something,] which is, on a deliberate and impartial view, attended with fewer difficulties. The law is good if a man use it lawfully; and no doubt but the whole work of God in the gospel was prefigured by the law in some respect, and all the ceremonies of the law had respect to the gospel; but the light of the gospel only can unfold these things with their proper application. For without the light of the gospel, no man had ever understood one of the legal ceremonies; and for the want of this light, by mingling the law and the gospel together, [which yet help to illustrate one another, each one being kept in its proper place,] or by seeking to the dead for the living, and to the darkness for light, men have such improper views of both the law and the gospel.

But the light of the gospel will sufficiently unfold the use of the law, and no doubt the design of many ceremonies of which worldly professors have no understanding. " Seeing then that we have such " hope, we use great plainness of speech; and not as Moses who " put a vail over his face that the children of Israel could not sted- " fastly look to the end of that which is abolished: but their minds " were blinded; for until this day remaineth the same vail untaken " away in the reading of the old testament; which vail is done away " in Christ. But even unto this day, when Moses is read the vail is " upon their heart. Nevertheless when it shall turn to the Lord, " the vail shall be taken away." [2 Cor. 3. 12 to 16.] When therefore men become acquainted with Christ by the gospel, they have a clear understanding.

The opinion therefore, that the Jews in offering their sacrifices, had respect to the blood of Christ, afterwards to be shed for them, and believed in it for their justification, is intirely without foundation. It was evidently not understood that he would be put to death, even by those who believed in him after he came, often as he had told them, until the fact proved it. Had those sacrifices then all typified Christ, (as no doubt they did point to him and concentrate in him, inasmuch as he was the leader, and the first who ever offered a perfectly acceptable sacrifice to God, after whom all others pattern,) the Jews did not know it; and neither did they know the substance to which they did relate, for they could not see the end of those things which were to be abolished. The partial, or ceremonial justification therefore which they found in those things, which were a figure serving for the time then present, was on the principle of their obedience to God in the things which they believed he had commanded them to do. And when any one offered an offering, in all things according to the law, it was imputed to him, and he was accepted; but if in any material point he failed, as in eating any of the sacrifice of a vow on the third day, it was not accepted, *neither was it imputed to him that offered it.* And again; " What man soever there be of the house of " Israel that killeth an ox, or lamb, or goat, in the camp, or that kil- " leth it out of the camp, and bringeth it not unto the door of the " tabernacle of the congregation, to offer an offering unto the Lord " before the tabernacle of the Lord, blood shall be imputed to that " man, he hath shed blood." To the same point is the law of the tithes of the Levites. When they offered the tenth of their tithes as a heave-offering to God and gave it to Aaron, it was reckoned, or imputed to them, " And this your heave-offering shall be reckoned " [Heb. imputed] to you as though it were the corn of the threshing- " floor, and as the fulness of the wine press." (Levit. 7. 18. and 7. 3, 4. Num. 18. 27.) So then under the law, and also in the gospel, as hath been already shown, that is imputed to any one, and that only, which he actually possesses or really performs: and this is the proper use of the word *impute*. Accordingly when Ahimelech was accused by Saul, as being an accomplice with David against him, he pleaded his innocence, saying, " Did I then begin to enquire of God

AND IMPUTATION.

" for him? be it far from me: let not the king impute any thing to " his servant." (1 Sam. 22. 15.) No atonement, therefore, or justification, in these things by imputation, from one to another; there was no substitution in the case; each man had to furnish his sacrifice at his own expense, and not the priest for him; so each one under the gospel is to offer at the expense of his own life, that is, the flesh, and not another for him. But as before stated; the high priest was no doubt a type of Christ; and amongst other things, in this, that he bore the names and the judgment of the people, and the sins of their holy things which they hallowed, or devoted to God, in all their gifts. For thus it is written; " And Aaron shall bear the names of the chil- " dren of Israel on the breastpiate of judgment upon his heart, when " he goeth into the holy place, for a memorial before the LORD con- " tinually—And thou shalt make a plate of pure gold, and grave " upon it, like the engravings of a signet, HOLINESS TO THE " LORD. And it shall be upon Aaron's forehead, that Aaron may " bear the iniquity of the holy things, which the children of Israel " shall hallow in their holy gifts: and it shall be always upon his " forehead, that they may be accepted before the Lord." (Exod. 28. 29, 30, 36, 38.) Thus the high priest bore the judgment and the sins of the peolpe before the LORD, that they might be accepted, when according to the law and appointed order of God, they had rolled their sins over on him, by confessing their sins and bringing their offerings to the ministering priests. For under the law, that which was offered to God was given to the priests. So did Jesus Christ bear the names, and the judgment, and the sins of his people, and still beareth them. " Nevertheless the foundation [or covenant] of " God standeth sure, having this seal, The Lord knoweth them that " are his." " He that overcometh, the same shall be clothed in white " raiment; and I will not blot out his name out of the book of life, " but I will confess his name before my Father, and before his holy " angels. By his knowledge shall my righteous servant justify ma- " ny; *for he shall bear their iniquities—And he bare the sin of ma-* " *ny;*" even of all those who roll them over on him according to the order of the gospel, by confessing their sins and bringing their offerings to God and presenting them to the ministers of Jesus Christ, and thus make covenant with God by sacrifice, and keep it. But neither did God nor Moses, whom the LORD made as God to the people, exact any punishment of Aaron in the execution of his office in the behalf of the people. Neither Aaron therefore, nor the under priests, bore the punishment of the sins of the people, or the reward of their iniquities; they only bore their sins away, and as it were, buried them out of sight, making atonement according to law. So neither did God exact any punishment of his Son, the great high priest of our profession, as a punishment for the sins of his people, or the reward of their iniquities, whom he came to save. But he and his holy priesthood, or he in them, and they in him, bear them away from the people and cover them in charity; for *charity covereth the multitude of sins;* and the priests make atonement and the sins of the people are forgiven them. No imputation of the sins of the people to the high priest, or of his righteousness to them: every one had to make his own offering. So neither is there any imputation of the sins of the people to Jesus Christ, or of his righteousness to them, only as they live his righteous life; *He that doeth righteousness is righteous, even as he is righteous; and he that doeth not righteousness is not of God. Let every one that nameth the name of Christ depart from iniquity.*

The sacrifices under the law were designed for the purification of the worshipers; and this end they answered ceremonially, but did not reach the conscience; for in the first tabernacle " Were offered " both gifts and sacrifices that could not make him that did the ser- " vice perfect, as pertaining to the conscience." " For the law having " a shadow of good things to come, and not the very image of the " things, can never, with those sacrifices which they offered year by " year, continually, make the comers thereunto perfect: for then " would they not have ceased to be offered? because that the wor- " shipers once purged should have had no more conscience of sins. " But in those sacrifices there is a remembrance again of sins every " year." (Heb. 9. 9. and 10. 1, 2, 3.) Thus the apostle fairly proves that they did not purge the conscience, nor in reality take away sin at all. But as those sacrifices, or the blood thereof, served to purify ceremonially, so doth the blood of Christ to those who drink it, purge the conscience before God. " For if the blood of bulls, and " of goats, and the ashes of an heifer, sprinkling the unclean, sancti- " fieth to the purifying of the flesh; (ceremonially;) how much " more shall the blood of Christ, who through the eternal Spirit of- " fered himself without spot to God, purge your consciences from " dead works to serve the living God." [Heb. 9. 13, 14.] This then was the end of those sacrifices, to cleanse the worshipers ceremoni- ally, and of the sacrifice of Christ now, to purge the conscience of the obedient believer, in the true spirit and substance; not by impu- tation of his blood to us, but by doing the will of God as he did it, as has been shown.

But it may be said that " Even Christ, our passover, is sacrificed for us," and this must surely mean, that he is the great Antitype of all the sacrifices, to whom they all pointed, who also was put to death in our room, that his blood sprinkled on us, or imputed to us, may save us from the curse, as the blood of the Jewish passover did the Jews. That he is our sacrifice, and that he was sacrificed for us, will not be denied. But it has been shown how, and to what end; even to be to us an example, and to lead us to God, while we are to follow his track, purifying ourselves, even as he is pure; and the connection of this text also corresponds with this view of the subject to confirm it. " Purge out therefore the old leaven, that ye may be " a new lump, as ye are unleavened. For even Christ our passover " is sacrificed for us: therefore let us keep the feast, not with the " leaven of malice and wickedness; but with the unleavened bread " of sincerity and truth." Thus faithful believers in Christ keep the feast; thus they eat the passover from day to day, eating his flesh and drinking his blood; that is, living as he did and in his spirit. For it is written that *the life of all flesh is the blood thereof;* and again Jesus testifies saying, " It is the Spirit that quickeneth, the flesh profiteth nothing." [1 Cor. 5. 7, 8. Levit. 17. 14. Jno. 6. 63.]

Another argument in defence of justification by the imputed righteousness of Christ, is the saying of Paul, " That I may win Christ, " and be found in him, not having mine own righteousness, which is " of the law, but that which is through the faith of Christ, the righ- " teousness which is of God by faith." [Phil. 3. 9.]

It might indeed, by this time be understood, that the doctrine of justification by faith and obedience, here contended for, is not, in any respect, intended or calculated to contradict the doctrine of justification by the righteousness of God, which is through the faith of Jesus Christ; but to deliver the people from the groundless notion of being justified by the good deeds and sufferings of another, or by the righteousness of another imputed to them, when God hath taught no such thing. For the righteousness of God by the faith of Christ is the same righteousness by faith and obedience, for which we contend; a righteousness and justification according to the faith of Christ, in opposition to the righteousness and justification by the law of Moses, or any other plan, partly or wholly separate from faith in Christ and obedience to him. For that righteousness which is obtained according to God's appointment, and to his acceptance, is *God's righteousness;* and it is always attained by faith in Christ, it is *The righteousness which is of God by faith, even that which is through the faith of Christ.*

A man's own righteousness is that in which he would justify himself, one side of the appointment of God; as the Jews, " Who be- " ing ignorant of God's righteousness, and going about to establish " their own righteousness, have not submitted themselves to the " righteousness of God." (Ro. 10. 3.) Zealous as they were of the law, it was not because they were so attached to the law, or so true and faithful in it, that they rejected Christ, but because, by their own traditions, they had made void the law, and were wanting in the true spirit of it. " For I bear them record," saith the apostle, " that " they have a zeal for God but not according to knowledge." But had they believed the law and understood it, they would have believed Christ. " For Christ is the end of the law for righteousness to " every one that believeth." Accordingly Jesus said to the Jews, " Do not think that I will accuse you to the Father: there is one that " accuseth you, even Moses, in whom ye trust. For had ye believed " Moses ye would have believed me: for' he wrote of me. But " if ye believe not his writings, how shall ye believe my words?" And again; " Did not Moses give you the law? and yet none of you " keepeth the law." And again; " Search the scriptures [or ye " search the scriptures] because in them ye think ye have eternal " life: and they are they which testify of me. And ye will not come " to me that ye might have life." (Jno. 5. 45, 46. 47. and 7. 19. and 39. 40.)

OF JUSTIFICATION

But after the law had served its day, and Christ had appeared, for a man to seek justification in any degree by the law, is to go about to establish his own righteousness, and not submit to the righteousness of God, for that is to go out of God's appointment. Therefore the apostle, although while the law was all he knew, he felt himself blameless, when Christ was made known to him, gave it up, with all his attainments in it, for the knowledge of Christ, " Touching the " righteousness which is in the law, blameless. But what things " were gain to me, those I counted loss for Christ. Yea, doubtless, " and I count all things loss for the excellency of the knowledge of " Christ Jesus my Lord : for whom I have suffered the loss of all " things, and do count them dung, that I may win Christ, and be " found in him, not having mine own righteousness, which is of the " law but that which is through the faith of Christ, the righteousness " which is of God by faith; that I may know him, and the power of " his resurrection, and the fellowship of his sufferings being made " conformable to his death." (Phil. 3. 6 to 10.) But in all this there is not a word of righteousness being imputed to him, especially any vicarious or surety righteousness of Christ. And who could have asked a fairer opportunity to have said, *The righteousness of Christ imputed to me*, had he believed any thing of such a plan? And what can be the reason that Paul, who shunned not to declare *all the counsel of God*, should never find an occasion to name in all his discoures, that which is esteemed one of the main branches *of all God's counsels ?*

But doth not the apostle here expressly disclaim his own righteousness ? Yea, his own righteousness which is of the law, now abolished in Christ. But although he gave up all other laws and attachments for Christ, that doth not imply that he must reject the law of Christ also, and disclaim that righteousness which is through the faith of Christ, even though it be called his own after he hath attained it. As said Jesus, " Except your righteousness shall " exceed the righteousness of the scribes and pharisees, ye " shall in no case enter into the kingdom of heaven. (Matt. 5. 20.) Your righteousness—not mine imputed to you. Now the righteousness of the scribes and pharisees, which is that of the law, is that which the apostle here disclaims, however perfect it might be, (for he was a pharisee as touching the law, and touching the righteousness which is in the law blameless,) that he might gain that righteousness which is through the faith of Christ. And what was the faith of Christ ? To do always the things which pleased God. " Lo, I come to do thy will, O God. He taketh " away the first, (the law,) that he may establish the second;" the doing of the will of God. This was the faith by which Jesus always maintained the union and protection of the Father, as he said ; " And the Father hath not left me alone, for [Greek, because] I al- " ways do those things which please him." (Jno. 8. 29.) And by this same faith believers maintain their union and access to God, as saith the apostle; " Beloved, if our heart condemn us not then have

AND IMPUTATION.

" we confidence towards God. And whatsoever we ask we receive
" of him, because we keep his commandments, and do those things
" that are pleasing in his sight." (1 Jno. 3. 22, 53.) And said Jesus;
" If ye keep my commandments, ye shall abide in my love; even
" as I have kept my Father's commandments, and abide in his love."
When therefore any man hath on him that righteousness which is
through the faith of Christ, it is his own righteousness, as truly as it
is the righteousness of Jesus Christ when on him, and on the same
principle; " He that doeth righteousness is righteous, even as he is
" righteous." But it is all of God; all things being done according
to his plan and appointment, and to his acceptance. " This is the
" heritage of the servants of the LORD, and their righteousness is of
" me, saith the LORD." (Isa. 54. 17.)

Much as is said of their righteousness, as being of God, and of the
righteousness of God by the faith of Jesus Christ, as being the righteousness of his people, it is remarkable that it is never once said to
be theirs by imputation, application, impartation, or any other way
contrary to that of doing righteousness, and so being righteous even
as he is righteous. Even in the epistle to the Romans, (3. 20 to 28.)
where the apostle has insisted so much on faith, he never once
names the righteousness of God, or of Christ, as being imputed to
believers, or Christ's satisfying divine Justice, appeasing God, or
working out a righteousness for his people, or any such thing; (neither any where else;) but shows clearly enough the work of Christ,
in *declaring, demonstrating, or exhibiting to view*, the righteousness of God, in a way different from the law, yet the very same
righteousness which was attested by the law and the prophets, and
is in the gospel manifested, not only to, but also upon all them that
believe, whether Jews or Gentiles. Thus Christ was set forth a
propitiation, [or ιλαστηριον mercy seat, being the same Greek word
which is so rendered in the epistle to the Hebrews (9. 5.) as expressing the place where God appeared to the people, and manifested his
glory: the same word also by which the seventy Jews have generally translated the Hebrew word which the English translators render mercy seat] to *manifest* or *declare* the righteousness of God,
not to work it out or to *make a righteousness for his people, by doing and suffering in their room,* but in a living example, at the expense of his blood, to *exhibit the righteousness of God to view,* for
the remission of sins that are past, even those transgressions which
were committed under the first testament, (Heb. 9. 15.) as well as
for those of the present time, that after such a demonstration of
God's righteousness, in his long-suffering, the way might be open
for him to be just and so to appear, and the justifier of those who
believe in Jesus and obey as he did. To this effect are his words;
" Therefore by *the deeds of the law* there shall no flesh be justified
" in his sight; for by the law is the knowledge of sin. But now
" without the law, the righteousness of God is manifested, being
" witnessed by the law and the prophets; even the righteousness of
" God through the faith of Jesus Christ, unto all and upon all them

P

"that believe; for there is no difference; for all have sinned and come short of the glory of God, being justified freely by his grace, through the redemption which is in Christ Jesus; whom God hath set forth a mercy-seat through faith in his blood, to *declare* [or Greek, for a demonstration of] his righteousness for the remission of sins, that are past, *through the forbearance of God,* (and not by the righteousness of Christ imputed;) to declare, I say, at this time, his righteousness: that he might be just and the justifier of him who believeth in Jesus," (or *of him who is by the faith of Jesus;* as it were a son of his faith; one who lives as he lives, doing the will of God in all things. For that was undeniably the faith of Christ which he kept and for which he came into the world. "Lo, I come to do thy will, O God;" and again, "The Father hath not left me alone, because I always do the things which are pleasing to him.") "Where is boasting then? It is excluded. By what law? of works? Nay; but by the law of faith. Wherefore we conclude that a man is justified by faith *without the deeds of the law.*" True enough; *without the deeds of the law; but not without the faith of Christ which worketh by love.* Disobedience to the gospel is as emphatically the character of the wicked who are not in Christ, as unbelief. "For the time is come that judgment must begin at the house of God; and if it first begin at us, what shall the end be of them that *obey not* the gospel of God?" "But to them that are contentious, *and do not obey the truth*, but obey unrighteousness, indignation and wrath, tribulation and anguish upon every soul of man that *doeth evil.*" "For which things sake the wrath of God cometh on the children of *disobedience.*" [1 Pet. 4. 17. Ro. 2. 8, 9. Col. 3. 6. Eph. 2. 2, and 5. 6.] Obedience is also as properly the character of a christian as believing. "But glory, honor and peace to every man that *worketh good.*" "And being made perfect he became the author of eternal salvation to all them that *obey him.*" (Ro. 2. 10. Heb. 5. 9.) Thus while the works of the law, and that righteousness which is of the law, are excluded from any part in justification, or in keeping union with God from beginning to end, that obedience which is after Christ is never excluded. "For in Jesus Christ neither circumcision, availeth any thing, nor uncircumcision; but faith which worketh by love," and again; "Circumcision is nothing, and uncircumcision is nothing, *but the keeping of the commandments of God.*" [Gal. 5. 9. 1 Cor. 7. 19.]

But on this view of the subject, it may be asked, how is boasting excluded? I ask in return, where is there any room for us to boast (except in God,) that God hath of his own free love and mercy given us a Saviour? and laid the whole plan of our redemption without our knowledge or our aid? and that too, not on account of any goodness in us, but of his own grace? "Not by works of righteousness which we have done, but according to his mercy he hath saved us by the washing of regeneration and renewing of the Holy Ghost." [Tit. 3. 5.] And what have we, which we have not received? If therefore we have received it, why should we boast, as though we had not received it? "So likewise ye, when ye have done "all these things which are commanded you, say, We are unprofit-"able servants; we have done that which was our duty to do." [Luk. 17. 10.] But all these things neither prohibit nor contradict a man's experience of justification, the approbation of his own conscience, and acceptance of God, in the performance of his duty, in making a right use of the things which he hath received, and submitting to the washing of regeneration, or rather in washing himself therein, (wash you, make you clean,) and so being renewed by the Holy Spirit. "Well done, good and faithful servant, thou hast "been faithful over a few things; I will make thee ruler over ma-"ny things: enter thou into the joy of thy Lord." [Matt. 25. 21.] But this subject will be noticed hereafter.

Another argument for justification by Christ's righteousness imputed, is, that Christ hath redeemed us from the curse of the law being made a curse for us. (Gal. 3. 23.)

By attending to the connection we may readily see that no great difficulty need be felt in this passage, it being susceptible, in its most natural construction, of an acceptation perfectly consistent with the doctrine which we are proving. The law here spoken of is the Mosaic, as is evident from the words a little before, "For "as many as are of the works of the law are under the curse; for "it is written, Cursed is every one that continueth not in all things "which are written in the book of the law to do them." Why under the curse by being of the works of the law which required obedience in all things and only cursed those who failed? Why not keep the law and be blessed? For it is written, "The man that "doeth them shall live in them." Why then not do them and live? Because there is no power. The law of Moses supplied not the people with power to keep it, except outwardly; and the man who did them lived in them; had a temporal life, and temporal blessings. But to love the Lord thy God with all thy heart, and with all thy soul, and with all thy strength, and with all thy mind, and thy neighbor as thyself, which things are written in that law, and thus to condemn sin in the flesh altogether, so as to fulfil the perfect righteousness of the law, purging the conscience from dead works to serve the living and true God, remained for the law of faith in Christ, that faith which worketh by love, that Christ, and not Moses, might be the first and have the pre-eminence in all things, having done, and opened the way, as our example, for us to do, that which was impossible for the law, or those under it to do, that the righteousness of the law might be fulfilled in us. This law is also that which was interposed between the promise and the inheritance, and was added because of transgression, until the seed should come to whom the promise was made, but could not justify as pertaining to the conscience; for justification was to be by faith which had respect to the promise. "But that no man is justified by the law in the "sight of God it is evident, for, The just shall live by faith. And "the law is not of faith; but the man that doeth them shall live in them," and therein shall be his life and not in Christ. " Is the law then against the promises of God? God forbid; for if there had been a law given which could have given life, verily righteousness should have been by the law. Christ hath redeemed us from the curse of the law, being made a curse for us: for it is written, cursed is every one that hangeth on a tree." How then did he redeem us from the curse of the law? By taking out of the way that law, or that dispensation of the law, which kept the people under the curse by making demands which it furnished no power to fulfil; " Blotting out the hand writing of ordinances that was against us, which was contrary to us, and took it out of the way, nailing it to his cross." " By wh..m we have received grace and aposticship, for obedience to the faith among all nations for his name." " For Christ is the end of the law for righteousness to every one who believeth." (Cor. 2. 14. Ro. 1. 5. and 10. 4.) But how was he made a curse for us? Rather than give place to the enemy; rather than fail or be discouraged in the work he came to do, until he should bring forth judgment to truth, for both Jews and Gentiles; rather than be lacking in any part of the example which he undertook to be, as the forerunner of his people who were sure to have to suffer for his name; and that he might in all things confirm the covenant of promise made to the fathers; he suffered himself to be taken and hanged on a tree, or crucified, and so by false accusation, endured the curse which the law of Moses prescribed for a malefactor: according to what has been already shown; " That the blessing of Abraham might come on the Gentiles through Jesus Christ; that we might receive the promise of the Spirit through faith." Christ therefore was made a curse by the malice of wicked men for doing his duty which he had undertaken for our redemption, and by becoming a curse in that way, put the seal to the covenant. But he was not made a curse by the Spirit of God; unless as before expounded; " For no man speaking by the Spirit of God calleth Jesus accursed." [1 Cor. 12, 3. B. W. Sto. p. 35.]

But fully to illustrate the above statement, let it be remembered, that the law, although it could not justify in the sight of God, as pertaining to the conscience, and the worshipers were always subject to a sense of being under the power of sin, nevertheless, did not necessarily leave them under the present burden of guilt for the omission of duty; for they were capable of complying with those statutes and ordinances which were enjoined upon them, that being all which was positively required of them for the time being; and in the performance of these institutions they were blessed, and found peace and prosperity; *For the man that doeth them shall live in them.* But as that obedience was mainly ceremonial and outward, so were the blessings which they received of a temporal nature. They had nothing which could minister life to the soul, or take away sin, which was the true spirit and end of the law. Their best ministrations left them in a state of condemnation and death; and the greatest work that whole ministration could do for them, was to waken them to some knowledge of their condition, (for by the law is the knowledge of sin, but not of salvation,) and hold out the promise (in the letter,) of a deliverance to come, so that it is called by inspiration, the ministration of *death* and of *condemnation*. (2 Cor. 3. 7, 9.) " For if there had been " a law given which could have given life verily righteousness should " have been by the law; As therefore the law, which was the only mean of life which they had in possession, could not give life, they could not be under guilt for not having it. But yet they were without that life which was spiritual, " Shut up to the faith which should af- " terwards be revealed." " For the law made nothing perfect, but " the bringing in of a better hope doth;* by the which we draw nigh " to God." (Heb. 7. 16.)

Another scripture, which may be considered as concurrent with the above, is in the epistle to the Hebrews, (9. 12.) " Neither by the " blood of goats and calves, but by his own blood, he entered in once, " into the holy place, having obtained [in the Greek, having found,] " eternal redemption for us." That he entered in by his own blood is not disputed; neither is it disputed, that he spent his life and blood in opening and consecrating the new and living way, that we might find redemption. But all this will not prove the doctrine of suretiship, or imputed righteousness. We have already seen, that there is another method for him to have entered in by his blood, (or through it, as the Greek word is very commonly and properly rendered,) that is, by spending his life and spilling his blood in overcoming the opposition of men and devils against him, as the captain of our salvation, that he might lead us to God, and through death, destroy him that had the power of death, that is, the devil, and deliver those who, through fear of death, were all their lifetime subject to bondage. In this way he obtained, or acquired, redemption; he gained his point, having found eternal redemption, as our captain; the first leader and perfecter of faith; being the first who ever gained full and immediate access to the throne of God. But this is a very different matter from purchasing, or obtaining by proper price, which is never applied by the Spirit of God to redemption, justification or salvation. A man may obtain the object in view by great labor, much sweat and blood, where there is no demand of an equivalent for the thing obtained, and where no one hath any right to make such demand. Thus Christ gained the point of overcoming the world, conquering the devil who had the power of death, and leading us to God, (1 Pet. 3. 18. Greek,) when the devil, who had the power of

---

* *The supplement here added by the translators seems rather to carry the sense to a different point from that of the Greek text, and might cause the writer to be understood as stating that matters were already perfected, whereas all that can be supported by the text, is, that the gospel, or the bringing in of a better hope, is the competent means of making perfect; the full effect to be obtained in due time: the sentence is eliptical.*

OF JUSTIFICATION

death and held souls in bondage, had no right to demand any pay for letting them go. And it was neither reasonable nor possible, that God could demand of him any pay for rescuing those souls whom he sent him to deliver. It is more reasonable that God should have given him a good reward. And this he hath done; for he hath *raised him from the dead—crowned him with glory and honor, and seated him on the right hand of the throne of God*—he hath *appointed him the heir of all things*—*made him the head over all things to the church, and prince over all the souls whom he redeemeth*—*hath highly exalted him and given him a name which is above every name, that in the name of Jesus every knee should bow, of those in heaven and those on earth and those under the earth ; and that every tongue should confess that Jesus Christ is Lord, to the glory of God the Father.* (Phil. 2. 9, 10, 11.) But the obtaining of this point cost him much labor and sweat, his life and blood; although God demanded nothing of him as payment for our redemption, and demands no less of us than before, but much more according to the greatness of our privilege. " Therefore we ought to give the more earnest " heed to the things which we have heard, lest at any time we should " let them slip. For if the word spoken by angels was stedfast, " and every transgression and disobedience received a just recom-" pense of reward: how shall we escape if we neglect so great salva-" tion; which at the first began to be spoken to us by the Lord and " was confirmed to us by them that heard him." (Heb. 2. 1, 2, &c.)

Once more; In defence of justification by the imputation of Christ's righteousness, it may be argued, that although the term *price, buy,* or *purchase,* is never applied directly to salvation or redemption, yet he certainly did pay a price for the people, as it is written ; " And ye are not your own for ye are bought with a price." " Forasmuch then as ye know that ye were not redeemed with cor-" ruptible things, as silver and gold, from your vain conversation re-" ceived by tradition from your fathers, but with the precious blood " of Christ, as of a lamb without blemish and without spot." And believers are called *The purchased possession.* (1 Cor. 6. 19, 20. 1 Pet. 1. 18, 19. Eph. 1. 14.)

I suppose little, if any thing, need be said to satisfy every man of liberal information, that *to purchase, to buy, to redeem,* and *to ransom,* are used as tantamount expressions. This may be more learnedly understood by those who can read the scriptures in their original languages, by comparing the different passages in which those terms are used. These terms all relate to liberating the people from their bondage to the devil, sin and death, and leading them to God to be his possession. " For ye were as sheep going astray ; but are now returned " to the Shepherd and Bishop of your souls." (1 Pet. 2. 25.)

That God's people are said in the scriptures, to be *redeemed, bought,* or *purchased,* will not be disputed ; and that the ransom, or price, of that redemption is said to be the blood, or life, of Christ, is frankly acknowledged. But the indisputed truth of these things makes nothing in favor of justification by the righteousness of Christ

AND IMPUTATION.

imputed to believers, or of his doing and suffering as their surety; for it is never once said that he paid his life, or his blood, to God, as a ransom, or price of redemption or purchase, or that by his life, blood, or any other means, he redeemed his people from the hand of justice, or of God, or any thing else, by which to prove that God held the people to punishment, and would not let them live and be happy, without an equivalent or payment; but on the contrary, that he redeemed them *to God*, and brought them back to him, from whom they had gone away, and become subject to another.

These things will appear in a clear point of view by a judicious consideration of the most conspicuous passages of scriptures, which teach in explicit terms *from whom* and *from what* Christ redeemed his people. And by these it will appear that he redeemed them from the enemies of God and man, as *from the devil; from sin and all iniquity; from vain conversation*, or an unprofitable manner of living; *from the carnal mind*, or from the fleshly principle which rules in men and holds them in bondage; and in a word, from every thing which is contrary to God and subversive of the true happiness of men. " Now is the judgment of this world: now shall the prince
" of this world be cast out. And I, if I be lifted up from the earth
" will draw all men to me." " That through death he might de-
" stroy him that had the power of death, that is, the devil; and de-
" liver them who through fear of death were all their lifetime subject
" to bondage." " And that they may recover themselves out of the
" snare of the devil who are led captive by him at his will." " Unto
" whom now I send thee, to open their eyes, and to turn them from
" darkness to light, and from the power of satan to God, that they
" may receive the forgiveness of sins." " But if I, by the finger of
" God, cast out devils, no doubt the kingdom of God is come upon
" you. When a strong man armed keepeth his palace his goods are
" in peace; but when a stronger than he shall come upon him, and
" overcome him, he taketh from him all his armor wherein he trust-
" ed, and divideth his spoils." (Jno. 12. 31, 32. Heb. 2. 14, 15. 2 Tim. 2. 26. Acts 26. 18. Luk. 11. 20, 21, 52.) Thus mankind are justly represented as being under the power of the devil, and led captive by him at his will, *for the whole world lieth in the wicked one*. But the work of Christ which he came to do, is to redeem them that obey him, from the devil, and destroy his power over them: " Wherefore he saith, when he ascended up on high, he led " captivity captive and gave gifts unto men." (Eph. 4. 8.)

Christ also redeems his people from sin and from all iniquity. This is the same as to redeem them from the devil, for " He that
" committeth sin is of the devil: for the devil sinneth from the be-
" ginning. For this purpose the Son of God was manifested that he
" might destroy the works of the devil. Whosoever is born of God
" doth not commit sin." " But if we walk in the light as he is in
" the light, we have fellowship one with another, and the blood of
" Jesus Christ his Son cleanseth us from all sin." " Who gave him-
" self for us, that he might redeem us from all iniquity, and purify

"to himself a peculiar people zealous of good works." "And he shall redeem Israel from all his iniquities." "This is the covenant that I will make with them. After those days, saith the Lord, I will put my laws in their hearts, and in their minds will I write them; and their sins and iniquities will I remember no more." (1 Jno. 3. 8, 9. and 1. 7. Tit. 2. 14. Psm. 130. 8. Heb. 10. 16, 17.) Mankind in their natural and fallen state, are all sinners, *servants to sin under its dominion, dead in sin, and obnoxious to wrath*, and the work of Christ is to redeem from all these things. "For all have sinned and come short of the glory of God; being justified freely by his grace, through the redemption that is in Christ Jesus." "For sin shall not have dominion over you: for ye are not under the law but under grace." "For when ye were the servants of sin ye were free from righteousness. What fruit had ye then in those things whereof ye are now ashamed? for the end of those things is death. But now, being made free from sin, and become servants to God, ye have your fruit unto holiness, and the end everlasting life. For the wages of sin is death; but the gift of God is eternal life, through Jesus Christ our Lord." "And you hath he quickened, who were dead in trespasses and sins: wherein, in time past, ye walked according to the course of this world, according to the prince of the power of the air, the spirit that now worketh in the children of disobedience: among whom also we all had our conversation, in times past, in the lusts of our flesh, fulfilling the desires of the flesh and of the mind; and were by nature the children of wrath, even as others." (Ro. 3. 23, 24, and 6. 14, 20 to 23. Eph. 2. 1, 2, 3.) Answerable to this work for which Christ came into the world, and which he accomplishes in his people, he hath his name; "And thou shalt call his name JESUS; for he shall save his people from their sins." (Matt. 1. 21.) Now to be redeemed from sin, the cause of death, of the curse and all evil, is to be redeemed from all these effects. *Sublata causa tollitur effectus*; take away the cause and the effect will cease. Again;

Christ redeems from vain conversation, or an unprofitable manner of living. "Knowing that ye were not redeemed with corruptable things, as silver and gold, from your vain conversation received by tradition from your fathers; but with the precious blood of Christ." [1 Pet. 1. 18, 19.] This vain conversation doth not relate merely to useless discourse, of which no doubt they, as well as people in these days, had a great deal; old wives' fables and endless genealogies, which are unprofitable and vain; but to the whole circle of active life, and with the utmost propriety, to the vain forms and ceremonies of religious worship, which they had received of their fathers by tradition, in which there was nothing saving, nothing of that godly edifying which is in the faith of Christ. The Greek word αναςροφης [anastrophees] in the connection in which it stands, fully justifies an acceptation thus extensive, and its common use in the scriptures is not contrary thereto. From this vain circle of life and religion then, in which is no true foundation of hope, christians

AND IMPUTATION.

are redeemed by Christ through his blood, or life, who set them a better example, to teach them and lead them to God in the new and living way, which he hath consecrated, at the expense of his life and blood, through the vail, that is to say, his flesh.

Christ having redeemed his people from this vain conversation, it follows as a necessary consequence that they are redeemed from the carnal mind, or fleshly principle, which rules in men and holds them in bondage; for that is the very core and foundation of the vain conversation of the world, as it is before written, " And you " hath he quickened, who were dead in trespasses and in sins ; " wherein in time past ye also walked according to the course of this " world, according to the prince of the power of the air, the spirit " that now worketh in the children of disobedience: among whom " also we all had our conversation, [αναςροφην] in times past, in the " lusts of our flesh, fulfilling the desires of the flesh and of the mind; " and were by nature the children of wrath even as others." Out of the wretched state, therefore, of death and carnality, Christ redeems his people, or which is the same, God in Christ, and quickeneth them together with him. " But God, who is rich in mercy, for [or through] " his great love wherewith he loved us, even when we were dead in " sins, hath quickened us together with Christ; (by grace ye are sav- " ed ;) and hath raised us up together, and made us sit together in " heavenly places in Christ Jesus." (Eph. 2. 1 to 6.)

That Christ hath redeemed us from the curse of the law, being made a curse for us, hath been already shown, as well as how he did it, that is to say, by suffering himself to be taken and by false accusation hanged on a tree, and thereby suffering the curse which that law announced against malefactors, which could inflict a curse, but could not give spiritual life, because it did not furnish its subjects with power or motive to keep it, except outwardly, and finally, by taking it out of the way, or putting it to death. And in so doing he delivers us from the law also, that imperfect law which worketh death, and also from that carnal mind which was patronised by the law : for, to be under the law seemeth unavoidably to imply being in the flesh. These things are taught in the following scripture. "Wherefore, my " brethren, ye are become dead to the law by the body of Christ ; (Christ therefore hath redeemed us from the law :) that ye should be " married to another, even to him who is raised from the dead, that " we should bring forth fruit to God. For when we were in the flesh, (under the law, or not married to Christ,) the motions of sins, which " were by the law, (thus the law could excite those motions, that is, " lusts, in the members, but could not extinguish them,) did work in " our members to bring forth fruit unto death. But now *we are de-* " *livered from the law, that being dead wherein we were held*, that " we should serve in newness of spirit, and not in the oldness of the " letter." (Ro. 7. 4, 5, 6.) Thus it was left for Christ alone to have the honor of redeeming us from the law and the curse which was in it, and the carnal mind, or sin in the flesh, which is the cause of the curse and the necessity of the law, which was added because of transgressions until the seed should come. For that the carnal mind, or sin in the flesh, was patronised by the law, and never condemned until Christ came, is evident from the apostle's words; "For God, " sending his own Son in the likeness of sinful flesh, and on account " of sin, (because it stood in the way and must be removed,) con- " demned sin in the flesh; that which the law could not do, [or the " impossibility of the law,] in that it was weak through the flesh:" for it suffered its subjects to live in the flesh, and never told them it was wrong, but adapted its injunctions to that manner of life, in meats and drinks and divers washings and carnal ordinances, that is, justifi- cations of the flesh, in the original Greek. [Ro. 8. 3. Heb. 9. 10. See B. W. Sten. Address, p. 29.]

Thus we have taken a compendious, though decissive view of the question, from whom and from what Christ hath redeemed his peo- ple, and still goeth on to redeem those who commit themselves to his guidance. And no evidence appears on which to ground our belief, that he ever redeemed them from God, or from the hand of justice, as some say, or that God at all required any payment of Christ in their stead, or any value, or satisfaction for what they had done, in order to his being willing to give them full salvation, or any thing of the kind. On the contrary, God, even that God who was in Christ reconciling the world to himself is their Redeemer and their purchaser. " Thus saith the Lord, the King of Israel, and his re- " deemer, the Lord of hosts; I am the first and I am the last; and " besides me there is no God. " Take heed therefore—To feed the " church of God which he hath purchased with his own blood." [Isa. 44. 6. Acts 20. 28.] Now God could not purchase or redeem his people from himself; but he could redeem them from the devil, from sin and iniquity, or from their vain conversation, at the expense of the blood of his own son; " For thus saith the Lord, ye have sold yourselves for nought; and ye shall be redeemed without money." [Isa. 52. 6.]

Several Greek words are used by the apostles on this subject, which are translated into the English words, *purchase*, *buy and re- deem*. But the word rendered, *purchased*, [περιεποιησατο, acquired,] where we read that God purchased his church by his own blood, is never by them used where an actual purchase was made or propos- ed by offering value for value. The same is to be said of the phrase *purchased possession.* [της περιποιησεως, the acquisition.] It is a word seldom used, and expresses the obtaining or acquiring of an object by perseverance in good conduct. Thus, " They that have used " the office of a deacon well, *purchase* to themselves a good degree, " and great boldness in the faith which is in Christ Jesus." [1 Tim. 3. 13.] But if the word be maintained to mean a purchase by a price paid, it will equally prove that christians purchase their own salvation by a price paid by them, as that Christ purchased them by a price paid by him. For the same word, excepting the distinction of noun and verb, is used to express the acquisition of salvation by them. " Whereunto he hath called you by our gospel, to the ob-

"taining [εις περιποιησιν] of the glory of our Lord Jesus Christ." "But we are not of them who draw back to perdition; but of them that believe to the saving [εις περιποιησιν] of the soul." [2 Thess. 2. 14. Heb. 10. 30.] Neither is the word *purchase, buy* or *redeem* ever applied to this subject, where it will justify the notion of a price paid for the redemption of the people. These words are used by the sacred writers on this subject in quite a different sense, and are universally figurative. "Remember thy congregation, which "thou hast purchased of old; the rod of thine inheritance which "thou hast redeemed: this mount Zion wherein thou hast dwelt." [Psm. 74. 2.] Now what did God ever give for this congregation which he purchased, or this inheritance which he redeemed? The history of their redemption shows, that he gave the Egyptians to death and destruction, and vanquished the Canaanites before them, that Israel might inherit the land. "I gave Egypt for thy ransom; "Ethiopia and Seba for thee." [Isa. 43. 3.] Thus God purchased his church and congregation redeeming them by conquest.

In like manner, when Christ redeemed his people from their spiritual enemies, as from the devil, or from all iniquity, what did he give to the devil for their redemption?—Destruction.—" *He led cap-*"*tivity captive, and gave gifts to men:* he gained their liberty by conquest, *Having spoiled principalities and powers he made a show of them openly, triumphing over them by the cross.*" [Col. 2. 15.] Thus Christ redeemed his people who are called *The purchased possession*, by the conquest of their enemies. But the difficulty will remain in the minds of some, that God's people are actually redeemed by price as well as by power. The church of God which he hath purchased by his own blood, is the explicit language of scripture; and the apostle in his first epistle to the Corinthians, hath these words in two places, *Ye are bought with a price.* [6. 20. and 7. 23.] Thus the blood of God, or of Christ, is counted the real price of redemption, which is also confirmed by other scriptures, as this, "For thou wast slain and hast redeemed us to God by "thy blood." [Rev. 5. 9.] If then this be considered as a real price given for the people, or for their redemption, a question will arise; Who received it? I have before proved that Christ redeemed his people from the common enemy of God and man. I have also shown what he gave to the devil for their deliverance—*Destruction*. The only sense then in which it can be said that the blood of Christ is the price of our redemption is, that he spent his life, or spilt his blood, in opposing the enemy, by which he finally overcame him. And this agrees with the words of the apostle; "Forasmuch then "as the children are partakers of flesh and blood, he also himself "likewise took part of the same; that through death he might de- "stroy him that had the power of death, that is, the devil; and de- "liver those who through fear of death were all their lifetime sub- "ject to bondage." [Heb. 2. 14, 15.] This statement of the apostle shows, that the taking of the life, or blood, of Christ, is no treasure of joy or consolation to the devil, but proves his destruction throughout all his dominions, wherever souls are turned from the power of satan to God. Such exclamations therefore, as " *That the precious blood of Christ was given by God to the devil in payment!*" That, " *God was so merciless, as to deliver up his only Son, to glut the malice of a blood thirsty demon!*" That, " *The Lamb of God was immolated on the altar of hell*," are only vain parade, becoming a mind infatuated with ungenerous prepossession, or insanity. [See Campbell's Strictures on Stone's letters.] This doctrine promises the devil no good thing, no satisfying acquisition.

That the Lamb of God, however, was immolated on the altar of hell, is true ; though not by God's appointment, but by the contrivance and malice of the devil and wicked men, as has been shown. And how much more consistent is this view of the subject ; that the devil should be offended against the Son of God who came to destroy his works and overturn his government, should hate him and put him to death, (seeing he was man and therefore capable of dying,) than that God should immolate his own Son on the altar of heaven, to spend on him, the relentless fury which glowed in his heart against the crimes of others ? But while the serpent bruised his heel, he bruised the serpent's head according to the promise. But neither Barton in his Letters, nor we, in any of our faith or ministrations, teach any such thing, as that the precious blood of Christ was given by God to the devil in payment ; although we teach it as much as the scriptures teach that, that same precious blood was given by God to God in payment for man's redemption! Neither do we, or Barton, teach, that " God delivered up his only Son to " glut the malice of a blood thirsty demon ;" although there would be as much reason and propriety in believing that he delivered him up for a season, that the people might escape from the devil, as in believing that he delivered up that same only Son to glut the revengeful fury of a blood thirsty Deity ! to render him propitious enough to agree that the people might forsake the demon and serve him, or be willing to give them aid to do so. May not a man of sober reflection say, that of the two plans, it would require an artist, a philosopher, or an angel, to determine which would be the worst demon, the devil or the Deity. When? O when will men discard such unscriptural notions ?

It hath been already proved that God is the Redeemer of his people, that they are redeemed to God, and not from him, or from his justice. " Thou hast redeemed us *to God* by thy blood," is the tribute of praise offered to Jesus Christ. It is therefore proved that no price was ever paid to God for man's redemption, for him or in his stead. Could God purchase his people from himself ? Or would he pay himself for their redemption ? Yet his people are bought with a price—the blood, or life, of Jesus Christ. For his life is as properly called the price of redemption as his blood. For the Son of Man came not to be ministered unto but to minister ; *and to give his life a ransom for many*. Thus the American colonies, now United States, were bought with a price from the British yoke ;

they were bought with the life and blood of the heroes of liberty, whom Britain slew, while America was contending for her freedom. But who paid Britain any price, as a reward for our liberation? Or what did Congress, or rather God by them, pay to Britain for our redemption from the British yoke? DEATH—BLOOD and CONQUEST—destruction of the British power wherever the American principles of liberty prevail. This may serve to elucidate the doctrine of Christ's people being bought with a price, in the only sense in which it can be supported by revelation.

But finally here. The concluding argument with some, for the death of Christ as a satisfaction paid to the justice of God, for our offences, the price of our redemption and the procuring cause of our justification, imputed to us, is, that had God forgiven the human race and restored to favor, without an expiating sacrifice, other worlds, perhaps the inhabitants of the planetary system, would have been exposed to take license to rebel in like manner against the government of God. This indeed appears like the last effort of despair in support of a tottering cause. Who hath ever told us that the inhabitants of other globes know any thing of our conduct more than we do of theirs? And if any of them be exposed to avail themselves of an occasion or a pretext to rebel, who can tell from which source they would draw the most flattering encouragement, provided they were informed of both, from God's forgiving without an expiatory payment, or from his demanding it and providing it himself, clear of all expense to the rebels, and so paying himself? Can any man be prevailed upon to build the hope of eternal life on such unscriptural arguments; too conjectural to enter the heart of any one who views matters as they appear according to evidence?

In the process of this inquiry however, it is found that there is no conclusive argument in favor of justification by the imputed righteousness of Christ. That doctrine also fails of proof from every quarter; because, without any forced construction, all the teachings of revelation are easily understood without implying it, and the burden of these teachings explicitly maintain the contrary: it is not found in the scriptures. We are therefore at full liberty to return to the doctrine of justification by faith and obedience, and find it unfoiled. And it is truly the only plan of justification which can leave a reasonable mind free from embarrasment, and in union with *The Father who, without respect of persons, judgeth according to every man's works.* [1. Pet. 1. 17.]

CHAPTER X.

Objections against the foregoing doctrines, stated and obviated.

ALTHOUGH some occasional objections may have been answered where they occurred, so many will be raised, and some of them so extensive, that it appears most advisable to include the most considerable of them in a chapter expressly for that purpose. Some of them will likely appear more like discussing other doctrines than answering objections; but as they all come in opposition to the doctrine heretofore stated, as well as what will follow, I have concluded to treat them all in the line of objections. And

1st. It is objected that the law must be magnified and made honorable—that mankind have broken the law and are unable to restore it—this therefore must be the work of Christ in their stead. " The Lord " is well pleased for his righteousness' sake; he will magnify the law, " and make it honorable." (Isa. 42. 21.) These words are read with application to Christ as obeying the law, magnifying and making it honorable, in the room of men, as their surety, so that God the Father is well pleased with them for the sake of his obedience, or righteousness.

But such a use of this text, evidently indicates a previously constructed plan into which it is pressed. A man must be hardly bested for support to a favorite scheme, if he will consider this scripture in its connection, and then employ it with confidence to defend the notion of justification by the righteousness of Christ imputed. For there is not one word, either in this text or its connection, to show that it relates to Christ in any part of the character peculiar to him as Mediator. The character described, in the immediately preceding part of the paragraph, is excessively wicked and disobedient, in no sense or respect applicable to Christ, who as a Son was obedient in all his Father's house. So far then are these words from speaking of any mediatorial or surety righteousness, that they are applicable to God only, or JEHOVAH, in the most absolute sense, as resting satisfied with his own righteousness, or justice towards that rebellious people, and proposing to vindicate his own law, without any intimation of the order, or plan, in which salvation is to be obtained, only that God will show it. Let us take a view of these words in their connection. " Hear ye deaf; and look, ye blind, that ye may see. Who is blind " but my servant? or deaf, as my messenger that I sent? (These " are not the characteristics of Christ; he was neither blind nor " deaf.) Who is blind as he that is perfect, (or according to Lowthe, " *perfectly instructed*, or as the Hebrew, *well compensated*. At all " events a perfect one is not blind,) and blind as the Lord's servant ? " (Israel?) Seeing many things, (the mighty works of God,) but " thou observest not; opening the ears, (as if to listen,) but he hear- "'eth not." [Heb. He will not hear.] These things do not bespeak the character of Christ, the obedient Son or servant of God. The prophet then breathes out this reflection concerning the faithfulness of God and the perfection of his work in the event. " The Lord is " well pleased for his righteousness' sake ; (JEHOVAH is satisfied and " enjoys his own good pleasure with regard to the justice of his " dealings towards his people; and in the event,) he will magnify the " law, (which he hath promulgated) and make it honorable ;" (let this people ruin themselves as they may.) This construction is confirmed by the Greek translation of the seventy Jews, who, it must be expected understood their own language.

But however true, that the law of God must be magnified and made honorable, and that Christ performed the same in the most perfect degree, the notion of his doing this in the room of others as their surety, is without foundation in the scriptures. The Lord is well pleased for his righteousness' sake. With whom ? No doubt with him who doeth righteousness. He shall magnify the law and make it honorable. But not a word of its being done by one in the room of another Obedience is confessedly the greatest honor which the law could receive ; and admitting that it received the first and most perfect obedience in the man, Christ Jesus, and was more honored and magnified, or set forth more gloriously, by the obedience of the Son of God, than it could possibly have been by the obedience of any inferior character, his obedience was not to release or prevent his people from yielding the same, or from honoring and magnifying the law in their place, as his true followers, but rather to lead them into a more perfect obligation, and more correct obedience, by his humiliating example. " Let this mind be in you which was also in Christ." " Purge out, therefore, the old leaven, that ye may be-
" come a new lump, as ye are unleavened. For even Christ our
" passover is sacrificed for us." " Forasmuch then as Christ hath
" once suffered for us in the flesh, arm yourselves with the same
" mind : for he that hath suffered in the flesh hath ceased from sin ;
" that he no longer should live the rest of his time in the flesh, to
" the lusts of men but to the will of God." " Be ye, therefore, fol-
" lowers of God, as dear children ; and walk in love, as Christ also
" hath loved us, and hath given himself for us, an offering and a sa-
" crifice to God for a sweet-smelling savor." (Phil. 2. 5. 1 Cor. 5. 7. 1 Pet. 4, 1, 2. Eph. 5. 1, 2.)

This argument is acknowledged in its main position in a book of great authority among a large class of professors. The words are these ; " The moral law doth forever bind all, as well justified per-
" sons as others, to the obedience thereof; and that not only in re-
" gard to the matter contained in it, but also in respect to the autho-
" rity of God who gave it. Neither doth Christ in the gospel any
" way dissolve, but strengthen this obligation." (See Presb'n. Conf'n. of Faith, Chap. xix. Sec. v.) There is not therefore, even a plausible pretext for justification by surety righteousness.

2d. Many have insisted that the idea of justification by obedience is agreeable to the carnal nature of men, and that their pride being opposed to salvation by grace, and justification by the righteousness of another, is the reason they reject that plan, counting it dishonorable and degrading to their own worth, to be justified without taking their own deeds and worthiness into the account. That men in nature are governed by a spirit of carnality, pride and self-will, is not to be disputed. But it is also undeniable that the spirit of carnality and pride leads men a very different way from obedience—quite the reverse; " So that when they knew God they glorified him not as " God, neither were they thankful," " Who were dead in trespasses " and sins (*these are the fruits* of the carnal mind, not *good works,*) " wherein in time past ye walked, according to the course of this " world, according to the prince of the power of the air, the spirit that " now worketh in the children of disobedience: (not in such as love to " do good works:) among whom we all had our conversation in times " past in the lusts of our flesh, fulfilling the desires of the flesh and " of the mind; and were by nature the children of wrath even " as others." " And you that were sometimes alienated, and ene-" mies in your mind by wicked works, yet now hath he reconciled." (Eph. 2. 1, 2, 3. Col. 1. 21.) This carnal mind, which is enmity against God, doth not lead men to obedience or good works, but to wicked works: and men are enemies to God by wicked works and not by good works or obedience.

It is unquestionable that men love carnal ease and the indulgence of their own natures, in the neglect of obedience to God, else why so little obedience, so few good works among those who hope for salvation? Whether they expect justification by their obedience or by Christ's righteousness imputed, (for both acknowledge the propriety of good works,) the name of God is blasphemed through them, for the want of the fruits of faith in good works. But true faith leads directly to obedience: it worketh by love, and by works it is made perfect.

And so far is the above objection carried by some, that the practical self-denial taught by Jesus Christ, for a man to deny himself and take up his cross and follow him, seems to be construed away into a denial of any capability to do what Christ proposed as the true method to partake with him; and for a man to deny that any of his most honest obedience or faithful services can be acceptable to God, so as to have any part in his own personal acceptance, or justification, is counted the true self-denial. A kind of self-denial this, unknown in the scriptures and unsupported by its authority, as well as expressly contrary to its dictates, " For by thy words thou shalt be " justified and by thy words thou shalt be condemned," (in the day of judgment.) " Ye see then how that by works a man is justified, " and not by faith only." " *Well done*—Yea, this is it; *Well done*, " thou good and faithful servant! thou hast been faithful over a few " things, *thou hast done thy duty*—I will make thee ruler over many " things: Enter thou into the joy of thy Lord—Be a partaker of the " joy of the Lord in his final appearing." (Matt. 12. 36, 37. Jas. 2. 24. Matt. 25. 21, &c.)

Never was there a doctrine more soothing to the carnal mind, which loves its own ease and its own ways, than that of justification by faith without obedience, or by the righteousness of Christ imputed—never a doctrine more congenial with the carnal heart, which hates obedience and duty to God, than that which is connected with that of imputation, *the necessary inability of the unregenerate man* to perform the duty which he owes to God; *to believe; to obey*, or to perform any thing acceptable, until God come and perform the saving work in his heart. When the alarm is sounded—*Escape for your lives—flee from the wrath to come—save yourselves from this untoward generation—work out your salvation.* O how agreeable the siren song: *It is all in vain—ye cannot save yourselves—the best ye can do is but sin, until God give you faith—your works cannot be acceptable until you get a new disposition—ye need not toil and slave yourselves for nought—ye may as well be at ease until God's time come, and he give you a new heart.* Hence the cold formality, the dull stupidity, the egregious insensibility towards spiritual things, which so abundantly prevail among the people of that faith. Hence also the painful labor of the apostle James, with those who had fallen into the notion of justification by faith without works, to prove to them that they were wrong, and did not bear the marks of true christians at all.

On the other hand; when the man is awake to a lively sense of his need of salvation, his soul ingulfed in sin and enveloped in the above doctrine with its concomitants, this produces another state of things. No justification without the righteousness of Christ imputed and received by faith alone; no faith without regeneration; no regeneration without imputation; no imputation without faith, and so on. No praying and crying to God, no seeking after God, no confessions and repentance, no attempts for deliverance, but what are all sin, because in unbelief—to call on God is sin, to neglect, say they, is no less—Inevitable death and damnation without faith and repentance; and these cannot be had unless God, by his irrevocable decrees, may possibly have fixed matters so, in the foundation of his own plan which never had a beginning. Of this matter the man has no knowledge; God hath never revealed the particulars of his decrees, and he is at least as likely to be left out of the happy number as not. Then all is hopeless; and after all his sufferings, alarms and cries for mercy, he must be condemned to hell, to suffer the eternal vengeance of God due to him for his sins, because God would not impute to him the righteousness of Christ—" Because " he hath not believed in the name of the only begotten Son of God;" because he hath not received that gift, or grace, which God from the origin of his own nature, which never had a beginning, hath decreed irreversibly not to give. Now the doctrines of justification by the righteousness of Christ imputed, of faith, as the direct and sovereignly free gift of God, and of absolute decrees, are all in one scale. But a gloom attends these doctrines of men, which so misrepresent the dealings of God, too distressing for the human mind to brook.

But tell me, ye who say mankind naturally love the plan of justification by their own obedience, and oppose the contrary because it hurts their pride ; Why do they not yield obedience ? For, corrupt as men are, they are intelligent beings, and by far the greater part expect, more or less, to stand or fall on that ground. It is the most consistent with rationality. Why then are they not found in daily obedience ? Why not saving themselves from this untoward generation ? But daily experience proves, in those who maintain the plan of justification by faith alone, as well as in those who look for it by works also, that the human heart is not so much opposed to any plan, as to real subjection to God in the obedience of faith.

3d. Another objection is, That many of the arguments employed to prove justification by the obedience of faith, more properly apply to sanctification, perseverance, and increase in the grace of the gospel. Thus men suppose justification is the immediate effect of one cause, and sanctification of another ; justification being instantaneous by faith, by taking hold of Christ and his righteousness imputed, and sanctification progressive by, as we may say, the obedience of faith, or obeying the truth. Some call the first an act of God's free grace, and the second a work of his Spirit.

But by the same act, or gift, of God, by which Christ becomes our righteousness, he also becomes our sanctification and redemption. " But of him are ye in Christ Jesus, who of God is made " unto us wisdom, and righteousness, and sanctification, and redemp- " tion." (1 Cor. 1. 30.) If then he is made, our righteousness, or justification by imputation, he is made our sanctification in the same way. For according to the scriptures, God's people are sanctified by faith as well as justified; " That they may receive forgiveness " of sins, and inheritance among them that are sanctified by faith, " that is in me." " And put no difference between us and them, " purifying their hearts by faith." " But ye are washed, but ye are " sanctified, but ye are justified, in the name of the Lord Jesus, and " by the Spirit of our God." (Acts 26. 18; and 15. 9. 1 Cor. 6. 11.) Thus justification and sanctification are attained by the same means, and uniformly go together, so that one cannot exist without the other. If then christians sanctify themselves in obeying the truth through the Spirit of Christ, they are also justified in the same way. If God sanctifieth them through the truth, which is his word, given to them in Christ, and which they also receive and obey, they are also justified in the same way, in the name of the Lord Jesus. " Sanctify " them through thy truth ; thy word is truth. And for their sakes " I sanctify myself, that they also might be sanctified through the " truth." (Jno. 17. 17, 19. Compare 1 Pet. 1. 22.)

Justification therefore and sanctification are attained by the same means, as well as promoted in perseverance, and in the increase of every grace of the Spirit to final redemption. " Whereto we have " already attained, let us walk by the same rule, let us mind the "same thing." "But he that endureth to the end shall be saved." (Pet. 3. 6. Matt. 10. 22.)

And in this view of the subject we may see how Christ is made of God to us, *Wisdom ;* because he revealeth to us God the Father, and teacheth us the things of God. "No man hath seen God at "any time ; the only begotten Son who is in the bosom of the Fa- "ther, he hath declared him." *Righteousness* or justification, *The Lord our righteousness ;* by declaring or demonstrating to us the righteousness of God as, he revealed the Father himself in his own life and example, "Whom God hath set forth a mercy-seat through "faith in his blood, (in that life which he lived, the character which "he sustained, and the end which he had in view in living such a life "at the expense of his blood,) to declare [Greek, for a demonstra- "tion of] his righteousness for the remission of sins, that are past, "through the forbearance of God ; (not through the righteousness "of Christ imputed,) to declare [for a demonstration of] his right- "eousness, that he might be just and the justifier of him that believ- "eth in Jesus," or who is by the faith of Jesus. *Sanctification ;* in the same manner, by becoming our example and leading us to God in the truth by which we are sanctified. "And for their sakes I sanc- "tify myself, that they also may be sanctified through the truth." "By a new and living way, which he hath consecrated for us through "the vail, that is to say, his flesh." (Jno. 1. 18. Ro. 3. 25, 26. Jno. 17. 19. Heb. 10. 20.) And finally, *Redemption ;* by leading us to God, from under the government of satan; turning us from dark- ness to light ; and from the power of satan to God ; that we may receive the forgiveness of sin, and inheritance among them that are sanctified by faith, that is in him. (Acts 26. 18.)

Thus the whole work of salvation, from the beginning, or first de- grees of justification, and finally, full redemption, is carried on by the gifts of God in Christ to men ; all which gifts are contained in the dispensation of the gospel which he hath committed to his peo- ple, "When he ascended up on high, he led captivity captive, and "gave gifts to men. And he gave some, (that is some of those "whom he gave were) apostles ; and some, prophets; and some, "evangelists, and some, pastors and teachers; for the perfecting of "the saints; for the work of the ministry ; for the edifying of the "body of Christ; till we all come in the unity of the faith, and in "the knowledge of the Son of God, to a perfect man in Christ, to "the measure of the stature of the fulness of Christ." (Eph. 4. 8, 11, 12, 13.)

It is a mistake to suppose that justification obtains in the mind of God, or in the records of heaven, as some would have it, and sanctification in the creature. Both are in the creature ; both in the heart and conscience. "Beloved, if our heart *condemn us not,* "then have we *confidence towards God,"* "Having our hearts "sprinkled from an evil conscience." [Jno. 3. 31. Heb. 10. 22.] And the sanctifying, or purifying of the conscience, and fitting it for the service of God, is also effected by the blood of Christ, as much as justification; (should we make a distinction;) "For if the blood "of bulls, and of goats, and the ashes of an heifer, sprinkling the "unclean, sanctifieth to the purifying of the flesh; how much more "shall the blood of Christ, who through the eternal Spirit offered "himself *without spot to God*, purge your conscience from dead "works to serve the living God." [Heb. 9. 13, 14.] This effect of the blood of Christ is justification as well as sanctification, which are both one work of God in Christ, to set us free from the power and nature of sin, and is called justification, as it delivers from the guilt and condemnation of sin, and sanctification, as it delivers from the pollution, and redemption, as it delivers from the power and dominion of sin. But these are all one work. Although to be a little more particular; justification may be considered as going before; not as being perfected before sanctification begins, but as being the ground-work and beginning of it, and so continuing in its progress until the work is completed. For it is also a mistake to suppose that justification is instantaneous, as by the sentence of a judge; but it is progressive, as men come to the knowledge of their sins, and put them away by confessing, repenting and forsaking. "Thou be-"lievest that there is one God; thou doest well:" Thus far then the man had justification, or the ground-work of it; but it was not perfect or saving for the want of good works. "But wilt thou know, "O vain man! that faith without works is dead." Faith not cultivated and improved by works will lose all its power to justify and produce the most piercing and distressing condemnation. When the publican and the pharisee went into the temple to pray, and the pharisee blessed himself in his outward, or legal goodness, and the publican smote on his breast and said, "God be merciful to me a "sinner, I tell you," said Jesus, "this man went down to his house "justified rather than the other." [Luke 18. 14.] But neither of them was justified to perfection. The one however was in a more favorable situation than the other.

But finally here; We may fairly conclude, that all arguments which prove sanctification, perseverance, or continued acceptance with God, by the obedience of faith, prove also justification by the same. "For by one offering he hath perfected forever them that are sanctified." And this is the same offering by which men receive justification or the forgiveness of sins; "Whereof the Holy Ghost also "is a witness to us: for after that he had said before, This is the co-"venant that I will make with them, After those days, saith the "Lord, I will put my laws into their hearts, and in their minds will "I write them; and their sins and iniquities will I remember no "more. Now, where remission of these is, there is no more offer-"ing for sins." (Heb. 10. 14 to 18.) And this view of the subject agrees correctly with the work of God in giving his Christ whom man despiseth as a covenant, or purifier, to the people. "I will pre-"serve thee, and give thee for a covenant [ברית: a purifier, from "בר to purify] to the people." "But who may abide the day of "his coming? and who shall stand when he appeareth? for he is

" like a refiner's fire, and like the fuller's soap." [ברית : purifier or covenant.]

4th. It will likely be objected by some, that the people of God in old time, did not plead justification, or acceptance with God for their good works, but for the Lord's mercy's sake. But observe; Never for the righteousness of another imputed to them. And to support this objection many scriptures may be adduced, some of which shall be noticed.

But let it be considered for what reason they never, or so seldom, pleaded their own good deeds, or faithfulness, even because they had nothing to plead on that ground, being continually disobedient. But wherever they had been up to their duty, they were not afraid to own it, and feel justified in what they had done. Thus the prophet Isaiah, (64. 5, 6.) " Thou meetest him that rejoiceth and worketh " righteousness; those that remember thee in thy ways:" (these stand accepted: but in the next place;) " behold, thou art wrath; for we have sinned." No wonder then that he saith, " But we are " all as an unclean thing, and all our righteousnesses are as filthy rags; " and we all do fade as a leaf, and our iniquities like the wind have " taken us away." This expression, *And all our righteousnesses are as filthy rags*, is greatly insisted on to prove that a man can have no acceptable righteousness, nor perform any acceptable obedience in his own person; as if the wickedness of the rebellious Jews were of the same nature as the obedience of a faithful christian. Daniel also (9. 18, 19,) saith, " For we do not present our supplications before " thee for our righteousness, but for thy great mercies. O Lord, " hear; O Lord, forgive; O Lord, hearken and do; defer not for " thine own sake, O my God: for thy city and thy people are called " by thy name." But he gives a good reason for not pleading their own righteousness—*because they had not done righteously*, but wickedly; (v. 11.) " Yea, all Israel have transgressed thy law, even by " departing, that they might not obey thy voice; therefore the curse " is poured upon us, and the oath which is written in the law of Mo- " ses, the servant of God, because we have sinned against him." But see on this occasion, the words of Nehemiah, (13. 14,) " Re- " member me, O my God, concerning this, and wipe not out my " *good deeds that I have done* for the house of my God, and for the " offices thereof; and of Hezekiah, (Isa. 38. 2, 3.) " Then Hezeki- " ah turned his face to the wall, and prayed unto the Lord, and said, " Remember now, O Lord, I beseech thee, how I have walked be- " fore thee in truth, and with a perfect heart, and have done that " which is good in thy sight;" and the Lord heard his prayer. See also the words of David; (Psm. 7. 8.) " Judge me, O Lord, accord- " ing to my righteousness, and according to mine integrity that is in " me." And the writers of that day throughout, exclude every prospect of acceptance with God on any other principle than obedience. " Who shall ascend into the hill of the Lord? and who shall stand " in his holy place? He that hath clean hands, and a pure heart; " who hath not lifted up his soul unto vanity; nor sworn deceitfully.

"He shall receive the blessing from the Lord, and righteousness
"from the God of his salvation." (Psm. 24. 3, 4, 5.) But in the
case of iniquity actually committed, the only method was to make
sacrifice to God according to the law, in repentance, with confession
and forsaking. "Blessed is he whose transgression is forgiven, whose
"sin is covered. Blessed is the man unto whom the Lord imputeth
"not iniquity, and in whose spirit there is no guile. When I kept
"silence my bones waxed old: through my roaring all the day long
"(for day and night thy hand was heavy upon me,) my moisture is
"turned into the drought of summer. I acknowledged my sin unto
"thee, and mine iniquity have I not hid. I said I will confess my
"transgressions unto the Lord; and thou forgavest the iniquity of
"my sin." (Psm. 32. 1 to 5.) Agreeable to these things are the words
of the apostle James, (4. 8, 9, 10.) "Draw nigh to God, and he will
"draw nigh to you. Cleanse your hands, ye sinners; and purify
"your hearts, ye double-minded. Be afflicted, and mourn, and weep:
"let your laughter be turned to mourning, and your joy to heaviness.
"Humble yourselves in the sight of the Lord, and he shall lift you
"up." And the testimony of Christ and his apostles, is clear enough,
that without obedience there is no acceptance with God, or justification in the conscience, and this testimony is sufficient for our purpose.

Nevertheless, it is not intended to argue that those who do righteousness in the obedience of faith, even the faith of Christ, have any right or any feeling to ask any thing of God as the reward thereof, as though they had done any thing more than their duty, or could be profitable to God, as a man may be profitable to a man; but death and the curse are the proper wages and natural fruit of sin, and as sin and disobedience stand in the way of the free love and blessing of God to men, that being removed and kept out of the way, the riches of God's free grace, and the communion and blessing of his nature have free access; and as there can be no guilt where there is no sin, justification in the conscience and before God is the natural fruit of innocence and obedience: and in these is true righteousness; "The "work, therefore, of righteousness, is peace, and the effect of righte-
"ousness, quietness and assurance forever."

5th. On this plan of justification by the obedience of faith in each one, some may conclude, that no grace is displayed in God, for each one receives just according to his works, and stands or falls according to his own proper character. Whether grace is displayed or not, God and his people will judge. But the fact is established by revelation, that God will finally judge every man according to his works, and that every one shall receive *according to the things done in the body*, whether good or evil; as before proved, "According to the
"revelation of the mystery, which was kept secret since the world
"began, but now is made manifest, and by the scriptures of the pro
"phets, according to the commandment of the everlasting God
"made known to all nations for the obedience of faith." (Ro. 16, 25, 26.)

And when people are truly affected by the salvation of God, and properly leavened into it, growing up into Christ in all things, they will not be disposed to deny or be insensible of the grace of God displayed through Jesus Christ, in the whole plan, from beginning to end. Was there no grace displayed in God's sending his Son into the world, with the generous proposals, that whosoever will believe on him, and receive him as their Lord, may not perish, but have eternal life? For to as many as receive him to them, gives he power to become the Sons of God, even to them that believe in his name. Or would it have displayed more grace, and have been more to the honor of God, to have sent his son with these fair proposals, while at the same time no one could possibly reach the terms of the offered salvation, but must inevitably perish in the additional crime of rejecting the gospel, trampling under foot the Son of God and counting the blood of the covenant wherewith he was sanctified, an unholy thing, together with his other sins, because he hath not done that which he could not do, unless God should do in him a work, in addition to the gospel provision, which he had never promised to any one individually, and in his own unalterable purpose and decree, had limited to a part, while all are equally invited and accounted equally guilty for not complying? Would such a plan have displayed more grace in God? When! O when will men let God be equitable, just and true? Is there no grace displayed in bringing about, and pursuing mankind with a gospel exactly fitted to their condition and necessity, into which they can come, according to their own faith, and have eternal life, by presenting themselves a living sacrifice to God, on such terms as are in their reach without farther aid than what is provided in the gospel? Or would it have displayed more grace to have made the gospel offers a mere parade, its proposals being such as no man can reach, in the condition in which the gospel first finds him? How deeply must the notion of such a gospel wound the character of its author, and aggravate the misery of man? Is there no display of grace in the gospel which furnishes every man with the full and unquestionable authority of God to him, as an individual, to believe and obey with the full confidence of eternal life, on no harder conditions than those which are in his reach, and nothing more required to be believed than those, the evidences of which are easy, and adapted to his physical powers? Or would there be more grace displayed in a gospel which would leave every man uncertain of his right or capability of believing, until a partaker of that salvation, or that Spirit which the gospel proposes as the fruit of his faith after he believes and not before? *In whom, after that ye believed, ye were sealed with that holy Spirit of promise.* Is there no grace displayed in the character of Christ, the author of this benevolent gospel, in whom are hid all the treasures of wisdom and knowledge, and out of whose fulness we may all freely receive grace, according to each grace treasured up in him? Is there no grace in the continued supplies of help, protection, strength and comfort which his obedient people receive from day to day? and in that earnest pursuit which the gospel makes to gain mankind and bring them into the number of the blessed? Or must it destroy all grace in the plan, because the blessings are in reach of the needy? What grace or goodness would appear in proposals of mercy, quite out of the reach of those who need it?

But the objection will be carried farther; That the greatest glory is ascribed to God, by leaving all the work to him, and waiting on him to do it. Some people affect to be so deeply devoted to the glory of God, that they seem as if they could not endure to have any one yield any practical honor to him, and feel conscious of having done his duty in obeying and serving God, lest God should be dishonored by the man's service and justified conscience? as if God disdained to have men serve him and feel conscious of having done their duty, after having taken so much pains to bring them to it. God hath done, and still doeth, all that is necessary for him to do. He hath introduced and established the everlasting gospel on a permanent foundation, against which the gates of hell cannot prevail, and hath his ministers always ready to minister to those who shall be heirs of salvation, even all those who will obey that gospel which includes all in the book of life, without farther restrictions, who do not voluntarily exclude themselves. How then shall we escape if we neglect so great salvation? With what color of truth can we withhold our consent under the pretext of that plan robbing God of his glory, which He hath devised? Or doth God require us to contrive a plan to glorify him, superior to his own? The way to glorify God is to worship him, and to order our life according to his directions without any scruples as to the propriety of the plan. " Whoso offereth " praise glorifieth me : and to him that ordereth his conversation " aright will I shew the salvation of God." (Psm. 50. 23.)

Should a noble prince, out of pure mercy and compassion to a perishing beggar, on the simple terms of putting away his rags and nastiness, coming into his premises, and doing what would be convenient for his comfort and health, of such things as the prince desired to have done, taking care not to dishonor the prince or injure any of his subjects or himself, and the like. Should this beggar object, that it would be dishonoring to the prince to suppose he could accept of these offers, unless the prince should first make him willing and able by some other method besides these offers, and so withhold his consent, would not every one pronounce him worthy to die? But should he be gained by the proposals without any other operations, enter into that comfortable manner of life, and receive from time to time increased benefits, as he became able to use them to profit, to whom would the honor be due? Would not he and all others ascribe it all to the prince? while in the mean time, the beggar would feel the conscientious satisfaction and justification, that he had accepted the generous offer and done his duty; the prince also would acknowledge the same, approve the kindness which he had shown, and perfect union would subsist between them. So is the gospel. God giveth to all who will come eternal life in Christ, or the just and equitable terms of faith and obedience, in such proposals as presuppose their capability of doing what is required, and a continual supply of aid to such, as fast as needed. To whom then is the glory due? to God or man? or wherein would it rob God of any glory, that the man should have the mental satisfaction, the conscientious justification, that he had yielded to the offers so generously made? Will it dishonor God for men to comply with his offers and receive the very benefits which he intends they should receive?

Who then glorifies God most? the man who believes the truth of God and submits to what he is taught, or he who declines, saying he cannot take God at his word? Doth not the man who rejecteth such offers under such pretence as incapability, impute fraud to God? Yea, surely. We are called upon to be actively employed; To awake out of sleep and arise from the dead, with the promise annexed, that Christ shall give us light; to save ourselves from this untoward generation; To glorify God with our bodies and spirits which are God's. And are we to suppose that God makes such proposals and demands, in the full knowledge that a compliance is out of our reach, in the condition in which the gospel finds us? If so, he is a mocker of our woes. For it is to be remembered, as before shown, that the gospel is sent to us as a remedy from our present misery, adapted to all our wants and equal to our full deliverance, in the full consideration, and knowledge of all our inability and all our guilt from the fall until now. No reasoning therefore can be supported against the plan of justification by the obedience of faith, and the doctrines connected therewith, as though it robbed God of any glory, or came short in the display of grace in God, seeing his grace is displayed in the whole plan from beginning to end, and the greatest glory is attributed to him by obedience; which cannot be denied :

And when on earth we've travell'd through, And done the best that we can do,

The glory all to God is due, We have but done our duty.

6th. Some may object; That, in all the discussions on this subject, we are led to view Jesus Christ as contending against the nature of sin in himself, like as other men; and this seems to derogate from the honor of the Son of God, *who is holy, harmless, undefil d, and separate from sinners.* Whereas Jesus was not born into the world by the works of ordinary generation, as other men are, but spoken into being by the WORD of God, the co-operating power of the Father and Spirit, as it was said to Mary; "The HOLY GHOST shall come " upon thee, and the power of the HIGHEST shall overshadow thee, " therefore, that *Holy One* when born, shall be called the Son of " God," it would be expected, that he came into the world, entirely disengaged and free, from the nature and fountain of sin. But the people need not be alarmed for the character of the Redeemer, lest while they are solicitous to vindicate and magnify, they diminish it: the knowledge and thorough investigation of truth, with answerable practice, will never disgrace the victorious Son of God. And;

OBJECTIONS

In the first place? It is clear, that notwithstanding he came into the world by an extraordinary work of God, he was " Born of a woman, " born under the law, to redeem them that were under the law, that " we might receive the adoption of sons." Thus it behoved him to be born [γενομενον, Gal. 4. 4.] as the beginning and parent of the new and spiritual creation and family of God, and in the position, or place of those whom he came to redeem; as it is written; " For both he " that sanctifieth, and they who are sanctified, are all of one; for " which cause *he is not ashamed* to call them brethren." By being born, therefore, of a woman, who was one of the same fallen family, whom he came to redeem, and according to the physical order of gestation and birth, the WORD became flesh; he was clothed in human flesh and blood, just such as the younger members of the family partook, who were to be gathered to him as their Redeemer, and in that process he assumed the same nature, stepped into their place and took their burdens on himself; *Surely he hath borne our griefs and carried our sorrows ;* and engaged by all means to *lead them* to God, being himself a fellow sufferer with them? *Made a little lower than the angels for the suffering of death.* All these things are clearly set forth in the scriptures, some of which are these; " Forasmuch " then as the children are partakers of flesh and blood, he also him- " self likewise took part [παραπλησιως μετεσχε, unitedly partook] " of the same; that through death," *or by dying to sin, For in that he died, he died to sin, once,* that " he might destroy him that had the " power of death, that is, the devil; and deliver them who through " fear of death, were all their lifetime subject to bondage. For, ve- " rily he took not on him the nature of angels; but he took on him " the seed of Abraham. Wherefore, in *all things* it behoved him to " be made like unto his brethren; that he might be a merciful and " faithful high priest, in things pertaining to God, to make reconcili- " ation for the sins of the people; for in that he himself hath suffered, " being tempted, he is able to succour them that are tempted." To wit, because he had experienced the same trials, and had learned to combat the enemy; for " Though he was a Son, yet learned he obe- " dience by the things which he suffered." Thus he was a subject of the same sufferings, temptations and feelings of infirmities, with his brethren. " For we have not an high priest who cannot be touch- " ed with the feelings of our infirmities; but was in all points tempt- " ed *like as we are,* yet without sin." For temptation is no sin; but yielding is sin; and in all his temptations he never yielded: he was therefore, *holy, harmless, undefiled, and separate from sinners,* from first to last: a victorious leader and example of his people.

Nevertheless, it remains true, that he held a sore conflict with the nature of sin in himself, like other men, as just now proved. And all this was necessary in fulfilling the commission with which he was sent: as the beginning of the new and spiritual creation of God, *the first born from the dead,* the first parent of the family who are saved, *the first leader and perfecter of faith,* the ONE who first, by a sore combat and complete victory, obtained access to the throne of

God, in his own behalf and in the behalf of his people; when there was no mediator, and the way to the mercy-seat was untrodden, having never been opened. The prophet Isaiah describes, in most pathetic language, the interesting scene—the engagement, the conflict, and the victory. " Who is this that cometh from Edom, with
" dyed garments from Bozrah? this that is glorious in his apparel,
" travelling in the greatness of his strength? I that speak in righte-
" ousness, mighty to save. Wherefore art thou red in thine apparel,
" and thy garments like him that treadeth in the wine-fat? I have
" trodden the wine-press alone; and of the people there was none
" with me: for I will tread them [in the Hebrew and Greek copies,
" have trodden them] in mine anger, and trample [have trampled them
" down, ואדרכם באפי וארמסם:] in my fury; and their blood shall
" be [hath been] sprinkled upon my garments, and I will stain [have
" stained] all my raiment." (And these things have given me the appearance which I exhibit to view.) " For the day of vengeance is
" in my heart, and the year of my redeemed is come. And I looked,
" and there was none to help; and I wondered that [I was brought
" into sore consternation, and yet] there was none to uphold;
" therefore mine own arm brought salvation to me; and my fury it
" upheld me." [There being no mediator, to whom to look for help, I gained the victory by the exertion of my own arm, and thus became foremost in the great work of salvation, gained the pre-eminence, and was made, through sufferings, a perfect mediator for the benefit of all who come after.) " And I will tread [have trodden]
" down the people in mine anger, and make [have made] them drunk
" in my fury; and will bring [have brought] down their strength, [or
" blood] to the earth." This prophecy is not alone, in speaking of future events as being already past, The following is descriptive of the same work, and includes both the past and the future. " And he
" saw that there was no man, and wondered that [was brought into
" sore consternation, because] there was no intercessor; (on
" whom to lean;) therefore *his arm* brought salvation to him, and
" his righteousness it sustained him. For he put on righteousness as a
" breastplate, and an helmet of salvation upon his head; and he put
" on the garments of vengeance for clothing, and was clad with zeal
' as a cloak. According to their deeds, accordingly he will repay,
" fury to his adversaries, recompense to his enemies; to the islands
" he will repay recompense. So shall they fear the name of the
" LORD from the west, and his glory from the rising of the sun: when
" the enemy shall come in like a flood, the Spirit of the LORD shall
" lift up a standard against him. And the Redeemer shall come to
" Zion." (Isa. 63. 1 to 6. and 59. 16 to 20.) These prophecies, as it is common, are metaphorical, and by the destroying and treading of the nations down, set forth the final and total overthrow of the nature which rules over the whole, the carnal mind, which is enmity against God, and must be utterly rooted out from all who are saved. All the nations have to be broken to pieces, before they will become subject to the government of Christ; but as fast as they are thus consumed, brok-

en off from the old creation and nature, *the Redeemer can come to Zion, and to them that turn from ungodliness in Jacob,* and to none else. Another prophecy will serve to elucidate this subject, and show, that the destruction of the old nature is represented by the overthrow of the people. "For, behold, the day cometh that shall burn as an "oven; and all the proud, yea, and all that do wickedly, shall be as "stubble: and the day that cometh shall burn them up, saith the "LORD of hosts, that it shall leave them neither root nor branch. "But to you that fear my name shall the Sun of righteousness arise "with healing in his wings; * * * And ye shall tread down the wick- "ed; for they shall be ashes under the soles of your feet in the day "that I do this, saith the LORD of hosts." It is not the Spirit of chris- tianity to use the sword or any carnal weapon, or to oppress or injure the persons of men, this prophecy, therefore, as well as the former, relates to the subduing of the people by the gospel, when the Sun of righteousness should arise, and the Redeemer come to Zion, and to those who fear God. And however weak and soothing some may suppose this prospect will appear to men in nature, it is found in ex- perience, that the prospect of being brought under the yoke of Christ, is of a more deathly nature to the people of the world, than the expectation of any of God's judgments: it takes their life.

But to return to the point in hand. The scriptures which we have been contemplating show clearly, that Jesus was a subject of warfare against the nature of sin in himself, and did actually overcome, and obtain salvation to himself first, as an individual man, (but the parent and example of his subjects,) and that he gained this conquest by overcoming the whole world, which bent its whole force right against him, so that he had to wade through the whole to reach the throne of God: hence the warlike and victorious appearances described by the prophet. He hath overcome the world: in himself therefore; for it was not yet overcome in others. Nevertheless:

That he is holy, harmless, undefiled, and separate from sinners from the beginning, and so remains, is not contested; but that is no proof that he had not to contend against the nature of sin in himself: such a conflict adds greatly to the lustre of his glory and his power in overcoming sin. For how did he support this character which he so honorably sustains? Not by having no trials or temptations, but by not yielding to them. He was holy, harmless and undefiled. By being wholly devoted to God; never doing any thing evil, injurious, or contrary to innocence, in the least instance; never uniting, consent- ing, or meddling with sin to defile himself in the smallest particle; and accordingly, was separate from sinners, because he never par- took with them, in *their ways,* who do *their own will;* but on the contrary directed his course towards God, according to his calling and commission.

To suppose that the man Christ Jesus, was separate from sin and sinners, in such a manner as to have no real contact with sin, real conflict against it, as assaulting him in his own person, nor real temptation to sin, is not only contrary to scripture, as already shown, but also tends to rob him of much of the honor of his victory, and of the glory due to his name, as well as to derogate from the glory of God in the great work of man's redemption. What honor is there in a combat and victory where there is no antagonist? Or if an antagonist be admitted, yet such an one, and in such a situation, as to have no room in his superior combatant, to ply his art or power against him, no place in him, no grip on him of which to avail himself? I say, what honor is attached to such a victory, compared with that over a powerful and subtle enemy who has full access and liberty to ply his heaviest artillery? The honor and glory of Christ's victory are predicated on the principle of his taking the enemy on his own ground, and there beating him, after he had become weak through the flesh which he assumed when he came on the battle ground, that is into the world, and thus exposed himself to the enemy, subject even to death. "For though he was crucified through "weakness, yet he liveth by the power of God." (2 Cor. 13. 4.) "But we see Jesus, who was made a little lower than the angels for "the suffering of death, crowned with glory and honor; that he by the "grace of God should taste death for every man. For it became him "for whom are all things, and by whom are all things, in bringing many "sons to glory, to make the captain of their salvation perfect through "sufferings." (Heb. 2. 9, 10.) "Who being in the form of God "thought it not robbery to be equal with God, [or as God,] but "made himself of no reputation, and took on him the form of a "servant, and was made in the likeness of men; and being found "in fashion as a man, he humbled himself, and became obedient un- "to death, even the death of the cross; wherefore God also hath "highly exalted him, and given him a name which is above every "name; that in the name of Jesus every knee should bow, of those "in heaven, and those on earth, and those under the earth; and that "every tongue should confess that Jesus Christ is Lord to the glory "of God the Father." [Phil. 2. 6 to 11.]

A man may in justice be counted honorable who abstains from drunkenness and every other vice, when he has no opportunity to be drunken, and no appetite for the intoxicating liquor; but his honor is greatly augmented, and the renown of his name magnified, who, being possessed with an insatiable thirst for spirits, in the midst of flowing liquors presented to him on every hand, faithfully bears his cross, overcomes his appetite, and out of a pure principle of goodness and propriety, leads a life of sobriety, to the conviction and conversion of many to the same honorable life. Not as though it were any direct honor to be possessed of a thirst for intoxicating spirits; but the honor is in passing through unfoiled when beset with an enemy or pestilence. God is essentially and intrinsically glorious in himself; but the brightest and most eminent display of his glory is in Christ, who as already seen, became man, was made in all things like his brethren, entered the list with the enemy, was tempted in all points like as we are, overcame by the cross, led captivity captive, and gave gifts to men, and thus in all things became our example, that we should follow his steps, that he might lead us to God by his own example, in the new and living way which he hath consecrated for us through the vail, that is to say, his flesh. In him the power of God is brought into contact with the enemy, that the real contrast between holiness and sin, between the obedience of faith and rebellion, might be manifested to the utmost, and the power of God, on the side of holiness and obedience, prevails. In like manner as the glory of God is displayed in Christ Jesus by the salvation which he wrought, and the victory which he gained over sin and death, and by the power of God in the great work of redemption, the same display of his glory is made in the whole body, the church, of whom he is the head. "For though he was crucified through weakness, "yet he liveth by the power of God: for we also are weak in him, "but we shall live with him, by the power of God." "And he "said unto me, My grace is sufficient for thee: for my strength is "made perfect in weakness." [2 Cor. 13. 4. and 12. 9.]

7th. It seems an insurmountable difficulty with some, against the foregoing doctrines, particularly that of the unrestrained privilege of all to believe and obey, *That faith is the gift of God*, it is therefore certain that none can believe or obey to acceptance until they receive that gift of faith from God. It might be surprising to find it asserted, that that gift is already made to all who hear the gospel. But so it is; for the gospel is not a mere rational scheme of morals, but the power of God. It is always ministered in the Spirit; for the Spirit of God is in those who minister it wherever they preach it, to convince the world of sin, of righteousness, and of judgment. [Jno. 16. 7, 8. 2 Cor. 3. 6.] That preaching which doth not minister the gift of faith, or the privilege of believing, unlimitedly to all who hear, is not the true gospel. Faith cometh, or is produced, by hearing, and hearing by the word of God; and this is *the word which by the gospel* is preached to you.

It is evident that the term, *faith*, is used in the scriptures, in a more extensive sense than that which is included in its simple meaning, which is, the believing or crediting of a report on sufficient evidence. But it is also evident, that the simple meaning of the term is included wherever it is used throughout the sacred writings. Thus, "Hast thou faith? have it to thyself before God;" (Ro. 14. 22.) where the term *faith*, evidently means *knowledge*, or the understanding of a certain matter; which was, that the eating of meat was innocent if done without offending others; but the simple meaning of faith is fairly included. "But before faith came we were kept un- "der the law, shut up to the faith which should afterwards be re- "vealed. Wherefore the law was our schoolmaster to bring us [or "pointing us,] to Christ. But after that faith is come we are no "longer under a schoolmaster." (Gal. 3. 22—25.) Now it is evident that the term *faith*, in this passage, includes more than its simple meaning; for Abraham and many others had faith before, but not the faith of Christ, or that faith in him by which men are finally and perfectly justified; for that faith had never come before. The term faith then in this passage is to be understood as including

Christ and all his benefits, or the gospel dispensation as contrasted with the Jewish, including believing, obeying and every thing pertaining to the life of a christian, " Whosoever believeth that Jesus " is the Christ, is born of God" [or hath been begotten, Greek, Jno. 5. 1. See Macnight on this text.] Here also it is evident that believing includes more than the simple meaning of the word, because many believe that point with an unshaken faith while ignorant of the spiritual truth, as hath been already shown. But in this place believing, which is acting faith, can include nothing less than following Jesus as the Christ, by living his life, without which no one is worthy of the name of a believer. But in this the simple meaning of the term *believe*, is included; for no man would follow Jesus without believing in him as the true Savior. Many other instances might be produced of the use of the term, *faith*, where it includes something more than its primary and simple meaning; but these are sufficient for our present purpose. That into which we are here inquiring, is faith in its primary and simple meaning, or that act or operation in the spirit by which a man acknowledges Christ in his heart, and by which he enters on the christian life.

Now that faith in this simple meaning is the immediate or direct gift of God, is not easily proved; it being no where unequivocally asserted in the scriptures that faith is the gift of God, at least in this sense, or directly so. Some have argued from these words, " Where" in also ye are risen with him (Christ) through the faith of the ope" ration of God, who hath raised him from the dead," that faith in the creature is produced by the same direct agency of God, by which he raised Jesus from the dead. But the most natural construction of that scripture is, that by the influence of believing that operation of God, they were also raised from the dead. (See Doddridge on this text.

But the almost universal scripture on this point, being, as I may say, the only one which comes near it, is this, " For by grace ye are " saved through faith; and that not of yourselves; it is the gift of " God." (Eph. 2. 8.) Now, waving the criticism which may be made on the original text, as it is certain the Greek language is not always correct to its common rules, let us consider in what respect faith can be the gift of God agreeably to the scriptures. That Christ is the primary and chief object of the faith of christians will be granted on all hands; and that he is the gift of God to men will not be contested by professed christians, " For God so loved the world, " that he gave his only begotten Son, that whosoever believeth in " him should not perish, but have everlasting life." (Jno. 3. 16.) Christ then, is the gift of God; and he is confessedly the true object of faith; and according to the scriptures he is given for the express purpose that the world of mankind might believe and have eternal life. He is not given for those to believe on him who are distinctly enabled one side of the preaching of the word; the scriptures make mention of no such matter, " For it pleased God, by the foolishness of preaching, to save them that believe;" (1 Cor. 1. 21.) but for the express purpose that every one who will may believe without mention or intimation of any other qualification, or authority, than what God hath included in the gift of Christ. If any man be of the world, if he belong to the fallen race of men, he hath a right to believe. "If any man thirst let him come to me and "drink." (Jno. 7. 37.) "And the Spirit and the Bride say, Come. "And let him that heareth say, Come. And let him that is athirst "come. And whosoever will, let him take the water of life freely." (Rev. 22. 17.) These offers are not made to a people incapable of complying with them, to increase their condemnation. "For God "sent not his Son into the world to condemn the world, but that the "world through him might be saved." (v. 17.) The matter is then decided that he is given that *the world*, not a part. but whosoever will, may believe and be saved. And this gift of God is actually made wherever the gospel is preached. "But faith cometh by "hearing and hearing by the word of God." (Ro. 10. 17.) This is in no respect different from what is already stated, that it is the unquestionable privilege and inalienable right of every man wherever the gospel comes, to believe and be saved. For that word by which faith cometh, or is produced, (for in the Greek the sentence is elliptical,) the word being the seed which begets faith, containing Christ in it, as it is written of those who preach the gospel, or word of God, "But we preach Christ crucified." And again, "For we "preach not ourselves, but Christ Jesus the Lord." (1. Cor. 1. 23. 2. Cor. 4. 5.) I say then, that the word by which faith cometh is the same word by which Christ is preached in the gospel, or in other words, it is Christ preached to the people; for, to preach Christ, and to preach the gospel, are tantamount. To these things also agree the words of Peter; (1. Pet. 1. 2, 5.) "But the word of the Lord "endureth forever. And this is the word which by the gospel is "preached unto you." These things show the order and line in which the gift of faith is made, and also prove, that that gift of God, *faith*, is already made indiscriminately to all who hear the gospel wherever it is preached. This then is the train of the gift of God; he sends out men to preach Christ for the belief of all men to their salvation; they preach, the people hear and believe; or those who reject the testimony or disbelieve, do it at their own option and voluntary choice. This train of faith, by the preaching of the gospel, is handsomely delineated by the apostle in the above quoted chapter to the Romans. (10. 13 to 19.) "For whosoever shall call upon the "name of the Lord shall be saved. How then shall they call on him "in whom they have not believed? and how shall they believe in "him of whom they have not heard? and how shall they hear with- "out a preacher? and how shall they preach except they be sent? "as it is written, How beautiful are the feet of them that preach "the gospel of peace, and bring glad tidings of good things! But "they have not all obeyed the gospel; for Esaias saith, Lord, who "hath believed our report?" Which by the way shows that obedience is the chief matter in the faith of the gospel, and that if one should believe in the simple and primary sense of the word, his faith would not be accounted of to his justification. After all therefore which can be said, a man's reception of the gospel to his justification, ultimately rests upon his own voluntary choice in the improvement of the gift of faith. "So then faith cometh by hearing and hearing "by the word of God." This then is the only sense in which faith can be said in truth to be the gift of God, that Christ, the object of faith, in whom is included salvation, for he is the salvation of God to the ends of the earth, and the preaching of the word which is the mean of producing faith, are the gift of God. And the Greek text of that solitary scripture which is so often adduced to prove that faith is the gift of God, will translate in perfect consistency with the same view; " For by grace ye are saved through faith; and that (method " of being saved) is not of yourselves; it is the gift of God." The word translated, *that*, being neuter gender, doth not correctly agree, according to the rules of that language, with the word translated, *faith*, which is femanine, but properly agreeth with the member of the sentence including salvation. Also tne words, " and not of yourselves," comprise a complete member of a sentence which is cliptical, leaving room for the verb, *is*, as it is common with that language.

But waving all reliance on the above criticism, however just, the scriptures teach clearly enough, that faith, as it exists in the creature, is there produced by the hearing of the word preached, and that it is the gift of God in no other sense than, that the object and means of faith are given. Thus also repentance may be called the gift of God; " Then hath God also to the gentiles granted repentance " unto life." And again ; " Him hath God exalted with his right " hand to be a Prince and a Saviour, for to give repentance to Israel, " and the forgiveness of sins." (Acts 11. 18. and 5. 5. 31.) But the act of repentance as well as faith, or believing, belongs to the man as his duty ; hence Christ and his ministers exhorted the people to repentance and faith, each of which was their particular duty according to the authority which God had given them by the gospel. Accordingly Jesus went forth " Preaching the gospel of the kingdom " of God, and saying, The time is fulfilled and the kingdom of God " is at hand : *repent ye, and believe the gospel.*" And Paul " Tes- " tifying, both to the Jews and also to the Greeks, repentance to- " wards God and faith towards our Lord Jesus Christ." (Mark 1. 15. Acts 20. 21.) But as the evidence of the things to be believed was laid before the people that they might believe, so were the motives to repentance, that they might repent. *Both* therefore are the gift of God in the first place, given or presented to all who hear the gospel, and *both* the proper duty and privilege of the same to be practised in receiving the gift so presented.

The gospel therefore, or word preached, is the proper evidence, authority, or power of believing, given of God to all mankind, wherever, and whenever, it is preached in truth, without the co-operation of any additional agency or power of God. There is, therefore, neither justification, excuse, nor even plausible pretext, for those who hear the gospel, to not believe and obey, saying they cannot for the want of the gift of God to enable them. For this is the sin of unbelief, or disobedience, by which a man makes God a liar and excludes himself from salvation, the not believing the testimony of God, that he hath given him eternal life in Christ. (As properly as a matter can be given before it is actually received.) " He that be-" leiveth not God, hath made him a liar; because he believeth not " the record that God gave of his Son." How doth he make God a liar ? by disbelieving an untruth ? Not so; for that could not make God a liar, unless he had first made himself a liar, by testifying a falsehood; but by disbelieving the true testimony of God toward us, concerning his Son. " And this is the record, [or testimony,) that " God hath given to us eternal life; and this life is in his Son." For a man, therefore to not believe, that God hath given him, as an individual, one among the rest, eternal life in Christ, is-the sin of unbelief, or making God a liar, (but especially his not laying hold of it in compliance with the gift,) and thus he excludes himself from eternal life ; because without the faith that eternal life is freely given to him in Christ, he will not, he cannot seek in faith ; " For he that " cometh to God must believe that he is, and that he is a rewarder " of them that diligently seek him. [Heb. 11. 6.]

On the other hand ; " He that believeth on the Son of God hath "the witness in himself;" he hath received it and findeth it true in experience, and as expressed by the same apostle in another place, from the mouth of John the baptist, " He that hath received his " testimony hath set to his seal that God is true." [Jno. 3. 33.] Such is the different influence of faith and unbelief, or disobedience. Such is the gift of God to us ; such is the gift of faith ; and such the gift of his Son, and eternal life in him, that we have no longer any excuse for remaining in sin, when once we are found by the gospel ; unless this be an excuse that we do not love eternal life in Christ, because of the cross ; and that rather than crucify the flesh with its affections and lusts, rather than confess our sins and forsake them, rather than deny ourselves and take up our cross, and follow Christ, not doing our own will but in all things devoted to the holy will of God, we will remain in death. But the objections are not done ;

8th. It will be alledged that some cannot believe, even of those who hear the gospel, for the want of authority, power or privilege, whatever it may be called, through the express appointment of God to that purpose ; in defence of which opinion the words of the evangelist John will come in good place. [12. 37 to 40.] " But though he " had done so many miracles before them, yet they believed not on " him : that the saying of Esaias the prophet might be fulfilled, " which he spake ; Lord, who hath believed our report ? and to " whom hath the arm of the Lord been revealed ? Therefore they " could not believe, because that Esaias said again, He hath blinded " their eyes, and hardened their heart ; that they should not see " with their eyes, nor understand with their heart, and be converted, " and I should heal them." The explication of this passage may by some, be thought arbitrary and forced; but those who are acquainted with the ancient manner of speech, of which there are many examples in the scriptures, as before shown, will, if free from prejudicial influence, have more correct views.

Now it is inconsistent in the nature of things, that these words of the evangelist should be understood literally, according to the most familiar forms of expression amongst moderns. It is impossible that those Jews should have rejected Christ and his doctrine, in the face of so many miracles and other evidences, for the sake of fulfilling that prophecy of Esaias, and laying themselves open to conviction as unbelievers. They had no such intentions; neither did they believe that saying of Esaias to be applicable in the case. To have believed that must have presupposed the belief that Jesus was the true Messiah, and that his testimony was the report which the prophet complained was not believed. Neither did God prevent them from believing the evidence which he had given them for the sake of fulfilling that saying, which had been fulfilled long before, among the disobedient Jews, and was then fulfilling daily, in its true import as relating especially to that day. But as it was common to the Jews to use the strongest language, and often in the figurative, these words, " That the saying of Esaias the prophet might be fulfilled;" import in strong terms, that that saying was fulfilled in them and with great justice applied. Again;

It was not possible that they could not believe because that Esaias said again, " He hath blinded their eyes and hardened their heart, " that they should not see, nor understand." For in the first place these sayings are not found literally in Esaias; the meaning therefore is not to be confined or understood in the letter of the language; but is clearly this; They could not believe, because they were possessed of that spirit of blindness and hardness of which Esaias spoke, to such a degree, as to blind their eyes and harden their heart, so that they could not see nor understand the things which pertained to their salvation. And this spirit of blindness and heardness which prevented them from believing was of themselves and not of God; as has been shown before. " For God cannot be " tempted of evil, neither tempteth he any man: but every man is " tempted when he is drawn away of his own lust and enticed." [Jam. 1. 13, 14.] But for God to give the people over to their own hearts' lusts, or to that spirit of blindness and disobedience which they had treasured up by their own doings, is a very different thing from laying it upon them by any direct agency, without any cause in them, and gives matters quite another aspect. And even the words of Isaiah, strong and awful as they are, do not necessarily bear any such meaning as that God had sent him to impose any such evil condition on the people, which they had not before, but to show them what kind of wicked people they were, as he had shown abundantly in the beginning of his prophecy. Thus, " Go, and tell this " people, Hear ye indeed, but understand not; see ye indeed, but " perceive not. Make the heart of this people fat, and make their "ears heavy, and shut their eyes; lest they see with their eyes, and hear with their ears, and understand with their heart, and convert, and be healed." [Isa. 6. 9, 10.] Make the heart of this people fat; make it so in thy language to them, that is, tell them that they have made it so; and so of the rest. I am very bold in this interpretation being supported by the apostle Paul who hath quoted this same prophecy in the same construction, correctly in the words of the Greek septuagint, and by no means foreign from the Hebrew; [Acts 28. 25, 26, 27.] and then the words are illustrated by the next quotation below, to the same purport. "Well spake the Holy Ghost by Esaias the prophet unto our fathers, saying, Go unto this people, and say, Hearing ye shall hear, and shall not understand; and seeing ye shall see, and not perceive: for the heart of this people is waxed gross, and their ears are dull of hearing, and their eyes have they closed: lest they should see with their eyes and hear with their ears." Thus they have done these things to themselves, by their own conduct to defend themselves from the galling evidence and influence of divine truth which they hated, and such people still hate, instead of that spirit's being imposed upon them by any judicial or sovereign act of God to prevent them from believing and being healed. The gospel with its evidence and influence, is not concealed from the people who hear it, in any such manner; for if it be concealed from any, it is only by the spirit of iniquity in themselves, the god of this world, to keep them from being constrained by its influence to enter that path of holiness which is so contrary to their nature and inclination; "But if our gospel be hid, it is hid to them that are lost, [in the lost state of sin,] in whom the god of this world, hath blinded the minds of them who believe not, lest the light of the glorious gospel of Christ, who is the image of God, should shine unto them." [2 Cor. 4. 3, 4.] Thus the god of this world conceals the light of the gospel from those who believe not, and not the God and Father of our Lord Jesus Christ, the God of mercy, truth and love: the testimony of God therefore remains unvailed for the belief of all.

9th. Another serious and heavy objection with some, in the way of the unlimited privilege to believe and lay hold on eternal life, on the authority of the gospel testimony, is, that Jesus said, "No man can come to me, except the Father who hath sent me draw him." [Jno. 6. 44.] And this drawing is supposed to mean some spiritual agency of the Father one side of the gospel testimony, or ministry, or in addition thereto, to give the gospel efficiency. Now the gospel is the power of God to salvation, and the admission of such a spiritual drawing necessarily contradicts its efficiency; though those of that faith do not acknowledge it. But it cannot consistently be denied that whatever needs additional agency to accomplish any certain effect is not itself equal to its intention. If therefore any agency or drawing of the Father, in addition to the gospel, or one side of it, be necessary to enable any one to come to Christ or to believe in him for salvation, the gospel is no longer the power of God to salvation; it is no longer an adequate remedy for the lost race.

It may be said that this necessary drawing of the Father is not in addition to the gospel or one side of it, but is a part of the gospel work which the Father hath reserved in his own hand as his prerogative: and such it is accounted. This however will by no means remove the difficulty; for if this drawing of the Father be considered as being a part of the gospel or pertaining to it, and is not contained in the ministration and commission committed to those who preach, Christ's ministers are no longer preachers of the gospel, and have no right to say, " We pray you in Christ's stead, be ye reconciled to God;" for the people are not able to be reconciled, and they are not able to help them or tell them the way; they are no longer able ministers of the new testament, not of the letter but of the Spirit; no longer sent to the people, To open their eyes, and to turn them from darkness to light, and from the power of satan to God, that they may receive forgiveness of sins, and inheritance among them that are sanctified by faith; all which are the express works of the ministers of Christ, which God hath committed to them.

Regeneration is attributed to God as his own work; and very justly; hence it is frequently called, being born of God, as " We know that " whosoever is born of God sinneth not." But it is effected by the preaching of that word which is committed to men, as it is written, " Of his own will begat he us by the word of truth." " Being born " again, *not of corruptible seed,* but of incorruptible, *by the word of* " *God* which liveth and abideth forever." " *And this is the word* " *which by the gospel is preached unto you.*" " For in Christ Jesus " I have begotten you through the gospel." (1 Jno. 5. 18. Jam. 1. 18. 1 Pet. 1. 23, 25. 1 Cor. 4. 15. Again; it is the work of God to call men out of darkness into the light of his kingdom. " Who hath " called you out of darkness into his marvellous light." " That ye " would walk worthy of God who hath called you unto his kingdom " and glory." (1 Pet. 2. 9. 1 Thes. 2. 12.) But he calls by that same gospel which he hath committed to his ministers; " Whereunto he " called you by our gospel to the obtaining of the glory of our Lord " Jesus Christ." (2 Thes. 2. 14.)

In like manner, it is the work of God to draw souls to Christ. But it is evident that he draws them by the gospel, or in other words, by Christ himself set forth in the gospel. Christ is the drawing of the Father, the loadstone by which the Father draws souls to himself; " For he is the way, the truth, and the life; and no man cometh to " the Father but by him." Accordingly said Jesus again; " And I, " if I be lifted up from the earth, will draw all men unto me." " And " as Moses lifted up the serpent in the wilderness, even so must the " Son of man be lifted up; that whosoever believeth in him should " not perish but have eternal life." (Jno. 14. 6. and 12. 32. and 3. 14, 15.) According to this view the gospel is all of a piece, and the plan which God hath laid for man's redemption is perfect, completely adapted to all his wants, an adequate remedy, " And all things are "of God, who hath reconciled us to himself by Jesus Christ, and hath given to us the ministry of reconciliation." (2 Cor. 5. 18.) Thus the drawing of the Father is treasured up in Christ and given to his ministers. And the words which follow as an explanation of the text quoted in the objection are by no means inconsistent with this view of the subject; "It is written in the prophets, And they shall be all taught of God. Every man therefore that hath heard, and hath learned of the Father cometh unto me." For not all who hear, not all who are taught, learn of the Father; some are untractable, and resist his Holy Spirit, as we shall consider shortly. "Not that any man hath seen the Father, (none therefore are taught by him immediately,) save he who is of God, he hath seen the Father. (The children have seen him.) Verily, verily, I say unto you, He that believeth on me hath everlasting life." In him then is the drawing of the Father, in him we may all hear and learn of the Father, and so be all taught of God, and he is found and known in the gospel a Savior near at hand and not far off, as before proved. "For the righteousness which is of faith speaketh on this wise, Say not in thine heart, Who shall ascend into heaven? (that is to bring Christ down from above,) or Who shall descend into the deep? (that is to bring up Christ again from the dead:) But what saith it? The word is nigh thee, even in thy mouth and in thy heart, that is the word of faith which we preach." (Ro. 10. 6, 7, 8.)

On this view of the subject, the drawings and teachings of the Father, are all in reach of those who hear the gospel; all things being ready on God's part, that whosoever will may come; and they who reject have no excuse because they do it of their own voluntary choice, refusing to be persuaded by the influence and authority of God. For it is proved by express scripture, that men can, and actually do, resist the Holy Spirit of God so as to prevent his saving operations on the heart. Thus said Stephen; "Ye stiff-necked and uncircumcised in heart and in ears, ye do always resist the Holy Ghost; as your fathers did so do ye." And Paul; "It was necessary that the word of God should first have been spoken to you; but seeing ye put it from you, and judge yourselves unworthy of everlasting life, lo, we turn to the Gentiles; for so hath the Lord commanded us, saying, I have set thee to be a light of the Gentiles, that thou shouldest be for salvation to the ends of the earth." (Acts 7. 51, and 13. 46, 47.) This word of God then, which those Jews put from them, contradicting and blaspheming, was that word which, though preached by men, contained in it everlasting life, with Christ the salvation of God.

But on the other hand; to suppose that God reserves that special drawing, or effectual calling, as it is frequently denominated, as a prerogative in his own hand, without which all other means and endeavors are ineffectual to faith and justification, they who do not believe and obey are not inexcusable, having no opportunity of complying. It is vain to plead that their duty is to believe in Christ, and they must necessarily be guilty in not complying with their duty;

for duty implies capability; it is no man's duty to do that which is out of his reach. If the duty of all is to believe the gospel when they hear it, that duty requires that the gospel be furnished with sufficient authority, even the authority of God, and ample provision for the faith and obedience of every man, the teachings and drawings of the Father, not excepted. But how weak! how preposterous is it, for men to insist on the duty of all men to believe in Christ, as many do, who believe; not only that it is impracticable for any, except those who receive that special drawing which they cannot resist, but also, that should any man suppose he would gain any thing towards acceptance with God, by complying with his duty, the duty of believing in Christ not excepted, it would be legality, he would be fallen from grace, and Christ should profit him nothing! For it remains true, that "Christ is become of no effect to you, whosoever of you " are justified by the law, ye are fallen from grace." (Gal. 5. 4.) And " Those whom God effectually calleth, he also freely justifieth," say they, " not for any thing wrought in them, but for Christ's sake " alone: not by imputing faith itself, the act of believing, or any " other evangelical obedience to them, as their righteousness." (See Conf'n. Faith. Chap. XI. Sect. I.) Strange language this, to be used by a people who profess to be directed by the scriptures, in which they never once read of any thing being imputed to any man except his own faith or works! " For we say that faith was reckoned, " [or imputed]to Abraham for righteousness." "Now, it was not writ- " ten for his sake alone, that it was imputed to him; but for us also " to whom it shall be imputed *if we believe* on him that raised up " Jesus our Lord from the dead." (Ro. 4. 9, 23, 24.)

But such plain declarations need not be misunderstood. The doctrines stated above relating to the unlimited privilege and duty of all to believe and obey, grounded in the authority of God as proclaimed in the gospel; and the impropriety of looking for any special operation or drawing of the Father in addition, beyond, or anywise abstractedly from the provision made in the gospel, and committed to those who are sent to preach it, as being necessary before souls can believe and set out to follow Christ; I say these doctrines, as often intimated, relate to those who hear the gospel, that is, those whom the true and perfect gospel hath actually found, and they know what it is and where, or at least have the opportunity of knowing by sufficient evidence. And by this also the gospel may be known. Whatever may be called gospel or the preaching thereof, which doth not relieve all honestly enquiring minds of all difficulty on these subjects, and set them at full liberty to make their choice for life or death, is not to be received as the true gospel: I say honestly enquiring minds; and there is no reason why those who are awakened enough to be honestly in quest of salvation should not be able to judge pretty correctly of their own honesty, when they hear the gospel. I give this rule as perfectly according with the scriptures; for according to these, the ministers of Christ are the ministers of the

Spirit; for the Lord is that Spirit; and where the Spirit of the Lord is, there is liberty. (2 Cor. 3. 6, 17.)

But some farther observations are necessary relative to the above doctrines. It will be alledged, that it is true enough, all may believe and come to Christ who will, on the authority of the gospel invitation; but here is the point on which the matter rests, that the people will not come, and have no power to will any thing of the kind, and those special drawings of the Father are unavoidably the pivot on which the whole matter finally must turn. And here it will be insisted that God is clear and the souls who perish guilty, because the reason why they do not believe and come to Christ is that they will not, and how can they be more completely without excuse? But this kind of reasoning affords no resolution of the attending difficulties, or relief to the mind; because man's incapability to be willing is confessedly as great as his incapability to believe or come to Christ, and his power as much out of his reach, being unattainable except by the aforesaid special drawing, which God gave to others and not to them, when there was no reason pertaining to the others why they should be preferred, and no reason in those who are left why they should not have received said special gift as well as those who received it. They are therefore no more inexcusable.

But it hath been alledged that God hath promised to make the people willing. Admitting that to be true, that he hath promised and will do it, unless he make all willing, after such unreserved invitations as are contained in the gospel offers, his character is by no means exculpated from the charge of injustice, while any one is condemned on the principle stated in the scripture; "*Because he hath not believed.*" But it is not true, that God promised to make the people willing to believe or come to Christ. especially by any such special gift or drawing. To prove that promise the words of David are often alledged. (Psm. 110. 3.) "Thy people (shall be) willing in the day of thy power." But these words have nothing in them from which such a promise can be inferred, being simply a prophecy expressing the character of God's people in the time of the gospel kingdom, as a willing people, who follow and serve him of choice. As to the words *shall be*, they are not in the Hebrew, and are simply expressive of futurity, as that which should take place in time to come. Another scripture alledged in defence of the aforesaid promise, or the doctrines connected with it, is the saying of the apostle, "Work out your own salvation with fear and trembling; for it " is God who worketh in you to will and to do of his pleasure." [Phil. 2. 12, 13.] But it is to be observed that this was not written to unbelievers as a promise of helping them into the faith, but to those in the faith, for the encouragement and help of those who had already complied with the gospel call, had believed and been sealed with the holy Spirit of promise. "In whom ye also trusted, after " that ye heared the word of truth, the gospel of your salvation : in " whom also after that ye believed, ye were sealed with that holy " Spirit of promise." They were also such as had kept their justification by obedience; the necessity of which we continually maintain. "Wherefore my beloved; as ye have always obeyed, not as in "my presence only, but now much more in my absence, work out "your own salvation with fear and trembling. For it is God who "worketh in you, both to will and to do of his good pleasure." Promises made to believers do not belong to unbelievers who refuse to comply with the simple and reasonable request of submitting to the gospel in the obedience of faith. Believers receive the Spirit; they keep the sayings of Christ; and the Father and the Son come to them and make their abode with them; they are the temple of the living God, and there he dwells according to his promise; *I will dwell in them and walk in them, and they shall be my people and I will be their God, and I will be a Father to them, saith the LORD Almighty.* These then, who believe and obey, are the proper subjects of his saving work and special power. These have the promise of eternal life, in Christ, in whom they have believed, and are kept by the power of God through faith to salvation. And others are freely welcome to the same privileges and blessings; whosoever will submit to the same door of access; faith and obedience: but without that submission they are excluded.

But I shall not dispute the fact, that God maketh the people willing, for the work is all of God. Not by any special agency or drawing beyond the ministry of the gospel, but by inducing them by gospel motives. Accordingly, that work is committed to his ministers; "And all things are of God, who hath reconciled us to himself "by Jesus Christ, and hath given to us the ministry of reconciliation; "to wit, that God was in Christ reconciling the world to himself, not "imputing their trespasses to them; and hath committed to us the "word of reconciliation. Now then we are ambassadors for Christ, "[or, in Christ's stead, or, in the behalf of Christ; υπερ Χριϛȣ;] as "though God did beseech you by us: *we pray you in Christ's stead*, "[or in the behalf of Christ, υπερ Χριϛȣ, as above,] be ye reconciled "to God. (2 Cor. 5. 18, 19, 20.) And saith Paul, in another place; "For though I be free from all men, yet have I made myself serv- "ant to all, that I might gain the more. And to the Jews I became as "a Jew, that I might gain the Jews: to them that are under the law, "as under the law, that I might gain them that are under the law ; "to them that are without law, as without law, (being not without law "to God, but under the law to Christ,) that I might gain them that "are without law ; to the weak became I as weak, that I might gain "the weak: I am made all things to all men, that I might by all "means save some." [1 Cor. 9. 19 to 22.]

Again ; I will not deny that God doth work a preparatory work among the people who know not the gospel, fitting and preparing their minds for its reception. Mankind are so far lost from God in ignorance of his true nature, and in the carnal mind which is enmity against God, because not subject to his law neither can be, that the gospel never could have access to them, without such a work, but would prove a curse instead of a blessing. "Behold, I will send you

"Elijah the prophet before the coming of the great and dreadful day of the Lord: and he shall turn the heart of the fathers to the children, and the heart of the children to the fathers, lest I come and smite the earth with a curse." (Mal. 4. 5, 6.) This preparatory work is carried on either more immediately by the Spirit of God through the ministration of unbodied spirits, or more ordinarily by communicating it from one to another by the ministration of those who are in the same work, while all the time, God is carrying on the work, making his angels ministers therein. Thus John the baptist was sent of God to do a preparatory work before Jesus Christ who brought in the true gospel, as it is written of him; "And many of the children of Israel shall he turn to the Lord their God. And he shall go before him in the spirit and power of Elias, to turn the hearts of the fathers to the children, and the disobedient to the wisdom of the just, to make ready a people prepared for the Lord." (Luk. 1. 16, 17.) Thus also Paul was convinced by a revelation from Jesus Christ to break him down in the midst of his opposition and prepare his mind for hearing the gospel by Ananias, a minister of Christ, and member of his body. Cornelius also had an angel sent to him, to tell him by whom he might hear the gospel, or hear words whereby he and his house might be saved; by which also many of his kinsmen and near friends were put into a situation to receive the same gospel. In like manner the eunuch had his mind awakened, and prepared by the Jewish worship, and the reading of the prophets, to receive the gospel by Philip the evangelist.

But this preparatory work is a very different thing from that supposed special work, or drawing of the Father, beyond the limits of that gospel which is committed to his ministers, to give it an application, and make it effectual. For this preparatory work is wrought in those who know not the gospel, although they live in the land where it is, as did Paul. Besides, in this preparatory work there is nothing saving; although in it there is often a ministration of much light and power from God. John was a burning and shining light, but was not the true, or perfect light; "The same came for a witness to bear witness of that Light, that all men might believe through him. He was not that Light, but was sent to bear witness of that Light;" [Jno. 1. 7, 8.] and led the people so far out of their old system, that they were able to reach the new dispensation, in Christ. Apolos also being an eloquent man, was mighty in the scriptures, was instructed in the way of the Lord, was fervent in the Spirit, and spoke and taught diligently the things of the Lord, knowing only the baptism of John. [Acts 18. 24, 25.] The seventy disciples also, who were yet in the preparatory work, returned from their mission, saying, "Lord, even the devils are subject to us through thy name;" [Luke 10. 17.] while entirely ignorant of the true spirit and inward work of the gospel. But Christ the salvation of God, is known in the *gospel alone*. *The gospel is the power of God to salvation.*

In this preparatory work then people often have great exercises, deep convictions, and much rejoicing. "John was a burning and a shining light; and ye were willing for a season to rejoice in his light." [Jno. 5. 35.] Many in the deep labor and travail of their souls, have felt the burden and guilt of their sins to an enormous size; have seen much of their lost estate by sin; have contemplated much of the contrariety and enmity of their nature against God, seeing much of their pollution and unholiness; have seen their pride in the things of the earth; have seen the pollution of the core and source of their existence and nativity, in their natural state, the work of natural generation, as being a work in which God is not known, in which there is nothing of God, nor any thing with which God can have any fellowship, and that they who live in it can have no savor for the nature of God; have been brought into the very borders of despair, and felt themselves as it were already eternally excluded from the notice and favor of God, on account of their own internal and practical wickedness. After such scenes of distress, some have returned to their former course of wickedness or rather worse, some have leavened down into an almost, or quite insensible stupidity, having none to show them the way of life. Some in the midst of their distress, or point of despondency, have been led to contemplate the freeness and fulness of the salvation of God in Christ, with which their hearts have closed in, and as far as they have understood it, they have delighted in the law of God in the inner man; with this their souls have been greatly releaved, and overwhelmed with a sense of God's goodness and love to them, not forgetting the freedom of the same to all who will come: for wherever any thing of this kind comes from the Spirit of God, it represents the true salvation of God unreservedly free to all who will come.

Much might be said, and has often been, on the exercises of those who have experienced such a change in the state of their mind; but this is not the object here. It is unnecessary to build up that which cannot stand. With all these exercises, though an hundred fold more than are here stated, the nature of evil is not destroyed; the soul is not renovated; the root of bitterness, the carnal mind, is still within. The man is still an old bottle, and though filled with new wine a thousand times, it would all run out in time. Hence the confession of indwelling sin, and the hardness and other plagues of an evil heart, with which those say they have to contend, who count themselves converted to Christ in some of those scenes which they have experienced. In these exercises people are apt to form their language greatly according to their previous education; (some however are led in them to a better understanding of things;) some thank God for his distinguishing love to them, (meaning that he hath included them in his special election,) rejoicing in the righteousness of Christ imputed to them, or that God hath forgiven their sins for Christ's sake, meaning, as their surety, who has paid their debt. Not considering that this is all unscriptural: but these are the impressions of their previous education. But whether they talk of the righteousness of Christ imputed, or applied, or of the benefits of Christ received by faith, while they expect, or believe they have received justification directly by faith, it amounts to the same thing in substance. No justification will stand the judgment of God, which hath already gone forth as the law out of Zion, only that which is built on the obedience of faith; or having the faith of Christ and living his life, walking even as he walked; as is proved in its place.

In this preparatory work, as before stated, many have had great light and power; clear views of many scriptures, so as to see things in the light of God, or in the light which the prophets and apostles had when they wrote them; or if they should in some cases even exceed in the gift of revelation, all this would not prove any thing more than a preparatory work. " And though I have the gift " of prophecy, (as many have had who were only in a preparatory " work) and understand all mysteries and all knowledge, and though "I have all faith, so that I could remove mountains, and have not " charity, I am nothing." (1 Cor. 13. 2.) Having these things given or revealed to them by the Spirit, they have been able to speak with great clearness, and to preach with great power and great success, so as to convert many into the same circle of light and beginning liberty.

Among these, some conclude they are in the safe path, they are now converted, are now in Christ and expect in the end to land safe in heaven; but not being ingrafted in the true vine, which is Christ, they are exposed to leaven back into the manners, the customs, the pride and lusts of the world, and by degrees lose their lively sense of sin, especially in the source of it, and can live after the course of the world with little or no remorse. If they can keep out of the commonly condemned, gross iniquities, can support a name in the church, can remember their conversion, and on some particular occasions have some lively, melting feelings of somewhat the same cast, although they find sin in them able to lift up its head from day to day, they hope to be saved in the end, and that Christ will make amends for all their failings.

But others cannot rest so; nothing will do them but full deliverance; nothing short of the clearest evidence of eternal life; nothing short of the death and final removal of that which they have found to separate their souls from God, which is sin in the very root and nature as well as its works. And though they may have been converted a thousand times as is commonly counted conversion; while sin is there, its wages are inevitably death; wherever it is, it unavoidably carries with it darkness, guilt and proportionate condemnation; and there is no peace saith my God, to the wicked, is the eternally haunting sound in those who commit sin, and are awake to see it: *these must have the truth and the substance.* Therefore as the prayers and alms of Cornelius came up for a memorial before God, and he sent him help, so doth God look on the condition of those who cannot do without the perfect and everlasting gospel, and send it to them. And when it cometh, it is with full authority for their faith, and full provision for all their wants, as already stated.

But not all who partake in the preparatory work receive the gospel when they hear it. Of the multitudes who followed John, and crowded after Jesus and his disciples, few would endure the doctrines of the cross. Hence it is said on a certain occasion, after he had been teaching the necessity of eating his flesh and drinking his blood, *" From that time many of his disciples went back, and walked no more with him."* (Jno. 6. 66.) And of those who have great anxiety to be saved, all do not obey the gospel when they find it : some stumble at the cross. Hence also the young man of whom the evangelists have spoken, who had such anxiety to be saved, when he heard of *the cross, the giving of all he had to the poor, and taking up his cross and following Christ,* was sad at the saying, and *though sorrowful,* yet he went away. In like manner, hundreds, not to say thousands of the people who were more or less partakers of the preparatory work in Kentucky, and the adjacent states, many of whom too, had great desires and earnest labors for eternal life, and cried with great anxiety for deliverance from *the last and least remains of sin,* yet when the gospel appeared and opened the way of deliverance by the cross, with full power to save, soon *descried the cross and turned away.* Some turning like the dog to his vomit, or the sow that was washed to her wallowing in the mire ; while others concluded they were on safe ground, and would there remain ; and some openly renounced the light which they had received and testified to be of God, that they might be furnished with a more plausible pretext for rejecting the testimony of the cross.

But on the other hand ; the true gospel, when it opens, is not confined to those who have been actual subjects of the preparatory work ; for after the way has been once prepared to let it among the people, and it hath made its entrance, its invitations are extended to all who have been awakened, or now will take the alarm, and its provisions are equally sufficient for all who will come. So that all being in the reach of salvation where the gospel comes, are left without excuse.

Farther ; It is true that men cannot believe without evidence ; and they cannot be expected to believe without understanding or seeing into the evidence of the gospel, so far at least, as to produce conviction of its truth, on fair and reasonable grounds. But this is so far from exculpating those who believe not, that on this ground they are fairly and readily criminated ; especially because they yield not so far as to give the evidence or testimony a fair investigation, having descried the cross of Christ on which they are to be crucified with him, and at which they stumble. Those who honestly contemplate the gospel testimony, receiving the word with an honest and good heart, and are willing to obey the truth wherever it is found, will not be lacking for evidence. Not only because the testimony of the gospel is rational and consistent with the understanding; but because God is always ready to assist those who honestly serve him to the best of their knowledge, whether Jews or Gentiles, whether after they have received the true gospel, or in a preparatory work, and yet in nature. Thus Cornelius being honest to the light which he had, God sent him farther instructions. Thus also Lydia being a worshiper of God, came to hear the gospel, "Whose heart the "Lord opened that she attended to the things which were spoken of "Paul;" and having heard she believed and was baptized. "So then "faith cometh by hearing and hearing by the word of God." (Acts 16. 14, 15. Ro. 10. 17.) But those who do not improve, but reject the light and opportunity which they have given to them, need not expect to receive farther help from God, but to lose what they have. "For to him that hath shall be given; and from him that hath not even "that he hath shall be taken away." (Luk. 19. 26.) In many other respects God works more remotely in the course of his providence, by afflictions, crosses, and distresses, or by setting bounds to men's habitations to prepare the mind for the reception of the gospel as it is written; "And hath determined the times before appointed and the "bounds of their habitation; that they should seek the Lord, if hap- "ly they might feel after him and find him." (Acts 17. 26, 27.) But none of these things amount to a saving work until the gospel is known, believed and obeyed; *for it is the power of God to salvation*.

10th. From the doctrines before treated of and the answers to the foregoing objections, another may arise; That the plan appears altogether legal, calculated to engage the attention of mankind to the gospel by motives of self-interest; whereas a true gospel motive is the glory of God—It is truly the work of antichrist to subvert order. But God is a God of order and not of confusion. That the glory of God is the ultimate and highest end of all his works is not contested; and that the happiness of his creatures is in subordination thereto. But the happiness of his creatures is also subservient to the glory of God. "*Praise waiteth for thee, O God, in Zion.*" "That we "should be to the praise of his glory, who first trusted in Christ." "And that every tongue should confess that Jesus Christ is Lord, to "the glory of God the Father." "And I will place salvation in "Zion for Israel my glory." (Psm. 65. 1. Eph. 1. 12. Phil. 2. 11. Isa. 46. 13.) Thus the Israel or church of God is his glory. If then the happiness of his creatures subserves the purposes of God's glory and is connected with it, their happiness is a justifiable motive and justifiable pursuit. And men must attain to the less before they can reach the greater; it is therefore justifiable and proper to invite and stimulate men to obedience with a view to their own happiness. But God of his own free mercy and love hath regard to the creature's happiness, "According to his mercy he hath saved us." "In this "was manifested the love of God toward us, because that God sent "his only begotten Son into the world, that we might live through "him." "We love him because he first loved us." (Tit. 3. 5. 1

Jno. 4. 9, 19.) To love God therefore in gratitude for his love to us is a justifiable exercise; besides, that the love of God to us hath paved the way and laid the foundation of our love to him. I must confess, I have no faith that I ever saw a christian legalist, a christian professor who depended on the excluded law of works for life or justification. No law instituted by God was ever excluded from the faith of a christian after the ceremonial law of Moses; and who ever saw any man, not a professed Jew, make the least attempt to gain life by that law? Or if in some countries some have endeavored to combine the Jewish law with christianity, or consolidate them into one, they are by no means on equal standing with those who expect justification and life, solely by the obedience of faith, even the faith of Christ.

But the dealings of God with men every where, show that he esteems it justifiable and proper to engage them to obedience, by a respect to their own safety and happiness. The truth of this will appear to all who will consult the scriptures without partiality; wherein, notwithstanding that the glory of God is preferred, as being the highest end and final result of all, yet the happiness of men is not only secured, but presented to them, as the first moving cause, to stimulate them to obedience. " Come now, and let us reason to-
" gether, saith the Lord; Though your sins be as scarlet, they shall
" be as white as snow; though they be red like crimson, they shall
" be as wool. If ye be willing and obedient ye shall eat the good of
" the land; but if ye refuse and rebel ye shall be devoured with the
" sword; for the mouth of the Lord hath spoken it." (Isa. 1. 18, &c.)

And to suppose it legal, or anti-evangelical, to use the rewards held forth in the gospel to influence men to consult their own happiness, *is wild and preposterous in the extreme*, if we consider but for a moment the manner in which Jesus and his disciples addressed themselves to the people. " Come unto me, all ye that labor and are
" heavy laden, *and I will give you rest*. Take my yoke upon you,
" and learn of me; for I am meek and lowly in heart: *and ye shall
find rest unto your souls*. For my yoke is easy, and my burden is
" light." (Matt. 11. 28, 30.) " Now when they heard, they were
" pricked in their heart and said unto Peter and the rest of the apos-
" tles, Men and brethren, what shall we do! Then Peter said unto
" them, Repent, and be baptized every one of you in the name of
" Jesus Christ for the remission of sins, and ye shall receive the gift
" of the Holy Ghost. For the promise is to you, and to your chil-
" dren, and to all that are afar off, even as many as the Lord our God
" shall call. And with many other words did he testify and exhort
" saying, Save yourselves from this untoward generation;" " Repent
" ye, therefore, and be converted, that your sins may be blotted out,
" that the times of refreshing may come from the presence of the
" Lord." (Acts 2. 37, to 41. 3. 9.) Thus the first counsel to mankind is to consult their own safety; not only to those who have just heard the gospel, to gain their attention and compliance, but to those also who have already believed and begun to partake of its grace.

"Wherefore they rather, brethren, give deligence to make your calling and election sure; for if ye do these things, (certain duties before enjoined,) ye shall never fall. For so an entrance shall be ministered unto you abundantly into the everlasting kingdom of our Lord and Savior Jesus Christ." (2 Pet. 1. 10, 11.) "Work out your own salvation with fear and trembling." But to instance all the examples, would be to recite almost the whole of all the exhortations and counsels given in the scriptures.

See also with what care and perseverance the Faith of Abraham and of Moses was fixed on the reward. "By faith Abraham, when he was called to go unto a place which he should after receive for an inheritance, obeyed; (he did not only believe;) and he went out, not knowing whither he went. By faith he sojourned in the land of promise, as in a strange country, dwelling in tabernacles with Isaac and Jacob, the heirs with him of the same promise: for he looked for a city which hath foundations, whose builder and maker is God." "By faith Moses, when he was come to years, refused to be called the son of Pharaoh's daughter; choosing rather to suffer affliction with the people of God, than to enjoy the pleasures of sin for a season; *esteeming the reproach of Christ greater riches than the treasures of Egypt*: for *he had respect to the recompense of reward.*" Thus that faith is recommended which had respect to the best recompense of reward, not only in Moses, but in Abraham and others who waited for the blessing contained in the promises; "These all died in faith, not having received the promises, but having seen them afar off, and were persuaded of them, and embraced them, and confessed that they were strangers and pilgrims on the earth. For they that say such things declare plainly *that they seek a country*. And truly if they had been mindful of that country from whence they came out, they might have had opportunity to have returned: but now *they desire a better country, that is, an heavenly: wherefore God is not ashamed to be called their God; for he hath prepared for them a city.*" Thus God approved their zeal in seeking a better country, a better inheritance, at the expense of that which was inferior; and he is not ashamed of them. "Wherefore, seeing we also are compassed about with so great a cloud of witnesses, let us lay aside every weight, and the sin which doth so easily beset us, and let us run with patience the race that is set before us, looking to Jesus the author and finisher [first leader and perfecter] of faith; *who for the joy that was set before him* endured the cross, despising the shame, and is set down at the right hand of the throne of God." (Heb. 12. 1, 2.) As we have the example of all the faithful and of Jesus the Lord and Master of all, the author and finisher of the true faith, in having respect to the recompense of reward set before, let us no more call it legality to invite and stimulate mankind by the hope of eternal life to fill up the number of the blessed—let us no more damp the zeal of those who would feel after God and seek eternal life, by persuading them that they must begin in the highest grade of a perfect man in Christ—or that all attempts to gain eternal life are useless, until that point is obtained. How weak would it be to feed with the strongest meat, the child who is scarcely able to use the mildest milk ? Mankind in their natural state, entirely pursue their own desires and their own will, until checked by some adequate cause, and have nothing in them, to influence them at all, to seek the glory of God. But when men have learned to know God in some good degree, to experience the benefit of his grace and salvation, and view him as being in reality superior to all other beings, his nature and will as being truly best, they are then capable of being led to seek the glory of God and feel interested in it. " We love him because he first loved us." But it is not possible that any man should love his enemy and seek his honor, in that character; it is therefore impossible that men should be induced to have a simple respect to the glory of God, until they come to know the real excellence of his character, God is love. " Greater love hath no man than this, that a man lay " down his life for his friend." " But God commendeth his love " toward us, in that, while we were yet enemies Christ died for us." Accordingly, the first proposals of God to men, towards bringing them to serve him and seek his glory, are those which respect their own happiness. In this way men are gained to subject themselves to the will of God, to deny themselves, renouncing their own wills, and to crucify the carnal mind which is enmity against God, that God may eventually be all in all.

To object, therefore, to the foregoing doctrines as being legal, because men are invited and urged to consult their own safety by believing and obeying, is altogether weak and unreasonable, worthy of those only who oppose the gospel, which calls for men to deny themselves and take up their cross and follow Christ.

I should now proceed to the last of the principal and most interesting objections to be stated in this place, relating to the election; but as it will require considerable scope to investigate it freely, I shall refer it to the next chapters, and close this with a compendious statement and vindication (partly by way of recapitulation) of some of the leading points against which these objections are raised. For we have so far answered the heaviest objections against the practical doctrine of justification by the obedience of faith, that we have full liberty to consider it unhurt. What therefore is now to be stated and proved, is, that obedience is as properly the character of a christian as believing. And in this part it will be considered that a man's justification before God, and in his own conscience, depends on the very same efficient cause, as the appellation of christian, in all cases where the term is justly applied. For no man hath any right to the appellation of *a christian*, unless he can show the grounds of his justification on all proper occasions; for the righteousness of God, without the law, which was attested by the law and the prophets, even the righteousness of God through the faith of Jesus Christ, is manifested, not only *to all* but also *upon all* them that believe. This is that righteousness which is declared, through the forbearance of God, and not by imputation, for the remission of sin. This righteousness then, is that which God will accept, which also consists in each one's doing the will of God as Jesus did it, as hath been already proved; for " He " that doeth righteousness is righteous even as he is righteous."

It is true, that faith, or believing, is more commonly used to express the character of christians, or rather to nominate them as a people distinct from the rest of mankind, as well as to point to the grounds of their justification; for which these obvious reasons may be given. That genuine faith, kept alive to the support of genuine christianity, always included obedience; and there could be no true obedience or christianity without faith; for without faith it is impossible to please God. Besides; No man could be induced to follow Christ bearing the cross and practising the self-denial which he taught, under all the persecution and reproaches which attached to that life without faith to support him. Faith is a true shield in the armor of God, which his people wear; " Above all, taking the " shield of faith wherewith ye shall be able to quench all the fiery " darts of the wicked." " And this is the victory which overcometh " the world, even our faith." [Eph. 6. 16. 1 Jno. 5. 4.] Add to these things, that the doctrine of justification and salvation, by the faith of Jesus Christ was contrary to the ceremonies of Moses, and so new and strange in the early days of christianity, to those who had been inured to that law, that there was in many a great propensity to turn back to those beggarly elements, it was therefore necessary to keep the sentiment alive.

And such was the necessity of supporting the doctrine of faith in Christ by those scriptures which the people believed, particularly the Jews, some of whom were found in all the churches, and were according to the order of their calling required to stand as it were the first pillars of the church of the Messiah, that the apostle collected almost every word in the writings of the old testament, which could subserve his purpose; and amongst them all did not find one to teach justification by faith without obedience. And indeed that was impossible; for the whole Mosaic dispensation stood in the principle of obedience; although faith was necessary then as well as after Christ appeared. But faith and obedience, in the christian dispensation, are in a different train from what they were in the Mosaic, being directed more towards the spirit and substance. But the apostle was ingenious enough, according to the wisdom given to him, to leave out the character and works of the persons justified, when he would prove justification by faith, without the deeds of the law, though these were the proximate and procuring cause of their justification, lest his hearers should thereby be induced to cleave to the same law, or lest his reasoning should not appear sufficiently plain to those who did not understand as clearly as he. But the apostles and the evangelists who recorded the words of Christ, have not left us in such penury of proof for the necessity of obedience to constitute us real christians, or as the grounds and maintenance of our acceptance with God. While not one word is said in all their writings of the righteousness of Christ being imputed to us for our justification, much is said of the necessity of obedience, and of their being acceptable and safe who render it to God. For in every nation, he that feareth God and *worketh righteousness* (not hath righteousness imputed to him,) is accepted of him.

A mighty outcry is raised against the notion of any one inheriting righteousness in himself, or in his own character and works, as though that man must certainly fail of being saved and be ultimately ruined, who expects God will accept him in his own personal works of righteousness, his own doings or obedience. But none of these things move the christian, who understands the law of faith in Christ Jesus. For he knows that without obedience no faith will justify any man before God; and supported by the words of Christ, he is not afraid to say, *Except your righteousness* (not the righteousness of another imputed to you,) *shall exceed the righteousness of the scribes and pharisees, ye shall in no case enter into the kingdom of heaven.* Thus Jesus who came to do the will of God as it was written of him in the volume of the book, and to establish the doing of the will of God, as that in which he would take delight, in the room of the sacrifices which were offered by the law, as before shown, hath not only set us that example, but hath taught by his words that he who doeth the will of God, (not who hath the doing of his will by another imputed to him,) shall dwell with God in the kingdom of heaven. " Not every one that saith unto me, Lord, Lord, shall " enter into the kingdom of heaven, but he who doeth the will of my " Father who is in heaven. " Well done good and faithful servant; " thou hast been faithful over a few things, I will make thee ruler " over many things: enter thou into the joy of thy Lord."

A christian is not afraid of being blessed in his doings, provided his deeds be (as those of a christian are) according to the perfect law of liberty; " But whoso looketh into the perfect law of liberty, " and continueth therein, he being not a forgetful heart, but a doer of " the work, this man shall be blessed in his deed." [Jam. 1. 25.] And of such importance is obedience and so essential to the very existence of christianity, that it is given by the apostle as the very criterion of the true christian. " Know ye not that to whom ye " yield yourselves servants to obey, his servants ye are, to whom ye " obey, whether of sin unto death or of obedience unto righteous- " ness. But ye have obeyed from the heart, that form of doctrine " which was delivered you." [Ro. 6. 16, 17.] And not only so; but the gospel was also sent and the apostles commissioned to the people to bring them to obedience, without which it is evident their faith would have done them no good. " By whom, saith Paul, we have " received grace, and apostleship, for obedience to the faith among " all nations for his name." " To make the Gentiles obedient by word " and deed." [Ro. 1. 5. and 15. 18.] Hence the increase of the gospel is marked by the numbers who obeyed; " And the word of God " increased: and the number of the disciples multiplied in Jerusa-

"lem greatly; and a great company of the priests were obedient to the faith." [Acts 6. 7.] And the gospel which is to bring all nations to obedience in Christ, even to the obedience of faith is expressly the mystery which was kept secret until Christ came, as taught by Paul to the Romans in the close of his epistle, after all he had said of the use of faith for justification. "Now, to him that is of power "to establish you according to my gospel, and the preaching of Jesus "Christ, (according to the revelation of the mystery, which was kept "secret since the world began, but now is made manifest, and by the "scriptures of the prophets, according to the commandment of the "everlasting God, made known to all nations for the obedience of "faith,) to God only wise, be glory through Jesus Christ for ever, "Amen." [Ro. 16. 25 to 27.]

Accordingly God, even the Father, judgeth every man according to his works, as saith the apostle; "And if ye call on the Father "who without respect of persons, judgeth according to every man's "works, pass the time of your sojourning here in fear." And the declaration of Christ is, "Behold, I come quickly; and my reward "is with me, to give every man according as his works shall be." [1 Pet. 1. 17. Rev. 22. 12.] And in that striking description which Jesus gave of the last judgment, a little before his crucifixion, the character and reward of each class, are determined by their works. [Matt. 25. 31, &c.] "When the Son of man shall come in his glo- "ry, and all the holy angels with him, then shall he sit upon the "throne of his glory; and before him shall be gathered all nations "and he shall separate them one from another, as a shepherd divideth "his sheep from the goats; and he shall set the sheep on his right "hand, but the goats on the left. Then shall the King say unto "them on his right hand, Come ye blessed of my Father, inherit "the kingdom prepared for you from the foundation of the world; "for I was an hungred, and ye gave me meat: I was thirsty, and "ye gave me drink: I was a stranger, and ye took me in: na- "ked, and ye clothed me: I was sick, and ye visited me: I was in "prison, and ye came unto me." To the best of my remembrance, the famous George Whitefield, in a sermon on justification, acknowledges this to be the most favorable argument for justification by works, which he had heard, but objects that it will not carry through, because the righteous disclaimed the performance of those deeds; "Then shall the righteous answer him, saying, Lord, when saw we "thee an hungred, and fed thee? or thirsty, and gave thee drink? "When saw we thee a stranger, and took thee in? or naked, and "clothed thee? or when saw we thee sick, or in prison and came un- "to thee?" But his objection is indeed weak enough, considering the light and abilities which he had, and shows the influence of systematic prepossession over the judgment. How easy is it to see, that what the righteous disclaimed was not the principle, or grounds of their acceptance, but that they did not understand, how or wherein they had done these good deeds? When did we see thee in these conditions and perform these things to thee? But the Judge unravels the mystery by letting them know, that to do good to his people is the same as to do good to himself. " And the king " shall answer and say unto them, Verily I say unto you, Inas- " much as ye have done it to one of the least of these my breth- " ren, ye have done it to me;" and on this they are silent, and the judgment is decided in their favor, on the principle on which it was first proposed. On the same principle the wicked are rejected as not having done those deeds of righteousness which the righteous had done, and which it was also their duty to do. These also object to the charge of treating him with such unkindness, as not knowing wherein. But the Judge shows them, that the neglect, the cold indifference, or cruelty, which they had showed to his people was shown to him. " Then he answered them say- " ing, Verily, I say unto you, Inasmuch as ye did it not to one of " the least of these, ye did it not to me. And these *(who had not* " *done righteousness,)* shall go away into everlasting punishment : " but the righteous *(who had done righteousness)* into life eternal." And these things are written for our edification, that we may have no want of information and evidence, on what principle our acceptance with God is finally to stand.

Therefore, however indispensable faith is to our acceptance with God, and being initiated into the gospel of Christ, in whom alone perfect justification is found, it is evident that faith cannot justify a single whit farther than it is accompanied by works : it is the obedience of faith, or a faithful obedience by which a man's acceptance, or safe standing in the sight of God, is secured from first to last; for " He that doeth righteousness is righteous even as he is righteous," and " In every nation, he that feareth God and worketh righteousness is accepted of him." " But without faith it is impossible to please him." Why ? Because without the belief that God will accept the man who seeketh him he will not seek, without the belief that God will accept him in the performance of his duty, there is no encouragement to perform : " For he that cometh to God must believe that " he is, and that he is a rewarder of them that deligently seek him." (Heb. 11. 6.) Again ; " It is impossible to please God without faith, because to discredit God is to blaspheme his name ; " He that believeth not God hath made him a liar :" This is offensive to God, and leaves the man under sensible guilt, by which his soul is separated from God. The principle, therefore, on which faith justifies is its being an act of obedience and subjection, and its being introductory to other acts of the same kind. Accordingly, although faith is so often mentioned as the mean by which men close in with Christ as offered in the gospel, and are introduced into the way of life, and indeed supported all along, being kept by the power of God through faith unto salvation, yet every man's character and final reward is decided by his works, according to what he hath done, and not according to what he hath believed ; " For we must all appear before " the judgment seat of Christ; that every one may receive the "things done in the body, according to that he hath done, whether it be good or bad." (2 Cor. 5. 10.)

Another consideration of great and serious importance presents itself; that every man will just get as much reward, or as much salvation as he gains by his own obedience to the gospel of God, and no more. Many are built up with an expectation, that although they live in sin all their days and do nothing truly acceptable with God, nothing that he will own as being fit to stand, and though they never know any thing savingly of Christ until about their dying day, they may be saved, and be as bright in the kingdom of God as any; for Jesus Christ will answer for all their deficiencies and their wrongs. But where do the words of revelation say that Christ will answer to God for the people? Christ will no doubt confess them that confess him; but they do not confess him who do wickedly; they may profess that they know God, but in works deny him. And as for those who commit iniquity he hath in plain terms declared that he will utterly disown them, no matter what their profession or works may otherwise have been. "Many will say to me in that day, Lord, Lord, have we "not prophesied in thy name? and in thy name have cast out devils? "and in thy name done many wonderful works? And then will I "profess unto them, I never knew you : depart from me, ye that "work iniquity." "But those mine enemies who would not that "I should reign over them, bring hither, and slay them before me." (Matt. 7. 22, 23. Luk. 19. 27.) These sayings show us how he will answer for those whose works are not in uprightness and obedience. But the scripture is also express enough, that every one will have to answer for himself. "So then, every one of us shall give account of himself to God." (Ro. 14. 12.) Those, therefore, who expect that Christ will confess them and answer for them and make good their character, while they are not doing the things which are answerable to the character of Christ, walking worthy of the vocation wherewith they are called, may surely lay their accounts to meet with a grievous disappointment.

For not only the character and reward of every man will in the classification among the righteous or wicked, be according to his works, but every degree of honor and glory in the righteous, or of death and the curse in the wicked, will be according to the works of each. "A good man out of the good treasure of his heart, bringeth "forth good things : and an evil man out of the evil treasure, bring-"eth forth evil things. But I say unto you, that every idle word "that men shall speak they shall give an account thereof in the day "of judgment." "Woe unto you, scribes, and pharisees, hypo-"crites; for ye devour widows' houses, and for a pretence make "long prayer : therefore ye shall receive the greater damnation." (Matt. 12. 35, 36. and 23. 14.) But on the other hand every thing done and suffered by the righteous according to the will of God, and for the gospel and name of Christ, shall stand in full account to them in their crown of righteousness and glory. "He that receiveth a "prophet in the name of a prophet, shall receive a prophet's re-

"ward; and he that receiveth a righteous man in the name of a right-
"eous man, shall receive a righteous man's reward. And whosoev-
"er shall give to drink unto one of these little ones a cup of cold
"water only in the name of a disciple, verily I say unto you, he shall
"in no wise lose his reward." "For God is not unrighteous to
"forget your work of labor and love, which ye have shewed toward
"his name, in that ye have ministered to the saints, and do minister."
"For this is thank-worthy, if a man for conscience toward God,
"endure grief, suffering wrongfully. For what glory is it, if when
"ye be buffeted for your faults ye shall take it patiently? but if,
"when ye do well, and suffer for it, ye take it patiently, this is ac-
"ceptable with God. For even hereunto were ye called: because
"Christ also suffered for us, leaving us an example, that ye should
"follow his steps." "But, and if ye suffer for righteousness' sake,
"happy are ye." (Matt. 10. 41, 42. Heb. 6. 10. 1 Pet. 3. 19, 20, 21.
and 4. 14.) But such is the superior excellence of that gracious reward, which hath respect to our union and communion with God in
eternal life, that all we can do and suffer in the cause hath no comparison or equality with it in that respect. "For I reckon that the
"sufferings of this present time are not worthy to be compared with
"the glory which shall be revealed in us." "For our light affliction,
"which is but for a moment, worketh for us a far more exceeding
"and eternal weight of glory; while we look not at the things which
"are seen, but at the things which are not seen; for the things which
"are seen are temporal, but the things which are not seen are eter-
"nal." (Ro. 8. 18. 2 Cor. 4. 17, 18.)

But finally here. This is the testimony which we have of Christ
Jesus, that "Being made perfect he became the author of eternal salvation to all them that obey him." (Heb. 5. 9.) Obedience therefore, as properly expresses the character of a christian as believing.
The same also is fairly inferred from disobedience, as being the
proper characteristic of the wicked. Accordingly Christ is declared,
as "Taking vengeance on them that know not God, and that obey
"not the gospel of our Lord Jesus Christ." And again; "What
"shall the end be of them that obey not the gospel of God?" (2
Thess. 1. 8. 1 Pet. 4. 17.) And the wicked are in different places
called the children of disobedience, and the wrath of God is said to
come on them for wicked actions. "Let no man deceive you with
"vain words: for because of these things cometh the wrath of God
"upon the children of disobedience." (Eph. 5. 6.) And by the
obedience of faith, even that faith which is in Christ, leading to obedience, we may in the freedom of God's righteous love, escape the
wrath of God and inherit eternal life in him, "Who will render to
"every man according to his deeds: to them who by patient contin-
"uance in well-doing, seek for glory and honor, and immortality,
"eternal life. But to them that are contentious, and do not obey the
"truth, but obey unrighteousness, indignation and wrath, tribulation
"and anguish, upon every soul of man that doeth evil; of the Jew first,
"and also of the Gentile: but glory, honor and peace, to every man

"that worketh good; to the Jew first and also to the Gentile: for there is no respect of persons with God." "Now, to him that is of power to establish you according to my gospel and the preaching of Jesus Christ, (according to the revelation of the mystery, which was kept secret since the world began, but now is made manifest, and by the scriptures of the prophets, according to the commandment of the everlasting God, made known to all nations for the obedience of faith,) To God only wise, be glory through Jesus Christ for ever. Amen" (Ro. 2. 6, to 11. and 16. 25, 26, 27.)

CHAPTER XI.

The Doctrine of Election, and the Foreknowledge of God.

THE sentiments which many professors entertain, relative to the doctrine of Election, furnish a serious objection against the foregoing doctrines, of the unlimited privilege of all men who hear the gospel to believe on its own evidence, and of justification by the obedience of faith. And to minister all the satisfaction possible on this subject, it will be necessary to investigate this doctrine with freedom; and the more so, because in it will be comprised the burden of what is to be said on the decrees of God, what has been said heretofore, being calculated to prepare the way, as being intimately connected with the main subject. For the decrees of God are considered as having a very special relation to the elect, who are finally to compose the church of God in its happy and glorified state, in whom the decrees are to receive their special and final accomplishment.

And here let us inquire; Who are the Elect? and what is their character? A twofold answer will be requisite to afford full satisfaction on this subject. And, in the first place;

The elect of God are they who worship him in the spirit, calling upon him day and night. "But the hour cometh, and now is, when the true worshipers shall worship the Father in spirit and in truth: for the Father seeketh such to worship him." (Jno. 4. 23.) And if the Father seeketh such, no doubt but these are his elect, whom he chooseth out from among others, even as they are expressly called his elect who call on him day and night, saying; "And shall not God avenge his own elect, who cry day and night unto him!" (Luk. 18. 7.) These therefore, are the elect of God, who are honestly devoted to his service, and have for that purpose come out from the rest of the world, and separated themselves from those who live in iniquity and defilement, as it is again written; "Wherefore, come out from among them, and be ye separate, saith the Lord, and touch not the unclean thing; and I will receive you, and will be a Father to you, and ye shall be my sons and daughters, saith the Lord Almighty." (2 Cor. 6. 17, 18.) These things show plainly enough who are the elect of God, and what is their character. They are such as live not as the world live, according to the course of this world, and are not of the world, but have come out from among them; according to what was said of old time; " Lo, the people shall dwell alone, and shall not be reckoned among the nations." (Num. 23. 9.) And as Jesus himself also said; " If ye were of the world, the world " would love his own: but because ye are not of the world, but I " have chosen you out of the world, therefore the world hateth you." (Jno. 15. 12.) From this view of these pointed testimonies of the scriptures, it is easy to see, that none are to be accounted God's elect while living in the practice of sin; none but those who deny themselves and take up their cross and follow Christ, denying all ungodliness and worldly lusts, and living soberly, righteously and piously, in this present world, while in it; and that as fast as any will thus deny themselves and take up their cross, God will own them as being of the number of his elect.

But it is asserted, that God's election is made unconditional and eternal, " Without any foresight of faith, or good works, or perseve- " rance in either of them, or any other good thing in the creature, " as conditions, moving him thereto." But as the scriptures speak so pointedly of God's elect as being " Elect according to the fore- " knowledge of God the Father," and of God, as predestinating those whom he foreknew, we shall not hesitate to conclude that he saw in them all something worthy of his choice, previously to his making it, whether we say from everlasting or after that excellence takes place. And as for the intimation often given, that it argues weakness in God to suppose that he hath any respect to the character or works of men in his purposes concerning them and his appointing of them to happiness or misery, as making his purposes and works depend more or less on the creature, none need be burdened with it, as long as it stands written that *In every nation, he that feareth him and worketh righteousness is accepted of him.* It reflects no dishonor on God to say that his acceptance of men now, as well as his final judgment and awards, rest on the character and works of each individual, for it is true that he judgeth every man according to his works. It argues no weakness in God to do justice. God is under no obligation, in his own nature, or from any other law, to do every thing which he hath positive or inherent power to do. This position can no man, with any consistency or plausibility, deny; neither doth this argue any weakness in him. But he is invariably fixed in all his purposes and works, not to say, bound by his own nature, to do in all things, that which is just, even to the meanest creature. And to fix any man's final state without respect to his personal character or works, can never be reconciled with justice. " And that the righte- " ous should be as the wicked, that be far from thee. Shall not the " Judge of all the earth do right? (Gen. 18. 25.) It argues no weakness in God; it reflects no dishonor on his character to have created and to govern a race of conscious beings, and accountable to him as free agents, and then to award them, each one according to his works; after giving them fair warning, as he hath done.

But for the sake of chasing the darkness out of every secret corner, the silencing argument, that God appoints men to life or to wrath without respect to their works, is, proposed, That with God is no succession of time, consequently no foreknowledge, because times, past, present and to come, are all present with him; therefore when he appoints or elects men to eternal life, from everlasting, it is not done according to his foreknowledge of their faith or good works, for they are all present to his view; or when he passes by, or appoints to wrath, it is not according to his foreknowledge of their unbelief or disobedience, for these also are all present to his view, with all their characters. This argument is indeed weak enough towards the defence of that point, as it implicitly, though effectually, confirms the contrary, that the reward of eternal life or death, and consequently, the justification of individuals now, rests on their works.

But the impossibility of justifying the principle of decreeing some men to eternal life and others to eternal death, without respect to their personal characters and works, leads those who believe it, or affect so to believe, to use weak and unreasonable measures. The above argument of no foreknowledge in God, hath been used with greater propriety on the other side of the question, to show that, admitting the state of all men to be fixed in the mind of God, even before their existence, that state is fixed by the just judgment of God according to their personal character and works, God having all these before him as the foundation of his judgment. And this view of the matter is infinitely preferable to that which supposes God to have from eternity fixed the state of all men, without respect to their works; as it exonerates the character of God from the charge of arbitrarily appointing some men to life and excluding others, and so ordaining them to wrath, without any possible opportunity of doing justice to God by obeying, or to themselves by laying hold on eternal life; God acting, in all these things, according to what men call his sovereign will: an attribute unknown to God. We read of *The purpose of him* (of God no doubt) *who worketh all things according to the counsel of his own will:* but counsel, in a wise being, implies rational deliberation and a reasonable conclusion. But to say there is no foreknowledge in God, is improper. It is contrary to the scripture, and represents God as an inconsistent being, always consulting and purposing to do things which are already done, or in the state of doing. For if no faturity, because no succession, then no anteriority; God is therefore represented as now, and for ever to remain, consulting and purposing to create this world and all others; to create man and all other works which are already done.

But in the second place. It is not unreasonable, neither is it unscriptural, that God hath an election of certain individuals to fill certain lots or places, to execute certain labors in carrying on the work of redemption for the whole. Every duty or work necessary for the edification of the whole, must be done by some one or more; and every man is not capable of filling every place. It is therefore no injury, but a real advantage to the whole, that God should select and furnish with suitable commission and gifts to lead the way and be helpers of the faith of others, those who are capable of performing such duties. These are often called to bear many burdens and to endure many sufferings, or to perform duties of which the physical powers of mind, according to natural creation, render others incapable. And whatever privilege such may be supposed to have, in being chosen to such duties, their election and calling cannot at all be any hindrance to the free access of others, to the same salvation, or to their receiving a full reward according to the utmost of their obedience of faith; but on the contrary, these are necessary to promote the good of the whole, and without them the church could not be built up in gospel order. "And he gave some, (that is, some of "those whom he gave were,) apostles; and some, prophets; and "some, pastors and teachers; for the perfecting of the saints, for the "work of the ministry, for the edifying of the body of Christ, till we "all come in the unity of the faith, and of the knowledge of the Son "of God, unto a perfect man, unto the measure of the stature of the "fulness of Christ."

Should God therefore send a special message or angel to these to waken them up and prepare their minds for the gospel, and so prepare the way for its introduction to any land or people, who are coming to a readiness for its reception; this could be no injustice to the rest but a real privilege; for the light which they would receive, they would unfold to others as being free to all : *Freely ye have received, freely give.* When the gospel is to be introduced among any people who are in readiness for it, that introduction must be effected through some means; there must be an instrument or more to bring it in, and room in the heart of some to receive it, a sanctuary where the testimony might rest, until borne to all, a people made ready and prepared for the Lord; as the few who first believed at Ephesus were a sanctuary to the gospel testimony, while Paul disputed for two years in the school of Tyrannus, until all they of 'Asia heard the word of the Lord Jesus. (Acts 19. 10.) It is not expected for a nation to be born at once. If God therefore should send a special message of the gospel to those who are the most likely to receive it, and give it room, among a people prepared for it; that could be no injury to the rest, neither could it at all stand in competition with their salvation, but on the contrary tend to promote it by establishing the gospel among them, "For therein is the righteousness of God "revealed from faith to faith." (Ro. 1. 17.)

But in all these things there is nothing to contradict that God should have respect to qualifications, natural and moral, to the character and works of those whom he thus elects, making choice of those who are best calculated to be of use to others while they secure their own salvation. And who can say there is any weakness or dishonor attached to God, by supposing that he fixes on the most capable instruments to perform so important a work, as leading the way in the gospel, and bearing it to others ? It would seem by the sentiments of some, that reasonable dealings in God, towards his creatures would be a disgrace.

But to constitute a real subject of the kingdom of grace and of glory, it is necessary to be called, and chosen, and faithful. Not all the called and chosen are found faithful on trial. " Have not I cho-" sen you twelve and one of you is a devil?" (Jno. 6. 70.) In like manner many who have been called, and chosen, and prepared, with great light and power, have tasted of the good word of God and of the powers of the world to come, in the preparatory work of the gospel, in Kentucky and the adjacent states, and some of them public teachers and leaders of the people, who were called to stand as doorkeepers to open to the true shepherd, on trial proved unfaithful, having stumbled at the cross, under which the shepherd appeared.

Further. It was necessary that a proper train should be laid, and the way prepared for the introduction of the gospel into the world at the first, against the fulness of time should come ; it was necessary that the name and worship of the true God should be preserved on the earth, among a people to whom promises should be made and proper testimony deposited with them, of the work which God was about to do, to be a witness of its truth when it should appear, according to the times and seasons before appointed and foretold; that men might believe on rational principles which they could also present to others for their conviction; principles established by their duration, their continued testimony, and their fulfilment, as well as the evidence which should attend the work when it should appear. For this purpose God chose Abraham, to be the father of the faithful ; that in him and in his seed through Isaac all nations might be blessed ; as it is written ; " And in thee shall all nations be blessed." and again ; " For in Isaac shall thy seed be called." [Gen. 12. 3, and 21. 12.] These are they, " Who are Israelites; to whom pertain the " adoption, and the glory, and the covenants, and the givings of the " law, and the service of God, and the promises ; whose are the " fathers, and of whom, as concerning the flesh Christ came, who is " over all, God blessed for ever. Amen." Thus the calling of Abraham and blessing him, furnished a people to preserve the name and worship of the true God, and also to be a figure of the work of the gospel when it should appear. " For they are not all Israel who " are of Israel, but the children of the promise are counted for the " seed." " And if ye be Christ's then are ye Abraham's seed, and " heirs according to the promise." [Ro. 8. 4, 5, 6, 8. Gall. 3. 29.]

These things being so, were a great advantage to the Jews who were the seed of Abraham according to the flesh, because they had the writings of Moses, and the other oracles of God to be to them a witness of the character of Christ when he appeared. " What ad-" vantage then hath the Jew ? or what profit is there of circumcis-" sion ? Much every way ; chiefly, because to them were committed " the oracles of God. For what if some did not believe ? shall their " unbelief make the faith of God without effect ? God forbid." [Ro. 3. 1, 2.] By this arrangement of things, the Jews were prepared to stand as the first living temple of God, in whom his Christ should appear and find an habitation, the first deposit of the treasures of the gospel of salvation among men. Accordingly the gospel is called the power of God to salvation to every one that believeth, but to the Jew first. But this first benefit to the Jew is no disadvantage to the Gentile; for the same gospel is the power of God to salvation to every one who believeth; To the Jew first, and also to the Gentile. And the special election and calling of Abraham and his family from among the nations who were all lost in idolatry, were no injury to any individual among them, but on the contrary prepared the way for the greatest blessings, *For in thee shall all the families of the earth be blessed.* This election, therefore, of Abraham is not partial to the exclusion of any one, Jew, or Gentile, from eternal life; and the passing by of any other man or men, or not choosing them into the lot into which Abraham was called, can by no means intercept their free access to eternal life in Christ, as being of Abraham's family; " For " they who are of faith are blessed with faithful Abraham." [Gal. 1. 3, 6.] This is that Abraham whom God foreknew, as he saith, " For " I know him, that he will command his children and his household " after him, and they shall keep the way of the Lord." [Gen. 18. 19.] Thus God found Abraham, a man according to his mind.

Now when Christ had appeared and the gospel began to be preached, if God, according to the purpose of his grace which he purposed in Christ, and according to the plan and order provided, called and chose Paul whom he had separated from his mother's womb for that purpose, and the rest of the apostles, together with the great number of Jews who at first believed, having predestinated them to the adoption of sons, whom he foreknew; this election and calling did not imply the rejection of any others, or that any others should not enjoy the same privilege of being called and predestinated to eternal life with them, but actually prepared the way for it; " That, in the " dispensation of the fulness of times, he might gather together in " one, all things in Christ, both which are in heaven and which are " on earth, even in him; (as fast as intelligent beings submit to the " faith of Christ, all things become subjected to that order;) in " whom also we have obtained an inheritance, being predestinated " according to the purpose of him who worketh all things according " to the counsel of his own will; that we should be to the praise of " his glory, who first trusted in Christ; *in whom ye also trusted, after* " *that ye heard the word of truth,* the gospel of your salvation; in " whom also, after that ye believed, ye were sealed with that holy " Spirit of promise, which is the earnest of our inheritance, until the " redemption of the purchased possession, to the praise of his glory." (Eph. 1. 10 to 14.) To carry the matter farther yet; Christ is the first elect of God; " Behold my servant whom I uphold! Mine " elect, in whom my soul delighteth." (Isa. 42. 1.) He was the elect of God when there were none besides him. But shall this election be to the rejection of any who believe in him, or put their trust in God as he did? Not one. But on the contrary; God in choosing and laying this foundation, hath made full provision for the eternal life of all who will put their trust in him, "For he that believeth on him shall not be ashamed." (Ro. 9. 33.) After Christ came his apostles, whom he chose, as he said, "Ye have not chosen me, but I have chosen you, and ordained you, that ye should go and bring forth fruit." Next come those who should believe through their ministry; "Neither pray I for these alone, but for them also who shall believe on me through their word." (Jno. 15. 16. and 17. 20.) Thus in the order of God's elect, from the man Christ Jesus to all that follow him, there is provision made for others to inherit the same salvation, and be united in the same spirit as long as one soul can be found that is willing to be saved.

These statements may be satisfying to the candid and unbiased, what is the true intention of God's election. But as many believe, or affect to believe, that God hath elected and ordained a certain number of the human race, who are individually specified in said election, to eternal life, and that these, and these only, will certainly be saved, and the rest consequently and inevitably left and ordained to destruction and wrath, without respect to character or works on either side, as the cause of such ordination, remote or proximate, and as many scriptures are adduced in support of this opinion, we shall consider the most conspicuous of them in order, as far as shall appear to be for edification and consistent with the limits of the present work.

Several chapters of the epistle to the Romans are viewed as containing silencing arguments to that effect; among which are the following words; "And we know that all things shall work together for good to them that love God, to them who are the called according to his purpose. For whom he did foreknow he also did predestinate to be conformed to the image of his Son, that he might be the first born among many brethren. Moreover whom he did predestinate, them he also called; and whom he called, them he also justified; and whom he justified, them he also glorified." (8. 29, 30.) In this place the apostle, as every unbiased mind sees, according to the plain order of the words, hath built the whole on the foreknowledge of God; *Whom he did foreknow he also did predestinate ;* to be conformed to the image of his Son: thus in God's foreknowledge. And whatever may be disputed as to the propriety of the word *predestinate*, in that use of it, the apostle, with all his learning and in the gift and inspiration of the Spirit hath so used it: And there is no more impropriety in this view of this subject, than for a man going to build an house, to look out suitable timber and mark it before hand: he hath thus predestinated that timber. Thus God predestinated to eternal life in Christ Jesus all who believe in him and obey him; and for the effecting of this purpose, and calling all who will come, he predestinated a people to answer this purpose, in the first entrance of the gospel, that he might gather together in one all things in Christ; as before shown. And in like manner he hath predestinated a people in every part under heaven, to give the gospel a full and free exhibition to all, wherever it cometh. These are in the

AND FOREKNOWLEDGE.

first place the elect of God, and in the next place all who call on him and obey him, as before described.

But granting that these are predestinated without any respect to their character or works, and as exclusively from all foreknowledge as any consistent hypothesis can admit, as in the epistle to the Ephesians, where nothing is said of foreknowledge, the apostle is express in the purpose of their predestination, one part of which is to gather others into Christ with them, that all might be one in Christ as their head; " That in the dispensation of the fulness of times he might " concentrate or gather into one head in Christ all things which are " in heaven and which are on earth." (1. 10.) These scriptures therefore afford no proof that any soul is reprobated by God's predestination or decrees, so as to be excluded from salvation, or finally passed by, who doth not exclude himself, by voluntarily rejecting that gospel which is as accessible by him as any other.

A little farther on, (Ro. 9. 9, &c.) the apostle shows that the elect are limited to Isaac and then to Jacob. " For this is the word of " promise, At this time will I come, and Sara shall have a son. And " not only this, but when Rebecca had conceived by one, even by our " father Isaac, (For the children being not yet born, neither having " done any good or evil, that the purpose of God according to elec- " tion might stand, not of works, but of him that calleth,) it was said " unto her, The elder shall serve the younger. As it is written, " Jacob have I loved, but Esau have I hated." These words are esteemed an incontrovertible proof that God hath unchangeably, predestinated, or elected, every man to eternal life, or eternal death, without any previous respect to his character. " For, doth not the " scripture say, the children being not yet born, neither having done " any good or evil, that the purpose of God *according to election* " might stand, *not of works*, (see how works have no part in the bu- " siness,) but of him that calleth, (just by the sovereign will and ap- " pointment of God,) it was said to her." And what was said? " The elder shall serve the younger." And because the elder, Esau, should serve the younger, Jacob, is that to prove that the person or soul of Esau, is by that election of God, without respect to his actions, as having done neither good nor evil, unalterably set off for eternal damnation? Or did Esau in person ever serve Jacob? Never; not a hint of any such thing in the history of the two men, but quite the reverse. The subject then must inevitably relate to something else; and the saying, *Jacob have I loved, and Esau have I hated*, relates to something very different from the persons of these two men, of which they were but the figure.

Now it is proved above, that the seed of the promise, or the true elect, are not found in the family of Abraham, Isaac and Jacob after the flesh, or in their natural line, even though Christ as pertaining to the flesh came of that family. " For they are not all Israel who are " of Israel: neither because they are the seed of Abraham, are they " all children: but, in Isaac shall thy seed be called. That is, They " who are the children of the flesh, these are not the children of

OF ELECTION

"God: but the children of the promise are counted for the seed." So that Abraham's natural seed are not, on that account, of the elect or seed of the promise, although he was one whom God chose and called in an especial manner and appointed him the father of the faithful. "As it is written, I have made thee a father of many nations." (Ro. 4. 17.) "For this is the word of promise, At this time "will I come, and Sara shall have a son." (So that even Abraham's seed separately from Isaac were not to inherit with Isaac.) "And not "only this, but when Rebecca also had conceived by one, even by "our father Isaac, it was said unto her the elder shall serve the "younger." Thus a part of the seed of Isaac is also rejected. And above; "For they are not all Israel who are of Israel, that is Jacob;" so that not even all the natural seed of Jacob are on that account of the true elect, as it is again written, "Israel hath not ob-"tained that which he seeketh for; but the election hath obtained it, "and the rest were blinded." (11. 7.)

And besides all this, some of the true elect of God, or children of the promise, are found among the nations who are not Israelites by nature, being uncircumcised, who are nevertheless the children of Abraham. "And he received the sign of circumcission, a seal of "the righteousness of the faith which he had being yet uncircum-"cised; that he might be the father of all them that believe, though "they be not circumcised; that righteousness might be imputed to "them also." (4. 11.)

It is therefore evident, that the rejecting of Esau from that certain lot to which Jacob was called, is so far from proving that his soul was reprobated of God to damnation, the whole affair will not prove that either Abraham, Isaac, or Jacob, or all of them together, were the true elect of God, or the true centre in whom the elect are found: it is even certain they were not, for none of them lived according to the faith of the promised elect when he came. They were, all of them, only types at best. For although Abraham is called the father of the faithful, as being himself faithful and called of God, to be the father of those among whom the name and worship of the true God were for a time preserved in the world, until the true elect appeared, he was not so in reality, but only in a figure, before him whom he believed. And though Isaac is called the promised seed, he was not so in reality, but Christ, as it is written, "And to thy seed which is Christ." He is the seed to whom the promise was made. And though Jacob is called Israel, or the prince of God, he was not the true substance, for his children were not all faithful. "For they are "not all Israel who are of Israel; that is, they who are the children "of the flesh, these are not the children of God." (Ro. 9. 6, 8.) If then Jacob was the elect of God, whom he loved in preference to Esau, "That the purpose of God according to election might stand," and he was that elect only in a figure, as it is proved, he represented that which God loved, in contrast with that which he hated, and which Esau represented. Now what are the things which are radically and essentially contrasted with each other before God, the one being an object of his love and the other of hatred? The Spirit and the flesh; "For the flesh lusteth against the Spirit and the Spirit against the "flesh; and these are contrary the one to the other." (Gal. 5. 17.) God therefore loveth the Spirit and all the spiritual seed, and hateth the flesh. And to this agree the words of the apostle, as he saith; "They who are the children of the flesh, these are not the children "of God: but the children of the promise are counted for the seed." That is, the children of Christ, who are born of the Spirit; for to him the promise was made. Jacob, therefore, is the Spirit in a figure, whom God loveth with all the seed, and Esau is the flesh in a figure, which God hateth with all its works.

Jacob and Esau, therefore, viewed as representing the Spirit and the flesh, or the children of God and the children of this world, are important characters, and set forth the condition of the lineages which they represent, in striking colors. But that Esau was consigned to eternal wrath by that election, without respect to his works, there is not one word in all the account, or any where else, to prove. For admitting the fact, that he lived wicked and died the same, his wickedness is not ascribed to his being reprobated on the principle of having done neither good nor evil. And when he is called a profane person, it is on the principle of neglecting that privilege which was his by right of inheritance. He had by birth a right to the blessing, and would not have lost it, had he not sold it as he did, for a morsel of meat. Thus many sell the spirit for the flesh: this was Esau's sin; "A fornicator, or profane person." (Heb. 12. 16.)

And the scriptures show plainly enough, that to love Jacob and hate Esau, (which the apostle quoted from the prophet Malachi,) had no respect to the persons of Jacob and Esau, much less to their being predestinated, the one to eternal life and the other to damnation without regard to their character and works. "Was not Esau Jacob's "brother, saith the LORD? yet I loved Jacob, and hated Esau, and "laid his mountains and his heritage waste for the dragons of the "wilderness." (Mal. 1. 2, 3.) But this desolating of Esau did not come to pass until Jacob and Esau had long deceased; and his posterity brought it on themselves by their own wicked and cruel conduct. "For thy violence against thy brother Jacob shame shall cover thee, and thou shalt be cut off for ever." (Ob. 10.) And the grand purpose which the quotation from Malachi serveth in the apostle's discourse, is to show that the election of God is permanently fixed, and that such also is the result, not in the person of Jacob and his posterity according to the flesh, to eternal life, and in the person of Esau and his posterity according to the flesh, to eternal damnation; but in the Spirit and the children of the Spirit, whom Jacob represented, to eternal life, and the flesh and all its works and children who so remain, to inevitable and eternal damnation. For as aforesaid, these things can never apply to Jacob and Esau in person; for Esau never served Jacob, but Jacob rather served him, being always afraid of him, until they were well advanced in years, when they were in good friendship together, and each one took his inheritance without any difficulty. But the fate of Esau's posterity outwardly, is a striking representation of the end of the flesh, which is to be utterly abolished. "Whereas Edom saith, We are impoverished, but we will return and "build the desolate places; thus saith the LORD of hosts; They shall "build, but I will throw down: and they shall call them, the border "of wickedness, and The people against whom the LORD hath indig-"nation for ever." (Mal. 1. 4.)

Now there was truly no occasion for God to have respect to the works of any individuals for a reason to condemn the nature of evil, or the flesh, which lusteth against the Spirit, and by consequence, all who would cleave to it. Neither was there any need, that God should wait until the children were born, or had done good or evil actions, before he should make a choice, according to his own wisdom, who should represent the flesh in a figure, and who the Spirit; "Not of works but of him that calleth." For in that election, Esau who was hated, as representing the flesh, was no more excluded, as an individual man, neither any one of his posterity, from the salvation of his soul, than Jacob. "That the purpose of God according to election might stand, not of him that calleth, it was said unto her, The elder shall serve the younger." Now the election of God was the upbuilding of the Spirit, and the rejection of the flesh. But the flesh is first; that is, all men have an existence in the flesh before they become spiritual. Adam, or the old creation, is foremost in the generation of men; afterwards Christ, in the regeneration, or work of the Spirit, as saith the apostle; "There is a natural body "and there is a spiritual body. And so it is written, The first man "Adam was made a living soul; the last Adam was made a quick-"ening Spirit. Howbeit that was not first which is spiritual, but that "which is natural; and afterward that which is spiritual." (1 Cor. 15. 44, 45, 46.) Accordingly the purpose of God was with great wisdom, that the elder should serve the younger; that the flesh should serve the Spirit, being in subjection to it, and not rule over it, as hath been the case in the family of the first Adam ever since the first transgression.

Jacob and Esau are not the only two who have been types of the Spirit and the flesh, in whom it may be seen that the elder serveth the younger, or that the Spirit will finally supplant the flesh and root it out for ever. Ishmael was the elder and Isaac the younger; but Ishmael was born after the flesh, of a bond woman, and Isaac by promise, of a free woman; and "What saith the scripture? Cast out the bond "woman and her son; for the son of the bond woman shall not be heir "with the son of the free woman." (Gal. 4. 30.) Saul was the first king of Israel, but David who kept covenant with God, took the kingdom. And in many things hath God shown that the old creation which is according to the flesh, is to be dissolved, and the new creation in Christ, which is according to the Spirit to remain for ever.

But the apostle proceeds; "What shall we say then? Is there "unrighteousness with God? God forbid." Doth God appoint any man to wrath without any cause in the man as the reason of it? or doth he select some to eternal-life, and leave the rest to perish, until they first make choice of the road to destruction? Never. God doeth no such things; for there is no unrighteousness in him. But is it unrighteousness in God to condemn the flesh which lusteth against the Spirit, and to promote the Spirit to eternal life? By no means; Who can gainsay him? Might not God purpose, without unrighteousness, in the first creation of man according to the natural order of the flesh, to bring that order to a close; but especially now when it and its children are corrupted, when it is become the cage of every unclean and hateful bird, may he not in righteousness have decreed its dissolution, and promote the Spirit as the superior state of happiness for men, in the new creation, to eternal glory? It is unexceptionable.

"For he saith unto Moses, I will have mercy on whom I will have mercy, [or on whom I have mercy, in the Greek,] and I will have compassion on whom I will have compassion, [or on whom I have compassion.] So then it is not of him that willeth nor of him that runneth, but of God that showeth mercy." And who ever thought any thing else than that salvation is all of God? Would any man, by his willing or running ever have found the way to be saved? Would any ever have thought of everlastingly condemning the flesh for the final redemption of the spirit? Not one. All would have gone their own way, in the flesh—they would all have willed its life.

With respect to the use which some make of this saying of God to Moses, as if in the hands of the apostle it proved, that God appoints men to life or to wrath, without respect to their proper character, it only exposes the weakness of such a plan. The work of the ministers of Christ is, after his own example, to set forth the righteousness of God to men, and show them that in all his dealings with them he is just, consistently with that reason with which he has endued them. *Come, saith the Lord, let us reason together.* But the argument is forced and arbitrary indeed to prove that it is righteousness in God to dispose of men in that sovereign or absolute manner, to say, *He said he would do it.* This kind of reasoning would not justify the character of a man, but highly criminate him as a wilful, unreasonable being, and how shall it justify that conduct in God, from whom more justice is expected than from men? And what is in that saying as delivered to Moses, to show that God would deal with the souls of men in that absolute manner? Moses had been pleading with him to continue his favors to the people of Israel, and to show him his glory, and he promised to do so; "And he said, I "will make all my goodness pass before thee, and I will proclaim "the name of the LORD before thee; and will be gracious to whom "I will be gracious, and will show mercy on whom I will show mer- "cy," (Exod. 33. 19.) as much as to say, What I have promised I will do—I will keep my covenant. Accordingly he kept covenant with Israel, wicked as they were, because he had made promise to their fathers, and they kept the remembrance of the name of God and his church, until out of them, as pertaining to the flesh, Christ

came, whose seed are the faithful only. But what have these things to do with appointing any man to eternal wrath, without respect to his real or personal character? Nothing at all. Hence when God came to make himself known to Moses according to promise, it was to this purpose; " The LORD, The LORD God, merciful and gra-
" cious, long-suffering, and abundant in goodness and truth; keep-
" ing mercy for thousands, forgiving iniquity and transgression and
" sin, and that will by no means clear (the guilty.") So in this proclamation of dread sovereignty, so reputed, to Moses, the guilty alone, and they only by remaining impenitent, are excluded from the favor of God; for he forgiveth iniquity, transgression and sin, and will not, clear certain who are called *the guilty*. The word *guilty* is not in the Hebrew, but seems to be a very proper supplement. (Exod. 34. 6, 7.) In like manner the apostle's reasoning will terminate, as we shall see, that they only are rejected who do not comply with God's offers in the gospel.

" For the scripture saith unto Pharaoh, Even for this same pur-
" pose have I raised thee up, that I might show my power in thee,
" and that my name might be declared throughout all the earth.
" Therefore hath he mercy on whom he will have mercy, and whom
" he will he hardeneth." And whom will he harden? the obedient and disobedient without discrimination? God forbid. But the disobedient and profane as Pharaoh was; and who could say, " Who is the LORD that I should obey his voice;" and who harden themselves as Pharaoh did. But who will produce an example of an obedient man, or one who doeth the best he knoweth, or can know, whom God hath set aside to wrath by this abetted sovereignty which men have palmed upon God? Where is the wise man? Where is the disputer of this world? Where is the philosopher? Who is able to establish such a notion of God's dealings with men. Hath not God in these last days confounded such wisdom? " The soul that sinneth, it shall die."

" Thou wilt say then unto me, Why doth he yet find fault? for
" who hath resisted his will?" True enough—if God appointeth every man to this condition or that, without regard to the faith or works of any one, who hath resisted his will? or who can? Come forth Paul, and vindicate the character of God, on that plan. But as thou hast no reason to give, I will give thee an answer according to truth and righteousness, and clear the character of God, before all men, until they shall all confess that the way of the Lord is equal. The soul that sinneth it shall die. And therefore doth he justly find fault, because all they who are not saved have resisted his will; for he is, " Not willing that any should perish, but that all should come
" to repentance." " Who will have all men to be saved and come
" to the knowledge of the truth." " Ye stiff-necked and uncircum-
" cised in heart and ears, ye do always resist the Holy Ghost; as your
" fathers did, so do ye." (2 Pet. 1. 9. 1 Tim. 2. 4. Acts 7. 51.)

" Nay but, O man, who art thou that repliest against God? Shall
" the thing formed, say to him that formed it, Why hast thou made

" me thus?" What now, Paul? wilt thou confound a man by sovereign mandates, without rendering him a reason? God forbid, that any man should be so foolish as to yield, so far as to conclude that God forms men for wrath until they first form themselves! " This " only have I found," said Solomon, (and that will relieve us now,) " that God made man upright; *but they*," (not God for them) " *have* " *sought out many inventions*." [Eccl. 7, 29.] " As I live saith the " Lord God, I have no pleasure in the death of the wicked; but that " the wicked turn from his way and live." [Esek. 33. 11.] Now Paul yield; and we also will grant to thee, that a man needeth not reply against God, until God doeth something unfair, which will never be.

" Hath not the potter power over the clay, of the same lump, to " make one vessel to honor and another to dishonor." Now Paul, I will answer thee again, out of the book of God. [Jer. 18. 1, 2, &c.] " The word which came to Jeremiah from the Lord, saying, Arise, " and go down to the potter's house, and there will I cause thee to " hear my words. Then I went down to the potter's house; and " behold, he wrought a work on the wheels. And the vessel that he " made of clay was marred in the hand of the potter; so he made it " again another vessel, as seemed good to the potter to make it." (such as it appeared to him fit to make.) " Then the word of the " Lord came to me, saying, O house of Israel, cannot I do with you " as this potter? saith the Lord God. Behold, as the clay is in the " potter's hand, so are ye in my hand, O house of Israel. At what " instant I shall speak concerning a nation, and concerning a king- " dom, to pluck up, and to pull down, and to destroy it: if that nation " against whom I have pronounced, turn from their evil, I will re- " pent of the evil that I thought to do unto them. And at what time " I speak concerning a nation, and concerning a kingdom, to build and " to plant; if it do evil in my sight, that it obey not my voice, then " I will repent of the good wherewith I said I would benefit them." So much power then hath the potter over the clay, to make a mean vessel of the clay which will not form into an honorable one. And so hath God power over the people (the mass was the whole house of Israel, and under the gospel, it is the whole world,) to do evil against those who do wickedness. Now Paul wilt thou not be satisfied; especially after thou hast thyself acknowledged that, " In a great house " there are not only vessels of gold and of silver, but also of wood " and of earth; and some to honor, and some to dishonor. If a man " therefore purge himself from these, he shall be a vessel unto honor, " sanctified, and meet for the master's use, prepared to every good " work." It is therefore decided by thy own words that the vessel to dishonor or to wrath, may purge himself from his connection with these vessels of wrath, and become a vessel to honor and mercy : for a man cannot purge himself from that which is not attached to him.

Nay; but let me plead once more, at least thus far; " What if " God, willing to shew his wrath, and to make his power known, en- " dured with much long-suffering the vessels of wrath fitted to des-

"truction; and that he might make known the riches of his glory on the vessels of mercy, which he had afore prepared unto glory, even us, whom he hath called, not of the Jews only, but also of the Gentiles." Yea, Paul, that reasoning will do. There is no unrighteousness in the thought, that God should endure long with those who are already vessels of wrath fitted for destruction, that he may show his wrath against sin, or the flesh which they serve, and make known his power eventually in their destruction, as in the case of Pharaoh, that his name may be known and feared throughout the earth; or that he should long preserve the vessels of mercy, and not remove them immediately out of the view of the world, that he might make known the riches of his glory and grace on those whom he hath afore prepared thereto. For God to manifest his grace and glory on the subjects of his grace, and to make known his wrath on the vessels of wrath, is rational and justifiable. But that is a very different thing from predestinating men to mercy or to wrath without respect to their faith or works. Let us then hear the conclusion in Paul's own words; "What shall we say then? That the Gentiles who followed not after righteousness, have attained to righteousness, even the righteousness which is of faith: but Israel, who followed after the law of righteousness hath not attained to the law of righteousness. Wherefore? Because they sought it not by faith, but as it were by the works of the law: for they stumbled at that stumbling stone." Thus when Paul bringeth the matter to a final conclusion, the principle on which any fail, is their not complying with God's terms. And a little after. (Ro. 10. 3.) "For they, being ignorant of God's righteousness, and going about to establish their own righteousness, have not submitted themselves to the righteousness of God."

I grant the apostle's language is somewhat abstruse, on this subject, yet not unintelligible; and the conclusion which he hath drawn from the whole in his own words decidedly proves the above exposition to be correct. But he did not write so without his reason; it being often necessary to give a subject a very awful cast, to impress the mind more deeply with a sense of how important it is to act in all things conformably to the will of God. "*It is a fearful thing to fall into the hands of the living God.*" (Heb. 10. 31.) Neither let it be forgotten that *Paul, according to the wisdom given to him, hath written some things hard to be understood, which they who are unlearned and unstable* (though not the honest and the wise toward God,) *wrest, as they do also the other scriptures to their own destruction.* Let people therefore beware how they tarnish the justice and glory of his character with whom we have to do. "For our God is a consuming fire." (Heb. 12. 29.)

CHAPTER XII.

The subject Continued.

WE have already seen concerning the election of God, that he hath reprobated the flesh, and by consequence all who cleave to it, and chosen his people in the Spirit. We have also seen it proved, that the natural seed of Jacob are not, on that account, elect in the Spirit; as well as that the Gentiles who receive the faith of Christ by the gospel, are of the true seed, and heirs according to the promise; so that Jews and Gentiles have equal freedom of access to the promised salvation in Christ. We have seen farther, that those Israelites who have not attained to the law of righteousness, have failed through unbelief; "For they stumbled at that stumbling stone; as " it is written, Behold, I lay in Zion, a stumbling stone and rock of " offence: and whosoever believeth on him shall not be ashamed." (Ro. 9. 32, 33.) But we have to enquire still farther concerning the elect of God both among the people of Israel and among the Gentiles. For although the Gentiles have become fellow heirs with the Jews, and partakers of the same covenant of eternal life, the middle wall of partition being taken away, God still remembers his covenant with Abraham, Isaac and Jacob, and in the seed promised in that covenant will include all the faithful, whether Jews or Gentiles. " God hath not cast off his people whom he foreknew." (Ro. 11. 2, &c.) " Wot ye, not what the scripture saith of Elias, how he " maketh intercession to God against Israel, saying, LORD, they have " killed thy prophets and digged down thine altars; and I am left " alone, and they seek my life? But what saith the answer of God " to him? I have reserved to myself seven thousand men, (even all " the men,) who have not bowed the knee to Baal, or have not kissed " him." (Compare 1 Kings 19. 18.) As these had not worshiped Baal, nor joined in killing the prophets, of whom Elijah alone seems to have been left at that time, God had reserved them from the destruction to be made by Haziel, Jehu and Elisha, which the apostle considers as a figure of the election to salvation in Christ. And very properly; because as they had their lives preserved by obedience to the true God and refusing to worship Baal, so the ingrafting into Christ and continuing there depended on complying with the gospel offers and continuing therein; as will appear in the sequel. Reader, understand.

But the apostle proceeds; " Even so then, at this present time " also there is a remnant according to the election of grace. And if " by grace then it is no more of works; otherwise grace is no more " grace. But if it be of works, then it is no more grace; otherwise " work is no more work." It hath been before shown that the works of the law are they which the apostle every where condemned as having no part in our acceptance with God, and which were a separating wall between Jews and Gentiles. But the language is here so decisive and absolute that it will certainly be understood to exclude works of every description from any part in our justification, or in numbering us among God's elect. But men who judge of the letter by short-sighted, carnal reason, are exposed to err. To view this passage as respecting the election of individuals to the exclusion of others, without contemplating the point at which the apostle aimed, it might seem to establish the notion that God absolutely appoints men to life or death, without making any account of their faith or works. But saith he, "There is at this time a remnant according to the election of grace." We have before seen what the election of grace is; That God having rejected the flesh and chosen the Spirit, chose Jacob to represent the Spirit, and confirmed to him the covenant made with Abraham and Isaac; according therefore to this election of grace, the blessing of Abraham, (now the gospel of Christ,) is continued with his seed, and some have believed; there was therefore a remnant according to the election of grace. It was by this grace of God the plan was laid, and by the same grace it was continued, and is now known among the Gentiles, since the Jews have so universally rejected the gospel.

Now those who believed are called the election in distinction from the rest. "What then? Israel hath not obtained that which he seek-
" eth for; but the election hath obtained it and the rest were blinded,
" (according as it is written, God hath given them a spirit of slum-
" ber, eyes that they should not see, and ears that they should not
" hear) unto this day. And David saith, Let their table be made a
" snare, and a trap, and a stumbling block, and a recompense unto
" them: let their eyes be darkened that they may not see, and bow
" down their back alway." We have before shown that this quotation from Isaiah is used of those who blind their own eyes and stop their own ears. And the words quoted from the psalm are by the author expressly spoken of the enemy, to point out the reward of iniquity. We have also seen that those who believe and walk in the obedience of faith are the true elect of God according the scriptures; so here they who have believed are called the election, in distinction from those who have stumbled at that stumbling stone. "I say then;
" Have they stumbled that they should fall? God forbid: but rather
" through their fall salvation is come to the Gentiles for to provoke
" them to jealousy." Then it seems these non-elect are not finally lost; they have not stumbled that they should fall; they have only staggered out of the way and may yet be gathered in and become a part of the election. "And they also, if they abide not still in unbe-
" lief, shall be graffed in: for God is able to graff them in again."
(v. 23.) This election then, to carry it to the utmost, is no more than that of which we spake before, a people chosen to go foremost to be an help, and to open the way to others. And in the mean time, God who is rich in mercy, having directed his ministers to avail themselves of every opportunity to gain souls, when the Jews rejected them, sent them to the Gentiles; for through their fall salvation is come to the Gentiles to provoke *them who had fallen*, to jealousy,

that they also might repent, and thus salvation work be promoted on every hand. " Now if the fall of them be the riches of the world, " and the diminishing of them, the riches of the Gentiles, how much " more their fulness? For I speak to you Gentiles; inasmuch as I " am the apostle of the Gentiles, I magnify mine office; if by any " means I may provoke to emulation them who are my flesh, and " might save *some of them.*" Of whom? Surely not of the election who have already obtained that salvation which they sought; *might save some of them only?* Nay, but of the rest who were blinded; the non-elect who had fallen, or stumbled: these then were yet in the reach of salvation, and might be added to the number of the elect.

The apostle proceeds to show farther, that the partial falling off of the Jews was the means of opening the door of faith and salvation to the Gentiles; (as he said in another place, " It was necessary that " the word of God should first have been spoken to you; but seeing " ye put it from you, and judge yourselves unworthy of everlasting " life, lo, we turn to the Gentiles: for so hath the Lord commanded " us, saying, I have set thee to be a light to the Gentiles." And again, " Be it known therefore unto you, that the salvation of God is " sent to the Gentiles and they will hear it." (Acts 13. 46, 47. and 28. 28.) And he shows besides that the return of the Jews will be the means of a still greater spreading of the gospel in the world, even as life from the dead. He nevertheless shows that the standing of the Gentiles in the blessing of the gospel, or God's covenant of salvation, depends on their perseverance in the faith and their continuance in that goodness which God had exercised towards them, and that the return of the Jews awaits their ceasing from unbelief. And thus he winds up the doctrine of election, as herein stated, that every man is to be added to the number of God's elect or people, or to the book of life, or excluded from it, according to his personal character and works, where both revelation and all reason leave it. But he remains confident that God will still remember his covenant made with their fathers, and that election which was first set forth in them, and that the children will yet be found partakers in that salvation which is in Christ, who is the true seed of the promise, the true elect in whom all others are found.

" For if the casting away of them be the reconciling of the world, " what shall the receiving of them be, but life from the dead ? For " if the first-fruit be holy, the lump is also holy;" (If the children of Israel who have already become believers in Christ are holy, and a sweet savor to God, as being the offering of the first-fruits, the remainder, when found in the same condition, can be no less valuable.) " and if the root be holy, (as a people covenanted to God,) so " are the branches." God will therefore yet remember them, and pursue them by the gospel, according to the promises of his covenant. " And if some of the branches be broken off, (for a time,) and " thou being a wild olive-tree, wert graffed in among them, (who " stand,) and with them partakest of the root, and fatness of the olive-

"tree; boast not against the branches; but if thou boast, thou bearest not the root, but the root thee. Thou wilt say then, The branches were broken off, that I might be graffed in. Well; because of unbelief, they were broken off, and thou standest by faith. Be not high-minded, but fear. For if God spared not the natural branches, take heed lest he also spare not thee. Behold, therefore, the goodness and severity of God: on them who fell, severity; (or cutting off;) but towards thee, goodness, *if thou continue in his goodness; otherwise thou also shalt be cut off.* (There is the pivot on which the matter turns; " The Lord is with you while ye be with him: and if ye seek him, he will be found of you; but if ye forsake him he will forsake you." 2. Chron. 15. 2.) "And they also, if they abide not still in unbelief, shall be graffed in: for God is able to graff them in again."

"For if thou wert cut out of the olive-tree which is wild by nature, (and therefore had no participation in the original covenant,) and wert graffed contrary to nature into a good olive-tree; how much more shall these which are the natural branches, be graffed into their own olive-tree?" When they come to understand that the gospel of Christ is the result of the promises of God made to their fathers, and the genuine fulfilment of his covenant; for they will then obey it as their proper calling and lawful inheritance. " For I would not, brethren, that ye should be ignorant of this mystery, lest ye should be wise in your own conceits," (as though ye were worthy to be more highly favored, or that God had more regard to you than others, or had cast off his people of Israel,) " that blindness in part (and not in whole, neither finally,) is happened to Israel, until the fulness of the Gentiles be come in." (At which time the Deliverer shall return in his glory to make an end of sin in his church.) " And so all Israel shall be saved; as it is written, There shall come out of Zion the Deliverer, and shall turn away ungodliness from Jacob. For this is my covenant to them, when I shall take away their sins. As concerning the gospel, they are enemies for your sakes;" (or for your benefit; for when they rejected the gospel it was sent to the Gentiles, as shown before;) " but as touching the election, they are beloved for the fathers' sakes. For the gifts and calling of God are without repentance." (He will always keep the mercy and truth which he hath promised to them that keep his covenant, and no breach can interfere except on the part of man. God therefore will remember his covenanted people and pursue them to the last.) " For as ye in times past have not believed God, yet have now obtained mercy through their unbelief; even so have these also now not believed, that through your mercy they also may obtain mercy." Because as the gospel of Christ was first opened among the Jews, who had the promises and the oracles of God, and of whom as concerning the flesh Christ came, in his first appearing, so it shall be and now is opened among the Gentiles to whom this promise was made, with the fulness of whom, in Christ's second appearing among them, Israel shall be redeemed. "For God hath concluded them all in unbelief, that he might have mercy upon all;" whether Jews or Gentiles, as fast as they receive the gospel. "O the depth of the riches, both of the wisdom and knowledge of God! how unsearchable are his judgments, and his ways past finding out! For who hath known the mind of the Lord? or who hath been his counsellor? Or who hath first given to him, and it shall be recompensed to him again. (God will not forget a man's works.) For of him and through him, are all things: to whom be glory for ever, Amen."

But other scriptures are proposed as proof of an unconditional election of a determinate number; among which is the following. "All that the Father giveth me shall come to me; and him that cometh to me I will in no wise cast out." (Jno. 6. 37.) I cannot help reflecting, on the difference which subsists between us and the first christians, with respect to quoting scriptures from the original text. In their day, the language in which their scriptures were written was mainly a living language, which no doubt made it much easier to satisfy the people, or rather prevented all difficulty from that quarter. Whereas the languages, in which the scriptures, which have come to us, were originally written, had many peculiarities, which have probably caused much difficulty, and likely, have been the cause of many passages being incorrectly translated. And I must confess it is rather a disagreeable task to propose an amendment of the translation to those whose faith is different from my own, and who are also unacquainted with the original text. But the acknowledgement of all denominations, that our scriptures are not the most accurately translated, is some alleviation. Amendments of the translation are in many places indispensable to giving the true and literal meaning of the words. But a greater consolation still is, that the same Spirit of God who helped the apostles and prophets to write the truth at first, now dwelleth in his church, and will surely guide the faithful into the truth and salvation of God, though they should never understand the literal meaning, or know the correct translation of many parts of the scriptures. Such knowledge is not necessary to salvation: it is enough for each one to know his duty and how to perform it. At the same time; it is no doubt the duty of every one to use the knowledge which he hath, prudently, and according to opportunity, to the charitable purpose, of edifying others.

There is a peculiarity of expression in the text last quoted from the apostle John, which, as translated elsewhere, would cause the sentence to read "*whatsoever* the Father giveth to me." Thus in the following words; "For, whatsoever is born of God, overcometh the world." [1 Jno. 5. 4.] According then to this translation, the propriety of which I see no reason to deny, the *All that the Father giveth*, cannot relate merely to any number of mankind, (for the word is singular neuter παν ο) but to the power, gifts, graces, and every part of the treasure which the Father gave to the Son, so that he had enough to receive all who would come to him, and to supply them with every necessary aid. And the connection in which the verse stands is by no means unfavorable to this view. "Whatsoever the Father giveth "to me, shall come to me; and him that cometh to me I will in no wise "cast out. (For I have enough to supply him.) For I came down "from heaven, not to do mine own will, but the will of him that sent "me. And this is the will of the Father who sent me, that of all, "which he hath given me, I should lose nothing, (not, *none*, or no "people,) but should raise it (not, *them* or *him*,) up again, at the last "day. And this is the will of him that sent me, that every one who "seeth the Son, and believeth on him may have everlasting life: and "I will raise him(not, *it*,) up again at the last day." All therefore, who believe in the Son, are given to him of the Father; it is the Father's will that he should take care of them and that they should have eternal life, and receive their portion of every part of the treasures of grace which he gave to the Son: for he shall raise all up again.

It is also written in the record of the prayer of Christ to the Father; "As thou hast given him power over all flesh, that he should give eternal life to as many as thou hast given him." [Jno. 17. 2.) This may be urged as a proof that the gift of eternal life in Christ, is limited to a definite number of the human race, who were given by the Father to him. In this verse also, the Greek phrase, rendered by, *as many as*, is singular neuter; [παν ο, all which, or whatsoever;] and it is considered, and not without reason, that a more correct and literal translation is thus; "As thou hast given him power over all flesh that he should give to them, all which thou hast given him—eternal life;" or "that he should give to them eternal life, all which thou hast given him." And that God hath given eternal life, or salvation in Christ to all the human race, is confirmed by other scriptures; as "All flesh shall see the salvation of God;" and, "I will pour out of "my Spirit upon all flesh; and it shall come to pass that whosoever "shall call on the name of the Lord shall be saved." (Luk. 3. 6. Acts 2. 17, 21.) So that in the event; they who have eternal life, are they who make it theirs by a right improvement of the gift. "Wherefore "the rather give diligence to make your calling and election sure," in the Greek, *firm*, or *permanent*, [βεβαιαν,] Accordingly, the testimony of God concerning his Son, is, "That he hath given to us eter- "nal life, and this life is in his Son;" that is, to all; for, "He that "believeth not God hath made him a liar, (and thereby excluded "himself from the benefit of the gift,) because he hath not believed "in the testimony which God hath testified concerning his Son; and "this is the testimony, That God hath given to us eternal life." Now it could not make God a liar to not believe that which he hath not said or done.

But according to the common translation of the verse before us all flesh, by which I conclude it will not be presumed that any thing else is meant than the whole human race, is given into the power of Christ or given to him, he must therefore give eternal life to all; consequently, all are to be saved, or the result must be according to every man's choice to improve or neglect the gift.

Again; it is written of the Gentiles who heard the gospel at Antioch; "And as many as were ordained to eternal life believed." It is useless to hesitate or conceal, that this translation is not sufficiently correct, and therefore subverts the spirit of the text, according to the common acceptation of the word *ordain*, relating to this subject·

Cornelius Schrevelius, whose Lexicon is in the hands of almost every pupil in the Greek, renders the clause in Latin, thus; "Quotquot seipsos paraverant ad vitam; *as many as had prepared themselves to life.* But he has produced examples out of ancient Greek writings which serve to confirm a still more elegible rendering, as pertaining to the gospel. In these examples the word translated *ordained*, is used to express the position which a chief commander took against his enemy, consequently, by the determination of his own mind, and his own exertion. These examples however, have not altered my own understanding of the text. Satisfactory evidence had determined my mind before I consulted the above author, to a translation from which I feel no temptation and see no reason to deviate; although I confess I felt comfortable to find the truth so well supported by Greek authority.

On consulting the well known works of Philip Doddridge, I found his translation, as I may say, not so materially different from my own. *as many as were determined for eternal life believed.* But liberal a man as he was, being deeply molded or imbued in what hath been called *high calvinism*, it was no doubt difficult for him to translate this text, so important to that cause, in the evangelical simplicity and spirit of the historian, and leave it so; or rather impossible, especially seeing he had never seen the living gospel in a living subject, and therefore could not understand it. "The meaning," saith he, "of "the sacred penman seems to be, that all who were deeply and seri-"ously concerned about eternal happiness, (whether *that concern* "began now or were of longer date,) *openly embraced the gospel.*" And a little after; "Wherever *this temper* was, it was undoubtedly "the effect of *a Divine Operation* on their hearts,and of God's gracious "*purpose* to call them, and *list them* (as it were) in their proper pla- ces *in his army.*" Thus he endeavoured to support the opposite doctrines of partial election and the freedom of choice in man. But he had never learned that *Divine Operations* are ministered by the gospel, and that the *purpose* of God is to call without exception and that whosoever will, may be determined, come and list with Christ.

The words [επιςησαν οσσοι ησαν τεταγμενοι, κ τ λ] translate with simplicity and ease; "As many as were determined on eternal life believed." This is the true state of the gospel wherever it is preached, in all the world; it is preached with the most unreserved liberality to all, and they who esteem eternal life in Christ above all things else, and are therefore determined to have it on all adventures, believe and lay hold. For wherever the gospel finds an entrance, there is nothing to hinder any one from believing, beside the cross or yoke of Christ which he requires all to wear; and which however good or easy, is truly offensive to the carnal mind, which is enmity against God, not subject to the law of God neither indeed can be. This

carnal mind, which is the God of this world, and rules in the children of disobedience, is that which renders the true gospel dark and mysterious, and obstructs its progress through unbelief, more than any deficiency of evidence attending it, any incapability in man to believe on the authority of God, exhibited in the gospel, or any decree of God respecting election or reprobation; " But if our gos-
" pel be hid, it is hid to them that are lost; in whom the God of this
" world hath blinded the minds of them that believe not, (and for
" this very reason) lest the light of the gospel of Christ, who is the
" image of God, should shine unto them." [2. Cor. 4. 4, 5.] Now who is adventurous enough to impeach the character of the true God, by saying that his decrees limit the faith of those who hear the gospel? or who will dare attribute thus directly to God, the works which properly belong to the devil?

" For there are certain men crept in unawares, who were before
" of old ordained, to this condemnation, ungodly men, turning the
" grace of God into lasciviousness, and denying the only Lord God,
" and our Lord Jesus Christ." [Jude 4.] If any conclude this text will prove that God appointed those wicked people to wrath, without respect to their character or works, or appointed them by any direct decree, to the perpetration of such wickedness, and then to consequent condemnation, let them at least consider that the translation hath been discovered to be erroneous, an age ago, if not more. The word translated, *ordained* [προγεγραμμενοι,] is by the learned Philip Doddridge, in his note on this passage rendered, *registered*. It simply expresses written before, and as it applies to evil works justly condemned, might be rendered by the English word, *proscribed*, " Who were of old proscribed to this condemnation;" in as much as ungodly men have long been known to be proscribed, or doomed to destruction, thus it had been long foretold that destruction would be the end of such.

" Who stumble at the word, being disobedient, whereunto also
" they were appointed." It is not strange that those who are disobedient should stumble at the word: this is according to the appointment and decree of God; the disobedient are all appointed to that issue. " And even as they did not like to retain God in their
" knowledge, God gave them over to a reprobate mind, to do those
" things which are not convenient." But my people would not hear-
" ken to my voice; and Israel would none of me. So I gave them
" up to their own hearts' lust; and they walked in their own coun-
" sels." [Ro. 1. 28. Psm. 81. 11, 12.]

" At that time Jesus answered and said, I thank thee, O Father
" Lord of heaven and earth, because thou hast hid these things from
" the wise and prudent, and hast revealed them unto babes. Even
" so, Father; for so it seemed good in thy sight." [Matt. 11. 25, 26.]

How great must be the thirst for partial, limited and absolute election in those who can feel any support for it in these words of our Lord, by which he expressly describes characters and not a limited or definite number of persons! It is argued that the will of God

AND FOREKNOWLEDGE. 191

once made known is enough to stop every mouth and silence every tongue into humble submission. True enough; for God cannot will any thing wrong; and whenever he shall tell us that it seemeth good in his sight that some men should not be saved, who are no more unworthy according to their own true character and works, than they who are to be saved, we will submit. But why should such a thought intrude itself into these sayings which teach us that it is God's will to save the humble, " But to this man will I look, even " to him that is poor and of a contrite spirit, and trembleth at my " word." [Isa. 66. 2.] Because it is good in the sight of God to stain the pride of all glory, that no flesh should glory in his presence, but that he that glorieth should glory in the Lord, and that men must be converted and become as little children, before they can inherit the kingdom, will that exclude any soul from disclaiming his own carnal wisdom and prudence, and stooping low enough at the call of God in the gospel, to learn the way of salvation? These words of Christ exclude none from an equal privilege in the salvation of God; but are indeed a solemn and gracious warning to all men to beware of the wisdom and prudence, or intelligence, of this world, and the men of the world, which leadeth them away from the humble path of the ministration and salvation of Christ.

" Nevertheless the foundation of God standeth sure, having this " seal, The Lord knoweth them that are his." [2. Tim. 2. 19.] These words seem to have been produced by Paul to Timothy, to support him against any discouragement or burden, which might be occasioned by the error of certain men who overthrew the faith of some, saying that the resurrection was already past. And afford weak support indeed to the doctrine of particular and definite election, for which they are used; as if because the Lord knoweth who are faithful to him, (for all such are his; and this cannot be reversed,) and will take care of them so that his foundation, or covenant, standeth sure, he must therefore have appointed a particular and definite number of the human race to eternal life, and unalterably left the rest to destruction, without respect to their obedience or disobedience on either side. Strange! into what wild subterfuges men will run to defend that which is indefensible. Thus say they, " These— " men, thus predestinated and fore ordained, are particularly and un- " changeably designed; and their number is so certain and definite, " that it cannot be either increased or diminished;" [Confess. 3. 4.] and the above scripture exhibited as proof. But that text taken in its connection, will not only admit, but defend a very different doctrine. " Nevertheless the foundation of God standeth sure, having " this seal; The Lord knoweth them that are his; and, Let every one " that nameth the name of Christ depart from iniquity." This latter clause is also the seal of God's foundation, (or covenant, for that is the only kind of foundation to which there is any propriety in fixing a seal,) as much as the former. The foundation of God therefore is secured by the people's departing from iniquity as much as by the Lord's knowing them that are his. But the apostle adds; " But in "a great house there are not only vessels of gold and of silver, but also of wood and of earth; and some to honor, and some to dishonor. If a man therefore purge himself from these, he shall be a vessel unto honor, sanctified, and meet for the master's use, prepared unto every good work." Now every vessel in the house is either to honor or to dishonor; and to pursue the figure, every man represented by these vessels, is either a vessel to honor or to dishonor, either a vessel of mercy or of wrath. If a man therefore purge himself from these, he shall be a vessel to honor. But a man cannot purge himself from that with which he is not defiled, or which doth not cleave to him. The man therefore who is encouraged to purge himself from these, is a vessel of wrath, or to dishonor, and yet he is admitted to become a vessel of honor fit for the master's use, and be added to that number. And thus according to this scripture, it is the privilege of any man and every man, to purge himself from these, to purify his soul in obeying the truth, and be added to the number of God's elect; and his being of that number depends, proximately and ultimately, on his thus purifying himself from these. *Come ye out from among them, and I will receive you.*

For why should such encouragement be given, or why such an injunction, as a part of the seal, or even attached to the seal of the foundation of God, as "Let every one that nameth the name of Christ depart from iniquity," if the elect of God, or those included in the covenant, be personally and definitely predestinated, and that too without respect to their conduct, with such precision that the number can neither be increased nor diminished? If all things be laid out by absolute decree of the unchangeable God, and every man's lot absolutely fixed in that decree, to what purpose are the warnings, the threatenings, the exhortations, the counsels, and the various awakening expostulations to men, to flee from the wrath to come, to escape to the refuge and lay hold on the hope set before them, to save themselves from this untoward generation, to give diligence, (even after they have believed,) to make their calling and election sure [βεβαιαν,] *firm*, and *not tottering?* I say, why: hese labors to secure that which is absolutely secured by unchangeable decree and irresistible power, to a definite, specified number, and unalterably out of the reach of the rest, ever to obtain or inherit?

Because, say they, the end being appointed, the means are also appointed to secure that end; and for elucidation the case of Paul in the shipwreck, hath been introduced. The angel of God stood by him, "Saying fear not, Paul, thou must be brought before Cesar; and lo, God hath given thee all them that sail with thee;" and Paul said to the people, "There shall be no loss of life among you." But when the shipmen were about to escape out of the ship, "Paul said to the centurian and to the soldiers, Except these abide in the ship ye cannot be saved." But cannot the people see, that the preservation of their lives depended absolutely on the proper means, so that a neglect would have cost their lives and forfeited the promise? "Except these abide in the ship *ye cannot be saved.*"

What! did not God promise to save all? Yea; but not without those exertions and attention to duty on which that salvation depended.

And again; What hath this instance to do with the promise of salvation by the gospel? Here was a promise of a certain number, without passing any by; all were to share alike; but in the promise of life by the gospel, although the gift is made, or tendered to all indiscriminately, every man's salvation depends eventually on his complying with the terms expressly stated: and in that condition the gospel is universally preached.

Querry. Did God appoint those means which are to effect the salvation of the elect, to effect the salvation also of the non-elect, which he knew never could be gained, according to his own absolute decree? If so why doth he strive against his own plan, and then charge his creatures with the sin of these strivings' not succeeding in their salvation? Nero like, who burned the city of Rome, and then charged it on the christians and destroyed them in revenge. But who can brook such thoughts of the Holy and Gracious God! But if those means are not sent to effect the salvation of the non-elect, why are such messages and expostulations sent to mankind indiscriminately, with the full assurance of salvation and eternal life to those who comply, and increased condemnation and wrath to those who, according to the real merits of that plan, are by the decrees of God excluded from believing.

Why did Jesus, the Son of God weep over Jerusalem? " And " when he was come near he beheld the city, and wept over it, say- " ing, If thou hadst known, even thou, at least in this thy day, the " things which belong to thy peace! but now they are hid from " thine eyes." " O Jerusalem, Jerusalem, thou that killest the pro- " phets, and stonest them, who are sent unto thee, how often would " I have gathered thy children together, even as a hen gathereth her " chickens under her wings, and ye would not?" [Luk. 19. 41, 42. Matt. 23. 37.] Say; would he have gathered them? He came down from heaven not to do his own will, but the will of the Father who sent him; and he sought not his own will, but the will of the Father who sent him; and would he have gathered them by the Father's will, when the Father had fixed by absolute decree, that all things should be with them just as they were? If he would not have gathered them, his lamentation was a mere hypocritical parade, inconsistent with the heavenly Spirit of him whom zeal for his Father's house had eaten up. But if he would have gathered them, of which there exists no cause to doubt, and they would not, their own will, choice, or determination, was the pivot on which their state was ultimately to turn, independently of any absolute decree in the case: and so of all others.

But some, to alleviate the matter, will grant, or rather plead, that the decrees of election are not so absolute, but that if any one of the non-elect would comply with the offers of salvation, God would accept of him; for, say they, whosoever will may come; but that they will not comply, the fault therefore is their own—they are not to be influenced by the secret decrees of God—it is their duty to close in with the gospel offers. And why will they not? Because they cannot without the special and saving agency of the Spirit of God, which he hath decreed, at least negatively, though absolutely, never to give them. This however is undeniable; That the elect of God and the decrees designating them, are either absolute, or they are not. If absolute, they are unconditional; and the man, who finally rejects the gospel, is condemned to eternal wrath, as a despiser of Christ and of the mercy of God in him, without respect to his works whether good or evil; and all his most assiduous endeavors to obtain salvation, are lost and worse, the primary and unalterable cause of which is, that God by his decrees hath not included him in the number of the elect. Nay, say some; the primary cause of his condemnation is his being a sinner. But is he primarily any more a sinner than the elect? And is not the avowed purpose of the gospel offers made to him, though he were the greatest of sinners, to save him from being a sinner? Should the gospel find any who are not sinners what would it have to do with them? The whole need not the phisician, but the sick. This therefore is a vain argument, as well as explicitly contrary to scripture; for he that believeth not is condemned *because he hath not believed*, and not because he was a sinner before. It is also vain to all intents to plead that they who honestly seek salvation will find it, while it is maintained that the elect only will be saved, the number of whom is definite and special, for it will ever return that man's compliance with the gospel is limited by God's decrees, and such a sentiment necessarily lays an embarrassment in the way of souls' seeking salvation. It is also preposterously begging the question, to plead that men ought not to be influenced in their practice by the secrets of God, and that it is the duty of all to close in with the gospel; for if the doctrine of particular election be true, and revealed as its advocates say, it is no longer a secret and ought to have its natural influence; else why do they preach it, and persuade others to believe it; And it will have its effects where it is believed; for a man's impression of mind and his works will be according to his faith. It will discourage the awakened, and harden them in unprofitable and melancholy distress, filling them with unnecessary terror, and benumb the careless into a stupid insensibility.

But it is not definitively revealed who are the elect, and therefore all ought to comply with the hope of being accepted. And what then? the non-elect must all eventually be sentenced to wrath, because not elected, after being vainly encouraged to hope by a message from God himself. For the fatal destiny of the non-elect is none the less certain by its being a secret to them, while the number of the elect is definite and cannot be increased.

I need not consume time to represent the horrid nature of such sentiments; the single glance is too horrid for any unbiased heart to brook—any heart not unaffected with the miseries of the human family. To suppose that God had selected a part of the human race

AND FOREKNOWLEDGE.

to eternal life and had given a definite account of them, so that the non-elect had never had any offer, neither been deceived with any vain hope, nor chargeable with the sin of rejecting Gods offers, would be to suppose that which is incompatible with his character; but as things are now represented, language fails to point out the enormity and the utmost sensibility of the heart to paint it.

On the other hand. If the decrees of God relating to election be not absolute and the number specified as well as definite, to the final exclusion of all the rest, they are conditional, and the numbering of every man among the elect of God rests on his own personal choice; and that choice to be made without any other aid than that which is ministered with equal fredom to all who hear the gospel. For there is no medium in the case; every man's election is either conditional or absolute. And the idea of absolute decrees of that nature is so horrid and gloomy, that I think no wonder that some, even of the abettors of the plan, have objected to the term. But where is the wise man? where is the philosopher? Where is the disputer of this world who can show the middle path between absolute and conditional decrees? The man, the angel is not extant.

The argument against a partial election, drawn from the inequality and injustice of God's dealings with his creatures, on that view, is commonly rebutted with this, That God was under no obligation to save any of the fallen race, and therefore the non-elect have no cause of complaint, no injustice being done to them. This method of reasoning is no doubt specious and plausible with many; but it is a most preposterous subversion of the truth; it lays, or supposes, an improper ground of argument, darkens counsel by specious words without knowledge misrepresents the character of God and contradicts revelation. For it denies any rule of right, any justice, any goodness, mercy or compassion, as being essentially in God: especially when we consider that they who use this reasoning, also assert, tht man fell into sin according to the determinate appointment and decree of God. It represents God as an arbitrary sovereign, or despot, whose volitions are only sovereign, without respect to any necessary and essential rule of rectitude, goodness or mercy to his dependent creatures. But the essential and unchangeable nature of God is to will the salvation of all; so that nothing can prevent any, except their own disobedience, or rejection of his grace, uninfluenced thereto by any of God's appointments or decrees. God is " Not " willing that any should perish but that all should come to repent- " ance." " Who will have all men to be saved, and to come to the " knowledge of the truth." And according to this his will, he sent the Mediator, Jesus Christ, " Who gave himself a ransom for all, " to be testified in due time." (2. Pet. 3. 9. 1 Tit. 2. 4, 6.)

But God in his own essential nature and according to his necessary existence, is under infinite and irresistible obligation, or to speak in language more appropriate to God, it is a necessary emanation of his nature to have compassion on his creatures, and therefore to provide a remedy and in the progress of the work to bring it within the reach of every individual, without partiality, preference or passing by, except in consideration of the real character or conduct of the subject, as much as to punish sin or to reward obedience. Neither doth this view of the subject make God accountable to his creatures; the perfect rule of rectitude is in himself, infinitely wise, holy, just and good; neither need any reply against God, nor will any of those who understand his ways which are just and equal.

But God is under no obligation to adapt the plan of salvation to the feelings of men. It is his own prerogative to lay out the plan and our province to obey. Although it is impossible that God should lay out any plan except that which is most wise, just and holy, and best calculated to effectuate the purpose. If, therefore, any ask, What plea or claim hath a sinner, or non-elect, on the justice of God? We answer; He hath a claim or plea, equal to all the justice which is in God, and to his own capacity to use it, provided he will use his plea according to justice—A plea, equal to all the justice contained in the overtures of peace and reconciliation set forth in the gospel—A plea, equal to all the justice, love and mercy, exhibited in the unlimited promises made to all who will comply with the terms, with full assurance that he died for all without exception; provided the sinner will submit to use his plea according to the condition of the promises, which requires every man to confess and forsake his sins, and live the life of Christ: a condition, not impracticable by those who have the gospel. It would seem from the writings of the abettors of a partial election, that they entirely forget that the gospel is a remedy provided for the express purpose of redeeming mankind from their fallen and ruined state, and is adapted in all things to their helpless and necessitous condition; provided for all, seeing all were dead and Christ died for all; and offered to all, without limitation distinction or preference, and that God hath pledged his veracity and his life for the safety of all alike, only let them submit to the gospel.

But might not God, consistently with the unsullied rectitude of his own nature, choose some, as his peculiar elect, and predestinate them to eternal life, and in the execution of his plan, give them, not only the ordinary means of grace, but that special aid, without which neither they nor any others would ever become subjects of salvation, and at the same time leave the rest without that special aid, as being by no means obliged to give it to any, to reap the fruit of their own doings in rejecting the offers made to them, so that they are without excuse, these things being done by the sovereignty of God without regard to character or works? The answer is decidedly in the negative in every part. For first. If God created man a fallible creature, as it could not be otherwise, and chose by his own sovereign appointment to not prevent his fall, but to leave him exposed to those trials which he knew would certainly effect his overthrow, it was impossible that he should not provide a remedy furnished with all the aid for man, necessary to his becoming a partaker, and bring it into his reach in his fallen state, before man can be inexcusable. And without such a remedy the rectitude and glory of God's character must have been for ever tarnished. And secondly. Those means of grace, so called, which are not sufficient to ensure the certainty of salvation, have no right to that name. To call the gospel the means of grace and salvation, and then say that sinners who are privileged with it are inexcusable when they are not saved by it, and then to presume that the special agency of the Spirit, some way distinct from the gospel, or in addition to it, is necessary, before any can believe and close in with the gospel offers, is to charge God with contriving a crafty scheme to destroy man under the specious pretext that he is guilty of rejecting his own life and neglecting his duty when he is not: for duty implies capability. Thus God is represented as a mocker of man's miseries and regardless of his sufferings. And man is represented as being without excuse wherein he is not; while under this specious pretext, cruelty is discovered in all, or at least the most important works of God, towards men.

Hear the language of a strenuous abettor of a partial election. " It " would be impossible to vindicate the honor of the divine govern- " ment in exacting duties by law from rational creatures which they " were naturally unable to perform. And it must be for ever incon- " sistent to say that a moral governor still has a right to demand obe- " dience in any one thing when the subject has no power to perform " it. A man never possibly can be under the least obligations to do " what he cannot do; and there is nothing in which rigorous austerity, " cruel tyranny and arbitrary and unreasonable injustice could appear " more evident than to require any such thing." But the pretext is that man's inability is moral, and therefore inexcusable. " It is " meant," says he, " that we are naturally as well as morally unable " to believe or to obey the gospel." And again; " Our moral power, " as it is called, or more properly our inclination or choice as to what " is good we have lost; and here lies the whole mystery. We are " really, fully and completely able to believe in Christ but we are " not disposed to do it. Inasmuch therefore as the non-elect will not " believe in Christ when he is freely offered unto them, when they " are really able to do it and nothing to hinder them but their own " evil disposition, they stand justly liable to condemnation and are en- " tirely inexcusable." (See Ges. Plan. P. 126, 127. By W. C. Davis.)

But this is only begging the question; for if my moral inability or evil disposition be immoveable by me, and I do not receive help sufficient to overcome it either by the gospel or some other way, and God who alone can, will not overcome it for me, I am as completely incapable of believing and obeying the gospel as if I were destitute of natural power or had none of the constitutional or moral faculties. It is therefore incompatible with God's perfect rectitude to appoint one man or some men to eternal life, by a sovereign purpose or decree, and to leave others to perish without regard to the character, faith or works of either class, and then condemn the non-elect on the principle of not believing and obeying the gospel. Besides,

Thirdly. It is a glaring inconsistency, a very contradiction of ideas, to say or suppose that God hath elected and predestinated to eternal life, a certain definite and exclusive number with all the means necessary to their inbringing and perfecting in salvation, by an act of his own sovereign will or purpose, and passed by others to remain under necessary condemnation and wrath, which they cannot escape without that necessary aid which he giveth to the elect but not to the rest, and all without making any account, in adjusting his decrees, of the faith, works or character of either, and after all will condemn the finally impenitent, that is, the non-elect, to eternal wrath because they have not believed and obeyed the gospel. That kind of election therefore is impossible, because inconsistent with the rectitude of God's nature, who is not only a God of truth but of propriety. Again.

Fourthly. If the loss which man sustained by the fall, or his present inability, or lack of power, be moral and not natural, the remedy or salvation from that inability must be moral also, or capable of furnishing him with moral power to obey God according to whatever he requires of man; otherwise the remedy is ineffectual and null. Now the gospel is either furnished with adequate power and efficacy to remove all moral inability and render men capable of believing and obeying, or it is not. If not, it is of no use to mankind, elect or non-elect; they must all die in their sins or be saved by some other means; and the gospel is a very mockery of the miseries of men by offering them life when it is not capable of effecting it. But if the gospel is furnished with all the necessary help to overcome or remove the moral inability or evil disposition and gain the souls of men to believe and obey to eternal life, including the sure promise to all such, of all necessary supplies on the way, which is the truth, and if it is preached to all without exception, reserve or preference, which is also truth, and if the justification of the one and the condemnation of the other turn on this pivot, he that believeth including obedience, is not condemned, but he that believeth not is condemned already because he hath not believed, (not because he was not elected,) there is no room for that partial and exclusive election for which men contend.

Fifthly. For God to have ordained some to eternal life, and others, if negatively yet certainly and unalterably, to condemnation and eternal wrath, without regard to the character faith or works of either class, is inconsistent with the overtures of the gospel as provided for fallen mankind in their ruined condition, and a specific remedy for their disease which was introduced by the fall. For these overtures declare that the grace of God bringeth salvation to all; (Tit. 2. 11.) according to the Greek text and the marginal reading; that Christ died for all; that he *tasted death for every man;* that he gave his life *a ransom for all,* and he inviteth *all* the needy to come, without preference or reserve.

But these things are not proposed or allowed to contradict, that God who knoweth the make of his creatures, and the effect of sin upon them, and what influence the gospel would have, being planned according to his own infinite wisdom, and well adapted to the recovery of mankind from ruin, should have recognised in his eternal counsels, (or decreed, if that phrase be more acceptable than recognised,) whom he would first apprehend by the gospel, it being exactly calculated to catch them in the condition in which it would find them, according to his counsel and appointment, (for I am by no means averse to God's working by a correct plan,) and whom he would first send forth to lead the way and be helpers to others, and then to whom he would adapt the ministration of the gospel to apprehend more, always recognising the condition of the inward man, and who would be most likely to receive the truth, as well as whom it will answer best to apprehend and take first, and so moving forward in his work until all have a fair and impartial trial of those means which furnish sufficient power of salvation, that is, sufficient authority and power to believe and obey the gospel : and the salvation of one, and condemnation of another must turn on the accepting or the rejecting of each for himself. "Whom he did foreknow "he also did predestinate to be conformed to the image of his Son, " and whom he predestinated he also called, and whom he called he "also justified, and whom he justified, he also glorified." And he hath "predestinated us to the adoption of children through Jesus "Christ to himself, according to the good pleasure of his will;" as hath been stated above.

The discerning will understand, that I am not speaking of any conditionality in the decrees of God respecting the sending of his Son to redeem lost men; or in the terms of redemption to which they have to come; as "He that believeth and is baptized shall be saved, and he that believeth not shall be damned;" or that salvation is in Christ alone, for those who come into him in truth and not in name, walking as he walked, and for none else. These and such like decrees are absolute and unconditional; for without an absolutely sure foundation, as well as special conditions unequivocally stipulated, the church could not be built with stability, neither could those who come find unshaken confidence. But the result of the gospel overtures, eventuating in each individual a savor of life or of death depends from first to last on his own choice; "Wherefore also it is "contained in the scriptures; Behold, I lay in Zion a chief corner- "stone, elect precious; and he that believeth on him shall not be con- "founded." (1 Pet. 2. 6.) This renders the whole equitable and fair; and opens to every man the pure fountain of the water of life, clear as crystal, whence flow these and the like unmingled streams of pure gospel; "If a man purge himself from these he shall be a "vessel to honor, sanctified, and meet for the masters use, prepared "to every good work." "Wherefore come out from among them, "and be ye separate, saith the Lord, touch not the unclean thing; "and I will receive you, and will be a Father to you, and ye shall be "my sons and daughters saith the Lord Almighty."

But the notion of the absolute election of a definite number of specified individuals, contradicts the breathings of the Spirit not only in the free, generous and unreserved calls and invitations of the gospel, but in the influence of the same Spirit in the hearts of all Gods children. Was it the spirit or faith of an absolutely definite election which led the apostles to preach as they did? "Warning every "man, and teaching every man in all wisdom: that we may present "*every man* perfect in Christ Jesus; whereunto I also labour, striv-"ing according to his working which worketh in me mightily." " For the love of Christ constraineth us; because we thus Judge, " that if *one died for all*, then were all dead; and that *he died for all*, "that they who live should not henceforth live to themselves, but to "him who died for them and rose again." (Col 1. 28,29. 2 Cor. 5 14, 15.) But I need not multiply examples; the breathings of the Spirit in Jesus, in the prophets, in the apostles, and in all who are born of the Spirit, and many who were not born of God, who have experienced a degree of the same influence, bear in direct opposition to the notion of a limited election, or an elect circumscribed by any thing one side of there being no more souls to be saved or their refusing to come in.

I doubt not but many of the circumstances which have been here stated, as unavoidably arising from the doctrine of an unconditional and limited election, will make many of the abettors of that doctrine recoil from them with abhorrence—no doubt, but many of them feel sensibly, according to their understanding of things, for the miseries of the human family—no doubt, but the operations of the Spirit of God which many of them feel at times, bear right against the beloved doctrine of a particular and limited election—but the pertinacity of education prevails against the Spirit of Christ. *Ye do always resist the holy Spirit.* No doubt but many will be inclined to reprobate us as being foremost in blaspheming God, because we have so freely shown how cruelly the doctrines which we oppose, tarnish his character. But we cannot help these charges; we endure all things for the gospel's sake, and that the purity of God's character may finally appear in glory, to the acknowledgment of all. If it is blasphemy to impute iniquity and cruelty to God, it is blasphemy to patronise those doctrines which imply these things. But it is not blasphemy to expose those doctrines which contain such implications. If it be iniquity to charge God falsely it is not iniquity to declare his righteousness and to show that the way of the Lord is equal.

No doubt many will plead that the enmity of the heart against God, and the want of reconciliation to his government, are the source of all the objections against this doctrine; for it hath been argued, that men will always object until the heart becomes reconciled to God, or until they find that they are of the number who are thus highly favoured by the distinguishing grace of God, but when that is effected they will understand the whole matter, see its consistency and its justice, be at peace with God and reconciled to his ways. Now, just consider what this plan teacheth—that when a man becometh a christian, he is regardless of the welfare of his fellow men—is reconciled that God should have elected a certain specified number to eternal life, and reprobated all the rest, the millions of the non-elect, to eternal damnation ;without previous regard to the

AND FOREKNOWLEDGE.

character of either! But by whom did God ever teach that men become reconciled to him by the most contracted selfishness? What heart can acquiess in the plan, and contemplate it without shuddering? Not one. Who of the advocates of the plan can view it without wishing it were not so? Not one; unless they who have no share in the divine character, whose hearts are relentless to the miseries or the happiness of the human race. And if any one feels any, the least pain or compunction in the contemplation, is he reconciled? Every man of discernment knows he is not. Thousands, through the pertinacity of education and prepossession, profess to be reconciled when they are far from it. And no wonder; when reconciliation cannot be gained unless by selfishness in the abstract. And is this the spirit which a man receives by becoming a christian?—infinitely selfish!—regardless of truth, justice or propriety towards other men or of their happiness, provided he is safe! And is this the Spirit of God which he hath received in Christ? Then, what a representation doth this give of God! Infinitely selfish! infinitely regardless of justice, or of the happiness of his creatures! But let us conceal the horrid prospect—let us cover the blasphemous thought—and veil the gloom from the heart of mortals—from the mind of all men whom we would invite to love and approve the character and works of God.

On the other hand. The advocates of this doctrine, accustomed to strain out a gnat and swallow a camel, often teach, that for a man to be moved to do the will of God by a respect to the recompense of reward is selfish, not evangelical, and that God will not accept it. But if so, God and his ministers, Jesus and his apostles, have taught mankind to be selfish indeed, who have always presented the crown of righteousness and glory, the reward of safety and eternal life, as a motive to obedience; as shown in its place. But there is no more selfishness in a man's seeking his own happiness on proper principles, or in having respect to the recompense of reward, than in God's claiming the honor justly due to his name. Selfishness envieth the happiness of others; claimeth the pre-eminence, even where there is no ground of preference; seeketh the same temper in God and calleth for a special election to the exclusion of others. But the mind of God is not so; his love is free to all; and he is not willing that any should perish, but that all should come to repentance.

Likely many other scriptures may be alledged in vindication of a limited and absolute election which I have not noticed; but I have intentionally considered those which appeared to me the most conspicuous, and which I have most commonly heard insisted on by the abettors of that doctrine. Other arguments also might be adduced on the other side; some of which have been stated in opening the doctrines of faith and the suitableness of the gospel, where they answer the same purpose. For, to maintain the incapability of mankind to believe the gospel on its own authority, or which is the same, on the authority of God therein contained, is implicitly, if not confessedly, to maintain an absolute and limited election; because, if no man can believe the gospel until God in his own appointed time, as they speak, give him faith, or do that work which will enable him to believe, that time must be definitively set for all who ever believe and the number becomes definite and limited.

But the carnally minded, willing to justify themselves, to shelter themselves from the edge of truth, and to ward off the necessity of entering on the path of obedience to God, and of vigorously laying hold on eternal life, will plead, that if God hath not unalterably decreed the character and final state of every man, it cannot be denied that he knoweth all things with certainty, and that the event with every man will be according to that knowledge which God hath of him from the beginning: some also are seriously difficulted on this subject. I have before stated that which is clear to the conscience of every man; that to admit that God's foreknowledge comprehendeth all the works of men and how they will eventuate, represents the character of God in a very different light from what is palmed on him by maintaining that all things eventuate as they do, the disobedience and consequent punishment of rational, conscious, and responsible agents not excepted, in consequence of those decrees of foreordination which have no respect to good or evil deeds. I have also shown before, the propriety of putting men to a thorough trial, that they might learn by a consummate experience to keep themselves from evil, to guard against danger, and to know the benefits of obedience. But some would have it that the foreknowledge of God is the primary and efficient cause of all events, evil as well as good. This is the same as unconditional decrees, and to be rejected on the same principle.

But let us consider soberly what is the foreknowledge of God, particularly as it respects our own estate. For however little we may be able to comprehend of God or his foreknowledge generally; it is reasonable, that according to the privilege granted to us, by the revelation which he hath made of himself, we should have a correct understanding of his foreknowledge as far as it is justly influential on our conduct and final estate. Then what doth God know concerning us? He knoweth that which he hath decreed; that "*He who be-* "*lieveth and is baptized shall be saved; and he that believeth not* "*shall be damned.* Or that, *In every nation, he that feareth him* "*and worketh righteousness is accepted of him. Thou meetest* "*him that worketh righteousness.* But doth not God certainly and absolutely foreknow the works and the final event of every man and every woman, whether they will believe and obey the gospel, and so be saved, or not? Without limiting, or desiring to limit the knowledge of God or any other of his perfections. I answer; That there is no such foreknowledge in God, as can have any direct influence, or any influence at all, without an undue use of it, to cause any man to fail, or to prevent any one from gaining the crown of righteousness in eternal life, who doth not deliberately, and without any necessity arising from foreordaining decrees, God's foreknowledge, or any other cause abstractedly from his own unnecessary choice, reject the gospel and its salvation. Thus I will ask; Doth not God know certainly whether this man and that will have a good crop of corn next fall? Deny his knowledge if ye can. God doth know this, making allowance for the goodness of the season, that if they plant their corn and give it proper cultivation they will receive their crop accordingly; but if they neglect they fail. To every man according to his works. But again; Doth not God know whether these men will plant and tend their corn and so receive their crop, or not? Deny it if ye can. Yet I say, there is no such foreknowledge in God as, directly, or at all, without an abuse of it, will cause one of them to fail, or prevent him from finding his crop in the way of his duty. God hath no foreknowledge to exercise in that way; and men in relation to natural things are not influenced by that kind of foreknowledge which God doth not claim, but by this, that he who doeth work shall reap the fruit; and they all find their account in doing their duty, except the indolent, whom there is no cause to prevent from sharing the blessing in the same line with others, only their own indisposition to submit to the order of God and the line of duty in the things of nature: the earth is as free to yield her strength to them as to others. Just so, the gospel will yield her fruits, the crown of righteousness and eternal life, to all who plant by faith, (which as already proved, is in the reach of those who hear the gospel,) and cultivate by obedience: and this is what God knoweth of these things. For in the gospel there is no unfruitful seasons, exclusively from the failings of the people towards their duty. Otherwise, wherever the gospel is there is always good seasons; and where it is not, men are as innocent in not cultivating it, provided they are upright in what degree of light they can acquire, as men who cultivate no corn where there is none to plant, in doing the best with what they have. But, *Woe to our land*, for the gospel is here and men are unwilling to cultivate it, because in so doing, it is indispensable, to cut down and destroy, all the wild weeds of the forest, the vine of the earth, the grapes of Sodom and the clusters of Gomorrah, which mankind love more than the holy fruits of paradise. But let the minds of the honest be released from difficulty; to such, having once found the gospel, there is no insurmountable cause of discouragement.

It is a matter of the greatest importance to keep the character of God clear in the view of men's consciences; for without this they will never see themselves in the wrong on right principles or feel proper compunction for sin. That law must be holy, just and good which can take occasion by a man's sin, deceive him and slay him. As long as a man conceives that any thing in God is the efficient cause, however remotely, of his being a sinner, whether decrees or foreknowledge, he can never feel clearly guilty, or justly condemned, neither while he conceives the cause to be any where exclusively of his own choice and doings. I am aware that some who presume to claim the name of preachers of the gospel talk otherwise, saying, They are not obliged to vindicate the character of God; God, say they, is able to vindicate himself; and thus represent him as a threshing tyrant who carries all before him by arbitrary power, and whose ways are not justifiable before his responsible creatures, who are required to obey him. And we have no right, say they, poor shortsighted mortals, to enquire into the justice or propriety of his plans or his executing them. It is enough for us that he hath said it and done it. True enough; a *Thus saith the Lord* is satisfactory to any consistent man. But we have no *Thus saith the Lord* for a partial and specified elect to the exclusion of others; they can show us no *Thus saith the Lord* for the foreknowledge of God amounting to an absolute decree, fixing the condition of men without respect to their faith and obedience, or in any wise limiting or cramping the certain prospects of eternal life for those who submit to keep the gospel in obedience on the authority implied in its proposals; there is no *Thus saith the Lord* for submitting to the dictates of arbitrary, or almighty power without a rational conviction in the judgment and conscience of the propriety of the requisition. But we have a *Thus saith the Lord*; Yea we have it, for enquiring into the consistency and propriety of God's dealings with men. " Come now, and let us reason together saith the Lord." (Isa. 1. 18.) What; men reason with God and God with men? Yea, even so; Come now, and *let us be convinced*, as if he had said, (thus in the Hebrew with a good color,) that we may see who are right, ye or I. And the prophets, Jeremiah and Ezekiel, had plain and familiar reasoning, by commission from God, to show to men the equity of his dealings towards them. These therefore found it an important charge committed to them to vindicate the character of God, to show to man, not his sovereignty about which some affect to be so much concerned, but his *uprightness*. For this is the work of a true messenger, one among a thousand (Job. 33. 23.) And this was the work of Jesus Christ the true messenger of the covenant *whom God hath set forth a mercy-seat*, through faith in his blood for *a demonstration of his righteousness*, that the people might come and obtain the forgiveness of sins, when they see before their eyes that *with him there is forgiveness, that he may be feared, that he is just and the justifier of him who is of the faith of Jesus*. But how will men be induced to render to God his due, to pay to him a reasonable service, unless they can understand the reasonableness of his plans, his doings and his requisitions.

Those preachers, therefore, who have such conceptions of the plans and purposes of God, as will not bear a fair and rational justification to the conviction and acknowledgement of all reasonable men, have a poor errand to the world of mankind, already lost in their enmity against him. So far as a messenger fails in showing to man the righteousness of God in all his ways, so far he comes short of the work of a minister of Christ. "For what if some did not be- " lieve? shall their unbelief make the faith of God without effect? " God forbid: Yea, let God be true (and faithful in all his ways to " the knowledge and understanding of men,) but every man a liar;

"(and so remain until he come to know the truth and righteousness of God;) as it is written, that thou mightest be justified in thy sayings, and mightest overcome when thou art judged." (Ro. 3. 3, 4.) But these few remarks must suffice; as a free and full investigation of this particular, would lead too far from the subject in hand as well as induce a repetition of much of what is already written.

We have now gone through the particular subject of election and reprobation, and shown clearly, that the decrees of God are absolute or positive, on those points only which were necessary to secure the foundation of the work, and to provide sufficiently for the salvation of men, and that the way is left open, for all who will, to come and be saved: and all to the glory of God. And although it should be objected, as no doubt it may, that on this plan the building will always be lacking in stability and glory, for the work and spirit of men will be mingled with the work of God and built on the foundation which he hath laid. This objection can arise from nothing but lack of understanding; for souls who are gained to the gospel by the authority of God therein made known, and yield that obedience which the gospel requires, live the same life and partake of the same Spirit with the foundation. *And out of his fulness have all we received, and grace according to grace.* Thus they become cemented or incorporated into one body by the baptism of the one Spirit, and the building is all of God who is above all and through all and in them all; for both he that sanctifieth and they that are sanctified are all of one.

I know it hath also been argued that such a plan leaves all in uncertainty and that God himself is implicated with uncertainty, whether he hath not sent his Son and done all the rest in vain; and that Jesus Christ also is involved in the same uncertainty; for if every man is to make his own choice, who knows who, or whether any, will obey the gospel, or whether Jesus will ever see of the travail of his soul and be satisfied! This is indeed a whimsical argument: and represents God as incapable of knowing any thing but what he determines to bring to pass at all adventures, without leaving his accountable creatures to any choice in the matter, except that which is produced, limited and circumscribed by absolute decrees, which is no choice at all, and the plan disannuls all responsibility, as proved in its place. What kind of being must we suppose God to be, if he hath so little understanding of the organization, faculties, and sensibility of the creatures whom he hath formed and endued with all these things, as not to know, with the utmost precission, what kind of a gospel would answer the purpose of gaining them to obedience, and what degree of energy, must be exercised to overcome them to make their choice? and how to encrease the energy of the call and pursuit until his house should be filled! It is indeed a poor conception of God to suppose or to admit, that he can be at any uncertainty how to adapt a gospel to the state of man even in his fallen condition. And what is to hinder, that God should bring men to trial a second time, even those who have rejected the first, the second being a deeper work? and if that will not do, a third! Thus while the obedient before the flood, were preserved in safe keeping ready for a greater day, and the wicked cut off, and so of all the rest in the days of Moses, and after until the perfect day; what is to hinder God from bringing them all forth and giving them a trial in a day when the work would reach deeper into the quick, and save some of them! For so it is written of Jesus Christ, that he was " Put to death in the flesh but quickened in the Spirit; by " which also he went and preached to the spirits in prison; who " some time were disobedient, when once the long suffering of God " waited in the days of Noe, while the ark was a preparing, wherein " few, that is, eight souls were saved." And again, " For, for this " cause was the gospel preached also to the dead, that they might be " judged according to men in the flesh, but live according to God in " the Spirit," if they will obey, and so have the same privilege of those in the body. (1 Pet. 3. 19, 20 and 4. 6.) Should God therefore in the great love wherewith he loved the world of mankind; in the great mercy and compassion in which he feeleth for their miseries; and in the abundant willingness which he hath expressed for their salvation, have given all those people a trial by the ministry of Jesus Christ in his first appearing; not even excepting Cain who slew his righteous brother, Esau who sold his birthright, (for when it is said That afterward when he would have inherited the blessing, he was rejected; for he found no place of repentance though he sought it carefully with tears; all this doth not imply that he would have come to repentance for his sins but could not get the privilege, but, that he found no room in Isaac to repent of having given that first blessing to Jacob, nor any disposition to recall it,) or Saul the wicked king of Israel, or Absalom the rebellious son of David, or Solomon, who after all his glory and after the LORD had appeared to him twice, had his heart turned away from the true God after idols, by his attachment to strange women, or Menasseh, Ahab, or Ahas, or Jezebel, who can gainsay or prove to the contrary? Is there any thing too hard for the LORD? " He that spared not his own Son, but delivered him up for us all, how shall he not with him also freely give us all things." (Ro. 8. 32.) For the gospel was preached to the dead; which signifieth those gone out of the body by being contrasted with men in the flesh; which flesh also signifieth the animal flesh, or the body, because men in the flesh, meaning men in a carnal nature would be no contrast with the dead, whether literally or morally understood. *To the dead,* is the exact rendering of the word which in the common reading is translated *to them that are dead.* And if Jesus Christ the charitable and forgiving Savior, as he cometh in his second appearing, (which is already commenced,) while he convinceth all, of their ungodly deeds, and hard, ungenerous speeches, should give all another trial to bring them to repentance, not even excepting Judas the traitor, or Pilate who basely through fear of the people, gave judgment against him, contrary to his own conscience, who can withstand, and say that our Lord and Savior hath done unjustly? And there is nothing to contradict the preaching of the gospel in the second appearing of Christ more than in the first; for that the time of the last judgment is a time of preaching the gospel is proved in its place. On this plan the gospel will have its full effect, God will have his house filled, and no man will be left to perish without first having a fair opportunity to escape.

The gospel is most liberal; God hath revealed himself therein a merciful God, generous, benevolent, and kind to the fallen race; but he is also just; this ought never to be left out of view. What security or propriety would be in the government of a prince whose life and institutions were not marked with decided justice in all respects? Many people appear to be highly entertained and delighted with the liberality of the gospel; they are pleased with hearing the liberal invitations, setting the door of salvation open to all, and making the way and end thereof, eternal life, free to all without respect of persons, in contrast with those contracted and selfish notions of some who believe in a partial election of some to life, with the consequent reprobation of others to perdition, without affording them any fair, or even possible opportunity to escape. But much as they are often gratified with hearing these things, their pleasure appears to be merely sentimental. In many of them no room is found for the least grain of the work of God's power to save the soul from sin; they savor not the inward workings and power of Christ, and have no relish for the holy, self-denied life of a christian, which is the prelude to eternal life and glory in heaven. It appears as though the more gracious and condescending God reveals himself to men for their salvation, the more confidently many claim to themselves license to treat the messages of grace with neglect or open contempt, and to affront his authority by disobedience: this is the effect with those who receive not the truth in the love of it that they might be saved, whose hearts are not governed by the Spirit of obedience in Christ. Can any people be in greater danger of coming into this condemnation, that " Even as they did not like to retain God in their knowledge, God " gave them up to a reprobate mind to do those things which are not " convenient: being filled with all unrighteousness." " Who being " past feeling have given themselves over to lasciviousness, to work " all uncleanness with greediness." " Oh that they were wise, that " they understood this, that they would consider their latter end." Will nothing do short of letting men rule and bringing God into subjection to their will? Will men refuse to submit until the door of heaven is opened wide enough to let them in with all their sins, and their own wills ruling in them; This would agree well with the nature of men; but it is impracticable. It is impossible even with God to effect it: sin cannot unite with holiness. It is unreasonable; man cannot rule the mind of God: he must either become subject or be unhappy for ever. " I have sworn by myself, saith the LORD, " the word is gone out of my mouth in righteousness, and shall not " return. That unto me every knee shall bow and every tongue shall " swear." (Isa. 45. 23.)

But the last time is the last. Every former dispensation spake of another to come. The first appearance of Christ bore witness to the second, but not to a third. That second having already commenced according to the scriptures, as proved in its place, proclaims the last opportunity for men to be saved. And shall not the goodness of God, lead to repentance? Or shall men finally persist in despising the riches of his goodness, and forbearance, and long-suffering! after he hath limited a certain time, Saying, *To-day, after so long a time,* as it is said, To-day, if ye will hear his voice, harden not your hearts. Whrefore (as the Holy Ghost saith) *To-day*, if ye will hear his voice harden not your hearts, as in the provocation, in the day of temptation in the wilderness, when he sware in his wrath, They shall not enter into my rest. For such a closing of the last dispensation, the last calling and offer of mercy, will be irrecoverable ruin. And let those who have any degree of light and conviction of the work of God which he is doing in these last days, by his Holy Spirit, remember these things, before their day pass and the work come to a close with them: for it will be cut short in righteousness. " For if we sin wil-" fully after that we have received the knowledge of the truth, there " remaineth no more sacrifice for sins, but a fearful looking for of " judgment and fiery indignation, which shall devour the adversaries." " And whosoever speaketh against the Holy Ghost, it shall not be " forgiven him, neither in this world, neither in the world to come·" " There is a sin unto death; I do not say that ye shall pray for it."

It hath been said, that by this plan which leaveth every man to make his own choice, God is subjected to his creatures; that every man may have a choice, down to the darkest savage or meanest Hottentot, but God must have no choice. Vain man would be wise; and by professing to be wise above what is revealed, he becometh a fool. Because God will only choose the thing which is good and just, because he hath chosen to himself the people who call upon him day and night, and who worship in spirit and in truth, is it therefore true that he hath no choice at all? But who ascribeth to man a power, or privilege of choosing, which is denied to God? a power to choose one man for good to the injury or neglect of another without any reason found in the men for such distinction? Surely not a friend of that God who judgeth every man according to his works—surely not a free man of America, a republican friend to human happiness. But is this to subjugate God to the will of man that every one may have a choice, according to God's appointment, to submit to God's plan or to die in his sins and to sink into irrecoverable perdition by rejecting the last offer of his grace? Could man reject God's terms with impunity, that would limit the power of the· Holy One and seem to subject God to men. But how many! O how many make bold strides, and show the fairest prospects to be added to the number of those whose end is destruction, who were of old proscribed to this condemnation, ungodly men, turning the grace of our God into laciviousness, and denying the only Lord God, and our Lord Jesus Christ, whose judgment now of a long time lingereth not, and their damnation slumbereth not?

CHAPTER XIII.

Of the Times and Seasons, or accepted time and day of salvation.

We shall close this subject relating to the decrees of God, with a few sayings on the Times and Seasons which the Father hath reserved in his own power. God who is most wise, and knoweth all his works from the beginning, hath the most correct knowledge at what time to introduce a new dispensation, or any new degree of light for the promotion of the great work of redemption. And what belongs to us is to be ready and obedient to his proposals. God never undertook so great a work without considering of his own power to carry it on, and his wisdom to govern in all things. "For he worketh all things according to the counsel of his own will." And no part of his work will ever come out of place: whatever is lacking or wrong will be on our part, and we must sustain the loss.

The principal point then, which ought to occupy the mind and the attention of all men, is to know the times and seasons, so far as to be in readiness, to open to every one his duty, and to make a proper use of the seasons as they pass along without being overly anxious about those which are not yet made known. When the apostles with great anxiety enquired of the Lord Jesus, "Saying, wilt thou at this time "restore the kingdom to Israel? He said unto them, It is not for you "to know the times and seasons, which the Father hath put in his "own power. But ye shall receive power after that the Holy ghost "is come upon you." (Acts 1. 6 to 8.) They were required to be obedient and in subjection, ready for what should come next. For the want of considering the day and attending to the duties of it in the proper time, many are exposed to great loss. This was the case with the Jews, over whose city Jesus wept, "Saying, If thou hadst "known, even thou, at least in this thy day, the things which belong "to thy peace, but now they are hid from thine eyes." (Luk. 19. 24.)

What is required therefore of every man, is to keep up with the time, fulfilling the duties as it passeth along: in so doing he is justified and accepted of God. Thus Cornelius was accepted of God, and his prayers and alms went up for a memorial before God, before he knew any thing of the gospel of Christ or had found the way to be saved. Thus the whole nation of the Jews in being obedient to the ordinances and statutes of God in that day, at all times when they were obedient in all these things, were accepted of God and had prosperity and peace. To keep up with the time is what is required and no more. It was not the duty of the Jews to believe in Christ in his proper character as the Son of God and their Redeemer until he appeared to them and began to make himself known in that character. They had the promises and believed them and were justified in so doing; but what things were contained in the promises it was not their duty to know, to understand, or even to believe, For eye had not seen nor ear heard, neither had they entered into the heart of man. And "The prophets have enquired and "searched diligently, who prophesied of the grace that should come unto you : searching what, and what manner of time the Spirit of Christ which was in them did signify, when it testified before hand the sufferings of Christ and the glory that should follow. Unto whom it was revealed, that not unto themselves, but unto us, they did minister the things which are now reported unto you." (1 Pet. 1. 10, &c.) Thus they were left to find their duty and their place in their own day. It was not the duty of Cornelius to believe in Christ until he had heard of him; neither was it the duty of the Eunuch to believe that Jesus Christ was the one of whom the prophet spake until he had a guide to give him an understanding of what he read. So neither is it the duty of the heathen at this day to believe in Christ who have had no knowledge or information about him. Neither is it the duty of professed christians under anti-christian darkness to believe that Christ hath made his second appearance, until they hear the testimony opened far enough to carry conviction to their consciences, if found honest. Until then they are justifiable in preaching and praying according to the best light which they can find—eating the bread and drinking the cup, showing forth his death until he come—looking for and hastening to the coming of the day of God. For according to any man's light and his obedience to it is his acceptance. For with God there is no respect of persons; but in every nation he that feareth him, and worketh righteousness is accepted of him, on the same principle with Cornelius.

But let it be remembered that ignorance of the truth, or not believing it, will not justify a man in neglect, who shuns the light because it is contrary to his former prejudice, but especially, who avoids the light, or wards off the conviction, because the things testified are contrary to the feelings and propensities of his nature. "The flesh lusteth against the Spirit and the Spirit against the flesh, and these are contrary the one to the other. Because the carnal mind is enmity against God for it is not subject to the law of God neither indeed can be." (Gal. 5. 17. Ro. 8. 7.) The gospel threfore is necessarily enmity against the carnal mind, which rules in natural men, whatever their profession may be. And it is not to be expected but the gospel will work in the people who hear it all manner of evil temper against it; as the apostle saith of that law which was holy and just and good; It wrought in me all manner of concupiscence: every kind of lust. Thus the gospel will stir up in men, lusts, murders, evil surmisings, maliciousness, blasphemies against God, hatred against men, hypocrisies, and every evil work, because it cometh directly against every such work and the nature which produceth them. Thus said Jesus, "The world cannot hate you :" (his brethren who did not believe and were therefore of the world :) "but me it hateth, because I testify of it, that the works thereof are evil." (John 7. 7.) And no matter what a man's profession is; that cannot be stirred up in him which is not there. If therefore such evil passions, lusts and blasphemies are stirred in any man it is undeniable that they have their home and residence there. And this is no evidence against the truth of such testimony, but rather in its favor because it stirreth up its enemies in oposition. For if it were of the world the world would love its own. Many, when they here the testimony of Christ in his second appearing, reject it, and forge many pretexts to excuse themselves, unwilling to disclose the radical reason, that it cometh against their lustful natures, testifying to them that the works thereof are evil, and the enjoyment impure. And they hate the Lord Jesus Christ who lived a self-denied life, and never indulged in the lust of concupiscence. Thus the Jews lost their justification, when the light appeared, by hating Christ and the Father. " If I had not come and spoken to them " they had not had sin; but now they have no cloak for their sin. " He that hateth me hateth my Father also. If I had not done " among them the works which none other man did, they had not had " sin; but now have they both seen and hated both me and my Fa-" ther." (Jno. 15. 22, 24.)

But however justifiable any are in unbelief, they are not saved, as hath been shown in the case of Cornelius and others; for there is no salvation out of Christ. " Neither is there salvation in any other: for there is none other name under heaven given among men whereby we must be saved;" (Act. 2. 12.) and Christ is not known without the gospel; for, to preach Christ is to preach the gospel, and to preach the gospel is to preach Christ. Thus the apostle saith of the Gentiles before they heard the gospel, that they were without God and had no hope. And in all the favorable language which he hath used towards them in the beginning of the epistle to the Romans, (2. 11 to 16.) there is not a word which can even imply salvation. " For " there is no respect of persons with God. For as many as have " sinned without law shall also perish without law; and as many as " have sinned in the law shall be judged by the law," and therefore be surely condemned, for cursed is every one who continueth not in all things which are written in the book of the law to do them, " (for not the hearers of the law are just before God, but the doers " of the law shall be justified. For when the Gentiles who have " not the law, do by nature the things contained in the law, these hav-" ing not the law, are a law to themselves; which shew the work " of the law written in thier hearts, their conscience also bearing wit-" ness, and their thoughts the mean while accusing or else excusing " one another,) in the day when God shall judge the secrets of men by " Jesus Christ according to my gospel." But not a word of their being saved on these terms.

Again. However justifiable any are in unbelief before they hear the gospel, the entrance of the gospel into the land and neighborhood, consumes all their justification on that ground; for the light will work in, and they have either to obey or strengthen themselves in their opposition, or to use the mildest term, their disapprobation of that gospel which strikes at the life of their sensual enjoyments and appetites. Now they have no cloak for their sin. " And the " times of this ignorance God winked at; but now commandeth all " men every where to repent." (Acts 17. 30.)

And as before observed, God will never introduce any dispensation out of time or place. When the Jews, who had the greatest privileges of any people, had been tried to the utmost in that dispensation, and were not saved or made a whit better than the Gentiles; for, "What then? are we better than they? No, in no wise; for we "have before proved both Jews and Gentiles, that they are all un- "der sin." (Ro. 3. 9.) When the Gentiles had done their best by their wisdom and philosophy, and could effect nothing; when the times were fulfilled according to the predictions of the prophets, and the people were in expectation, after John had preached that the kingdom of heaven is at hand, the Christ of God appeared and opened the way of salvation by the way of the cross, to be preached to all people; yet quite contrary to the expectations and feelings of all. "For after that, in the wisdom of God, the world by wisdom "knew not God, it pleased God by the foolishness of preaching to "save them that believe. For the Jews require a sign, and the "Greeks seek after wisdom: but we preach Christ crucified to the "Jews a stumbling block and to the Greeks foolishness; but to those "who are called, both Jews and Greeks, Christ the power of God "and the wisdom of God." (1 Cor. 1. 21 to 24.) And after the falling away, to which Jesus and his apostles bore witness, had prevailed in the earth, in the power of anti-christian darkness, and the people had long looked for the better day of deliverance, many having borne witness that the time is at hand, the true gospel of Christ is again made known in his second appearing, tendering salvation to all who will confess and forsake all sin in nature and works, and thus follow Christ bearing his cross in the faith of his second appearing. This second appearing is without sin to salvation, to those who look for him, and are willing to have him and his salvation on any terms which are safe and effectual: all these can see him. But others can no more see him, than the Jews could see Christ in the man Jesus, who, they said, had a devil, or than the disciples, while yet carnal, could see the Father in the Son. And this gospel of Christ's second appearing, is so contrary to the nature and carnal feelings of men, as well as their expectations, who are of the earth and savor the things of the earth, that it is inferior, if possible, to the foolishness of God, and its followers meaner than the filth of the world and the offscouring of all things. But they seek that honor which cometh from God only.

Now while God is thus attending to the great work of redemption, it is not contrary to his wisdom, nor to the equity and love in which he so much aboundeth to his creatures, to call them by many providential movements, from one country to another, or from one condition of life to another, where they will be more likely to receive the gospel, and subserve the great end, knowing at what period it will be proper to introduce the gospel into certain places. "For he "hath made of one blood all nations of men for to dwell on the face "of the whole earth, and hath determined the times and seasons be- "fore appointed, and the bounds of their habitation; that they "should seek the Lord, if haply they might feel after him and "find him." (Act. 17. 26, 27.) This then is the purpose of God in all his providential movements, that men may be brought to seek after God and find him to their salvation. And when the gospel is sent to any country or people, they who are obedient will be blessed and will prosper, but the disobedient will fall under the curse and be destroyed, for God will dispose of the people according to their doings, as freely as the potter doth his clay, forming of it such a vessel as it is fit to make. " Then I went down to the potter's house; " and, behold, he wrought a work on the wheels. And the vessel " that he made of clay was marred in the hand of the potter; so he " made it again another vessel, as seemed good to the potter to make " it. Then the word of the LORD came to me, saying, O house of " Israel, cannot I do with you as this potter? saith the LORD. Be-" hold, as the clay is in the potter's hand, so are ye in mine hand, " O house of Israel. At what instant I shall speak concerning a na-" tion, and concerning a kingdom, to pluck up and to pull down, " and to destroy it: if that nation, against whom I have pronounced, " turn, from their evil, I will repent of the evil that I thought to do " unto them. And at what instant I shall speak concerning a nation, " and concerning a kingdom, to build and to plant it: if it do evil in " my sight, that it obey not my voice, then I will repent of the " good wherewith I said I would benefit them." (Jer. 18. 3 to 10)

I have heard it argued that the man who was hired into the vineyard at the eleventh hour, received equal wages with those who entered in the morning, and it seems to be used as a plea that any time will do to enter into the work of Christ. And it is no doubt a pleasing cloak to those who hate to serve God in the Spirit, or to follow Christ bearing his cross and his reproach, and are glad of a pretext to keep out of the narrow way, as long as they dare. But it is a wretched and horrible deception, like the rest of the devil's fabrications, who is subtle enough to appeal to the scriptures with great dexterity. And who is so blind, unless wilfully so, as not to see in a moment, that the account ministers no kind of pretext for any delay in those who hear the gospel? or any ground of hope, that matters will eventuate as favorably with those who delay as with those who enter in at the first call? So did they who went in at the eleventh hour; they made no delay, but went in immediately. Had they been invited in the morning early, and stayed away until then, the event would not have been so favorable as it was. And to what doth this parable relate? to the people entering into heaven, or final glorification? Can any one suppose that they who are finally redeemed in the evening of the day of redemption, will feel or make any murmurings against their Lord and Master, for making others as happy as they? Never. This is a crooked serpent, found in some of those who have gained but little if any thing in the work of the gospel, and envieth that others should participate in the same blessings equally with them, especially those who are called in much later than themselves: they are high-minded and love the pre-eminence. But the good-man of the house will give the last, who come in at his call, an equal privilege with the first. But woe to them that neglect the call, to wait for another time : they shall be found in the company of the foolish virgins who neglected to provide oil in their vessels until the hour had passed.

The natural conclusion therefore of all these things is, that wherever the gospel is opened in any land, and the people hear and receive faith, it is the immediate duty of each one to repair to the standard and put his faith into practice by obedience, for the time is come. Like Paul, who when he first believed, immediately conferred not with flesh and blood. For however true, that God hath kept in his own power the times and the seasons for the opening of the gospel, he hath laid no injunction, given no liberty, nor left the least ground of encouragement to make any delay after believing; after hearing the gospel and feeling any conviction or apprehension of its truth, but on the contrary, " *To-day* if ye will hear his voice harden not your hearts." " For he will finish the work and cut it short in righteous-
" ness: because a short work will the Lord make upon the earth."
All they who believe in the heart, as Paul hath expressed it, or with *all the heart*, as Philip said to the eunuch; that is, they whose faith worketh by love and is accompanied with the determination of the heart to the gospel when believed, will not delay. He that in an honest and good heart heareth the word of the kingdom bringeth forth fruit. The work of Christ is to bring in everlasting righteousness and to make an end of sin. And in doing this he will make havoc with the wickedness of the world; and with the wicked who will not forsake their sins. " According to their deeds accordingly he will repay." The Hebrew text is emphatical and very strong; [בעל גמלות כעל ישלום:] " *Recompensing according to works according to works he will repay ;* fury to his adversaries, recompense to his enmies ; to " the islands [or nations] he will repay recompense." Every man therefore may expect to receive in full proportion according to his works.

How long will men weary the patience of God; It would seem as though some encourage themselves in sin, because the judgments of God have been so long announced against sin, and yet they are not cut off. But cannot the ungodly consider, that these judgments have been executed on the multitudes of the disobedient from age to age, who have felt the weight of their iniquities and sunk under the curse, and that they also will soon experience the same destruction, without a prompt repentance. But some see others in the ungodly and indifferent situation with themselves, and yet not cut off, and why should they fear? " Because sentence against an evil work is not " executed speedily, therefore the heart of the sons of men, is fully " set in them to do evil." (Eccl. 8. 11.) Thus men may look one on another, and wait to see what will become of each other until both are ruined, as many are doing at this day. But the wise will remember, and the disobedient must know, that " He that being often re-
" proved, hardeneth his neck, shall suddenly be destroyed and that

"without remedy." "What if God, willing to shew his wrath and "make his power known, endured with much long-suffering the "vessels of wrath fitted to destruction." It appears as though many conclude according to the proverb, *While there is life there is hope*, that as long as life lasts they may at any time become obedient and be saved; and thus they get some ease. But these are blinded, snared and taken by the enemy. These can be no better than wilful sinners, wilfully and wantonly provoking God. And what saith the scripture? "If we sin wilfully after that we have received the know- "ledge of the truth, there remaineth no more sacrifice for sins, but a "certain fearful expectation of judgment and fiery indignation which "shall devour the adversary." It is then evident that people may, by sinning against light, shut the door of heaven against themselves, while they have yet years to live, and heap up wrath against the day of wrath. Behold, now is the accepted time, behold, now is the day of salvation. *To-day*, if ye will hear his voice harden not your hearts.

And for the same reasons, it is the duty, the indispensable duty of all those who hear the gospel testimony, to open their ears with freedom and without prejudice, while its ministers reason with them: to be like the noble Bereans, who searched the scriptures daily to see whether these things were so. The leading cause of unbelief, as before shown, is an unwillingness to receive salvation by the way of the cross—an unwillingness that this should be the true gospel—an unwillingness that the spirit should be saved at the expense of the life and very existence of the flesh, or carnal mind—an unwillingness to forego the present sensual fleshly enjoyments and pursuits, to obtain future blessedness and glory in the spirit, as well as present peace with God. People would rather salvation could be had some other way. But God is most wise; gracious, and not cruel. He maketh the way as strait and narrow as it ought to be, and no narrower. Let the people consider these things, and feel into their own consciences; whether the oposition in their own breasts be not that which renders the gospel of Christ's second appearing, dark and objectionable, more than any lack of evidence or conviction.

This is the will of the Father, that whosoever seeth the Son and believeth on him, may have everlasting life. If it be not the will of God, or if he doth not require, that they who have never heard the gospel should believe, until the gospel is sent to them, it is the will of God that they who hear and believe should obey without farther neglect. Therefore, "Sow to yourselves in righteousness: "reap in mercy, break up your fallow ground; for it is time to seek "the Lord till he come and rain righteousness upon you." (Hos. 10. "12. "Blessed are they who hear the word of God and keep it."

THE

MANIFESTO.

PART II.

THE ORDER AND POWER OF THE CHURCH OF CHRIST;

Including certain MARKS *and* EVIDENCES *whereby it may be* KNOWN *and* DISTINGUISHED *from all others.*

CHAPTER I.

The appointed and correct Order of God for the Confession and Forgiveness of Sins.

It will readily be granted that it is just and proper to confess our sins to God, against whom all have sinned, and who is Judge of all. And none who correctly believe the scriptures will deny, that confession is necessary to obtain God's forgiveness. For, " He that cover-" eth his sins shall not prosper; but whoso confesseth them shall find " mercy." And, " If we confess our sins he is faithful and just to " forgive us our sins." But if we confess to God we must have access to him; and that access must be in a way of his own laying out, as we shall prove.

Some imagine that God may be found in any place and every where, because he fills immensity. And it is true God may be found in all places and in all things, but not to the same purpose and effect. Thus God is seen in the sun, the moon, the air and the water. But the sun doth not shine by night, nor the moon by day; the fowls cannot fly in the water nor the fish swim in the air; the air doth not supply men with drink, nor the water with breath; every thing hath its own time, order and place, in which it is acceptable with God and profitable to men. And God is no less orderly in things of a Spiritual nature, than in those of a more temporal; as saith the apostle; " There are differences of administrations, but the same Lord, and " there are diversities of operations but it is the same God who work-" eth all in all."

Among other requisitions of God from fallen man, the confession of sins hath its proper place and order; and in that order alone God is accessible to hear and forgive. This is manifest from both the law and the gospel. For the law, though an outward dispensation, and did not save from sin, or cleanse the people as pertaining to the conscience, was a just and correct shadow, and pattern of the saving work of Christ in the gospel. " The Holy Ghost this signifying, that " the way into the holiest of all was not yet made manifest, while as " the first tabernacle was yet standing: which was a figure for the time " then present, in which were offered both gifts and sacrifices, that " could not make him that did the service perfect, as pertaining to " the conscience; which stood only in meats and drinks and divers " washings, and carnal ordinances [or Justifications of the flesh] im- " posed on them until the times of reformation. But Christ, being " come, an high priest of good things to come, by a greater, and " more perfect tabernacle, not made with hands, that is to say not " of this building, neither by the blood of goats and calves, but by his " own blood, he entered in once into the holy place, having obtained " [Greek, *having found*, being the first who ever did,] eternal re- " demption." (Heb. 9. and 1. 10 &c.) The law of Moses then, being a pattern of the gospel, we will take a view of the order of confessing sins under that dispensation; by which it will appear, that God had but one medium in all the earth, and that in only one place appointed for that purpose, through which he was accessible for the confession of sins and obtaining forgiveness.

After the departure of the children of Israel from Egypt, the Lord commanded Moses to build a tabernacle and to put therein the ark of the covenant, the mercy-seat and other implements of service, and to build an altar for burnt offerings, and sacrifices for sins, and for cleansing the unclean. That tabernacle was called the tabernacle of the congregation. And that congregation was the first church which God ever had on earth, formed, and constituted in order; so that these institutions were the beginning, or first principles of order among the people of God. To the door of that tabernacle God commanded them to bring all their sacrifices and sin offerings, that they might be offered on the altar. And when they sinned by breaking any of the commandments of God, if they made their offer- ings in the appointed place and according to the law, there was an atonement made, and their sin was forgiven. And that there was no other place on earth in which they could be accepted in these things, appears evident from the following scriptures. " What man soever " *there be* of the house of Israel, that killeth an ox, or lamb, or goat " in the camp, or that killeth *it* out of the camp, and bringeth it " not unto the door of the tabernacle of the congregation, to offer an " offering unto the Lord before the tabernacle of the Lord; blood " shall be imputed unto that man; he hath shed blood; and that " man shall be cut off from among the people: to the end that the " children of Israel may bring their sacrifices which they offer in the " open field, even that they may bring them to the Lord, to the door " of the tabernacle of the congregation, to the priest and offer them " for peace offerings before the Lord. And they shall no more of- " fer their sacrifices to devils, after whom they have gone a whoring. " This shall be a statute for ever to them, throughout their genera- " tions. And thou shalt say unto them, Whatsoever man there be

OF SINS.

"of the house of Israel or of the strangers who sojourn among you, that offereth a burnt offering or a sacrifice, and bringeth it not to the door of the tabernacle of the congregation, to offer it to the LORD, even that man shall be cut off from among his people." (Levit. 17. 3, &c.) And again, "These are the statutes and judgments which ye shall observe to do in the land which the LORD God of thy fathers giveth thee to possess it, all the days that ye live upon the earth. Ye shall utterly destroy all the places wherein the nations which ye shall possess served their Gods, upon the high mountains, and upon the hills and under every green tree. Ye shall not do so to the LORD your God. But to the place which the LORD your God shall choose out of all your tribes to put his name there, even to his habitation shall ye seek, and thither thou shalt come: and thither ye shall bring your burnt-offerings, and your sacrifices, and your tithes, and your heave-offerings of your hand, and your vows, and your free-will-offerings. Ye shall not do after all the things that ye do here this day, every man whatsoever is right in his own eyes. Take heed to thyself, that thou offer not thy burnt-offerings in every place that thou seest: but in the place which the LORD shall choose in one of thy tribes, there thou shalt offer thy burnt-offerings, and there thou shalt do all that I command thee." (Deut. 12. 1, &c.) Thus we see that God had one appointed place in which alone the people could find access to him in offering their sacrifices, and performing the service which he required. And the same order was continued in the temple which superseded the tabernacle in the days of Solomon, as is manifest from his own words, "But will God indeed dwell on the earth: Behold, the heaven, and the heaven of heavens cannot contain thee; how much less this house that I have builded? Yet have thou respect to the prayer of thy servant, and to his supplication, O LORD my God, to hearken to the cry and to the prayer which thy servant prayeth before thee to day: that thine eyes may be open towards this house night and day, even towards the place of which thou hast said: My name shall be there, that thou mayest hearken to the prayer which thy servant shall make towards this place." (1 Kings 8. 27, &c.)

When the children of Israel came to the door of the tabernacle, where the whole congregation might come, they could not even there have immediate access to God. They could neither confess their sins nor offer their sin-offerings, nor perform any other part of their service, immediately to him; but all these things were done through the priests, who were a medium ordained of God for that purpose. Accordingly, if any man offered an offering to God, he must bring it to the priest, and if he would confess his sin to God, he must tell it to the priest. And that this was the correct and true order of God, by which he communicated his will to the people and was accessible by them, is fairly and conclusively proved by the instructions given to Moses on that subject. First, God saith to Moses concerning Aaron, "And he shall be thy spokesman, [in the

"Hebrew, for a mouth,] to the people: and he shall be, even he
"shall be to thee instead of a mouth, and thou shalt be to him in-
"stead of God." And again, " See, I have made thee God to Pha-
"raoh, and Aaron thy brother shall be thy prophet." (Exo. 4. 16.
and 7. 1.) This is the exact purport of the Hebrew text. Moses
was not made *a god* distinct from the one true God, but was made to
be God to Pharaoh; he stood as God, and was as it were the exhibition of God, to Pharaoh, to show him God's will, and to execute
his judgments. And *Aaron thy brother shall be thy prophet*. God
must have a prophet. When JEHOVAH made Moses God to Pharaoh, and when he made him God to the children of Israel his brethren, Aaron was in both cases his prophet, or spokesman, for without prophet and priest there is no communication from God, and no
access to him. Thus Aaron was ordained the God, or the mouth of
God to the people of Israel as well as to Pharaoh and his subjects.

The same Aaron and his sons were afterwards consecrated a continual priesthood before God, to stand between God and the people,
to minister to the LORD from their hands, and to enquire of God for
them and to make atonement. For thus the LORD commanded Moses; " Take unto thee Aaron thy brother, and his sons with him,
"from among the children of Israel, that they may minister to me
"in the priest's office, even Aaron, Nadab and Abihu, Eleazar and
"Ithamar, Aaron's sons. And thou shalt make holy garments for
"Aaron thy brother, for glory and for beauty. And thou shalt put
"them upon Aaron thy brother, and his sons with him; and shalt
"anoint them, and consecrate them, and sanctify them, that they may
"minister to me in the priest's office." And again; " And thou
"shalt put upon Aaron the holy garments, and anoint him, and sanc-
"tify him; that he may minister to me in the priest's office. And
"thou shalt bring his sons and clothe them with coats. And thou
"shalt anoint them as thou didst anoint their Father, that they may
"minister to me in the priest's office: for their anointing shall sure-
"ly be an everlasting priesthood throughout their generations."
" And Aaron shall bear the names of the children of Israel in
"the breastplate of judgment upon his heart, when he goeth in
"unto the holy place, for a memorial before the LORD continually.
" And thou shalt put in the breastplate of judgment the Urim and the
"Thummim; and they shall be upon Aaron's heart when he goeth
"in before the LORD; and Aaron shall bear the judgment of the
"children of Israel upon his heart before the LORD continually."
" And thou shalt make a plate of pure gold, and grave upon it, like
"the engraving of a signet, HOLINESS TO THE LORD. And thou
"shalt put it on a blue lace, that it may be upon the mitre: upon the
"fore-front of the mitre it shall be. And it shall be upon Aaron's
"forehead, that Aaron may bear the iniquity of the holy things,
"which the children of Israel shall hallow in all their holy gifts: and
"it shall be always upon his forehead, that they may be accepted be-
"fore the LORD." (Exod. 28. 1, &c. and 40. 13, &c.) Thus Aaron
and his sons were consecrated a continual priesthood, and their duty
and burden clearly delineated.

OF SINS.

To this priesthood the Israelites were commanded to bring all their offerings for sin, and all other gifts which they presented to God; and the priests were commanded to receive and offer them, and to make atonement. For thus it is written; " And he (who hath trespassed) " shall bring his trespass-offering *unto the Lord*, a ram without blem- " ish out of the flock, with thy estimation, for a trespass-offering *unto* " *the priest.* And the priest shall make an *atonement* for him before " the Lord; and it shall be forgiven him, for any thing of all that he " hath done, in trespassing therein." It is however to be remembered that in the case of trespassing against men a restoration was to be made to the owner of the article, of the principal with one fifth part in addition. But it is written farther; " And when any will offer a " meat-offering unto the Lord, his offering shall be of fine flour; " and he shall pour oil upon it, and put frankincense thereon. And " he shall bring it to Aaron's sons, the priests." Once more. " And " if a soul sin, and commit any of these things which are forbidden to " be done by the commandments of the Lord; though he wist it not, " yet is he guilty; and shall bear his iniquity. And he shall bring a " ram without blemish out of the flock, with thy estimation, for a " trespass-offering, *unto the priest:* and the priest shall make an " atonement for him concerning his ignorance wherein he erred, and " wist it not; and it shall be forgiven him. It is a trespass-offering; " *he hath certainly trespassed against the Lord?*" and yet we see, his offering was brought to the priest. These things, together with many in the beginning of the book of Leviticus confirm the fact, that all their gifts, as their meat-offerings, peace-offerings and sin-offerings, were to be presented to the priests. And out of this line of order no acceptable offerings could be made to God, nor any forgiveness obtained as already proved. For whether the whole congregation had sinned, or an individual, whether a ruler or one of the common people; and whether a sin of ignorance brought to knowledge, or whatever was the sin, or of whatever nature in the reach of pardon; in a word, whether one only had sinned or all; it was expressly commanded, that they should bring their offerings to the door of the tabernacle of the congregation, to the priest, and the priest should offer them before the Lord, upon the altar, and make an atonement for them. Not the Lord shall make an atonement, but the priest, who ministered at the time, he shall make an atonement; he shall bring about a reconciliation. Now the high priest bore the sins and the judgment of the people and of their offerings which they brought to the ministering priests.

But not only were they required to bring their offerings to the priests, which they offered to God, but also in the same order and by the same medium to confess to God the sins which they had committed against him. This was the exclusive order under the law, whereby to obtain forgiveness. The confession had to be made before the offering was presented, or as it was first presenting to the priest; as it is written concerning the trespass-offering; " And it shall be, when " he shall be guilty in one of these things, that he shall confess that he "hath sinned *in that thing*. And he shall bring his trespass-offering "unto the LORD, for his sin which he hath sinned, a female from the "flock, a lamb or a kid of the goats, for a sin-offering: and the priest "shall make an atonement for him concerning his sin." Now that the confession was to be made to the priest, or to God in him is made evident thus. The priest was the minister of God, the only Mediator, [משיח the Messiah, or Christ of that day,] through whom the people had access to God, as proved. The conclusion therefore is rational and just that the confession was made to the priest.

But farther. Inasmuch as the priest's office was to receive the sacrifice and make the atonement for, or to cover the particular sin for which the offering was made, an irresistible necessity existed that he should be made acquainted with the sin and all the criminal circumstances which attended it. The ritual also was different in the atonement for one sin from that of another; which adds to the evidence, that the confession of every sin was to be made particularly to the priest, that he might know with clearness and certainty for what sin he had to atone and therefore what ritual he had to perform. Accordingly it was commanded, that "When a man or woman shall commit "any sin that men commit, to do a trespass against the LORD, and that "person be guilty, then they shall confess their sin, which they have "done." (Num. 5. 6, 7.) And again; "He shall confess that he "hath sinned in that thing." Every sin therefore which men committed in that day, had to be exposed to the priest, God's minister and witness, before there could be any forgiveness or atonement. Even in cases where no actual sin was committed or known, but only the tokens and effects of the sin, or corruption and depravity of nature; as in the case of leprosy, the whole matter must be exposed to the priest. "When the plague of leprosy is in a man, then he shall be "brought to the priest:" and he must show himself to him; as Jesus said to the man whom he had cleansed, "Go, shew thyself to the "priest, and offer the gift which Moses commanded for a testimony "unto them." (Lev. 12. 9. Mat. 8. 4.) And let them see that thou also walkest uprightly according to the law. Or if the plague of leprosy was in a house, (now the house could not sin but the inhabitants or owners,) the whole matter must be exposed to the priest. "And he that owneth the house shall come and tell the priest, saying, "It seemeth to me there is as it were a plague in the house:" and so of other things. So that in that day and under that dispensation, no sin could be forgiven, no atonement made, no reconciliation could exist between God and the sinner, until the sin was first exposed to the priest, God's minister and witness. "Here is a transgressor; he brings a lamb to the altar; lays his hand upon its head; and confesses his sins." (See B. W. Stone's Letters on Atonement. Page 30.)

Another convincing proof that the confession of sins under the law was made to the priest, or minister of God, is found in the account given by Ezra the priest, of the events which took place when the Jews returned to Jerusalem, from the Babylonish captivity. Their sin was no secret; there was therefore no need of confessing it to make it known: it was already public. But to remove the sin, confession was necessary as well as forsaking. And this must be done according to the law. (For they were now beginning to be restored to their ancient privileges, and it was necessary to keep the law.) Their sin was in taking wives of other nations. This was the sin to be removed, " And let it be done according to the law." Now the law required a confession as the first step. " Now therefore," said Ezra the priest, " make confession to the LORD God of your fathers, " and do his pleasure: and separate yourselves from the people of " the land, and from the strange wives. Then all the congregation " answered and said with a loud voice, As thou hast said so must we " do. But the people are many, and it is a time of much rain, and " we are not able to stand without, neither is this a work of one day " or two : for we are many that have transgressed in this thing." Had the confession been to God, without a mediator, or priesthood, or certain men to serve in that office, as God's ministers or witnesses, a hundred thousand of them could have confessed as soon as one man. On that supposition there would have been no propriety in their saying, *Neither is this a work of one day or two ; for we are many that have transgressed in this thing*. Neither was there any cause why they must wait about the temple, or stay in Jerusalem to put away their strange wives, they could have done that at home, would it have sufficed to have done that privately, or before God without a witness. But all these things must be done or agreed upon and the confession made, in the presence of men—God's witness. Hence they continued: " Let now our rulers of all the con- " gregation stand, and let all them who have taken strange wives in " our cities come at appointed times, and with them the elders of " every city, and the judges thereof, until the fierce wrath of our " God for this matter be turned from us." Thus we see they understood that the fierce wrath of God could be turned from them by coming to these men who should stand to wait on them, and by no other method. " And the children of Israel did so. And Ezra the " *priest* with certain chief of the fathers, after the house of their " fathers, and *all of them by their names*, were separated, and sat " down in the first day of the tenth month to examine the matter." To see that the people did as they had promised to do, *To make confession to the LORD God of their fathers*. Thus they confessed to him and told Ezra and those who were separated with him, what they had done. Now Ezra was the priest. This was confessing to the LORD God of their fathers, and so they accounted it. " And " they made an end with all the men that had taken strange wives " by the first day of the first month." A work of three full months, because all had to be done according to law. (Ezra 10 chapter.)

Another example of the manner of confessing sins to God under the law, is set forth in the history of Achan. " And Joshua said un- " to Achan, My son give, I pray thee, glory to the LORD God of " Israel, and make confession unto him; and tell me [open up to " me] now what thou hast done: hide it not from me. And Achan

" answered Joshua, and said, indeed I have sinned against the LORD
" God of Israel, and thus and thus have I done: when I saw among
" the spoils a goodly Babylonish garment, and two hundred shekels
" of silver, and a wedge of gold of fifty shekels weight, then I co-
" veted them, and took them; and, behold, they are hid in the earth
" in the midst of my tent and the silver under it." Thus Achan gave glory to the LORD God of Israel and made confession to HIM, by giving to Joshua a particular account of the things which he had done, even to the thoughts of his heart. " And Joshua sent messen-
" gers; and they took them out of the midst of the tent, and brought
" them to Joshua, and to all the children of Israel, and laid them out
" before the LORD." But how were they laid out before the LORD? were they not as much before the LORD in Achan's tent as after they were brought out? No doubt they were. But they were not before the LORD in the order of his judgment, until they were laid out before *his congregation, his witnesses, and the judges* that were appointed in those days. To this agree the words of Solomon. " He
" that covereth his sins shall not prosper: but he that confesseth and
" forsaketh them shall have mercy." That confession which is connected with the promise, is contrasted with covering, and therefore implies uncovering. But as nothing can be hid from the eye of God, nothing can be laid open or uncovered before him except as he is revealed in his witnesses.

It is true, the confession of Achan was not in the established order, for Joshua was not of the priesthood; but it is also true that his case was not an ordinary case, his sin being such as did not admit of legal atonement or forgiveness, but when he was detected by extraordinary means, and brought to an open confession, he was first stoned and then burned, with all that pertained to him. But the order of confessing sins to God is not at all obscured by the extraordinary nature of the case, but rather elucidated. For although Joshua was not a priest, he was the minister and witness of God to that people; and whereas he was required to tell, or as in the Hebrew, [הגיד] *to often up*, or *make manifest*, to Joshua all his sin, in a case which did not admit of confession and atonement by the priest, it serves to confirm the fact, that nothing was accounted confession to God either in pardonable or unpardonable cases, but that which was made to a man in whom God was revealed. And should it be still objected that Achan's confession could not be a type of the confession of sins in the gospel, because his life was taken away notwithstanding? Let it be considered that it is an illustrious exhibition of the order of confessing to the LORD God of Israel: and that is the point which we are now investigating. We shall enquire into its application to the gospel afterwards. But consider farther; there is also a sin which hath no forgiveness in the gospel, either in this life or in that which is to come. And yet the perpetrators of such sin will undoubtedly be finally brought to confession. For, " As I live, saith the LORD.
" every knee shall bow to me and every tongue shall confess to God.'
(Mat. 12. 32. Ro. 14. 11.)

If the dispensation of the law consisted mainly in types and shadows of things to come, and those types were outward and temporal, no such benefit, as the result of Achan's confession, can be considered as pertaining to him, but to the congregation of Israel, from whom the curse was removed, when he was separated from them. His confession therefore is not to be considered as a type of the confession of sins in the gospel for the deliverance of the individual confessors. For in that case, to make the type complete and consistent, he must have received a typical salvation answerable to that in the gospel; and congenial with that dispensation under which he lived—his life must have been preserved. Whatever benefit Achan might acquire to his soul, by his honest and punctual confession, after he was detected; no such benefit can consistently be reckoned a figure, or type, as that would be making the substance a shadow of the substance.

The valley in which Achan was made an example is called the valley of Achor; and to that memorable event the prophet Hosea had respect when he spake of the future restoration of the church, and said; "Therefore, behold, I will allure her, and bring her into "the wilderness and speak comfortably to her. And I will give her "her vineyards from thence, and the valley of Achor for a door of "hope." (2. 14.) It is not said, I will give *them* as of individuals, but I will give *her* as of the church collectively. The typical Achor was in that day made a door of hope to the congregation of Israel; for as soon as Achan, with the pledges of his wickedness was consumed in the valley, their drooping hope was revived; and whereas they had been smitten before their enemies, they immediately after went up and prospered and took the inheritance which answered to the heavenly Canaan. So shall the church of Christ triumph in glory when all the Achans, with all the accursed things are purged out; as it is written; "The Son of man shall send forth his angels, "(or ministers,) and they shall gather out of his kingdom all things "that offend, and them that do iniquity; and shall cast them into a "furnace of fire; there shall be wailing and gnashing of teeth. "Then shall the righteous shine forth as the sun in the kingdom of "their Father. Who hath ears to hear, let him hear." (Mat. 13. 41.) This view of the case of Achan doth not contradict its being an illustration of the practice of confessing sins under the gospel, as it confirms the necessity of universal confession. And it shows that in all cases, unpardonable as well as pardonable, confession is not made immediately to God, but through his witnesses.

The Israelites might seek God upon the mountains and hills, or in any place or manner, besides the place and order appointed by himself, and confess and make sacrifices, but there was none to hear or regard. If on extraordinary occasions some might have transient visions of God in those places, there was no forgiveness or atonement. Not even the name of God was found in that work, except in the place where he had the ark of his covenant, his mercy-seat, his altar, his holy fire and his priesthood. And even in that place none could be accepted, either in their offerings or confessions, except in the appointed order: all must be done through the priesthood; and that was offering and confessing to God according to his own appointment; and so they esteemed it. Accordingly the priest was not only the mouth of God to the people but the ear of God also; a mediator between God and man. And every man was accepted of God in being accepted of the priest; for the priest made the atonement; the reconciliation was effected between the offender and the priest, God's minister, who covered the sin that it might be done away; and it was forgiven. But whoever spoke or rebelled against the priest, or any of God's ministers, rebelled against God; as it is written; " And the whole congregation of the children of Israel " murmured against Moses and Aaron in the wilderness : and Moses " said ; The LORD hath heard your murmurings which ye murmur " against him : and what are we? your murmurings are not against " us, but against the Lord." (Ex. 16. 2, 8.)

But when the Israelites transgressed the law and covenant of God, and were given to captivity ; when the temple at Jerusalem, where he had placed his name and covenanted to dwell between the cherubim, was destroyed ; his altar thrown down, the ark of the covenant and the mercy-seat removed; the holy fire extinguished and the priesthood dispersed ; in these circumstances there could be no acceptable offering according to the law. Yet God did not wholly cast off his people, but noticed for good, all who came as near the mark as was in their reach, while the true order was impracticable. In this state of things the prophet Daniel kneeled down and prayed three times a day, with his face towards Jerusalem, as he could not go to the spot. By this he showed his regard to the true order ; and the more so, as his observing it was directed against his own life, by the decree of the king of Babylon. Had it been according to true order to seek God and find him any where, Daniel might have turned his face another way as well as towards Jerusalem. But that was not Daniel's faith ; nor was it the faith of any except those who chose to run their own way, and go a whoring after their own idols, on the mountains and hills and under every green tree ; which the law of God solemnly forbade. (Dan. 6. 10, &c.)

While in Babylon also, Daniel made a general and serious confession of the sins of the house of Israel ; and it is a reasonable conclusion, that he then also turned his face to Jerusalem in obedience to the established order of God's worship : according to the words of Solomon at the dedication of the temple. " If they shall bethink " themselves in the land whither they were carried captives, and re-" pent, and make supplication to thee in the land of them that carried " them captives, saying, We have sinned, and done perversely, we " have committed wickedness; and so return to thee with all their " heart, and with all their soul, in the land of their enemies who led " them away captive, and pray unto thee toward their land, which " thou gavest unto their fathers, the city which thou hast chosen, " and the house which I have built for thy name : Then hear thou "their prayer and their supplication in heaven thy dwelling place, and maintain their cause, and forgive thy people." (1 Kin. 8. 47, &c.) Thus their prayers and their confessions were all to be made towards Jerusalem and towards that house where God had placed his name, in those times when they could not come before the altar and the priest in the correct order of God's appointment. But when they were released from captivity, and the temple, the altar and the priesthood became accessible, they could no longer be accepted unless they observed the prescribed order, as in the case of those who had taken strange wives as already shown.

My reason for dwelling so much on the confession of sins among the Jews and Israelites is to show that there never was any confession of sins from the beginning, which was acceptable to God, unless in the appointed order in the presence of his witnesses, except when the thing was impossible; and that in that case, it was only acceptable for the time being in coming as near to the mark as it was practicable to come; and also that as the law was an appointed pattern or shadow of the gospel, and was so considered by the inspired apostles, the confession of sins under the law, in a perpetual order, is a confirmed reason that we may look for it in the gospel; but especially when we find, not only John the forerunner of Christ, but christians themselves confirming and practising it. It may appear strange to some, but not the less true, if it be found, on a strict examination, that no people ever pretended to confess their sins with any hope of pardon and acceptance, either under the law or the gospel, without bringing them to the witnesses of God, until after the falling away, spoken of by the apostle, took place, and the reign of the beast commenced, and the doctrines and works of Anti-christ were promulgated and adopted.

We have now gone through the dispensation of the law and the prophets, which continued until John, to whom was given a new and farther revelation from God, which was preparatory to the gospel dispensation. "The law and the prophets," said Jesus, "were until John; since that time the kingdom of God is preached." (Luke 16. 16.) But though the old dispensation then began to come to its end, the article of confessing sins, was not disannulled, but continued with an increase of light and energy; so that they who had been long acquainted with the law and its order, and no doubt, had confessed according to that order, came and confessed to John. As it is written; "John did baptize in the wilderness and preach the baptizm of repentance for the remission of sins. And there went out unto him all the land of Judea, and they of Jerusalem, and were baptized of him in the river of Jordan, confessing their sins." (Mar. 1. 4, 5.) From these things it appears that the matter of confessing sins was not a ceremony, although performed among the ceremonial observances, but a direct act of duty and worship to be continued throughout the work of salvation, as prayer, praise and other duties of perpetual obligation. The Hebrew term [תודה] which signifies *confession*, signifies also *thanksgiving*, importing the laying open to God, of the blessings received as well as the sins committed.

Now the people had sinned, not against John, but against God; the confession, therefore, was not due to John, but to God. But as John was the medium of the revelation of God to them for the work to which they were called, they came and confessed to God in his presence and hearing, or to God in him. Thus God continued to show his regard to order, as a God of order and not of confusion: he still had a witness; and as the ministry of John was preparatory and introductory to that of Christ who was one, John was for a time the only ministering witness: all the faithful went to him. And in acknowledging that order of God and that minister of order, they acknowledged God in the only acceptable manner then extant, and confessed their sins to him in the only acceptable method. Probably the most rebellious man would be willing to acknowledge God in some manner; he might acknowledge his name and authority at a distance; but the disorderly nature of man is opposed to order. Korah, Dathan, Abiram and their company, rebelled against the appointment and order of God in Moses and Aaron, and at the same time professed to be God's people—all holy. The pharisees also, who rejected John's baptism and the confession of sins accompanying it, and thereby rejected the counsel of God and refused to justify God; and who also said of Jesus Christ, " Who is this that speak- " eth blasphemies? who can forgive sins but God only?" (Luke 5. 21. and 7. 29, 30.) nevertheless made a high profession of being God's peculiar people, having faith in the coming of both Elias and Christ that were to come. Many also in these days who have cast off almost every trace of the true order of God in the gospel, still profess to be christians.

He who confesseth his sins in secret is not certainly conscious that any being hears or regards him, or if he believes he is heard, he hath no idea, that any thing more is known after his confession than before. He may say it is his choice to confess to God whom he fears and regards more than man. But that he hath more fear toward a man like himself, than towards God is evident; because when he is confessing his sins to God in secret without dread, were he conscious that a man of like passions with himself, especially, a hater of sin, were in hearing, he would be alarmed, or filled with consternation. And why so; only because the fear of man is deeper in his heart than the fear of God out of man? It is infinitely more mortifying for a man to confess his sins in faith and honesty, in the hearing and presence of God's witnesses, than to confess to God, as they say, abstractedly from men; which conclusively proves that to confess to God in men, is the deepest work, and the nearest possible approach to God. It fills up what is written, " He that covereth his sins shall " not prosper: but whoso confesseth and forsaketh them shall have " mercy." " For every one that doeth evil hateth the light, neither " cometh to the light, lest his deeds should be reproved." [discovered, or convicted, in the Greek, that is, lest he should be convicted of them, they being laid open in their true colors to his conscience,] "There is nothing covered that shall not be revealed; neither hid that shall not be known." But to confess secretly, brings nothing to light; it makes nothing known. These hate the light, and come not to the light; they seek deep to hide counsel from the LORD; for no man will imagine he can hide from God absolutely, or attempt to do it; but many seek with profound subtlety to hide from him in his witnesses. And Woe to them, saith the LORD. But he that confesses to God in the true and established order, knows and sensibly feels, that he is heard and understood; that what he hath done is made known. This is coming to the light and uncovering; it is coming to truth and honesty; it is contrary to the spirit, or principle, which inclines men to commit sin; for that spirit can never lead a man to confess and expose his sins in so open a method, in so near an approach to God, until satan can be divided against satan. By thus confessing in the light, the spirit of sin and of darkness which rules in the corrupt and deceitful heart, is sensibly detected and exposed; this is coming to a light and a judgment of which the sinner is sensible; and this shows the necessity and propriety of God's having a witness. This is coming to the living God, on his living throne and in his living temple. As it is written; "Ye are the temple of "the living God," and again; "The place of my throne; and the "place of the souls of my feet; where I will dwell in the midst of "the children of Israel for ever." And again; "To whom coming "as unto a living stone disallowed indeed of men; but chosen of "God, and precious, ye also, as living stones, are built up a spiritual "house, an holy priesthood to offer up spiritual sacrifices (not legal "types, but sacrifices in the spirit, or of a spiritual nature,) accepta- "ble to God by Jesus Christ." (Ezek. 43. 7. 2 Cor. 6. 16. 1 Pet. 2. 4, 5.) Now we have already shown that the priesthood were God's ministers to the people, and the people's ministers to God; that the people presented to the priesthood what they offered to God, and confessed to God in them, or to them in God's stead, the sins which they had committed against him. Thus believers in Christ are (not now a legal or ceremonial, but) an holy priesthood. Not that each one of them is an appointed ministering priest; but the true priests of God are all among them, Jesus Christ being the high priest: and separately from them, there is no access to God for salvation.

CHAPTER II.

The subject continued, as it respects the work of God in the Gospel.

THAT the confession of sin is necessary, and so remains, under the dispensation of the gospel, it is evident, from the consideration, that the whole order of the law was typical of the gospel, and the baptism of John figurative of that of Christ, but also by the express teachings of the ministers of the gospel. "If we confess our sins, "he is faithful and just to forgive us our sins, and to cleanse us from "all unrighteousness." (Jno. 1. 9.)

After the introduction of the gospel, God continued to show himself a God of order; and continued, or renewed, the direct line of order for his people. For although the priesthood was transposed from Aaron to Melchizedec, that is, to Christ, and the law transposed also, neither the law nor the order thereof was lost. (See page 73.) God had prepared a Mediator, a merciful and faithful high priest, in things pertaining to God, a shepherd of the sheep; the great antitype of all that had been before exhibited, the beginning of the new and spiritual building of God, the Judge of quick and dead. None, therefore, could approach God, or confess their sins to him, or receive forgiveness, except through that Mediator: no attempts of the kind, in any line or way, detached from him as the medium could succeed. Accordingly he said, "I am THE WAY, the truth and the life; no "man cometh to the Father but by me." (Jno. 14. 6.) But as the office of Christ was represented by that of the levitical high priest, we are not to look for much confession of sins made immediately to him; for there was another medium, subject to him, and through which to approach him. "Now, when these things were thus or- "dained, the priests went always into the first tabernacle, accomplish- "ing the service: but into the second went the high priest alone, "once every year." (Heb. 9. 6, 7.) It was not the manner under the law, for the people to come with their sacrifices immediately to the high priest who went alone once a year into the most holy place, but to the second order of priests, who went always into the first tabernacle, accomplishing the service for the people. This is made evident by the commandments which were given directly after the tabernacle was reared up in the wilderness. Aaron's sons, the subordinate priests were they who received the offerings at the hands of the people, and of course heard their confessions, as before shown. And the same order obtains with Christ and his ministers. The priests of Levi were not ordained and qualified as priests in their order, until the tabernacle was reared; so neither were the gospel ministers, until the gospel was given; as said Jesus; "Behold, I send "the promise of my Father upon you: but tarry ye in the city of "Jerusalem, until ye be endued with power from on high." (Luke 24. 49.)

The rearing up of the Jewish tabernacle consisted in bringing the different parts together, on an appointed day, sometime after they had been formed, and joining them one to another, so as to make one tabernacle. So the rearing of the spiritual tabernacle also consisted in uniting the parts, in that day when God, and Christ, and the church, became united in one according to the words of Christ; "In "that day ye shall know, that I am in my Father, and ye in me, and I "in you." "For where two or three are gathered together in my "name, there am I in the midst of them." (Jno. 41. 20. Mat. 18. 28.) This took place after Christ ascended to the right hand of power, and his disciples were baptized with the Holy Spirit, that cement of love and union, by whose influence they became of one heart and one soul. It was then Christ Jesus properly became an high priest of that living tabernacle; as saith the apostle; "We have such an high priest, who is set on the right hand of the throne of the majesty in the heavens; a minister of the sanctuary and of the true tabernacle, which the Lord pitched, and not man. For every high priest is ordained to offer gifts and sacrifices: wherefore it is of necessity that this man have somewhat to offer. For if he were on earth he should not be a priest, seeing that there are priests that offer gifts according to the law; who serve unto the example of heavenly things. But *now hath he obtained* a more excellent ministry," or priesthood. [Heb. 8. 1. to 6.] By this view of the subject, it is evident, that while Christ Jesus was on earth, he was not properly qualified to execute his office, as it respected the offerings of the people to be made through him, any more than Aaron was before the tabernacle was reared and he anointed. As Aaron then became a medium, for others to make their offering through him, so did Jesus Christ; the one being the type and the other the antitype.

Abundance was spoken concerning the office and duty of Aaron, and the offerings of the people, through them, long before the tabernacle was set up. A great part of the book of Exodus is taken up in treating on these subjects; but the last chapter gives the first account of the actual setting up of the tabernacle, and the eighth of Leviticus of Aaron's being actually anointed. And then his sons were also consecrated with him; and at the same time also, the tabernacle with all its utensils, and the altar with all belonging to it, were anointed, sanctified and prepared, for the use long before prescribed. When this was done, Aaron entering through the vail into the most holy place of the tabernacle, found immediate access to God, and his throne, or mercy-seat, there placed; and the priests, standing in the first apartment of the tabernacle, and fulfilling their part of the service, in union with the high priest, found their access to the mercy-seat through him, in their gifts and offerings; and the congregation, meeting the priests, at the door of the tabernacle, with their gifts, found access to God in his mercy-seat, through the whole priesthood. And thus they all found access to God, and were accepted, and received blessings; but each in his own order. In these things the priests of Levi *served to the example and shadow of heavenly things ;* and answerable to that example, or pattern, were the gospel order and ministry established. Therefore, as the confession of sins and offering for sins went together, under the law, as before shown, and as they were not presented immediately to the high priest, but to the subordinate priests, so after the gospel day and work took place the confession of sins was not immediately to Christ Jesus, but to his ministers, who are the gospel, or christian priests, and his church, or people, are the temple, or house, where the offerings are made to God in order, as it is written; "To whom coming as to a "[ζωντα] living stone, disallowed indeed of men, but chosen of God and precious; ye also as [ζωντες] living stones, are built up, a spiritual house; an *holy* priesthood, to offer up spiritual sacrifices, acceptable to God through Jesus Christ;" "But ye are a chosen generation, a royal priesthood, that ye should show forth the praises of him who hath called you." (1 Pet. 2. 4, 9.) These words embrace the whole Jewish order, with manifest application to the christian church and ministry. But this subject will be farther considered hereafter.

I am aware of the objections of some, against the appointed order of confessing sins, on account of the evil conduct, or heretical name of a certain people, who have maintained it the nearest of any, in the outward form, and say they have preserved it down from the apostles. But the abuse of the order of God is no exception against the order itself. If any abuse it, they are criminal; but that is no cause why others should neglect it. No truth is to be neglected or condemned because a wicked people profess it.

Now as the ministering priests of the law, offered up their own sacrifices and those of the people through the high priest, so the priests, or ministers, of the gospel, offered up their own sacrifices and those of the people through Christ, the great high priest of the gospel. To this these words agree and are justly applicable; *Ye also as living stones are built up a spiritual house, an holy priesthood, to offer up spiritual sacrifices acceptable to God through Jesus Christ.* They were not to offer up material sacrifices, as the Jewish priests, but those which pertained to the spirit—those which were calculated to purge the conscience from dead works, and make it fit to serve the living God. And as the people under the law could not make an acceptable offering to God, except in the appointed place, the temple, or house of God, and through the priesthood, so neither can any in the gospel make an acceptable offering to God to purge the conscience from dead works, or offer themselves up a perfectly acceptable sacrifice in the spirit, unless in this spiritual house, built up of living stones, on Christ the living stone. *Whosesoever sins ye remit, they are remitted to them; and whosesoever sins ye retain, they are retained.* And as Aaron bore the sins of the people, even of their holy things, or things devoted to God in sacrifice, (not the punishment or reward of sins, for there was no punishment or reward of iniquity laid on Aaron, in the performance of his duty in the behalf of the people,) and these sins were first borne from the people by the subordinate priests, to whom the confessions were made; so in the gospel, Jesus the high priest bears the sins of those things, that is, persons who devote themselves to God, making covenant with him by sacrifice, and sins are first removed from the people, by the ministers of the gospel, to whom confession is made, while they minister in the name of Christ and in his behalf. Thus I say Christ and his people bear the sins of those who make covenant with God by sacrifice, or who confess and forsake their sins according to the true order of God for that purpose. Not the punishment of sins, or reward of iniquity. No punishment was inflicted on Christ Jesus in the execution of his office in the behalf of the people ; neither is there on his ministers, except that which is inflicted by the enemy, who waged war against Christ and his people for doing their duty. But the sins of those who faithfully make their offerings to God are borne by Christ who is in the people, and by his people in charity to those who offer them, and for the destruction of the sins, to bury them out of sight. *Charity covereth the multitude of sins.* And this is the substance of the atonement made by the priests of Levi under the law. And as Jesus Christ bore the sins of many ; as he took our infirmities and carried our sorrows; so it is written concerning christians ; " Brethren, if a man be overtaken in a fault," [τινι παραπτωματι, any offence ; the very word which is used by the same apostle to express our *offences* for which Christ was delivered. Ro. 4. 25.] " Ye that are spiritual restore such an one in the spirit " of meekness; considering thyself lest thou also be tempted. Bear " ye one another's burdens, and so fulfil the law of Christ." " Con- " fess your faults one to another, and pray one for another, that ye " may be healed. Brethren if any one of you do err from the truth " and one convert him ; let him know, that he who converteth the " sinner from the error of his way *shall save a soul from death, and* " *shall cover a multitude of sins.*" (Gal. 6. 1, 2. Jas. 5. 16, 19, 20.) And as quoted above ; "Whosesoever sins ye remit, they are remitted " to them." An objection hath been made against the use of the saying of James, " Confess your faults one to another," in proving the true order of confession ; and the same exception may be taken at the above quotation from the epistle to the Galatians : but it will be obviated in a convenient place.

As the priesthood under the law of Moses included both the high priest and the second order, so in the gospel of Christ, the church, or body of Christ, is composed of the head and the members, and there is no true church, or body, without both. But as under the law, when Aaron was anointed, he was the priest, and the only anointed one on earth, though incapable of serving at the altar, until he had offered a sacrifice, and then his sons were anointed with the same oil ; and yet the service could not be all performed in order, in behalf of the people, until the high priest went into the Most Holy place and returned. So when Jesus was anointed with the Spirit, he alone was the only anointed priest of the gospel; the only true habitation of God on earth, the true tabernacle, which the Lord pitched and not man, until he had made his sacrifice, and then his disciples were anointed with the same Spirit and became one with him ; for he breathed on them, and said, receive ye the Holy Ghost. Howbeit they were not fully commissioned nor qualified to minister the gospel to the people, until he had ascended to the Father and returned in the gift of the Holy Ghost, on the day of pentecost? They were then fully empowered, according to the work of that day, to preach repentance and the remission of sins in his name, and to do all that work in the spiritual house, which was set forth in a shadow, by the service of the tabernacle. They were then one with Christ and with the Father, according to the work of that day; and these in their proper order and power are the true body of Christ, and the true Christ, having received the same anointing of the Father, as Jesus himself, while he stood alone, and of the people there was none with him. Accordingly it is written, "He that hath seen me hath "seen the Father." And again; "At that day ye shall know that I "am in my Father, and ye in me, and I in you." (Jno. 14. 9 to 20.) And again; "But ye have an unction from the Holy One, and ye "know all things—But the anointing which ye have received of him, "abideth in you; and ye need not that any man teach you: but as "the same anointing teacheth you of all things, and is truth, and is "no lie." Further.

To prove that the church is one with Christ, they being one body and constituting the true seed and true Christ to whom the promise was made, the words of the apostle Paul may be introduced. "Now "to Abraham and his seed were the promises made. He saith not, "And to seeds, as of many: but as of one, And to thy seed, which "is Christ." (Gal. 3. 16.) Now all the faithful are the seed; not seeds, for they are one, as it is again written; "The children of the "promise are counted for the seed." (Ro. 9. 8.) And, as it were, to put the question beyond a doubt, the following words are to the point. "For as the body is one, and hath many members, and all "the members of that one body, being many, are one body: so also "is Christ. For by one Spirit are we all baptized into one body: "whether Jews or Greeks, bond or free; and have been all made to "drink into one Spirit. For the body is not one member but many." (1 Cor. 12. 12 to 14. See the chapter throughout. See also B. W. Stone's Reply to Dr. J. P. Campbell. Let. 4. Pag. 19.) The apostle calls the church, Christ, by name. So then wherever the true church of Christ is, there is the true Christ of God, the light of the world, the light of men, and the salt of the earth; as said Jesus to his disciples; "Ye are the salt of the earth;" "Ye are the light of "the world." (Math. 5. 13, 14) And wherever a true church of Christ is found, having regained the communion and unity of the Spirit, after the falling away by anti-christ, there is Christ in his second appearing without sin to salvation. Such was the light into which honest believers brought their deeds, by confessing them, in the apostolic dispensation, according to the work of that day: and such is the light to which all souls, who esteem Christ and his salvation above all inferior enjoyments, bring their deeds and expose them in the judgment, in his second appearing for a last and finishing work of salvation.

As it was the anointing of the Holy Ghost that constituted Jesus the Anointed, or the Christ, which is the same; so the church being anointed with the same, they were constituted the anointed, the Christ. And the same authority, power and office ascribed to and possessed by Jesus, the Christ, as such, was also ascribable to and possessed by the church, as will be seen by and by. But to Jesus were given other names or titles besides *Christ*, or in addition to that, as, " The mighty God, the everlasting Father," which are not ascribable to the church. Nor is it to be understood that any one member of the church received that anointing in its fulness which constituted Jesus the Christ, but the church collectively. " The " glory which thou gavest me, I have given them ; that they may " be one even as we are one ; I in them, and thou in me." (Jno. 17. 22, 23.) " To one is given by the Spirit, the word of wisdom ; to " another, the word of knowledge by the same Spirit ; to another, " faith by the same Spirit ; to another, the working of miracles ; to " another, prophecy ; to another, discerning of spirits : to another, " divers kinds of tongues ; to another, the interpretation of tongues : " but all these worketh that one and the self same Spirit, dividing to " every man severally as he will. For as the body is one and hath " many members, and all the members of that one body, being ma- " ny, are one body." " For we are members of his body, of his " flesh, and of his bones." " Know ye not that your bodies are the " members of Christ?" " Touch not mine anointed, [:משיחי my " christs,] and do my prophets no harm."

Thus the true church of Christ is very Christ and possesses all the power of Christ as a Savior and a Judge. First ; Jesus saith, (Jno. 5. 22.) " The father judgeth no man ; but hath committed all judg- " ment unto the Son." And then, in his address to his Father, (Jno. 17. 22.) " The glory which thou gavest me, I have given them." What glory then was it which his Father had first given to him, and he afterwards gave to his disciples, but that which included the pow- er and office of judgment ? What else did he mean when he told his disciples, (Jno. 20. 22.) that what they did on earth with respect to binding and loosing, remitting and retaining sins, was done in hea- ven ? And what else is meant by the following language ? " Do " ye not know that the saints shall judge the world ? Know ye not " that we shall judge angels ?" (1 Cor. 6. 2, 3.) " And I saw " thrones, and they sat upon them, and judgment was given to them." (Rev. 20. 4.) " Behold, the Lord cometh with [or in, Greek,] ten " thousand of his saints to execute judgment upon all." (Jude. 14. 15.) " I beheld, and the same horn made war with the saints, and " prevailed against them ; until the Ancient of days came, and judg- " ment was given to the saints." [Dan. 7. 21, 22.] This last is the same that is shown in Revelations, as quoted above ; " And I saw " thrones, and they sat upon them, and judgment was given to them ;" which shows it to be the final judgment which is there intended, and not any thing that took place in the apostle's time ; as the book of the Revelations was written by the last of the apostles near the close of his life. And if the final judgment is in the saints, how much more any judgment prior to that ?

An objection may arise against the idea of the final judgment be- ing in the saints, because it is thus written ; " When the Son of man " shall come in his glory, and all the holy angels with him, then shall " he sit upon the throne of his glory : and before him shall be ga-

"thered all nations; and he shall separate them one from another, as a shepherd divideth his sheep from the goats: and he shall set the sheep on his right hand, but the goats on the left." But this is not to be understood literally, any more than the righteous and wicked are literally sheep and goats. Compare the above text with the following one. "Verily, I say unto you, that ye which have followed me, in the regeneration, when the Son of man shall sit on the throne of his glory, ye also shall sit upon twelve thrones, judging the twelve tribes of Israel." [Mat. 19. 28.] This makes it evident that the apostles have part in the final judgment: and it is evident by the same, that the description is symbolical; for the apostles are there represented, not only as having part in the judgment, but as having the first and principal place in it, instead of Jesus, the twelve tribes of Israel being given to them to judge, leaving only the Gentile nation for him; or rather none, as the twelve tribes of Israel, seems to be a phrase designed to include the whole number of the saved. Besides, Jesus and his apostles are here represented as occupying thirteen separate thrones, and all these distinct from the Father's, which would make the fourteenth; whereas the Father and Jesus and the saints are elsewhere represented as all sitting in one throne. "To him that overcometh," says Jesus, "will I grant to sit with me in my throne, even as I also overcame, and am set down with my Father in his throne." [Rev. 3. 21.] If Jesus sits with his Father in his throne and the saints sit with Jesus in his, all at the same time, then they must all sit in one throne, which would contradict the other passage, if the two bear a literal acceptation.

Now what man is there that doth not know that a throne is the place and seat of judgment, and that if two sit together in one throne they both sit in judgment jointly? To say, He that overcometh shall sit with me in my throne, is as much as to say, He that overcometh shall sit with me in judgment. And if the Father and Jesus and the saints all sit in one throne they are all united in the judgment. And where they are represented as sitting in different thrones, it only means the different degrees of power and authority which they possess, or the different stations and grades which they fill in the one judgment. The saints judge nothing of themselves but Christ in them; and Christ judges nothing of himself but the Father in him. "I in them, and thou in me." "I can," said Jesus, "of mine own self do nothing: as I hear I judge." [Jno. 5. 30.] And to his disciples, "My Father is the husband-man—I am the vine, ye are the branches—without me ye can do nothing." [Ver. 1 to 5.] "He that receiveth you, receiveth me, and he that receiveth me, receiveth him that sent me." [Mat. 10. 40. and Ver. 29.] "It is not ye that speak, but the Spirit of your Father which speaketh in you." God the Father worketh all things and judgeth all things, but he worketh and judgeth in and by his ministers, of whom Jesus Christ is first and Lord of all. The root bears the vine, the vine the branches, and the branches the fruit.

It may be asked, If there is no judgment but in the saints, then by whom are the saints judged? With the same propriety it may be asked, If the saints preach the gospel and minister it to the world, then who ministers it to the saints? It is well known that Jesus chose and prepared certain individuals as the first pillars of his church, and that to them he ministered the Holy Ghost on the day of pentecost, after his ascension. And as he was thus their minister of course he was their judge. But the Holy Ghost was never given to any afterwards in the same manner. None afterwards could receive it immediately from heaven, but by the ministration of those on earth who had received it before. But this gift and office was not confined to the first apostles alone; for when they had ministered the Holy Ghost to some, these again could minister it to others. And the judgment was in the same order, in proportion to the work of that day.

I will now prove what I have said of the order of the ministration of the Holy Ghost. How the apostles first received it is manifest as follows. " It is expedient for you that I go away : for if I go not " away the comforter (the Holy Ghost,) will not come unto you; " but if I depart, I will send him unto you." Again, after he rose from the dead, " And when he had said this, he breathed on them, " and saith unto them, Receive ye the Holy Ghost. Whosesoever " sins ye remit, they, are remitted unto them ; and whoseso- " ever sins ye retain, they are retained." " And when the day of " pentecost was fully come, they were all with one accord in one " place. And suddenly there came a sound from heaven, as of a " rushing mighty wind, and it filled all the house where they were " sitting. And there appeared unto them cloven tongues, like as of " fire, and it sat upon each of them." (John 16. 7. and 20. 22. Acts 2. 1.) Thus the apostles received the Holy Ghost immediately from heaven without the interposition of any on earth. But that it was not so afterwards is manifest by the following. " Now when the " apostles who were at Jerusalem heard that Samaria had received " the word of God, they sent unto them Peter and John; who when " they were come down, prayed for them, that they might receive " the Holy Ghost [For as yet he was fallen upon none of them; " only they were baptised in the name of the Lord Jesus.] Then laid " they their hands on them, and they received the holy Ghost." [Acts 8. 13. 14.] " Paul having passed through the upper coasts, " came to Ephesus ; and finding certain disciples, he said unto them, " have ye received the Holy Ghost since ye believed. ? And they " said unto him, We have not so much as heard whether there be " any Holy Ghost. And when Paul had laid his hands upon them, " the Holy Ghost came on them; and they spake with tongues and " prophesied." [Acts 19. 1. to. 6.]

And furthermore it is found that even Paul himself though called to be an apostle, yet, as his conversion to the faith was after the Holy Ghost had been committed to the church, he could not receive it but by some member of that anointed body. By the vision he saw going to Damascus he was struck blind and converted, but could in that way neither have his sight restored, be filled with the Holy Ghost, nor told what he must do. For, when he asked saying Lord what wilt thou have me to do? the answer was, " Arise and go into " the city and it shall be told thee what thou must do." And when he had done so Ananias a member of Christ, having received a commandment of him, entered into the house, and putting his hands on him, Said, " Brother Saul, the Lord, even Jesus, that appeared unto " thee in the way as thou camest, hath sent me that thou mightest " receive thy sight and be filled with the Holy Ghost." [see Acts 9. chapter.]

It is worthy of particular consideration, that before Ananias came Saul had remained three days without sight and under the manifest marks of God's displeasure; by which it is the more evident that men cannot be initiated into union and fellowship with Christ, except in union with his body the church. Angels cannot minister it. Even the Angel that met Saul in the way, although he came in the name of Jesus and spake in that name could not minister it. Christ is the Savior of the souls of men not angels; and Christ was not to be found save in his temple. The Holy Spirit that was sent in Christ's name as he had promised, and had taken its abode in the church, acted and judged in the name and authority of Christ on earth. And none could obtain judgment or atonement in any other line. The treasures of the gospel were commited to earthen vessels, these were the light of the world and the salt or savior of the earth; there was the tabernacle of God, his altar and his holy fire, so clearly prefiguered in the law of Moses—there were the keys, and the power to bind and to loose, to remit and retain, there was the enterance into the kingdom—and there could be no other, so long as God continued to be a God of order and not of confusion.

The case also of Cornelius the Centurian serves eminently to prove the same thing. It is written (Acts 10. 3.) that " He saw in " a vision evidently about the ninth hour of the day, an angel of " God coming in to him, and saying unto him, Cornelius. And " when he looked on him, he was afraid, and said unto him, What is " it Lord? And he said unto him, Thy prayers and thine alms are " come up for a memorial before God. And now send men to " Joppa, and call for one Simon, whose sirname is Peter; he lodgeth " with one Simon a tanner whose house is by the sea-side: he shall tell " thee what thou oughtest to do." Peter himself afterwards relates the same; " And we entered into the man's house. And he shewed " us how he had seen an angei in his house, who stood and said unto " him, Send men to Joppa, and call for Simon, whose sirname is Peter, " who shall tell the words whereby thou and all thy house shall be " saved. And as I began to speak, the Holy Ghost fell on them, as " on us at the beginning. But why could not the angel have told Cornelius words whereby he and his house should be saved, and ministered to them the Holy Ghost? Had not Jesus ascended to the throne of God in the heavens? and had not Cornelius seen an angel

OF SINS.

from heaven and conversed with him? What need then of sending all the way to Joppa, and waiting several days for a mortal man like themselves, before they could know what to do, or receive the unction? The reason is plain, as shown above. "No man," saith Jesus, "cometh to the Father but by me." And saith the apostle; "For as the body is one, and hath many members, and all the members of that one body, being many, are one body; so also is Christ." Christ in his body was the way the truth and the life, and none could be taught the way or receive the truth and the life separately from that body. I am the vine, ye are the branches—As my Father hath sent me into the world even so send I you into the world—He that receiveth you receiveth me, and he that receiveth me receiveth him that sent me. As ambassadors of Christ therefore, we pray you in Christ's stead be ye reconciled to God—For judgment am I come into the world—And when he [the Holy Ghost] cometh he shall convince the world of sin, of righteousness, and of judgment—Know ye not that the saints shall judge the world? Receive ye the Holy Ghost. Whosoever sins ye remit they are remitted unto them; and whosoever sins ye retain they are retained—And many that believed came and confessed and shewed their deeds—Confess your faults one to another and pray one for another. (Jas. 5. 16.)

This effect of coming and confessing and showing their deeds, seems to have been the genuine influence of divine truth on the heart, to turn the man's inside out, and expose him in the light in his true colors. Thus Christ is the true light which lighteneth every man who cometh into the world; and every honest, faithful man feels at once the propriety of exposing the dark works of iniquity in the light, and of putting every man in his own proper place according to his proper character. When therefore the light has found its entrance into any man who heareth the gospel, he may bring his deeds into the light, and expose himself, in the regular line of God's judgment, and find mercy, or he may, in many cases, shrink from the light, and cover up from the judgment of God for a time, until he shall be arraigned in person, (for none can escape the judgment,) with all his sins following him to his greater condemnation; as it is written, "Some men's sins are open beforehand, going before to the judgment: and some they follow after." [1 Tim. 5. 24.] But this influence of divine light, leading people to confess their sins, was not limited to the primitive church; it hath been experienced in modern times, in divers cases, among those who had no understanding of the line of God's judgment, or the order of confession.

Some may suppose that the confession here spoken of is not absolutely necessary for all, because it is not written that *all that believed* came and confessed and shewed their deeds, but only *many of them*. But since it is clear that many did it, what reason is there to suppose that any did not who were sound and honest. It is evident a great part who professed in that day were far from being real christians. For a proof of this see the following plain and honest testimonies to the point. "From whence come wars and fightings among you?

" Come they not hence, even of your lusts, that war in your mem-
" bers? Ye lust, and ye have not: ye kill, and desire to have, and
" cannot obtain: ye fight and war, yet ye have not, because ye ask
" not: ye ask, and receive not, because ye ask amiss, that ye may
" consume it upon your lusts. Ye adulterers and adulteresses."
[Jas. 4. 1.] " For many walk, of whom I have told you often, and
" now tell you even weeping, that they are the enemies of the cross
" of Christ; whose end is destruction, whose God is their belly, and
" whose glory is in their shame, who mind earthly things." " These
" are spots in your feasts of charity, when they feast with you, feed
" ing themselves without fear: clouds they are without water, car-
" ried about of winds; trees whose fruit withereth, without fruit, twice
" dead, plucked up by theroots." " This thou knowest that all they
" which are in Asia are turned away from me." [Phil. 3. 13, 19.
Jude. 12. Tim. 1. 15.]

These false professors were not real members of the church of Christ. They received the gospel only as seed sown on stony ground, or among thorns, and very likely such as never honestly brought their deeds to the light, as those did who received the word into good and honest hearts. But that is no proof that it is not necessary for all in order to acceptance with God. The orderly work of the gospel in one or a few, showeth its nature and tendency as correctly as in many, or in all. Moreover, the phrase, *many*, is used more than once, when all are intended, particularly who belong to a certain class, or are the subjects of a certain work, as, " If through the of-
" fence of one *many* (that is, the whole family of Adam,) be dead,
" [have died]; much more the grace of God, and the gift by grace,
" by one man, Jesus Christ, hath abounded to *many*"—to the whole family of Christ. " And *many* of them that sleep in the dust of
" the earth shall awake, some to everlasting life, and some to shame
" and everlasting contempt." That is, *all*, both good and bad, in the day of final rewards. [Ro. 5. 15, 17, 19. Dan. 12. 2.] Thus we understand that " Many of those who believed came, and confessed,
" and shewed their deeds"—all those whose conviction was deep and whose hearts were honest, and who were intent on having the gospel in its fulness and purity, who were willing to endure the cross despising the shame.

Respecting the words of James quoted a while back, where he teacheth the people to confess their faults one to another, it hath been argued that they cannot relate to the necessity or utility of confessing sins to God, or for the purpose of obtaining the forgiveness of God, because the word is, *faults;* and a criticism hath been introduced on the Greek text, that the word is not [αμαρτιας] sins, but [παραπτωματα] faults, errors, blunders, or the like. This is however a flimsy criticism for a man of learning, a mere evasion to blind the weak and unlearned. But every honest man, acquainted with the Greek text, can easily discover the cheat by observing that it is the same word, by which the apostle has expressed the sin, or offence, of him by whose offence judgment came upon all men to condemnation, and by whom death reigned, as well as the numerous offences committed afterwards, all productive of condemnation and death. These, therefore, appear to be doleful and pernicious offences, or faults, well deserving the name of sins.

We will not deny that, [αμαρτια] the word commonly translated *sin*, is the proper word to communicate the notion of sin, in its nature and inward principles, as, "Behold the Lamb of God who taketh "away the sin [αμαρτιαν] of the world." [Jno. 1. 29.] Neither will we deny that it is commonly and very properly used to express sinful actions. But it is also certain that the apostle Paul uses the same word [παραπτωμα] which the apostle James uses, and which is translated faults; this same word, I say, Paul uses to express those acts of iniquity which Adam first, and his children after him, committed, which bring condemnation and death; and these are the proper burden of confession; these are sins. "For if, through the of- "fence [παραπτωματι] of one, many be dead," [απεθανον, have died;] "For if by one man's offence [παραπτωματι] death reigned by one." "Therefore, as by the offence [παραπτωματος] of one, judgment "came upon all men to condemnation." The same apostle also a few verses before (Rom. 4. 25.) hath used precisely the same word [παραπτωματα] to describe the sins for which Christ was delivered to death who was delivered for our offences or faults according to the same word, as used by James. That the apostle James had a direct view to the confession of sins, properly so called, is confirmed by the history of the church in the first century, which was that in which the apostles lived and wrote. "Those who were visited with violent "and dangerous disorders, sent, according to the apostle's direction, "for the rulers of the church, and, after confessing their sins, were "recommended by them to the divine mercy." (Eccl. His. V. 1. P. 127.) The same historical accounts show us that the practice of confessing sins was always kept in the church; among the various classes who professed the christian name, whether those who were counted the orthodox church and held the power of law in their hands, or those who were counted heretics, and suffered the persecution of their lordly oppressors. The above extract gives us a moderate intimation of the state of things in the first century, as being sanctioned by the apostle's counsel to the sick, which is in immediate and direct connection with the counsel to confess one to another, as a part of the same instructions; and this relation showeth that the primitive church understood it of the confession of sins properly so called. And in the seventh we have an account of the confession of sins spoken of as a common matter known to all, and not as an innovation; but like other apostolic instructions, after the apostacy got in, suffering the modifications and regulations of men. Thus the following extract states, "This zealous prelate, (Theodore,) formed and executed se- "veral pious and laudable projects; and among other things reduced "to a regular science that branch of the ecclesiastical law, which is "known by the name of *penitential discipline*. He published a *pe- "nitential* which was entirely new to the Latin world, by which the "clergy were taught to distinguish sins into various classes, according as they were more or less heinous, private or public; to judge of them and determine the degrees of their guilt by their nature and consequences; the intention of the offender; the time and place in which they were committed; and the circumstances with which they were attended. This new *penitential* contained also the methods of proceeding with respect to offenders; pointed out the penalties that were suitable to the various classes of transgression; prescribed the forms of *consolation, exhortation* and *absolution ;* discribed in an ample and accurate manner, the duties and obligations of those who were to receive the confessions of the penitent." (Eod. V. 2. P. 177.) We need no plainer testimony that this penitential of Theodore embraced the universally acknowledged practice and indisputable propriety of confessing sins to the gospel ministry, that is to God in them, or in their presence.

In the twelfth century, there seems to have existed a dispute or controversy, with respect to the confession of sins, between the Waldenses, a people justly esteemed for their piety and good faith, and the Roman church; not relating to the propriety or duty of confessing sins, for that was granted on both sides, but whether confession must of necessity be made to the priesthood, or whether it would be sufficient if made to a private christian. Of the Waldenses it is said; "They, at the same time, affirmed, that every pious christian was qualified and entitled to prescribe to the penitent the kind and degree of *satisfaction*, or expiation, that their transgressions required; that confession made to priests was by no means necessary, since the humble offender (sinner) might acknowledge (confess) his sins and testify his repentance to any true believer, and might expect from such the counsels and admonitions that his case and circumstances demanded." (Eod. V. 3. P. 120, 121.) No doubt but the Waldenses were led to this view of confessing to believers in common, from two considerations. The first was, that in the days of primitive christianity, the business of ministering the gospel, and taking a part in the edification of others, was not confined to the priesthood, or the appointed ministry, as it was in after times among those who have assumed the character of orthodox or orderly christians. And the second, to resist the abuses which were introduced by the Roman priesthood in that with every other christian institution. But that a proper ministerial order, or priesthood, belongs to the church of Christ, it is evident, not only by the scripture testimony, as shown before, but by the attempts which anti-christ has made in his various branches to imitate and keep it up: by arbitrary authority after the apostacy took place.

The following extracts are taken from the history of the thirteenth and fourteenth centuries, and support the evidence that the same practice of confessing sins to God in his ministers was universally approved, though some disputes existed relating to this point; Who were the proper persons? But that they were in the true church, wherever that was, hath been always granted; for in that is the power of forgiveness and salvation, and of necessity those who keep it. Accordingly, in the following extracts this power is granted to exist in the church; but a controversy existed with respect to the order of communicating it. They are taken from the history of the mendicant friars, who are said to have received such uncommon privileges as to excite discontent and opposition against them. " Such, " among many other extraordinary prerogatives, was the permission " they received from the pontiffs, of preaching to the multitude, " hearing *confession*, and pronouncing *absolution* without any license " from the bishops." (Eod. V. 3. P. 194.) " But JOHN DE POLLIAC set " himself openly against them, publicly denying the validity of the " absolution granted by the Dominicans and Franciscans to those " who confessed to them, maintaining that the Popes were disabled " from granting them a power of absolution by the authority of the " *canon*, entitled, *omnis utriusque sexus*, and proving from these " premises, that all those who would be sure of salvation, ought to " confess their sins to their own parish priests, even though they had " been absolved by the monks." (Eod. V. 3. P. 322.) And so universally was the practice acknowledged and authenticated that the Lutheran church kept up the practice, notwithstanding the great opposition between them and the Catholics, and the casting off by the former, of so many things practised by the latter. But the professed principles of all who dissented from the church of Rome in many centuries, or bore testimony against her, being to reform the church or restore the primitive simplicity of the gospel, would naturally include the confession of sins in the living temple or house of God, which was unquestionably known to be a practice and an order descending in direct line from the apostles and primitive christians. It is related in history, that a certain JOHN CASPAR SCHADE, near the close of the seventeenth century, " Inveighed with the greatest bit-" terness, against the custom that prevails in the Lutheran church of " confessing privately to the clergy." (V. 5. P. 317.) Thus by these few testimonies, as well as by the testimony of the scriptures, it is sufficiently evident that no people ever had any correct order or form of the christian profession without embracing in it the universal practice of confessing their sins to God, and that too before his witnesses, or those who were so reputed, or in his living temple, the proper place to offer up sacrifices according to the gospel, acceptable to God through Jesus Christ.

The Catholics are acknowledged to have universally made use of confession. And I know of nothing which the people believe concerning the Catholic faith, which discovers more brutish ignorance of God and man, than the supposition that they invented it themselves, or introduced it from any other source than the revelation of God or apostolic authority: except the supposition that they or any other people, ever invented the testimony or the faith and cross against the sexual intercourse in the flesh, or ever received such a faith except from God. The Catholics and others who were counted heretics by them, agree in the authenticity and utility of the practice; and they could never have held the people to it so long, not only the ignorant and the superstitious, but the learned, the judicious, and the most pious, had it not been of God and well authenticated. For there is nothing in it so agreeable to nature, that men would invent or cleave to such a practice for nought. And whatever earthly emoluments may have accrued to the Roman priesthood, and however they might have duped the laity, to the practice for their own interest, this could have been no motive to those who, from time to time, testified against the Roman Catholic practices, and thereby exposed themselves to persecution and to death. But the corruptions and abuses with which the Catholics have murdered all the christian institutions, give this one a poor appearance in their hands, and may have been one cause why Calvinists and other dissenters from the Roman church cast off the practice with the abuses. Nevertheless the Roman church, in connection with those of a more commendable practice, and who are called heretics, is an abiding and swift witness in vindication of the true order of God in the confession and forgiveness of sins. For although they have long been entirely destitute of the true Spirit and power of Christ, "Having a form of god-" liness but denying the power," they have preserved the form, or rather the skeleton of it, the most correctly of any other people, likely, on earth, and are the best able to prove their descent in a direct line from the apostles.

But the nature of the gospel work is such as to show, as I may say, in explicit terms, that the power of salvation, including the confession and the forgiveness of sins, is in the church on earth. " For " we preach not ourselves, but Christ Jesus the Lord; and ourselves " your servants for Jesus' sake. For God, who commanded the " light to shine out of darkness, hath shined in our hearts, to give the " light of the knowledge of the glory of God in the face of Jesus " Christ. But we have this treasure (God and his Christ,) in earthen " vessels, that the excellency of the power may be of God, and not " of us." And again; "But the righteousness which is of faith " speaketh on this wise. Say not in thine heart, Who shall ascend " into heaven? (that is to bring Christ down from above :) or, Who " shall descend into the deep? (that is, to bring up Chris again from " the dead.) But what saith it? The word is nigh thee, in thy " mouth and in thy heart; that is, the word of faith which we preach. " That if thou shalt confess with thy mouth the Lord Jesus, and " shalt believe in thine heart that God raised him from the dead thou "·shalt be saved. For with the heart man believeth unto righteous-·" 'ness," (or acknowledges and contemplates the way in which it is to be obtained; and so his faith is imputed to him for righteousness thus far, εις δικαιοσυνην. The same phrase is used which is rendered *for righteousness*, when Abraham's faith, or believing, is said to be imputed to him.. But to obtain salvation, more than believing has to be done.) " and with the mouth confession is made unto salvation." (εις σωτηριαν, for salvation, as setting out to obtain it: for salvation is the end, or result, and perfecting of faith and obedience and not the

OF SINS.

beginning.) For the scripture saith, "Whosoever believeth on him "shall not be ashamed. For there is no difference between the Jew "and the Greek." (2. Cor. 4. 5, 6, 7. Ro. 10. 6, &c.)

In these scriptures we are clearly taught that Christ, the salvation of God, and the power of God to salvation, dwells with men on earth. *We have this treasure in earthen vessels.* What treasure? The power of God to salvation—God himself who first commanded the light to shine out of darkness, and who also hath shined into our hearts to give us the light of the knowledge of the glory of God in the face, or person, [εν προσωπω] of Jesus Christ, or as it shineth in him—that is very Christ the Savior. Again; The WORD is nigh thee; the LOGOS, [λογος] the eternal WORD. So that there is no need to say in thine heart, even once to think, Who shall ascend into heaven, to bring Christ down; for he hath already come and taken up his abode with men; or Who shall descend into the deep, or into *hades*, the place of departed spirits, to bring up Christ again from the dead, for he is already risen, and we are quickened together with him by the same Spirit; for he dwelleth in us. The word which we preach say the men of God. The word of faith; the word of God by which faith cometh, or is produced, when it is preached and heard, as well as that WORD which is the object of faith, the word of God, which is Christ. Seeing then that Christ the salvation of God hath his habitation in his church with the fulness of salvation, and he is the head of the body; no reasonable doubt can exist but there is the correct and orderly place to confess sins, and find forgiveness and salvation. And as Christ the power of salvation is known only in his body, the church, which is Christ, no man can confess Christ the Lord with his mouth in any other order or way disconnected from this body. *To confess with thy mouth the Lord Jesus*, is more than a verbal acknowledgment that he is the Christ, and that God hath raised him from the dead; for many make this verbal confession, and believe in their hearts that God raised him from the dead, and yet know not the way of salvation. In strictness of language all who believe this fact at all believe it in their hearts; for they have no other method or place to believe it. But the phraseology, both here and by Philip to the Eunuch, is no doubt intended to be very special and emphatical, implying sincerity of conviction and honesty of intention with confession, or that believing which taketh the heart, and the heart chooseth the thing believed: the faith and confession must go together. And this confession must indubitably be such as to comprehend the whole character and commission of Christ, as the messenger of the covenant, or covenant of salvation, itself, from God to men, with full subjection and obedience, according to what is written. "I will give thee for a covenant of the people," [ברית, a purifier, or Savior.] If then Jesus Christ is the forgiver of sins, in whose name remission, or pardon of sins is preached; which is indubitably true; and if confession is necessary to forgiveness; which is also true, as already proved; it remains true and proved; That without confessing our sins to him in his body, where alone he is known, there is no confessing *the Lord Jesus* with the mouth to salvation. It therefore remains true, That the Son of man hath power on earth to forgive sins, and a people in whom that power resides and operates; and the saying is fulfilled, which is written; "Mercy and truth are "met together righteousness: and peace have kissed each other. "Truth shall spring out of the earth; and righteousness shall look "down from heaven. Righteousness shall go before him, and shall "set us in the way of his steps." (Psa. 85. 10, 11, 13.) They who dwell on the earth and in earthly tabernacles, practise on the principle of honesty and truth; and the LORD OUR RIGHTEOUSNESS, looks down from heaven and takes his abode with men: they who in an honest and good heart receive the word, bring forth fruit.

The words of the apostle Peter, which have already been introduced, perfectly accord with what is here stated. "To whom com-"ing, as unto a living stone, disallowed indeed of men, but chosen of "God, and precious, Ye also, as living stones, are built up a spiritual "house, an holy priesthood to offer up spiritual sacrifices, acceptable "to God by Jesus Christ. Wherefore also, it is contained in the "scripture, Behold, I lay in Sion a chief corner stone, elect, precious: "and he that believeth on him shall not be confounded." "But ye "are a chosen generation, a royal priesthood, an holy nation, a pecu-"liar people; that ye should shew forth the praises of him who "hath called you out of darkness into his marvellous light: Which in "time past were not a people, but are now the people of God: which "had not obtained mercy, but now have obtained mercy." (1 Pet. 2. 4, 5, 6, 9, 10.) Accordingly we have the united testimony of the apostles in their writings, that Christ with his whole salvation dwells in his church on earth; the church is his peculiar people, a people for a possession, or acquisition; [λαος εις περιποιησιν;] that is, his temple, or house, wherein to offer sacrifices, make confession, and offer praise; therein are his priests to receive the offerings and make atonement; this same church is his kingdom, the people, the members of which, show forth the praises of him who hath called them out of darkness into light. These are the inhabitants of the kingdom of God, the kingdom of heaven on earth, as it is written in another place; "For our conversation is in heaven," or [πολιτευμα] citizenship is in the heavens; we are the free inhabitants of that kingdom; *we are come to Mount Zion, the city of the living God, the heavenly Jerusalem;* and there Christ dwelleth; the same who hath power on earth to forgive sins. "From whence also we look "for the Lord Jesus." [Phil. 3. 19.] From the same heaven of which we are the citizens.

Now in all these things it is evident that Christ Jesus the Lord is acknowledged, to be the substance and fountain of the salvation of God to men, even to the ends of the earth; the Great High Priest, the hearer of confessions, and the forgiver of sins, through whom we receive the atonement. But Christ is in his temple according to the established order of God; and there he is a stumbling-stone and

rock of offence; " As it is written, Behold, I lay in Sion a stum-
" bling stone, and rock of offence: and whosoever believeth on him
" shall not be ashamed." [Ro. 9. 33.] The people can endure to
worship a Christ far off whom they cannot see, and whose habitation
is unknown; but Christ in his living temple, which is visible and accessible, and he accessible and visible in it, is too much for natural
men to endure—*he is a stone of stumbling and rock of offence.*

" But such an high priest became us, who is holy, harmless, un-
" defiled and separate from sinners, and made higher than the hea-
" vens." [Heb. 7. 26.] It was necessary that one should find access
to the throne of God first, as a forerunner in the behalf of the rest;
and he must necessarily be one who was separate from sinners, for
no sinner could have obtained access to the throne, for the want of a
Mediator, and especially because he would have been in an agreement with other sinners, and therefore could never have overcome
the carnal mind which is enmity against God and ruleth in the wicked,
nor have trodden the wicked under his feet. But Jesus our GREAT
HIGH PRIEST, kept himself separate from sinners; for " He did no
sin, neither was guile found in his mouth;" and he gained access to
the throne of God and to his mercy-seat, when he had no Mediator,
and thus became a Mediator for sinners in their lost estate. And
this he did through consummate sufferings and the most painful labors.
" And he saw that there was no man, (to stand between him and the
" throne of God,) and he wondered that there was no intercessor;"
(or, he was brought into consternation; ישתולם from שלם a root
importing, wasting or consumption—*The zeal of thine house hath
consumed me ;)* because there was no intercessor; " Therefore his
" own arm brought salvation to him, and his righteousness it sustain-
" ed him." " I have trodden the wine-press alone; and of the peo-
" ple there was none with me; for I have trodden them in mine an-
" ger and trampled them in my fury; (the nature of men and all the
" people who abide in it;) and their blood hath been sprinkled upon
" my garments, and I have stained all my raiment. For the day of
" vengeance (against evil) is in my heart, and the year of my redeem-
" ed is come." (I am determined to find eternal redemption.) " And
" I looked and there was none to help; and I wondered that there
" was none to uphold: (or I was brought into consternation, as above,
" and yet there was none to uphold:) therefore mine own arm
" brought salvation to me; and my fury it upheld me." " But Christ
" being come an high priest of good things to come, by a greater
" and more perfect tabernacle not made with hands, that is to say,
" not of this building, neither by the blood of goats and calves; but
" by his own blood, he entered in once into the holy place, having
" obtained (Greek, found, ευρομενος) eternal redemption," for us;
having first gained it himself, according to the words of the prophet
just quoted. Thus he is become our great high priest, who is
made perfect through sufferings, and is the head of the body, in
whom all the priesthood are comprehended, who minister in the name
and by the authority of the great high priest, receive the offerings

of the people, hear their confessions, and make atonement, according to the true order of God in the gospel, *the fulfilment and substance of that* which was set forth by shadows under the law. "As "thou hast sent me into the world," said Jesus, "even so have I sent "them into the world. And the glory which thou gavest me I have "given them; that they may be one, even as we are one: I in them "and thou in me, that they may be made perfect in one." So that wherever his people are, there is Christ, and there is the Father; and whatever commission Jesus the Christ had to the world, the same have his ministers; provided always, that he is the head and forerunner, who opened the way, and always hath the pre-eminence. Is it given to him of the Father to execute judgment; so is it to his people. "Know ye not that the saints shall judge the world." Is he the high priest of his people, to whom it is proper and necessary to make confession of sins; so are his ministers his subordinate priests, as hath been fairly stated and proved. Had the Son of man power on earth to forgive sins, by the commission and gift of the Father; so have his ministers by the commission and gift of the Son. "Then "said Jesus to them again, Peace be unto you; as my Father hath "sent me, even so send I you. And when he had said this he breath- "ed on them, and said unto them, Receive ye the Holy Ghost. "Whosoever sins ye remit, they are remitted unto them; and "whosoever sins ye retain, they are retained:" and so in other respects, as shown in its place.

Once more, Jesus said to his disciples; "He that receiveth you "receiveth me"; and he that receiveth me, receiveth him that sent "me." And that saying is true, not only as it respects the first disciples, but of all his ministers. "Verily, vesily I say unto you, "He that receiveth *whomsoever I send*, receiveth me; and he that "receiveth me, receiveth him that sent me." [Mat. 10. 40. Jno. 13.] 20.) Therefore, seeing the Son and the Father are in his ministers, or ambassadors, to that effect that he who receiveth them receiveth both the Son and the Father who sent him; no reasonable objection can be raised; yea, it is undeniable and irresistible, that they who confess their sins to them whom he hath sent, that is, to any faithful and true minister of Christ, in the faith of his authority and his commission to his ministers, do in reality confess to him and to the Father who sent him. And on the other hand; "He that despiseth you, "despiseth me; and he that despiseth me, despiseth him that sent "me." (Luke 10. 16.) It is therefore evident, that they who reject or despise the ministers of Christ, refusing to confess their sins to them, or to God in them, and in their hearing, will be esteemed by Christ as refusing to confess to him. Without this confession therefore, no real or acceptable confession of Christ in his true character and commission, can be made: and they who deny it deny Christ; and he will deny them before his Father and before the holy angels. He is no finished minister of Christ, who will refuse to stand in the place of Christ as his witness, or living temple, and hear the honest confession of those who are intent on having salvation. "Now then,

OF SINS.

"we are ambassadors for Christ, [υπερ Χριςȣ; in Christ's stead, or in the behalf of Christ,] as though God did beseech you by us: we pray you, in Christ's stead, [or in the behalf of Christ, υπερ Χριςȣ as above,] be ye reconciled to God." [2 Cor. 5. 20.] And on the same principle of receiving Christ and rejecting him, confessing him and denying him, serving him and neglecting him in his people, the final judgment of all men is eternally decided. "And the King shall answer, and say, unto them, (the righteous who have done good deeds, to their brethren,) Verily I say unto you, Inasmuch as ye have done it to one of the least of these my brethren, ye have done it to me." Again; "Then shall he answer them, (the wicked who have not done good to his people,) Verily, I say unto you, Inasmuch as ye did it not to one of the least of these ye did it not to me. And these shall go away into everlasting punishment: but the righteous into life eternal." [Mat. 25. 31. &c.

It is objected by some, as being of great weight, against the order of confessing sins to God in his ministers, or to men, as they call it, that it sets men in the place of God, and robs God of the honor due to him, transferring it to the creature. To remove this difficulty from the minds of the honest, let it be observed, that what God requires is *obedience*, which is better than sacrifice, and *to obey*, than all whole burnt offerings. The true way to honor and glorify God, is to yield a willing and hearty obedience to his order and appointments, and his order is to do his work through the medium of men, or by men, who are his ministers, appointed to that office. "Now then," saith the apostle, "we are ambassadors for [in the behalf or in stead of] Christ, as though God did beseech you by us; we pray you in Christ stead, be ye reconciled to God." And saith Jesus; "He that receiveth whomsoever I send receiveth me"

Now the question is; Doth it honor God most to submit to his institutions and receive his ambassadors in their full and proper character, or to pass them by, saying, We will go directly to God, or to Christ, and treat with him, and so make our peace? When the American Government sent ambassadors with full powers, (or plenipotentiaries, as the modern term is: and such are all Christ's ministers,) to treat with Great Britain, did Great Britain do most honor to the American government by consenting to treat with her ministers and thus acknowledging the validity of her instructions; or would it have been more honorable still to the American government, for Great Britain to have said, "We acknowledge you as the true ministers of the American government, and we joyfully receive all the tidings which ye bring, relating to proposals of peace; nevertheless, it is not sufficient to sign a treaty with you, but we will receive and obey you so far, that we will go to the American government and to the President and Congress, and there make peace with them." Will not every one understand, in a moment, that the last proposition would have been an affront on the government, by disallowing the validity of her instructions? Or on the other hand; had the American ministers told the people or ministers of Great

Britain, saying, "We are indeed American ministers in as full pow-
"er as any such can be, so that if ye receive us and make a treaty
"of peace with us, ye do the same with our government; neverthe-
"less, if ye would be at peace with America, ye must go immedi-
"ately to the president, or to the congress, and there make your of-
"ferings and come on terms." Would not every one see, at first
view, that they had dishonored their mission, and no longer deserved
the name of ministers-plenipotentiary?

Thus it is sufficiently plain to be understood, that any man who
cometh forth, in the character of a minister of Christ, called and sent
of God, and saith to the people, "I am sent to preach to you the
"gospel of Christ, for your peace and salvation; nevertheless, I can-
"not help you, ye must go to God, or to Christ, [be it in secret, or
"where it may be except through the ministry,] and make your
"peace with him;" he dishonors God, and forfeits the character
of a minister of the gospel of Christ. And the people who will acknowledge the ministers of Christ, as such, but are too incredulous
to risk making their peace with God through them, or hope to find
God in some other way, are evidently unacquainted with God, ignorant of his true order of salvation, and do dishonor him, by discred-
iting and rejecting his institutions and instructions.

The embassage, or ministry of reconciliation, with which the ministers of the gospel are intrusted, is indeed a more finished commission than any such thing among the nations. God's terms with which
he furnishes his ambassadors, and by which he limits them, are the
most equitable, and the most profitable which can be proposed, so
that there is no need or room for men to propose any alteration to
suit their inclinations or abilities: it is for them to take him on his
terms or remain enemies; whereas nations have no natural right to
such power over one another. Besides as the nations have their governments, or centres of power, ministers from one to another, treat
with the nation through that centre, and not with each individual
separately; whereas God's ministers are sent to each and every individual, separately and collectively, and if a nation or neighborhood
will not receive them, each individual who will comply with the proposals, is noticed of God and taken into the number of his family, as
freely and safely as if all had complied, and none have any right or
power over him, to hold him back. For "God is no respecter of
"persons: but in every nation he that feareth him, and worketh
"righteousness, is accepted of him." (Acts 10. 34, 35.) In every
nation or neighborhood where the ministers of the perfect gospel of
Christ come, whosoever will keep treaty with them, as the ministers
of heaven, confessing and forsaking their sins, shall find mercy, and
experience the pardon of their sins and established peace with heaven, without the labor of sending their treaty to London, or to the
Federal City, or up to heaven to have it ratified.

The gospel brings salvation to the sinner's door, puts it into his
mouth and his heart, and calls on him to keep it and use it. "But
"the righteousness which is of faith speaketh on this wise, Say not

"in thine heart, (do not even think,) Who shall ascend into heaven? (that is to bring Christ down from above;) Or who shall descend into the deep? (that is, to bring up Christ again from the dead:) But what saith it? The word is nigh thee, even *in thy mouth*, and *in thy heart;* that is, the word of faith which we preach." (Ro. 10, 6, 7, 8.) And again, as stated above; "Now then we are ambassadors for Christ, as though God did beseech you by us; we pray you (and others) in Christ's stead: be ye reconciled to God." We are ambassadors for Christ, in Christ's behalf, or in Christ's stead, it being the same Greek phrase which is so rendered in an after clause of the verse. Christ Jesus is the first true ambassador of God to men, and next his true apostles and ministers are God's ambassadors in Christ's stead, to do his work, according to God's established order: to these he hath committed the word and ministry of reconciliation. Other arguments might be introduced, and other objections raised and answered; but the foregoing will satisfy the honest, who weigh matters candidly, and are willing to obey the truth when they know it.

CHAPTER III.

Evidences relating to the Church of Christ, mainly Negative.

THE two former chapters show the order and power of the true church, with respect to the confession of sins. A question may arise; How are we to know who are the true church of Christ, and where shall we find them? So many divisions of professors claim a relation to Christ that something clear and definite is necessary, satisfactorily to show with whom to cast our lots.

Such clear and definite knowledge is indispensably necessary; because out of that body salvation is unknown, and wherever it is there is salvation. As it is written; I will place salvation in Zion for Israel "my glory." (Isa. 46. 13.) To the same effect are the words of Christ; "Whatsoever ye shall bind on earth, shall be bound in heaven; and whatsoever ye shall loose on earth, shall be loosed in heaven." And again; "Whosoever sins ye remit, they are remitted to them, and whosoever ye retain they are retained." (Matt. 18. 18. Jno. 20. 23.) So that what the church do in relation to the forgiveness of sins, is by Christ counted valid, to all intents. That none can be saved in a disunited state, or separate from the only true church, is farther evident, because there is one Christ and one way. "I am *the way*," said he: and there is not another. As under the law of Moses, which was a pattern of the gospel, there was one high priest, and also one law and one way for all. Thus it is written; "One law shall be to him that is home-born, and to the stranger that sojourneth among you." [Exod. 12. 49.] So under the gospel there is one body and one Spirit, one faith, one Lord Jesus

Christ; one High Priest; one faith and one way, for the Jew and Gentile, the professor and non-professor, whosoever will eat of the bread of life. And disunited from the *one body and one faith*, no man can keep the faith of Christ. For in the first place; He cannot have a sufficient motive. Every man is influenced by motive; no man, therefore, can perform any great work, or effectuate any arduous and important purpose, without an adequate motive. But no man's motive can exceed his faith: *By faith we stand*. And no faith, in whole or in part, separate from *the one faith of the one body*, the church, can furnish and maintain sufficient motive to overcome all sin, root and branch, because as long as any one hath any hope or expectation that salvation can possibly be found without the full cross, his faith is inadequate. In connection therefore with the various denominations of professors whose faith is so indefinite and precarious, no man can keep the faith of Christ, or walk in him. And again; No man can stand alone. Not only the strength, but the life of the body and of each member depends on union: and without it all is lost. No one member can live disconnected with the body. So is Christ, and so is the gospel church. " For as the body is one, and " hath many members, and all the members of that one body, being " many, are one body; so also is Christ. For by one Spirit are we " all baptized into one body; whether we be Jews or Gentiles, whe-" ther we be bond or free; and have been all made to drink into one " Spirit. For the body is not one member, but many." [1 Cor. 12. 12, 13, 14.] Could any man, therefore, have the true faith of Christ, mentally, while separate from the body, he could not keep it practically, he could not have it in *the truth and the substance*, for the want of union: he could not be saved. And take away the visible union of the member with the body, and the member must perish; for there can be no invisible union extant, so as to support life, without a visible. The knowledge therefore of the true church, and an open profession of *the one faith*, are indispensable in attaining to final salvation, and full redemption.

To those, therefore, who enquire as stated above, if candid and intelligent, a reply to the following purport, will be satisfactory; That nothing more is necessary to distinguish the true church, than to understand the order of the church and to see the people who keep it. For as the order of the true church, is that which no other people can keep, (as will be shown hereafter) among whomsoever that is seen, it will sufficiently evince that these are the true body of Christ. A sufficient evidence, therefore, to any one honestly in quest of salvation, is for a people to be able to tell what are the true order and power of the church of Christ, and to keep that order and power themselves, as far as can be discerned: for where these things do not exist in reality, the disguise can be detected, as will appear in the sequel. It is therefore an invincible truth, that no man who knoweth the true character of the church of Christ, will remain at any loss where to find it. But it is also true that, it is easier to get satisfactory information than to submit to it, when offered; " Because "the carnal mind is enmity against God; for it is not subject to the "law of God, neither indeed can be." [Ro. 8. 7.]

But considering the great importance of being able to discriminate, between the anti-christian and the christian church, we will state the evidence, or character of the christian church in the following propositions, that the honest man may be informed, and occasion cut off from those who desire occasion. Not that we expect what is here stated to be cordially received by all, or by a majority; the testimony of Christ has always been opposed, and we look for it to be so still; there are yet those who stumble at the word being disobedient, and the way of life is narrow as well as heretofore: but truth must prevail in the end.

The first general proposition is this; Wherever the church of Christ exists, it is accompanied with such discriminating characteristics as are sufficient, satisfactorily to distinguish between those of whom it consists, and all other people or professions on the earth. Now unless this be true, all the marks of the true church, given by Jesus Christ and his apostles, fall to the ground; but God doth nothing in vain, and his word shall not return empty, but shall prosper in the thing whereto he sent it. But if the body of Christ cannot be known with certainty, all men are left in uncertainty whether they are united to it or not, and therefore whether they are in the way of life or death; consequently every man is at full liberty to make his own choice his rule, and no one has any authority to dispute his being in the path of life, be his practice almost what it may; for scarcely any iniquity is too great to be patronised by some, as being within the limits of a christian's blunders, though not comprehended in the line of his duty. One may indeed scruple the standing of such an one, saying, It is my opinion thou art not in Christ, or if he should say, I know thou art not, What of it? The self-determined professor hath as good a right to his opinion, as the opiniative accuser. Thus all restraint on sin produced by the fear of coming short of salvation is removed, and yet that is the highest restraint of which the unregenerate are susceptible.

Nothing can be effected to correct and undeceive the erroneous, unless an appeal can be made to an intelligible line of demarkation. In vain therefore is an appeal to revelation unless it exhibiteth such a line, and if it doth, the argument is closed; it can be known who are united to the body of Christ, and who are not. Thus by an appeal to scripture, it is evident, that the church is known, and cannot be unknown, according to the language of Christ to his disciples, whom he was then training up as the first members of his body; "Ye are the light of the world. A city that is set on a hill cannot "be hid." [Matt. 5. 14.]

But this truth will be farther illustrated and confirmed while we consider the second general proposition; That whereas the true church can be certainly known, the next subject to be considered is, What are those discriminating characteristics by which that body can be distinguished from all others. And here let it be considered;

That it is not known by local situation. The body of Christ is not limited to any part of the earth as the Jews were under the law of Moses; As said Jesus, " The hour cometh, when ye shall nei-" ther in this mountain, nor yet at Jerusalem, worship the Father— " But the hour cometh, and now is, when the true worshipers shall " worship the Father in Spirit and in truth; for the Father seeketh " such to worship him." " For, where two or three are gathered " together in my name, there am I in the midst of them." [Jno. 4. 21, 23. Matt. 18. 20.] From this, however, it is evident, that wherever the body of Christ is, its members are all gathered into one, as will be farther shown in its place.

The body of Christ doth not depend on any name which its members may bear, or by which they may be called; for many have a name to live and are dead; and it is no uncommon thing for the enemies of the cross to fix terms of reproach on those who live nearest to God— *They shall revile you, and shall cast out your name as evil.*

In discribing the body of Christ, we would not be understood, as rejecting any real light from God which any people may have received, because it has been at first short of full measure, but as acknowledging every degree of the light and power of God to its full extent. But at the same time, we cannot consider any measure of light and power sufficient to characterize the church, which cometh short of that character which Christ hath given. It is not by any means intended to cramp or restrain the spirits of men from improving every degree of light to the best advantage, to increase in the knowledge of God and the true christian life, but we are perfectly willing to own the work of God wherever it appears, and to acknowledge the members of Christ wherever they are found and under whatever name, provided they are furnished with that evidence which is indispensably necessary to constitute their real character. The object of our labor is not to create parties and divisions in the body of Christ, but to be in the number of his real followers, and to use our faithful endeavors as far as our knowledge and duty extend, that others also may partake of the same blessedness. But it cannot be uncharitable, to require, in every man, the genuine evidences of christianity before he be encouraged to consider himself one of the body; for evidently, it can do no man any good to be seated in the guest chamber without the wedding garment, much less can it avail to any good effect, to betray mankind with the notion of having already obtained it, until the time is past; but in these cases it is by all means best, to honestly point out the way, as opportunity may serve, faithfully maintaining what is the real character of the christian, and what the genuine marks of the body of Christ, and leave all men under the most forcible impression possible, as to these points—*who are the body of Christ; what the true marks*, and *not to stop short of an inheritance with them:* for, that these are attainable and free to all, is just as certain as that they exist. *Whosoever will let him take the water of life freely.*

EVIDENCES. 255

The power and existence of miracles are frequently pleaded as forming a prominent part of the character of the true church, and particularly in these days when men are wakened up by the report of a new and last dispensation; and so far is this particular urged by some, that they appear to overlook, with neglect and even contempt, every other part, even those which the scriptures state as superior, and in which the main force of evidence consists, according to the inspired writers: like the Jews who paid tithe of mint, anise and cummin, and neglected the weightier matters of the law, judgment, mercy and faith.

The power of miracles no doubt belongs to the church, and we have no idea of any true church of God without such power. But before we proceed farther, it will be proper to consider the nature of miracle, in a few particulars. First. A miracle is something out of the ordinary course of nature, and which must necessarily proceed from superior agency. Hence the term miracle; something wonderful, or calculated to excite wonder. Secondly. As miracles are not ordinary or natural events, but extraordinary, it follows that they cannot be the product of any ordinary and established medium, for that would destroy their nature, and they would become common occurrences. This however relates especially to the subjects in whom the miraculous power appears, and also those events commonly included in the term miracle, and is by no means intended to deny the abiding power of miracle in God, who ministers it when expedient, according to his own wisdom. The true source of miracles then is the power of God, and they are to be considered as the effect of the present agency of that power. Thirdly. It cannot therefore be denied that miracles are wholly at the disposal of God, who is the most competent judge, when they are necessary and when not. Fourthly. One thing more cannot be denied, That miracles are at God's disposal also, with respect to the kind and form of them, in what order and with what appearance it may be most expedient to minister them. Accordingly the attentive reader may readily discover, that in the dispensation of Jesus and his apostles, miracles were greatly changed in these respects, from what they were in the days of Moses.

This change in dispensing miracles may be considered necessary for three reasons. First. That their proper effect might not be destroyed by the commonness of them, and at the same time, the necessity of carrying them to an improper length be prevented. Secondly. Because when impostors understand that certain miracles have been wrought by the true ministers of God, they will endeavor to imitate them, as the magicians in Egypt. And though they may in many respects be outdone and overcome, as those were finally, and as the sons of Scheva, in the days of the apostles, yet such is the thirst of many for miracles, that frauds might in many cases be practised: "For false Christs and false prophets shall arise, and shall "show signs and wonders, to seduce, if possible, even the elect." "For such are false apostles, deceitful workers, transforming them-

"selves into the apostles of Christ And no marvel; for satan him-self is transformed into an angel of light. Therefore it is no great thing, if his ministers also be transformed as the ministers of right-eousness; whose end shall be according to their works." [Mar. 13. 22. 2 Cor. 11. 13, 14, 15.]

Now in what respect were these deceitful workers transformed into the apostles of Christ and ministers of righteousness? Not by teaching and doing righteousness after the example of Christ and his apostles, for that would have constituted them true ministers of Christ; and to say they taught and did righteousness as the true apostles, is to say that a corrupt fountain can bring forth a pure stream, and an evil tree good fruit, contrary to the rule of Christ. Besides, their end was to be according to their works; if therefore their works were good, their end must be good also, contrary to evidence. But the matter is plain enough, that those deceitful workers, presumed to vie with the true apostles or even to surpass them, in a fair and ostentatious appearance of piety and power, while they artfully taught things contrary to the gospel, corrupting the minds of the hearers from the simplicity which is in Christ.

Thirdly. Another necessity of this change is to check the pride and vain glory of mankind, who are prone to turn the grace of God into wantonness, and serve the purposes of a fleshly mind, by the knowledge which they obtain of the work of God; by disappointing them in their views, and carrying on his work in a manner unknown to them, that all may be taught to wait on God, and receive of him in the present tense, that no flesh should glory in his presence, and that he may lead his people in a way which they knew not: Vain man would be wise.

Another fact relating to what are commonly called miracles, is that whatever purpose they may answer in their own place, they are not saving. Salvation is not necessarily connected with them, they save no souls, and are not a proof to any man, that those who perform them have the power of salvation, for persons may have them and not know Christ or be known of him. "Many will say to me in "that day, Lord, Lord, *have we not prophesied in thy name? and* "*in thy name have cast out devils? and in thy name done many won-* "*derful works?* And then will I profess to them, I never knew you: "depart form me, ye that work iniquity."(Mat. 7. 22, 23.) " Though "I speak with the tongues of men and of angels, and have not chari-"ty, I am become as sounding brass or a tinkling symbal. *And* "*though I have the gift of prophecy, and understand all mysteries,* "*and all knowledge, and though I have all faith, so that I could re-* "*move mountains, and have not charity, I am nothing.* And "though I bestow all my goods to feed the poor, and though I give "my body to be burned, and have not charity, it profiteth me no-"thing." (1 Cor. 13. 1, 2, 3.) Thus every thing is set aside in making proof of the christian, but that which cannot be imitated or forged—charity; of which hereafter.

It is therefore utterly improper, in searching for the church of God, to give these a first or main place in its character; and especially when it is farther considered that if found, they can prove nothing to the point unless accompanied by such evidence as confirms the matter without them; so that were the greatest possible external and visible miracles discovered amongst any people called christians, these would not prove them to belong to the body of Christ, until confirmed by those testimonies which cannot accompany any other people. Thus it is written of the prophets of old. "The prophet "who prophesieth of peace, when the word of the prophet shall "come to pass, then shall the prophet be known, that the Lord hath "truly sent him." (Jer. 28. 9.) But this could only be admitted in case of promoting the worship of the true God which had been taught before, for on the other hand, it is written; "If there arise "among you a prophet, or a dreamer of dreams, and giveth thee a "sign or a wonder, and the sign or the wonder come to pass, where- "of he spake unto thee, saying, Let us go after other gods which "thou hast not known, and serve them; thou shalt not hearken to "the words of that prophet or that dreamer of dreams; for the Lord "your God proveth you to know whether ye love the Lord your God "with all your heart and with all your soul." (Deut. 13. 1, 2, 3.) Thus we see that signs and wonders were no proofs of a true prophet even in that dark day when they were so common and so necessary in the true prophet, unless corroborated by the end to be promoted by them. Obedience is better than sacrifice, and to love is more than to prophesy, or to do miracles. In like manner, the false apostles mentioned above, were known, at least in part, by their wicked doctrine and works, corrupting the minds of the people from the simplicity of the gospel, and preaching, in effect, another Christ, whom Paul had not preached." (2 Cor. 11. 3, 4.)

Those miracles, therefore, which are commonly understood by the term, however necessary they have been, in their proper place, or may yet be on certain occasions, serve but an inferior part in the great work of salvation, or in characterizing the church. And it is not to be wondered at that God, the wise dispenser of his grace, should discontinue them, for the most part, in the present arrangement of things, and introduce in their room, that which is spiritual, pure and heavenly—the substance instead of the outward sign; especially considering that the work of God increases in the ministration of light and power, becoming more spiritual in each additional dispensation; so that men who fear God, are capable of seeing his work, and understanding its nature and evidence to their satisfaction, without those figurative representations, calculated to arrest the physical man, which were necessary in former dispensations; having in addition to the weight of evidence attending those dispensations, transmitted to us by the scriptures and already prepossessed by all professed christians, the increasing light of the present day.

And it is here to be especially noticed, that introducing a new dispensation of the gospel and testifying it to the world, are very differ-

ent matters from emerging out of the dispensation of Moses and the prophets, and planting and establishing that of Christ; for as the foundation-stone had not been laid, salvation had not appeared, or Christ been made known, all that had been in possession before, stood in meats and drinks and divers washings and carnal ordinances, which served for the time then present, as shadowy representations of a substance to come, there was a necessity of overturning the whole Jewish ecomony, so that, as it is written;. " The priesthood being chang-
" ed [or transposed,] there is made of necessity a change [or trans-
" position,] also in the law;" but in the present case there is a transition from the corruption and darkness introduced by the man of sin, in the time of the falling away, into the life and light of Christ which was revealed in the beginning; so that notwithstanding there is a difference in order and economy, in several particulars, it is the same gospel, as much as a renewed portion of physic out of the same mass, with additional quantity and more perfect instruction, is of the same nature with the former; the same Christ, same self-denial and same cross, insomuch that whosoever honestly apprehends and embraces the faith and life of Christ and his apostles, and other real followers, in the first dispensation, will be in nowise difficulted to embrace the present: the same demand therefore for miracles is not requisite in the present dispensation as in the former, because all the miracles which were wrought to establish that, contribute to the support of this also.

Farther to elucidate this subject, let it be remembered that to do miracles in the sight of men, is a principal characteristic of the beast, or anti-christ; "And he doeth great wonders, so that he maketh fire
" come down from heaven on the earth in the sight of men, and de-
" ceiveth them that dwell on the earth by those miracles which he
" had power to do in the sight of the [first] beast." (Rev. 13. 13, 14.) It may be objected, that this is figurative language. But this answer is at least justifiable, that the things which the figure most resembles, are most likely to be those which it represented, unless good evidence is obtained to the contrary; and it is more than justifiable, even forcible, to argue, that no good reason can be offered for reversing the figure, and concluding that it represents the body of Christ doing wonders in the sight of men and gaining them over to the truth, instead of the beast deceiving them. The strongest evidence therefore is that to do miracles in the sight of men is eminently the character of the beast. And to this agree the words of Christ, which are not so metaphorical; " For there shall arise false Christs and false prophets, and shall show great signs and wonders,
" insomuch that, if possible, they shall deceive the very elect."
(Matt. 24. 24.) Thus concurring testimonies evince, that it is the proper character of the beast, or anti-christ, to show great signs and wonders, or to work miracles, in the sight of men. And this is the character which the world try to impose on the church of God in these days, and then reproach them as deceivers and impostors, because they do no miracles and show no signs.

It is also worthy of notice, that Jesus or his disciples, never wrought a miracle to satisfy the inquiries of the curious, or to obviate the cavils of adversaries. "A wicked and adulterous generation seek- "eth a sign; and there shall no sign be given to it, but the sign of "the prophet Jonas;" the sign of the cross which they do not desire. "But whereto shall I liken this generation?—For John came neither "eating nor drinking, and they say, He hath a devil. The Son of man "came eating and drinking, and they say, Behold a man gluttonous "and a winebibber, a friend of publicans and sinners." (Mat. 16. 4. and 11. 16, 18, 19.) The same generation rejected Christ demanding of him a sign from heaven, because in their carnal sense, the miracles which he wrought were not equal to those of Moses, or more truly, because the life which he lived and the doctrines which he taught were offensive to them; as they said, "This is an hard saying; who "can hear it?" (Jno. 6. 60.) He taught the destruction of the flesh, and the promotion and upbuilding of the spiritual work and kingdom of God. And for the same reason do men reject the testimony of Christ in these days, because it is offensive to their nature, being for the destruction of the flesh and the edification of the Spirit.

Were all the signs given, in support of the spiritual work of Christ, which the men of this generation ask, they would be no better satisfied, for all would tend to promote the same work of God by the cross, and they would resist still, as was abundantly proved by the first ministers of the present testimony. The Jews asked signs, but when they saw them they were not relieved; these signs did not alter the nature of Christ's work, and they stubbornly resisted, saying, "What "do we? for this man doeth many miracles." (Jno. 11. 47.) And when the apostles had done so notorious a miracle on the lame man that they could say nothing against it, and had no prospect of concealing it by denying, they endeavored to crush its effects by violence, for they hated the name, work and cross of Christ, as much as ever. [Acts 4. 13 to 17.] In vain therefore do carnal professors call for miracles, for the nature of Christ and his work remain the same, and ever will: But wisdom is justified of all her children: honest souls have always found evidence enough in the work of Christ to satisfy them.

That Jesus and his apostles wrought miracles in confirmation of their doctrine is a fact not to be denied, according to the testimony of those who, in many cases, were eye witnesses of the facts; but it is also undeniable that the use of them gradually subsided, no doubt, as the necessity for them ceased, and their use was superseded by the more permanent, substantial and genuine fruits and evidences of the gospel—charity, union and good works. Accordingly in the latter part of the apostle's ministry there is much less said about working miracles than in the beginning: not denying but that the church in that day had the power of miracles until the falling away. In like manner, the first ministers and witnesses of the second appearance of Christ, wrought miracles in the gift and power of God, in confirmation of their testimony, as it is attested to us by those who were in many cases living eye witnesses of the facts, and many such witnesses are living to this day. But these things have greatly subsided, the use of them being superseded by the gathering together of the church, and the manifestation of those fruits and evidences which are more substantial, genuine and abiding. At the same time, every necessary gift and power remain in and with the church at this day, and she is not left destitute of that power of miracle which is able to silence the adversary and confirm the faithful.

CHAPTER IV.

More Negatives. The absence of Christ. Christians do not commit Sin.

GREAT contentions and animosities have subsisted, for ages, among professed christians, respecting the church of Christ, who they are and with what limits circumscribed; and all about sentiments and speculative doctrines, and such other things as were in all respects foreign from real christianity; and while these were carried on, professors, like the Jews who would strain out a gnat and swallow a camel, have missed the mark altogether—an humble submission and obedience to the example and precepts of Jesus Christ, in which it could be said, and in which alone, *To me to live is Christ, and to die is gain* " Now the end of the commandment is charity, out of a " pure heart, and a good conscience and faith unfeigned; from which some having swerved have turned aside to vain jangling." " Ye are " my friends, if ye do whatsoever I command you." [1 Tim. 1. 5, 6. Jno. 15. 14.]

While men have been saying, Lo here! and lo there! and the inquiry hath been made, *Who of them all are the true church?* they have overlooked the simple and plain answer of Jesus Christ—*None of them.* " And he said to his disciples, The days will come, when " ye shall desire to see one of the days of the Son of man, and ye " shall not see it, And they shall say to you, See here, or see there, " go not after them, nor follow them." " Then if any man shall say " to you, Lo here is Christ, or there, believe it not." [Luk. 17. 22, 23. Matt. 24. 23.] These things prove unequivocally that the days were to come, in which Christ should not be known on the earth, and no people were to be followed, or believed—not any man, because no man in those days knew the truth or kept it: for a man of truth is to be believed, and the true followers of Christ are to be followed. " Brethren, be followers together [Greek, fellow imitators,] of me, " and mark them who walk so, as ye have us for an example." (Phil. 2. 17.) Neither did Jesus ever say any thing to the contrary of this, but confirmed it: " He that heareth you, heareth me." But such were the days of the false Christs and false prophets, who say, Lo here! and lo there! And the very nature of the language shows that all should be in confusion; no one knowing what was the truth.

or what to tell another; none knowing where to find Christ, or where to direct the inquiring soul. This total falling away hath been spoken of by the prophets, by Christ and his apostles, and by some of them, as having already begun in their days.

To discuss this subject at full length would not comport with the present purpose. A few observations, however, may be for edification. As a man can receive nothing except it be given him from heaven, so the church having once fallen as to its true order, purity and power, and the power of the holy people having been scattered, could no more be restored without a renewed revelation and manifestation of the same power, the same Christ who first gave them birth. And this agrees with the statement of the apostle, when speaking of the man of sin, who sat in the temple of God there to remain until the coming of the Lord, that is, until his second appearing, for this was written after the first. Now this mystery of iniquity, or man of sin, was to sit; in the temple of God, Christ therefore was not in it.

But what is the temple of God? are not his people? As it is written, " Ye are the temple of the living God; as God hath said, I " will dwell in them and walk in them." " Know ye not that ye are " the temple of God, and that the Spirit of God dwelleth in you." [1 Cor. 6. 16. and 3. 16.] While therefore the mystery of iniquity sat in the temple of God, or church, all was in confusion, the power of the holy people was scattered, and this beast made war with the saints and overcame them, as the scripture expressly said he should. [Rev. 13. 7.] Here also this *wicked* was to sit, making and continuing this havoc, until the second coming of the Lord and the day of our gathering together to him, as the apostle expressly states, speaking of that day, that it should not come, unless there came a falling away first, and also that that wicked should be revealed. Then after describing him, and telling that he was then working, he also states the time when he should be revealed, consumed and destroyed—at the appearing of the Lord. " And now ye know what with- " holdeth, that he might be revealed in his time. For the mystery " of iniquity doth already work : only he who now letteth will let, " until he be taken out of the way, [or let him who detaineth come " forth out of the midst; or be born;] and then shall that wicked " [ανομος, lawless,] be revealed whom the Lord will consume with " the Spirit of his mouth and will destroy with the brightness of his " appearing." [2 Thes. 2. 7, 8.] Thus it is stated by Christ Jesus in the parable, that the time of the kingdom's being made clean is at the end of the world, which can be none else than his second coming; " So shall it be in the end of the world. The Son of man shall send " forth his angels, and they shall gather out of his kingdom all things " that offend, and them that do iniquity." [Matt. 13. 40, 41.]

Notwithstanding, the scriptures speak abundantly of a kingdom on the earth already clean, extending itself over the whole earth, and abiding for ever, even for ever and ever; Yet this pure kingdom could never commence until the coming of Christ the second time, as already stated, which statement is corroborated by another saying of the apostle concerning Christ, "Who shall judge the quick and "the dead at his appearing, and his kingdom." Here it is evident the coming and kingdom commence together. [2 Tim. 4. 1.] For the church, after being once scattered, to arise again to its proper purity, order and power before the revelation and appearing of Christ, would be as inconsistent as for the salt which hath lost its savor to become good without the restoration of the saltness, or for a dead man to perform the functions of life without reanimation. Accordingly it hath been found by experience, that all the labored attempts to restore the church to its primitive purity and order, by gathering up the scattered fragments and putting away destructive errors, have proved abortive; and they always will to all people, until they find the renewed revelation of Christ from heaven, in his second appearing. For when any remarkable outpouring of the Spirit of God is known, it comes in such a manner as to show it does not spring forth out of any or all the established professions or churches, as the law coming forth of Zion, or the word of the Lord from Jerusalem, but on the contrary, tends to demolish, rather than upbuild those churches of long standing. For not unfrequently new denominations or parties of some renewed cast spring up in remarkably great revivals, carrying off the weight and Spirit of the work and leaving the old denominations in barrenness, and in a short time those who keep the revival longest are barren also, so that nothing of the kind hath ever been found abiding. These things however only serve to confirm a painful truth which is the natural inference from what hath been before stated; for inasmuch as the power of the holy people hath been once scattered, the daily sacrifice once taken away, and the salt, which is the church, has once lost the savor, which is the anointing, no church can have the anointing or Spirit, who is Christ, abiding in them, until Christ is again revealed from heaven; therefore all those churches who claim their standing as being in an uninterrupted succession from the apostles, are nothing but antichrist, and false prophets, who have lost the true Christ and know not where to find him: hence they say, Lo here! and lo there! in the desert and in the secret chamber. They preach and pray with such uncertainty that it can be felt by their hearers; and though they presume to be ministers of Christ, and can borrow, or more properly steal the words of his true ministers, not one amongst the thousands of them can tell any one soul who inquires, What shall I do to be saved? the way to find Christ and salvation, so as to prove by fact, that he is a minister of Christ indeed: this truth is felt by themselves, as far as they are awake, and when weighed in the balance they are found wanting.

That Christ is absent and not present with them their own words and works declare; for they are continually preaching and praying about his yet coming the second time. The same is farther confirmed by their perpetual fastings before eating the Lord's supper, and at other times, a practice, expressly predicated to be observed in the absence of Christ. It is not the habit of the followers of Christ to fast while he is present with them. " And they said unto him, Why " do the disciples of John fast often, and make prayers, and likewise " the disciples of the Pharisees; but thine eat and drink? And he " said to them, Can ye make the children of the bride-chamber fast " while the bridegroom is with them? But the days will come, " when the bridegroom shall be taken away from them and then shall " they fast in those days." [Luk. 5. 33, 34, 35.] It would be doing violence to these sayings of Christ to limit them to his going out of the tabernacle; for until after he had ascended and sent the Comforter they never really knew him, or began in truth to rejoice in him; with great propriety therefore they relate to that period, when the daily sacrifice was taken away, and the power and presence of Christ not known—he is absent, therefore they fast.

Eating the Lord's supper also, proves the absence of Christ; " For " as often as ye eat this bread and drink this cup, ye do shew forth " the Lord's death till he come," not afterwards. (1 Cor, 11. 26.)

An objection will here be raised, that eating the Lord's supper and fasting can afford no argument of the absence of Christ, because Jesus himself instituted the supper, and it was practised by the apostles and primitive christians, in those times when it is not pretended that the apostacy had actually commenced, and that fasting also hath the sanction of the same authority But this objection is sufficiently obviated thus; That Jesus and his apostles knew and foretold the apostacy which actually began to appear before the close of the apostles' labors; and as it was necessary that some animating memorial of the true Christ and his gospel should be left with the children, or friends of the Bridegroom, during his absence, to encourage them in the prospect of his return, and be a warning to his enemies, nothing could be observed with so good grace as that which had received the sanction of his own hand and his own words, " Do this in remem-- " brance of me." And, " When the Bridegroom shall be taken " away from them, then shall they fast in those days."

No allegation of insincerity is here intended against those whose real faith it is to fast or to eat the Lord's supper in remembrance of Christ, and who have not seen any farther; it is perfectly consistent with the faith of those who do not believe, that he hath come the second time, and it is, by no means unaccountable, that the sincere lamenters of degeneracy should keep up the remembrance of former times as accurately as possible. But the most genuine sincerity, admitting it were found in all who have not the faith of Christ's second appearance, which is far from being the fact, cannot at all invalidate the argument, that these memorials of his coming prove his absence. Neither can it avail any thing for them to plead that he is with them in Spirit; for Christ is the Spirit, and where he dwelleth in Spirit, there he dwelleth in reality. The disciples knew little of Christ while they could see his body of flesh and bones, but when that was out of the way, and they received him in Spirit, they had him in power, and could call him Lord by the Holy Ghost. But with the denominations in these days he is not present in Spirit, as their own words and works evince; because their most spirited cries and prayers are to this effect. That he would come and take up his abode with them; by which it would be absurd to suppose they intended any other coming than in the Spirit.

But the church and ministers of Christ are not so; they run not as uncertainly; they know Christ, and where he dwells, and can say with Jesus himself, and with Philip, his young disciple. Come and see. Christ's ministers are not sent without tidings; they can direct any honest inquirer to Christ and salvation, so certainly and safely that none such can ever fail.

This brings us again to the point in hand; That the members of Christ are known, and how they are distinguished from all others. And as the church is a select people, and a collection of many into one, the body being one and having many members, and all these members but one body, we shall first inquire into the subject as it respects each one individually. The people of God then, are known and distinguished by the fruits which they bear.

Here it will be expedient to clear up a little farther a difficulty which may possess the breast of some who are honest to the best of their understanding; it having been so universally taught, that real christianity is so great a secret, that no one can certainly be known whether he is a christian or not; yea farther it is even taught that none certainly know themselves whether they are christians or not. Some lay great stress on those words of the prophet Jeremiah, "The "heart is deceitful above all things, and desperately wicked; who "can know it?" (17. 9.) These words are considered as an unreserved description of the character of all men, christians as well as others. And indeed without such an acceptation, the inference drawn from them, that christians cannot be known, must fall; for it will readily be granted that if any one can be free from the charge of a deceitful heart, it must be one who is a christian indeed. But it is father to be remembered, that the prophet in that paragraph, of which these words are the beginning, spake particularly of the wicked man who gets riches not by right.

It is also to be considered as a matter of great consequence, though little understood heretofore, that the language of a Jewish prophet, respecting the people in his day, is not to be taken as a proper discription of a christian. What the law saith it saith to them that are under the law, but that by no means makes the sayings of the law a rule for those who have the gospel. It was necessary for them to speak the truth according to the day in which they lived; it is therefore no wonder if they often complained of the wickedness of the people and the scarcity of the truth in those days of darkness, when salvation was not known; when all they had in possession consisted in carnal ordinances, weak and beggarly elements; and they were encouraged and supported mainly by the promise of that which was afterwards to be possessed. Before faith came they were kept under the law, shut up to the faith which should afterwards be revealed; for nothing could be brought forth to perfection until faith came, and that could not be until the author of it came, who is Christ; "For the law made nothing perfect, but the bringing in of a better "hope (doth.) by which we draw nigh to God." (See note, page 117.)

The gospel of Christ therefore goes on a very different footing from the law; and though deceitfulness never could be acceptable with God, it is especially reprehensible where the light of Christ has appeared, so that all those who harbor it, are entirely excluded from Christ. Hence the doctrine of Christ, in the parable of the sower; none could bring forth fruit, but those who received the word in an honest and good heart. And it is a fact to be received with the utmost certainty that none but the honest and good, who keep judgment to the line and righteousness to the plummet, will ever be able to stand before him or partake with him. To the same effect is the saying of the apostle John who appeals to the decission of the heart as a witness to give confidence before God; " Beloved, if our heart condemn " us not, then have we confidence towards God." [1 Jno. 3. 21.]

What is here stated in a few words, could be illustrated to much greater fulness in a suitable place; and it obviates all the objections introduced from the writings of the old testament, against the truth of christians' being known, and also living without sin. And we conclude that no reasonable man will count it improper in us to reject all arguments to that effect, drawn from that quarter, until it can be proved that salvation was as real, not to say as full, in the days of the prophets as after the coming of Christ, that is, in plain terms that Christ came in vain and died in vain. "For if righteousness come "by the law Christ hath died in vain." "If therefore perfection " were by the Levitical priesthood (for under it the people received " the law,) what further need was there that another priest should " arise after the order of Melchizedec, and not be called after the " order of Aaron?" [Gal. 2. 21. Heb. 7. 11.]

But another text hath been named, to prove that christians cannot be known. "The wind bloweth where it listeth, and thou hearest "the sound thereof, but canst not tell whence it cometh and whither "it goeth: so is every one who is born of the Spirit." (Jno. 3. 18.) If it be argued that the Spirit is here compared to the wind, and the operations of the one to the movings of the other, and therefore that, as no man can understand accurately the moving cause and secret windings of the wind, so as to know whence it cometh and whither it goeth, so neither can any one know the manner of the Spirit's working, nor the christian who is the subject of it: So is every one who is born of the Spirit. It is answered, that this argument is forced and inconclusive; for let it be granted that the secret method of the Spirit's working is unknown, it no more proves the operations of the Spirit and the subjects of those operations to be unknown, than the secrets of the wind being unknown, proves that no man can know *when* the wind bloweth or *where*. The text therefore in consideration proves unquestionably, that as certainly as a forest or grove can be known to have the wind in it, by hearing the sound and observing other effects, just so certainly can the subjects of the Spirit's operations be known: *so is every one who is born of the Spirit.* By their fruits ye shall know them. And however the operations of the Spirit may be disputed and called the works of the devil; when men see the operations of the wind by its effects, (which are otherwise unknown,) they are obliged to acknowledge them to be beyond the reach of men, and are from the most rational evidence induced to attribute them to the proper cause, because there is no other power known to produce such; in like manner when the effects of the Spirit's operations appear, every man is by the most rational evidence invited to attribute them to their proper source. The only hindrances to this conclusion are found mainly in the adversaries to the gospel; as, First; An unacquaintance with the Spirit's operations through inattention, or want of opportunity. This may be easily removed in the honest. Secondly; Unwillingness to yield to the truth. This is so far from being a justifiable objection, that it is a proper foundation for guilt, and also a strong argument in favor of said operations' being of God, because offensive to the carnal mind. But I would not anticipate what is to come in another place.

The church is so far from being an unknowable, that nothing is more expressly and clearly testified in the scriptures than that it is known. Christians know themselves to be of God in Christ, by the work of God in them and the fruits which they bring forth. " Here-
" by know we that we dwell in him, and he in us, because he hath
" given us of his Spirit." " He that believeth on the Son of God hath
" the witness in himself." " And hereby we do know that we know
" him, if we keep his commandments. He that saith I know him,
" and keepeth not his commandments, is a liar, and the truth is not
" in him. But whoso keepeth his word, in him verily is the love of
" God perfected: hereby know we that we are in him." " My lit-
" tle children, let us not love in word, neither in tongue, but in deed
" (work) and in truth. And hereby we know that we are of the
" truth; and shall assure our hearts before him." [1 Jno. 4. 13. and 5. 10. and 2. 3, 4, 5. and 3. 18, 19.]

Christians also know others, and are able to distinguish who are in Christ, and who are of anti-christ, by their being of the same faith or not, by their embracing or not embracing the same Spirit and work which they have received. Accordingly the apostle John speaking of the anti-christs and christians, distinguisheth thus; " They are of the world, therefore speak they of the world, and the
" world heareth them. We are of God: he that knoweth God hear-
" eth us; he that is not of God heareth not us. Hereby know we the
" Spirit of truth and the spirit of error." [4. 5, 6.] Thus there is union in all the work of God, and among all the souls who serve him; no matter in what country they live, or by whatever reproachful names they may be called, or whatever other circumstantials may attend them. If any therefore are uncertain who are members of Christ's body and who not, or in other words, who are the true church, it proves in the first place, that they are not christians.

But the children of God are not only known to themselves and to one another, but the evidence is sufficiently plain to those about them. Not as though the internal and spiritual nature of the work can be known and understood by the mass of mankind, or any one in the state of nature. " But the natural man receiveth not the things of " the Spirit of God, for they are foolishness to him; neither can he " know them, because they are spiritually discerned. But he that is " spiritual judgeth [or discerneth] all things (or every one,) yet he " himself is judged [discerned] of no man." (1 Cor. 2. 14, 15.) But the fruits which appear are so rational that the understanding of natural men can apprehend them, so far at least, as to be sufficiently convinced of the source whence they come. These fruits consist in the performance of their duty towards God, towards one another, and towards mankind: and in the performance of these duties they cannot neglect a duty to themselves.

1st. The first description of the church which we shall here state, by which they are known, is their doing the will of God. " Circum-" cission is nothing, and uncircumcission is nothing but the keeping " of the commandments of God." " Not every one who saith unto " me, Lord, Lord, shall enter into the kingdom of heaven, but he " who doeth the will of my Father who is in heaven." (1 Cor. 7. 16. Matt. 7. 21.) This too is the language of Christ Jesus and his apostles who well understood the nature of the gospel, and not the mistakes of a formalist or hypocrite. But as Christ Jesus is he who first revealed the Father, and all Christians own him as the head of the body, receiving all their knowledge of God, and paying all their duty to God, in obedience to him, we here proceed to state. That,

2d. The fruits of the members of the church by which they are known and distinguished from all other men are found in keeping the commandments of Christ and doing his will: short of this in vain do any pretend to be members of Christ's body. " Ye are my " friends if ye do whatsoever I command you." " If ye keep my " commandments ye shall abide in my love, even as I have kept my " Father's commandments and abide in his love." " If a man love me " he will keep my sayings." " Therefore whosoever heareth these " sayings of mine, and doeth them, I will liken him to a wise man, " who built his house upon a rock: and the rain descended, and the " floods came, and the winds blew, and beat upon that house; and it " fell not: for it was founded upon a rock. And every one who " heareth these sayings of mine, and doeth them not, shall be likened " to a foolish man, who built his house upon the sand." " Blessed are " they who do his commandments, that they may have right to the " tree of life, and may enter in through the gates into the city." " He " that saith, I know him, and keepeth not his commandments, is a " liar, and the truth is not in him." [Jno. 15. 15. V. 10. and 14. to 23. Matt. 7. 24, 25, 26. Rev. 22. 14. 1. Jno. 2. 4.]

These are the terms and these only which Christ proposes to any man who would be a partaker with him; and all other plans or schemes, however specious and flattering, are nothing but the works of anti-christ, contrivances of men who know not God or Jesus Christ whom he hath sent; and therefore have no power over sin, yet claim a share in the kingdom of God. Thus through such false apostles, deceitful workers, it has been so universally taught that christians transgress the commandments of Christ as well as others, that the law and rule of Christ are made void by tradition, and it is esteemed a gross heresy, a pernicious enthusiastic flight, for any man to teach that christians correctly keep the commandments of Christ. This however was not esteemed a heresy by the apostles who wrote thus; "For though we walk in the flesh, we do not war after the "flesh: (for the weapons of our warfare are not carnal, but mighty "through God to the pulling down of strong holds,) casting down im- "aginations (Greek, reasonings,) and every high thing that exalteth "itself against the knowledge of God, and bringing into captivity "every thought to the obedience of Christ." [2 Cor. 10. 3, 4, 5.] How different is the language of those who maintain that they and all others transgress the commandments of Christ every day, in thought, word and deed! Will any one suppose they serve one and the same Lord?

3d. But no man who committeth sin can keep the law of Christ, as he saith, "Whosoever committeth sin is the servant of sin." Again it is written, "Know ye not that to whom ye yield yourselves "servants to obey, his servants ye are to whom ye obey, whether of "sin unto death, or of obedience unto righteousness?" [Jno. 8. 34. Ro. 6. 16.] This then is the unequivocal distinction between the members of Christ's body and the rest of the world, "In this the "children of God are manifest and the children of the devil." [Jno. 3. 10.] Now that which is manifest is no longer a mystery, no longer unknown. This is the sweeping rule of Christ and his apostles, which puts a period eventually, to all the contentions and debates, about Who is a christian and who is not.

All therefore which is required of any man, in searching for the true church, is in the first place to find the people who bear a bold and living testimony against all sin, and confirm the same by their works: and he is fully authorized of Christ and his apostles, to set aside all others, whatever zeal, light, or power they may have, as being yet short of the mark. We would not be understood as condemning or rejecting any society of professed christians, on account of the misconduct or iniquities of some who may be called by their name, and have some agreement with them in sentiment, but are not living in union with the body, and are not owned by them as honest subjects of their faith. Neither on account of those who are so young in their faith, as not to have had time to gain power over sin. For the disciples were subject to error in the beginning of their discipleship; but after they received the Holy Ghost, and became experienced in the gospel, they set another example, and taught another doctrine. The work of regeneration is an increasing work; in it men cease to do evil and learn to do well.

EVIDENCES.

But if any man, in quest of the true church, find a people whose leading characters, or those members who have professed long enough to have become of age, yet commit sin, he must violate the law and rule of Christ, if he consider them the church of God. Or if he find a people whose acknowledged faith it is, that no man can live, and not sin; or that people may commit sin, and be christians notwithstanding; such a people are avowed enemies to the rule of Christ, and in honor to him are obliged to be rejected as not belonging to his body. " For he that saith, I know him, and keepeth not " his commandments is a liar, and the truth is not in him. He was " manifested to take away our sins : and in him is no sin. He that " saith he abideth in him, ought himself also so to walk, even as he " walked." [1 Jno. 2. 4. 6. and 3. 5.] Or if a people be found who cannot show a united body of one faith, (for in the church there is one faith) who have gained power over all sin; and if they do not reject all who have not gained full power over all sin, as not born of God, but at best, even if of their own faith, as no more than learners, such people are to be set aside as not being the body of Christ; for the true church are the temple of God, and that temple is holy.

Finally, Whatever work, under the name of christianity, doth not in its progress, give power over all sin and the darkness which leads to it, so as to produce a people who are saved in the present tense, falls short of being the true gospel, and the subjects of it are all under the power and government of anti-christian darkness. " This " then is the message which we have heard of him, and declare to " you, that God is light and in him is no darkness at all. If we say " that we have fellowship with him, and walk in darkness, we lie and " do not the truth. But if we walk in the light as he is in the light, " we have fellowship one with another, and the blood of Jesus Christ " his Son cleanseth us from all sin." (1 Jno. 1. 5, 6, 7.) Not will cleanse us when we die, or sometime hereafter; it is present tense; as it is written again, " How shall we that are dead to sin live any " longer therein." (Ro. 6. 2.) This then is the character of the true church; they have fellowship with God, fellowship with one another, and commit no sin. " In this the children of God " are manifest, and the children of the devil; whosoever doeth " not righteousness is not of God, neither he that loveth not " his brother." But, " He that doeth righteousness is righteous, " even as he [the Son of God] is righteous." And, " He that loveth " his brother *abideth* in the light, and there is none occasion of stum- " bling in him," (1 Jno. 3. 10, 7. and 2. 10.)

CHAPTER V.

Some objections against the sinless life of a christian answered and the point confirmed.

BUT the thought of God's having a people on earth, in whom he dwells as his holy temple, and who do not commit sin, is so far out of the sight and remembrance of professors, that the very idea will appear to many of them romantic, and the most explicit declarations of scripture appear to have lost their edge, and a few undefined old phrases to which they have been accustomed, partly scriptural and partly not, are sufficient with them, to counterbalance all the testimony of Christ and his apostles. Some also who possess a respectable degree of honesty and feeling, may through the influence of prepossession and the deficiency of information, be not altogether clear in their judgment. We shall therefore take notice of some of the most plausible objections.

The apostle John hath written; " If we say we have no sin we de-
" ceive ourselves, and the truth is not in us." Hence it is argued that no man can be free from sin; for if any man, be who he may, should say, I have no sin, or I am saved from all sin by the blood of Christ, this text, say they, would prove that he is deceived and the truth not in him; for the apostle said *we*, If *we* say we have no sin *we deceive ourselves* and the truth is not in us; and surely if any man could become free from sin, it would be an apostle, and if any amongst them, the beloved disciple John. To a man unacquainted with the nature of language, this is a considerably specious objection; I have therefore stated it in as strong terms as I could, that it may be effectually removed.

The apostle had just stated the condition of those who walk in the light as he (the Son of God) is in the light, that the blood of Christ cleanseth them from all sin. But he well knew the enmity of the Jews and others against Christ and the doctrine of his blood, as saving them, as well as their pride in presuming they were not sinners, and therefore had no need of being cleansed. He therefore adds;
" If we say we have no sin we deceive ourselves, and the truth is not
" in us." If we, or any of us, or any man (let it go to the full extent,) should say we have no sin, and therefore have no need of Christ, he deceiveth himself. That this is the purport of the apostle's statement, is sufficiently plain, if we attend to the following words.
" If we confess our sins he is faithful and just to forgive us our sins,
" and to cleanse us from all unrighteousness." And then the matter is changed from the present to the past; " If we say we have not
" sinned, we make him a liar, and his word is not in us." But no more talk of being deceived by saying we have no sin, after the confession, forgiveness and cleansing. It would nevertheless be false to say *we had not sinned ;* for one who is saved from sin ever so completely, connot say but that he hath sinned, because *all have sinned.* The apostle therefore, by saying, in such a connection, " If

we say we have no sin we deceive ourselves," no more proves that to be the case with christians, than it proves that if a man is once a sinner he must so remain: but Christ is manifested to take away our sins. Besides; to understand this passage as proving that christians commit sin, excludes the apostle's testimony on this subject by exposing him to a contradiction; because he hath so boldly stated at length, that they who are born of God do not sin.

As to his saying, *we*, it is no more than a familiar mood of speaking common to the apostles. Thus James, speaking of the tongue, saith, " Therewith bless we God, even the Father; and therewith " curse we men, who are made after the similitude of God. Out " of the same mouth proceedeth blessing and cursing. My breth- " ren, these things ought not so to be." Likely none will insist that the apostle James was one of those who took part in such cursing, and yet he says *we*, in as pointed terms as John. (See 3. 9, 10.)

Another portion of scripture which many ply with great confidence to maintain that christians commit sin, or live in it, is that of Paul, where he saith, " For we know that the law is holy, but I am carnal " sold under sin," and more to the same purport. (Ro. 7. 14, &c.) This however is a disputed text among the denominations of professors; so that their own testimony on this point doth not agree.

John Wesley and his followers have maintained vigorously that the apostle did not there speak of himself or describe the christian, but the convinced sinner.

Doctor Philip Doddridge, notwithstanding he was possessed of the common error, that christians commit sin, though unwillingly, in his notes on the scripture under consideration, observes that, " The " *apostle* here, by a very dexterous turn, changes the person and " speaks as of himself. This he elsewhere does, when he is only " personating another character. And the character here assumed " is that of a man first *ignorant of the law*, then *under it*, and sin- " cerely desiring to please God, but finding to his sorrow, the weak- ' ness of the motives it suggested, and the sad discouragement un- '' der which it left him; and last of all, *with transport discovering* '' *the gospel* and gaining pardon and strength, peace and joy by it. " But to suppose (continues the Doctor,) he speaks all these things " of himself, as the confirmed christian, that he really was when he " wrote this *epistle*, is not only foreign, but contrary to the whole " scope of his discourse, as well as to what is expressly asserted " Chapter 8. 2."

Osterwald says. " This is a chapter which ought to be well under- " stood, and which must not be misapplied. For this purpose it " must be observed, that the apostle represents in his own person, in " a figurative way of speaking very usual with him, the condition of " a man who is under the law; and who not having faith and the Spi- " rit of Christ is a slave to his passions." Thus this scripture is judiciously taken out of the hands of the abettors of the doctrine that christians are not free from sin, by men of their own faith.

It is indeed inconsistent, that any one of understanding should build with any confidence on the apostle's expressing himself after that manner in a figure so common to him as well as others. As thus, " For if the truth of God hath more abounded through my " lye to his glory, why yet am I also judged as a sinner? And not " rather (as we are slanderously reported and as some affirm that we " say,) let us do evil that good may come." [Ro. 3. 7, 8.] This is the language of others whom he personates, whose damnation is just, and yet he says, *my lye*, and why *am I* judged as a sinner, as though it were his own. But to the chapter under consideration.

In the chapter before, the apostle had shown at length that they, christians, were *dead to sin and could not live any longer therein; free from sin and servants of righteousness;* and it is worthy of particular consideration, that he finds, knows, or admits no middle station between being servants of sin and servants of righteousness. But in the beginning of this chapter, he proceeds to elucidate the state of christians, as being delivered from the law, by the case of a married woman whose husband is dead; in consequence of which she is at liberty to be married to another, which she could not be had he been yet alive; and to show, that as their first husband, the law, to which they had been in bondage, was dead, (or they were dead to it, which is the same, for he uses the phrases as being tantamount,) they were at liberty to be married to another, even to Christ, which could not have been while the first lived and they were bound to it. " Wherefore, my brethren, ye also are become dead to the law by " the body of Christ; that ye should be married to another even to " him who is raised from the dead, that we should bring forth fruit to " God. For when we were in the flesh, the motions of sins, which " were by the law, did work in our members to bring forth fruit unto " death; but now we are delivered from the law, that being dead " wherein we were held; that we should serve in newness of spirit, " and not in the oldness of the letter." This shows the event of what had taken place in them to be an effectual change from bondage to liberty, from the service of sin to the service of righteousness, as above; " Being then made free from sin, ye became the servants of " righteousness." And again; " Therefore if any man be in Christ " he is a new creature: old things are passed away, behold, all things " are become new. And all these things are of God." (Chapter 6. 18. 2 Cor. 5. 17, 18.)

The apostle next proceeds to show that the law is not sin, neither the proper cause of death; but that it discovered sin, or revived it; for without the law sin was dead; and that sin works death by that which is good, which is the law; " *Wherefore the law is holy, and " the commandment holy, and just, and good.*" He herein also shows the workings of the mind, in one under the law; and among other things says, " For I was alive without the law once." This cannot apply to the apostle, who was not only trained up in the law from his infancy, long before he could have any understanding of the life of which he here speaks, and which he lost by the law and the reviving of sin, but was so exceedingly zealous of the law, long before his conviction and conversion, that in the Spirit of inspiration, after he became a christian, he could refer back to those times and say, " *Touching the righteousness which is in the law, I was blameless :*" he therefore was not without the law.

But as all this is in the past tense, and therefore cannot, with any plausibility, be considered as Paul's own exercise, except at some former period, when he might be supposed to be in convictions, I shall proceed to where he commences in the present tense; " For " we know that the law is spiritual, but I am carnal sold under sin." Now if this be true of one born of God, then the following consequences are true. First. That Christ and sin are one; for no man can serve two masters, but this character serves sin. Secondly. That to be carnally minded is not death; for sin has no mechanical or coercive power, but can only prevail by influencing the mind, therefore this person's mind has yielded to the power of sin, and yet he is esteemed as alive in Christ. Thirdly. That to be carnally minded, and to be spiritually minded imply no important distinction; for this character is both; therefore the apostle is wrong in saying, " To be carnally " minded is death, but to be spiritually minded is life and peace." Fourthly. That a slave to sin can be a free born son of God at the same time; " For if the Son make you free ye shall be free indeed," but this character is made free by the Son and yet sold under sin: now one sold under another against his will is what common language calls a slave. So is it with this character, " For that which I do I " allow not; but what I would I do not: but what I hate that do I." " If then I do that which I would not, I consent to the law that it is " good." Like the impious heathen, *Video meliora proboque, deteriora sequor.* I see better things and approve them, but pursue the more pernicious. Then out of thine own mouth will I judge thee, thou wicked servant. Thou knowest thy Lord's will, and approvest it, but dost not perform it: thou shalt be beaten with many stripes. And yet this character is called a christian. But if a slave to sin be a christian who is not?

But hear his reasoning. " It is no more I that do it but sin that " dwelleth in me." This man then is the temple and agent of sin; it dwelleth in him, and he acteth it out. But christians are the temple of the living God, and the Spirit of God dwelleth in them; and if any man defile the temple of God him will God destroy. (1 Cor. 3. 16, 17.) Therefore, " Whosoever sinneth hath " not seen him neither known him." (1 Jno. 3. 6.) This person therefore is not a christian, but an assumed character, under the power of sin, convicted, but not acquainted with Christ.

The next verses are only a kind of repetition of the same workings, expressing the man's anxiety about his condition. But he adds, " I find then a law, that when I would do good evil is present with " me. For I delight in the law of God after the inward man." This is counted an infallible proof that this whole description applies to the christian, not considering the essential deficiency which would attach itself to this verse with all the rest—that of not doing. " If " a man love me he will (unexceptionably) keep my words;" (not he would if he could,) and " He that loveth me not keepeth not my " sayings." [Jno. 14. 23, 24.] This is the test of the christian; and in vain doth any man presume to be a christian without it. Christ makes no apology for those who are not able; neither do his apostles; that is, where the gospel is heard and known. If many shall seek to enter in and shall not be able, he hath no more compassion on them, than on those who do not seek at all. And why should he, seeing no man will ever experience the fatal calamity except those who waste their day and strength in pursuing unjustifiable ways, and rejecting the only true way and time of entrance?

Who therefore is to believe that a man has the inside of his cup and platter clean, unless the outside be clean also? Who is to believe that there is a good and pure fountain within, unless the stream be also clean and pure? Who is to believe that any man delights in the law of God in the inward man, and yet walks, or at all acts contrary to it in his life, on any other principle, than that he is merely a natural man, having never known the power of Christ? It is a most audacious impeachment of the character of Christ, for any man to say, that he, or any other, hath received Christ, hath submitted to his instructions, and hath not received power to overcome sin. Or are these sayings true or false? " He that committeth sin is of the de- " vil: for the devil sinneth from the beginning;" and " For this " purpose the Son of God was manifested that he might destroy the " works of the devil. Whosoever is born of God doth not commit " sin; for his seed remaineth in him: and he cannot sin because he " is born of God." I say, are these sayings true or false? And is it true or false, that " To as many as receive him, to them he giveth " power to become the sons of God, even to them that believe on his " name?" [Jno. 1. 12.]

People who pretend to be christians on the presumption that they delight in the law of God after the inward man, while they find such a law, that when they would do good evil is present, and they do not keep the law of God, are little, if at all, superior to the heathen mentioned above, who said, Video meliora proboque, deteriora sequor; or those mistaken Jews whom Paul describes, Who approve the things which are more excellent, and yet the name of God is blasphemed among the Gentiles through them. [Ro. 2. 18, 24.] Multitudes of such people profess the name of Christ and in works deny him, neglecting the christian signal, " Let every one that nameth the " name of Christ depart from iniquity," [2 Tim. 2. 19.] and by so doing bear the boldest testimony they can readily do, to support infidelity, and prove the gospel a blank, and their profession of it a farce. " Blessed are they that hear the word of God and keep it." [Luk. 11. 28.]

Much stress seems to be placed on the phrase, *Inward man*, as if this character had some new or distinct part, or faculty, some physical, moral, or intellectual power, distinct from other men, which must constitute him a christian, so that his delighting in the law of God after the inward man, must prove him to be a christian let him be ever so unable to do what he ought. Thus I remember to have heard a preacher of considerable rank, when preaching expressly on this subject, boldly assert that, the unregenerate man *has no inner man.* But when people become intelligent enough to know, that the regenerate possess no physical or intellectual faculties, but such as are common to them with the unregenerate, and that the *inward man,* is no other than the intellectual spirit which we commonly call the soul, they need not be surprised that men should approve, be pleased and delighted with the law of God after the inward man, and yet be only natural men. God's works have a beauty and order which are fit to attract the approbation and delight of intelligent men in an unprejudiced state of mind, and especially when conviction of duty, sense of necessity, and the hope of salvation all press toward the same point: but these come far short of that renovating work of the Spirit, in which the man receives power to become a son of God, and improves it to that effect.

" But I see another law in my members warring against the law of " my mind, and bringing me into captivity to the law of sin which is " in my members." This decides the point that this is the character of one yet under the power of sin, for the law in his members is too strong for the law in his mind; therefore he is either not a christian, or the opposing law in the members of a christian is superior to the law or Spirit of Christ, for christians have the mind of Christ, [1 Cor. 2. 16.] and " If any man have not the Spirit of Christ he is " none of his." [Ro. 8. 9.]

" O wretched man that I am! who shall deliver me from the body " of this death? I thank God through Jesus Christ our Lord." This is the first expression in the whole description which savors of the gospel. When in the last extremity, and would probably have sunk without some relief, he is at last shut up to the faith of Christ, and finds the prospect of deliverance which gives him some courage. But that until now he had never known the way of deliverance, and especially that he had never experienced it, is still farther proved as follows. First. Until now he complains of that opposing law having power over him and keeping him in bondage. But of the christian it is said, " For sin shall not have dominion over you: for ye are " not under the law; but under grace." [Ro. 6. 14.] Secondly. Those who are in Christ are not at any loss about who shall deliver them from the body of death; they both know him and his work and have found it to be sufficient and complete. " And ye are com-" plete in him who is the head of all principality and power, in whom " also ye are circumcised with the circumcission made without " hands, in putting off the body of the sins of the flesh by the circum-" cission of Christ: buried with him in baptism, wherein also ye are " risen with him (Yea! already risen,) through the faith of the ope-" ration of God, who hath raised him from the dead." [Col. 2. 10, 11.] Thirdly. This character under consideration doth not even pretend to be an overcomer yet, notwithstanding he hath gotten some discovery of the way, but remaineth just as he was excepting the prospect. "So then. with the mind, I myself serve the law of God; "but with the flesh the law of sin." He is therefore not yet in Christ; for they that are in Christ do not serve the law of sin with the flesh itself, They have crucified it with its affections and lusts. "I say "then walk in the Spirit, and ye shall not fulfil the lusts of the flesh." "For if ye live after the flesh, ye shall die; but if ye through the "Spirit do mortify the deeds of the body, ye shall live." "But I "keep my body under, and bring it into subjection." [Gal. 5. 24. 16. Ro. 8. 13. 1 Cor. 9. 27.] Now that which is crucified, mortified, or brought into subjection by the christian, cannot have power to serve the law of sin.

But the christian again comes into view. "There is therefore "now no condemnation to those who are in Christ Jesus, who walk "not after the flesh but after the Spirit." [8. 1.] This is an inference from the sixth verse of the seventh chapter, where the apostle left the subject and made a digression to speak of the man under the law, before he proceeded to the full description of a christian. Objections have been made against the division between the seventh and eighth chapters, as being in an improper place, considering the first verse of the eighth an inference from the last of the seventh : but a man of discernment must see the weakness of such reasoning. To say there is no condemnation to those who are in Christ Jesus who walk not after the flesh but after the Spirit, because I serve the law of God with my mind, but the law of sin with my flesh, is at best inconclusive, not to say absurd. But that justification should be the consequence of becoming dead to the law and living to Christ in the Spirit is rational, and according to the gospel. "But now we are delivered from the "the law, that being dead wherein we were held; that we should "serve in newness of Spirit and not in the oldness of the letter." [7. 6.] "There is therefore now no condemnation to those who are in "Christ Jesus, who walk not after the flesh, but after the Spirit. "For the law of the Spirit of life in Christ Jesus hath made me free "from the law of sin and death. For God sending his own Son in "the likeness of sinful flesh, and for sin, (on account of sin, to put it "away by the sacrifice of himself;) condemned sin in the flesh; "(where it hath its source,) that which the law could not do in that it "was weak through the flesh; that the righteousness of the law "might be fulfilled in us, who walk not after the flesh, but after the "Spirit." [8. 1, &c.]

Here is a christian indeed; one who doth not walk after the flesh, but after the Spirit; one who is set free from the law of sin, by the Spirit of life in Christ Jesus; one who hath a work done in him, which the law could not do, and which no man under the law ever experienced, or ever could, until God's own Son appeared to do it; that is, to condemn sin in the flesh. It is worthy of observation, that in all the description of a christian, there is no account that he would do good, and cannot.

NOT SINNERS.

But Paul is again introduced by some, as an instance of a christian who is plagued with the power and vigorous efforts of sin, as in these words; "And lest I should be exalted above measure through the "abundance of revelations, there was given to me a thorn in the "flesh, the messenger of satan to buffet me, lest I should be exalted "above measure." (2 Cor. 12. 7.) This thorn in the flesh, it is pleaded, was remaining sin, with which he had to contend. But it might be asked, Why is it said to be given to him; for if it was remaining sin it was with him all along. Besides; A thorn in the flesh must be painful to the flesh, as this no doubt was, for the purpose intended; but sin in nature or works, is not painful to the flesh, it is what it loves, as being its own kind, its own offspring. Paul was no better than Jesus his Lord; who, "Though he was a Son, yet learn- "ed he obedience by the things which he suffered;" and by his own account this thorn was given for the purpose of humiliation, contrary to any effect of sin. Should this thorn be understood to be the judaizing, and otherwise corrupt teacher, who gave Paul so much distress and tribulation, the Greek text would not by any means contradict the idea, "There was given to me a thorn in the flesh, the mes- "senger of satan, that he might buffet me, lest I should be exalted "above measure." But it would be beside the present purpose to enter into a full investigation of what this thorn was: it is enough to be satisfied it was not sin in him.

It would also be endless to enter upon all the contentious arguments and objections against the faith of a sinless life in christians. I have purposely noticed those which are most commonly offered, and which appear most plausible. As for those frequently introduced from the Mosaical dispensation, I have already dismissed them as coming from a source incapable of furnishing the example or pattern of a christian. The law made nothing perfect, but the bringing in of a better hope doth. By the law was the knowledge of sin, but not of salvation.

It remains now to be observed that in all the arguments proffered in support of the sentiment, that christians live in sin, or commit sin, no scripture asserts the fact. All that can be done is to argue by inference, and such as is very precarious; such as can easily be understood differently without distortion; such as must necessarily be received in a different sense or set the scriptures to clash one part against another, and the more feeble and precarious evidence to confront and overturn the more plentiful, most pointed, connected and forcible. For in proof of the sinless life of the christian, all and every one, stands connected and pointed work, such as is not found on the other side, and which will not admit of any acceptation contrary to proving, as expressly as language can do it, that the regenerate sons of God do not commit sin, but are saved from it. "There- "fore if any man be in Christ, he is a new creature; old things "are passed away; behold, all things are become new. And all "these things are of God, who hath reconciled us to himself through "Jesus Christ." (2 Cor. 5. 17. 18.) It may be inquired; Is sin of the old fallen creation, or of the new? If it be of the old it is passed away from those who are in Christ; but if sin be the whole, or any part of the new creation of God in Christ, it may abide for ever. Christ came to save his people from their sins; and if an end to sin be not the certain concomitant of being in Christ, it may be asked, What hath the new creation effected? If he be yet a sinner, he was that before, and thus the new creation is made a mere sound, a name without substance, a true description of the religion of the bulk of professors. But,

Paul, in his epistle to the Romans, hath in the most explicit terms declared, that they who are in Christ, are dead to sin, so as to live no longer therein, and are already free from it. " What shall we say " then? Shall we continue in sin that grace may abound? God " forbid, [It cannot be]: how shall we who are dead to sin live any " longer therein? Know ye not that so many of us as were baptized " into Jesus Christ, were baptized into his death? Wherefore we " are buried with him by baptism into death; that like as Christ was " raised up from the dead by the glory of the Father, even so we " also should walk in newness of life. For if we have been planted " together in the likeness of his death, we shall be also in the like- " ness of his resurrection." Here the end of Christ's death and resurrection is stated in plain terms to be *our dying with him*, that is, to sin as he died, and rising with him, or walking in newness of life; if therefore we be in Christ, and not dead to sin, and consequently do not walk in newness of life, the end of his death and his rising again is lost, Christ hath died in vain, we are yet in our sins, and he hath failed in his undertaking.

It is vain to argue that these happy effects are to take place at some future period, for the apostle brings the matter right down to the present tense, to take effect now and henceforth, as the foundation work of future increase and glory. We who *are dead* to sin—*are buried* with him—"Knowing this that our old man *is* (already) *crucified* " *with him*, that the body of sin might be destroyed, that *henceforth we* " *should not serve sin*. For he that *is dead is freed from sin*." That is, as we are. And then on that position, *that we are dead with him*, he grounds the argument of our living as he lives; that is, *to God—in the Spirit—in the resurrection*, or *in newness of life*. " Now if we be dead " with Christ we believe that we shall also live with him. Knowing that " Christ being raised from the dead, dieth no more; death hath no " more dominion over him. For in that he died, he died to sin once; " but in that he liveth, he liveth to God. *Likewise reckon ye also* " *yourselves to be dead indeed to sin*, (not in name, or in prospect,) " *but alive to God* through Jesus Christ our Lord."

It might be asked, Why should he counsel them to reckon themselves dead to sin and alive to God, if they were not so in truth? Did he want them to be deceived? Or did he expect that to esteem themselves what they were not, or could not be, would be for their edification? But it was reasonable to encourage all who believed, to inherit their privilege.

reviving of sin, but was so exceedingly zealous of the law, long before his conviction and conversion, that in the Spirit of inspiration, after he became a christian, he could refer back to those times and say, " *Touching the righteousness which is in the law, I was blameless:*" he therefore was not without the law.

But as all this is in the past tense, and therefore cannot, with any plausibility, be considered as Paul's own exercise, except at some former period, when he might be supposed to be in convictions, I shall proceed to where he commences in the present tense; " For " we know that the law is spiritual, but I am carnal sold under sin." Now if this be true of one born of God, then the following consequences are true. First. That Christ and sin are one; for no man can serve two masters, but this character serves sin. Secondly. That to be carnally minded is not death; for sin has no mechanical or coercive power, but can only prevail by influencing the mind, therefore this person's mind has yielded to the power of sin, and yet he is esteemed as alive in Christ. Thirdly. That to be carnally minded, and to be spiritually minded imply no important distinction; for this character is both; therefore the apostle is wrong in saying, " To be carnally " minded is death, but to be spiritually minded is life and peace." Fourthly. That a slave to sin can be a free born son of God at the same time; " For if the Son make you free ye shall be free indeed," but this character is made free by the Son and yet sold under sin: now one sold under another against his will is what common language calls a slave. So is it with this character, " For that which I do I " allow not; but what I would I do not: but what I hate that do I." " If then I do that which I would not, I consent to the law that it is " good." Like the impious heathen, *Video meliora proboque, deteriora sequor.* I see better things and approve them, but pursue the more pernicious. Then out of thine own mouth will I judge thee, thou wicked servant. Thou knowest thy Lord's will, and approvest it, but dost not perform it: thou shalt be beaten with many stripes. And yet this character is called a christian. But if a slave to sin be a christian who is not?

But hear his reasoning. " It is no more I that do it but sin that " dwelleth in me." This man then is the temple and agent of sin; it dwelleth in him, and he acteth it out. But christians are the temple of the living God, and the Spirit of God dwelleth in them; and if any man defile the temple of God him will God destroy. (1 Cor. 3. 16, 17.) Therefore, " Whosoever sinneth hath " not seen him neither known him." (1 Jno. 3. 6.) This person therefore is not a christian, but an assumed character, under the power of sin, convicted, but not acquainted with Christ.

The next verses are only a kind of repetition of the same workings, expressing the man's anxiety about his condition. But he adds, " I find then a law, that when I would do good evil is present with " me. For I delight in the law of God after the inward man." This is counted an infallible proof that this whole description applies to the christian, not considering the essential deficiency which would deed give themselves wholly to God and yield to nothing else. "For "though we walk in the flesh, we do not war after the flesh: (for the "weapons of our warfare are not carnal, but mighty through God to "the pulling down of strong holds:) casting down imaginations, "[reasonings] and every high thing that exalteth itself against the "knowledge of God, and bringing into captivity every thought to "the obedience of Christ." (2 Cor. 10. 3, 5.)

The conquered are not conquerors. If a man contend against the flesh, and be at all overcome, so as to commit sin or be defiled in his spiri, he cannot be said to be free from sin, "For of whomsoever "a man is overcome, of the same is he brought into bondage." (2 Pet. 2. 19.) And though his freedom may have been proposed to him, and he may have engaged in the war, he has not yet gained his point—he is not born of God. "We know that whosoever is "born of God sinneth not; but he that is begotten of God keepeth "himslf, and that wicked one toucheth him not;" (Jno. 5. 18.) therefore to be brought into captivity to the law of sin is incompatible with being a christian indeed. (Ro. 7. 33.)

Enough is said to satisfy any man, who doth not yield to prejudice and the carnal mind, more than to truth, that they who are christians indeed do not sin, and are in no degree subject to serve sin. But knowing the force of education and the strength of prepossession on the mind, that the unwary, though intentionally honest, may be liable to overlook the evidence, we shall here add a series of scriptures in connection, so plain and pointed, that nothing but wilful dishonesty can easily ward off the conviction, in those who value the truth of the scriptures. "And every man that hath this hope in him purifieth "himself even as he [that is Christ] is pure. Whosoever commit- "teth sin transgresseth also the law: for sin is the transgression of the "law. And ye know that he was manifested to take away our sins: "and in him is no sin. Whosoever abideth in him sinneth not: who- "soever sinneth hath not seen him neither known him. Little child- "ren, let no man deceive you: he that doeth righteousness is right- "eous even as he (the Son of God) is righteous. He that committeth "sin is of the devil: for the devil sinneth from the beginning. For "this purpose the Son of God was manifested, that he might destroy "the works of the devil. Whosoever is born of God doth not com- "mit sin; for his seed remaineth in him: and he cannot sin, because "he is born of God. *In this* the children of God are manifest, and "the children of the devil: whosoever doeth not righteousness is not "of God, neither he that loveth not his brother." Thus boldly and unequivocally do the scriptures testify, that sin is not found in those who are born of God, or are the true followers of Christ.

The learned student of Edinburgh, Macknight, on the passage; "Whosoever is born of God doth not commit sin;" which he renders; *Whosoever is begotten of God doth not work sin;* hath the following remark. "By translating *ε ποιει αμαρτιαν* [ou poiei amar- "tian] doth not work sin according to the true import of the phrase, "the argument drawn from this text in favor of the sinless perfection

NOT SINNERS.

of the saints in the present life, is precluded." By this gloss he hath aimed to prove that all a christian can gain in the present stage of action is to not make a trade or business of sinning, or perhaps to not sin willingly, as often expressed: for should we take his comment in an acceptation more favorable to him, it must lose all its force; because, to understand his phraseology, *Doth not work sin*, as meaning, *Doth not sin*, or *doth not commit sin* at all, would be to make him acknowledge the fact which he aimed to overturn. But the nakedness and impotency of his criticism might have appeared to himself had he been critic enough to inspect with some dis.ce.nment, the next clause of the verse; " For his seed remaineth in him: and *he cannot sin* [ȣ δυναται αμαρτανειν] because he is born of God." Or this; " Whosoever sinneth [πας ο αμαρτανων] hath not seen him neither known him." Or had he attended, without prepossession to another phrase of the same apostle on the same subject. " We know that whosoever " is born of God sinneth not: [πας ο γεγεννημενος; *every one* who is " born, or hath been begotten, ουχ αμαρτανει, sinneth not, or doth not " sin: real sin is not chargeable or applicable to him in the minutest " sense;] but he that is begotten of God *keepeth* himself, and *that* " *wicked one toucheth him not*: [ο γεννηθεις, one who is a subject of " that birth or begetting which is of God."] According to our author's reasoning we may conclude that a christian is about on equal standing with the devil with respect to the commission of sin; " For the devil sinneth from the beginning; [αμαρτανει;] but *whosoever is begotten of God*; every christian; *doth not work sin*; [αμαρτιαν ου ποιει;] yet according to him, he sinneth; [αμαρτανει;] that is, he is just equal to the devil, except that the devil may be the oldest and most deliberate. Such labored and unnatural turns; such forced constructions, in the writings of studious and learned men, show the amazing influence of systematic prepossession, and the indispensable necessity for the light of the Spirit in those who would give a genuine and liquidated explication of the holy scriptures. The language of the apostle is explicit, plain and simple, that they who are born or begotten of God, (for the Greek word is the same) *do not sin*.

Where can the abettors of sin in God's children, find such express and pointed testimony? Until they can, it is time for them to cease to sow pillows to all armholes, to daub with untempered mortar, to soothe and flatter souls with the notion of eternal life, while they come short of the mark which Christ and his apostles have given. But such testimony is not to be found: not a single text of holy scripture saith, that those who are born of God commit sin, or have sin in them, or any thing tantamount. Other scriptures might be adduced, but the above are sufficient here: the evidence is as pointed as language will admit.

It is indeed the greatest absurdity to suppose that christians commit sin, or are subject to sin; for there is no supposable cause for such a state of things, unless they either choose to sin, or God chooseth they should, or they cannot avoid it. The two first are too absurd to be avowed. If the last be true; it is either because God is unable, or unwilling to save them; which involves the same absurdity, as no violence to the conscience or agency of man, is requisite to caue them to do what they desire to do. To argue that chiistians sin through the strength and subtlety of the temptations of the devil, notwithstanding the will of God and their own chcice to the contrary, as many are weak enough to say, this at once acknowledges the devil to possess more power and influence over christians, than God himself possesseth, consequently, that the devil is most wise and most powerful.

After all; people are so fond of a pretext for sin, of a name to live while they are dead *in* sin and not *to* sin, and especially so unwilling to take the conviction, that they are the true body of Christ, and they only, who are free from sin, that some will likely raise objections, saying, May not people be deceived, and think they do not commit sin when they do? This objection, weak as it is, I have heard from the mouth of professors of great zeal, and no contemptable degree of respectability. But be that objection as it may, there can be no deception in the strongest confidence that they who are visible sinners, they who are conscious to themselves that they are sinners, and they who acknowledge they are sinners, and under that impression are habitually praying to God to forgive their daily transgressions, are none of them christians. Neither can there be any deception in setting aside those bodies of people, whose faith it is, that all men commit sin, even after they are born of God, as being none else than branches of anti-christ. If people may be deceived where no sin appears and none is acknowledged, no deceptions need be dreaded where it is manifest, or where it is acknowledged to exist. If wolves may appear in sheeps clothing, sheep do not appear in wolves' clothing.

But let it be considered against whom this objection is leveled: not man but God—not a scheme of men but the teaching of Christ. If the rule of Christ and his apostles be deceptious, if his teaching be unsafe, it is time to look out for another head of the body But if Christ is a true teacher, there is no deception in the case; his word and those of his apostles put the matter out of doubt; " If a man " love me, he will keep my word—He that loveth me not keepeth " not my sayings." " Either make the tree good and his fruit good, " or else make the tree corrupt and his fruit corrupt: for the tree " is known by his fruit." " He that followeth me shall not walk in " darkness, but shall have the light of life." " He that loveth his " brother abideth in the light and there is none occasion of stumbling " in him." [Jno. 14. 23, 24. Matt. 12. 23. Jno. 8. 12. 1 Jno. 2. 10.] Now who will pretend to be christians and not love the brethren? yet many, if not all of those who profess in the various denominations called christian, complain of getting into darkness, and being in great darkness. Let all men spedily determine who are the true witnesses, Christ and his apostles, or these dark souls.

But perhaps it will be pleaded, that the rule of Christ and his apostles is true and safe enough, but the danger is in the weakness and inability of men to comprehend it. Men are very apt to plead thus, saying, He is true, but we are false—the wrong is all in us. This objection reflects just as much dishonor on Christ, and is just as weak as in any other form; for Christ gave his instructions for the use of men just such as they are, their weakness, darkness and loss being all included, that they might be delivered, walk in the truth, and know it to their satisfaction; "For the Son of man is come to "seek and to save that which was lost" And again, "The Spirit "of the Lord, is upon me, because he hath anointed me to preach "the gospel to the poor; he hath sent me to heal the broken-hearted, "to preach deliverance to the captives, and recovering of sight to "the blind; to set at liberty them that are bruised; to preach the "acceptable year of the Lord." [Luke 19. 10. and 4. 18, 19.] Now to suppose any danger from the weakness and blindness of men respecting the law of Christ, (except in those who are wilfully ignorant and disobedient,) is to impeach the character of Christ as an unsafe and incapable teacher, that is, an impostor, inasmuch as his avouched commission is to relieve those in that very condition. Cease then to contend against the benevolent and condescending king of heaven, who makes the way so plain, that he may run that readeth it—that way in which the wayfaring man though a fool shall not err, and acknowledge the truth—Lay aside all pretensions to be christians, until ye get the faith and works which will stand the test.

Ignorance of the life and power of the gospel may lead some to conclude, that deceivers may live so like true christians, that they cannot be known, or fully distinguished. This argument will be granted to be valid, provided nature can equal the gospel, or the fruits of the gospel are not such as cannot be imitated by the strictest rules of morality, or greatest exertions of wisdom and prudence of natural men. If the life of christians is not such as cannot be imitated, they cannot be distinguished from others; for if any deceivers, or any other class of the children of this world, can produce as good fruit, and consequently as good evidence of ceristianity as the truehearted christian, they will have as good a claim to the character as he, consequently Jesus Christ and his apostles must be found false witnesses, in proposing a rule, and giving instructions, which are insufficient, and by consequence dangerous. But as this will not redily be granted by professors, we shall persist in proving according to their words, that the true church can be known and distinguished from all others.

CHAPTER VI.

Inimitable Love and Union obtain in the Church of Christ, and are manifested in a Joint Inheritance in things temporal as well as spiritual.

THE same rule of judgment, and the same marks by which christians know themselves, and know one another, so as to apprehend the body of Christ collectively, serve in the main, to prove to the world and to all men, who are the true church. For notwithstanding the wicked may call them devils, and reproach them as deceivers, because of the very evidences of Christianity which they manifest, such are these same evidences, that they must be confessed to proceed from a source superior to human wisdom and human art. Therefore, "Beware of false prophets, who come to you in sheep's " clothing, but inwardly they are ravening wolves. Ye shall know " them by their fruits. Do men gather grapes of thorns or figs of " thistles? Even so, every good tree bringeth forth good fruit; but " a corrupt tree bringeth forth evil fruit. A good tree cannot bring " forth evil fruit; neither can a corrupt tree bring forth good fruit— " Wherefore by their fruits ye shall know them." [Matt. 7. 15 &c.] No doubt false prophets may appear with great zeal, and make a fair show; but they can nevertheless be known; *for by their fruits ye shall know them*. Now these fruits can be known and distinguished from all others, else an appeal to them as the criterian by which to distinguish the true prophets, or church, from the false, would be useless. Thus it is written; " In this the children of God " are manifest, and the children of the devil: whosoever doeth not " righteousness is not of God, neither he that loveth not his brother." Here then is the evidence; " Love is the fulfilling of the law." [Ro. 13. 10.] So also the substance and work of the gospel appear to concentrate in nothing so much as love; " For in Jesus Christ nei- " ther circumcission availeth any thing, nor uncircumcission, but " faith which worketh by love." [Gal. 5. 6.] " And now abideth " faith, hope, charity [love,] these three; but the greatest of these is " charity [love."] "If a man love me he will keep my words: and my " Father will love him, and we will come to him and make our abode " with him." (1 Cor. 13.-13. Jno. 14. 23.) " God is love; and he " that dwelleth in love dwelleth in God and God in him." " Behold, " if God so loved us, we ought also to love one another." (1 Jno. 4. 16, 11.) These scriptures, and a multitude more, show that the substance and work of the gospel dwell in love. Therefore said Jesus Christ, "By this shall all men know that ye are my disciples, if ye have " love one to another." (Jno. 13. 25.)

Men are so tenacious of that kind of sense that the life of a christian is so hidden a matter as not to be known by any means, that many will probably conclude, that nothing can be determined by this love, for who knows whether a man's love to the brethren be genuine or not? But the scripture cuts this matter short; for *by this shall all men know*; they are not left to guess at it, but *they shall know* that ye are my disciples; love therefore must be satisfactorily manifested to all candid men, where ever it existeth.

But let it be granted that love is not known by intuitive knowledge, that the gift and sensation, or internal affection of love is not visible, or in the abstract, to the natural man, it can nevertheless be discovered in its operations; for as faith without works is dead, being alone, so love without effects would be a contradiction of terms. " But " whoso keepeth his word, in him verily is the love of God perfect" ed : hereby know we that we are in him." (1 Jno. 2. 5.) " But " whoso hath this world's good, and seeth his brother have need, and " shutteth up his bowels of compassion from him, how dwelleth the " love of God in him? My little children, let us not love in word, " neither in tongue, but in deed, [or work] and in truth, and hereby " we know that we are of the truth and shall assure our hearts before " him." (1 Jno. 3. 17 to 19) Love therefore is manifested by its operations as the cause by the effect. But as the love of the body of Christ is peculiar to his members, separate and distinct from all love of the children of this world, (otherwise it would not distinguish them) so its operations must be such as do not pertain to any rank or class except the aforesaid body of Christ so as to prove the present agency and indwelling of the Spirit of God.

Now the immediate production of love, in the members of Christ's body, and that also by which the world are to know and believe them to be the people of his love, is union—such an union as the world know not. " That they all may be one; as thou, Father, art in me, " and I in thee, that they also may be one in us: that the world may " believe that thou hast sent me. And the glory which thou gavest me " I have given them; that they may be one, even as we are one. I " in thee, and thou in me, that they may be perfect in one; and that " the world *may know* that thou hast sent me, and *hast loved them*, " *as thou hast loved me*." (Jno. 17. 20, to 23.) This then is the state of the body of Christ here on earth, in sight of the world, that they might know and believe the work of God—Perfect in one. This evidence, in the estimation of Jesus Christ, is sufficient to convince the world, Who are the people of God's love—and who is he that will scruple the propriety of his judgment? But where such an union doth not subsist, as evidences the present agency and indwelling of the Spirit of God, as being his holy habitation, the true evidence of christianity is wanting.

This union is of a different nature, separate and distinct from all the union which can possibly subsist among the children of the flesh, professed christians or others: " The unity of the Spirit in the bond " of peace." (Eph. 4. 3.) Therefore it is that true believers are able to maintain and increase in that union which the world cannot teach; gathering together more and more as they increase in the work of God in Christ Jesus, as it was prophesied of them; " There" fore they shall come and sing in the height of Zion, and shall flow "together to the goodness of the Lord, for wheat, and for wine, and for oil, and for the young of the flock and of the herd: and their soul shall be as a watered garden; and they shall not sorrow any more at all. Then shall the virgin rejoice in the dance, both young men and old together: for I will turn their mourning into joy, and will comfort them, and make them rejoice from their sorrow. And I will satiate the soul of the priest with fatness, and my people shall be satisfied with my goodness, saith the Lord." (Jer. 31. 12, to 14.) "Now, therefore, ye are no more strangers and foreigners, but fellow citizens with the saints, and of the household of God; and are built upon the foundation of the apostles and prophets, Jesus Christ himself being the chief corner-stone; in whom all the building, fitly framed together, groweth unto an holy temple in the Lord; in whom ye also are builded together for an habitation of God through the Spirit." (Eph. 2. 19, to 22.)

Numerous other passages might be quoted to prove that christians are united by one Spirit into one body, as the habitation or temple of God. And as like cause produceth like effect, the unity of Spirit within, produceth unity of operation without, for as is the fountain so are the streams. Therefore it is that believers are united in a manner and degree which the world cannot imitate, and the rule of Christ is proved true by experiment. Thus also it took place in the days of the apostles; "And the multitude of them that believed were of one heart and of one soul: neither said any of them that ought of the things which he possessed was his own; but they had all things common. And with great power gave the apostles witness of the resurrection of the Lord Jesus: and great grace was upon them all. Neither was there any among them that lacked: for as many as were possessors of lands or houses sold them, and brought the prices of the things which were sold, and laid them down at the apostle's feet: and distribution was made to every man according as he had need." (Acts 4. 32, &c.)

Not only the example of the primitive christians, in whom dwelt the Spirit of Christ, but the doctrine of the apostles afterwards teaches the same union and disinterested benevolence and charity. "Let no man seek his own, but every man another's wealth." "Fulfil ye my joy, that ye be like minded, having the same love, being of one accord, [Greek, one soul,] of one mind. Let nothing be done through strife or vain glory; but in lowliness of mind let each esteem others better than themselves. Look not every man on his own things but every man also on the things of others. Let this mind be in you which was also in Christ Jesus." "Let the brother of low degree rejoice in that he is exalted: but the rich in that he is made low." (1 Cor. 10. 24. Phil. 2. 2. to 5. Jas. 1. 9, 10.)

Thus the church and people of God are united in one body and in one Spirit and have all things common, a common interest and common inheritance in all good things, whether temporal or spiritual. And all those who yield to the truth of God, impelled by the same Spirit, know nothing better to do with all they have and are then to give all up to God; that is, to his people; for this is to give it to him, as it is written; " Inasmuch as ye have done it to one of the " least of these my brethren, ye have done it to me." (Matt. 25. 40.) This fulfils the word of the Lord by the prophet, to his church, in the day when her deliverance should come. " Arise and thresh. O " daughter of Zion: for I will make thine horn iron, and I will make " thy hoofs brass: and thou shalt beat in pieces many people: and I " will consecrate their gain unto the Lord, and their substance unto " the Lord of the whole earth." (Mic. 4. 13.)

The world have no such union, neither can have, because they are governed by a different principle incapable of producing it; not a principle of purity in the Spirit, but a fleshly principle of lust, as it is written; " All that is in the world, the lust of the flesh, the lust " of the eyes, and the pride of life, is not of the Father, but is of the " world." (1 Jno. 2. 16.) God is Spirit; and when man fell from God, he fell from the Spirit into the flesh; hence the flesh is considered as being in opposition to the Spirit. God is love; and therefore when man fell from God, he fell out of love into lust. The love of God unites, but the lust of the flesh separates and divides. " From " whence come wars and fightings among you? come they not " hence, even of your lusts that war in your members?" (Jam. 4. 1.) The world therefore cannot live in a joint union; jealousies and divisions arise too easily, because they are in the flesh, and walk as men, that is, in the fleshly, fallen nature of men. " For whereas there is " among you envying, and strife, and divisions, are ye not carnal and " walk as men." (1 Cor. 3. 3.)

To avoid these things therefore as much as possible, and partake such comfort as Esau's portion, the earth, affords, the world find it expedient to keep a convenient distance apart, at least so far, that every one can have his own moiety separate and unmixed with that of his neighbor, or even his brother. And if at any time, two or more remain in conjunction for a time, it is on the principle of each one advancing his individual profit, better than in any other method, still keeping the dividing line marked. And whatever small digressions from this general state of things, may happen in a few instances, these do no honor to the profession of christianity, and are no proof of the reality of those who profess it; for those who make no pretense to the profession, and some of them even to the belief of it at all, equal, if not exceed, the boldest professors amongst the denominations of reputed christians. This proves that all those professors have gotten, falls short of the mark, because it can be equaled, and in many instances, exceeded by men who do not pretend to be influenced by any thing more than natural reason.

Thus father and son must divide as soon as one, particularly the latter, concludes it is for his individual advantage. Brother and brother must part, lest one should oppress the other, or take some undue advantage of him: or perhaps their families are in danger of disagreeing—their love is warmest at a distance. Professors and their brother professors must be apart; and count it a great matter, if they live in one neighborhood and have no jars; and perhaps boast of what brotherly love is among them—that they love their brethren as themselves. But let them come into contact; let them take each other's property, and minister it to their families indiscriminately, as every one hath need; or let one come to another, and ask favors of value from day to day, and say nothing of any retribution; or let them enter into a stipulation to be thus liberal and disinterested with each other, and the scale will soon be turned; jealousies will arise and all their christianity cannot prevent them.

Or if professed christians are able to come together and inherit jointly, and so prove in fact, that they possess the character of Christ's disciples, or body, in having love one to another, and having the same care one of another, why do they not put it into practice, and so do honor to their profession, and wipe off reproach from the name of christianity? Or will they presume to say, that their love is sufficient in strength, to overcome every barrier, and bring them together, and keep them so, but is not so great, as to render such a situation desirable? Many have acknowledged that, it is the true and proper order of christians, and that possessing separately is selfish and corrupt. Some have tried it in vain. Others have acknowledged it to be the most comfortable and proper method of living, and some even of those who profess no christianity. But how shall it be effectuated? No human wisdom—no philosophy—no philanthropy—no degree or order of godliness, short of crucifying the flesh with its affections and lusts, each one denying himself, taking up his cross, renouncing the old generation and following Christ in the regeneration, can ever lay a proper foundation for this union. Now when a man is not as willing that his brother should use his property, as he is to use it himself, in the same circumstances, he cannot be said to love his brother as himself. But the members of Christ's body have the same care one of another. And whether one member suffer, all the members suffer with it; or one member be honored, all the members rejoice with it. (1 Cor. 12. 26.)

Any people may live in a manner esteemed peaceable, in their towns and neighborhoods, each one pursuing with eagerness, those measures which he thinks best calculated to subserve his own selfish purposes, and saying to his neighbor, *Touch not mine, and I will not touch thine:* and if occasion require, they can call on the civil authority to settle their disputes. But if the followers of Christ do not exhibit an union, superior to any thing found among other people, how shall all men know them by their love one to another?

That the primitive believers at the day of pentecost and afterwards, did exhibit the most incontestable evidence of their love one to another, when they were of one heart and one soul, having all things common, and dividing their substance as every one had need, and that this love was superior to any love or union found among any other people, no man of understanding and truth will pretend to deny. And by parity of reason it will be granted, that where the same love and union are found, there the same Spirit rules.

At this instant, the same essential and distinguishing characteristics, once exhibited by the primitive believers, are exhibited by the believers of the present day, who have received the faith of Christ's second appearing. Hundreds! Yea thousands in America, happy land of liberty, live together in large families, to the number of thirty, forty, and sometimes sixty or more, like brethren and sisters, or like a company of harmless lambs. And a number of such families form societies, and live in peace and harmony, bound together by no other bond than that of love. On what principle can such a work be effected, except that superior love of the gospel which influenced the primitive christians by a divine unction to become of one heart and one soul?

At the day of Pentecost and afterwards, there were Jews, Greeks, Barbarians, bond and free, bound together by the bonds of love, visibly manifested by union and agreement, to the astonishment of the beholders. Here are the same visible works of that superior love, manifested in colors equally striking. People in large collections, living in peace and harmony; people brought up in different countries; naturally different in their dispositions; different in their educations, their manner of living, their plans of economy, their degrees of industry and degrees of wealth; naturally covetous, proud and self-willed, tenacious of their own plans, and possessed of every other disposition which prompts the children of men to hatred, variance, and the perpetration of evil actions. How are these fashioned alike? On what principle are they united? Let conscience answer, and it will say; *On no other than the present operation of the Spirit of the one and only true God.* This is the work which carries the palm. And we may victoriously say of it; " Where is the wise " man? where is the scribe? where is the disputer of this world? " hath not God made foolish the wisdom of this world?—For after " that in the wisdom of God, the world by wisdom knew not God, it " pleased God by the foolishness of preaching to save them that be- " lieve. For the Jews require a sign, (and so do our nominal profess- " ors,) and the Greeks seek wisdom; but we preach Christ crucified, " to the Jews a stumbling block, and to the Greeks foolishness; but " to those who are called, both Jews and Greeks, Christ the power of " God, and the wisdom of God." This then is the work in which the wisdom of their wise men shall perish, and the understanding of their prudent men shall be hid. (See Isa. 29. 16. Compare 1 Cor. 1. 18, to 24.)

If people therefore in these days demand a miracle, here it is; a work, even a marvellous work, out of the ordinary course of nature, contrary to it, and which cannot proceed from any other source than the present agency and indwelling of the Spirit of God, as in his own living temple—a miracle which cannot be imitated—of a spiritual nature—an abiding miracle, containing the essence of the gospel of the kingdom of God—a miracle confessedly superior to all miracles of another kind. " Charity never faileth: but whether there be pro- " phesies they shall fail; whether there be tongues they shall cease;

"whether there be knowledge it shall vanish away—and now abideth faith, hope, charity, these three; but the greatest of these is charity." [1 Cor. 13. 8, to 13.]

It is a question with some, whether the Spirit of Christ leads to so great an union as to possess a joint interest in all things, as well outward as spiritual; or whether it is necessary to practise such an union to be christians indeed? This question can exist in that heart only, where selfishness prevails above every other principle; for out of the abundance of the heart the mouth speaketh; and where the Spirit of Christ prevails it saith, Look not every one to his own things, but every one also to the things of another.

But the very existence of such an union proves it to be of God and in the Spirit of Christ. For fact proves principle; or the existence of any effect proves the existence of the cause producing it. And the existence of any effect which cannot be produced by any cause save one, proves invariably the existence of that cause. But it is proved in fact, that the aforesaid union in a joint interest cannot be supported by any cause separate and distinct from the Spirit of Christ dwelling and acting in the people who are thus united. Yet said union doth exist in a joint interest: it therefore proves the agency and indwelling of the Spirit of Christ, and that said union is according to the mind of Christ and proceeds from him as his own work.

A candid attention however to a few portions of scripture, in addition to those already considered, will sufficiently dissipate all doubts on that point. Jesus said, "There is no man who hath left house, or brethren, or sisters, or father, or mother, or wife, or children, or lands, for my sake and the gospel's, but he shall receive an hundred fold now in this time, houses, and brethren, and sisters, and mothers, and children, and lands, with persecutions, and in the world to come eternal life." [Mark 10. 29, 30.] But how can they who forsake all for Christ's sake and the gospel's, receive an hundred fold in this present time, except only on the principle of a joint union and gospel equality? How could a believer possess an hundred fold of houses and lands, except only on that principle in which he could possess all that which his brethren possessed, while they also possessed the same in joint union? For an hundred fold of private interest is out of the question; not only in fact, but even in theory; common sense forbids it.

If any argue, that the promise of Christ relates to the superior degree of comfort enjoyed in their former relations and possessions; it may be asked, Where are the society of professors who are not heard to complain, murmur and fret, at their temporal inconveniencies, wants, losses and disappointments, as much as other people? Where are the professed christians who enjoy an hundred fold more comfort, union and peace with their kinsfolk? And if they have not, according to their own method of reasoning, it is either because Christ has not been faithful to his promise, or they have not complied with his conditions by forsaking all

But that this cannot be the meaning of this promise is proved from this, that when any man forsakes all for Christ's sake and for the gospel's, he incurs the enmity of his kinsfolk on that account. "Think not, said Jesus, that I am come to send peace on earth: I " came not to send peace but a sword. For I am come to set a man " at variance against his father, and the daughter against her mother, " and the daughter-in-law against her mother-in-law. And a man's " foes shall be they of his own household." [Matt. 10. 34, 35, 36.] This shows that to forsake all for Christ, is something real, not in word and in tongue, but in work and in truth, something manifest to the family and kinsfolk, which engages their resentment; and therefore, that the brethren and sisters, and mothers, and children, as well as houses and lands, are not according to the old order at all, but according to the order of Christ, whose kindred are those who do the will of his Father in heaven: Accordingly the promise includes no wife, though the forsaking does, and for this plain reason, that the works which are appropriate to a wife according to the old order, have no part in Christ: their place is not found with him. But farther; How can any be said to forsake all for Christ's sake and the gospel's, while they continue to hold them as formerly, at their individual disposal, and there is no discoverable difference between their claim to the same kind of possessions, and the same claim in those who make no pretence to have forsaken all for Christ?

These things show what the truth is; that those, and those only, who have forsaken all, according to the true order of the gospel, can and do enjoy an hundred fold more satisfaction than formerly, and that there is no way in which a man can forsake houses and lands, brethren and sisters, father and mother, and at the same time receive an hundred fold according to the promise of Christ, but by renouncing his former selfish disposition and claim, in *heart and practice*, with all the gratifications pertaining to said claim, and coming into a joint union, in which what is possessed by an individual, is possessed by the whole, so that a just and impartial equality reigns among the whole, and the rich and the poor share an equal and universal privilege. Granting therefore, that the promise in consideration is expressed in language somewhat figurative, it admits and requires, an acceptation as literal as can be expected in representing spiritual things by natural.

Another passage of scripture which will not admit any acceptation except such as supports the faith of an union in joint interest, and is as free from figure in itself and in its connection as perhaps any language can be, is this ; " It remaineth that both they that have " wives be as though they had none ; and they that weep as though " they wept not; and they that rejoice, as though they rejoiced not; " and they that buy, as though they possessed not; and they that " use this world as not abusing it: for the fashion of this world pas- " seth away." [1 Cor. 7. 29, to 31.] How can this scripture be fulfilled in any people except those in whom an union in joint interest subsists, and an impartial equality reigns? How can a man buy, and be as though he possessed not, and the fashion of this world pass away, when he buys for himself distinctly from his brethren? or to hold at his own individual disposal? for though he should be somewhat liberal in the use of his possession, it is all within the compass of the fashion of this world.

Some argue that the apostle had respect to the state of men after the dissolution of the body. But what concern have disembodied Spirits with buying and selling? or with using this world? And if the argument be stated thus, that those who *now* buy, will *then* be as though they possessed not. That is not what is said; and his meaning is best known by what he said. It also represents the apostle's language weak and futile to make him say of those in a world of spirits, that they are as though they possessed not, when it cannot be said they either use or possess this world in any sense whatever. Besides the reason annexed for that state of things which the apostle describes, is by no means favorable to its having its accomplishment in the disembodied state—not, because we go out of the world, but, *for the fashion of this world passeth away.*

Now the fashion, the known fashion of this world, is, for those who have wives to be as though they have them, using them in that which it would be unjustifiable to make common; for those who buy to possess, and be as though they possessed, holding their possessions as their peculiar right; and for those who use the things of this world, to do it according to their own pleasure, without proper regard to the fear of God and the promotion of his cause. Whereas in the church of God, those who come into union, if they have wives, with Peter, they forsake them, and no longer make any use of them which would be unjustifiable in any case. So that they are literally as though they had none. And in them is fulfilled the scripture which saith, "Marriage is honorable in all, and the bed undefiled," because they abstain, most rigidly, from all works pertaining to marriage, which are dishonorable, (according to the practical testimony of all people by their concealment,) and which alone ever defiled the marriage bed. And this is the only admissible acceptation of that scripture, because it is manifest from the law, that no married Jew kept his bed undefiled.

Also, in the church those who buy are as though they possessed not, because they only possess in common with their brethren, and claim no private property: as having nothing yet possessing all things. Charity seeketh not her own: Let no man seek his own but every man that of another. For the man who has forsaken all for Christ, has taken up his cross and followeth him, and hath found that treasure which is with Christ and endureth to eternal life in heaven, is not careful, or even willing, to inherit any separate treasure or estate, either real or personal. Nevertheless it is not the faith or practice of the church to require any man or people, to make a sacrifice or surrender of their temporal interest to the common use of the society, contrary to their own faith and best understanding. It is only the practice of those whose faith it is so to do; who have maturely considered the subject, and believe such sacrifice and common inheritance to be for the honor of God and his gospel as well as for their own best interest, because they desire to inherit substance. Until their faith is thus ripe for a joint interest, believers are admitted to a free privilege in things spiritual, their separate interest notwithstanding.

Again, if in the order of a joint union in Christ they use the things of this world, that is, material things, they do it to the noble and superior purpose of subserving the work of God in Christ, to the edification of his church. Whether ye eat or drink, or whatsoever ye do, do all to the glory of God: this therefore is using so as not abusing.

On the whole therefore we conclude that this language of the apostle is properly descriptive of a time and work which should take place on earth, when God, according to his promise, should create new heavens and a new earth, wherein dwelleth righteousness.

A consideration of the new heavens and new earth may serve as a farther confirmation and illustration of the order of the church in a joint union and interest. For what can mean these new heavens and new earth, but a new state and order of things, both in outward things, and in things relating to the Spirit. Or will any be so weak as to suppose they mean the literal creation of another heaven and earth? or if this language be supposed to relate to a time and state of things when all shall be heaven, and the earth put out of the account, what then is the meaning of the new earth?

But the truth may be illustrated in this particular, by the case of a man in Christ. He is said to be a new creature; not because there is any change in the identity of his existence; he is the same person as before, having the same soul and body. The change is not physical; he has new objects and pursuits, is converted from the flesh to the Spirit, from the old order of things in Adam, to the new order in Christ, having renounced and put off the old man with his deeds which are corrupt according to the deceitful lusts, and put on the new man who after God is created in righteousness and true holiness. So when Christ possesseth that kingdom on earth which is promised, and every individual in it is thus renewed, such an happy change in spirit will be produced, and as the effect thereof, in outward economy, as is fitly represented by new heavens and a new earth. For that such a state and order of things must and will take place on the earth cannot reasonably be doubted by those who believe the scriptures and pay due respect to them: after the reign of the beast is finished—when the sanctuary is cleansed, and when the kingdom, and the dominion, and the greatness of the kingdom under the whole heaven, shall be given to the people of the saints of the MOST HIGH. But once more.

Another promise is. " *He that overcometh shall inherit all things.*" This promise is also made to every individual overcomer; and therefore showeth that a joint union and equality is the very order of heaven itself, and is therefore the true character and proper order of that kingdom for which Christ taught his disciples to pray, in which the will of God is done on earth as it is in heaven. For short of such a state of things no true distinction can be made between the false prophets and the true, or between the wolves and the sheep: neither can there be a true distinction between the churches of anti-christ and the church of Christ.

Thus we have stated, in some leading particulars, the true character of the church, or body of Christ, according to the scriptures, and shown the evidence by which they are to be certainly known and distinguished from all other people, which consists of love and union not to be imitated or counterfeited. No doubt many of the carnally wise and learned among the professing world, will sneer at this evidence and these statements, as being inferior and trivial, because out of the line of their high sense and exalted notions of christianity, according to their own minds, and not according to Christ. But the city of God's people is low in a low place, and the inhabitants are meek and lowly in their spirits; let those therefore who are disposed to sneer and contemn, cease from so doing, until they can disprove by experience the evidence here stated.

It is here stated that a joint union and interest, with an impartial equality, reigns at this instant among the believers, who have the faith of the second appearing of Christ; and it is proved by scripture testimony, in conjunction with plain reason, as clearly as any unbiased man can ask, to be the effect of the Spirit of Christ in the gospel, and the necessary product of that Spirit, without which there can be no true church. It is also stated that this inimitable love and union are miraculous in the most noble sense of the word, as being superior to all philosophy, philanthropy, or any other science or order of knowledge, exclusive of the wisdom of God by the cross, and as being truly spiritual and comprehending the very essence and treasure of the gospel, and therefore evincing the present agency and indwelling of the Holy Spirit. If this consequence be denied by those who scoff, let them prove by experiment, that the same consequences, that is, the same love and union, with the same united interests, can be produced from some other source. Until that is effected, they will leave us and all judicious men, in possession of this faith, that the above premises and conclusions have their foundation in that immoveable rock, TRUTH.

I shall therefore close this chapter with removing an objection or two. The first is, That other people live in common interest and joint union as well as we. And particularly the monastic orders of the Roman Catholic church have been alledged as an example equally evidential of the faith of Christ on the score of unity of Spirit and community of interest. I have no dispute in my mind, but some may obtain partially the order of the church of Christ by possessing partially the same form of faith. And whatever hath any part of the truth of God ought so far to be approved; and where there is an increase of light, producing an increase of order and good fruits, it is still more hopeful: but to produce good fruits in perfection a full and correct faith is requisite. No doubt but every man will find a measure of justification, in proportion to the honesty and perseverance with which he bears his cross against all evil in his knowledge and denies himself, for the truth's sake. And if the Catholic monastic orders retain something of the form of godliness, from the apostolic dispensation, (as no doubt they do, and are almost the only church that can exhibit plausible evidence for such a pretension,) that cannot disannul the propriety of the order of the true church, nor invalidate its testimony wherever it is found; neither can it prove the Roman Catholic church, or their monastic orders, to be in equal possession of the truth and unity of the Spirit with the believers in Christ's second appearing, unless the fruits of the former be in all things equal to those of the latter, when all attending circumstances and apparent hindrances are taken into the account. It still remains true that the tree is known by its fruit; and that the existence of an effect which can subsist by one cause only proves the existence of that cause.

But the Roman monastic orders bear a very distant resemblance indeed to the believers in Christ's second appearing. They are a select number professing greater sanctity than the church in general, and consequently greater than is indispensably necessary to perfect salvation, for they do not dispute the justice of the hope of salvation in those members of the body who are not monks and nuns. But these believers aspire to no more sanctity than that which is sufficient to perfect salvation or full redemption, knowing no perfect salvation short of a full and perfect cross. Those are an excepted and dependent branch of the body supported mainly by the gratuities and other contributions of the church. These support themselves by their own industry, working with their own hands doing the thing which is good, to satisfy their own necessities and to have to give to those who need. These are free from the incumbrance of wife, husband or children to embarrass the mind in their first entrance. These include all classes of people, married and unmarried, old and young, rich and poor, who are willing to have salvation by the cross of Christ. Those are bound by oath or solemn vow to maintain their life of celibacy. These have no bond but their faith and choice, or love to the truth. Those are patronised by public approbation and authority; while these are marked out as enemies to mankind and dangerous to society. But with the faith and power which those have, let them attempt, like these, to unite into one body, and advance with the same celerity—let them include in their community of interest, the old and the young, the rich and the poor, the married and the unmarried—let them bring into one, whole families, with their various wants, and other diversities of situation—and let parents labor equally for the support of the children of others as for their own, so that things may appear in their true effects, and they will find themselves as weak as other people.

But another objection or difficulty may be, That to come into this order of common interest, to dispose of family and property in this manner, intermingling in the common mass, with an unknown people, their manner and spirit also greatly unknown, is too great a sacrifice: God cannot require it. But God requires all; for said Jesus, Whosoever he be of you who doth not forsake all that he hath cannot be my disciple.. (Luke 14. 33.) Yet not unreasonably; as I have just stated above that it is the faith of believers so to do, and that one side of such faith there is no requisition of that kind. It is not to be expected that people in common circumstances will unite with them at all, unless moved by the faith that these have the truth and know the way of salvation; neither is it required or expected of any to undertake any degree of community of interest beyond what their own faith approves, and their own understanding and choice sanction. Accordingly some live more years and some fewer in their private families and private interest; and still hold their union to the body, keep their justification and find salvation from all sin in proportion as they keep an effectual and uniform cross against sin in their knowledge. But the testimony of Christ's second appearing excells in this, that it effectuates the gathering into one, those whose faith it is to come into that heavenly order—The unity of the Spirit in the bond of peace.

CHAPTER VII.

Without the cross of Christ no power over sin. The Abomination that maketh desolate, or Man of sin.

FARTHER to elucidate the true character of the church of Christ, and to evince the impossibility of supporting the character without being possessed of the real faith of Christ in obedience, that is, the impossibility of appearing to be christians without being so in reality, let it be considered, That the real faith of Christ cannot be kept without bearing his cross. " If any man will come after me, " let him deny himself, and take up his cross, and follow me." (Matt. 16. 24.) He doth not say follow Adam, or Moses, or David, but *follow me.*

A fundamental error among those who profess the christian name, is in not distinguishing properly and radically, between Christ and Adam, or the old creation and the new, and between Christ and Moses, or the law and the gospel. Therefore, in stating the character and duty of christians, they are as likely, if not more so, to introduce those things which pertain to the law, or to the first Adam, as those which belong to Christ and his followers. This error is the supporter of many more. But the scriptures make it evident, that the order of Christ is not the order of the old creation in any of its different forms, insomuch that those who follow Christ are no more of this world. " They are not of the world, even as I am not of the world." (Jno. 17. 16.) Those who follow Christ, follow him, not in the generation, but in the regeneration. " The first man is of the earth, "earthy; the second man is the Lord from heaven. As is the earthy, "such are they also that are earthy; and as in the heavenly, such are "they also that are heavenly." (1 Cor. 15. 47, 48.)

Now a proper understanding of the order, cross and work of Christ, will greatly assist in discriminating between the body of Christ and other people. Some particulars have been already stated relating to the order of Christ, by which his people are distinguished from others, as their being free from sin, their love and union. But as every effect must have its cause, it will not be improper to inquire, and assign some reasons, why no people can live in the same union of the Spirit, except those who believe that Christ hath made his second appearance.

It will be remembered, that it is written, that the power of the holy people should be scattered, and that the abomination of desolation spoken of by Daniel the prophet should stand in the holy place. Now if it can be found that the abomination of desolation is standing where it ought not, that will give satisfaction that the faith and participation of the second appearance of Christ are necessary to keeping the unity of the Spirit in the bond of peace, because that abomination was to remain in the holy place, or temple of God, until the coming of the Lord, as hath been before shown. So that when the abomination had once gotten in and obtained a possession where it ought not, the true order of that holy place could never be kept again, until the Lord came, to turn it out, or to destroy it. It is therefore indispensably necessary that they who are able to keep the true order of God, be possessed of the faith, and do actually partake of Christ in his second appearing. And if it can be shown what that abomination is which was spoken of by Daniel, and afterwards by Jesus Christ, that will give satisfaction, as to the correctness of the views of those who have the faith of Christ in his second appearance, and also that none can keep the unity of the Spirit in the bond of peace, without the same faith.

I have already shown, that the church, or people of God, are his temple, and that that temple is holy, and an habitation of God through the Spirit, as it is written; "Son of man, the place of my throne, and "the place of the soles of my feet, where I will dwell *in the midst* "*of the children of Israel for ever, and my holy name shall the house* "*of Israel no more defile.*" And again; "For ye are the temple of "the living God; as God hath said, *I will dwell in them, and walk* "*in them;* and I will be their God, and they shall be my people." (Ezek. 43. 7. 2 Cor. 6. 16.)

Now if it can be made appear what the abomination of desolation is, that will more clearly decide, whether it is now standing, and also where it stands. But that it is now standing is already proved, unless Christ hath made his second appearance long enough to consume it; for it was to continue until he came. The business therefore which remains, is to find what is that abomination which maketh desolate, and is the cause why people cannot be united in one body, who have not the faith of Christ in his second appearing.

And 1st. The first character of that abomination, of which I shall take notice, is that it stands in the *holy place*, where it ought not. To put any thing where it ought not to be, is corrupt, but to put into the *holy place*, or temple of God, an unclean thing, that which ought not to be there, is supremely corrupt. Now by inquiring into the order in which the professors of christianity live, and comparing it with the order of Christ, we may find what that is, which keeps its residence *in the place where it ought not*, which doth not belong to the order of Christ, and yet resides uninterruptedly among the professors of his name, who have not the faith of his second appearing. There are, at most, but a few exceptions of those with whom the same Spirit of Christ hath some influence.

"The children of this world marry and are given in marriage: "but those accounted worthy to obtain that world and the resurrection "from the dead, neither marry nor are given in marriage." Now all the true followers of Christ are accounted worthy to obtain that world and the resurrection from the dead. It is therefore proved, logically, and to a demonstration, that the true followers of Christ neither marry nor are given in marriage. Observe. It is not said, They will not, as at some future period; but it is said in the present tense, They neither marry nor are given in marriage. But professed christians of nearly all denominations, except those in the faith of Christ's second appearance, marry and are given in marriage. This therefore affords a lively presumption, that this same work of marrying and being one flesh, as a man and his wife are, is the very thing which at least contains the aforesaid abomination; and especially considering, that nothing besides this and what pertains to it, is said by the revelation of God, to be of the world, or of the old creation, and yet approbated by professed christians.

That this is peculiarly the order of the first Adam and his line, is sufficiently evident by the very words of the scripture. "Therefore "shall a man leave his father and his mother, and shall cleave to his "wife; and they shall be one flesh." "Have ye not read that he who "made them at the beginning, made them male and female, and said, "For this cause shall a man leave father and mother, and shall cleave "to his wife: and they twain shall be one flesh." (Gen. 2. 24. Matt. 19. 4, 5.) But no such appointment was ever made by God to Jesus Christ the Father of the new creation and Head of the church; no such order or appointment was ever made by Jesus Christ to his followers. And no impropriety can be alledged against recollecting in this place the contrast between Christ Jesus and the first Adam, and the consequent contrast between their posterities. "The first man "is of the earth, earthy; the second man is the Lord from heaven. "As is the earthy, such are they also that are earthy; and as is the "heavenly, such are they also that are heavenly." If therefore the posterity of Adam are in their proper order, to marry, and cleave each man to his wife and be one flesh with her, after the example of their earthly head, by parity of reason, the followers, or children of Christ are in their proper order to marry not, after the example of their heavenly Head, that they may be one Spirit with him: for "He "that is joined to the Lord is one Spirit."(1 Cor, 6. 17.)

To introduce marriage therefore, or natural generation, into the church of Christ, is to put it out of its own order and place it where it ought not to be. Marriage and natural generation are indisputably the order of the flesh and of the first Adam; and the flesh lusteth against the Spirit; therefore, to introduce the generation into christianity, or into the church, is to put into the holy place that which ought not to be there; for the temple of God, which is his church, is holy, as before shown.

2nd. Another mark of the abomination is, that it maketh desolate. To all those who are able to perceive spiritual things, this is self-evidently true of the order and works of the flesh, that they scatter the works of holiness and make all desolate wherever they find a residence. But that which is visible, as a living evidence to all men, natural as well as spiritual, is, that those only who, walking in the faith of Christ, neither marry nor are given in marriage, but renounce the order of the flesh wholly, are able to keep *the unity of the Spirit in the bond of peace*, and to live together in a joint interest, in things temporal as well as spiritual: this is a living and perpetuated proof that the said order of the flesh is the abomination of desolation; or at least contains it, as before observed.

3d. That which maketh desolate is called an abomination—something hateful and to be hated. No doubt the subjects of Adam's line are difficult to persuade that the order and works of the flesh are abominable: "They who are according to the flesh relish the things "of the flesh." But on the other hand, they who are according to the Spirit savor the things of the Spirit; and as the flesh lusteth against the Spirit, and the Spirit against the flesh, it is unavoidable, that the flesh is an abomination to the Spirit, and that all the works of that fleshly order, are an abomination to all those in whom the Spirit resides; "For that which is highly esteemed among men is "an abomination in the sight of God." (Lu. 16. 15.)

But that the works of said order of the flesh are an abomination, all men of common decency bear witness, by scrupulously concealing them; and however they prize them, or for their sake, marriage, as that which legalizes them, their estimation instead of justifying them, only illustrates the truth of that scripture which saith, *Their God is their belly, and their glory is in their shame;* and again, that *It is a shame to speak of the things which are done of them in secret:* these are literally they.

4. I conclude few, if any, deny that the abomination of desolation is the same with the son of perdition spoken of by Paul; not only because their works are tantamount, *desolation* and *perdition*, but also because they are both represented as having their residence in the same holy place, or temple of God; thus the entrance of each is attended with the banishment of the true worship of God, the falling away in the one description, and the taking away of the daily sacrifice in the other. But that this son of perdition, called also, in the

same place, the mystery of iniquity, and that wicked or [Greek] lawless, is the order of the flesh, or at least the nature of that order, it needs only a moderate statement to prove.

1. His first character is that he " *Opposeth and exalteth himself* " *above all that is called God or that is worshiped.*" (2 Thes. 2. 4.) Which very naturally admits this acceptation, that this son of perdition, whatever it is, claims the worship and estimation of all, in preference to any other God, or any conception concerning God. Now observation and experiment prove, that this is strictly true with the order and nature of the flesh. A man may worship what God he pleases, or have what faith concerning God and his worship, he thinks most appropriate to his character, provided he scrupulously maintains an unrestrained license to the works of natural generation.

Although some may think the man is wrong, and sometimes try to convince him by argument, that is the extent; he remains in good credit, is reputed a good citizen, and all hold as great familiarity with him as if his sentiments were more congenial with their own. Thus professors of various denominations and contrary sentiments, and those who profess no christianity at all, nor even give credit to the reality of it, can live together in good civility, good neighborhood and sociality, as freely as if they all possessed one common faith. The husband also, or wife of the unbeliever may be a professed christian, this difference makes no material jar between them, notwithstanding such professors generally agree that such unbelievers are all finally damned. This good christian husband or wife seldom feels any distress of moment about his or her unhappy infidel companion as long as he or she unfailingly adheres to the offerings of the flesh. Thus thousands agree, and live in as much peace as is common among men, while nothing is between them of greater importance than, what they count the worship of God: but difference in matters esteemed of the greatest consequence must by parity of reason produce the greatest disunion and separation. Whence then this agreement amidst such diversity of sentiment and practice? They all agree in the chief matter; *that which demands the estimation of all men, and stands superior to all objects of worship.*

But let any man once receive the faith of Christ in the regeneration, and once begin to testify and practise it, and the sociality is interrupted, and especially with the professed christians; his wife complains that he has awfully fallen, he has forsaken Christ, because he has taken up his cross against the flesh; his neighbors say he is deluded, they are sorry for him, grow shy of him, and soon begin to tell of some evil he hath done, and wish him out the neighborhood; for they count him a troublesome man, or a dead man to them. Thus the separation grows wider and wider, as soon as all their efforts to reclaim him from the faith of Christ, and regain him to the flesh, are found to be of no avail. And what hath he done? He hath determinately engaged in following the footsteps of Christ, and abstaining from those things which they all know Christ never touched, and which they also believe it would be a base impeachment of his character to suppose he touched : therefore the man is deluded and hath forsaken Christ. These things represent the general nature of the consequences of a man's taking up his cross to follow Christ, though the effects are more violent on some occasions than others.

The abettors of the flesh may object a thousand other matters; but fact proves that no religious sentiments make any interruption of moment amongst relations or neighbors, so long as the nature and order of the flesh, or works of natural generation are preserved sacred or inviolable ; but let a man or a woman take up the cross of Christ, and follow him in the regeneration, and the spirits are all around up in arms: this shows that the flesh is in higher estimation than any other God I here speak of matters as they exist in a free government; in those which are incorporated with religious sentiments the true source of division might not be so palpable.

2. This son of perdition also sitteth in the temple of God. This hath already been shown to be the case with the generation.

3. He also showeth himself that he is God. This is also proved to be the case with the generation. The people may call it marriage, which is considered as legalizing the generation ; which is said to be honorable in all, and in its own order without abuse had nothing evil in it; but doth not belong to the order of Christ ; the works also to which it is considered accessory, are dishonorable, as it is also proved above ; for they always blush at the light, which honorable and good deeds do not; " He that doeth truth cometh to the light, *that his deeds may be made manifest*, (not concealed,) that they are wrought " in God." (Jno. 3. 21.) Or they may call it the order of the flesh, in which are included the correspondent union and co-operation of the male and female who are one flesh, which in its own place without abuse was innocent and very good, but doth not belong to Christ or the order of the Spirit—God therefore is not in it.

These remarks introduce an occasion to observe, that the evil is not originally or primarily in the order of the flesh, or the corresponding union between the male and female, but is that nature of the serpent received in and by the fall, consisting in a spirit of disobedience to God and subversion of his order and appointments, which nature hath its seat in the flesh, is incorporated with it, and operates in its order where it chiefly presides, so that the works of the flesh are the works of that nature, which is itself become the very nature of the flesh. On account of this nature and its productions, the flesh is degenerated and degraded even in its own order, but is especially inimical to Christ and the order of the Spirit. Add to this, that the order of the flesh, in its best estate, is not the order of Christ, or the Spirit, but much inferior, inasmuch as the earthly man is inferior to the heavenly. These things account for the irreconcilable contrast and enmity subsisting between the flesh and the Spirit, so abundantly confirmed in the scriptures.

But the flesh or its order, by whatever name it is called, has the nature of the serpent in it; its works also are every where known, and esteemed by all whose faith approves them, as at all belonging to the christian, above God, and Christ and all things, as is proved by that faith which rejects them from christianity being more offensive to them, than any other faith which embraces or rejects any thing else. As therefore this order of the flesh shows itself to be God, so it is in truth god, even the god of the world, set up in the holy place.

What farther proves this same to be the god of those who approve it, is the sacred reserve with which its works and its nature are kept from public contemplation, in being concealed not only from the eyes, but also from the ears. No language is so offensive as that which represents these things in naked colors. Now the sources of unbecoming and offensive language are two. First; When language communicates the ideas of things in themselves unbecoming and offensive. If this is the case with the above order, or its works, that decides the argument that it is not according to Christ or the order of his church; and as it is abetted as being innocent, by the professed church, and has its full and undisturbed residence there, it is hereby proved to be the son of perdition, the abomination of desolation.

But if it be argued, that language descriptive of the works of the flesh, is not offensive because of any thing unbecoming or loathsome in them, its offensiveness must be attributed to the other source of offensive language, which is, The common and irreverend use of language pertaining to God, or some character, too sacred to be named in a common or indifferent manner. According to this view, the generation is proved to be God, much more sacred than any other, and its peculiar names as sacred at least as JEHOVAH, the incommunicable name of the true God, was among the Jews; for it is experimentally true, that the man who blasphemes the name of the true God most freely is not so odious and offensive to the abettors of the flesh, as he who uses with unbecoming freedom, language which expresses their secret works; the only secret works under the whole heavens, or within the reach of man's conception, of which it is ashame to speak.

It is vain to plead that this can be true of illegitimate actions only; for lawful or unlawful, the actions are the same, the nature the same, and language descriptive thereof as offensive in the one case as the other. No doubt therefore remains to the judicious, but this same is the very man of sin, the son of perdition, the abomination of desolation.

4. Another of its characters is, *That wicked*, in Greek, lawless. This is a very proper description of a wicked thing; for nothing can be counted wicked which is subject to any good law; for sin is the transgression of the law; but that which is subject to no law but its own caprice, is necessarily wicked. Thus the carnal mind is proved to be enmity against God because it is not subject to the law of God, neither indeed can be. (Ro. 8. 7.) Thus the above, which in truth, is but the same, is known to be subject to no law, except in its own ungovernable sallies; not the law of nature, because its operations are abundantly frequent in those circumstances which make it impossi

ble for the fruits appointed by nature to succeed—not the law of Moses, because it is not kept within the limits and purifications prescribed by that legislator—not the law of Christ, who never cherished it in a single instance, but appointed it to be crucified with its affections and lusts: for that which cannot exist and be subject, is necessarily wicked, and its ultimate fate is certain destruction—Whom the Lord will consume with the Spirit of his mouth, and will destroy with the brightness of his coming.

Should any suppose so free a discussion of a subject so delicate and secret, to be contrary to propriety or decency, let them duly consider, what idea is to be entertained of a gospel which would patronise and cherish in secret, such works as are unfit to receive the most liberal investigation. " Every one that doeth evil hateth the light, neither " cometh to the light lest his deeds should be discovered (margin) or " (in Greek) convicted. But he that doeth truth, cometh to the " light, that his deeds may be made *manifest* that they are wrought " in God." (Jno. 3. 20, 21.)

CHAPTER VIII.

The order and works of the Generation do not appertain to Christ or his Church.

THAT marriage and the order of the flesh have neither part nor lot in Christ, is farther proved by this doctrine of Christ; " If " any man come to me, and hate not his father, and mother, and wife, " and children, and brethren, and sisters, yea, and his own life also, " he cannot be my disciple." (Luk. 14. 26.)

Some however are quite apt in qualifying the sayings of Christ, so as to accommodate them to their own views. But it is at least necessary not to explain the teaching of Christ all away; his words are not mere wind, but contain an important meaning, and an energy not to be neglected. This hatred, of which he speaks, cannot be leveled against the soul or the body, or intend any injurious feeling towards either: this will be granted. Yet the words of Christ mean something of great importance, for on it depends our discipleship and consequently, our acceptance with God. I conclude therefore that these energetic words were not delivered for a deception; and that when he said *hate*, he did not mean *love*, notwithstanding, that the purest and most genuine love, is strictly consistent with that hatred; and as the man's nearest relations, together with his own life, are singled out, as peculiar objects of hatred, I conclude, that when he says father and mother, wife and children, brethren and sisters, yea, and his own life also, he means these especially, inasmuch as these stand nearest to self, and therefore, are most closely connected with that self-denial and cross-bearing so indispensably necessary to partaking with Christ; " If any man will come after me, let him deny himself, and take up "his cross, and follow me." But as aforesaid, it is not required to hate the person; but to be a disciple of Christ a man must hate his father and his mother, and his wife, and his children; not the man and the woman, but the father and the mother; not the woman, but the wife. Now every one knows, that what constitutes father and mother, wife and child, is the flesh, operating in its own line and order. *They twain shall be one flesh;* and, *That which is born of the flesh is flesh.* Therefore a man born of his father and mother, who are one flesh, is born of the flesh, and according to Christ, he is flesh, and accordingly so are the whole connection and relation: and in all this work Christ is not known. "But that which is born of the Spi-"rit is spirit," and therefore hath part with Christ.

A man is not required to hate his own personal existence, or physical life, but his carnal life, and that which supports it—that by which he hath his existence in a fleshly fallen nature. What therefore Christ requires us to hate is the flesh, which lusteth against the Spirit and is contrary to it; which also is partial, leading a man to esteem, regard and befriend his own fleshly relations more than others, contrary to Christ who said, "Whosoever shall do the will of God, "the same is my brother, and my sister and mother." (Mar. 3. 35.) When it is considered that men esteem their own relations after the flesh more than others, and are more closely attached to them, notwithstanding that others are as respectable and as worthy as they, and often more so, every man of real intelligence must grant, that such estimation and attachment are merely the partialities of the flesh. Yet such estimation and attachment, or these partialities, are as necessary to the support of marriage and the line of the flesh therein, as the junction of the members to the existence of the body. This proves that marriage and the order of the flesh have neither part nor lot in Christ, whose love is impartial, and where each one is esteemed according to his real character, without respect to persons, and in whom all crucify the flesh with its affections as well as its lusts.

This view of the subject leaves no room for any part of all the inhumanity, cruelty and distress, about which the children of this world make such an outcry against the followers of Christ, but leaves the christian under every sacred obligation of humanity and charity, necessary to the existence and comfort of society. For as the first creation in its own order, is necessary to the existence and increase of the new in its own line and order, so every duty between the members of the old, as husband and wife, parent and child, not subversive of the new, remains sacred and inviolable, until they all arrive to that state wherein they have no need of such good offices from such relations. "If any man have not the Spirit of Christ he is none of "his;" But the Spirit of Christ esteems all those who do the will of God, brethren, and sisters, and mothers; these therefore who truly belong to Christ, are in no want of relations or their good offices.

Some indeed believe, or affect to believe, the hating and forsaking required in the disciples of Christ, to be merely mental and comparative, and to produce no material separation or visible cutting off from the fleshly connection and intercourse; because it is written; "He that loveth father or mother more than me, is not worthy of "me; and he that loveth son or daughter more than me is not wor- "thy of me." [Matt. 10. 37.] But nothing is more certain, than that these words imply a contrast between Christ and the man's kindred; so that his love cannot be divided between them, or at all imparted to both; which makes it plain, that the love which men have to father and mother, son and daughter, wife or child, is a rival to the love of Christ, and that both cannot dwell in one heart. The words therefore are precisely the same as to say, He that loveth father or mother, is not worthy of me, and he that loveth son or daughter, is not worthy of me. The sentence therefore is just tantamount with that above; "If any man come to me and hate not "his father, and mother, and wife, and children, and brother and sis- "ter, yea, and his own life also, he cannot be my disciple:" for what any man hateth he doth not love.

Farther. If the hating and forsaking requisite in the followers of Christ be only comparative and mental, or even verbal also, and the heart as fully therein as the nature of the case would admit, Whence all those divisions and enmities of which Christ speaks, as the certain and inevitable attendants of his gospel? "Think not that I am "come to send peace on earth: I came not to send peace but a "sword. For I am come to set a man at variance against his fa- "ther, and the daughter against her mother, and the daughter-in- "law against her mother-in-law; and a man's foes shall be they of "his own household." [Matt. 10. 34 to 36.]

Or if the gospel of Christ requires no more than a mental or comparative forsaking of the line and members of the flesh, wherein was the necessity, or even propriety of the apostle's stating a provision especially and specifically for a man and his wife, in the case of one being a believer and the other not. Let not the believer put away or leave the unbeliever; "But if the unbeliever depart let him (or "her) depart. A brother or a sister is not under bonds in such cases." (1 Cor. 7. 15.)

Now where was it ever known that a man put away his wife because of her being a believer in Christ, or that a woman departed from her husband on account of his being a believer, provided the faith of such believer did not extend to the demolishing of the works of the flesh and disannulling its claims, in christians? It is true as stated above, that infidels and professed christians, or professed christians of divided faith, can live together in as much agreement as where their faith is one, provided the claims and works of the flesh be preserved inviolate.

Or where was it ever known, particularly in a free country, where temporal interest or privilege can be no object, as being connected with the profession, that a man is at variance against his father, the mother against her daughter, and the daughter against her mother, so as to make a man's foes to be those of his own household, on account of his faith in Christ, so that it could be said, he came to do this, unless where the believing part have that real and genuine faith of Christ, which leads to the crucifying of the flesh with its affections and lusts, and excluding the order of the flesh and its works, (the sexual intercourse, lawful or unlawful) from all share in Christ? Although it is not to be denied, that partial jars have sometimes taken place between those of the same household, on account of the faith of some towards Christ; particularly in those times when God hath been pouring out on the people a Spirit of grace and supplication and spreading light abroad in some uncommon manner, as in the Kentucky revival. But as all these revivals fall short of the perfect work of salvation by the cross, these partial divisions may be removed, and civil peace and agreement restored. For although such revivals burn with vengeance against the flesh, they do not reach far enough to purge it out of the temple.

It is also to be granted, that variances, enmities, feuds and animosities are frequent enough among professed christians; but it is too evident, that they spring from a very different source than the abounding of the faith of Christ and a tenacious adherence to it—the want of genuine faith and obedience; for the Spirit, or faith of Christ persecuteth none, envieth none, banisheth none, nor causeth any divisions, except what are produced by his people's testifying and living that truth which is necessary for salvation.

On the whole. To suppose the denying, forsaking or hating requisite in being a disciple, to be mental, verbal, comparative, or in any respect short of a total demolishing of the order of the flesh and its works, depreciates the words of Christ, and renders them weak and indeterminate; not to say false.

When men make resistance and become foes to others, it is on the principle of considering themselves injured or aggrieved; but why should the children of this world complain of injury or grievance, against the gospel of Christ, or become foes to those who practise it, if they can partake of its benefits, and keep their beloved works unhurt, and the body and core of them unmolested. But the work of Christ proceeds immediately to life and death. "He that findeth "his life shall lose it; and he that loseth his life for my sake shall "find it." [Matt. 10. 39.] This makes a thorough and final separation between those who bear the cross and those who remain enemies to it.

As for the notion of dividing the love between Christ and the wife, children and others, allowing Christ the greatest portion, it is too weak to merit a serious answer, were it not so much set by of many. In the first place; it is granted, that Christ requires the whole heart, love and affections; consequently, whosoever interferes to prevent any part is a rival to him, because no man can serve two masters. But whosoever practiseth the generation doeth the work of the first Adam, and thereby serveth him, and therefore cannot serve Christ.

But if this be counted an unfair statement, and it be argued, that as Christ demands the whole heart, love and affections, which being given to him comprehend in the same relation, parents, children and others. This is granted, provided those parents, children and others are in Christ, and the love embraces them in that character; and this is the very love for which we contend, which effectually supplants, and utterly excludes all that love which is partial, fixing on those who are nearly allied in the line of the flesh. For it is before stated in evidence, that the love which men bear to their natural relations as such, distinctly from others, is a rival to the love of Christ—partial and unjust. But,

Once more; By an appeal to the conscience of those who have had their mind and feelings wakened up to a consideration of the testimony of Christ in his second appearing, it may be farther proved to their satisfaction, that those who love wife or children for instance at all, in the order of that relation, and refuse to forsake them, do necessarily love them more than Christ, and consequently come short of genuine love to Christ. For let it be considered, that when the gospel is presented to such with these terms of hating and forsaking, father and mother, wife and children, and others, their ultimate objection is, that Christ doth not require such terms, and on that plea reject the whole. This proves that these relations and enjoyments are by them loved more than Christ; for if they esteemed Christ above those, they would make sure of their part in him, come of other matters what would; not doubting, at the same time, but that wife or husband, or children, will be all restored, provided such a state of things be compatible with genuine christianity. "For no "good thing will he withhold from them that walk uprightly." (Psm. 84. 11.) "Seek first the kingdom of God and his righteous- "ness, and all these things shall be added to you;" (Matt. 6. 33.) that is, all those things of which your heavenly Father knoweth ye have need, as is stated in the preceding verse.

Should any object that the above argument is not conclusive, because many reject that testimony of the gospel which requires such sacrifices, because they do not believe it true, whereas did they actually believe it true they would submit, and make all the sacrifices which could be required to obtain salvation. To these it is replied; that no sacrifices are required to be made in the gospel for which we plead, more than what are very expressly taught in the words of Christ; and no way appears to get round them only to plead that he did not mean what he said, and also to contrast one saying against another to weaken the force of his doctrine. *Poor subterfuges*, for those who acknowledge Christ as a true teacher. This testimony of the gospel, goeth no greater length than these words, "So likewise "whosoever he be of you that doth not forsake all that he hath, he "cannot be my disciple;" and many more, as it hath already appeared.

Besides; The ultimate and cogent reason why people disbelieve, or affect to disbelieve, is their unwillingness to make a sacrifice of all for Christ—their enmity against the cross which the gospel requires, and instead of being an evidence against the truth of the gospel in this day, is really in its favor. But they stumble at the cross being disobedient.

But to set this subject in a still clearer point of view, let us once more have recourse to the words of Christ. It is stated above, that whatever is compatible with the genuine gospel of Christ and necessary for those who are called into it shall be restored or given to them. Now the Spirit and words of Christ are the best testimony of these things, what they are and what not. He saith. " There is no man " that hath left house, or brethren, or sisters, or father, or mother, or " wife, or children, or lands, for my sake, and the gospel's, but he " shall receive an hundred fold now in this time, houses, and breth-" ren, and sisters, and mothers, and children, and lands, with persecu-" tions ; and in the world to come eternal life."

It is worthy of observation, that there is no wife in the premise of Christ, (Why cannot the people see it?) for this plain reason, no doubt, that the works and office commonly attributed to a wife, do not belong to the gospel. People may have parents and children, brethren and sisters according to the Spirit, houses and lands to subserve the work of the Spirit, and enjoy them when devoted to that use, but a wife pertains to the order of the flesh and in that respect is not known in the gospel. Other scriptures speak of those who are called fathers in relation to the work of Christ, that is, in the Spirit.

This will be no improper place to introduce another scripture which draws the line of distinction, and shows to what class marriage belongs. " The children of this world marry and are given in mar-" riage: but they which shall be accounted worthy to obtain that world, " and the resurrection from the dead, neither marry, nor are given in " marriage. Neither can they die any more : for they are equal un-" to the angels, and are the children of God, being the children of the " resurrection." (Luk. 20. 34, 35, 36.) Now the children of this world are not the children of God, or followers of Christ, as he said, " They are not of the world, even as I am not of the world." Those therefore who marry and are given in marriage, are not the children of God, or followers of Christ. Again ; It is not to be denied, that all the true followers of Christ are and shall be accounted worthy, and have been from the period when they became such, to obtain that world and the resurrection from the dead. But those accounted worthy neither marry nor are given in marriage ; therefore none of the true followers of Christ marry, or are given in marriage.

I am aware of the flimsy objection of carnal 'men, to evade the force of this text ; That the question proposed to the Sadducees, to which this answer was given, related to the resurrection of men literally dead. And what if it did? Must the ignorance and carnality of those Sadducees compel Jesus to talk of carnal things as well as they, or make his words false? It was a business not unknown to Jesus, to lead people out of their inferior care and gross conceptions, into things spiritual. So did he with Nicodemus, whom he led immediately to the subject of being born of the Spirit; a subject of which Nicodemus had never thought or heard before, and by no means a direct reply to the proposition which he had made.

In like manner he dealt with Martha, on the occasion of the death and resurrection of Lazarus. " Jesus saith to her, thy brother shall " rise again. Martha saith to him, I know that he shall rise again in " the resurrection at the last day. Jesus saith to her, I am the re- " surrection and the life; he that believeth on me, though he were " dead yet shall he live; and whosoever liveth and believeth in me " shall never die." (Jno. 11. 24, 25, 26.) Martha believed the resurrection, the Sadducees did not, but her conceptions of its nature accorded with theirs. But Jesus availed himself of the opportunity to lead her into something of its true nature, showing it to be a spiritual work, and that he is the resurrection and the life; so that to be in him is to be in the resurrection and in the life so as never to die. Now notwithstanding that Martha, in what she stated, had respect to literal death and literal resurrection, the answer of Jesus related ultimately to neither; for in that relation it would be false, because it is an uncontested truth, that believers in Christ die the common literal death as well as others; and Jesus well knew, that even Lazarus himself after being raised as an instance of his power and truth, was subject to literal death as well as others. But in Christ shall all be made alive; (1 Cor. 15. 22.) those who are truly in Christ who is the resurrection and the life, are in the resurrection, and can die no more.

These Sadducees it is true, proposed their question as it related to men literally dead; but the answer of Jesus was not confined to these individuals, but included the subjects of the resurrection in general; it also excludes from marriage, those who are worthy of the resurrection. The proposition therefore remains true, That the children of God, or true followers of Christ, neither marry nor are given in marriage; for it cannot be denied that they are all accounted worthy.

The parallel texts in the other evangelists farther evince, that the resurrection of which Christ here speaks, is not corporeal but spiritual. Thus Matthew, " In the resurrection, (observe, Christ is the " resurrection,) they neither marry, nor are given in marriage, (pre- " sent tense,) but *are* as t e angels of God in heaven." [22. 30.] And Mark; " When they shall rise from the dead they neither marry, " nor are given in marriage; (present tense,) but *are* as the angels " which are in heaven." [12. 25.] As Christ is the resurrection and the life, when any come into Christ they rise from the dead. " If " then ye be risen with Christ, seek those things which are above." [Col. 3. 1.]

Thus by comparing these parallel texts, it is evident, that to be in the resurrection, to rise from the dead, and to be accounted worthy, are one and the same thing; for the three evangelists, speaking by the same Spirit, use these different phrases in describing precisely the same state; which could not be true of any resurrection of the body literally, but is strictly applicable to that moral or spiritual change, which is effected in the soul by becoming one with Christ in the Spirit, and so passing from death to life. Add to this, that Luke's account expressly limits the resurrection here intended to that by which its subjects become children of God. " They are the chil-" dren of God, being the children of the resurrection." Here the resurrection is stated as the medium whereby they become children of God, which is confessedly no other than receiving Christ and being made alive in him.

To prove that the resurrection here intended is incompatible with remaining in the tabernacle, and therefore that this scripture teaches nothing, contrary to christians marrying like the rest of the world, some avail themselves of this argument. *That the characteristic terms used in describing those who do not marry, are such as cannot be applied to men on the earth.* Such as, " *Neither can they die any* " *more.*" But it has been already shown that this is applicable to all those who are truly in Christ. Another part of their character is ; " *But are as the angels of God in heaven,*" or " *For they are equal* " *to the angels.*" Now query ; Is this any more than that for which Christ taught his disciples to pray ? *Thy kingdom come ; thy will be done on earth as it is in heaven.*" This kingdom can be no other than the kingdom or church of Christ on the earth, for to that the prayer limits it : those therefore who are true members of Christ's church on earth, are as the angels of God in heaven, for they do the will of God on earth as it is done in heaven. And what do angels more ? Besides ;

The nature of language is to be limited in a certain degree to the subject under consideration when it is used. The subject in hand is the resurrection, as it stands connected with marriage. In the first place then ; Those who are in Christ, the resurrection and the life, though they have once died in Adam are now where they can die no more, and herein are equal to the angels. Also, Those who are in Christ, *are counted worthy to obtain that world and the resurrection from the dead,* therefore they neither marry nor are given in marriage, and are therefore as the angels of God in heaven, who do not marry.

These things show, that the whole description of those who neither marry nor are given in marriage, is strictly applicable to men on the earth ; and though the language be too spiritual and heavenly for those who are after the flesh, and therefore savor only the things of the flesh, it is no wise inconsistent with the faith and feelings of those who are in Christ Jesus, who walk not according to the flesh but according to the Spirit. They can ask no better condition, and they know that angels are incapable of any thing superior to being free from the fetters of the flesh, the bondage of corruption, and doing the will of God according to the order of Christ, " *Of whom the whole family* " *in heaven and in earth is named.*" [Eph. 3. 15.]

An appeal to the learned. The Greek word used by Mark, which the translators have rendered, " *They shall rise,*" is the present of the subjunctive mood. Now can any reason be assigned why they should translate it, by a future tense, except to accommodate it to their own understanding, being at the same time, ignorant of the import of the text and the subject to which it related? The phrase in Luke, which is translated, " *Shall be accounted worth*," is a participle of the second indefinite, importing past tense, though imperfectly. On what principle could the translators make such a bold adventure, as to render that phrase by a future verb, except the same arbitrary determination to translate to their own views? The literal translation of the phrase used by Mark is, " When they rise ;" and it properly expresses the situation of those who hear the gospel, with respect to the resurrection; which, though it had never been perfected in any case, was then working, and would be accomplished in an increasing progressive succession. Thus the sentence will read; " For when they rise (that is, as fast as any rise,) from the dead, they " neither marry, nor are given in marriage." The phrase used by Luke, though used in a different tense, communicates the same information, by a different form of expression. It may be translated, " Those accounted worthy ;" or, in its connection, thus ; " But they " who are (or have been) accounted worthy to obtain that world and *"* the resurrection from the dead, (that is, as fast as any are accounted " worthy, or come into the number of God's children, they) neither " marry, nor are given in marriage." Thus the whole matter is applicable to those who keep the gospel on the earth ; as much as the commission which Christ gave to his disciples, to preach the gospel and to baptize those who should believe ; both of which, the believing and baptizing, are expressed in the same tense, or division of time, as the being accounted worthy ; " He that believeth, (or hath believed,) and is, (or hath been,) baptized, shall be saved " When the people believed they were baptized ; and when they were baptized, they received the promise of salvation, and began to be saved from that hour ; for they were baptized into Christ and into his death, or baptized by the Spirit, as it is again written ; " After that ye believ- " ed, (or having believed, the word being a participle, expressing " the same division of time as above,) ye were sealed with that Holy " Spirit of promise." [Eph. 2. 13.] So when the people are (or have been) accounted worthy to obtain, they cease to marry in the present tense.

A farther proof that marriage is inconsistent with christianity, is the saying of the apostle, " Now concerning the things whereof ye " wrote unto me; It is good for a man not to touch a woman." [1 Cor. 7. 1.] This point he hath treated at considerable length and in a manner which appears to be little understood by professors in general ; who in their appeals to it, seem to forget the proposition which is laid down as the foundation point to be discussed and maintained, that, *It is good for a man not to touch a woman*, and to build all their arguments on the exceptions and permissions which are made to answer cases of necessity and inability ; and thus they subvert the whole of the apostle's meaning. It is expected of an honest writer, that the proposition which he undertakes to defend will meet the approbation of his own best judgment and so remain until he is convinced of the contrary. But the apostle was so far from giving up his position, that he hath maintained it to the last, and confirmed it with an appeal to his having the Spirit of God and that he spoke as one who had obtained mercy of the Lord to be faithful. Accordingly, all he hath said in favor of marriage or of living in natural generation by those who were already married is on the principle of permission and necessity, contrary to the desire of him who had the Spirit of God and had obtained mercy of the Lord to be faithful.

"It is good for a man not to touch a woman. Nevertheless, to avoid fornication," (or, but because of the fornications, δια δε τας πορνειας, for the words *to avoid*, are not in the Greek, but for no other cause, as to marry is not after Christ; but for the reason offered;) "let every man have his own wife, and let every woman have her "own husband." If those entersexual works must be carried on let every one have his own, and not meddle with another. And in the mean time let the best possible deportment be observed towards each other. "Let the husband render unto the wife due benevo- "lence; and likewise also the wife to the husband. The wife hath "not power of her own body, but the husband; and likewise also the "husband hath not power of his own body, but the wife. (This is "according to the law of marriage.) Defraud [or deprive] ye not "one the other, except with consent for a time, that ye may give "yourselves to fasting and prayer; (for if ye touch wife or husband "ye can neither fast nor pray in the Spirit. (See Exod. 19. 15.) and "come together again that satan tempt you not through your incon- "tinancy. But this I speak by permission, (because of your car- "nality and weakness in the faith, ye being unable to receive the un- "mingled truth of Christ,) not of commandment. For I would that "all men were even as I myself; but every man hath his proper gift "of God, one after this manner and another after that." So that some were able to bear a heavier and more perfect cross than others, having received a greater gift of God according as they were better able to exercise and improve it. Thus he gave to every one accord- ing to his ability to improve. And that this is the true meaning of the apostle's words is proved by this, that the Spirit doth not contra- dict itself; for to suppose as some have whimsically done that some men had received a gift of God to marry and some not, would con- tradict the same Spirit in the apostle, saying, "I would that all men "were even as I myself;" who confessedly was unmarried. "I say, "therefore, to the unmarried and widows, *It is good for them* if they "abide even as I. But if (through the violence of their lusts and "their lack of power in the Spirit of Christ) they cannot contain, "let them marry: for it is better to marry than to burn." And thus it is through the whole discourse, as every man of a discerning mind can see; the only countenance given to marriage is permission, to avoid a greater evil, or, which is the same, through inevitable ne- cessity. But he maintains his position, that *It is good for a man not to touch a woman;* or wife, as the word is rendered every where else in that discourse; neither is there any kind of reason for not rendering it *wife*, in this proposition, as wife and husband are the special subject-matter of the whole chapter. Accordingly in his last sentence, after he had considered the matter through and on every side, he hath confirmed his proposition, that the *good way* is not to marry. " But she (the widow) is happier if she so abide, after my judgment: " and I think also that I have the Spirit of God." If therefore Paul was not mistaken—if he was under the guidance of the Spirit of God—if he understood the genuine Spirit of christianity—if his writings have any validity on this subject, it is not good, it is not according to genuine christianity for a man to touch a woman, or a woman a man, in the line of marriage or its works. But the apostle did not enjoin it on them absolutely to abstain, but urged it as far as they were able to bear, and left them to make their own choice for the time being, after having shown them what is the best way.

Neither were they who married absolutely disowned nor excluded from the number of believers, in that day, although they were not able to come into that close spiritual and pure union with the unmarried, and suffered many disadvantages, for the time being, and also must finally come to that point, bearing a full and perfect cross before they could find full redemption. Hence he, urges them with great earnestness, and yet with that tenderness and forbearance which their situation required. They were just called and likely most of them out of heathenism. They were yet carnal and walked as men; [1 Cor. 3. 3.] and it became necessary to deal with them as they were able to bear, to feed them with milk and not with strong meat. " Now, concerning virgins, I have no commandment of the Lord, " yet I give my judgment, as one that hath obtained mercy of the " Lord to be faithful, I suppose, therefore, that this is good for the " present distress, [or, αναγκην, necessity,] I say, that it is good for a " man so to be. Art thou (already) bound to a wife? seek not to be " loosed, (for the present. But) Art thou loosed from a wife seek not " a wife, (but being free remain even as I, and thou wilt find thy ad-" vantage in so doing.) But and if thou marry, thou hast not sinned ; " and if a virgin marry she hath not sinned :" for sin is the trans-" gression of the law, and there is no commandment to not marry; abstinence is only a matter of faith in Christ. This is quite an accommodating expression, to ameliorate the edge of truth, in tenderness to those who were not able to digest sound doctrine in its naked simplicity. It was also well calculated to prevent contentions and evil surmisings against each other, to which the Corinthians were very subject. In this view we may consider many of his expressions, and amongst others, that in the epistle to the Hebrews; " Mar-" riage is honorable in all, and the bed undefiled." [12. 4.] A saying which cannot apply to any except those who faithfully abstain from the flesh. A short saying dropped, in an unconnected dress, to relieve from difficulty : Lest they who were unmarried should surmise evil against those who were married, as though they corrupted the faith of the gospel. He could say thus far ; It is honorable in all; cast no disgrace upon them. But he adds; " Nevertheless, such shall have trouble in [or θλιψιν τη σαρκι tribulation by] the flesh: (being plagued by its lusts; because by the law of marriage they have not power over their own bodies being bound to others by the flesh:) but I spare you. (Having said as far as ye can well bear.) " But *(I must do my duty*, therefore,) this I say, brethren, the time is short: it remaineth, that both they that have wives be as though they had none; and they that weep as though they wept not; and they that rejoice, as though they rejoiced not; and they that buy, as though they possessed not; and they that use this world, as not abusing it: for the fashion of this world passeth away." All these customs of the world therefore must cease in the church.

In vain do men plead that these things relate to the state of christians after the dissolution of the body, or natural death, because in that state there is no kind of evidence that they will either buy or use this world, or that they will have wives to be as though they had none. Besides, the reason of this state of things is not because we go out of the world but because its fashion or form passeth away. In vain do they alledge that the distress, which made it most proper to omit marriage was the persecution which lay on the church, making the times difficult; for had that been the distress the time might have come when they might marry with more convenience. But instead of that the only prospect he lays before them is, that the time was fast approaching when all such things would entirely cease. The distress therefore, or necessity, was on the other side. They were so lost in the flesh, and had so little power over it, that he found a necessity to leave those who had wives to live in that order for the time being. " Art thou bound to a wife? seek not to be loosed;" and only to entreat of those who were not married to remain in that state. " Art thou loosed from a wife? seek not a wife." And that only by request as they could bear no more. But his care for them, seeing the danger to which they were exposed, holds him to expostulate with them yet more, and show them still farther the advantages of the single life. " But I would have you without carefulness. " [Or free from perplexing cares, αμεριμνους, which is a state incompatible with the married life, for] He that is unmarried careth for the things that belong to the Lord, how he may please the Lord. But he that is married careth for the things of the world, how he may please his wife. There is difference also between a wife and a virgin. The unmarried woman careth for the things of the Lord that she may be holy both in body and in spirit, (a privilege incompatible with the married life, else why not the married woman have it also?) but she that is married careth for the things of the world, how she may please her husband. And this I say for your own profit, (or convenience, from the conviction of its truth and propriety, with great tenderness,) not that I may cast a snare upon you, (or bring you under any unnecessary trial or sufferings,) but for that which is comely (and suitable to the life of a christian) and happily

" corresponding with the Lord [ευπρσεδρον τω Κυριω] without (offer-
" ing any thing by) violence ;" as I would much rather gain you to the
best way, by inviting motives than by violent means. Observe ; the
words, *That ye may attend upon the Lord,* are a forced translation
without any regular foundation in the Greek. " But (he still gives
" permission in case of real necessity,) if any man think that he be-
" haveth himself uncomely toward his virgin, if she pass the flower
" of her age, and need so require, let him do what he will (marry or
" not,) he sinneth not; let them marry," (if they conclude that is
best.) " Nevertheless he that standeth stedfast in his heart, having no
" necessity (the word translated distress above) but hath power over his
" own will, and hath so decreed in his heart that he will keep his vir-
" gin, (and let her remain in virginity) doeth well. So then, he that giveth
" in marriage (when imperious necessity requireth it) doeth well; but
" he that giveth not in marriage (where the necessity is not imperious)
" doeth better." So that, after considering the subject through and on
every hand, he hath maintained his position, that " It is good for a
" man not to touch a woman." Add to these things, that marriage
is entirely a matter of law and not of christianity, those therefore who
marry, being professed christians, are under the law and serve another than Christ. " The wife is bound by the *law* (not by the gospel)
" as long as her husband liveth ; but if her husband be dead, (or hath
" fallen on, sleep, κοιμηθη,) she is at liberty, (according to the same
" law,) to be married to whom she will; *only in the Lord*." Let
her at least observe this caution ; and submit thus far to the gospel.
For if those who made any profession of christianity would marry at
all, it was best not to marry with infidels, lest they should be entirely
lost, but to keep as near the mark as possible until the day of greater
power should come. But still it was better not to marry at all ;
therefore he adds ; " But she is happier if she so abide, after my
" judgment : and I think also that I have the Spirit of God."
But as before stated, those who married were not wholly rejected,
but left to keep their own order in the outer court. What was certainly required of every one, was to keep faithfully that which he
professed. For although there was no finished salvation or perfect
justification to be obtained in living according to the course of this
world, or in a married life, yet some were acknowledged as believers
in the outer court, who lived in that manner, while others bore a full
cross against the flesh, and composed the inner court, or temple.
And not unlikely some even at Corinth ; for it is quite a reasonable
conclusion that some would be found so far devoted to Christ and his
beloved apostle as to feel the propriety of yielding to his great anxiety for their spiritual advantages, and of living as he lived ; when he
said, I would that all men were even as I myself—Art thou loosed
from a wife ; seek not a wife—and, I would have you without carefulness. And a still clearer proof of these two orders of believers,
as well as that marriage, in no respect belongs to the faith of Christ
or the life of a christian, is found in the apostle's words to Timothy.
[1 Epist. 5, 9, &c.] " Let not a widow be taken into the number
" under three score years old, having been the wife of one man, (not

"twice married) well reported of for good works: if she have brought up children, if she have lodged strangers, if she have washed the saint's feet, if she have relieved the afflicted, if she have diligently followed every good work." Now this could not be merely the number of widows to be maintained by the church; for it would be too poor a reason for not taking in one who was in need, that she was not sixty years old, or that in the days of her ignorance of Christ she had been a wife to two husbands. But the following words show plainly who were the number; They whose faith was not to marry but to live in continence and virgin purity after the example of Christ and his apostles. Which faith any one who professed it, would necessarily violate and give an occasion to the adversary to reproach the profession, by marrying, or showing any such inclination. " But the younger widows refuse: for when they have begun to wax wanton against Christ they are willing to marry; [γαμειν θελουσιν] having damnation because they have cast off their first faith." Those passions therefore which incline people to marry, especially in those who profess to follow Christ bearing a full cross, are *wantonness against Christ*. Else why not be willing to marry without waxing wanton against Christ? And why not marry without casting off their first faith, if that first faith had not been contrary to marrying? And why have *damnation* because they cast off their first faith, if that first faith had been unnecessary or improper? For who can be condemned by the truth for doing what is right? Not one. No solid arguments can be offered against this reasoning, or in support of marriage as being consistent with pure christianity. And when they became willing to marry, having cast off their first faith, they were exposed to run into greater evils than those who never pretended to any such faith; "And withal they learn to be idle, wandering about from house to house, and not only idle, but tattlers also, and busybodies, speaking things which they ought not. I will, therefore, (to avoid the extravagant and greater evils,) that the younger widows marry, (there is no authority in the Greek text for the term *women*, it not being in the text, which is exclusively of *widows;)* bear children, guide the house, (or family, in a manner suitable to that order which they are able to keep,) give none occasion to the adversary to speak reproachfully," (by acting contrary to what they have professed, or marrying after coming into the number of those who profess a contrary faith.) "For some have already turned aside after satan," having consented to marry after professing to be of *that number*, which is the true church, bearing a full cross, therefore receive no more of them except the aged and pious characters above described. And as for the younger, "If any man or woman that believeth have widows, let them relieve them, and let not the church be charged; that it may relieve them that are widows indeed." " Now, she that is a widow indeed, and desolate, trusteth in God, and continueth in supplications and prayers night and day. But she, that liveth in pleasure, is dead while she liveth." Now it could be no ground of reproach to a church who have no faith that marriage is contrary to genuine christianity for one of their young widows to marry, because in so doing she would violate no profession of faith, and might thereby relieve the church of expenses, if she had to be maintained.

The reason therefore that the apostle gave counsel for the young widows to marry is clearly to avoid more distressing evils—It is also evident, all who were in that day called believers did not keep the faith in a full cross, as did the apostles and some others who were more properly the church—and finally that marrying or living in the works thereof is inconsistent with the life of the true followers of Christ.

CHAPTER IX.

Marriage a civil right and carnal relation of the world, therefore doth not belong to the church of Christ.

THAT the children of this world, distinctly from the followers of Christ, should marry, is quite natural. And this shows what marriage is, and to what class it belongs; that it is a civil right and civil institution, properly belonging to the citizens of the world, and therefore the privilege of every man who chooses to use it.

That it properly belongs to the civil department is not only proved by the doctrine of Christ, but acknowledged and confirmed by the usage of civil governments, who constantly assume the sole power of regulating marriage among all classes of people, determining who may perform the ceremony and who may not, who may be married and who may not, and annexing penalties on those who transgress the prescribed limitations. And this is the case, not only in those governments who usurp an authority over the conscience, but in those wiser and more happy governments, who declare, as being part of their constitution, or bill of rights, That no civil power hath, or can have, any right to control or at all to interfere with the rights of conscience.

Thus the civil department supports this position, That marriage is a civil right and civil institution, and maintains its prerogative in it. And professors of christianity also acknowledge this prerogative, being all careful to regulate their marriages according to the limitations prescribed by law.

The act also of marrying, which is only a ceremonious rite, is properly of a civil nature; for, notwithstanding the civil department, at least in free governments, leaves every class of people, or every individual, to his own choice, in what manner to perform it, it is nevertheless the confirming and guarantying of a civil right, between the parties, and he or they who officiate therein, do it by the sanction of the civil department, and are thereby properly civil officers. Certain of the ministerial order have had light to see into this so far, as to have serious reflections about giving up the business of marrying people, (thus far at least in one of my acquaintance,) but the next natural consequence is, that provided it is improper for a preacher of the gospel to marry others, it is also improper for him to be married: but this is too crossing to the flesh, to be sanctioned by the example of those who prefer the flesh to the Spirit.

Marriage being the privilege of all people who choose to use it, no one man, or association of men, have any right to forbid or require any one to marry: in this respect every man's faith is his law; if he marry, he shall deprive no other man or people of their equal civil rights, and if not, it remains the same. If therefore any man choose to marry, and so be of the children of this world, none have any right to forbid him: his faith is his law. And on the other hand, if any one choose to omit marrying, that he may follow Christ in the regeneration, (every one knows this is not contrary to the example of Christ,) and be counted worthy to obtain that world and the resurrection from the dead, none have any right to interfere or control him, or on that account to interrupt him in the use of any other civil right or privilege: his faith is his law. It is an evident truth, that no one, by omitting the use or enjoyment of any civil right, gives any just occasion to be deprived of another. For instance; The possessing of landed property is a civil right; but should any man or people believe it contrary to the Spirit of christianity to hold personal or private landed property, and so refuse to do it, for conscience' sake, would it be presumed that, on that account, he could justly be deprived of the liberty of worshiping God according to his own faith, which is a civil and natural right, or of buying and selling common property, which is a civil and natural right, or even of marrying, which is also a civil and natural right? I trow not.

But the unquestionable privilege of all men, according to the very nature of their civil rights, to marry and be of the children of this world, can never introduce a civil right or civil institution, into the church of Christ, or incorporate it with his law and order. Neither can that or any other reason make it criminal or unchristian, in the church and ministers of Christ, who preach by commission from him, to maintain that marrying or living in that order according to the course of this world, is contrary to the faith and order of Christ, or to require, by the faith of Christ, not by civil authority, that all those who unite with them and profess to be of the body of Christ, conscientiously and scrupulously abstain from every thing of that nature. It is just for a man to profess to be what he is. Each man is left to his own choice, whether he will follow Christ or the world, and at liberty to act his own faith; but no man's faith or choice, can alter the faith and order of Christ; it may and must finally determine the man's own condition, but the faith of Christ must remain inviolable; which whosoever possesseth, is counted worthy to obtain that world and the resurrection from the dead, and those accounted worthy neither marry nor are given in marriage.

No matter what any man professeth, as belonging to the faith of Christ or worship of God, which doth not interfere with the rights of others, so as to be any just cause of grievance, no civil or arbitrary power hath any right to molest him; but to require the people or ministers of Christ, preaching under commission from him, to acknowledge as belonging to the faith or work of Christ, any thing or every thing which any man should propose, as agreeable to him, or to cede any part of the faith or doctrine of Christ, or which they preach as by commission from him, to accommodate the gospel testimony to the feelings or choice of others, is in effect to give every man the pre-eminence over Christ, and subjugate the gospel testimony to the will of man. Whatever therefore belongs to the gospel of Christ, his church, not only have a right, but are under the most solemn obligation to God to maintain; and if any man or people hold errors, and call them truth, arguments according to scripture and sound reason, or the gift and power of God in the Spirit of the gospel of Christ, are the only justifiable weapons with which to oppose said errorists; and these the faithful have a right to ply with freedom.

No man can serve two masters—The flesh lusteth against the Spirit, and the Spirit against the flesh; and these are contrary the one to the other. "He that soweth to the flesh, shall of the flesh reap "corruption; and he that soweth to the Spirit, shall of the Spirit "reap life everlasting." Thus every man hath to make choice for himself, and be rewarded accordingly.

If marriage be not a civil right and free to all citizens, or if it be a christian institution, none but christians have any right to it. But on the contrary, if it be a civil right and civil institution, which few if any will deny, it is no part of the christian faith or economy, unless introduced by the author of christianity, which it hath not been, but expressly excluded, as hath been shown. It may then be inquired with the utmost propriety; What authority or pretence have any who profess christianity, to introduce into the church, a civil institution, or ceremony, which Christ hath not required at their hand? Who have a right to require any class of professed christians, to use any civil right, which they consider improper for them and inconsistent with their calling? What power hath any right to assume the prerogative over the consciences of any class of professed christians, to subject them to inconveniences or deprive them of their civil rights, because they choose to omit one or more, as being inconsistent with their calling, while at the same time, they leave all people to an equal freedom of choice, and neither usurp nor claim any authority or influence over any individuals contrary to their own faith and choice? If therefore any people, for the sake of following Christ more perfectly, choose not to marry, or if married, choose not to live after the flesh, because they believe such a life to be inconsistent with the faith and order of Christ, in the mean time considering and maintaining it a matter of free choice and faith with all others, according to their natural and civil rights, whether to be one with them or not. On what foundation of justice, or according to the free and happy principles of American government, can they be accused or subjected to oppressions or grievances by giving their opposers legal advantage against them ? as hath been attempted by some, who savor the spirit, not of Christ, but of anti-christ, in his European tyranny. An additional and very striking proof that marriage doth not belong to the church of Christ but is entirely of the world is contained in the measures taken by the apostates in the latter times to establish their reputation, and perhaps their hope as christians. " Now the " Spirit speaketh expressly that in the latter times certain shall apos- " tatize from the faith, yielding [προσεχοντες] to seducing spirits [or " πνευμασι πλανοις, erroneous spirits,] and doctrines of demons, who " speak lies in hypocrisy [or through the hypocrisy of liars,] who " have their own consciences seared as with a hot iron, who forbid to " marry, (and require or command) to obstain from meats which God " hath created to be received with thanksgiving of those who believe " and know the truth." (1 Tim. 4. 1, &c.) A material point in affecting a well concerted plan of forgery is to retain all the most noted and conspicuous characters of the true. When therefore the antichristian church prevailed, having lost the true Spirit of Christ, and having for that reason no longer any power over the spirit of the world, and their members being all carried away with the lust of concupiscence, so as to lose every appearance of the followers of Christ, and the reputed church or rather chief bishop now reigning with absolute power, nothing appeared more eligible or better calculated to maintain some resemblance of the christian church, than to forbid to marry, and to require to abstain from meats, or to keep fasts, which was also a practice of the anchient church, that they might restrain by the force or energy of law, those passions which they had no longer any power of the Spirit to crucify. But as the apostles bore with many in a certain degree and acknowledged them as believers, though in a more distant relation as the outer court, and they only abstained from marriage and the works of the flesh entirely, who lived in the first order as did the apostles and others who were the true church in that day, so the law prohibiting marriage extended only to the foremost class of professors, to the whole of the priesthood, to which they are bound by law, who undertake to live in that order, and also by oath, with all the rest of the monastic order. Thus arbitrary measures became substitutes for the faith and Spirit of Christ since these have been lost, to preserve as much as possible, the resemblance of the christian church. These things having taken place early in the apostacy while the order of the church of Christ was yet known, are a striking proof that marriage hath no part in that church, but is of the world. The following Extract from an Epistolary Discussion on religion, between a Protestant and a Catholic, which fell into my hands a few days after I had written the above statement, elucidates and confirms it by the Catholic's own words. In his reply to the Protestant, who complained that the law of the monastic orders was arbitrary and cruel, he saith; " The promoters " of the disciplinary law that prescribes it, had undoubtedly a com- " mendable intention : they wished them to be angels—like, who " angelical functions exercise ; but considering its inconveniences, "they had better perhaps been ruled by St. Paul's doctrine, satisfied with giving it as a counsel, not as a command."

A proper understanding of this subject, at one stroke exonerates the people who refuse to marry for the sake of Christ and his cross, from the charge of *forbidding* to marry, inasmuch as what they teach and practise amounts to this, That every thing ought to be kept in its proper place and treated according to its own order, so as to stand or fall therewith. Or will any suppose that this is to depart from the faith of Christ, To do as he did, for the purpose of obedience to him? Or is a man guilty of speaking lies in hypocrisy for living up to what he believes and testifies is right? and not rather he who testifies one thing and practises another? as all those do who profess to be of the family of Christ, and to follow him in the Spirit, while they live after the flesh, according to the first Adam, marrying and giving in marriage, as it is written of that order, *They twain shall be one flesh.* Or do a people forbid to marry, or intrude on the rights of others, by testifying that marriage doth not belong to the followers of Christ, and living according to that testimony, declaring all the time, that it is a matter of pure faith, without force or commandment, in every one who chooses to walk in that order? If this be the case, by parity of reason, whatever any people profess, be it false or true, and maintain it to be necessary to christianity, living accordingly, they by so doing, forbid all others to practise contrary to that profession, and thus the faith of Christ is turned into a law of commandments, contrary to the whole nature and plan of gospel invitation—Whosoever will, Let him. For let truth be what it may, those who are christians indeed must have it, not only in profession but possession, holding the truth in righteousness, and according to the aforesaid conception of forbidding, they necessarily forbid all others to deviate from them, even those who make no pretentions to christianity, as well as those who differ from them in the profession of it.

It will be granted on the principle of equal rights, that all orders of professed christians, have a right to institute their own order of worship, or to speak more consistently with giving Christ the preeminence, to learn of him what is the true worship of God, and to require all who undertake to be of that body, and of the same faith with them, to live according to that faith, otherwise to not pretend to be of them. Those therefore whose faith is not to marry or live after the course of this world, because of its being contrary to the faith and order of Christ, have an indisputable right to require all those who profess their faith and desire to be joined with them, to live according to that faith, and to abstain from every thing contrary thereto, or else not pretend to be of that people. And this is perfectly consistent with the faith and law of Christ, as well as the utmost natural freedom of every man's conscience. Neither has it any relation to the forbidding of others to do what they in substance practised themselves, or enjoining on others that abstinence and self-denial which they themselves did not keep; to which may be added as contained in that forbidding, the subverting of the Spirit and faith of the gospel, by undertaking to effect by arbitrary measures, what they were unable to do by the faith of the gospel, having lost the Spirit and power by apostatizing from the faith of Christ. " Speaking lies " in hypocrisy, having their conscience seared with a hot iron, for- " bidding to marry." But when people live according to what they teach and profess, bearing a living testimony against the flesh and all evil, they neither speak lies in hypocrisy, nor have their conscience seared.

Seeing that marriage is a civil right of the world and not a christian institution; for professed christians to marry or claim it as their province, involves, amongst other things, the following absurd principles. In the first place, it reflects disgrace on the gospel of Christ and charges God with affording only a scanty and insufficient portion to its subjects; and alledging that the inheritance of God's people, by the gospel, including the promise of the life that now is, and of that which is to come, is so unsatisfying, that it can be made more perfect by the addition of fleshly pleasures, they therefore count it expedient for the completion of their happiness to add the pittance of pleasure which belongs to the world. Secondly; It is an attempt to rob the world of the pittance of inheritance which is allowed to them, as it is said, the fatness of the earth shall be thy portion, but not of heaven, and thus claim, ungenerously, an inheritance which is not theirs. Thirdly; It is an attempt to serve two masters, Christ and Adam, contrary to the express words of Christ; (for Christ and Adam are not one;) to serve Adam by doing his work, multiplying and replenishing the earth, or propagating the people of the world while presuming to serve Christ, whom the world hateth.

Now Christ is of the Father and not of the world; for if he were of the world it would love him. And if his people were of the world it would love them; but according to his own words, they are not of the world even as he is not of the world, and therefore the world hateth them. As really therefore, and as correctly, as Jesus Christ is not of the world, but of the Father, so really and correctly are his people, the children of God, not of the world, but of the Father, being born, not of blood, nor of the will of the flesh, nor of the will of man, but of God. Jesus Christ is the first, the foundation on which others are built, the head of the body, to whom his people are joined in one body and one Spirit, and are therefore no more of their first father Adam, but have renounced him and all relation to him, and are of God, the Father of our Lord Jesus Christ.

But the pressing, heavy objection with the advocates for christians marrying, comes in the following train; That those who maintain that marriage is inconsistent with the faith of Christ, by so doing exclude all who differ from them, from the salvation of Christ, and thus condemn the whole world, except themselves. Let this consequence be granted for a moment; does that prove the testimony false, or that those who bear it prohibit others from living according to their own faith? Or was Noah in an error, when By faith being warned of God, of things not seen as yet, he was moved with fear, and prepared an ark to the saving of his house; by the which he condemned the world, and became heir of the righteousness which is by faith? Had the testimony of Noah been false, what injury could it have done the people? Those who had no faith at all in him, no doubt, made themselves easy. In like manner the testimony of those who have the faith of Christ's second appearing, if not true, needeth not disturb any, because none are required to obey it, contrary to their own faith. The great uneasiness therefore and vigorous opposition to said testimony, must spring mainly from the evidence and conviction of its truth, especially in those who know what it is, and still oppose.

If christianity must not be professed in that order or to that degree, that it will condemn the world, it cannot exist on the earth; for Christ is not of the world, and the world hate him, because he testifies to the world, that their works are evil; and if they have hated him they will hate his followers also, for as he is not of the world, even so they are not of the world. And this is their testimony; " We know that we are of God, and the whole world lieth in wicked-" ness." [1 Jno. 5. 19.] Christianity therefore and truth condemn the world; not men, by their own power or holiness, or by any thing which they can arrogate to themselves, but the faith and work of Christ which they possess, and the testimony of truth which they bear. And this condemnation is not for the injury of mankind; it is really necessary that men be condemned by the truth as it is in Jesus; for unless condemned by it, they will never seek or obtain justification and life in faith and obedience to it. This condemnation therefore is not final to any except those who make it so by disobedience; but perseverance in disobedience during the accepted time and day of salvation, which none know how soon will end as to them, must prove final condemnation. Once more;

It is alledged, that to testify that marriage or living after the course of the world is not after Christ, implies forbidding to marry, because those who testify it, maintain they do it according to the mind of God, and by commission from him. Therefore, say the adversaries, these people forbid to marry by the authority of God. I have already opened this matter, and answered this objection. But why cannot people understand, that these people alledge no commission from God, to require any to submit to their testimony, contrary to their own faith and consequent choice, always declaring it a matter of the most free choice with every one whether to follow Christ or not? There is no arbitrary force or compulsion in the gospel ministry. Christ's people are *a willing people* in the day of his power. [Psm. 110. 3.] Probably no word in the Hebrew language, could more amply express the uncompelled, fair and deliberate choice of a people, than that which is here translated *willing*. And though every one who makes choice of the gospel, is compelled, or rather constrained and engaged by motive, contrary to his fallen nature, his choice is in the event most free.

Yea, saith the disputer, ye say people may act their faith, but ye maintain that out of the faith which ye have, no man can be saved. What then? Must any people renounce their faith to please others? For why is my liberty judged of another man's conscience? Or must the cross and self-denial of Christ be removed out of his gospel, that it may be adapted to the lovers of pleasure? Is the way of Christ too straight? or must it be widened to procure the carnal mind and the order of the flesh, admittance into heaven? Is any thing under the heavens more reasonable or just, than that every man should have his free choice, when the consequences on each hand, are laid before him? Those who are offended with believers in Christ's second appearing, for renouncing the first Adam and his works, if they believe there is salvation for them in Adam, let them cleave to him. But as we believe that Christ, and none else, is the salvation of God to us, let us at least have the privilege of cleaving to him. It is our unshaken faith that in Adam, or any where one side of the faith of Christ, salvation is not known.

I have looked; my spirit hath inquired; Is there no access to the children of the flesh, who dote on the perishing and polluted fancies of the earth, as if there were no better inheritance? But can that old serpent, called the devil and satan, be convinced of the propriety, and subjected to the duty of obeying God? They are his children and he is their father and governor. They have no room for God in all they do. But if the serpent cannot be convinced of the propriety, or subjected to the duty of obeying God, the wisdom of God is able to supplant him, and will do it, and the power of God in the gospel is able to overthrow and dispossess him, and to redeem his subjects from his slavery into the glorious liberty of the sons of God, *that they may inherit substance.* And the work is begun which will effectually dethrone the old serpent, and bring those who willingly yield obedience to him now, and contemptuously neglect and spurn at salvation by the cross of Christ, to beg with remorse of heart and bitterness of spirit, for an interest and a privilege in the same gospel which they now despise, and those who come not too late, to be humble, contrite and thankful when they are admitted.

Those who are determined on the pleasures of the flesh, at the risk of salvation, have their liberty to proceed accordingly; and those who are determined on salvation, at the expense of all, according to the doctrine of Christ, are not going to put themselves out of the way because of a testimony against the flesh, or against christians marrying. They have respect to the recompense of reward, and are not afraid of being losers by giving up all for Christ. They receive faith in God and in his promise. *That no good thing will he withhold from them that walk uprightly.*

Those who know the way of God and keep it, are able to talk like the people of God; " We know that we are of God, and the whole world lieth in wickedness;" [εν τω πονηρω, in the wicked one]. " We " are of God: he that knoweth God heareth us; he that is not of " God heareth not us. *Hereby* know we the Spirit of truth and the "spirit of error." Those who cannot adopt such language, are their own witnesses, that they lack an unshaken confidence that they know the truth and keep it.

There is one Christ, therefore one way to the Father, one truth, one life; one faith, one body and one Spirit; to pretend therefore to be in the way, and in the truth, and yet to believe that others are in the same way, who have a different faith, and consequently a different life, in matters of so great consequence as to cause a separation, is too absurd to find a residence with reasonable men. But as it remains true that the tree is known by its fruit, and the true gospel is best known by the fruits which it must unfailingly bring forth wherever it is, let all those who would deal honestly with themselves cease to contend about smaller matters, and no longer reject truth for fear of the cross, but lay hold of that gospel which produces its proper fruits—love, union, righteousness and peace.

CHAPTER X.

Christ's people not of this world.

TO bring this subject to a close, and to show as in one compendious view the discriminating line of separation between the church of Christ and all other people, whether professors or not, the last characteristic which I shall here state, and the pre-eminent, in which all others are included, is this, *That his people are not of this world.* " *They are not of the world even as I am not of the world.*"

It is generally granted in loose terms that the people, or church, of Christ, are not of the world, but few consider in what respect and how distinguishably, they are not of the world. The distinction is viewed, or contemplated, as being internal in the Spirit and therefore invisible, so that the people of God cannot be known, or distinguished by physical or merely natural men: as if an internal work would not be clearly manifested by its visible effects. " *They are* " *not of the world even as I am not of the world.*" As clear a line of distinction therefore as there is between Christ and the world, so clear is the same line of distinction between his church and the world: for they do as he said; *Deny themselves, take up their cross daily, and follow him*, in his footsteps where the world cannot go. And this discriminating line is so manifest that the world can see it, and discern the people of God from the world, and know that they are not of them or of their order, that they have put off the old man with his deeds, and have forsaken the world for Christ's sake. No matter if the world call them devils, or impostors and deceivers, as they did their master, they know them, and can discover that they have gone away from them. They cannot always discover in every case, who will follow Christ to the end; but they can observe the course which people must take, to come out of the world and follow

Christ, or be his chosen. The world can know the church of Christ distinctly enough to see that they are not of them, and to hate them for that only reason, because they are not of the world. Thus they hate his people as they hated him—*without a cause.* " If the world " hate you, ye know that it hated me before it hated you. If ye were " of the world, the world would love his own: but because ye are " not of the world, but I have chosen you out of the world, therefore " the world hateth you." [Jno. 15. 18, 19.]

Now it was not the man Jesus whom the world hated; " For he " increased in wisdom and stature, and in favor with God and man." [Luk. 2. 52.] But they hated the doctrine of the cross; so that when he 'showed the way of the cross they hated him for that—they hated and reproached that God, even the Father who dwelt in him, as it is written. *The reproaches of them that reproached thee are fallen upon me.* Thus the world or the spirit of the world in all men hateth the cross of Christ because it is not of the world and requireth those who would be saved to deny themselves, to cease from their works as God did from his, to walk not according to the flesh or works of the world, but according to the Spirit of God in Christ Jesus. In like manner, the world do not hate the men and women who follow Christ, abstractedly, but they hate the Spirit and cross of Christ: were it not for the cross, they could love them as well as other people; for take away the cross and all men would be of the world. The followers of Christ are courteous and comely in all things were it not for the *hated cross.* But the spirit of the world can never be reconciled with the cross of Christ, therefore the men of the world can never have fellowship with the people of God.

The church of God therefore have a living testimony, which is the word of God preached, and which draweth a discriminating line of separation between them and the people of the world, so that not only they can see it, but the world can see and feel the separation, and hate the church of Christ. " I have given them thy word; and " the world hath hated them, because they are not of the world, even " as I am not of the world." [Jno. 17. 14.] The man therefore, or the people of whatever name or denomination, however zealous or bold in the profession of christianity, and however great degrees of power they may have experienced or witnessed, who have not such a living testimony in word and works, as to let the world see and know by their preaching and their lives, that they are not of the world, but are called or chosen out of the world to follow Christ, fall short of the mark of Christ's church: in vain do men profess christianity without possessing the substance. *Our God is a consuming fire.*

But on what principle are the church of Christ not of the world, as really so as he is not of the world? In the first place; Because they have rejected the first Adam, the father of the world, with all his works, and have put on Christ, being all baptized by one Spirit into one body, of which Christ is the head. " Seeing that ye have " put off the old man with his deeds; and have put on the new man, " who is renewed in knowledge after the image of him that created " him." " For as many of you as have been baptized into Christ

" have put on Christ. There is neither Jew nor Greek, there is
" neither bond nor free, there is neither male nor female : for ye are
" all one in Christ." [Col. 3. 9, 10. Gal. 3. 27, 28.] In the next
place ; They who are baptized into Christ, or by the one Spirit into
the one body, of which he is the head and they the members, are
baptized into his death, and thus die, or become dead with him even
as he is dead or hath died. " Know ye not, that so many of us as
" were baptized into Jesus Christ were baptized into his death?
" Therefore we are buried with him by baptism into death." [Ro. 6.
3, 4.] Moreover; the church of Christ are raised to life in him and
live with him even as he liveth. " For ye are dead, [or, απεθανετε,
" ye have died,] and your life is hid with Christ in God." " There-
" fore we are buried with him by baptism into death; that like as
" Christ was raised up from the dead by the glory of the Father,
" even so we also should walk in newness of life. For if we have
" been planted together in the likeness of his death, we shall be also
" in the likeness of his resurrection; (having the same death and
" resurrection with him ;) knowing this, that our old man is crucified
" with him, that the body of sin might be destroyed, that henceforth
" we should not serve sin. For he that is dead, [dieth] is freed [is
" justified, δεδικαιωται] from sin. Now if we be dead, [απεθανομεν, have
" died,] with Christ, we believe that we shall also live with him : know-
" ing that Christ being raised from the dead, dieth no more; death hath
" no more dominion over him ; for in that he died, he died unto sin
" once ; but in that he liveth, he liveth unto God. Likewise reckon
" ye also yourselves to be dead indeed unto sin, but alive unto God
" through Jesus Christ our Lord." [Col. 3. 3. Ro. 6. 4, to 11.] Thus the
church of Christ are dead with him and alive with him so as to be
quite separated from the world ; and the world see and feel that it is
even so, and think it strange that they run not with them into the
same excess of riot, or same pursuits, speaking evil of them and
hating them because they are not of the world even Christ Jesus is
not of the world.

But if Christ died to sin and liveth to God, and his people do the
same, there can be no good reason why the world should hate either
him or them, or be at all disaffected with them on that account. But
they hate them as they hated him—without a cause, that is, without
any just cause. The world had a reason for hating him, *Because,*
said he, *I testify of it that the works thereof are evil.* So it is with
his people. Could they die to sin and live to God, and pursue the
course of this world as other men do, that is, live as the world do,
the world could not hate them. For said Jesus to his brethren who
did not believe on him ; " The world cannot hate you, but me it
" hateth ;" and to his disciples; " If ye were of the world, the
" world would love his own; but because ye are not of the world,
" but I have chosen you out of the world therefore the world hateth
" you." And again ; " I have given them thy word ; and the world
" hath hated them, *because they are not of the world even as I am
" not of the world.*" [Jno. 7. 7. and 15. 14. and 17. 19.] Thus it

is evident, that the separation between the world and the church of Christ who are baptized into his death and who also live with him, is effectual and real, and that the baptism with which they are baptized into Christ is an effectual work cutting them entirely off from the world, and also manifest, so that the world perceive it and look upon them who are thus baptized, or who take up their cross to follow Christ and once become established in his faith, as dead men. *For ye are dead, and your life is his hid with Christ in God.*

The world follow their former conversation which they had of old, walking after the course of the world, fulfilling the desires of the flesh and of the mind; but the children of God, the church of Christ, enter in with him into his rest, " By a new and living way, which he " hath consecrated for us through the veil, that is to say, his flesh." " For we who have believed do enter into rest." And again, "For he " that hath entered into his rest (the rest in Christ according to " God's promise to his people,) he also hath ceased from his own " works as God did from his." [Heb. 10. 20. and 4. 3, 10.] If then he hath ceased from his own works he doth not still practise them. The children of God therefore have rejected the former conversation, the manner of life which this world pursue, and live a new life with Christ in God, as he lived, and the world see it and hate them. " But ye have not so learned Christ ; (to live as the world ;) if so be " that ye have heard him, and have been taught by him, as the truth " is in Jesus; that ye put off, concerning the former conversation, the " old man which is corrupt according to the deceitful lusts; and be " renewed in the spirit of your mind ; and that ye put on the new " man, which after God is created in righteousness and true holi- " ness." [Eph. 4. 20 to 24.] Thus as the scion which is to be grafted into another tree of a different kind, must be cut entirely off from its original stock, before it can become one with the new, so must the children of Adam if they will be saved through Christ, be entirely cut off from the first Adam and become one with Christ so as to be no more of the world even as he is not of the world.

Now, " The children of this world marry and are given in mar- " riage : but those accounted worthy to obtain that world and the re- " surrection from the dead (and undeniably God's children are all " accounted worthy, these therefore) neither marry nor are given in " marriage : neither can they die any more ; (for having been once " dead in Adam in whom all die, and having died with Christ they " have their life securely hid with him in God :) for they are equal " unto the angels ; (having the life of Christ which is equal to that " of any angel ;) and are the children of God, being the children of " the resurrection." [Luke 20. 24, 25, 26.] The sum of this discourse is, that the world, or the children of this world marry and are given in marriage, but the children of God do not. For *the children of this world* are set in contrast with another class or character of people who neither marry nor are given in marriage ; and when their character is fully developed, they are found finally to be *the children of God,* being the children of the resurrection ; which resurrection is set forth as the medium or principle by which they become children of God, and this can be none else than coming into Christ. For to as many as receive him to them he giveth power to become the sons of God—He is the resurrection and the life. As Christ Jesus therefore did not marry as the children of this world do, neither took any participation in their peculiar works, so neither do his church. And this is the centrical and radical point in which both he and they are not of this world. This is the ground work of the separating line between Christ, including the whole church, and the world—in this centres that cross of Christ which the world hate, and without which no man can be saved from sin.

And that this is the radical point in which Christ was dead to sin and to the world, and his people dead with him, the words of the apostle are plain and pointed. " Wherefore, if ye be *dead with* " *Christ from the rudiments of the world*, why, as though living in " the world, are ye subject to ordinances?" Why submit yourselves to those ordinances of which I have been speaking which are a shadow of things to come, weak and beggarly elements imposed on those who live after the flesh and were alive to the rudiments of the world? [Col. 2. 20.] The body or substance is of Christ; and, if ye be dead with him from the rudiments of the world, ye have no need of these carnal ordinances; for ye are complete in him. Now the rudiments of any thing are the first principles, out of which it springs and according to which it is continually supported or hath its subsistence, as the first principles of a language, are called the rudiments of that language. Accordingly, the rudiments of the world are its first principles, by which it is continued through succeeding generations, and the place of the deceased is continually supplied with a multiplied increase. These rudiments are found in the order and works of the generation among those who marry and are given in marriage. These are the rudiments of the world, on which the children of the world live, and which they pursue, and from which Christ is dead and his people with him. These are the life of the world, which to forsake in the faith of Christ and to follow him, renders a man dead and hateful as death to this world; so that he is no more of this world even as Christ is not of this world.

On this principle a man is dead and yet living, even as Christ lived, " Because, as he is so are we, in this world." [1 Jno. 4. 19.] " And if Christ be in you, the body is dead because of sin;" (sin is found to have its seat in its appropriate works, it is therefore devoted to death with Christ, from all these works and their nature, that the whole body of sin might be destroyed;) " but the spirit is life " because of righteousness. But if the Spirit of him that raised up " Jesus from the dead dwell in you, he that raised up Christ from " the dead shall also quicken your mortal bodies by his Spirit that " dwelleth in you. (That they may be living temples for God while " they remain.) Therefore, brethren we are debtors, not to the flesh, " to live after the flesh. For if ye live after the flesh ye shall die:

of the world, and the rejection of that which is their life and necessary to their being in their own order, otherwise a man might be of Christ and of the world too. It must moreover include that which can make it manifest who are of the world and who are of God, and belong to the church of Christ. Now no profession of christianity, or possession either, consistent with marriage and ordinary generation, can include the necessary causes of the separation. For it is well enough known that all such possession of inward piety may be made in hypocrisy, where correspondent works do not accompany the profession sufficient to prove it genuine. Such profession therefore as is not accompanied with such correspondent works cannot carry conviction to the world, that such a man or people are of Christ and not of the world, nor cause the world to hate them because they are not of them. And where correspondent works attend any profession compatible with living in the state of marriage and ordinary generation, such profession and such works cannot carry conviction to the world that such people are not of them, nor cause them to hate them on that account; for notwithstanding, they may abstain from certain matters of less importance to the pursuits and enjoyments of the world, which yet pertain to their order, as from avenging injuries, or from taking a legal oath, or from shedding human blood; yet while they pursue or approve the generation the world will acknowledge them, although they may view them for a time with a degree of zeal and power which burns hot against a carnal nature. But this burning degree of zeal and power will abate in time with those who live in the generation, being consumed on their lusts, and they and the rest of the generation who live in the generation can retain that none of those churches who live in the generation can retain their separation from the world even as far as they sometimes gain it; neither can they keep a day of power and revival in religion more than a short time.

Besides; The men of the world do not hate a man or people, nor count them dead men, or not of themselves, because they pursue a profession and show correspondent works, provided that profession and those works be in the approbation of the generation of this world. Men esteem others the more for living up to what they profess. If a man will practise what they esteem as virtue; if he be just in his dealings, rendering to all men their due; if he be upright in his deportment, chaste in his outward conversation, humane towards mankind, kind to his family, generous to the poor, merciful to the afflicted and hospitable to strangers; and if he show the same goodness in other respects, although he should profess to be a christian and therefore not of the world, as long as he will support the generation of this world and acknowledge it as being consistent with the life of a christian, the world will never hate him nor count him out of their class; they will but esteem him the better for his consistent deportment. That which separates a man from this world so as to make him not of the world even as Christ is not of the world, and causes the world to hate him, cannot be his abstaining from ido-

" but if ye through the Spirit do mortify the deeds of the body, ye
" shall live." [Ro. 8. 10 to 13.]

I am aware that it will be contended, that the only necessary discriminating line between Christ and the world, or at least between his church and the world, (for clearly as it is taught few seem to have any conception that it is true, that they are not of the world even as he is not of the world,) and that line by which they are not of the world even as he is not of the world, consists in being obedient to commanded duties and abstaining from all things unlawful or expressly forbidden (or believing in Christ and having his righteousness imputed to them and thus being entitled to a reward in heaven, according to some,) but all in a perfect consistency with living in the works of the first Adam, as if Christ and Adam were completely at one. Thus many profess to be dead with Christ from the rudiments of the world, and are as continually and successfully employed as any of the children of the world in procreating the living subjects of the world, by its own rudiments and in the fulness of its spirit: for their offspring are as corrupt as any others. Many profess to have renounced the first Adam, to have put him off and to have come into Christ, to be baptized into his death and to live his hidden life in God, and yet are from time to time, begetting and bringing forth Adam's sons and daughters in all his fallen nature, as corrupt as the children of the infidel world or the fruit of illegitimate intercourse. And when they are asked for a reason to justify such works in christians, they will directly appeal to the commandment or law originally given to Adam, notwithstanding that as professed christians they claim an entire disunion with Adam, his family and his law, with all its consequences, to have put off the old man with his deeds, and to have put on the new, even the Lord Jesus Christ, who never incorporated himself with the first Adam, except by such conjunction as was necessary to put him to death, and lead the people out of his order and nature to God in the resurrection of life. O how inconsistent are the lives of professed christians! They make no radical or effectual distinction between Christ and Adam—no marked or discriminating line between the flesh and the Spirit—none between the living and the dead—none between the Church of Christ and the world.

But if it be the province of christians to propagate their species by natural generation, and if they may perform this who are dead with Christ and not of the world, how comes it to pass that they do not propagate their own likeness? Or is there any discriminating difference between their children and those of other people? Are they any more holy, or any easier to initiate into the faith and life of Christ? When Adam begat a son he was in his own likeness, and a lost, corrupt creature, and his posterity ever since, through successive generations have done the same; for *by one man sin entered into the world and death by sin; and so death passed upon all men, for that all have sinned.* How then cometh it to pass that christians do not propagate an offspring in their own likeness, or in the likeness of Christ, saved in Christ their living head? For Adam's sons con-

by nature children of wrath. Why then hath not the op-
the same influence at least over his seed and their posterity as the spirit of Adam over him? How cometh it to pass that they all have to be converted by the Spirit of Christ in the gospel and experience a regenerating work, before they are like Christ their Father and their head? It is proved by scripture, as above quoted, and by a painful experience, that the corruption of Adam's fall hath carried death to the remotest generations. But it is written, That where sin abounded grace did much more abound. Why then cannot this superabounding grace in Christ eradicate the abounding corruption of Adam's fall in the children of God, so that christians may propagate a legitimate and christian offspring, if it be their province to procreate their species by ordinary generation? Shall this only *abounding* sin or corruption of Adam's fall maintain its ground against the *superabounding* grace of God in Christ, and banter the followers of Christ and their offspring, struggling under its oppressions, and held by it all their life time subject to bondage through fear of death? Can this be all the fruit of Christ's delivering them, by his through *death destroying him that had the power of death?* It cannot be. Or can they be dead with Christ and not of the world even as he is not of the world; can they be separated from the fall, who do the same work, liberated from the deadly effects of the fall, and suffer the same corrupting influence of the which the world do, and fall with other people? It cannot be. Cease then to contend that the work of propagating the species by ordinary generation committed to the first Adam, is at all the province or work of the church of Christ, who are dead with him and not of the world. "*If the root be holy so are the branches.*" If that work could by any means be grafted into Christ, and be made the province of his people, it would be holy and its fruit holy; but all these attempts fail, so that when introduced into the church it is found to be *the man of sin,* as shown in its place. The church of Christ, the branches of the holy root, are brought forth by a very different process, not the generation but the regeneration, *being born, not of blood, nor of the will of the flesh, nor of the will of man, but of God.* Again;

If that separation from the world, or that Spirit or standing by which Christ's people are not of the world even as he is not of the world, consists in any thing compatible with marrying and practising those works which make that separation, with sufficient clearness to mark it out to the men of the world, and so disagreeable to them that they hate Christ and his disciples for its sake? The separation must evidently include something which the world highly disapprove and abhor, or the rejection and condemnation of that which they pre-eminently love, or both. It must also include that which is the death latry or the worship of false gods, from profaning the name of the Lord, from murder, manslaughter or otherwise taking the life of a man, from theft or fraud, from false witness or slander, from adultery or fornication, from drunkenness or debauchery; for all these things and the like the world themselves disclaim and disapprove according to their own profession as good citizens of the world, and those who practise them are more or less esteemed unworthy of countenance. These therefore cannot be the works of the world to which Jesus alluded when he said, " But me it hateth because I testify of it, that the works thereof are evil;" neither can these be the things which his followers do not practise, so that they are not of the world even as he is not of the world, and the world hateth them on that account.

But let a man once deny himself and take up his cross and follow Christ; let him once maintain that gospel which teacheth us to deny all ungodliness and worldly lusts, lawful or unlawful; (for many things are lawful which are not christian;) let him support the testimony of Christ in his own words, *That the children of this world marry and are given in marriage; but those accounted worthy to obtain that world and the resurrection from the dead, neither marry nor are given in marriage,* and live according to that testimony, showing that he is not of the world even as Christ is not of the world, and it will soon be seen what maketh the separation—it will be seen what ailed the world at Christ Jesus, why they hated him and why they hate his disciples, even as he said, *Because they are not of the world even as he is not of the world.* They who take up their cross and follow Christ reject that which is the life of the world, and are of course dead men in their view, as well as in reality, dead with Christ from the rudiments of the world, and as added a little after; *Ye are dead and your life is hid with Christ in God.* No wonder therefore that the world hate them, that is, the death and the life which are in them; they are dead, and no creature ever yet loved its own death but hateth it, and they live a life with Christ in God, a life which the world abhor, a life of self-denial and the cross of Christ; *I am crucified with Christ; nevertheless I live; yet not I, but Christ liveth in me;* a life which speaketh death to this world and the rudiments of it, which the children of this world love more than all things besides; for by these things men live and in these they glory. Well said Jesus; *I have given them thy word; and the world hath hated them, because they are not of the world, even as I am not of the world.*

It hath been supposed that the hatred and opposition of the world, particularly of the Jews, against Jesus, arose from his teaching a doctrine which overturned and superseded their law, disannulling their system of service, and leading them in new and unknown paths. But the world hated him because he testified of it that the works thereof are evil; and he did not teach that that law or service was evil; that therefore could not be the cause of the world's hatred. Besides; The disannulling of the Jewish law was not understood by the disciples, much less by the unbelieving Jews until after the giving of the

Spirit: this therefore could be no part of the cause of their hating him and putting him to death. That his doctrine led them in new and unknown paths is indeed true. The doctrine of self-denial and the cross, to eat his flesh and to drink his blood, or to live his life, to cease from the generation of the world or have no part with him, was to them an offensive doctrine: it struck directly against the lusts of the flesh, the lusts of the eyes and the pride of life, the all that is in the world. (1 Jno. 2. 16.)

The Jews, it hath been presumed, were offended with Jesus, and hated him, because he said that God was his Father. But why should this offend them? Did they not call themselves the sons of God? *We have*, said they, *one Father, God.* (Jno. 8. 41.) And could it be offensive to them to hear their Messiah say, *My Father worketh hitherto, and I work?* But the truth is, they hated him for another cause; his denying himself, and bearing his cross, as he also taught them to do, against all ungodliness and worldly lusts; the lust of the flesh, the lust of the eyes and the pride of life, including all covetousness and the claiming of worldly possessions. And their charge against him, for saying that God was his Father, was only a pretext to support their quarrel against his holy and self-denying life which was not according to this world.

In the same manner they contended with him, for breaking the sabbath. Not because they cared for keeping the law in truth; for they made void the law by their traditions; neither because he did break the sabbath, or violate the law in any case; for he was always able to put them to confusion and to vindicate his own works on the sabbath, by their own law and their own practice, and thus to show, that they only sought an occasion against him by such accusations, because they hated his doctrine and his holy, self-denying life. He did not gratify the lust of the flesh and of the world; he did not marry and hold private possessions. The world hated him because he testified of it that the works thereof were evil.

Again; One of their heavy charges against him to ensure his crucifixion, was that he made himself a king and was therefore an enemy to Cesar: as if they had been friends to Cesar. When it is evident that nothing would have pleased them better, than that he would have taken the command and established them in the kingdom and glory of this world, at the expense of the life of Cesar and all his power. And such was their opposition to Cesar and his government, that no man was by them counted a greater sinner than he who held the office of a tax gatherer, called a publican, under Cesar's government. But they hated him, not because he did any evil, but because he denied himself, as they also do his disciples, and say all manner of evil against them falsely for his name's sake, whom they follow in the same self-denial.

It is also true that the branch cannot bear fruit of itself except it abide in the vine, no more said Jesus, can ye, except ye abide in me. Now as true as this similitude is when applied to Christ as the vine and his people as the branches, so true is it when applied to the world as the vine and the children of the world as the branches, and illustrates the subject as correctly in the one case as in the other. For as no man can bring forth the appropriate fruit of Christ, or of his body, the church, unless he abide in him, so neither can any man or woman or both, bring forth the appropriate fruit of the world, unless they are of the world and abide in it. But the whole world lieth in wickedness; those therefore who are of the world and abide in it, even those who bring forth the fruits or do the appropriate works of the world, are lying in wickedness, [εν τω πονηρω] in the devil, and not in Christ. But they that marry, or in any relation propagate the children of the world serve the world, and therefore do not serve Christ; they bring forth the appropriate fruit of the world and are therefore of the world and abide in it. Thus it is logically proved, by undeniable premises and correct conclusion, that they who marry, or do the works of natural generation, are of the world and not of Christ.

After taking this view of the subject the common silencing objection will present itself, that if this is the true gospel, and all should believe and obey it, as all ought surely to obey the truth, the world would soon come to an end. To obviate this let it be considered in the first place that the very work of Christ is to bring the world to an end in his people as soon as they become his. A work unknown to the church before the coming of Christ, as saith the apostle; " Now, all these things happened unto them for our example ; and " they are written for our admonition upon whom the ends of the " world are come." (1 Cor. 10. 11.) Accordingly, as before shown, his people are not of the world even as he is not of the world.

Now let us ask, on what principle can the end of the world be effectuated by the abstinence of those who are not of it? The world is to be served and continued through its own subjects and is sufficiently organized for that purpose. But the objection includes this also, that the call is to every one to come into the same faith, and should this be so, the world must inevitably come to a period. It is true; the call is to every one wherever the gospel comes; but it is also true, that few are disposed to obey. There is a heavier objection in the way than the fear or the prospect of the world's coming to an end; their unwillingness to deny worldly lusts is of more weight with them, than the prospect of the world's being at an end, the hope of salvation or the fear of damnation. Now the deciding question is simply this, Which is the most momentous work; to continue building up the world in its present order in which the salvation of Christ is not known and keep every individual to that work, or to build up the church of Christ in eternal life for all souls who are willing to come out of the world and be joined to Christ? They that prefer the latter will confirm the wisdom of their choice by making a speedy escape from the course of the world and all its fetters, and uniting themselves to the body of Christ, the church. And those that make choice of the former may solace themselves in their short lived and paltry inheritance, the portion of Esau, while we consider the second answer to the objection in the words of Jesus Christ.

"And this gospel of the kingdom shall be preached in all the world, for a witness unto all nations; and then shall the end come." (Matt. 24. 14.) This prophecy was not fulfilled in the apostolic dispensation, nevertheless it will surely come to pass. Now what can they effect who are so deeply interested in keeping this world from running out? Can they rebuke the purpose of God which is to publish to all nations that everlasting gospel of Christ which he hath already introduced amongst men to make a finishing work of salvation in all who will receive it? Can they withstand the decree of God saying, let the finishing, the everlasting gospel be published to the men who dwell on the earth, saying, " Fear God and give glo-" ry to him for the hour of his judgment is come?" Or can they prevent the faith and obedience of honest souls who seek a kingdom which hath foundations, whose builder and maker is God? Can they support the world in its present course and order when the testimony is fulfilled and the end is come, any more than the disobedient in the days of Noah could by their eating and drinking and marriages, keep the flood from drowning them when it came? " For as " in the days that were before the flood they were eating and drink-" ing, marrying and giving in marriage, until the day that Noah en-" tered into the ark, and knew not until the flood came and took them " all away; so shall also the coming of the son of man be." (Matt. 24. 38, 39.) They will not yield until the end is come.

As God in the days of Noah gave the people warning long enough to prove them and give them a fair opportunity to repent, before he brought the flood, so when the everlasting gospel hath been preached to all the world for a testimony to all nations until the time is fulfilled and all have heard, then cometh the end : and whether many or few have believed the world can support its cause no longer.

In every dispensation, except the christian, marriage was justifiable and consistent; for in Christ alone the people are called to leave the world and its works. And the practice is so common, that mankind are hardly convinced that Christ is at all distinct from Adam. Hence some after all will plead the instruction or permission given to Noah ; as if Noah had been Christ, and had the pre-eminence, or had even been a follower of Christ, many hundreds of years before he opened the way; or as if Noah were the pattern and example of believers, whose steps they are to follow. Neither do all the permissions, commandments and regulations, under the law of Moses and the whole levitical priesthood, although they contained every commandment from the beginning, afford any support to the faith or practice of marrying and living in the generation after coming into Christ, in whom there is neither male nor female. " For (in Christ) there is " verily a disannulling of the commandment going before, for the " weakness and unprofitableness thereof. For the law (called the " commandment going before,) made nothing perfect, but the bring-" ing in of a better hope doth ; by the which we draw nigh to God." When the priesthood was in the hands of the tribe of Levi and of Aaron, and the first born of the high priest was his heir, they all married and begat children in the flesh. But the priesthood being transposed, from Aaron to Christ, who is made priest, not after the order of Aaron, but after the order of Melchizedec, who was without father, without mother, and without descent; so is the Son of God and so are his people, without father, without mother and without descent after the flesh: these neither marry nor are given in marriage. For the priesthood being changed or transposed there is a transposition or change made also in the law. There is one law and one rule.

The thought is in itself inconsistent and preposterous, that christians should count it their province or privilege to occupy the old ground of the generation of the first Adam, after they are called out to be a separate and devoted people to God. That any people should be redeemed from death and initiated into life, and yet be participators in the appropriate works of him in whom all die; or should be regenerated from the first Adam into the second; transplanted from the world into the church, the body of Christ; from the ruined state of fallen nature into a state of salvation by the grace of God in Christ; from union and relation to the men of the world, who all lie in wickedness, to a relation and union with the general assembly and church of the first born whose names are written in heaven; or in a word, from Adam to Christ, and from earth to heaven, and yet occupy the same ground from which they were transplanted, and cultivate the same old polluted soil of the fleshly generation, is too absurd to admit of a supposition: these different states are incompatible with each other. It is utterly unreasonable, that they who believe they were conceived in sin and shapen in iniquity, as well as all others who have been thence produced, should cleave to the former ground and cultivate the old soil wherein they were thus conceived and shapen, after (they say) they have been called with the holy calling of the gospel into Christ, to be a people devoted to God, to serve him in the newness of the Spirit, and no more in the oldness of the letter. Can it be that such people have any real understanding of the character of Christ the quickening Spirit, the Lord from heaven? Or of the nature and work of Christ, in the redemption of souls? Or can they have any just conceptions of the greatness and reality of that change which is experienced by those who are called in Christ to put off the old man with his deeds which are corrupt (so that all his fruit even the most legitimate, is conceived in sin and shapen in iniquity,) according to the deceitful lusts, and to put on the new man who after God (and not after the fleshly works of the old generation) is created in righteousness and true holiness? Can they be the circumcission who worship God in the Spirit and rejoice in Christ Jesus and have no confidence in the flesh, to whom it is like cutting the heart strings and rending the cords of life, to renounce the fleshly works and fleshly relation of the first Adam for the sake of Christ and eternal life in him? Do they love him more than these?

But some will yet say, Did we not all come forth into life by natural generation? And without it how could there be any people to be saved? And what then? Because we are all born into the world by natural generation, born of blood, of the will of the flesh, and of the will of man according to his desires and propensities, must we on that account, or can we, remain on the ground and in the works of natural generation after we are called out to be of the number of the new born chidren of God in Christ, who are born, not of blood, nor of the will of the flesh, nor of the will of man, but of God, and are not of the world even as Jesus is not of the world? Can any man be in Christ and remain where he was before? Can a man put off the old man with his deeds, and put on the new, and be a partaker of the nature and a practiser of the works which are the very core of the old man's life and the foundation of his existence? Let the dead bury their dead; and let the world propagate its members; but Let not God's people return to the beggarly elements, *the rudiments of the world*, wherein some desire to be in bondage.

But some will argue, that to put off the old man with his deeds, implies nothing more than to put off or renounce, and not practise or approve, the evils which have attached themselves to him, and which he hath practised, as drunkenness, murder, theft, adultery, fornication, covetousness and other unlawful works and lusts. But this plan in its utmost extent is only to dress the old man in goodly attire, to sweep and garnish the house, and let him live. These are no part of the old man. They are unmanly things, as well as unchristian. Unlawful deeds were never committed to him to do; neither was he ever allowed to indulge in unlawful lusts; they are none of his appropriate works even in nature, unless by that appropriation which he himself hath made by deviating from his proper line, without any authority from God. And although these and such like are the works of the flesh, they pertain to it in its fallen condition only, in its fallen nature as opposed to the Spirit. And the flesh is not to be redeemed from its loss, purified and saved, but to be crucified with the affections and lusts, whether appropriate or self-made. So also, the old man is not to be renewed and redeemed by Christ, but put off with his deeds, whether appropriate by God's appointment or self-made. And Christ is to be put on, the new man who is renewed in knowledge after the image of him who created him in every follower, in whom he is formed. " Put ye on the Lord Jesus " Christ; and make no provision for the flesh to fulfil the lusts there- " of, [do not make the provision of the flesh towards its desires. Ro. 13. 14.]

As Jesus was a partaker of a human body and soul as other men are, that he might be the elder Brother of his redeemed brethren, the Father of his spiritual children, a fellow partaker and leader in their sufferings and tribulation, and thus be made like them in all things, while he opened for them the new and living way through the vail, that is to say, his flesh, his own being part of the same which they had, and by the cross which he taught them also to bear. In that situation, I say, he used the proper means of support for the animal life of the natural body, but took no part in the generation of the world, nor made any provision, by laying out or submitting to any method for the fulfilling or satisfying of the desires or lusts of the flesh; so it is justifiable and consistent with christianity to provide things necessary and convenient for the support of the body, to make a vessel for God's service, subject to the Spirit, which mortifies the deeds of the body, but not to feed it for the indulgence of fleshly lusts or the performance of the first Adam's works, after being called into Christ. We have an altar whereof they have no right to partake who serve the tabernacle. (Heb. 13. 10.)

Farther to illustrate the doctrine of Christ and show that the world will hate and oppose the people of Christ as they also do himself, I will introduce the saying of Christ to the Jews. " I am come in my " Father's name, and ye receive me not: if another shall come in " his own name, him ye will receive." (Jno. 5. 43.) Could any thing more strikingly exhibit the enmity of the world against God and his Christ, than the rejection and abuse which Jesus received at the hand of the people among whom he wrought so many miracles, spake so many gracious words, did so many kind offices and good works, and in all his works revealed the Father so clearly ? But, *I am come in my Father's name, and ye receive me not : if another shall come in his own name, him ye will receive.* Query: If any man should come professedly in his own name and propose to be a teacher to lead men to life, not even pretending that God had sent him, or that he had any commission from God, would even the world receive him? I trow not. These words then are figurative; and the phrases, *In my Father's name,* and *In his own name,* are to be understood as containing more than words.

When Jesus spake of the false prophets and teachers, he said, *Many shall come* in my name, saying, *I am Christ. Saying but not doing according to Christ,* not walking in his Spirit or works. Now if any man will come in the name of Christ, *not saying but doing according to* Christ, walking in his Spirit and works, him the multitude will not receive. But if another shall come in his own name, as almost all do, not saying but doing also, walking in his own ways and teaching out of his own spirit, him they will receive. For when a man cometh in his own name, or according to his own spirit, and will promise the people salvation in that spirit, he cometh in the name and spirit of all the world, and they will receive him and close in with the plan. A Christ, or his ministers, who will preach salvation to the flesh or in the flesh, bring the most acceptable news to mankind, and they will receive them.

Now it is according to the name and the spirit and the practice of this world to marry and live in the generation, therefore it is that all those preachers of the various denominations who approbate that work as being consistent with christianity find so hearty a reception among mankind. They bring them no cross against their own life. These are they who promise the people liberty while they themselves are the servants of corruption. But it is not according to the spirit of this world for a man to deny himself and take up his cross and follow Christ, bearing his yoke and his reproach, to crucify the flesh with the affections and lusts and lose his life for Christ's sake and the gospel's. Therefore it is that those preachers and people who follow Christ bearing his cross and his reproach and teach the necessity of coming out from among them and not being of this world even as Christ is not of this world, as the true way to be saved, find such poor reception among professed christians as well as others. These are they who truly come in the name of Christ and of the Father, and the people prove it by their so generally rejecting them.

The foregoing doctrine, bears hard against the children of this world, whose only dependence is the flesh, who trust in it for their existence and continued succession here and finished happiness in heaven. For, cut off the flesh and the world is ruined; its children are enervated; they have no longer any source of existence, no longer any comfort or any lively spring of action or pursuit, in this stage of action; and their grand concentrating hope and prospect of perfected happiness (most of them) in the next world is the resurrection and reanimation of the flesh, or natural body; so that their great confidence is in the flesh, without which they have no hope. " But " we are the circumcission who worship God in the Spirit, and re- " joice in Christ Jesus, *and have no confidence in the flesh,* (Phil. 3. 3.) neither for life nor happiness here, nor for any part, much more the perfecting of happiness in heaven. For notwithstanding we had our confidence in the flesh when we were of the world, having renounced the world and its appropriate works, to follow Christ and be of him, we have that confidence no more, neither stand in relation to those who live according to the flesh. " For the love of Christ con- " straineth us, because we thus judge, that if one died for all, then " were all dead: And that he died; for all, that they who live, should " not henceforth live unto themselves, but unto him who died for " them, and rose again. Wherefore, henceforth know we no man " after the flesh: yea, though we have known Christ after the flesh, " yet now henceforth know we him no more." (2 Cor. 5. 14, &c.) Once Christ was known as a man descending from the loins of Abraham, Isaac and Jacob according to the flesh, but he is now known in the Spirit as the Lord from heaven and Head of the new and spiritual creation, the true Father of the faithful; the former kindred or relation, therefore, according to the flesh, with all its knowledge is forgotten, and men become known and united in the Spirit. " There- " fore, if any man be in Christ, he is a new creature: [or, there is a " new creation, Greek,] old things are passed away, behold, all things " are become new. And all things are of God." He hath new motives, new prospects, new works, a new parentage, and all new kindred, in the Spirit and according to Christ, in the room of the old in the flesh and according to the first Adam, new springs and a new life. He drinketh out of a new fountain, serveth a new master, and finally walketh with him in the new and living way which he hath consecrated through the vail in which he vailed himself that we might hold a relation to him and follow him ; that is to say, his flesh. For he is dead with Christ from sin, from the world and its rudiments, and alive to God in the Spirit. His brethren, and his sisters, and his mother, are the same as Christ's are, those who do the will of his Father in heaven. He is a subject of the same death which Christ died, *to sin*, and of the same life which Christ lived, *to God*. He no more looks to Adam as his head or his root, or his law-giver, but to " Jesus the author and finisher [or, the first leader and per-" fecter] of our faith ; who, for the joy that was set before him, en-" dured the cross, despising the shame, and is set down at the right " hand of the throne of God." Thus he is eventually an overcomer with Christ and sitteth with him on his throne, even as he overcame and hath sat down with the Father on his throne.

But all this work of dying with Christ, of suffering with him, and of losing the life for Christ's sake and the gospel's, is considered by some and argued with obstinacy, as consisting in an inward work, reforming indeed, and regulating the life and manners of men, as well as softening their hearts, but not cutting them off from the original stock so perfectly, but that they may do the appropriate works of the first Adam while they also serve Christ—may propagate and do the other appropriate works of the world while they are not of the world even as Christ Jesus is not of the world. But besides the impossibility of a man's serving two masters, and the impropriety or rather absurdity of any man's propagating the world and doing the appropriate works of the world and of the first Adam the father of the world, when he himself is not of the world, which are silencing considerations with men of discernment; it may be asked, How cometh it to pass that by the faith, or work of Christ, the son is divided against the father, and the father against the son, the mother against the daughter, and the daughter against the mother, the daughter-in-law against the mother-in-law, and the mother-in-law against her daughter-in-law, and that a man's foes are (emphatically) those of his own house, or family ; and how cometh it to pass, with an emphasis, that the kindreds of the earth (or earthly kindreds, relations) shall wail because of him; unless the faith and work of Christ cut the cords of the kindred of the earth and took the life of the fleshly or Adamic relation ? According to the promise of God to his Israel, even to Christ, so it is coming to pass. " Thou art my " battle-ax and my weapons of war : for with thee will I break in " pieces the nations, and with thee will I destroy kingdoms ; And " with thee will I break in pieces the horse and his rider ; And " with thee will I break in pieces the chariot and his rider ; With " thee also will I break in pieces man and woman; and with thee will I " break in pieces old and young; and with thee will I break in pieces " the young man and the maid ; I will also break in pieces with thee " the shepherd and his flock ; and with thee will I break in pieces " the husbandman and his yoke of oxen ; and with thee will I break " in pieces captains and rulers," (Jer. 51. 20, to 23.) even all the connections and the whole order of the flesh and the world. Again;

The promise of God for the work of Christ is as follows. " And it
" shall come to pass in that day, that I will seek to destroy all the
" nations that come against Jerusalem. And I will pour upon the
" house of David, and upon the inhabitants of Jerusalem, the spirit
" of grace and supplications: and they shall look upon me whom
" they have pierced, and they shall mourn for him, as one mourneth
" for his only son, and shall be in bitterness for him, as one that is in
" bitterness for his first born. In that day shall there be a great
" mourning in Jerusalem, as the mourning of Hadadrimmon in the
" valley of Megiddon. And the land shall mourn, every family
" apart; the family of the house of David apart, and their wives
" apart; the family of the house of Nathan apart, and their wives
" apart; The family of the house of Levi apart, and their wives
" apart; the family of Shimei apart, and their wives apart; All the
" families that remain, every family apart, and their wives apart."
(Zec. 12. 9, to 14.) Men and wives are in the course of this world;
for its children marry and are given in marriage; but the work of
Christ will rend them all asunder for the destruction of the flesh,
that the Spirit may be saved—that they may be as angels of God in
heaven, all joined to the Lord in one Spirit.

But it is argued that this work of dying with Christ was all done
in him, that is by him in our room when he suffered once in the end
of the world, and that the actual loosing of the life for Christ's sake
and the gospel's is limited to those who are called to suffer martyrdom, or give up the natural life in the cause of Christ. But if this
be true, none besides those martyrs can be saved: for whosoever
will save his life shall lose it; and in all the revelations of God to
men where do we read of any who ever arrived to finished salvation
except those who arrived through great tribulation, suffering and
death, in a word, any but martyrs who loved not their lives unto the
death?

No affliction so great; no death striketh so deep and deadly a blow
against human nature, its hope, its life and its prospects in its fallen
state as the piercing call of God to come out of the world into
Christ: this death is to both the male and female; for both are partakers of the ruin which is in the flesh by sin. But as the woman
was first in the transgression, was deceived, and first obeyed the serpent, (and the man obeyed through her means,) she is exposed to an
increased death and torture in coming out of the world into Christ.
But both have to be torn up from the foundation or never be saved.
The nature of the serpent, which is the source of all iniquity, hath its
life and subsistence in the works of natural generation, and liveth under cover of marriage first instituted by God, or that appointment
according to which a man was to forsake his father and his mother
and be joined to his wife, and they twain were to be one flesh. This was
the original order of the first creation, and was in its own time and
place correct and innocent; until the serpent beguiled the woman,
and she became obedient to him and partook of his nature, which she
hath retained ever since, with much obsequiousness; and the woman

ingeniously occupying the same bait, enticed the man, and decoyed him into the same transgression; to whom he hath yielded himself a servant, and to the serpent through her, ever since, to the production of all the real evils which are extant, or ever have been on the earth. For that original order appointed and fixed by God, wherein the blessing of God would have been found in peace, had it been kept according to the original calculation and design, *that God might seek a godly seed*, (Mal. 2. 15.) when it became subverted over to the devil, became the fruitful womb of the contrary evils, *and the earth was filled with violence*. (Gen. 5. 13.) According to this view Solomon, notwithstanding he lived in a dark day, when the light of the gospel had never appeared, and therefore could not find out all the truth, as he confessed, when he applied his heart *to know, and to search, and to seek out wisdom, and the reason of things, and to know the wickedness of folly, even the foolishnsss, and madness*, exclaimed, " And I find more bitter than death the *woman* whose heart is as " snares and nets, and her hands as bands;" (Eccl. 7. 25.) thus esteeming the woman as the ground work, or productive soil of all the evils, the folly and wickedness, under the sun. According to what was seen and written before; " That the sons of God saw the daugh- " ters of men that they were fair; and they took them wives of all " whom they chose. And God said my Spirit shall not always strive " with man, for that he also is flesh. And God saw that the wicked- " ness of man was great in the earth, and that every imagination of the " thoughts of his heart was only evil continually." (Gen. 5. 2, 3, 5.) This was the fruit of their being one flesh, after the first order of creation became subverted by the serpent; and so it remained, not only until the days of Solomon but ever since. I would not be understood by the strong language here used, that the woman is alone in the transgression: the man is as really guilty as the woman. But as the woman was first deceived and first in the transgression, she appeareth foremost in the production of evil and in the affliction to be felt in the work of redemption. " Woe to them that are with child and " to them that give suck, in those days." (Mark. 13. 17.) Why not as directly to them that beget; unless because the woman standeth in the front of the afflicted? For the work of redemption cometh with death to the fallen nature of the human family: and this fallen nature is the life of the lost world.

From the same source may we account for the greater and if possible more universal opposition in women than in men against the gospel and cross of Christ in these last days; that gospel which is especially adapted to redeem the woman from all her woes in consequence of the fall. The woman was created an helper meet for the man. But when the order between the man and woman was subverted into the nature of the serpent, the woman obeying him instead of the man, her appointed head, they were both lost in the flesh together; and the woman, viewing the flesh to be cut off by the cross of Christ, and the work of generation to cease, considereth herself as rejected and stripped of her all—dishonorable, disesteemed and useless—a mere nuisance on the earth: for if called out from the work of propagating the species, she seeth no other work which the man cannot perform without her. For in nature, she hath no understanding more than the man, of the honorable and happy lot she is to fill in the work of redemption. Besides, since the day when the sons of God saw the daughters of men that they were fair, and took them wives of all whom they chose, the woman hath found that the only peculiar attachment or regard which a man in nature, (or in what common professors call grace, or the gospel,) hath to a woman, hath its root and subsistance in the work of generation, which being cut off by the faith of the gospel, her estimation and glory in nature are eternally sunk, and she is degraded and ruined: for her consequence with all her glory is in the flesh, and the glory of the man, the fleshly glory is in the woman; but the gospel calleth them both to worship God in the Spirit and rejoice in Christ Jesus, and have no confidence in the flesh. Thus the unhappy woman, led by the nature of the serpent, whom she hath so long obeyed, unhappily rebelleth against the messenger of her peace and redemption, and the man led by the same spirit received from her, rebelleth also. And thus it will be until they become acquainted with the nature of the redemption in Christ; in whom the man is emphatically, the glory of God, comely and honorable, and the woman is truly the glory of the man, comely and amiable; and the union in the Spirit is safe, innocent and pure.

This statement is not intended to cast any disparagement on the woman in her proper order, but if possible to bring her to sober reflection and convict her judgment and conscience of her lost estate; and to let her know that her art of pleasing, as the idolizing world delicately term it, however noble and amiable the faculty in its proper use, is subverted into the serpentine skill of beguiling and decoying, being abundantly used to that effect; which if not crucified by the cross of Christ, will eventuate in her destruction. " I find, (saith " Solomon,) more bitter than death *the woman* whose heart is as " snares and nets." It may be objected; as it already hath been, that the woman here exhibited or characterized, is not the whole sex in contradistinction from the man, but the dissipated or lecherous woman of exceptionable conduct. This objection may arise from two causes. First; The unwillingness of the man as well as the woman, to be convicted of the egregious ruin which hath overtaken the woman by her obedience to the serpent, and which is by her dispersed amongst her admirers; and secondly, an unacquaintance with the construction and force of language, *I find more bitter than death the woman whose heart is as snares*, importing the same as if it read, *for her heart is as snares and nets*. Surely the man, lost as he is, will not agree that the woman of an exceptionable character is the only one who can environ him with her snares and nets. But it is the appropriate power of the woman, in her fallen state, to allure by the flesh in the nature of the serpent; and Solomon was led astray, no doubt, by the most worthy in his knowledge. The Hebrew text is correctly translated thus. " I find more bitter than death, the wo- " man, (or as the seventy have translated it, I find her out; and I say

NOT OF THE WORLD.

" that there is somewhat, more bitter than death, with the woman)
" who is as snares, and her heart as nets, and her hands as bands."
No doubt, according to the words which follow, " Whoso pleaseth
" God shall escape from her; but the sinner shall be taken by her,"
but Solomon, who then knew not fully the seat of depravity (but the
Spirit knew,) might have cherished the idea that the evil lay in the
exceptionable conduct of nearly all women, and that if the good woman
could be found, it might be remedied. But unhappily he never could
find her; and no wonder; for the earth had not yet been honored with
her person, nor the church been blessed with her Spirit. The Good woman is she that hath forsaken and crucified the flesh, and hath borne her
cross after Christ Jesus her Lord: the good woman could not be found
before the good man. The flesh must be crucified; for it is of the world
and not of God; and its fruits have always been in iniquity and in sin;
as saith the Psalmist; " Behold, I was shapen in iniquity; and in sin
" did my mother conceive me." As our common translation reads.
But no English language occurs to me, calculated to express the
force of the original, without lengthening the description. The
Psalmist, pressed with the sense and weight of his corruption and
depravity, which he brought with him by descent from the rock
whence he was hewn and the hole of the pit whence he was digged,
and laboring to make a clear communication of his impressions, used
the most energetic expressions, it is probable, his native language
could afford, " I was conceived* in *the act of* iniquity, and in *the act
" of* sin my mother inclosed me, in the lust of coition;" evidently
making the whole work and production, the fruit of sin, and that neither the fellowship nor nature of God was therein—that God was not
known therein.

Would time and the limits of the book admit, there is abundant
testimony in history to prove by that authority, that it hath been the
faith of all professed christians since the days of the apostles, to renounce the generation of the first Adam, as being included in the

* הוללתי. *For what reason the English translators have rendered
this word by*, I was shapen, *I know not, unless, being unable to find
any phrase by which to render the following* יחמתני, *which they have
rendered by* conceived, *they substituted the word shapen for the first,
that a gradation, or increase in strength of expression, somewhat
answerable to the original, might appear in the description; the last
phrase being the strongest and most expressive of the root and nature of human depravity. The Septuagint, though only a translation from the Hebrew text, and therefore cannot demand implicit
reliance, yet as its authors were Hebrews, and at least ought to have
understood their own language correctly, renders the first of the
above phrases by a Greek word,* [συνελήφθην] *which properly and
naturally reads,* I was conceived, *and the latter by* [εκισσησε] *a remarkable word, which by a secondary meaning signifies* to conceive,
*but primarily, according to derivation is indicative of pertness, or
wantonness.*

cross of Christ, which every christian is required to bear. And although all did not bear a full cross in that point, they who did were esteemed the best christians. At this day all those faithful and zealous disciples of Christ are counted heretics; and as such their mangled characters have been handed down to us, by historians who were enemies to the cross of Christ. But enough is siaid to prove the point in hand; neither have we any good evidence that the notion of christians' marrying and doing the works of the first Adam, was ever patronised with full fellowship in any professed christian church until in modern times: it is entirely an innovation; the work of men, who are lovers of carnal pleasures, more than lovers of God, or real friends to the cross of Christ. I say the mangled characters of the most zealous and faithful disciples, who have denied themselves for the sake of Christ and his gospel, have been handed down to us under the name of heretics; and such are all those esteemed by the professing part of the world, who correctly adhere to the doctrine and example of Christ in obedience. It is esteemed the worst kind of heresy; the worst kind of apostacy from Christ, to renounce the world, or the first Adam the father of the world, and put all confidence and all dependence in Christ; rejoicing in Christ Jesus and having no confidence in the flesh. So that after all the mighty outcry of heresy, delusion and presumption against the believers in Christ's second appearing, our faith is not so different from that of other people, as many represent it, or as prejudice and opposition say. Do we believe that the old generation is not the work of Jesus Christ? So do they. Do we believe that his real followers do not practise it? So do they; as many as have kept a direct line of faith from the primitive church. Do we believe that God's purpose is to put a period to the world and the old generation? So do they. Do we believe that God will put an end to the world by fire, that the earth and the works thereof shall be burnt up, and that the elements shall melt with fervent heat? So do they: and so in many other points. The erroneous notion among professors, that prophetic language can be understood by them before it is explained by the accomplishment, is productive of many more. By that they are exposed to take metaphorical and symbolical language in a literal acceptation. The fire of God by which the earth is to be consumed, is preposterously maintained to be elementary fire, notwithstanding so many scriptures speak differently. But what that fire is, the gospel, or the Spirit of God in the gospel, is the best expositor, and showeth those who keep the gospel, that it is God himself, who is a consuming fire; or the Holy Spirit; who is the fire in Zion; or Christ who is like a refiner's fire. By this fire the earth and the works that are therein shall be burnt, and the elements shall melt with fervent heat; " And the world passeth away and the lust there-" of: but he that doeth the will of God abideth for ever." It is before shown and every where known that the lust of the world, or the works of the generation of the world, are the elements of the world. " Nevertheless, we, according to his promise, look for new

" heavens and a new earth, wherein dwelleth righteousness;" in the earth as well as in the heavens, after the great burning hath come to pass, and the heavens and the earth have passed away with a great noise. (1 John 2. 17. 2 Pet. 3. 10, &c.) It is also a question with some, and with many a matter of obstinate unbelief, whether the times and seasons are come, in which the old heavens and earth shall pass away by the fire of God. The mistaken notion that the prophecies can be understood before the day of their accomplishment or without the gift of the same Spirit who gave them at first, and also the notion that they are to be literally fulfilled, operate, strongly in support of their not believing that the times are come, while they do not see those literal accomplishments, not considering that the work of the kingdom of Christ is spiritual, and that " None of the wicked shall understand: but the wise shall understand;" that is the pious. But these things will be more fully considered hereafter.

CONCLUSION OF PART SECOND.

Thus we have performed what was proposed, to show what are the distinguishing characteristics of the church, or body, of Christ, by which they can be known and distinguished from all other people— They are found to be a people in the possession of that gospel which giveth them power over all sin, so that in the progress of the work they cease to commit sin, or do any iniquity—a people living in the exercise of such love and union as no other people can imitate, being the product of no other cause, no other spirit than that of which they are possessed—the Spirit of God—*the unity of the Spirit in the bond of peace*—a people who are not of this world, and therefore neither marry nor are given in marriage as the children of this world do, but live as the angels of God, who are devoted to the work and service of God in the Spirit and serve not the flesh. *Therefore, brethren, we are debtors, not to the flesh, to live after the flesh. For if ye live after the flesh, ye shall die: but if ye through the Spirit do mortify the deeds of the body, ye shall live.*

It may appear to some a very improbable thing, or rather impracticable, for a society of people to subsist on the earth from year to year, and from age to age, in the practical rejection of the physical order of procreation. But God hath begun the work and he will carry it on. It is not the work of man, or it could not stand; for said Jesus, " Every plant, which my heavenly Father hath not planted, shall be plucked up from the root." It hath been shown that the flesh is not the source of confidence in the people of God, but the Spirit—That the flesh is the source of divisions, of wars and contentions; but that the church and people of God are united in one Spirit. " Jerusalem is builded as a city that is compact together." The church of God, the new Jerusalem, is built in a new order of things after the Spirit; in Christ, " Of whom the whole family in heaven and earth is named." So said John, in the Book of Revelations; " And I saw a new heaven and a new earth: for the first heaven and

"the first earth were passed away; and there was no more sea. The material heaven and earth could not subsist in their present order, without the water of the sea, to supply both the animal and the vegetable creation. But the language is prophetic and symbolical. The sea is the source and treasure of *many waters* on the earth; which are used in this same book of the Revelations, as a symbol of Peoples, and multitudes, and nations, and tongues; a divided and immense multitude over whom the great whore; THE MYSTERY BABYLON THE MOTHER OF HARLOTS AND ABOMINATIONS OF THE EARTH presideth, with noise, tumults and divisions, like the roaring waves and commotions of the sea. But none of these things are in the church of Christ; in whom *there is neither Greek nor Jew, neither bond nor free, neither male nor female ;* neither confusion, nor division, nor tumult; for in that church God hath his dwelling. "And I John saw the holy city, new Jerusa-
" lem, coming down from God out of heaven, prepared as a bride
" adorned for her husband. And I heard a great voice out of heaven,
" saying, Behold, the tabernacle of God is with men, and he will
" dwell with them, and they shall be his people, and God himself
" shall be with them, and be their God. And God shall wipe away
" all tears from their eyes; and there shall be no more death, neither
" sorrow nor crying, neither shall there be any more pain: for the for-
" mer things are passed away." (Rev. 21. 1, 2, 3, 4.)

THE MANIFESTO.

PART III.

OF THE RESURRECTION AND JUDGMENT.

CHAPTER I.

Of the Resurrection; more particularly as it relates to the person of Jesus Christ.

THE belief of the resurrection is acknowledged by all who profess christianity, as an inseparable article in the profession of the gospel of Christ. "For if the dead rise not, then is Christ not raised; "and if Christ be not raised, your faith is vain; ye are yet in your "sins." (1 Cor. 15. 16, 17.)

The gospel of Christ hath a special relation to a future state of existence, as the time and place of the most glorious fulfilment of its most precious promises. And that future state of happiness is unattainable without the resurrection of the dead; because death, without restoration, is the issue with all in the first order and state of things, since the fall. For to this day, "In Adam all die," according to the threatening; "For in the day that thou eatest thereof thou "shalt surely die." (Gen. 2. 17.) And again; "In the sweat of thy "face shalt thou eat bread, till thou return to the ground; for out of "it wast thou taken; for dust thou art and to dust shalt thou return." (3. 17.) The only method therefore, of restoration to life, and the only true foundation of hope for a future state of happiness, are to be found in Christ, who is the resurrection and the life, and who saith to his followers, Because I live ye shall live also. The certainty of the resurrection therefore, is not a matter of dispute, being granted by all.

The inquiry relates rather to such questions as these; What is the resurrection from the dead? How is it effected? What is the state of those who have attained to the resurrection from the dead? Or in the language of scripture; "How are the dead raised? and with "what body do they come?" But the whole of the differences on this subject will naturally be presented to view for investigation in the discussion of this simple inquiry; Is it necessary to the accomplishment of the resurrection, taught by Jesus Christ and his apostles, that the material body, which men inhabit during their natural or physical life, be raised again, restored to life, and confirmed in eternal life; or can that resurrection be accomplished in the spirit, without the reuniting of the spirit with the natural body?

In treating this subject, my purpose shall be, In the first place—To collect and examine the evidences alledged in favor of the resurrection of the same body. And secondly—To consider some passages of scripture, which cannot be understood with good sense if considered as speaking of the resurrection of the same material body. And thirdly—To show that the true resurrection promised in Christ, is the passing from the first Adam into the second.

I am not unaware, that to satisfy the mind and conscience of natural men, and to stop the mouth of gainsayers, on this subject, will be a more difficult and arduous undertaking, than on almost any other particular pertaining to the gospel. And no marvel, when it is considered that the gospel is a spiritual topic, pertaining to spiritual things and a spiritual work, and that the resurrection is the very substance and marrow of the gospel, and as it were the basis on which it stands or with which it falls—No resurrection no gospel. It is also that rudiment, or first principle, according to which the whole work of the gospel is carried on, and the whole building framed together, and finally accomplished, in the Spirit of Christ—He is the resurrection. It is therefore not strange, that it is out of the reach and comprehension of natural men. "For the natural man receiveth not the "things of the Spirit of God; they are foolishness to him; neither "can he know them, because they are spiritually discerned." [1 Cor. 2. 14.] Nevertheless, candid inquirers are not incapable of receiving such evidence, adapted to their intellectual faculties, as will satisfactorily evince, what the true resurrection of the saints is, and how to attain to it.

Now according to the proposed plan, the first business is, To collect and examine the evidences alledged in favor of the resurrection of the same body. And as the resurrection is entirely dependent on revelation, for its confirmation and elucidation, our examination shall have immediate respect to the scripture testimony. And as life and immortality were brought to light by the gospel, and the resurrection was not known with any certainty to the Gentiles, and but imperfectly known or understood by the Jews, being first taught explicitly and fully by Jesus Christ and then by his apostles, the principal attention shall be paid to the apostolic writings, with such of the Jewish as Jesus and his apostles have quoted.

It is peculiarly necessary in treating this subject, to consider the great darkness and ignorance of the Jews respecting the resurrection; for although it was believed and looked for by some, yet such was the darkness on this subject, and particularly respecting the resurrection of Jesus Christ, that it could be said of his disciples and followers, "For as yet they knew not the scriptures that he must rise "again from the dead." Being natural and accustomed to a carnal dispensation, they understood natural and carnal things, but were ignorant of the spiritual. This state of things made it necessary, to use expressions and representations to the Jews, in the introduction

RESURRECTION.

of christianity, very different from those used by christians who were instructed in the nature of the spiritual work and kingdom of God. Accordingly the apostles used very different language, different representations, and on the whole, a very different statement of facts in their first public ministrations, proving the certainty of the resurrection of Jesus Christ, from what they afterwards used in the progress of christianity, showing what that resurrection is in its nature and effects. And it ought by all means to be considered, that the statement and proof of the fact, of the resurrection of Jesus Christ, and consequently of his people, are very different matters from the illustration of its nature, showing how the dead are raised and with what body they come. By not attending to this distinction, the mind is liable to be led quite astray, and to substitute the natural in the room of the spiritual, and so err from the truth not knowing the scriptures neither the power of God.

Before we enter fully into the discussion of this subject, it will be expedient to premise, that the term BODY admits, and necessarily requires, different acceptations, in the holy scriptures as well as in other writings and in the common use of language, to the present day. Sometimes it means the animal body in distinction from the spirit—Sometimes, an individual person including body and spirit—At other times, a number of persons collectively, as when we speak of a body, or corps of soldiers, and also the church, or body of Christ, and the like. Respect will be had to what is here premised, in the sequel.

The arguments in proof of the resurrection of the same natural or animal body, generally concentrate in the resurrection of Jesus Christ. The advocates of this sentiment plead, That the resurrection of Jesus Christ was a real fact—That there could be no resurrection of Jesus Christ without the resurrection and reanimation of the same material body which he inhabited before his crucifixion; because the resurrection of that body is the grand point in which his resurrection consisted, so that to deny the resurrection, reanimation and ascension of that material body, is the same as to deny the resurrection of Jesus Christ altogether—That the resurrection of Jesus Christ is the example and pledge of that of his people; therefore, the resurrection of the material body of the saints is an undoubted fact to be expected in the fulfilment of the promises of God in Christ; as the grand point in which the resurrection of his people consists, consequently, it is considered erroneous to teach that the resurrection is come, until those material bodies actually arise. These considerations render the subject serious.

With respect to the first particular here stated, as pleaded by the abettors of the resurrection of the material body—That the resurrection of Jesus Christ was and is a real fact; It is granted without hesitation. And also that his resurrection is the example and pledge of that of his people, is freely acknowledged. But the second proposition is not granted, neither can it be proved, neither the inference drawn from it. For in the first place ;

It is no where explicitly stated in the scriptures, that the same material body of Jesus arose, or had any part in his resurrection. Had that been the case, it was quite natural for it to have been mentioned, as that was the particular object of the disciples' attention, for which they sought, and of which alone they seemed to have any real knowledge or understanding: for as yet the Holy Spirit had not been given, to lead them into the knowledge of spiritual things. Accordingly, both Peter and Mary and those with them, made their search for the body. And Mary, because she saw not the body, said "They have taken away my Lord." And the angel, adapting his language to the understanding of the women, said, "Come see the place where the Lord lay." This manner of speech was no doubt common in those days, as it is also in these. Nothing is more common than to say such a man was buried there, or he lies there, when at the same time, no one believes the man is there at all, but the visible part, the body, or carcase, is there, and that serves as a reason for such language; but the most essential constituent of the man is believed to be some where else, so that professors do not hesitate to talk of such an one's being in heaven. In the next place,

With all that is said on the resurrection of Christ and in confirmation of the fact, there is no language used in the scriptures, but what is capable of being consistently understood, without implying that his material body had any share in the true resurrection or ascension. Yet it is not to be denied that he appeared to his disciples invested with a body which could be apprehended by their senses. Of which hereafter.

Now if all the expressions used in the scriptures, in proving and describing this fact, be capable of a consistent acceptation without implying the resurrection, reanimation and ascension of the same material body, to the right hand of the Father, that view of the resurrection fails of being established. For no language can prove or establish any fact, except that which cannot be consistently understood in a different light, especially when pointed language, of equal authenticity, teacheth the contrary: which will be inquired into hereafter.

It is farther to be considered here, and kept in mind through the whole inquiry and argumentation, that unless the ascension of the same material body to the right hand of the Father can be established, the above plan, of a literal resurrection, must fall to the ground. For he is the life as well as the resurrection, and that which arose, must also have ascended, and live for ever, else not be a participator in the resurrection of Christ; and to consider the resurrection of the same body as an example and pledge of that of the saints, and then to suppose that body not to ascend as aforesaid, would render the resurrection of the saints a blank.

In the histories of the evangelists we find the following remarkable language, which is argued as an unequivocal proof of a real material body, consequently the same which was crucified. "And "they came and held him by the feet, and worshiped him." [Matt.

RESURRECTION.

28. 9.] " And as they thus spake, Jesus himself stood in the midst
" of them, and saith unto them, Peace be unto you. But they were
" terrified and affrighted, and supposed that they had seen a spirit.
" And he said unto them, Why are ye troubled? and why do thoughts
" arise in your hearts? Behold my hands and my feet, that it is I
" myself: handle me and see: for a spirit hath not flesh and bones as ye
" see me have. And when he had thus spoken, he showed them his
" hands and his side." [Luk. 24. 36, to 40.] " Then the same day
" at evening, being the first day of the week, when the doors were
" shut where the disciples were assembled for fear of the Jews, came
" Jesus, and stood in the midst, and saith unto them, Peace be unto
" you. And when he had so said he showed unto them his hands
" and his side. Then were the disciples glad when they saw the
" Lord." " And after eight days again his disciples were within,
" and Thomas with them : then came Jesus, the doors being shut,
" and stood in the midst, and said, Peace be unto you. Then saith
" he to Thomas, Reach hither thy finger, and behold my hands; and
" reach hither thy hand, and thrust it into my side ; and be not faith-
" less but believing. And Thomas answered and said unto him,
" My Lord and my God." [Jno. 20. 19, 20, 26, 27. 28.] Here it is
argued, was a real, material body.

It hath been granted above, that he appeared in a body which
could be apprehended by the senses, seen and felt. But it is argued
that it was a body of flesh and bones: so be it; therefore a body
which could not inherit the kingdom of God, and consequently did
not ascend thither. For flesh and blood cannot inherit the kingdom of God ; and it is known that flesh and bones do not live without
blood, because the life of all (such) living is the blood thereof; and
it is evident that the phrases, flesh and blood and flesh and bones literally mean one and the same thing—the animal constitution distinctly
from the spirit ; the latter of which is capable of inheriting the kingdom of God, but not the former.

But this body had the wounds in the hands, feet and side, and therefore must be the same body. If the wounds prove it to have been
the same body which was pierced with the spear and the nails in the
crucifixion, they also prove it to have remained in the same material
state as when he was crucified and buried ; but that was not possible,
because he had appeared to some in a different form once or twice,
on that same day, in the evening of which he came and stood in the
midst, and showed himself, on the first occasion of which John hath
related these circumstances. This appearance was in the evening of
the first day after the resurrection, as particularly stated by both
Luke and John, who both relate the same interview between Jesus
and his disciples.

Now to have preserved the wounds safe through such changes, or
to have restored them to their former state for the disciples to see
them, implies an accommodation of his appearance to their prejudices and natural senses as really as an assumption of the whole body, or the accommodating of himself to their senses while the ani-

mal body constituted no part of the representation; the existence therefore of those wounds proves nothing in favor of that being the same body which had been crucified. Add to this the remarkable fact of his coming and showing himself to them when the doors were shut, so carefully related by John, in his narrative both of the evening of the first day and also of the eighth after, when Thomas was present. Unquestionably the evangelist, in relating this fact so carefully on each of these occasions, intended to indicate something extraordinary or miraculous in it. If then the miracle consisted in the same material body's being found in the house, or coming in, when the common avenues adapted to the entrance of such bodies were all closed, it proves unequivocally that these wounds were also miraculously preserved or restored, to accommodate the appearance to the prejudices and carnal weaknesses of the disciples. The discovery therefore, or the existence of these wounds, is no proof of its being the same body, for it was as natural according to the view here stated, to show them in one body as another. With respect to the silly plea which I have heard, that Jesus had gone into the house and concealed himself, while the doors were yet open, it implicates him in the commission of a fraud, or the disciples in an uncandid statement of facts; or both. For him to come into the midst of them, the doors being shut, if he had come in before, was no more extraordinary than for any other man to step into a company; and the supposition gives the whole narrative the appearance of fiction and affectation, and not a relation of simple facts: the notion is chimerical.

As for the objection which some make, that this view of the subject represents Jesus as putting a cheat on the disciples, persuading them it was the same body when it was not, it is easily obviated. This reply is plain and simple. That he was the same Jesus Christ who had before conversed with them and had been crucified, and that was the point to be proved; but that he was then clothed with the same animal body in which he had formerly dwelt, the disciples never tell us that it was the same or that they thought it was. And admitting that in their ignorance of spiritual things and the earthly conceptions relative to the kingdom of God, which they then had and retained until after the ascension and the giving of the Holy Spirit, they had no other apprehension or conception, than that he appeared to them in the same body as before, that being the extent of their knowledge or prospects, this being an admissible case, (which I would not peremtorily contradict,) is no proof, either that the former animal body was a partaker of the true resurrection, or that the disciples were imposed on by any fraudulent or deceptious measures. They received such evidences of the truth as their weaknesses required, and their infancy in spiritual things admitted; for they were yet unacquainted with the distinction between the natural and spiritual creation—between the old man and the new. And there could be no deception in his appearing to them in the old creation, or body, or an assumed body in the appearance of the old, until they were convinced of his resurrection, his being alive and his really appearing to them, and until they obtained more correct knowledge of his true character in the new creation, more than in any man's putting on a coat which he had been accustomed to wear, or one resembling it where the people were not sufficiently acquainted with him to know him without such coat, and yet the necessity of his being known were indispensable.

If it was an imposition or cheat for Jesus Christ to show himself to his disciples in a form adapted to their senses and apprehension, when he was not clothed in the same flesh and blood, which he had formerly taken on him, it was no less an imposition, to intimate that the wounds had remained as they were, after having passed through that which rendered it impossible. And no reason can be produced, why he should carry those wounds, after he arose, had he even inhabited the same body, except to accommodate himself to the senses and understanding of his disciples, so as to gain their consent to the truth of his being alive, or the truth of his resurrection. Figures and shadowy representations are not the substance; yet they are not false or fraudulent, when they subserve the purpose of conveying evidence to the understanding and of establishing truth. The disciples were yet in nature, the Holy Spirit being not yet given, and needed natural and perceptible representations, to confirm them in the faith of that substance which is spiritual.

But the advocates for the resurrection of the animal body argue farther; That as the body had now become spiritual, it could be put into any form, or removed to any place, on any necessary occasion, with the utmost ease, a spiritual body being unresisted by matter. Without this expedient there is no accounting for the various appearances which took place, as passing into the house, the doors being shut, disappearing in the open light, and the like. But this argument militates directly against the common plea, that it was properly flesh and bones, and the same in which he was crucified. Thus the arguments on that side of the question destroy each other, and like the witnesses against Christ in old time, agree not among themselves. For the arguments adduced to prove the resurrection of the same material body, assert that it is yet material, flesh and bones, consequently that which cannot inherit the kingdom of God, and therefore can have no participation in the resurrection of Christ, as already proved. But if to avoid this difficulty, it be argued, that the body which was raised was spiritual, the one argument invalidates the other, and there remains no proof of its being the former material body. And if it be said that the body of Jesus is not asserted or believed to have been proper flesh and bones after the resurrection, but that which had been such, now become a spiritual body. I ask what peculiar faculty, or ability, such a spiritual body would possess to favor the appearance of flesh and bones, or what claim it would have to be so denominated, above that which was originally spiritual? Spirit is spirit; and that which is of the spirit is also spirit. And flesh is flesh, and that which is of the flesh is also flesh. So that all such notions of flesh and blood, or flesh and bones, becoming spirit, or being so modified as to constitute a spiritual body, are without foundation. But the crowning argument with some may be, that the body of Jesus was not transformed into a spiritual body, as long as he conversed with his disciples, but was thus translated when he ascended to heaven. But this proposition lacks proof. It also militates against the scripture testimony, and even contradicts it, concerning the resurrection of the dead, of which the resurrection of Christ is maintained, not improperly, to be an example, It is raised a spiritual body: of this hereafter. Neither is the above proposition free from the former difficulty, that flesh and blood cannot inherit the kingdom of God. And the scripture makes no provision for any qualification of that unequivocal expression; for neither is there any doctrine in revelation, nor any principle in natural reason, philosophy or morals, to teach us that matter can, by any method or degree of modification, be transformed into spirit : all such conceptions therefore, are at best vague and groundless.

This sentence. " A spirit hath not flesh and bones as ye see me " have," contains no real proof that it was the same body, when two things are considered. First; the intention of the expression; which was to convince the disciples that he was a real man, the same Lord Jesus whom they had formerly known, and by the way to dispel their fears, and so bring them to be composed and conversable. For they were terrified and affrighted and supposed they had seen a spirit. This shows that he had not the common appearance : for why should they be terrified at the sight of a man with whom they had been so long conversant or suppose him to be some unknown spirit, having already heard that he had risen ? The answer however was well calculated to soothe their minds, until they should become better acquainted with him in his true order.

The terror with which the disciples were seized on that occasion and the reason assigned, strongly indicate the necessity which existed, that he should show himself to them a man in full form with flesh and bones. , They were terrified and affrighted, and supposed that they had seen a spirit. From this it appears they knew very little about spirits : they had not yet understood, that their Lord and Master was a spirit. But they were now in a kind of deserted forlorn condition—their Lord had been crucified—the Jews were their enemies, for fear of whom they were gathered together into that house— and in the midst of these calamities, as if to perfect their misery, behold ! a spirit—an evil spirit, or demon, as they supposed—a messenger of evil. For why should they have been afraid of an heavenly spirit—an angel of peace ? But their understanding was small on these subjects. No method therefore was so proper, to calm their fears, as to present himself to them, a man in full form, and perfect in all his members, and give them a fair opportunity to examine him, together with the wounds which he had wisely retained for this purpose, until they were satisfied that THIS IS HE. It hath been already evinced that such representations imply no fraud. Observe;

It is not said, I am flesh, or I have flesh and bones; but, a spirit hath not flesh and bones, as ye see me have—as ye behold or [θεωρειτε.] contemplate me as having. A form of expression perfectly consistent with an accommodating appearance, or an assumed body for accommodation's sake. For the Lord, even Jesus Christ, is a Spirit, and therefore hath neither flesh nor bones.

Secondly; We are told by the learned, that according to the idiom or manner of the Jews, whose language Jesus and his disciples used, they said any thing is so, when it appeared to be, and there are examples in the scriptures to confirm this observation. Accordingly it is said. (Gen. 5. 24.) " And Enoch walked with God, and he was not: " for God took him." He did not cease to be, he only disappeared from the earth. " And (Jno. 1. 14.) the Word was made flesh;" that is, was clothed with flesh, or took on him flesh and blood such as the children had. Again; (2 Cor. 5. 21.) " For he hath made him " who knew no sin, sin for us." For our sakes he prepared him a body, and clothed him in flesh and blood such as the children had, sinful as it was, thus laying on him the iniquity of us all. But who is dark enough to believe that the Word which was God, was also proper flesh, or that Jesus Christ was really sin? Again; (Ro. 5. 20.) " Moreover the law entered that the offence might abound." That it might be seen how much it did abound, for by the law is the knowledge of sin. Once more; (Ro. 6. 17.) " But God be thanked " that ye were the servants of sin." That ye have seen that ye were servants and taken the conviction. These examples are sufficient to confirm the observation, that it was according to the Jews' manner to say on many occasions, that such a matter is, when it appeared to be. The saying of Jesus therefore, after the fullest examination contains neither assertion nor conclusive proof that he then possessed the same animal body which he had formerly inhabited.

The saying of Matthew, " And they came and held him by the " feet," contains no decisive proof that it was the same body. Before any such fact can be established from that saying, we must have it proved that the body which Jesus possessed when divested of the clay tenement, and which saints also possess eventually, is incapable of perceptibility and form, and also that he was unable to assume perceptibility for the satisfaction of those women.

Another particular related by Luke of that first memorable evening, was his eating. (24. 41, to 43.) " And while they yet believed " not for joy, and wondered, he said unto them, Have ye here any " meat? And they gave him a piece of a broiled fish and of an honey- " comb. And he took it, and did eat before them." It is presumable, that few, if any, will be so weak as to suppose this was done for any thing else than a sign, to take off their excessive commotion of mind, to render them more conversable by becoming more familiar with them, and eventually to confirm their faith in the resurrection, and in him as their Lord and Master. Now if this sign could not have been given without the use of the same body which he formerly inhabited, it must undoubtedly have been there. But I presume none will say that Jesus had not power to give it through some other medium; it therefore fails of proving the presence of the same body.

CHAPTER II.

The subject continued; with some attention to prophetic scriptures.

SEVERAL other particulars are recorded by the evangelists in confirmation of the fact, that Jesus rose from the dead; but I have purposely selected those which had the greatest appearance of favoring those who plead that the same material body arose, and ascended, and that the same material bodies of the saints must also arise. My object in selecting these hath been, that the labor might be shortened, both in writing and reading; for these comprehend every evidence contained in the other particulars, and so present the whole in a shorter view than could have been done by quoting every passage which speaks of these things. And in all these, and all the rest, although there is sufficient proof that Jesus rose from the dead, yet none either by express testimony or by necessary consequence, that the same body arose; because all the language is capable of a different acceptation consistently with truth. For as before intimated, it is perfectly just to plead, that as long as the language alledged in proof of the fact, is capable of a different acceptation, it cannot pass for proof, especially considering that other scriptures of equal authenticity more explicitly teach the contrary. Uncertain consequential arguments, and these partly analogical, however plausible, without explicit testimony, must not be allowed to overbalance proposed and explicit teachings of equal authority; neither can literal and natural representations of a spiritual work, adapted to the understanding of natural men, be admitted as being capable of communicating the knowledge and understanding of said work, as well as the work itself, or the language and experience of those who travel in it.

The subjects of every new dispensation require the light and teachings of that dispensation, before they can understand the nature and order of its works. The apostles were just emerging from a dispensation which consisted in outward things, In meats and drinks and divers washings and carnal ordinances, and which had only a shadow of good things to come and not even the real image of the things, (Heb. 9. 10, and 10. 1.) and were properly in a carnal state, and had earthly conceptions of the work of Christ and kingdom of God, as their works and language every where show. At one time they were inclined to command fire to come down from heaven, to consume those who did not receive their master. [Luk. 9. 54.] At another time they undertook to defend him with the sword. [Jno. 18. 10. Matt. 26. 41.] And at another time Peter undertook to rebuke Jesus himself because he showed them what should befall him,

RESURRECTION.

"That he must go to Jerusalem, and suffer many things of the El-"ders and chief Priests and scribes, and be killed, and be raised again "the third day. Then Peter took him, and began to rebuke him, "saying, Be it far from thee, Lord: this shall not be unto thee." No doubt but he intended to fight courageously. But Jesus ordered him to get behind him, as one who stood in his way, and called him satan, an enemy, telling him in plain terms that he savored the things of men, who seek ease and protection to the flesh, and not the things of God, whose way is to crucify the flesh that the spirit may be saved, "Get thee behind me, satan; thou art an offence to me: for thou "savorest not the things that be of God, but those that be of men." [Matt. 16. 21, to 23.] And so deeply were they all lost in a carnal sense of things, and in ignorance of the work and kingdom of God, that when Jesus was taken and crucified, they felt themselves forsaken, and became disconsolate, as though all had been lost. For notwithstanding all the teachings which they had received from his own mouth, and the writings of their own prophets they knew not that he was to be put to death and to rise again, "For as yet they "knew not the scripture, that he must rise again from the dead," [Jno. 20. 9.] and when it came to pass, they were with difficulty prevailed on to believe, by the plainest testimony of their own senses, as their history shows. And even after he had risen and they had believed and conversed with him about forty days, their carnal sense greatly remained, and they still expected an earthly kingdom. And hoping, that as he was risen from the dead to their full conviction and satisfaction, the time had come when he would commence his reign with them for ever, "They asked of him, saying, Lord, wilt "thou at this time restore again the kingdom to Israel? And he "said unto them, It is not for you to know the times or the seasons, "which the Father hath reserved in his own power. But ye shall "receive power after that the Holy Ghost is come upon you." [Acts. 1. 6, to 8.] They asked him, if he would at this time restore the kingdom, as though they had once had it, (when that which they had had was only carnal,) after he had so plainly taught them long before, that the kingdom is within, and cometh not with observation, or outward show. But knowing their earthly conceptions and their shortsightedness in spiritual matters, he referred them to the teachings of the Holy Spirit, shortly to be given to them, whose office it was to guide them into all truth, and to take of the things of Jesus Christ and show to them; whom after they had received, they began to understand the spiritual nature of the work and kingdom of God.

Now it could not be expected, that the disciples, under the influence of those earthly views with which they were so strongly prepossessed, according to the works and teaching of the dispensation in which they had been educated, could suddenly receive the knowledge and understanding of a spiritual kingdom and of the resurrection to eternal life in that kingdom, without such evidences and representations, adapted to their senses and their understanding, as were sufficient to establish the fact, that Jesus did arise, and confirm them in the belief of it, the true nature of which they had afterwards to learn, by a farther experience under the guidance of the Holy Spirit. And for the same reason, it behooved these disciples, in preaching the gospel to others, who labored under the same disadvantages, or greater, to present to them, such evidences as were calculated to beget in them the faith of the fact, that Christ arose from the dead, by addressing them in such language, as they could understand, although by so doing, they were obliged to dwell greatly in the letter, and leave the true spiritual substance to be learned by future experience. All people must be children in grace, as well as in nature, before they can be men and women of full age, grown up into him in all things, who is the head, even Christ.

It will likely be objected that it is unfair to make a studied labor of explaining all these facts in such a manner as to exclude the resurrection of the animal body, when a simple attention to the narrative would certainly fix that impression. Thus it hath been objected to me, that a child would receive the understanding of the natural body as being raised, by just reading or hearing the account. I acknowledge the truth of the observation, but not the propriety of the argument. And no doubt a child or minor, previously to better information, being necessarily ignorant of the nature and order of spirits, or spiritual existence, would readily receive the impression of a natural body, as well as others who know nothing beyond nature; but the argument is disingenuous, for although Jesus enjoined it on all, to become as little children, that requisition did not relate to the understanding of the spiritual nature of his work and kingdom, but to simplicity of manners teachableness, and the like. Hence the apostle's exhortation, " Brethren, be not children in understanding; howbeit " in malice be ye children, but in understanding be men." [1 Cor. 14. 20.] It is also granted that the narrative of facts given by the evangelists would readily fix the impression of the resurrection of the animal body, were there no testimonies to the contrary, and were not the subject better understood by the gift of the Spirit in those who have traveled in their spirits into the same work with Christ, as the apostles began to do after the Spirit descended on them; or could the resurrection of the animal body, be once established by unquestionable testimony, the different facts recorded by the evangelists would be strong corroboratives, naturally coinciding with such testimony. But such unequivocal testimony is wanting. And it cannot be unfair, in a subject of so serious a nature, to examine the evidences with the utmost scrupulosity, and give them no more weight than they necessarily and justly claim.

Another objection is, That if the same body did not rise, it could not be the same Jesus Christ, for he could not properly exist as the man Jesus without it. I would ask, What imperfection, inability, or deficiency, existed in Jesus the Son of God above other men, that he could not exist and be the same Jesus Christ without a body of clay? Abraham, Isaac and Jacob had laid off the tabernacle of clay, ages before the ministration of Moses, and yet they existed in his days, the same Abraham, Isaac and Jacob, and the Lord remembered them and was their God. But God is not the God of the dead, but of the living. Moses also, though he had been dead hundreds of years, and his body buried in one of the hills over against Beth-Peor, was alive in the days of Jesus Christ, and came in company with Elias, and talked with him in the mount, and the disciples saw him, *and it was Moses:* so saith the evangelist. If these and many more could exist, and retain their personality and name, before the resurrection was completed, and while their animal bodies were in the dust, how much more the Son of God who is the resurrection and the life? a true Spirit of divine origin?

Another objection stands thus; If the animal body did not rise, there was no resurrection in the case, for none but that body died. This objection originates in ignorance of what the true resurrection is. Jesus laid down the tabernacle and descended into the common state, or place, of the dead, and returned again to be seen among the living, " Now no more to return to corruption." And the scripture was fulfilled, " Thou wilt not leave my soul in hell, neither wilt thou " suffer thine Holy One to see corruption."

Jesus Christ the first born Son of God was a man, and lived a Jew, being born under the law. In the character of man, he was invested with the whole of human nature in its fallen state, according to the order of the first Adam, that he might be a suitable leader to lead them out of their lost estate, who were subjected to death by reason of sin. " For both he that sanctifieth and they who are sanctified " are all of one, for which cause he is not ashamed to call them bre- " thren. For as much then as the children are partakers of flesh " and blood, he also himself likewise took part of the same ; that " through death he might destroy him that had the power of death ; " and deliver them who through fear of death were all their lifetime " subject to bondage. For verily he took not on him the nature of " angels ; but he took on him the seed of Abraham. Wherefore " in all things it behoved him to be made like unto his brethren ; that " he might be a merciful and faithful high priest in things pertaining " to God, to make reconciliation for the sins of the people. For in " that he himself hath suffered, being tempted, he is able to succour " them that are tempted." [Heb. 2. 11, 14 to 18.] " All we, like " sheep have gone astray ; we have turned every one to his own way ; " and the Lord hath laid on him the iniquity of us all."—" By his " knowledge shall my righteous servant justify many ; for he shall " bear their iniquities." [Isa. 53. 6, 11.] " Behold the Lamb of " God who taketh away [or beareth away] the sins of the world." [Jno. 1. 29.]

As a Jew, he was a true minister of that dispensation to fulfil it, and to open the door for the salvation of the Gentiles as well as the Jews. " For he is the end of the law for righteousness to every one " who believeth." " Now I say that Jesus Christ was a minister of " the circumcission for the truth of God, to confirm the promises " made to the fathers; and that the Gentiles might glorify God for

" his mercy. (Ro. 10. 4. and 15. 8, 9.) And he not only kept the Jewish law, or law of Moses perfectly, but also the intermediate dispensation committed to John as his forerunner, submitting to his baptism, and saying, " Thus is becometh us to fulfil all righteousness," and so putting an end to that. And this was consistent with the views which John had of these things, that the ministry of Jesus Christ would supersede his, as he said, " He must increase, but I must decrease." [Jno. 3. 30.]

Thus keeping his way fully cleared on every hand, and in every character which he filled, he stood on fair ground to commence the work of his supreme character, as the Son of God, the first born among many brethren, to introduce the new and spiritual family, the kingdom of God. Now in accomplishing this work, the labor of Jesus was to renounce all the works and travel out of all the nature of the first Adam, to die to sin and live to God according to the law of the new creation : for he is the beginning of the creation of God. So it is written, " In that he died, he died to sin once ; but in that he liveth, he liveth to God." [Ro. 6. 10.] And this is the true resurrection of Christ and of his people, of whom he is the example, captain and leader, of which all other resurrections are but the sign. But this remains to be more fully stated in the third general proposition.

Now to return more immediately to the point in hand. Having thus far examined the history of facts, relating to the resurrection of the man Jesus, I shall next proceed to enquire into the import of some portions of scripture of a prophetic nature, relating to the same subject.

When the Jews had asked a sign, " Jesus answered and said unto " them, Destroy this temple and in three days I will raise it up. " But he spake of the temple of his body." (Jno. 2. 19, 21.) This scripture will likely be considered as an explicit and decisive testimony, that the same material body arose and ascended. And it might be so considered were it not for two reasons. The first is that other scriptures more copiously teach the contrary, as will be shown hereafter. And secondly. We are not without example of the same form of expression, in the teachings of Christ, wherein the same is not intended : that is where the demonstrative pronoun IT which commonly implies the same as the antecedent noun to which it stands related, doth not in these instances imply the same, but that which succeeds in the room thereof. " For whosoever will save his life " shall lose it : but whosoever will lose his life for my sake, the same " shall find it." [Luke. 9. 24.] This text is a plain example of what is stated above ; for the life which the man is here said to save, is not the same which he would lose by so doing ; the one being carnal, the other spiritual and eternal. And the life which is here stated as being lost for Christ's sake, is not the same which is found by so doing, the first being carnal and the last spiritual and eternal. Yet it is said he that loseth his life shall find IT ; which IT, doth not signify the same life which is lost, but that which succeeds. So, destroy this temple, or body, and in three days I will raise it, doth not necessarily signify the raising of the same body, but of that which succeeded, or it is applicable to any body which answered the purpose of his being raised ; as much as to say, Kill me, and in three days I will be alive and have a living body.

Another argument, vigorously maintained, for the resurrection and ascension of the same material body, is grounded on the words of the Psalmist (16. 10.) " For thou wilt not leave my soul in hell; nei-"ther wilt thou suffer thine Holy One to see corruption." This prophecy is twice quoted by the apostles, with express application to Christ and his resurrection. Peter, speaking of David, saith, " He, " seeing this before, spake of the resurrection of Christ, that his " soul was not left in hell, neither his flesh did see corruption." [Acts 2. 31.] And Paul on the same subject, saith, " And we declare " unto you glad tidings, how that the promise which was made to " the fathers, God hath fulfilled the same to us their children, in that " he hath raised up Jesus again; as it is also written in the second " Psalm, Thou art my Son, this day have I begotten thee. And as " concerning that he raised him up from the dead, now no more to re-" turn to corruption, he said on this wise, I will give you the sure " mercies of David. For David after he had served his own genera-" tion by the will of God fell on sleep, and was laid unto his fathers, " and saw corruption : but he whom God raised again saw no corrup-" tion." [Acts 13. 32 to 37.]

It is remarkable, that in all which is said by both these apostles, it is not once said that the material body, or flesh, was that which arose. Paul, in all he said while commenting on the remarkable prophecy, did not once name the body, or flesh of Jesus Christ, but simply stated that he was raised from the dead, as God had promised to do ; a fact acknowledged on all hands. And that Jesus could be raised from the dead, and exist, the same Jesus, without the same material body, had been already proved.

But much stress hath been laid on the words of Peter, " Neither " his flesh did see corruption." That this is figurative language is evident ; for a dead body of flesh in no case seeth. That there was a marked difference between Jesus and David with respect to death and resurrection is not denied ; for David was buried, and as other men do, remained among the dead, waiting for the day of resurrection and redemption, while his body remained in the sepulchre and returned to its native dust ; but Jesus, who was the resurrection and the life, though he expired and was laid in a tomb, on the third day was found among the living, God having raised him from the dead, having loosed the pains of death, because it was not possible he could be holden of it. But that all this could take place without the material body constituting any part of the true resurrection, hath been already shown, and remains to be farther illustrated in its proper place.

This phrase therefore, " Neither his flesh did see corruption," doth not positively prove more than what is not disputed, that he did not remain under the power of death as others had done, and that his material body did not remain in the tomb and moulder to dust as others did: for when they looked into the tomb, they saw not the body of the Lord.

People appear as intent for the resurrection of the animal body of Jesus, as if they thought the resurrection disannulled, and Christ and his salvation made of no effect without it. But it may with propriety be asked on the contrary, What use had he for that body, after the end for which he took it on him was accomplished? That end according to the scripture was, " That through death he might de-" stroy him that had the power of death and deliver those who, " through fear of death, were all their lifetime subject to bondage." [Heb. 2. 14, 15.] He had now travailed through death and conquered it, with him that had the power of it; he had finished the work, which the Father had given him to do, even before he had altogether passed through that natural death of the animal body on the cross. What use therefore had he for that body any longer? Or was that body so much superior to the spirit, that without it he could not be glorified with the Father himself, with the glory which he had with him before the world was? How then did he partake of that glory before he had put on said body?

Was the assumption of that body of flesh and blood the work of glorification or humiliation? Not of glorification, but of humiliation: this needeth no proof. And having once stooped to the work of humiliation, must he forever remain under it? By parity of reason, because he once submitted to death, he must forever remain under its power, or lose the reward of victory through death and exaltation through his humiliation. [See Phil. 2. 6, 7, &c.] When he had passed through death and risen from the dead, the foundation was completely laid, he being the chief corner stone; he had opened the new and living way, had set us an example that we might follow his steps, was made perfect through sufferings, and had become a complete forerunner and captain of his people. And what now remained, but to convince his disciples of the truth of what he had done, and lead them into an understanding of its nature and design? And as the work and kingdom of Christ are spiritual, what need for the animal, or material body?

But some may object, that this reasoning arraigns the work of God, and inquires into matters which are not our concern; that the work of God is evidence enough for us, and that the fact of Christ's being raised from the dead ought to silence all our objections. God's works are not arbitrary; and it is not contrary to true obedience and real faith, for us to inquire into the reason and nature of the works of God, as far as will be profitable for the ministration of light. But let the fact be once established, that Jesus Christ rose from the dead, and disputing on that point is at an end: this is the undisputed fact among christians. And let it be established by the authority of inspiration, that the resurrection of Jesus Christ from the dead consisted in the raising again of the material body, or that it could not be accomplished without it, and disputing is at an end on that point also: but that is the point in debate, and which cannot be proved in the affirmative, until it be first proved, that that material body constituted the true Jesus Christ, so that he could not exist without it—the negative of which hath been already proved.

It may, as hath already been done, be objected; If the material body did not actually rise, or is not the proper subject of the resurrection of Christ, what was done with it? for it was not found in the tomb, neither did it see corruption. Let me use the liberty assumed above, but with more propriety, and say, What is that to us? Have we any right, or any occasion to search into the unrevealed method of God's working, and that too in a matter which doth not materially affect our salvation? "It is the Spirit that quickeneth; the flesh "profiteth nothing." (Jno. 6. 63.)

But to obviate this objection more fully, for those who count it weighty, or even plausible; let me ask; Was there not as much reason for removing the body of Jesus from the tomb as for concealing the body of Moses from the Israelites, so that no man knew of his sepulchre? If the fathers were in danger of worshipping the body or tomb of Moses, as hath been supposed, (or what other reason can be assigned for his concealment?) on account of his great character and mighty works, how much more might the body of Jesus, who so far exceeded Moses in the glory of his character and works, have become a snare to his followers, and a real hindrance to their belief of the resurrection, and to their understanding of his spiritual character and work, in the carnal condition in which they still remained? They have taken away my Lord, said Mary, because she found not the body. And could they have been readily convicted of idolatry, or any wrong procedure, in offering adoration to their Lord? while all the time their sense would have been cleaving to the flesh, to the neglect of the Spirit. Neither is it probable, that they could have been readily convinced, or easily satisfied, with respect to his resurrection, or his being actually alive, his ascension and glorification, and other things pertaining to his work and kingdom, while they could, at any time, by going there, have seen him to their sense, dead in the tomb. Besides; How much more difficulty must have attended the ministry of the disciples, after they had come to believe, to convince others, who either had no faith in the resurrection at all, or had carnal and natural views of it, that he had risen from the dead and was actually alive, while his body could at any time have been seen, or had it been commonly known how it was removed? The report, common among the Jews, that his disciples had come and stolen him away by night, while the soldiers were asleep, was fabricated to prevent the people from believing, and what plausibility would have been attached to that fabrication, could the body have been found? From every consideration therefore it was necessary that the body should be removed as it was, out of the reach or knowledge of any of them.

Upon the whole; From a consideration of the real character and condition of the disciples—the literal and carnal sense of things which they had by nature and according to the carnal dispensation to which they had been accustomed—their slowness of heart to believe on the plainest testimony, it appears to have been necessary to represent to them, the work of God in the resurrection and ascension of Christ, in such a dress as that they could at least apprehend it, and be convinced of its truth in the sense and understanding of things, in which they then were, while in the mean time every possible hindrance was taken out of the way, that being confirmed in the truth of facts which had actually come to pass, they might the more easily be led into a better understanding of their true nature, after they became more fully able to receive correct information; which was after they had received the Holy Spirit. "I have yet many things," said Jesus, "to say to you, but ye cannot bear them now. Howbeit, when he, the Spirit of truth, is come, he will guide you into all truth—He shall glorify me: for he shall receive of mine, and shall show unto you." (Jno. 16. 12, 13, 14.)

The removal of that material body required, that the stone should be rolled away from the mouth of the sepulchre, because material substance requireth space to move in, free from other obstructing materials. But what was to hinder the soul of Jesus, replete with the resurrection power of God, to enter the grave, reanimate the body, and bring it forth, a spiritual body, without removing the stone, or even cracking the seal, any more than to enter the house where the disciples were, the doors being shut?

Thus far of the resurrection as it immediately relates to the person of Jesus Christ. And herein I have taken notice of the principal and most prominent passages, as being most calculated to comprehend the whole and bring them all into full examination, which are pleaded in favor of the resurrection of the same material body, and have found none but what are capable of a consistent and sufficiently free acceptation without including the belief of that fact. That point therefore of the literal resurrection of the same animal body remains unestablished; untaught in explicit language of the scriptures, unproved by fair and necessary inference. But in the mean time it is proved that Jesus Christ was capable of existing and being the same Jesus Christ, without inhabiting that same body; consequently the resurrection and reanimation of that body, is not the point in which the resurrection of Jesus Christ consists, as commonly insisted; therefore to deny the resurrection, reanimation and ascension of that material body, is not the same as to deny the resurrection of Jesus Christ altogether, seeing that the resurrection can exist in fact, according to the scriptures, without the aid of that body: he was quickened in the Spirit.

In perusing these sheets, it may frequently be suggested to those of a different sentiment, that it is uncandid to labor proposedly after a method of understanding these scriptures and all others, so as to exclude the faith of the resurrection of the animal body. But a method of arguing which is open and above board is not uncandid. I proposed in the beginning of this branch of the subject to show that all these scriptures could be understood consistently without implying that fact; and it is not an unfair method of arguing, to show that any fact is not established by the arguments advanced for that purpose and particularly with respect to the subject now in consideration, or others of the same nature, it doth not so properly belong to us who disbelieve the resurrection of the animal body, to prove it did not rise; what belongeth to us, is the negative part; and that cannot require proof, according to any philosophical or logical method of reasoning. But to those who believe the resurrection of that body, and consider it an essential part in the resurrection of Jesus Christ, it belongs to establish it in the affirmative, by unquestionable testimony, while it is not disingenuous in us to analyze every argument with the strictest scrutiny, and to invalidate, as far as honesty, truth and reason, will admit.

I have hitherto kept up the idea of the resurrection and the ascension as being so closely connected together that that which arose must also have ascended, and that which ascended must also have arisen. This idea needs no farther proof, being evident from the most simple view of the subject. But that the material body was not that which ascended, either in whole or in part, (at least that it is not necessarily included, the point now under consideration,) is fairly argued from this, that that which ascended was the same which descended first from heaven. "He that descended is the same also "that ascended." [Eph. 4. 10.] Now the animal body was not that which descended, being produced of the substance of Mary's body, and brought forth like those of other men. Add to this, that the apostle hath explicitly marked the difference between his dying and rising, applying the first to the flesh,, " Put to death in the flesh," and the second to the Spirit, " But quickened in the Spirit." It is observable that he is never said to be quickened in the flesh, or his flesh to be alive: It is already proved that the man could be alive without it.

I take the liberty to appeal to the learned for the consistency and correctness of the translation which I have prefered in the text last quoted, while I ask if any reason can be proffered, for rendering the one phrase *In* the flesh, and the other *By* the Spirit, when the grammatical construction and government of both are precisely the same? Add to this, that the similar expression, a few lines after, which relates to the above as a kind of recapitulation, is in the same grammatical construction and government, and is necessarily rendered *in* the flesh. "For as much then as Christ hath suffered for us *in* the "flesh.". [1 Pet. 3. 18. and 4. 1.]

The following propositions appear necessary to be believed by the abettors of the doctrine of the resurrection of the same material body, before their plan can be complete. First. That the body of Jesus was raised a spiritual body; consequently it was a spiritual body on that evening when he appeared to the disciples in the house, the doors being shut. For they insist (not improperly) that his resurrection is a true example and earnest of that of his followers, and also, that their body is raised a spiritual body. It is sown a natural body, it is raised a spiritual body. Secondly. That when he appeared on that same evening, and at the same instant of time, that same body of his was a material body, a proper body of flesh and bones, such as a spirit hath not. " Handle me, and see, for a spirit hath " not flesh and bones, as ye see me have," is to them an unequivocal argument that he took with him the same body of flesh and bones. Therefore thirdly. That the same body was a spiritual body, and a proper material body of flesh and bones at one and the same time. The necessity of believing these propositions in support of that plan, their glaring inconsistency notwithstanding, is sufficient to convince the abettors of it, if they would be reasonable, not only that these, and the tantamount phrases in the scriptures, are susceptible of a different acceptation from that in which they receive them, but that a more consistent one is indispensably necessary to the support of truth. They may however argue, that it is urging the matter too far, to charge them with calling it a proper material body, that the sense and meaning of their language is not to that extent. But it must be either matter or spirit, material or immaterial—Let them tell us decisively which they mean.

CHAPTER III.

The Resurrection, with more immediate relation to the Saints.

I PROCEED in the next place to carry the examination to the resurrection of the saints, and therein to show, That there is no language used in the scripture to prove or explain the resurrection of Christ's people, but what is capable of an easy and consistent acceptation, without including the resurrection of the animal body, as being the proper subject of the resurrection, or constituting any necessary part of it.

I have hitherto treated of this subject, with particular relation to the person of Jesus Christ; but as it is pleaded and granted, that the resurrection of Christ is a true earnest and example of that of his people, the certainty of the latter depending on the certainty of the former, and the nature and manner of the one serving to elucidate the nature and manner of the other alternately, the subject becomes essentially one, according to the scriptures. We may therefore with propriety proceed to examine the language of the scriptures relating to the resurrection of the saints, to see if it cannot be understood consistently, without including the resurrection of the animal body.

I have spoken of said body, as not being the proper subject of the true resurrection, neither participating in it. My reason for such communications is, that I would have the understanding and sense of the people fixed on the abiding substance, and not confined to the shadow. Not doubting but there have been resurrections of animal bodies, of men who were under an indispensable necessity of experiencing a resurrection entirely distinct, before they could inherit the kingdom of heaven; as the widow's son and Lazarus, Neither would it materially affect the subject in hand, were it admitted that Jesus assumed the same body for a time, and used it as occasion required, as a medium of access to his disciples, for their conviction and information. But the true resurrection of which the apostles spake, and to which they looked for substance, was quite another thing; as will be shown in its place.

It hath been already stated, that there is no principle in nature, or in the most profound philosophy; neither any doctrine in the revelation of God to men to prove that matter is converted into spirit, or material physical bodies into spiritual. And to these things agree the words of a late writer; " As no possible combination of the " elementary parts of matter, however diversified, and extended, " can produce a result which is *immaterial*, or which is destitute of " the properties, and qualities of matter; so no reduction of com- " pound bodies can be carried beyond the elementary forms out of " which, or by which they were produced." [See Philos. hum. mind Page 18.]

Unwilling however to cede their pretentions to a favorite plan supported by tradition, prepossession and the allurements of the flesh, the abettors insist, that God hath actually taught by revelation, that the material body is converted, by the power of Christ into a spiritual body, so far at least, as to be the proper subject of the resurrection. In defence therefore of the favorite plan, the words of Paul to the Philipians are introduced; [3. 20, 21.] " For our conversa- " tion [in the Greek, citizenship] is in heaven, from whence also we " look for the Savior, the Lord Jesus; who shall change our vile " body, that it may be fashioned like unto his glorious body, accord- " ing to the working whereby he is able even to subdue all things to " himself." According to the common use and meaning of words, there is no difficulty in understanding this passage, without any relation to the resurrection, or reanimation of the material body, or any conversion of the natural into the spiritual. The ordinary and natural use of the active verb, *to change*, is properly to put away one and receive another. Accordingly a man is said to change his garment, when he puts off one and puts on another; and to get his money changed, when he giveth to some other man a large piece, and reciveth small to answer his purpose, or giveth paper money and receiveth silver; or the contrary. But a man will hardly conclude he hath got his money changed by having it taken away for a time and given back again. So to put off the body and put on the same, is no change. That is not therefore the work which Christ has to do at his coming, but to finish the redemption of his people, delivering them completely and finally from the *old man*, and clothing them in the new, fashioning them like himself, according to the working [ενεργιαν, energy, or inward working] whereby he is able even to subdue all things to himself.

With respect to the demonstrative, IT, commonly understood to mean the same as the noun to which it points, (on which account it would be argued, that this language, Who sh il change our vile body, that IT may be fashioned like his glorious bod means the refitting of our same animal body for the inheritance of eternal life,) it hath been already shown and exemplified, that such phraseology is used when identity, or sameness is not intended. It is also to be considered, that the term, *body*, doth not always mean the animal body, or carcase, separately from the spirit, but the man, or person, as intimated in the beginning. Thus a certain Greek author speaks of *wicked bodies*. And the same use of the word is quite common in our day. Thus it is often said, I see some *body* coming, some *body* told me, I want some *body* to do a piece of work, there was no *body* there, and a thousand other instances, in all which the undeniable meaning of the term *body*, is *man*, or *person*.

Some may suppose that an argument advantageous to the favorite plan, may be had by a critical attention to the Greek text. And it must not be denied that a literal translation of the text might be considered more favorable, at least in the word translated *change*; Thus, " Who shall transform the body of our humiliation [or hum-" ble body] that it may be conformed to the body of his glory [or " glorious body] according to the energy whereby he is able even, to " subdue all things to himself." But when we consider the use of the term, *body*, as already stated, with the other remarks on this text, pertaining to the nature of its language, as also that the energy or power by which the body is to be transformed and fashioned like his glorious body, is an inward working, we shall find nothing in this text sufficient to establish the resurrection, reanimation and glorification of the same material body. For, to transform our humble body cannot necessarily imply any thing different from transforming our humble person, by removing finally all the evil and useless incumbrances and increasing the true and valuable substance, by the working of his spirit. Besides,

It is farther to be considered, that the term, *body*, may very properly be understood of the church collectively, in the same manner as in the words of the apostle in another place, (Ro. 8. 23.) " Wait-" ing for the adoption, to wit, the redemption of our body," and is with propriety called *our body*, as being that body of which we (christians) are all members. This view of the subject properly comports with the body's being called *our humble body*, or the *body of our humiliation*, expressing the oppressed and afflicted state of the body, or church, from which it will be entirely redeemed in the progress of the work of Christ at his coming, and translated into that which is perfect and glorious. His work is before him, and his reward is with him. There is neither absurdity nor contradiction in expounding these and many other scriptures with the latitude here allowed;

notwithstanding the fabricated maxim among systematics, That the meaning of scripture is not various but single; a sentiment from which all denominations justly as well as necessarily deviate in practice, it being as groundless as whimsical. Variety is not tantamount with contradiction: but it is necessary to teach and to expound according to [αναλογιαν] the analogy of the faith of Christ. (Ro. 12. 6.) The account giv 1 by Matthew (27. 52.) of the bodies raised at the crucifixion, is alledged by some, in favor of the notion of the general resurrection of the material bodies of all men. A free consideration however of the relation there given, and the attending circumstances will fully evince that it affords no proof of such a fact. For admitting the fact there stated, to be the proper resurrection to life, of corpses which had been buried in those graves; the simple existence of the fact is no proof of the general resurrection of all dead bodies, or corpses, any more than the resurrection of the body of Lazarus or the widow's son, although both these had to die again, and also to experience a very different resurrection, or never inherit with Christ. But further;

The dessign of the historian seems to have been, to give a statement of the signs which appeared when Jesus expired. It is not therefore probable that the narrative relates to companies of invisible spirits only, or to many spiritual bodies, for the centurian and others around could not have seen them, of course they could not have been signs to them. What is said of the spirits of those saints, or in other words, of those saints in their true order, took place afterwards, that is after the resurrection of Christ. Neither can that resurrection of bodies, which took place when Jesus expired, be considered as the first fruits of his resurrection and thus be proffered as an example and proof of the general resurrection of bodies, for two reasons. First. That view of the subject supposes these saints to have the pre-eminence over Christ, in that very particular in which he is specially said to have it; "Who is the beginning, the first born from the dead; that in all things he might have the pre-eminence." "Christ the first fruits." (Col. 1. 18. 1 Cor. 15. 23.) Secondly. The time had not yet arrived for the fruits of his resurrection, even the first fruits to appear. " Christ the first fruits (observe, he is foremost;) afterwards they that are Christ's at his coming." The apostles, not excluding other christians of their day, were according to their own testimony, *a kind of first fruits*. But *the first fruits to God and to the Lamb*, or the first resurrection, was to appear long afterwards, as shown to John in the revelations made to him.

The true state of the facts related by Matthew appears to be this; That when Jesus expired, there was such a miraculous and extraordinary commotion in all nature, by the special providence of God, that the vail of the temple was rent in twain, from the top to the bottom; this was a fact visible to all; and the earth did quake and the rocks rent; these facts were also visible to all; and the graves were opened; this also was visible; and many bodies of the saints which slept arose; that is, were thrown out by the commotions in the earth. These bodies were also visible, being kept, at least some of them measurably in form, by means of the embalming which was practised by the Jews. Thus far the narrative may be considered as relating to the things which were visible; and here is a period to the relation of the signs which appeared at that time.

What is written immediately after is separated from those visible facts by two particulars, in the Greek text, according to the proper order of language. First; A full period denoting the end of a sentence; and secondly; The disagreement of the parts of speech describing the two facts, the one of which was visible to the merely physical man, the other not. The first of these particulars depending on the position of a single point, is liable to be varied; but the other, depending on correct orthography and due grammatical construction, is free from that liableness, and is also a strong reason for the correctness of the first. The Greek word translated *came*, is not a verb, as it is made to be in the English, but a participle, and so constructed as by no means to agree with the word translated *bodies*, according to the construction of that language, but agrees correctly with the term *saints*. Besides; as before observed, the sentence closes with the word *arose*, and a different subject is touched on in few words, relating to that which was not visible to all: This will be still farther manifest by the following considerations.

First. It is not a reasonable supposition that these dead bodies of the sleeping saints were reanimated by the return of their spirits to them, in the power of Christ as their life, at the time when Jesus expired, and yet remained among the tombs until after his resurrection from the sixth day in the evening until the first day in the morning. To which we may add, that had this been the case, they must have been seen by many Jews and Romans, without going into the holy city. But secondly. It is stated that the bodies arose at the time when Jesus expired, and that they who went into the holy city, whatever they were, came out of the graves, after his resurrection. This would imply that these saints were confined, or to use the easiest terms, remained in the tombs until the third day after their bodies arose. To such absurdities the notion of the resurrection of dead bodies necessarily leads. But no difficulty attends the plan here stated; That the bodies of the sleeping saints were raised, or thrown out, by the quaking of the earth, by which the rocks were also rent; but the saints, undisturbed by the commotions of material nature, remained at rest, until after the resurrection, when in their proper order, Christ having gone before, as their proper head and forerunner, they arose, or awoke, and coming forth, went into the holy city, (not bloody Jerusalem) and appeared to such as had eyes to see them. "And the graves were opened; and many bodies of the saints who "had slept were raised. And (these saints) having come out of the "graves, (residence of the dead,) after his resurrection, went into the "holy city, and were manifested to many."

One passage out of the book of Job seems proper to be noticed, before this part of the subject be closed, because urged by some with a degree of confidence. The words are these, (19. 26.) "And "though after my skin, worms destroy this body, yet in my flesh

RESURRECTION.

"shall I see God." These words indicate the firm confidence which Job had in God, that he would yet deliver him out of all his troubles, and appear on the earth as his redeemer, and that his eyes should see him while yet in the flesh. All which came to pass according to his faith and expectation. (42. 5.) " I have heard of thee, " (said he) by the hearing of the ear; but now mine eyes see thee." And in the event Job was delivered, after the Lord appeared to him, and he ended his days in peace and prosperity. But all this proves nothing towards the resurrection of the body of flesh and bones, after it is actually dead. To say that, *Yet in my flesh shall I see God*, means, I shall see him in my flesh at the final resurrection of the just, contradicts the grand doctrine of the resurrection so confidently urged, that it is raised a spiritual body: now flesh is not spirit. These remarks are made on the common translation.

But the marginal translation, which is often much the best, gives quite a different and more noble view of the subject, and properly accords with the faith of the gospel of Christ in his second appearing. In their connection the words stand thus, "For I know that " my redeemer liveth, and that he shall stand at the latter day upon " the earth: After I shall awake, though this body be destroyed, " yet out of my flesh shall I see God: Whom I shall see for myself, " and not another; though my reins be consumed within me." These words whether Job understood them or not, being the words of the Spirit of God, show in bold terms the important change which should take place in the latter day, when the redeemer should stand on the earth, to accomplish his work of redemption, from a natural and fleshly state into that which is all spiritual. When I awake from my long sleep, after all these sufferings and troubles are over, although this body be then destroyed, and I see it no more, I shall then be in comfort, for yet *out of my flesh* I shall see God. Let this scripture therefore be received as it stands in the common reading in the text, or in the margin, it affords no proof of the resurrection of the material body. But although there is nothing false or contrary to the doctrine of revelation in either of the two translations, a more correct and literally unexceptionable one is that which I shall here give, after remarking that the words *after my skin*, are the best confirmed reading in the Hebrew copies which use the points, and perfectly consistent with the omission of them. But the phrase, *in my flesh*, is contrary to the Hebrew text in every form; as the proper use or signification of the particle there rendered, *in*, is out of, from, by and the like. The correct translation therefore is, " And though " after my skin *(worms)* devour this *body*, yet out of my flesh I " shall see God;" when I am in my spiritual state, having got free from this burdensome and afflicting condition.

I have now taken a plain and particular view of most, if not all, of those scriptures which I have found to be alledged in favor of the resurrection, reanimation and glorification of the animal body, except those which will more naturally be presented to view in considering those branches of the subject which are yet to come. And in all these which have been noticed, I have shown, that they, and all such, should there be any remaining, can be understood in a sufficiently natural meaning, without doing violence to the common and free use of language, and yet by no means prove the resurrection of the material body, or any change of it from matter to spirit.

This negative part claimed the priority in the discussion, for two reasons. First; Because in establishing any point by evidence, positive proof is not required on the negative side, but on the affirmative. It doth not therefore belong to those who deny the resurrection of the animal body to prove by positive evidence that it will not rise, but to the advocates of that scheme, that it will; therefore to obviate all their arguments, goeth a great length, not to say the whole, towards bringing the subject to a decision. And secondly; After the arguments in favor of the resurrection of the animal body are removed, those testimonies which show positively, what the resurrection is, and that the animal body hath no part in it, will be introduced with better efficacy and more lasting impression.

Some may object, and those too of serious minds, that to spend so much labor to show that the foregoing and other such scriptures may be understood, without including the resurrection of the animal body, is dishonest and unchristian, and carrieth the appearance of wilfully blinding and misleading the people. This objection hath been sufficiently obviated already; and I presume it will not be made by any candid persons who understand the nature of reasoning and know the use of a negative part.

Should it be objected farther, that it is needless to be at the expense of such labored arguments and replies, to disprove the resurrection of the animal body; for if the people can be brought to believe in Christ and to follow him in the regeneration, all will be well in the end; for should the same body be raised, it will be so modified that it will be no real incumbrance or other injury, and should it not rise God will so order matters, that no loss will be sustained for the want of it. This may be considered plausible reasoning. Would the people be wise enough for their own good, to follow Christ in the regeneration bearing their daily cross, we would not be desirous of contending with them about this or any other subject out of their sight, but rather to let them obtain a correct knowledge of the work of God by a faithful travel, walking in the obedience of Christ; "If any man will do his will, he shall know of the doctrine." [Jno. 7. 17.]

But herein is discovered the craft of the spirit of wickedness which ruleth in carnal men, professors and profane. While the grand matters essentially pertaining to the work of regeneration and following Christ therein, as the self-denial and the cross which he requires all to bear, who follow him, or would partake with him, are alledged to belong to those only who are actual partakers of the resurrection of the just, it is no small labor to convince those who believe in the resurrection of the animal body, of the necessity of bearing such cross and of partaking such self-denial, while that resurrection doth not appear, or as long as they can maintain any hope of salvation however flimsy, supported by the prospect of any thing yet to come: natural men do not love the self-denial and the cross of Christ, necessary to traveling with him in the regeneration. These things however make it necessary, that people should understand something of the nature of the resurrection of the just, which is the resurrection in Christ, that they may the more easily be gained to that faith and obedience which are necessary to salvation. And it may be not unavailing towards preparing the mind for the reception of what is yet to come, to add here that the resurrection of the just, as they are raised in Christ, is the same in its nature, as the regeneration in which men follow Christ to salvation and eternal life. Accordingly they are used in the scriptures as being tantamount, or nearly so.

For the sake of better clearing the way for what is yet to come, I take this opportunity to notice a very common and prevalent error pertaining to the subject of the resurrection; which is that there are two resurrections of the just, or which they experience—the one spiritual, and the other natural, or literal—the one the resurrection of the spirit from the state of death in sin, into Christ who is the resurrection and the life, and the other the resurrection, reanimation and glorification of the earthly tabernacle—the one the regeneration of the spirit, the other the regeneration of the body—or according to some, it appears that regeneration includes the resurrection of both spirit and body, and is not complete without both—the one is called the first, the other the second resurrection.

That the scriptures speak of a first resurrection, the partakers of which are blessed and holy, and over whom the second death hath no power, is not denied. But they are silent with respect to a second resurrection, especially with this predication annexed to it, that the subjects of it are blessed and holy, and free from the second death; no mention is made, any where in the scriptures, that they are blessed and holy who have part in the second resurrection. It is therefore most rational and correct to understand the first resurrection as belonging to the just, who are blessed and holy, and the second (when we use the term at all: it is not in the scriptures,) as pertaing to the wicked. For there shall be a resurrection, both of the just, and also of the unjust; for all must come forth in their proper order, and fill up their proper character, and stand in their proper lot; those who have done good, (who have been obedient to the will of God as far as made known to them, and have also come into Christ who is the resurrection and the life, of whom they have learned to do good all the time,) to the resurrection of life, and those who have done evil (and continued so to do; for all have done evil more or less;) to the resurrection of damnation. [Acts 24. 15. Jno. 5. 22. 28.]

A second implies a first; but a first doth not necessarily imply a second; at least of the same kind and pertaining to the same order of things. Two cannot be without one, but one may be without two, and that one is the first. The second death therefore necessarily presupposes a first; but the first resurrection for those who are blessed and holy, no more implies a second for the same characters, than Jesus' being called the first begotten, implies that God has a second begotten, according to the same extraordinary generation: here the first begotten is also the only begotten. [Jno. 1. 18. Heb. 1. 6.] Besides; that which is by the Spirit of inspiration, called the first resurrection, fills the place and time commonly assigned to the second, even the day or time of judgment; and in it the souls of the faithful are spoken of as being seen, but not a word of any other bodies being united to them, or in anywise connected with them; thus in the resurrection of the just, the old body, or tabernacle is left out of the question, as will be more fully shown in its place.

CHAPTER IV.

Of some scriptures incapable of a proper acceptation on the principle of their relating to the resurrection of the animal body.

SECONDLY. I am now to consider some of those passages of scripture, which cannot be understood with good sense, if considered as speaking of the resurrection of the same material body. This short branch of the subject is nearly allied to that which is next in course; and by a careful perusal and diligent digestion of what is here stated, the mind will be profitably prepared for the reception of what is to come, in which the subject of the true resurrection in Christ, will be treated of to a still greater extent.

The first passage to be introduced here is the following; [2 Cor. 5. 1, 2, &c.] " For we know that if our earthly house of this taber-" nacle were dissolved, we have a building of God, a house not made " with hands, eternal in the heavens. For in this we groan, earnestly " desiring to be clothed upon with our house which is from heaven." Were the resurrection of the same animal body an object of the apostle's faith and expectation, no more favorable opportunity could have been asked to bear his testimony to the fact, and to express his confidence in it, as a source of encouragement against the thoughts of its dissolution. But without the smallest intimation of a resurrection or restoration of the body, (for so he terms it afterwards,) or earthly house of this tabernacle, he directs the mind to quite another source of recompense and comfort—*We have a building with God, a house not made with hands, eternal in the heavens— our house which is from heaven.* And this is the more remarkable, as this part of the apostle's discourse is a manifest descant on what he had just before stated of the confidence which he had, that they would all be raised up by Jesus, by the agency of the one who had raised up the Lord Jesus himself. So that what he here speaks of receiving after the dissolution of the tabernacle, is to be considered as the fruit of Christ's resurrection in its influence on them, and its equivalent in them; and yet nothing is said of the resurrection, or restoration of the tabernacle or body. [Chap. 4. 14, 16, 17, 18.] " Knowing that he who raised up the Lord Jesus, shall raise up us " also by Jesus, and shall present us with you—For which cause we " faint not : but though our outward man perish, yet the inward man " is renewed day by day. (The new continually supplanting the old, " but no account of the old being restored.) For our light affliction " which is but for a moment worketh for us a far more exceeding " and eternal weight of glory; while we look not at the things which " are seen, but at the things which are not seen; for the things which " are seen are temporal, but the things which are not seen are eter- ". nal. For we know, that, if our earthly house of this tabernacle " were dissolved, we have a building with God, an house not made " with hands, eternal in the heavens." (Yea, we have it ready at any time whenever this is dissolved without waiting for a restoration of the old.) " For in this we groan, earnestly desiring to be clothed upon " with our house which is from heaven : if so be that being clothed " (with our house from heaven,) we shall not be found naked. (The " dissolution of our earthly house notwithstanding.) For we who are " in this tabernacle do groan being burthened : not that we would be " unclothed, (clean dissolved) but clothed upon, (fixed in a more du- " rable and comfortable existence in the true substance,) that morta- " lity might be swallowed up of life." (That new dwelling wherewith we shall be clothed upon, and which is the true and eternal life, may supplant and for ever supersede the old earthly house, which is mortality in the abstract.) " Now he who hath wrought us for this " self-same thing is God, who also hath given to us the earnest of the " Spirit. (While yet in the tabernacle.) Therefore we are always " confident, knowing that whilst we are at home in the body we are " absent from the Lord: (for we walk by faith not by sight,) we are " confident I say, and willing rather to be absent from the body, and " to be present with the Lord. Wherefore we labor, that, whether " present or absent, we may be accepted of him. For we must all " appear before the judgment-seat of Christ; that every one may " receive [bear or carry] the things done in [by] his body, according " to that which he hath done, whether good or bad." Yet not one word or intimation of the same old body being raised, or of the tabernacle being restored, at the judgment-seat of Christ, or any where else.

But the following is, if need be, still more imcompatible with reason and good sense, on the supposition of the resurrection of the same body. (For that is acknowledged by the advocates of that plan, to be common to both the righteous and the wicked, as that which will unavoidably come to pass in all who rise at all.) The place alluded to, is in the epistle to the Philipians, (Chap. 3.) where the apostle shows what he had counted loss for Christ, and what labor and care he underwent, that, " If, saith he, by any means I might attain to the " resurrection of the dead, [or τήν εξαναςασιν των νεκρων, the resur- " rection from among the dead]." Now upon the supposition of the resurrection of that body's being the object with the apostle, his language is either improper, or his great labor and care in vain, because he was certain to attain to it, labor for it or not. But to rise into the perfection of life in Christ Jesus; to enter into that circle of life in the Spirit of Christ which would leave behind all the dead and every thing pertaining to death; thus to attain to the resurrection from among the dead, was quite another matter: this being his object, his language is correct, and his labor and care exceedingly proper.

And what farther proves that he had no respect to the resurrection of the animal body, is, that he speaks of the resurrection as attainable at least to a good degree, in the present tense, and therefore takes an occasion to state, that he had not attained to it: which had been utterly unnecessary on the supposition of his speaking of the resurrection of the animal body, which they all knew had not taken place. "If by any means I might attain to the resurrection of the "the dead. Not as though I had already attained, or were already "perfect; but I follow after, if that I may apprehend that for which "also I am apprehended of Christ Jesus. Brethren, I count not "myself to have apprehended: but this one thing I do, forgetting "those things which are behind, and reaching forth to those things "which are before, I press toward the mark, for the prize of the "high calling of God in Christ Jesus." These words show farther what is the resurrection of which he speaks, that for which he was apprehended of Christ Jesus, which can be nothing short of a finished resurrection, perfection or final redemption. And this is evidently the object which he was laboring to obtain and in the attainment of which he was making some progress, and which he expressed by the different names of the resurrection from the dead; perfection, that for which he had been apprehended of Christ Jesus, and the prize of the high calling of God in Christ Jesus: and yet in all this the animal body hath no part, as already shown.

Should it still be alledged that, although the resurrection of which the apostle here speaks, is granted (which cannot be denied with any plausibility,) to be that which hath no respect to the natural body, yet that is not to exclude the resurrection of that body at an after period. This allegation is effectually refuted, if we consider, First; that the resurrection of which the apostle here speaks is, as already stated, the perfection of that for which he was apprehended of Christ; there is therefore no further use for the natural body, the work being perfected without it; and therefore secondly; that the resurrection is a gradual, or progressive work, the same as regeneration, and not instantaneous. For the apostle was evidently in the resurrection, and might be said with propriety, according to the work of that day, to be risen with Christ from the dead, when he forsook his opposition to Christ, and betook himself to the work of preaching the gospel, and to the labor and travel of which he here speaks, and yet he frankly acknowledges he hath not yet attained to the thing, or in other words, is not yet perfect. "But one thing, "(says he,) I do; forgetting those things which are behind, and "reaching forth to those things which are before, I press toward the

" mark, for the prize of the high calling of God in Christ Jesus." He had therefore heard the high calling of God in Christ Jesus, obeyed it, and set out to obtain the prize to which it directed—he had awaked and risen from the dead, and Christ had given him light, and he was now in full pursuit of the prize, perfect deliverance, or full redemption—the fulness of the resurrection to life in Christ Jesus. His aim therefore to attain to the resurrection while he was actually in it, being alive in Christ, proves the resurrection to be progressive, and the fulness of it being the grand object at which the apostle aimed, cannot fail to obviate every argument for the necessity of an after resurrection of the body.

Farther to refute the allegation of a future resurrection of the animal body, without repeating what hath been already stated of the inconsistency of the apostle's anxiety and care on that supposition, I observe, Thirdly; That I have already considered the most forcible and plausible scriptures to favor that plan, known to me, (if any are more favorable, I am willing to have them produced,) and have not found the fact established. Not to anticipate therefore in this place what is more properly to be contained in the next general head, I drop the subject here, after just observing, that it may be kept in remembrance in the sequel, That what has been stated shows, that whenever the term resurrection is found in the scriptures, as belonging to the christian, none else is to be understood but the resurrection to life in Christ, as will be farther illustrated in the following pages.

CHAPTER V.

The resurrection the same as regeneration; and a progressive work.

THIRDLY. I now come to show, That the true resurrection promised in Christ is the passing from the first Adam into the second. It hath been intimated, that the resurrection of God's people, and the regeneration are the same. That point will be proved in the discussion of this head, which is in the substance the same position. Not denying that *regeneration*, may with propriety be used in a more extensive sense than that which is common to the term resurrection, as comprehending the final restitution. It will be granted on all hands, that regeneration is the work of passing, or being transplanted, from the first Adam to the second, or in other words, of becoming the sons of God in Christ, and so partaking spiritual life in him. And that this is the amount of the resurrection, the scriptures are plain enough. " For as in Adam all die, even so " in Christ shall all be made alive"—" And are the children of God, " being the children of the resurrection." But more particularly.

1st. Resurrection is used by the sacred writers instead of regeneration; or in other words, they are said to be risen with Christ, who, it is evident, had experienced nothing farther than being regenerated into Christ. Thus the apostle, [Col. 3. 1, 3.] " If ye then be risen " with Christ, seek those things which are above, where Christ sit- " teth on the right hand of God—For ye are dead, and your life is hid " with Christ in God." Their being risen with Christ is, too evi- dently to need proof, the same as being regenerated into Christ, or as it is stated a little after, having put off the old man with his deeds, and having put on the new.

See also the words of Christ, recorded by Luke, as quoted above. " And are the children of God being the children of the resurrec- " tion." To be the children of God by regeneration, or being the children of the regeneration, would be quite intelligible language, very naturally conveying the idea of those who are born again, or regenerated into Christ; because it is by regeneration, or being born again that men become the children of God. But here the term *resurrection* is used to express that by which men become the children of God, which proves that the resurrection is the same with regeneration—at least thus far.

2d.. To be risen with Christ; or to be alive with him from the dead, which is the same, is the proper predicate of regenerate men; and it is perfectly correct to apply it to them while yet in the body, having never laid it down, much less having reassumed it. This is evident from the above quotation, taken, from the epistle to the Colossians; to which may be added the language of the same apostle to the Romans, whom he addresses " As those who are *alive from the* " *dead*," advising them to consider themselves of that character and to act becomingly to their privilege.

It hath been already objected, and the objection obviated, to this amount, that there are two resurrections pertaining to the saints, and that all these statements in the sacred writings, which represent the resurrection as being tantamount with regeneration, relate to the first, which is indeed the same as regeneration, but that the second, or last, is the resurrection of the material body: I say this objection hath been already obviated. It may however be argued, that the resurrection of the body is that in which alone we can ever resemble Christ, and his resurrection be a proper pledge and example of ours, inasmuch as he committed no sin, and therefore was not a sinner, and consequently could not die to sin and live to God as a proper and correct example of men who thus die and rise in the regeneration.

That Jesus Christ ever committed sin, or that he was a sinner, is not pretended; but that he stood in the tract where sinners stood; took on him the same flesh and blood, so that it is said he, the Word, became flesh; that he also assumed the very nature of those who were sinners, as it is written that Both he who sanctifieth and they who are sanctified are all of one, when the Lord prepared him a body, and laid on him the iniquity of us all, so that it is said he made him to be sin for us; and that he was by that nature exposed to temptation, being tempted in all points like as we are; as well as that he was made like unto his brethren in all things, are characters and facts in his history and life, too prominent ever to be concealed. And that one thing in which it became him to be made like his brethren, and to be their proper example, was that of his rising, or living to God a life of holiness, while he daily died to all sin, in the midst of the most subtle temptations, is taught at length by the apostle to the Hebrews and also to the Romans in the context of the last quotation from that epistle. In that chapter the apostle shows, and correctly illustrates these points; That the death which Jesus Christ died was dying to sin; and that the life which he lived, or the resurrection in which he rose, so that death could have no more dominion over him, was living to God a life of holiness; That for us to die to sin, is that wherein we are planted together with Christ in the likeness of his death, being the effect of his death to us and its equivalent in us; and that for us to live in newness of life, or to be alive to God in holiness, is that wherein we shall be in the likeness of his resurrection, which is the effect of his resurrection to us and its equivalent in us. By a proper attention therefore to that chapter, the argument in behalf of a second resurrection, that of the animal body, drawn from the likeness of our resurrection to that of Jesus Christ, will be sufficiently obviated. It will also be understood more clearly, that whatever death Jesus Christ died was either comprehended in that of his dying to sin, or inflicted on him by the enemy because he would die to sin, or else served as a sign or representation of his so dying; as the natural creation which he assumed, is in many respects a figure of the spiritual; and that whatever other life, or resurrection, he experienced, was only a sign or figure, to represent the true resurrection and life in the Spirit, to those who were in the state of nature, to lead and confirm their minds in the truth of future and spiritual things, until they should travel into an understanding of them in their true order, as before taught. Thus the first Adam, whose fashion Christ assumed, to be conversant with his offspring and for the suffering of death, is the figure of him who was to come.

These things will be made more apparent, while we consider part of that chapter in discussing the leading point now in hand, That the true resurrection promised in Christ, is the passing from the first Adam to the second—the dying to sin and living to God—being born again, born of God, born of the Spirit, or regenerated in Christ, and becoming the children of God in him: for many phrases of this kind are used by the sacred writers to express one and the same thing.

Now that this regeneration, or passing from death in Adam to life in Christ, is the amount of the resurrection promised in Christ, hath been already shown, being a necessary inference from statements previously made. But as the subject is important, and somewhat intricate to the natural mind, we shall prosecute it to some length. And it is enforced with great perspicuity by the apostle in the sixth chapter of his epistle to the Romans. That those believers at Rome, to whom he wrote were yet living in the natural body, having never put it off, and therefore could not possibly have reassumed it—that he addressed them in the character of those who were born again, and that he considered them risen with Christ, being dead and alive again, are facts not to be controverted. "How shall we that are "dead [have died] to sin live any longer therein? Know ye not that "so many of us as were baptized into Jesus Christ were baptized "into his death?" Thus the life of the christian commences with death, even the death of Christ; this is the beginning of their spiritual race or warfare, they are baptized by the Spirit of Christ into his death; as it is said in another place, [1 Cor. 12. 13.] "For by one "Spirit are we all baptized into one body."

It would be an unnecessary labor, as well as improper, to enter into disputations on the subject of water baptism, so much controverted and so highly esteemed by professors, and which at best cannot be considered with any plausibility, as any thing more than a sign, or shadow: it cannot introduce or baptize souls into the death of Christ. The baptism of which the apostle here speaks is that of the Spirit; that one baptism which obtains in the church which is the body of Christ; for as many as were baptized therewith, were baptized into his death: this could not be said of any other than the baptism of the Spirit. And it is evident the apostles made no account of the sign, or water baptism, in the matter of salvation, neither do they ever speak of it as any part of real christianity; but always that of the Spirit, into Christ and into his death. There is one body and one Spirit, one Lord, one faith, one baptism; for by one Spirit are we (who are in Christ) all baptized into one body. Now all they who are baptized in water are not baptized into one body, but those baptized into Christ or into his death are. This is the baptism which accompanieth salvation, but not the baptism of water. As saith the apostle Peter, when speaking of the ark, "Wherein few, that is, eight "souls, were saved by water. The antitype to which, baptism, doth "now save us (not the putting away of the filth of the flesh, but "the answer of a good conscience towards God) through the resur- "rection of Jesus Christ:" [1 Pet. 3. 20, 21.] not water but the Spirit.

John baptized with water, but Christ with the Spirit; and he sent his disciples and commissioned them to do his work and to receive his glory, "As the Father hath sent me, even so send I you." "He "that believeth on me, the works that I do shall he do also." "And "the glory which thou gavest me I have given them." [Jno. 14. 12. and 17. 22. and 20. 21.] And this is in the Spirit and truth, the baptism with which Christ commanded and commissioned his apostles to baptize all nations, saying, "Go ye, therefore, and teach [or dis- "ciple] all the nations, baptizing them [εις το ονομα] into the name "of the Father, and of the Son, and of the Holy Spirit," (not into or with water, but initiating them into the doctrine, life and death of Christ in whom the Father and the Spirit dwelt.) "Teaching them "to observe all things, whatsoever I have commanded you." [Matt. 28. 19, 20.] Or as another evangelist hath it; "Go ye into all the "world, and preach the gospel to every creature. He that believeth "and is baptized shall be saved; but he that believeth not, (such can- "not be baptized with the baptism of Christ,) shall be damned."

[Mark. 16. 15, 16.] Accordingly saith the apostle; "Not that we "are sufficient of ourselves to think any thing as of ourselves; but "our sufficiency is of God; who also hath made us able ministers of "the new testament; not of the letter, but of the Spirit." [2 Cor. 3. 5, 6.] This is the true christian baptism whereby men are baptized into Christ or into his death; while many are running in his name, *Saying*, I am Christ, (but not doing his works, nor walking in his Spirit,) baptizing the people with water, and cursing them with deception, persuading them that this is the true christian baptism, and that they are herein following Christ, while they experience nothing of his death or his resurrection. But all true christians are baptized into Christ and into his death and raised with him. "Therefore we "are buried with him by baptism into death; that like as Christ was "raised up from the dead by the glory of the Father, even so we also "should walk in newness of life. For if we have been planted to- "gether in the likeness of his death, we shall be also in the likeness "of his resurrection." What was that likeness of his death to which the apostle referred them? The same death in them which had been in him, as the after context shows. Not disputing the probability that he had a reference to baptism in water as a figure, as he sometimes spake of circumcission for the same purpose. But as there was the likeness of his death, so also there must be an equivalent likeness of his resurrection, and they be planted together with him in both. This could not be the case with any outward baptism, for that cannot continue with them until the perfecting of the saints in the resurrection: neither is there any such sign appointed.

What then is that likeness of his resurrection, in which believers are planted together with him? The same resurrection in them, the likeness of that which was in him, and which they began to receive in the same baptism, by which they were (and now are, as many as receive him,) baptized into his death. For the baptism of the Spirit abideth the same, even to the completion of the work of redemption, in those who receive it, and keep it. Accordingly the apostle proceeds; "Knowing this, that our old man is crucified with him, that "the body of sin might be destroyed, that we should not serve sin. "(Here is the crucifixion with Christ and death to sin.) For he that "is dead (or hath died, not in sin, neither who hath laid off the bo- "dy, but to sin, as Christ also died,) is freed [or justified] from sin. "(Here is the beginning of life.) Now, if we be dead with Christ, "we believe that we shall also live with him. Knowing that Christ "being raised from the dead, dieth no more; death hath no more "dominion over him:" And such is the blessedness of his people, as he said, [Jno. 11. 25, 26.] "He that believeth in me, though he "were dead, yet shall he live: and whosoever liveth, and believeth "in me, shall never die."

And what was the death which Jesus died? To sin. And what was the life which he lived? A life to God—a life of holy obedience. "For in that he died, he died unto sin once; but in that he liveth, "he liveth unto God." Now what are the effects toward us, of the death and life of Jesus Christ? The same death and life in us, as many as live worthy of their privilege. " Likewise reckon ye also " yourselves to be dead indeed unto sin, but alive unto God through " Jesus Christ our Lord. Let not sin therefore reign in your mortal " body, that ye should obey it in the lusts thereof. Neither yield ye " your members as instruments of unrighteousness unto sin : but " yield yourselves unto God, *as those that are alive from the dead*, " and your members as instruments of righteousness unto God. For " sin shall not have dominion over you: for ye are not under the " law but under grace." Thus by a proper attention to the apostle, it is not difficult to see, what is the true resurrection in Christ, to which those attain who are in him and for which they strive. Freedom from sin, and from the law, with power to serve God in righteousness and holiness. All which are the proper fruits and effects of the work of regeneration, or coming out of the first Adam into the second. And this is the resurrection promised in Christ ; as will yet more pointedly appear from an investigation of the subject as stated in the fifteenth chapter to the Corinthians, first epistle.

In this part of the epistle the subject is treated in an orderly and masterly manner. The subject is introduced with a statement of the apostle's preaching, when he first introduced the gospel among that people, and the fact which he testified as a fundamental truth, in the reception, confirmation and establishment of the gospel, that fact without the faith of which the gospel could not subsist in the world— this fact is the resurrection of Christ, as subsequent to his death. " For I delivered unto you first of all, that which I also received, " how that Christ died for our sins, according to the scriptures ; and " that he was buried, and that he rose again the third day, according " to the scriptures ; and that he was seen of Cephas, then of the " twelve. (and others afterwards)—Whether I or they, so we preach, " and so ye believed." These facts were and still are received and acknowledged by all true believers.

He next proceeds to show the inconsistency of their having received the gospel on these principles, and yet some among them, who were accounted believers, denying the resurrection of the dead, and to prove that either the dead must rise and live in a future and superior state, or the testimony of the resurrection of Christ be proved false. On this part of the argumentation, two things are to be observed. First. That the arguments are all proffered to those who believe the gospel, and in it the·resurrection of Christ, as they are all built on the credibility of that fact, and no appeal is made to any principles or data, acknowledged by unbelievers, so that they could have no direct influence on such : and this is the method of all the apostolic writings ; they were written to believers, and not to unbelievers. Secondly ; The next observation is, that none of the apostle's arguments in this discourse, minister any support to the notion of the resurrection of the animal body, being all such as can be answered without any appeal to that as a fact, or having it necessarily involved with the subject, but aim to prove a future state of existence, or a life to come, in Christ after the present hath come to a close; as, "If in this life only we have "hope in Christ, we are of all men most miserable;" and "As in "Adam all die, even so in Christ shall all be made alive;" that is believers as I have before shown that he wrote to them exclusively. But these things will be more evident by a view of his argumentation.

"Now if Christ be preached that he rose from the dead, how say "some among you, that there is no resurrection of the dead? But "if there be no resurrection of the dead, then is Christ not risen: "and if Christ be not risen, then is our preaching vain, and your "faith is also vain. Yea, and we are found false witnesses of God: "because we have testified of God that he raised up Christ; whom "he raised not up, if so be that the dead rise not. For if the dead "rise not then is not Christ raised; and if Christ be not raised, your "faith is vain; ye are yet in your sins. Then they also who are "fallen asleep in Christ are perished. If in this life only we have "hope in Christ, we are of all men most miserable." It would be imposing on the good sense of the judicious reader, to take up each of these arguments and show, how ineffective they would all be towards an unbeliever. For what efficacy can an inference have with one who hath no faith in the premises?

The apostle, by a well constructed plan, adapted to those who believed the first principles, enforces the subject, by showing how it comes to pass, that the dead are raised, and inherit new life. "But "now is Christ risen from the dead, and become the first fruits of "them that slept. For since by man came death, by man came also "the resurrection of the dead. For as in Adam all die, even so in "Christ shall all be made alive. But every man in his own order: "Christ the first fruits: afterwards they that are Christ's at his com-"ing." A little after, he resumes the subject, with arguments somewhat diverse from the former; to wit, the unreasonableness and improbality that he and other christians, should suffer such things as they did, were the resurrection of the dead and future state of retribution, not true. Of this class of arguments, it may be remarked, that although directed immediately to believers, as being founded on the hope of eternal life, ministered and nourished in the gospel, which hope must fail without the resurrection, they are not very improperly, though somewhat indirectly calculated to beget faith in the natural man; because it will be justly considered an unreasonable thing, and very improbable, that christians, who are naturally men of like passions with others, would endure such privations, and undergo such sufferings, which are real and distressing, in the hope of a life to come, unless supported by good evidence. "Else what shall they "do, who are baptized for the dead, if the dead rise not at all? Why "are they then baptized for the dead? And why stand we in jeo-"pardy every hour? I protest by your rejoicing which I have in "Christ Jesus our Lord, I die daily. If after the manner of men, "I have fought with beasts at Ephesus, what advantageth it me, if "the dead rise not? let us eat and drink, for to-morrow we die. Be not deceived; evil communications corrupt good manners."

The violent attachment of christian professors to the notion of the resurrection of the natural body, will be a sufficient apology for my imposing on the good sense of the judicious reader, so far as to observe, that there is nothing in any of these arguments, of the former or latter class, to confirm or support that doctrine, because every argument in favor of the resurrection of the dead, can be amply satisfied by the spirit's inheriting eternal life. For example; "If in " this life only we have hope in Christ, we are of all men most mise- " rable." But says the Sadducee, or disputer against the resurrection of the body; (if that were the point in debate;) I do not mean that we shall not exist after death, neither do I mean that we shall not have an eternal life in futurity; I only mean that these same bodies will not rise again, to be the habitation of our spirits in that eternal state. And this argument the apostle hath said nothing to rebut: and so of the rest. And it cannot be concealed that he was too profound a reasoner (one side of the consideration that he spake in the gift of the Holy Spirit,) to leave so material an argument in such a free discussion of so fundamental a subject, unanswered.

The same is true of the other class of arguments; as " Why stand " we in jeopardy every hour?" and " If after the manner of men I " have fought with beasts at Ephesus, what advantageth it me, if the " dead rise not? let us eat and drink, for to-morrow we die." Let us take pleasure and ease while we can get it; for to-morrow, or very shortly at least, we die and there is no more of us; but especially we are exposed to a short life, while we maintain the faith of Christ, by which we are continually kept under the lash of persecution. Why therefore need we be thus exposed to danger? And what profit will my sufferings at Ephesus be to me, which I endured for Christ, if the dead rise not? Are not all these things in vain to me and to us all? Nay, says the Sadducee, For your spirit shall live, or ye shall live in the spirit, and inherit a full compensation for all these sufferings and abuses, in that eternal life which shall be your final portion, when for ever done with this earthly body: this argument, as before observed, the apostle hath said nothing to rebut; which could not have passed without notice, had the resurrection of the body been the point in dispute. It is therefore logically true, that all which the apostle hath proved, and therefore all he intended to prove, was, that the spirits of men exist hereafter, or that men exist in the spirit, inheriting spiritual bodies.

While on this particular, it will not be foreign from the main subject in consideration, to introduce the words of Jesus to the Sadducees, as being collateral with those of the apostle. " Now that the " dead are raised, even Moses showed at the bush, when he called " the Lord, the God of Abraham, and the God of Isaac, and the God " of Jacob. For he is not a God of the dead, but of the living; for " all live unto him." Now these three men were long since dead, and yet they were alive, for God was their God, and he is not a God of the dead but of the living. They were also the same men, Abraham, Isaac and Jacob; and yet had not on their earthly bodies; for the time had not yet commenced for them to rise, even if such an event had been expected.

Again; The words of Jesus show, that these three men were either then in the resurrection, or in a situation capable of it. If the first; they were risen, and the material body had no participation in it. If the second; the situation, in which they then were, proved them capable of coming forth, among those who had done good, to the resurrection of life, without any relation to the old dust. But, say the Sadducees, we are convinced, by this reasoning from the words of Moses, (for they were at least put to silence, Matt. 22. 23.) that the dead shall live again; but these bodies are not to rise and live again; Moses hath said nothing of that, and thou hast brought us no proof of it from his words, but rather of the contrary, for he maketh them alive without their former bodies. This argument, there is nothing in the words of Jesus to obviate. If therefore the resurrection of the same body was the point in question, or at all necessary to the existence of the true resurrection, Christ, the Wisdom of God, hath left the grand point, in this fundamental doctrine, without any proof, or even an assertion, as his great apostle did after him; to whose discourse we now return.

The apostle having stated the fact, together with such argumentation as he judged it expedient to use on the occasion, proceedeth in the next place, to show more fully what the resurrection is, and the manner of its coming forth. He in the first place compares it to a crop of grain, which is sown in the seed or bare grain, but is brought forth another body, which God giveth it, and then applies it to what it really is, a spiritual body, which is first sown in the first Adam, and is perfected in the second. " But some man will say, How are " the dead raised up; and with what body do they come? Thou " fool, that which thou sowest, is not quickened except it die: and " that which thou sowest, thou sowest not that body that shall be; " but bare grain; it may chance of wheat, or of some other grain. " But God giveth it a body, as it hath pleased him, and to every seed " his own body." These words pointedly and unequivocally declare, that the resurrection body, or that body which is the subject of the resurrection, is not that body which is sown, or the first body, as afterwards called.

But as this is a part of scripture, so frequently contradicted by many professors, with peremtory and bold assertions, that the apostle here teacheth expressly, that it is the same body, the candid reader will bear with me, while I impose so far on his patience as to make a few remarks, for the sake of elucidation. I grant that these remarks are, some of them, so minute, and at the same time so evident on the simple reading of the text, were it not for the influence of education and prepossession, that they would almost need an apology, to preserve the author of them from the suspicion of being non compos mentis, or of an officious fondness for writing. However, from the foregoing considerations it may be necessary to remark, First; That the body which is sown, is not quickened except it die. That is after the sowing; for let the grain die, or undergo any change, which can with any propriety be called dying, and it is useless to sow it, because it will not grow or produce a crop. This therefore cannot apply to the case of the natural body, or cold lump of flesh and bones, which is deposited in the grave, being previously dead, (for the body without the spirit is dead,) and therefore cannot die again: that which is absolutely dead, cannot become more dead. But what is here affirmed of the grain when sown, is truly applicable to the natural body, or to the physical man, as originated in the first Adam; for as the bare grain cannot be quickened, or bring forth its proper crop, unless it be put into the ground, or covered with manure, which is its proper soil for prolification, so neither can the natural man ever come forth in the resurrection, or be raised to a new and glorified state, unless he be planted with Christ in the gospel, which is the proper and only soil, in which the spiritual body can be produced. For as the bare grain, planted in the soil of the earth, dieth; that is giveth away its spirit, or that part of which its vegetable life and usefulness consist, to enable the earth to produce a new and more valuable crop after its proper kind, a body proper to that sort of grain, (for as the body without the spirit is dead, so the grain without its vegetable spirit is dead also,) so the natural man, or child of the first Adam, when planted in the gospel of Christ, dieth with Christ, being planted together with him in the likeness of his death; he becometh dead to that to which he once lived, and giveth out his spirit which constitutes his life, so far at least that without it he can have none, and converts it away from his former life in the first Adam, and devotes it to Christ in the gospel, to enable the gospel, to bring forth a new and more glorious body, or man, in Christ the beginning of the new creation of God—a body peculiar to that rank or order of beings. "Therefore if any man be in Christ, he is a new creature, " old things are passed away: behold, all things are become new." " Now, if we be dead with Christ, we believe that we shall also live " with him." [2 Cor. 5. 17. Ro. 6. 8.]

But as the earth can produce no crop of grain, unless the seed be first deposited in it, so the gospel cannot produce a new body, or regenerated man, in the order of Christ, without a natural man in the order of the first Adam to be regenerated. And as in the production of a crop of grain, there are always two productions, (not to say a continued succession; for in all crops of grain in its proper order, the crop exceeds the seed in quantity only, being a continued succession of the same kind, but inferior or superior in quality, according to the influence of adventitious causes,) so in the resurrection of men to eternal life in Christ, there are two productions or births, the first originating in the first Adam, and (to trace the subject from the beginning) taking its origin from the act of generation; and the second originating in Christ, being begotten by the word preached and received by faith and obedience; which is the same as to be planted in the gospel. But each of these births is produced in its proper order; and a man in the Spirit, work, or union in the one hath no participation in the other. Accordingly the children of this world, or of the first Adam, marry, and are given in marriage; but those in the resurrection, which is Christ, or those accounted worthy to obtain the resurrection, neither marry nor are given in marriage. So of the first Adam it is said. They (the man and his wife) shall be one flesh; and again, They are therefore no more twain but one flesh. But of Christ it is said, He that is joined to the Lord is one Spirit.

But again. " Thou sowest not that body that shall be." When a man begets a son, in the order of the first Adam, he doth not plant that body which shall be raised glorious in Christ, being a subject of the resurrection, but bare animal seed. But as every kind of animal, in prolification, communicates to its issue, the rudiments, or constituent first principles of its species, so man also, who is an animal, though of the superior order on account of the superior rational spirit, communicates to his physical offspring, in the process of prolification, the rudiments of his species. So that man is begotten entire man in embryo; is born and grows up entire man in the first body; out of that first body or seed, which was produced by the first Adam, cometh forth in the work of regeneration, or the resurrection, by the power of Christ in the gospel, that **spirit** of which is formed the new body, or the new man with such **body as** it hath pleased God to give him. Hence it will follow, that the **regenerated**, or resurrected man, is the same as before, as to identity of **person**, or the most essential constituent parts; but is a new man as being regenerated into a new and superior order, having laid aside the first order pertaining to the first Adam with the natural body, before the work is completely finished, and put on the spiritual which is of Christ. All such put off the old man with his deeds, and put on the new, who is renewed in knowledge after the image of him who created him.

" But God giveth it a body, as it hath pleased him, and to every " seed his own body." On the authority of this last clause of the verse, I suppose it hath been, that some, not to say many, have asserted with great confidence, that the apostle here teacheth that the same body which was sown, is that which also cometh forth in the crop, and consequently that the same material body which is interred, is that which is raised to eternal life in the resurrection, notwithstanding his express declaration to the contrary. " Thou sowest not that " body which shall be." But if by saying, " And to every seed his " own body," he meant that every seed receives the same body which was sown, here is a pointed contradiction, his testimony hath in this instance invalidated itself—he hath taught nothing. But it is plain enough to be understood, that *To every seed his own body*, meaneth, *To every seed a body peculiar to that kind of seed*, which is properly its own body; and then the contradiction is avoided, and no violence is done to the language. The candid among the learned can help to confirm this statement, by noticing that the Greek phrase there used, is very justly rendered in English, *a proper body*, or *a body peculiar to it*, and contains nothing in it to require any translation, or acceptation, which would at all contradict or weaken what is before asserted, That it is not the same body. The learned Philip Doddridge saw the propriety of this criticism; and, in his critical notes on the text, hath acknowledged, that there appears to be a reference in the apostle's words, to the bodies peculiar to the different kinds of grain; but for the want of better testimony to support his favorite plan, or not having a right understanding of the subject, he hath pressed this text into his scheme, the glaring contradiction above stated, notwithstanding.

There are various kinds of bodies on the earth, and every species of animals hath its peculiarities of body; so also may there be divers degrees of glory among the subjects of the resurrection; but every individual subject must have a spiritual body agreeing in nature and lineage with all the rest. "All flesh is not the same flesh: but there "is one kind of flesh of men, another flesh of beasts, another of "fishes, and another of birds. There are also celestial bodies, and "bodies terrestrial; but the glory of the celestial is one, and the "glory of the terrestrial is another. There is one glory of the sun, "and another glory of the moon, and another glory of the stars: for "one star differeth from another in glory. So also is the resurrec- "tion of the dead. It is sown in corruption, it is raised in incorrup- "tion." What is sown? Not the same body which is raised as some adventurously and preposterously assert, through prepossession and prejudicial education, or an unacquaintance with the subject in the true spirit of it, and perhaps also, for the want of considering the plain connection of the different members of the sentence—Thou sowest not that body that shall be. But it is sown. What is it? The resurrection; or that crop which cometh forth after the sowing of the first seed, or its being planted and dying; "So also is the re- "surrection of the dead; it is sown in corruption." In that corrupt nature found in that corrupt work, which hath always been shown to be unclean since the days of Moses, and all whose fruits are in corruption and death, until finally dissolved: As in Adam all die. Or, in plain terms, it is sown in the flesh, which is *corruption* as though in the abstract; or as though there were nothing pertaining to the flesh but corruption absolutely. Accordingly, "He that soweth to "the flesh shall of the flesh reap corruption;" but the crop, or fruit of the flesh is flesh again, for "That which is of the flesh is flesh." The fruit therefore which those reap who sow to the flesh is flesh, or it is corruption as though in the abstract, for corruption is so combined with the flesh that wherever the flesh is, there is corruption, and whatever is done by the instigation of the flesh is done in corruption: "It is sown in corruption, It is raised in incorruption;" In the incorruptible Spirit and likeness of Christ, and by the power of his word, which is incorruptible seed, and liveth and abideth for ever. "It is sown in dishonor;" in that work which for the very dishonor of it, even when sanctioned by the broad seal of law authority, all men who have the smallest sense of shame are constrained to conceal: for men are not want to conceal honorable deeds; " I " was shapen in iniquity and in sin did my mother conceive me." [Psm. 51. 5.] " It is raised in glory;" fashioned in the glorious likeness of Christ. " It is sown in weakness;" of which all are partakers in the first Adam, more or less, from their conception to the grave. " It is raised in power." " It is sown a natural " body," (according to the first Adam) " it is raised a spiritual body. (According to the order of the last Adam.) " There is a natural " body, (which is the first Adam and according to him,) and there " is a spiritual body, (which is the last Adam and according to him,) " And so it is written, The first man Adam was made a living soul, " the last Adam a quickening spirit." These last words are unequivocally to the point; and conclusively put the matter beyond doubt, with every judicious inquirer, that the sum of the resurrection is regeneration, or becoming new creatures in Christ, that is coming out of the first Adam into the last, in spiritual union and relation; which was the point to be proved.

But the apostle proceeds to a father illustration of the subject. " Howbeit, that was not first which is spiritual, but that which is na- " tural; and afterwards that which is spiritual." The spiritual body therefore is not the same which was once natural, else it had been first, yea, both first and last, (a title which belongs to none in all the church, Christ excepted,) but he saith it was not first. Our existence in Christ, or our spiritual body, is not our first existence, but that in Adam, which is natural, and afterwards that in Christ which is spiritual. Accordingly it is added, that, " The first man is of the " earth, earthy; the second man is the Lord from heaven. As is " the earthy, such are they also that are earthy; (Adam's sons are " like himself;) and as is the heavenly, such are they also that are " heavenly. (The people of Christ are spiritual and walk in the " same way with him.) And as we have borne the image of the ear- " thy we shall also bear the image of the heavenly." These words are satisfactorily to the point, that this is the meaning of the natural body which is first, and of the spiritual which is last, to wit, that the first pertaineth to the first Adam, according to his order, and the last to the second Adam, who is Christ, according to his order, and consequently, that to come out of the first Adam into the second, is the true resurrection promised in Christ, for in this point the apostle's arguments all concentrate. I have before shown that the regeneration, or resurrection, is not an instantaneous work, but progressive. Accordingly the apostle speaketh of it, as being yet to come, although he and other faithful believers had actually begun to partake of it, and were alive in Christ according to the work of that day, being alive from the dead.

But to put the matter still farther out of doubt, if possible, that the material body hath neither part nor lot in the resurrection, he hath added. " Now this I say, brethren, that flesh and blood cannot inhe-

"rit the kingdom of God; neither doth corruption inherit incorruption." He hath left no room nor possibility for the entrance of flesh and blood, on the principle of any alteration or refinement which they might possibly undergo, but accounts them corruption, as it were, in the abstract. Neither, as before stated, is there any principle in nature, or any doctrine of revelation to prove, that flesh and blood, or any other material substance, can be converted into spirit, or the material body become a spiritual body, although there is authority enough in revelation, and not contrary to natural reason, that that spirit, which inhabits the material body during the physical life, will be glorified in the likeness of Christ; this is the true resurrection. According to this plan, the people of God resemble their forerunner, and are the true followers of Christ, who was born into the world, of a woman, as the children also are; and so took on him the same flesh and blood with them, that through death (by dying to sin and so setting them an example to follow his steps,) he might destroy him that had the power of death, that is, the devil, and deliver those who through fear of death were all their life time subject to bondage. For he was not only born into the world of a woman, as other men are, but was also born out of the world to God, by the Spirit of regeneration, that he might therein be a forerunner to his people. Or he was born from the dead, and is the first fruits of them that slept; " The first born from the dead; that he might in " all things have the pre-eminence;" that he might in all things be a leader and be acknowledged and honored as the head over all, and that his people might follow him through, receiving of his fulness, grace answering to grace. " Christ the first fruits; afterwards they " that are Christ's at his coming."

It is indeed true, that in the strictness of language, Jesus Christ, the son of God, never did either die, or fall asleep; neither was he ever dead in sin, or alive to sin; his spirit, or soul, was always too deeply immersed in the knowledge of God, and too devoutly submissive to his will, to admit of any such things. But that he stood in the place of sinners, partook of the same flesh and blood, as they exist in the order of nature, fallen as it is, when God prepared him a body, and laid on him the iniquity of us all; that in this state of existence he experienced all that intimate physical union between soul and body, which is common to other men, and was thereby exposed to suffer all the temptations and allurements of the fleshly, or natural appetites, so as to be tempted in all points like as we are; that he suffered the ordinary dissolution of that physical union, in the most painful and ignominious manner, being numbered with the transgressors, and making his grave with the wicked and with the rich in his death, and so passed into Hades, the receptacle or state of the dead, or departed spirits, and was thus counted of those who slept; and that he thence ascended and became the first fruits of them that slept and the first begotten from the dead, are facts too well established to be forgotten. These statements comprehend the only principles, on which it was possible for Jesus Christ the Son of God to die to sin, being perpetually beset with temptations of the devil through the flesh, and as perpetually and successfully resisting and overcoming, until he arose to God in newness of life, having completely vanquished the tempter, disappointing him on every hand, and having subjugated and completely mortified every source and principle of temptation, having abolished the enmity in himself, until the enemy had no more room to work. These statements also contain the only principles on which the Son of God can be said to have been dead, or numbered with the dead, or those who slept; but so far was he from being dead, or asleep, as had been the case with many others, that he was in the mean time actively employed, preaching to the spirits in prison, who had been disobedient in the days of Noah, and had been dismissed to hades [the state or receptacle of the dead,] in bondage for their disobedience.

That the spirits of men, dislodged from the body, are variously situated according to their proper state and character at their exit, is no doubt a reasonable and equitable truth: but their situation was in general termed a sleep, particularly as it respected the righteous under the law, as signifying that state in which they were neither properly saved nor irrecoverably lost—neither properly alive to God, nor finally dead in sin; neither of which they could be until the salvation of God appeared, and they either accepted or rejected it. For the law making nothing perfect, and opening no possible way of salvation from all sin, because it was impossible that the blood of bulls and of goats, and the ashes of an heifer a year old, or all their meats and drinks and divers washings and carnal ordinances, should take away sin ; so neither could it sanction a final and confirmed state of condemnation. As finished salvation can be obtained by the gospel only, so absolute and complete condemnation is the lot of those only who reject it. " And this is the condemnation, that light " is come into the world, and men loved darkness rather than light, " because their deeds were evil." [Jno. 3. 19.]

The same term of sleep was continued by Jesus and his apostles in the gospel dispensation, with special application to believers in Christ, who laid down the tabernacle in the faith, and waited for the day of final and full redemption at his second appearing. Agreeably to this acceptation of the term sleep, the apostle speaketh concerning the deceased, denominating them, *Those who are asleep*, and again saying, *Those who sleep in Jesus will God bring with him*. And of the same characters he saith in the same discourse. *The dead in Christ shall rise first*. So said Jesus Christ; "Our friend Lazarus sleepeth;" and afterwards said plainly, " Lazarus is dead."

That there were divers degrees in the faith, light, power and travel among the believers from the beginning, is not only rational but scriptural ; consequently some were farther advanced in the spiritual life than others, and therefore could not be expected to fall so deeply on sleep, as those who were less acquainted with God and more lost in the earth. Besides, the apostles looked for a day, and spoke of it, in which all believers should be entirely awake, and arise to that eternal life in which they should receive their full reward. So saith Paul; "Henceforth there is laid up for me a crown of righteous-"ness, which the Lord, the righteous judge, shall give to me *in that* "*day*: and not to me only, but to *all them also that love his appear-* "*ing*." [1 Tim. 3. 8.] Until that day should appear many would sleep, but in that day, none can fail of being waked up.

In relation to this day speaketh the apostle, bearing forward in his discourse on the resurrection. [1 Cor. 15. 31.] "Behold, I shew "you a mystery; We shall not all sleep, but we shall all be chang-"ed." And a little after he showeth what that change is; "For "this corruptible must put on incorruption, and this mortal must put "on immortality." That all men in this imbodied state are mortal and corruptible, being subject to the dissoluton of the physical constitution, or the separation of the spirit from the body, is granted by all, and confirmed by perpetual experience. But according to the faith of the gospel, all true believers expect to grow up into Christ in all things until they all come in the unity of the faith and of the knowledge of the Son of God, to a perfect man, to the measure of the stature of the fulness of Christ; or in other words they expect (and not in vain,) to arise with Christ and in him, to that eternal life which is incorruptible, undefiled, and that fadeth not away. And this eternal life is begun, and can make its advances, in those who are in the body, as assuredly as in those who are out; as said Jesus; "He that believeth in me, though he were dead, yet shall he live: "and whosoever liveth, and believeth in me, shall never die." And again; "If any man keep my sayings, He shall never see death." [Jno. 11. 25, 26. and 8. 51.] This work therefore of growing up into Christ in all things, or of rising in him to a new, spiritual and eternal life in immortality and incorruptibility, may be begun while living in the earthly house of this tabernacle, and proceed with uninterrupted success, from one degree to another, until perfected.

But especially in the day of Christ's second appearing, (the true testimony of which is now gone forth, and the last trumpet begun to sound,) in the progress of which all are to come forth, those who become properly awake to righteousness and the knowledge of God, and travel into the true life and spiritual work of Christ, far enough to go through the dissolution of the physical constitution, or death, in common language, without interruption, or the suffering of loss, shall not sleep, but go right onward in their spiritual travel, standing as living members of the living body, and in union with the head, and so pass through the change from Adam to Christ, or of putting on incorruption and immortality, as well as those who had slept before they were perfectly acquainted with the finishing work of Christ, and had to be awaked by the last trumpet, for the perfecting of the work in them. This was a mystery, a subject beyond their reach and out of their sight in that day, in the degree of travel which obtained with them, until opened to them by the Spirit of revelation. But to suppose that all not sleeping meaneth, that some would be alive in the natural body, when the last trumpet should sound, and call all to judgment in a moment, and that these should proceed to the judgment without the formality of dying and rising again, is, on that plan, were that the truth, no mystery at all, but a natural consequence, naturally deduced, by natural or common sense, from plain premises, perceptible and intelligible to the natural senses. But some may insist, that the mystery consisted in the sudden and great change which they should pass through in the whole constitution, fitting the bodies as well as the spirits for being inhabitants of heaven. But the context and connection will not warrant such an explanation; for he had just before asserted, " That flesh and blood (by which we are " inevitably to understand, that substance of which the animal body " consists,) cannot inherit the kingdom of God; neither doth corrup- " tion inherit incorruption." In this sentence flesh and blood, or the animal body, is put on a par with corruption, as though they are both one, or at least, that wherever the first can be, the last may also be expected, accordingly they are both equally excluded from the kingdom of God, without appeal.

To maintain therefore that the saying, " We shall not all sleep, " but we shall all be changed," means that all men shall not put off this earthly tabernacle, but that some shall experience a change equal to putting it off and on again, and so having it glorified in heaven, while they remain constitutionally or physically the same beings which they were before, consisting of the same body as well as spirit, is utterly unwarrantable. For, that we may take a compendious view of some of the reasons which might be extracted from what is already written. In the first place; Such a construction of that sentence destroys the apprehension of what is there taught being a mystery as before stated. Secondly, It contradicts the doctrine so fully taught in the former part of the discourse, that the resurrection promised in Christ, is the passing of the creature from the first Adam to the second. To which add thirdly, That when the first Adam sinned, he was nominated dust, and sentenced to the dust as his proper place, since which time to the present, there hath never appeared any satisfactory, or convincing proof, that he should ever be recovered, much less be released from suffering the dissolution : " It is " appointed to men once to die." That that denunciation was specially against the animal body is evident, for the spirit is not dust, and is not consigned to it, but remaineth susceptible of a renovation and resurrection in Christ the second man. But to return to the argument;

It is unwarrantable in matters of the last importance, to build on the figurative language of prophecy, without more satisfactory testimony; especially where the language bears a proper and consistent meaning without teaching such things as are sought for from it. Therefore add fourthly; That this sentence bears a very proper acceptation without meaning simply or mainly the death of the body. For although the term *sleep*, when used metaphorically in the scriptures, frequently means the death of the body, yet not universally; as in these words, [Eph. 5. 14.] " Awake thou that sleepest, and " arise from the dead, and Christ shall give thee light ;" it is evident that the sleeping hath no respect to the death of the body, but to the insensibility and inattention of the mind to spiritual affairs—to being asleep, or dead, in trespasses and in sins. At the same time, it is not a reasonable supposition, that the apostle had respect merely to being asleep in sin, when he said, We shall not all sleep; for in that sense it would not be in all respects true, as that is the natural state of all; and also, as he saith, *We* shall not all sleep, he hath evidently a particular respect to believers, and to that state into which those pass at the dissolution of the natural life, who have not become sufficiently alive to God and experienced in the regeneration to travel directly onward with those who were in the holy city before them. And as the work of Christ was justly expected to be a deeper and more thorough work, in the sounding of the last trumpet, or in his second appearing, than at any time before, all should not sleep, but all should then be changed.

In defence of the resurrection of the earthly body and its translation into the kingdom of heaven, by an instantaneous and mechanical exertion of divine power, great stress probably will be laid by some, on these words, " In a moment, in the twinkling of an eye, at " the last trump : for the trumpet shall sound, and the dead shall be " raised incorruptible, and we shall be changed." It cannot be denied with any plausibility that the change which those experience who do not sleep is the same which those also experience who have been dead, or asleep, (for the two words mean the same characters,) or in other words, they undergo such a change as to make them equal, and set them in the same situation with those who had been dead. " We " shall not all sleep, but we shall all be changed—the dead shall be " raised incorruptible, and we shall be changed. For this corrupti- " ble must put on incorruption, and this mortal must put on immor- " tality ;" consequently must put off the contrary, for in that day the work is to be finished and perfect. The dead shall be raised incorruptible—alive in the Spirit of Christ, in whom there is no corruption —free from the flesh and all its inherent and attendant corruption— to be for ever with Christ and like him, now no more to return to corruption.

The apostle hath not, in this place, shown, whence the dead arise, as to locality, or whence they shall come, who have been asleep, but in another description of the same period and of the same events, [1 Thess. 4. 13, to 17.] he hath shown whence they come, that when Christ cometh, they come with him. " But I would not have you " ignorant, brethren, concerning those who are asleep, that ye sorrow " not, even as others who have no hope. For if we believe that Je- " sus died, and rose again, even so them also who sleep in Jesus will God " bring with him. For this we say to you by the word of the Lord, " That we who are alive, and remain until the coming of the Lord, " shall not prevent [go before] those who are asleep. For the Lord " himself shall descend from heaven with a shout, with the voice of " the archangel and with the trump of God: and the dead in Christ " shall rise first. Then [επειτα, afterwards] we who are alive and

" remain, shall be caught up together with them in the clouds to meet the Lord in the air: and so shall we ever be with the Lord." This statement doth not well accord with the common notion, that Christ must first come and raise the saints out of the earth before they can be with him in the execution of judgment, but it accords with the Spirit of inspiration, and all sentiments and notions must yield to that. Those then who had slept in Jesus, or the dead in Christ, are raised to life in Christ, before those who are alive and remain are called forth into the same work and by the sounding of the same trumpet, and sit with him and act for him in the prosecution of his work, toward those who are alive and remain, as well as with those who slept in sin. As it is also written in another place, " Do ye not " know that the saints shall judge the world;" [1 Cor. 6. 2.] for " The dead in Christ shall rise first, and afterwards we that are alive " and remain shall be caught up together with them to meet the Lord " in the air." But " Those who sleep in Jesus will God bring with " him ;" which showeth how they are raised ; in the spirit as Christ also was, and thus they are like him : as he was put to death in the flesh and quickened in the Spirit, so are they. These things also show, that there is a progressive work in the resurrection, for the dead in Christ shall rise first. Neither is there any thing in this whole description, at all inconsistent with the statement made above, That the true resurrection in Christ, is the passing out of the first Adam into the second. The shout, the voice of the archangel and the trump of God, are bold prophetic figures, aptly expressing the vigorous and zealous propagation of the gospel, calling the human family out of the flesh into the Spirit—out of the first Adam into Christ—out of death into eternal and incorruptible life. The first Adam is corrupt and mortal, without any promise of ever being better; consequently, all those who stand united with him in his peculiar order, in any part, spirit or matter, are proportionably corrupt and mortal. But Christ Jesus, the second Adam, is life and immortality as in the abstract; those therefore who are perfectly renewed into Christ in all things, have put on incorruption and immortality ; " For as in Adam all die, even so in Christ shall all be made alive."

With respect to the peculiar phraseology, " In a moment, in the " twinkling of an eye, at the last trump ;" nothing special or definitive can be inferred from it, as to the length of the time in which the work will be accomplishing. For although the peculiarity of the apostle's genius, the Spirit of the day and dispensation, being full of the elevated strain, or style of prophecy, and the peculiar gift of revelation made to him, justify such bold figures in his writings, (For although the indolent, earthly and contracted mind, may announce that mysterious, symbolical and abstruse method of writing, unfair, even in an apostle, it remaineth true that according to the *wisdom given to him* he hath written in all his epistles, speaking in them of these things ; in which are some things hard to be understood, which they that are unlearned and unstable, but not the wise towards God, the faithful and self-denying, wrest, as they do also the other scriptures, to their own destruction.) nothing can be known definitively by such language in a gift of prophecy, how long, until the same Spirit who gave it, open it up in the fulfilment of the work, or by other suitable explication from himself. We read of a moment, an hour, half an hour, a day, three days and an half, and a thousand years, but all are mysterious and symbolical expressions, unknown, as to the certainty of the time designed thereby, until unfolded by the same Spirit. And although it be granted as a reasonable thought, that a moment or the twinkling of an eye, means a much shorter time than a day or a year; and not saying how suddenly the work may be understood to commence in its introduction, or with each individual in its progress, these things cannot prove any thing definitively, as to the space of time during which the last and finishing work of Christ, the work of the resurrection and the judgment, will progress and continue.

I know of no principle in all which hath been said, in the nature of the work itself, or in the various scripture accounts of it, to contradict its being introduced suddenly; every work however durable must have a beginning; but that is not to contradict its after increase; and to suppose that the words In a moment, in the twinkling of an eye, are a literal proof that the resurrection and consequent change are to be accomplished literally in that period of time, is probably more than any man will believe on a deliberate view of the subject. Besides, such an acceptation of those words would set this verse at variance with itself; for, in perfect agreement with the other scripture which we lately considered, it giveth the dead in Christ the foreway in the resurrection. It would also set this text at variance with almost, if not entirely, every other text on that subject, which it would be too great a digression from the subject in hand to show at length in this place. One passage however, I think it expedient to notice here, which the aforesaid acceptation would contradict. I notice it here, because it is in this chapter, on which I am now treating, and was omitted in treating of the sentences immediately connected with it, with the peculiar impression of introducing it here. The words are in connection with some which have been freely used already; " For as in Adam all die, even so in Christ shall all be made " alive. But every man in his own order; Christ the first fruits; " afterward they that are Christ's at his coming. Then cometh the " end, when he shall have delivered up the kingdom to God, even " the Father; when he shall have put down all rule and all authority " and power. For he must reign till he hath put all enemies under " his feet. The last enemy that shall be destroyed is death." Here is evidently a succession of events described by the same language as one part of the successive appearances of Christ to his disciples; " After that [επειτα] he was seen of James; then [ειτα] of all the " apostles;" So here, " Christ the first fruits; afterward [επειτα] " they that are Christ's at his coming. Then [ειτα, after, not, τοτε, " at that time,] cometh the end, when he shall have delivered up the " kingdom to God, even the Father, when he shall have put down all " rule and all authority and power. For he must reign, (to wit, after he

" hath come,) till he hath put all enemies under his feet. The last
" enemy that shall be destroyed is death. And when all things shall
" be subdued unto him, then shall the Son also himself be subject to
" him that did put all things under him, that God may be all in all."
How long his reign will be, before he hath conquered all his enemies
and fitted out the kingdom to deliver it up to the Father, is yet to
learn, but we have sufficient reason to believe it will be longer than
a moment or the twinkling of an eye. It is once stated, though still
in the language and style of prophecy, that it will be a thousand years
or more. But all this will not contradict the expectation, that the
work will be short and speedy in deciding the case with individuals
as they come forward in their own order—a short work, cut short in
righteousness, giving every one an offer, a fair trial, and when he hath
made his choice dealing with him accordingly. But to return;
  " So when this corruptible shall have put on incorruption, and this
" mortal shall have put on immortality, then shall be brought to pass
" the saying that is written, Death is swallowed up in victory." It
hath been sufficiently proved, that this great and happy change is effected by the gospel in the work of regeneration, or coming out of
the first Adam where is mortality and death, into Christ who is immortality and life. Accordingly it is written in another place;
" Whatsoever is born of God overcometh the world : and this is the
" victory that overcometh the world even our faith." [1 Jno. 5. 4.]
  Not foreign from this point are the words of Christ to the Jews,
[Jno. 5. 25, &c.] " The hour is coming, and now is, when the dead
" shall hear the voice of the Son of God : and they that hear shall
" live." According to these words the time of raising the dead had
then come, and also the time of executing judgment, as the following words show : but these things only in part, as a prelude and example of that which was to come ; for the time was coming as well
as then present. " For as the Father hath life in himself, so hath he
" given to the Son to have life in himself, and hath given him autho-
" rity also to execute judgment, because he is the Son of man."
Thus wherever the gospel is there is the judgment. " Now is the
" judgment of this world, now shall the prince of this world be cast
" out. And I, if I be lifted up from the earth, will draw all men
" unto me." [Jno. 12. 31, 32.] And again ; " For the time is come
" that judgment must begin at the house of God." [1 Pet. 4. 17.]
But, " Marvel not at this ; (which is now doing, which is only the
" beginning,) for the hour is coming, in the which (the work by the
" same word of power shall be so extensive that) all that are in their
" graves shall hear his voice, and shall come forth, they that have
" done good to the resurrection of life, and they that have done evil
" to the resurrection of damnation." Each to be judged and receive
his reward according to his doings. But observe, They shall come
forth to the resurrection, so that each one as he cometh forth hath
a fair and decisive choice to make, into which resurrection eventually
to enter ; according to what is again written ; " And I saw another
" angel fly in the midst of heaven, having the everlasting gospel to

"preach to them that dwell on the earth, and to every nation, and kindred, and tongue, and people, saying with a loud voice, Fear God, and give glory to him ; for the hour of his judgment is come : and worship him that made heaven and earth, and the sea, and the fountains of waters." [Rev. 14. 6, 7.] Here the gospel is expressly announced as going forth with the judgment ; accordingly every one who is waked up and called forth hath an equitable opportunity to make choice, whether he will fear God and give glory to him or not. Herein is the work of the first resurrection ; and blessed is he whosoever is prevailed upon to enter into it. It may be objected, as it hath been done already, that this text is prophetic and metaphorical. But the reply is natural and easy ; That as this is, prophetic and metaphorical, so is that which is alledged in defence of the suddenness of the change by a mechanical agency.

When the apostle had proved out the truth of the resurrection, shown the manner of it, and such other things as he saw proper to state in conjunction with it, he breaks out into an exultation. " O death! where is thy sting? O grave !" (Hades, the receptacle of departed spirits, not the tomb into which the body is laid) " where is thy victory." (Thou takest the spirits of all men, but being in Christ who is our life, and with whom our life is hid securely in God, we arise to a better and more glorious life which is eternal and free from corruption.) " The sting of death is sin ; and the strength of sin is the law. But thanks be to God, who giveth us the victory through our Lord Jesus Christ," who was born of a woman, born under the law, that he might redeem them that were under the law, that we might receive the adoption of sons—who hath also borne our sins on his own body on the tree, and opened the new and living way through the veil, that is to say, his flesh, that he might lead us out of all sin and the wages of it, into the new and spiritual life in himself—The last enemy that shall be destroyed is death. When sin is all removed and death is destroyed, then the resurrection and the life shall reign triumphantly, and remain forever.

Other scriptures might be introduced to illustrate the same point ; that the resurrection promised in Christ is the same work of the regeneration, or passing from the first Adam into Christ who is the Lord from heaven, a quickening Spirit, in whom all his people are made alive, and become spiritual. That which is of the flesh is flesh ; or it is corruption ; for that which a man soweth shall he also reap ; but he that soweth to the flesh shall of the flesh reap corruption, or flesh : the body of flesh therefore cannot produce a spiritual body. But that which is of the Spirit is spirit ; they therefore who are born of the Spirit, or are regenerated into Christ who is a quickening Spirit, are spiritual and inherit spiritual bodies, of incorruption and immortality. Should any feel dissatisfied with the application which is made of Paul's discourse on the resurrection and think they could apply it more correctly ; they may consider that if the day is come, they who are in the work, may begin to understand ; for *the wise shall understand ;* but they who are not in

the work, in the true spirit, cannot; for *none of the wicked shall understand*. But if the day and time of the resurrection be not come; no man can understand the things which are written of it; for it never was the intention of prophetic language that it should be understood until the time of the fulfilment, and by those who possess the same Spirit of God by whom it was given and by whose operations the work is accomplished. " Knowing this first, that no pro-
" phecy of the scripture is of any private interpretation. For the pre-
" phecy came not in old time by the will of man; but holy men of God
" spake as they were moved by the Holy Ghost." Without the teachings, therefore, of the same Spirit, no man can understand the scripture prophecy; and just where that Spirit applieth it, the application is correct, and can be seen to agree with the prophecy: for the Spirit is truth. Should any inquire; On this view, how cometh it to pass that any can venture to make so bold an application as the above, of that prophecy written by Paul, on the resurrection? I answer; Because the day is come; the resurrection hath begun; many hath risen with Christ and walk with him in white; To those who look for him and are willing to receive him, he hath appeared the second time without sin unto salvation. To them that fear God, the Sun of righteousness hath arisen with healing in his beams, and is shining as clear as the noon-day sun. This Sun of righteousness showeth us what is the mystery—that we shall not all sleep; and in what manner the spiritual body, which was not first is obtained in Christ; and what is the nature of that resurrection to which the apostle strove, that if by any means he might attain.

CHAPTER VI.

Of the last judgment; by way of APPENDIX to the foregoing chapters.

THE resurrection and judgment are so intimately connected, that a full discussion of the first is not to be expected without including many things pertaining to the last. Accordingly, in the preceding discourse, to interfere with the judgment was unavoidable. But it being inconsistent with the purpose of that discourse, to say as much on some parts of scripture which naturally come into view, in discussing those subjects, as would give satisfaction, without digressing too far from the leading proposals, I have concluded to add a few pages by way of appendix, descanting on the resurrection or judgment as either may interfere, but intending to touch mostly on the latter. And no scripture appears better adapted to introduce the subject than that on which so much hath been already written. " In
" a moment, in the twinkling of an eye, at the last trump; for the
" trumpet shall sound, and the dead shall be raised incorruptible
" and we shall be changed." (1 Cor. 15. 52.)

In this text are to be noticed; First, The transaction to take place; The trumpet shall sound—the last trumpet. Secondly, The effects to follow; The dead to be raised incorruptible; or the sleeping awaked; and the living to be changed. Thirdly, The time and space in which these matters are to be effected; In a moment, in the twinkling of an eye. And,

First. Of the transaction to take place—the sounding of the last trumpet.

This is the only place in scripture, where the phrase, last trumpet, is used in relation to this scene. And I know no reason beyond conjecture, or the combination of human conceptions transferred from one to another, to fix any impression on the minds of professed christians, why this last trumpet should be any other than the seventh, spoken of in the Apocalypse. It is evident from the manner in which the sacred penmen have written, that they did not judge it necessary, to describe minutely every circumstance attending that scene, on every occasion when they spake of it, neither always to describe it in the same words: or in other words; It did not appear necessary, to the Spirit of God, to show them all things minutely and at all times.

In the text now before us there is no mention of whose trumpet it is, or by whom sounded. But other scriptures descriptive of the same scene, afford information on that particular. In the epistle to the Thessalonians it is announced by these terms; "For the Lord " himself shall descend from heaven with a *shout*, [κελευσματι; ex- " pressing the exhortation or command given by sailors,] with the " *voice of the archangel* and with the *trump of God*." In the description of the same scene by Jesus himself, (Matt. 24. 31.) it is said; " And he shall send his *angels with the sound of a great trumpet*." Thus by a comparison of those scriptures, which speak of Christ's coming attended by the sound of a trumpet, it appears that the trump of God, or of Christ, is that which the angels sound. And that these angels are messengers of God to the people, and that the message which they bring is the gospel of Christ for the salvation of all whosoever will hear and obey it, (for that is no gospel which doth not contain the privilege and power of salvation,) will appear by comparing the above with another scripture descriptive of the same tremendous scene—the commencement of the last judgment. (Rev. 14. 6, 7.) " And I saw another angel fly in the midst of heaven, hav- " ing the everlasting gospel to preach to them that dwell on the " earth, and to every nation, and kindred and tongue, and people, " Saying with a loud voice, Fear God, and give glory to him; for " the hour of his judgment is come; and worship him that made " heaven, and earth, and the sea, and the fountains of waters." In this description the vision is of one angel. Thus an angel with a message, angels with the sound of a great trumpet, the voice of the archangel and the trump of God, as well as the Lord with a shout, are all introduced to communicate the same information. On which we may unhesitatingly observe, that no man can produce the smallest authority, that any one of them, or any other prophecy of that day, is a literal description of the appearances and transactions to which they relate. But as they are all apt figures to represent the publication of the gospel, as before hinted, and whereas the scene of the last quotation was last shown, in late days, consequently nearest the time of the accomplishment, and to one to whom future events were shown in a singular manner, and as this testimony is expressly, that this loud voice, shout, or trumpet, which ever it be called, is the everlasting gospel, (and can we expect the tidings of the last day to be any thing less favorable than God hath said?) may we not with confidence and safety conclude, from these premises and in perfect consistency with an acquaintance with the work in the present day, that all these symbolical representations uniformly point to the Spirit of Christ in his church, and going forth to the people on the earth, in his angels or ministers? And as in the first dispensation of Christ the judgment went with the gospel, as before shown, it is not unreasonable that the last judgment of the world—the final casting out of the prince of this world, should usher in with the everlasting gospel. At least, such is the statement of the scriptures; and I must be allowed to believe them until I find more competent authority. And in addition to the truth of God, that judge of all the earth, who will do all things right, and who inviteth mankind to reason with him on fair and equitable principles, I can appeal to the common sense of every man; to the unbiassed feelings of every heart; to the receptacle of light and evidence, and the comparer of evidences in every man, whether it be not more equitable than any thing which can be proposed to the contrary, to give every one a fair trial by ushering in the gospel as a concomitant of the judgment, allowing to every one the pirvilege of confessing all his sins, laying down his rebellion, and bearing his cross in obedience and self-denial; and whether any thing could be imagined more unequal, than to arraign a man and condemn him finally and irrecoverably, for having not done his duty, in a situation in which he could neither know nor have any power to do it, or for doing that which he had no power to avoid, or knowledge of its being evil; and his inability all this time invincible in his situation. And it is abundantly evident, that by far the majority, thousands and millions of those who are and who have been, knew not the will of God, and had no possible way to know it, and therefore could not possibly do it: and at the same time, none can enter into the kingdom of heaven except those who do the will of God. "Not " every one that saith unto me, Lord, Lord, shall enter into the king-" dom of heaven; but he that doeth the will of my Father who is " heaven." "But he who knew not (his Lord's will), and did com-" mit things worthy of stripes, shall be beaten with few stripes;" Yet he is beaten, and therefore not clear.

Now let us inquire, what there is, in any or all the representations of the last day, or judgment, by which they can be proved to be at all different from the sounding of the seventh trumpet in the Apocalypse. Nothing can be argued from the suddenness and quick accomplishment in any of those representations; for although in this no mention is made of a moment or an hour, the work is described as being as instantaneous and momentary as language can point it out; even as quick as the trumpet gave the blast. " And the sev-" enth angel sounded; and there were great voices in heaven, Say-" ing, The kingdoms of this world are become the kingdom of our " Lord, and of his Christ; and he shall reign for ever and ever." (Rev. 11. 15.) Neither can any thing be shown in the sounding of this seventh trumpet, by which it can be proved to fall short of the general and last judgment; for no language could more forcibly paint that important day, in respect to the things which were shown to take place in the time of it; as the setting up of that kingdom of God in which he is to reign for ever and ever; and added to this, The wrath of God on the nations, the dead raised, his servants rewarded and his enemies destroyed. " And the four and twenty El-" ders, who sat before God, on their seats, fell upon their faces, and " worshipped God, saying, We give thee thanks, O Lord God Al-" mighty, who art, and wast, and art to come; because thou hast " taken to thee thy great power and hast reigned. And the nations " were angry, and thy wrath is come, and the time of the dead, that " they should be judged, and that thou shouldest give reward to thy " servants the prophets, and to the saints, and them that fear thy " name, small and great; and shouldest destroy them that destroy " the earth."

At the same time, there is nothing in the sounding of this seventh angel, to contradict its being the ushering in of the everlasting gospel, to make final settlement with all people, and to reward them according to their works; and in the mean time, to give every one a fair trial of access to God in his holy temple, to obtain forgiveness on the same principle with others: with God is no respect of persons. " And the temple of God was opened in heaven, and there was seen " in his temple the ark of his testament; and there were lightnings, " and voices, and thunderings, and an earthquake, and great hail."

According to the general representations given of God, by professed christians, he is the most unjust of all judges, who will take a man to an account, and condemn him irrecoverably, for not having done his duty, when he had neither knowledge nor power to do it. Whereas it is always honorable in a judge, or potentate, to publish an universal amnesty to those who have been in rebellion, although with the fullest knowledge of it, on the condition of confessing their wrongs and becoming obedient subjects; and it is justly esteemed cruel to do otherwise.

On the contrary; Some seeing in a measure, the unreasonableness of the prevalent notions concerning the judgment of God, and at the same time ignorant of the terms of pardon and acceptance, or unwilling to submit when informed, have fallen into the opposite extreme; and believe, or affect to believe, that men will all be accepted of God in doing what they conclude is right, each one for one, and thus annul the will of God and his judgment altogether, subjecting him to the judgment of every man, and requiring him to sanction whatever course of life each man saith in his mind is right. This scheme serveth for a temporary plaster on the conscience; but that only partial, because none of that faith are able to lead such a life, as to have the unreserved approbation of their own consciences in all things. I speak especially of those who acknowledge the truth and necessity of christianity. This scheme therefore must fall to the ground, and make way for the doctrine of Christ, That nothing can include the title to eternal life, short of knowing the will of God and doing it, as stated above.

Another matter maketh it appear reasonable, not to say unavoidable, that the judgment should be in union with the gospel or included in it, and consequently that the everlasting gospel should usher in, together with the last judgment, which is, that the gospel cannot have its proper and full effect without it. The effect, or end, if the gospel is a full acquittal, or remission of sins, with acceptance with God in justification and peace. But as no man can be justly condemned until he is tried, so neither can any be justified, or acquitted; and no man can be tried before the time of trial, or day of judgment. This showeth the inconsistency and the flimsy foundation of those professors, who boast, or even hope, that they are justified of God, and yet expect to come to the judgment and have their character examined and their final condition fixed, according to an order of judgment yet unknown.

But the sounding of the seventh angel is acknowledged to have been going on a considerable time already; consequently, it will not be denied, that the gospel is preached during that time. So likewise it will have to be granted, that the gospel is preached during the time of which Christ spake, saying, " And he shall send his angels " with a great sound of a trumpet, and they shall gather together " his elect, from the four winds, from one end of heaven to the " other." " But of that day and hour knoweth no man, (before its " commencement,) no, not the angels of heaven, but my Father " only." (This is acknowledged to be the day and hour of judgment.) " But as the days of Noah, so shall also the coming of the " Son of man be. (or, And as it was in the days of Noah, so shall it " be also in the days of the Son of man." (Luk. 17. 26.) " For as " in the days that were before the flood, they were eating and drink-" ing, marrying and giving in marriage, until the day that Noah en-" tered into the ark, and knew not until the flood came and took them " all away; so shall also the coming of the Son of man be." (24. 31, 36, to 39.) Now in the days of Noah he was a preacher of righteousness to the people; so in the coming or days of the Son of man, the gospel shall be preached until the work is finished, and the angels, or ministers of Christ, have gathered in the elect, the faithful and obedient, from under the whole heaven, and he hath fitted out the kingdom ready to be delivered up to the Father.

Observe; It is not said, as in the day that Noah entered into the ark, so shall the coming, or days, of the Son of man be; but it is expressly stated, as in the days that were before the flood; and this continued *until* the day of entering in, when he had fulfilled to them his commission, and the people being disobedient were swept away; so shall it be in the day of the Son of man; those who are obedient to the everlasting, or finishing gospel, shall be kept safe in the ark, as Noah and his family were, while the disobedient and impenitent shall be swept away.

However energetic the language which describeth the day of judgment, there is no description of it at all incompatible with preaching the gospel successfully in the time of it. For although in the process of the time, the judgment is certain; and it will also come as a snare on all the earth, and there can be no escape; when the nature of the language used in the scripture, relating to that day, is considered, it cannot be proved, that the process will be too swift for the successful preaching of the gospel. Thus when it is said, " That the day of the Lord so cometh as a thief in the night. For " when they shall say peace and safety, then sudden destruction com- " eth upon them, as travail upon a woman with child; and they shall " not escape." (1 Thess. 5. 2, 3.) This is very forcible language; but any one of moderate understanding may see, that it doth not describe a momentary, or instantaneous accomplishment. For however suddenly and surprisingly the travail of a woman with child may, in some cases, commence, it is not suddenly over; and the woman hath the encouraging prospect of being delivered from the distress after the birth, and of being more happy than before her travail came on. " A woman when she is in travail hath sorrow because " her hour is come: but as soon as she is delivered of the child, she " remembereth no more the anguish, for joy that a man is born into " the world." (Jno. 16. 21.)

So also when the judgment of the last day commences and brings destruction to the wicked, it is not without the gospel announcing pardon and life to the penitent, but to the impenitent, inevitable, and most aggravated destruction. For while to the one it is the savor of life, unto life, to the other it is the savor of death unto death. Besides; as travail is the certain lot of a woman with child, in the ordinary nature of things, so judgment is sure to overtake all, and destruction the finally impenitent, and that speedily. " Because sen- " tence against an evil work is not executed speedily, therefore the " heart of the sons of men is fully set in them to do evil." But " He " that being often reproved hardeneth his neck, shall suddenly be " destroyed, and that without remedy." " And shall not God " avenge his own elect, who cry day and night to him, though he " bear long with them? I tell you, that he will avenge them speedily. " Nevertheless, when the Son of man cometh shall he find faith on " the earth?" (Eccl. 8. 11. Prov. 29. 1. Luke 18. 7, 8.) The elect therefore are then to be searched out and proved, before they are avenged, and before the wicked are destroyed with a swift destruction.

It is peculiarly common to the Spirit of prophecy, to paint in strong colours, and to express with great energy, insomuch that matters of long continuance appear to be accomplished in an instant, or nearly so. Thus of the fall of Babylon; "And a mighty angel took "a stone like a great milstone, and cast it into the sea, saying, Thus "with violence shall that great city Babylon be thrown down, and "shall be found no more at all." And again; "For in one hour "so great riches is come to nought." And again; "For in one "hour is she made desolate." [Rev. 18. 17, 19, 21.] And yet this fall of Babylon is acknowledged to fill up many years, not to say ages. In like manner the sounding of the seventh trumpet hath been confessedly going on for many years, and it is yet a secret with God, how long it is to sound. And the fall of Babylon evidently commences with the sounding of the seventh, or last trumpet; for immediately therewith, "The kingdoms of this world are become "the kingdom of our Lord and of his Christ; and he shall reign "for ever and ever." But the fall of Babylon, or of the beast, or of the man of sin, (for I suppose few, if any, of the informed, will dispute these being all one, in the real spirit and substance of the matter,) is not until the last appearing of Christ, or day of final judgment. Neither will it any less agree with the sounding of the seventh trumpet; for that judgment is plainly taught as commencing with the sounding of that trumpet, as already stated. But that the fall, or destruction, of this beast, is not to take place until the commencement of the day of final judgment, is plainly enough taught by the apostle Paul in his second epistle to the Thessalonians; where he speaketh in such explicit terms, that I know not if any dispute its being the last judgment of which he is treating, and in a few sentences introduceth the man of sin, or beast, in such plain terms that they have been long acknowledged to apply to the same beast, or spiritual Babylon; and after showing that that day of the Lord, of which he had been speaking, would not come except there should be a falling away first, and that wicked, or man of sin, should be revealed; he then announceth in unequivocal terms, that the Lord will consume him with the spirit of his mouth, and destroy him with the brightness of his appearing. "Seeing it is a righteous "thing with God to recompense tribulation to them that trouble "you, and to you who are troubled, rest with us, when the Lord "Jesus shall be revealed from heaven with his mighty angels, in flam- "ing fire, (He maketh his ministers flames of fire, and by his gos- "pel shall judgment be executed in the world,) taking vengeance "on them that know not God, and that obey not the gospel of our "Lord Jesus Christ; who shall be punished with everlasting des- "truction from the presence of the Lord and from the glory of his "power; when he shall come (in the progress of that day,) to be "glorified in his saints, and to be admired in all them that believe "(because our testimony among you was believed) in that day." (Thus there will be a real privilege of believing *in that day*, that being the time to gather in the elect, or to gain men to the true and perfect faith; For when the Son of man cometh shall he find faith on the earth?) "Now we beseech you, brethren, by [concerning] "the coming of our Lord Jesus Christ, and our gathering toge- "ther to him, that ye be not soon shaken in mind, or be troubled, "neither by spirit, nor by word, nor by letter, as from us, as that the "day of Christ is at hand. Let no man deceive you by any means: "for (that day shall not come) except there come a falling away first, "and that man of sin be revealed, the son of perdition; who oppo- "seth and exalteth himself above all that is called God, or that is "worshipped; so that he as God, sitteth in the temple of God, show- "ing himself that he is God—And then shall that wicked be reveal- "ed, whom the Lord shall consume with the spirit of his mouth, and "shall destroy with the brightness of his coming." Thus clearly doth the apostle show, that the destruction of the beast is conjoined with the last appearing of Christ to judgment; for the brightness of his appearing cannot be seen, or have its effects, in the destruction of the son of perdition, until his appearing hath commenced. Besides; His consuming him with the spirit of his mouth is an apt expression to designate the preaching of the gospel to the world— the sharp two-edged sword which goeth out of his mouth; "For "the word of God is quick and powerful [living and efficacious,] "and sharper than any two-edged sword, piercing even to the divid- "ing asunder, of soul and spirit, and of the joints and marrow, and "is a discerner of the thoughts and intents of the heart." [Heb. 4. 12.] And as to his being revealed in flaming fire, it is no unapt phraseology to indicate the flaming Spirit of Christ in his ministers and people, in whom he will be glorified and admired. "For our "God is a consuming fire," and he dwelleth in his people. "For "all the earth shall be devoured with the fire of my jealousy, saith "the Lord, whose fire is in Zion, and his furnace in Jerusalem." [Zeph. 3. 8. Isa. 31. 9.] For observe, That in his saints he com- eth (that is, in his people or Zion where he dwelleth, and hath pro- mised to dwell for ever,) as the apostle Jude also hath it; "Be- "hold the Lord cometh in myriads (Greek) of his saints." But to pursue the subject;

From the above statements it appeareth that, the seventh trumpet in the Apocalypse, is the same as the last trumpet spoken of by Paul, and that it commenceth conjointly with the downfall of Babylon, the setting up of the kingdom of Christ, or Millennial reign, and with the last judgment of the quick and the dead. And to these things agree the words of the apostle Paul in another epistle, (2 Tim. 4. 1.) speaking of the appearing of Christ, "Who shall judge the quick "and the dead at his appearing and his kingdom." And if any scripture testimonies inevitably contradict the expectation of the gospel's being successfully preached to them that dwell on the earth, in the day and hour of judgment, or if any are incompatible with the execution of ample vengeance on the finally impenitent, the preach- ing of the gospel notwithstanding, I should be glad to see them. When men hear the testimony, that the day of God's judgment hath

JUDGMENT.

commenced, let them beware that they be not found among the scoffers, who walk after their own lusts and say, Where is the promise of his coming? and who speak evil of the things which they know not. Although the proposed limits of this appendix are too contracted to admit of considering minutely, many of the numerous scriptures which relate to this important period, one or two more seem necessarily to present themselves. The prophet Daniel hath spoken very pointedly of the same period, and the same work in his vision of the last beast, his destruction, and the kingdom of God, or of the saints, succeeding everlastingly. [7. 21 to 27.] " I beheld, and the same " horn made war with the saints, and prevailed against them ; until " the Ancient of days came, and judgment was given to the saints " of the Most High and the time came that the saints possessed the " kingdom. Thus he said, The fourth beast shall be the fourth " kingdom upon earth, which shall be diverse from all kingdoms, " and shall devour the whole earth, and shall tread it down, and " break it in pieces. And the ten horns out of this kingdom are " ten kings that shall arise : and another shall rise after them ; and " he shall be diverse from the first, and he shall subdue three kings. " And he shall speak great words against the Most High, and shall " wear out the saints of the Most High, and think to change times " and laws : and they shall be given into his hands until a time and " times and the dividing of time. But the judgment shall sit, and " they shall take away his dominion, to consume and to destroy it " unto the end. And the kingdom and dominion, and the greatness " of the kingdom under the whole heaven, shall be given to the peo- " ple of the saints of the Most High whose kingdom is an everlast " ing kingdom, and all dominions shall serve and obey him." Here is a very remarkable description of the beast in the Apocalypse ; and also of his judgment, agreeing with the sounding of the seventh trumpet ; as also the kingdom to last for ever, as in the seventh trumpet, " And he shall reign for ever and ever." It is also observable that the work is progressive, for the dominion of the beast is not destroyed at once, But the judgment shall sit, and they shall take away his dominion, to consume and to destroy it to the end. Once more ; This kingdom and dominion and the judgment were all given to the saints, and the kingdom is the LORD's, with all things which pertain to it. Thus it is perfectly correspondent with the reprsentation in the Apocalypse, which was shown to John in vision, and is " called the first resurrection. " And I saw an angel come down " from heaven, having the key of the bottomless pit, and a great " chain in his hand. And he laid hold on the Dragon, that old ser- " pent, which is the devil, and Satan, and bound him a thousand years, " and cast him into the bottomless pit, and shut him up, and set a seal " upon him, that he should deceive the nations no more, till the thou- " sand years should be fulfilled : and after that he must be loosed a " little season. And I saw thrones, and they sat upon them : and " judgment was given to them : and I saw the souls of them that " were beheaded for the witness of Jesus, and for the word of God, "and who had not worshipped the beast, neither his image, neither had received his mark upon their foreheads, or in their hands; and they lived and reigned with Christ a thousand years. But the rest of the dead lived not again until the thousand years were finished. This is the first resurrection. Blessed and holy is he who hath part in the first resurrection; on such the second death hath no power; but they shall be priests of God and of Christ, and shall reign with him a thousand years." [Rev. 20. 1 to 6.]

In this vision Christ and his saints are represented as reigning a thousand years. But that phraseology in prophecy is by no means inconsistent with the continuance of the kingdom for ever. And as other prophecies, concerning the same work and kingdom, (for the kingdom of God is one, there cannot therefore be an universal and everlasting kingdom for each distinct representation in prophecy) assert that it shall be everlasting, it is entirely safe to conclude the same in this place, inasmuch as this relateth to the coming of Christ to judgment: and we read of his second coming, but not of his third; and therefore have but one coming to expect after the apostolic dispensation; of which more hereafter. Accordingly saith Daniel, [7. 18.] "But the saints of the Most High shall take the kingdom, and possess the kingdom for ever, even for ever and ever." No difficulty needeth arise from satan's being loosed a little season, at the accomplishment of the thousand years; for although some remarkable events may be expected then to take place, not only with the wicked, but even towards the holy city, or church, there is nothing said which in the least resembleth disinheriting them, even for a time, or even interrupting their reign; for when Gog and Magog compass the camp of the saints and of the beloved city, fire cometh down from God out of heaven and consumeth them, and the saints appear to suffer no loss nor interruption. But it is time to say something.

Secondly; Of the effect to follow on the sounding of the last trumpet; The dead shall be raised incorruptible; or the sleeping awaked; and the living be changed.

Having shown in the preceding discourse, what the true resurrection promised in Christ is; that it is a spiritual work, effected in the spirit by the gospel; and having just done showing, that the gospel is preached in the sounding of the seventh, or last trumpet, or in the day of judgment; I need only take time in this place, to show why this is called the first resurrection, which cometh in the last day, and what is immediately implied in that saying. And it is so called in simplicity and plainness because it is the first which is finished and completed. These are the first inheriters of the kingdom and glory of Christ when he setteth up his everlasting kingdom; or in other words, they are the true and real inheriters distinctly from the wicked, and have now got into the possession, at least in its commencement. "The dead in Christ shall rise first."

The apostles in their day had received the first fruits of the Spirit, and were a *kind of first fruits* to God; yet the first fruits to God and to the Lamb, who had come to be fully ripe and perfect, were seen as having come long afterwards, with the Lamb on Mount Zion, contemporary with the fall of Babylon. So likewise, although the apostles were risen with Christ, and traveled in the work of the regeneration, according to the dispensation and gift of the day in which they had lived, the fulness of the work was to come in another day, which they also foresaw and testified, though not always by the same terms. And this first resurrection in its perfection, was that which the apostle so earnestly sought, " That if by any means he might " attain to the resurrection from among, or from the dead, as before " shown." Nothing therefore appears in the account of this which is called the first resurrection to prevent any one of all those who have believed in Christ and been obedient from the beginning, from being amongst those who partake of it; the account seems actually to favor the impression that they are all there, and eventually all mankind except the wicked who exclude themselves by rejecting the gospel offer. " And I saw thrones, and they sat upon them, and " judgment was given to them : and I saw the souls of them that " were beheaded for the witness of Jesus, and for the word of God, " and who had not worshipped the beast, neither his image, neither " had received his mark upon their foreheads, or in their hands; " and they lived and reigned with Christ a thousand years. But the " rest of the dead lived not again until the thousand years were " finished. This is the first resurrection. Blessed and holy is he " who hath part in the first resurrection; on such the second death " hath no power ; but they shall be priests of God and of Christ, and " shall reign with him a thousand years." It is here worthy to be noticed, that there is no mention of a second resurrection, and that whatever may be said in proof of its existence, there is nothing said of any blessedness or holiness as the portion of those who partake of it. We may observe farther; That the resurrection and the judgment are intimately connected, as before stated; those who lived again, and participated in the first resurrection, are the same, and at the same period, who sat on the thrones and had judgment given to them. Once more ; From what hath been shown, it will naturally be understood, as formerly stated, that the resurrection is a progressive work ; to such a degree that those who believed in Christ in the apostles' days or after, and kept their faith in obedience, entered into that resurrection which is finished in the second appearing of Christ, then called the first resurrection; and that with what they had gained and faithfully kept, they are ready to enter into the increased and finishing work of the resurrection to eternal life in Christ, in his second appearing, " Who are kept by the power of God through faith " unto salvation, ready to be revealed in the last time." " That the " trial of your faith, being more precious than that of gold that " perisheth, though it be tried by fire, might be found to praise, " and honor, and glory, at the appearing of Jesus Christ." [1 Pet. 1. 5. 7.]

The multitude of symbolical representations exhibited in the Apocalypse, and the strong allegories used in this particular vision, seem to have led some to conclude that this is not properly a resurrection, which is here called the first, but that the phraseology is wholly symbolical. But without endeavoring to crowd the understanding of any man beyond measure, I would make free to remark, that, To count all the phraseology in this narrative, so symbolical, as to exclude its being intelligibly applicable to the real substance, seems to be an error: good symbols have an aptness to represent the things signified. And whatever may be the rules among the learned, to disapprove of metaphorical and appropriate forms of language being mixed, it is certain these rules have not always been rigidly observed. And it is evident that prophecies are sometimes so far mixed, that the fulfilment cometh out so exactly according to the letter of the prophecy, that it may be called at least nearly literal, while part of the same is metaphorical. But especially; Some parts of the symbolical representations in the Apocalypse, appear evidently to have literal explanations. The vision of the Lamb on Mount Sion with the hundred and forty-four thousand, though highly symbolical, is immediately explained in language as free from metaphor as most of the prophecies, which are accounted the most literal; so free as to be in no wise embarrassing to honest minds under the gospel. [Rev. 14. 1, to 5.] So in this place, the vision is quite symbolical; but the explanation, " This is the first resurrection—Blessed and " holy is he who hath part in the first resurrection; on such the se- " cond death hath no power," is sufficiently plain, when once men come to know what the resurrection is. And thus it will be found in the issue with many prophecies.

The notion of a literal resurrection of the animal body, so strongly prepossessed, seems to lay a foundation for difficulty respecting the first resurrection. But whatever remarks are necessary to be added here may come in place after a quotation from a late learned author. (See Dr. Tim. Dwight on Isa. 21. 11, 12. Pag. 40, 41.) This author, among other remarks on the first resurrection, hath the following. " But, should we construe this part of the passage, lite- " rally, our difficulties, instead of being lessened, will be increased. " It is said, that *the souls* of the martyrs *lived again;* and that *the* " *rest of the dead lived not.* This, literally construed, teaches us " irresistibly, that the souls of the martyrs, antecedently to the Mil- " lennium, were dead, as well as their bodies; and implies, that the " rest of the souls of mankind were also dead. * * * Unfortunately, " however, this construction makes St. John contradict himself: for " in the 6th chapter and 9th verse, he informs us, that he saw these " very souls living, clad in white robes, and employed in prayer to " God.

" Nor are we yet at the end of our difficulties. St. John says, *this* " *living again of these martyrs is the first resurrection:* η πρωτη " αναστασις, [anastasis,] *the first future existence.* The word, αναστα- " σις, signifies, not a *resurrection,* but a *future existence:* as is un-

"answerably evident from our Savior's use of it in his reply to the Sadducees, concerning the situation of the woman who had seven husbands: (Matt. 22. 28, &c.) Here he adduces the declaration of God, (Exo. 3. 6.) *"I am the God of Abraham, the God of Isaac, and the God of Jacob,"* as unanswerable proof of the αναςασις; not a *resurrection*, but a *future existence*. *"God,"* he says, *"is not the God of the dead, but of the living."* As, therefore, God declared at that time, that he was the God of Abraham, Isaac, and Jacob; it was certain, that these men were living beings, when this declaration was made. The declaration was therefore a complete proof of the αναςασις, or *future existence;* but it was no proof at all of the *resurrection;* because Abraham, and Isaac, and Jacob, were not then raised. According to this very interpretation, it is here said, that *the souls* of these martyrs *lived, and reigned, with Christ a thousand years;* and that *this is the first* ανςασις, or *living again*. Were this intended literally it could not be true; because St. John, as has been mentioned, saw the souls of martyrs having the same future life, many ages before; and because our Savior asserts the same thing, under the same Greek name, concerning Abraham, Isaac, and Jacob; and applies it generally to mankind. Besides, Moses had this life on the mount of transfiguration; and *many of the saints arose*, after our Savior's resurrection, *and were seen of many:* they were therefore living beings.

"But what puts this matter out of all doubt is this: the scriptures positively assert, that Christ will never again appear in this world until the judgment. Thus says St. Paul:—*"Christ was once offered to bear the sins of many; and unto them, that look for him, shall he appear, THE SECOND TIME, unto salvation."* Thus, also, in many other places. This declaration, repeated in a variety of forms, places it beyond a debate, that Christ will never appear again personally, in this world, until he comes to the final judgment. As, therefore, the appearance and reign of Christ, here, are symbolical; it follows irresistibly, that that of the martyrs is symbolical also." I do not intend to inquire minutely into the correctness of every idea in this quotation, but only to make some use of its leading features.

The burden of difficulty in the way of understanding this account of the first resurrection, appears to be the same prevalent notion of the literal resurrection of animal bodies, and the want of the understanding that the true resurrection pertains only to the soul—That a future existence is the cardinal point to be confirmed in proof of the general resurrection; and that to make that future existence an happy existence in Christ, is the sum of the resurrection of the saints; while to have that future existence rendered completely miserable, by remaining under sin, in the nature of the first Adam, in whom all die, and receiving its full wages, is the sum of the resurrection of damnation, and to which the wicked eventual come forth. From this view of the subject, there is no difficulty in allowing this first to be a real resurrection. Neither is there any argument, that *the souls of these martyrs*, or of *the rest of the dead*, were *literally dead*, from its being said, *The rest of the dead lived not again until the thousand years were finished*, but only, that they had not come forth to their final reward. This view of the subject also escapes the charge of a contradiction in John's two accounts, as having seen these same souls alive long before, notwithstanding the acknowledgment of a real resurrection. For it is evident from the account which he there giveth, that these souls had not then come forth to their reward, or in other words, to the uninterrupted fruition of an happy future existence, or the first resurrection. " And when he " had opened the fifth seal, I saw under the altar the souls of them " that were slain for the word of God, and for the testimony which " they held: and they cried with a loud voice, saying, How long, O " Lord, holy and true, dost thou not judge and avenge our blood on " the men that dwell on the earth ? And white robes were given to " every one of them; and it was said unto them, that they should " rest yet for a little season, until their fellow servants also, and their " brethren, who should be killed as they were, should be fulfilled." [Rev. 6. 9, to 11.] These therefore, although they had not come into the fulness of the resurrection of life, or first resurrection, were kept in safety and in readiness to enter in, as soon as they should open, having kept in faithfulness that measure of life and salvation which they had already found, according to their day and privilege. And, as before observed, the account is quite favorable, that they have now come, and are partakers of the blessedness of the first resurrection.

But the above author has made a bold stand towards proving the point, on which I am here insisting, when he asserts that the Greek word, αναςασις, signifies, not a *resurrection*, but a *future existence*. This is materially true as it is used in the new testament, and particularly with respect to the final event of those who hear the gospel; which he has also learnedly proved, by the language of Christ to the Sadducees, relating to Abraham, Isaac, and Jacob. Now a future existence is the lot of all, both righteous and wicked; of the first happy in Christ, and of the last miserable, being separated from Christ and from all good; for they shall come forth; they who have done good, to the resurrection (future existence) of life, and they who have done evil, to the resurrection (future existence) of damnation.

Besides; The word, which he says, signifies, not a *resurrection*, but a *future existence*, is the same word which is almost every where, in the new testament, translated, *resurrection*, and with the exception of a solitary instance, the only word so translated. In the narrative given by Matthew, of certain saints, who came out of the tombs after the resurrection of Jesus, the Greek word translated, *resurrection*, is not αναςασις, but εγερσιν; [egersin] which is the only place where I remember to have seen it used, in that sense; and in the connection in which it there stands, it evidently signifies the very same with the other which is the word commonly and freely used on all such occasions, and is therefore tantamount with it. The two verbs also, from which these two words are respectively derived, are used, as it would seem by their examples, as being equivalent. And it is remarkable, that our author in his reference to the aforesaid narrative of Matthew has included the whole in the future existence. But the common word, αναςασις, is used on all occasions in relation to that subject; if then it doth not signify or imply a `resurrection, the Greek writings of the apostles, which have come down to us contain no word which signifies it. According then to our author's own explanation of the word, no other resurrection than a future existence, is proved, or even spoken of, by Christ and his apostles, with this only distinction of happy and miserable.

Consistently with this view, the word is once used by Paul, compounded with a syllable which signifies, *from among*, or *out of.* " If " that by any means I might attain to the resurrection from the " dead"—[εις την αναςασιν των νεκρων] to that future existence in Christ, which is free from death and all who are dead. For as in Adam, where is the first, or present existence, all die, even so in Christ, where is the second, or future existence, which is the resurrection, all are made alive—He is the resurrection and the life. As in the first Adam men are physically raised to life, or brought, into the first, or present existence; so in Christ they are re-raised to life, or brought into a future and happy existence in the Spirit; not only redeemed from the fall which they have suffered in the first Adam, from their original rectitude, but advanced into a grade of life and existence superior to any thing which could have been experienced in the first creation: and this is a real resurrection or re-raising. Accordingly, to bring forth into life for the purpose of filling up an appointed place which ought to be filled according to order, is the same as to resurrect, or raise again, according to the use of the word by the apostles, in relating the proposition of the Sadducees. " If a " man die, having no children, his brother shall marry his wife, and " raise up [αναςησει, by Matthew, εξαναςηση, by Mark and Luke; *he* " *shall resurrect*,] seed unto his brother."

That this description, in the Apocalypse, of the judgment and first resurrection, is highly symbolical, is not to be denied. But that is no proof that it cannot be understood in its proper time, although that understanding may be gained by slow degrees. Neither is it any proof that the allegories are not well adapted to represent the substance, so that the likeness may be clearly seen in the fulfilment. Besides; The symbolical representation of the judgment and resurrection as commencing with the Millennial reign of Christ and his saints, is no proof that those things are not real at that time; nay, it is a positive proof of their reality, to all who have unshaken faith in the scriptures, as undoubtedly as if the facts were announced in the most appropriate language; for on any other view of this, and all such representations, the final coming of Christ to judgment, and his rewarding the righteous and the wicked, according to their several characters and works, might also be considered symbolical and not real. Nevertheless, it is not to be controverted, that these symbolical representations render such matters obscure, as prophecies commonly and designedly are, until the time of the fulfilment.

The aforesaid author has acknowledged, according to the prevailing belief for many years, that the seventh angel has commenced his sounding, and that Christ has come to the judgment of the great whore, or Babylon. Part of his words are, (Pag. 20.) "We may, I think, fairly " consider the *great voice* as already uttered *out of the temple of* " *heaven from the throne, saying, It is done.*" " In the mean time, " Christ has come to this work of judgment *as a thief:* in a manner " the most sudden, the most astonishing, the most terrible." The only objection then, against believing that Christ has come in the Millennial reign, and that the first resurrection, or future existence in happiness, has commenced, and consequently that some, even those who are in it, have an understanding of what it is, seems to be contained in the notion, that the coming of Christ to the judgment and fall of Babylon and his coming to reign with his saints, are two different comings in succession, otherwise he, with others, must acknowledge that the Millennium has already commenced. And indeed this seems to be virtually acknowledged by him, though cautiously: of which in its place.

But the inquiry yet remains with them, When will the Millennium commence? Our author, after laboriously examining the prophecies of Daniel and John, concludes, " The probality is that we shall " find *the words closed, and sealed up unto the time of the end.*" (Pag. 43.) True enough; but at the end, or when the finishing work has commenced, the words are to be unsealed. Thus the prophet Daniel, (12. 10.) " And none of the wicked shall understand; " but the wise shall understand." On these words our auther observes, " He (the interpreter to Daniel,) then mentions that men of " piety shall hereafter understand this subject; that is, I suppose, " (says he,) after the prediction shall have been fulfilled." (Pag. 43.) If then this author, and others of the same faith with him, are of the pious, or wise, why need they be at any loss to understand, so far at least, as to know that the time is come, and when it commenced, or nearly.

The aforesaid author acknowledgeth, that the Millennium cometh on by successive steps. [Pag. 42.] He also acknowledgeth the probality that it hath actually commenced, at least in some degree. His words are, [Pag. 44.] " There is no improbability in the opinion, " now extensively embraced; and in my own view it is just; that " this happy period has, in the sense which I have specified, already " begun." So much are men of exquisite literature and profound study perplexed in a subject which it is expressly said, The wise shall understand—the wise towards God, or pious, as is evident from the wise being contrasted with the wicked. This remark is agreeable to the aforesaid author's own words, who calls those *wise* ones, men of piety. It is then a fact, supported by the opinion of those who study the scriptures, an opinion now extensively embraced, that the Millennial reign of Christ has dawned. The same also is supported by the testimony of scripture prophecy, which fixes its commencement, in about, the year 1747, agreeing to the end of Daniel's one thousand two hundred and ninety days or years. [12. 11, 12.] " And from the time that the daily sacrifice shall be taken " away, and the abomination that maketh desolate set up. there shall " be a thousand two hundred and ninety days. Blessed is he who " waiteth, and cometh to the thousand three hundred and five and thirty days." Here is an addition of forty-five days or years, at the close of which some additional blessedness was to be found. These forty-five years added to one thousand seven hundred and forty-seven, make one thousand seven hundred and ninety-two. And it is remarkable that the aforesaid author has noticed that year as a memorable Epoch in *the great day of God Almighty*, for the destruction of Babylon. [Pag. 18.] It is also remarkable, that he has mentioned a powerful prevalence of vital piety, which had lasted twelve or fiteen years, and began to decline about the year 1752, and consequently included the year 1747. Likely the very revival in which the reign of Christ began to dawn, according to the prophecy, and the testimony of those who say Christ is come, and they have found him; while in the mean time, many walk after their own lusts and scoffingly say, Where is the promise of his coming, for since the fathers fell asleep all things continue as they were from the beginning of the creation; and others are sorrowfully looking out between hope and despair. But these will not be forgotten, if they persevere: as it is written, [Hab. 2. 3.] " Though it tarry, wait for it; be-" cause it will surely come, it will not tarry." [לא יאחר it will not be slack.] Other revivals also, are no doubt preparing the way for the spread of this glorious work, as well as the continued exertions of those societies which are formed for the purpose of spreading the knowledge of salvation. And it is still farther remarkable, that the same author hath noticed the same remarkable year 1792, as the year in which those missionary societies had their commencement, first in England, which are now become so common. Thus, while God in his providential government pursued the destruction of the beast, making havoc of his secular power, by the wasting and distressing wars in Europe, and the more serious and piously disposed of the nations, who looked for the coming of the Lord, made vigorous efforts, to spread the knowledge and savor of his name, among those who lay in greater darkness, and thus to prepare the way of the Lord; the people who had waited for him and found him of whom Moses in the law, and the prophets, and after them the apostles, did write, were making their advancements in the work of the everlasting gospel, and beginning to learn the blessedness of him who waiteth, and cometh to the thousand three hundred and five and thirty days. A judicious consideration of all these matters must produce forcible conviction that the Millennium hath unquestionably dawned on the earth. For, taking a compendious view of the whole matters together, men of reason and information cannot but see and acknowledge, that the light is much greater than it was a century ago, and that it has been on the increase, at least gradually for many years, not to say ages. The consideration therefore of these things afford a conclusive argument that the total darkness is past and the day hath begun to open.

But difficulties will ever remain on this subject, as long as people separate and divide that work which God hath made one. The destruction of Babylon and the building up of the kingdom of Christ, are evidently only counterparts of the same work and accomplished in the same period of time. Admitting, nevertheless, that the destruction of Babylon precedes, so as to prepare the way for Christ to enter; and also that when the destruction of Babylon is finally completed, the reign of Christ will continue: for his kingdom is everlasting. Thus it was shown to the prophet. (Dan. 7. 16, 26, 27.) " But the saints of the Most High shall take the kingdom, and pos-
" sess the kingdom for ever, even for ever and ever." " But the
" judgment shall sit, and they shall take away his dominion, to con-
" sume and to destroy it unto the end. And the kingdom and domi-
" nion, and the greatness of the kingdom under the whole heaven,
" shall be given to the people of the saints of the Most High, whose
" kingdom is an everlasting kingdom, and all dominions shall serve
" and obey him." Thus the work of God is begun by smaller measures at first and increased to perfection; or more correctly with respect to the present subject, It is according to the dispensations of his grace to men, to send a forerunner, or preparatory work, to prepare the way for that which is perfect; as it is written, " The voice
" of him that crieth in the wilderness, Prepare ye the way of the
" Lord, make straight in the desert a high way for our God. Every
" valley shall be exalted, and every mountain and hill shall be made
" low: and the crooked shall be made straight, and the rough places
" plain: and the glory of the Lord shall be revealed, and all flesh
" shall see it together." (Isa. 40. 3, 4, 5.) Thus the coming of the Lord in his glory is announced by a preparatory voice. And however applicable this prophecy was to the first appearing of Christ, being fulfilled, for that day, in John the Baptist, it is no less applicable to his second appearing; yea, more especially it belongeth to the second; for all flesh must see his glory together, which did not come to pass in the first, and therefore must be fulfilled in the second, when he shall come in the clouds, and every eye shall see him and they also who pierced him: and all kindreds of the earth shall wail because of him: when his reward is with him, and his work before him; " And whosoever shall exalt himself shall be abased: and he
" that shall humble himself shall be exalted."

There is no possible rule by which the wisest or most learned can distinguish between the time of the destruction of Babylon and that of Christ's reigning with his saints in the Millennium, otherwise than as here stated. Neither can any distinguish the scriptures which relate to the one from those which relate to the other. Together, therefore, with the judgment of Babylon, commence the Millennium and the first resurrection. But it is the nature of human language, that one thing must be expressed before another. Thus the binding of the old serpent, or dragon, is related before the appearance of the thrones, the judgment, and the living of the martyrs, although all these were comprehended in one vision, and are to be actually accomplished in the same time, going forward together.

But its being granted, that the coming of Christ to the destruction of Babylon and his coming to the Millennial reign, are one coming, is not enough to unravel the difficulties on this subject. Here is the first resurrection; and we read of no other, or second resurrection for the saints. "Blessed and holy is he that hath part in the first resurrection; on such the second death hath no power." But no such promise to him that hath part in the second. The first resurrection and the second death seem to be counterparts of the work of the judgment, the first being the lot of the righteous, and the second the lot of the wicked. This being the case, it is evident that the first resurrection, is that which is accomplished in the final appearance of Christ to judgment, and that the vision shown to John, of the binding of satan, and of thrones, and of judgment, and of the first resurrection, was nothing less than a vision of the commencement and process of the last judgment, which in its progress, is to make decisive work, and to fix the eternal condition of every individual. Again; That kingdom of God which immediately succeeds the reign of the last beast, or kingdom of Babylon, is an everlasting kingdom, having no end, consequently can never be supplanted by the enemy, never superseded by any other kingdom or work of God, however it may be increased and advanced into different and successive grades of glory and blessedness: for "Of the increase of his government and peace there shall be no end." This kingdom therefore can be no other than that which Christ will deliver up to the Father, after he hath put down all rule and all authority and power, and hath put all enemies under his feet, in that day when those who are his shall be made alive at his coming. Now that that kingdom, which immediately succeeds the reign of the beast, commonly called the Millennium, is endless, as here stated, hath been shown, once and again, by the accounts given of it by the prophet Daniel, and the description of the seventh trumpet in the Apocalypse; which scriptures the judicious reader may consult.

The thought may be novel to some, and on that account exceptionable, that the coming of Christ to the last judgment, to raise the dead, and fix the final condition of all, is the same as his coming to destroy the kingdom of Babylon, and set up his kingdom on earth. The novelty however of the thought, by no means maketh it justly exceptionable. Every increasing degree of light is new in its commencement; and so is every increasing dispensation of God to men, for their salvation. After Christ had performed his ministry, and ascended, in the days of the apostles, we are told he will come again, the second time, but not the third or fourth time, "But now once in the end of the world hath he appeared to put away sin by the sa-

"crifice of himself—and to them that look for him shall he appear "the second time without sin to salvation." (Heb. 9. 26, 28.)

This text is adduced by the author quoted above, (as may be seen by reverting to the place,) to prove that this second coming of Christ is personal, and, I suppose, literal, as being contrasted with all those descriptions of his coming which are symbolical, and are considered generally to relate to his coming in the Millennial reign, which coming and reign he seems, on that account, to conclude, are not literal or perhaps even real. But the result of an investigation of that plan of reasoning will be, completely to expose the weakness of that whole system, which contemplates the coming of Christ to the Millennial reign, and his coming to the last judgment, as being two different comings, and the work of each a different work, the one from the other. For in this second coming, of which the apostle speaks to the Hebrews, there is not a word of its being literal, or personal, more than any other coming, or in any other place. It is simply said he will appear to those who look for him, the second time, without sin to salvation. It might be asked, If this appearance be literal, or personal, why appear to those only who look for him and are saved? for the wicked, who look not for him, can see personality, or a literal object as well as the righteous. But none of the wicked shall understand; but the wise shall understand. It may also be inquired, Whether a literal or personal appearance of Christ be necessary to being saved? If so, surely none have ever been saved, since he ascended out of their sight, ten days before the Holy Spirit was given.

But farther. These accounts of the coming of Christ, which are inevitably acknowledged to relate to his final appearing to judgment, are as far from being communicated in literal language, as any of those which are thought to relate to the Millennial reign, insomuch, that none of the advocates for two comings, the one symbolical and the other real, are able to draw the line between the two accounts, or to show any narrative, which designates the one appearing, and is necessarily incongruous to the other. The result then of this inquiry is, that we have no authority to expect more than one appearing of Christ after that of the apostles' days, either symbolical or real. (For that which is merely symbolical is not real.) But symbolical predictions are not inconsistent with real accomplishments, although they leave the subject obscure until the time of the fulfilment. This coming then, in which we have authority to believe, is that same, in which all that are in their graves, shall hear his voice, and shall come forth, *those who have done good, to the resurrection of life, and those who have done evil, to the resurrection of damnation.* Or as the prophet Daniel hath it; "And many of them that slept in the "dust of the earth shall awake, some to everlasting life and some to "shame and everlasting contempt." The term, *many,* which the apostle here useth concerning those who slept, is no exception to this being a prophecy of the general resurrection and judgment, for *many,* meaning *all,* is an acceptation of the word, not unknown in

the scriptures, in language less symbolical than this. "For if through
"the offence of one, *many* be dead;" and, "For as by one man's
"disobedience, *many* were made sinners; so by the obedience of
"one, shall many be made righteous." (Ro. 5. 15, 19.) And it is
conclusively true, that the prophet here spake of the work of the
final judgment, from two considerations. First; The universality of
the deliverance of the righteous; "And at that time thy people shall
"be delivered, every one that shall be found written in the book."
And secondly; That both the righteous and the wicked are taken
into the account, and receive their appropriate rewards, *everlasting
life*, or *everlasting contempt*.

Some may alledge, that the disquisition is lame in this part, for the
want of proof, that only one coming of Christ is meant by the various
representations recorded in the scriptures, and that to give satisfaction on this subject, which is of so great importance, it would be
necessary to examine the different accounts separately and minutely.
This however doth not comport with the limits here proposed; neither doth it comport with propriety, without the most obvious necessity, to make the most laborious efforts, to disprove that which is no
where taught, known, or promised. We conceive the subject will
here be carried far enough in that respect, until greater necessity
shall appear. It belongs to those who believe in two appearings of
Christ, the one symbolical and the other real, to produce their evidence, and to discriminate sufficiently, what scriptures designate the
one and which the other, and to show what is said of the one, which
is incompatible with the other, making proper allowance for the
prophetic style. When the advocates of that scheme agree on these
things I presume there will be little difficulty remaining, on this
subject.

I have however noticed some of the most bold and forcible descriptions of the coming of Christ to the last judgment, and shown
that they are entirely applicable to the Millennial reign, or in other
words to a day of ministering the gospel with good effect. But to
open the subject a little more clearly to the understanding, I will here
take notice of one other passage which has been viewed as an awful discription of the last judgment and the destruction of the wicked; and so it is, as will eventually appear. "And Enoch also, the
"seventh from Adam, prophesied of these, saying; Behold, the
"Lord cometh with ten thousand ($εν$ $μυριασιν$, in myriads) of his saints,
"to execute judgment upon all, and to convince all that are ungodly
"among them of all their ungodly deeds which they have ungodly
"committed, and of all their hard speeches, which ungodly sinners
"have spoken against him." [Jude. 14. 15.] Now what is here
stated is, that all impious sinners shall be convinced, thoroughly; such
being the literal import of the Greek language used. What then?
Is conviction incompatible with repentance and salvation? Or is not
conviction the most necessary forerunner of repentance? The whole
need not the physician, but they who are sick. "I came not,"
said Jesus, "to call the righteous, but sinners to repentance."

A plausible objection to this doctrine, with some, will be, that on this plan, that men have an opportunity of repentance and salvation, in the day of judgment, all people will be saved, for none are such fools, as not to avail themselves of that last opportunity. What then, O man! Art thou envious against God because he will give to men, even to the rebellious, a favorable opportunity to repent and be renewed, who have never had it before? Or would it be any advantage to mankind, or any additional honor to God, that those who have never had the privilege of knowing the way of salvation by the cross of Christ, or those whose knowledge hath been partial and imperfect, should be excluded from all possible hope or prospect of salvation, without any, the least offer or trial, to prove what they would do, if brought to the knowledge of the truth? Art thou, O man! whoever thou art, in fatal deception with respect to salvation, and wouldst thou be unwilling to have a fair trial, when fully convinced of thine error? And wouldst thou have God to be a respecter of persons?

But be not in haste to conclude, that times will be too easy. It is found by painful experience, that men have no fondness for repentance and turning to God, in true faith and obedience. Scarcely, if at all, any choice, lawfully proposed to mankind, is more difficult for them to decide upon, than whether to endure the pain of repentance and of bearing their cross, in the faith of Christ, to salvation, or the pain of eternal damnation. I suppose if all the people saw hell opened, and themselves going to be ingulfed in immediate damnation, irrecoverably, in such a view as would take with their sense and feelings, they would submit, though irksomely, to take up some measure of a cross, and come to some repentance, would that save them. But this is not God's method of working. A forced obedience is not well pleasing to God. He requires the heart. Neither are forcible means of lasting benefit to the creature: the people who come to Christ in the day of his power are a willing people. When these things are considered, instead of fearing lest too many be saved, each one ought to take the alarm, lest a promise being proposed of entering into rest, he, or she should seem to come short of it. Many in that day will find the gate too strait and the way too narrow to suit their taste, and refuse to enter and to walk therein. "For the time "is come, that judgment must begin at the house of God: and if "it first begin at us, what shall the end be of them that obey not "the gospel of God? And if the righteous scarcely be saved, where "shall the ungodly and the sinner appear?" Therefore, "Strive "to enter in at the strait gate: for many, I say unto you, shall seek "to enter in and shall not be able." Doubtless, because they have spent their privilege and their strength, doing their own will. Thus will many even in the last day, when the wrath of God is clearly revealed against all ungodliness and unrighteousness of men, by obeying their own carnal mind, spend that privilege which they will never be able to recover. Awake therefore, thou that sleepest, at the sound of the last trumpet, and arise from the dead, and Christ shall give thee light—light to know thy duty and to make thy escape. To day if ye will hear his voice, harden not your hearts. But it is time to consider,

Thirdly ; The time or space in which certain transactions are to be performed : In a moment in the twinkling of an eye. Having previously spoken so fully on this point, I shall introduce what is here to be said with this proposition. That although there is sufficient reason to believe ; that the whole work of the resurrection and judgment will not be accomplished in so short a time, as is here described, yet there is no evidence that said work may not be begun in a period so short as that which in the language of prophecy is marked by, *a moment or the twinkling of an eye.*

After what hath heretofore been stated, relative to the resurrection, and the preaching of the gospel in the last day, or time of the last judgment, it will not be foreign to our present purpose to introduce the saying of the apostle, " Awake thou that sleepest, and " arise from the dead, and Christ shall give the light," as a suitable description of the work of the last day, or time of the resurrection and judgment. We read of *the day of judgment ; the day of the Lord ; the day of God ;* and *the day of the Son of man,* or *the day when the Son of man is revealed ;* all denoting the time when God will bring the world into judgment. Every day also hath its morning, which is the proper time to awake and enter on the work of the day. " Therefore, let us not sleep as do others ; but let us watch and be " sober. For they that sleep, sleep in the night ; and they that be " drunken, are drunken in the night. But let us who are of the day, " be sober, putting on the breast-plate of faith and love ; and for an " helmet the hope of salvation. For God hath not appointed us to " wrath, but to obtain salvation by our Lord Jesus Christ, who died " for us, that whether we wake or sleep (being in the earthly taber- " nacle or out of it,) we should live together with him."

The dispensations of God towards men have an increase ; and in each one something is made known, which had not been known in the former. It is therefore impossible for the people in one dispensation to know what is to be in the next ; but each one must be understood by its own light. Accordingly the Jewish prophets, or those who consulted their writings, could not know what was to be in the days of Christ in his first appearing, but believers learned it in the light and revelation of that day. And for the proof of these things, the words of the apostles are in point. Paul, referring to the prophet Isaiah, saith ; " But as it is written, Eye hath not seen, nor " ear heard, neither have entered into the heart of man, the things " which God hath prepared for them that love him." Thus far the prophet : to which the apostle adds, as what had come to pass in his day, and by the superior light of the gospel of Christ. " But God " hath revealed them to us by his Spirit : for, the Spirit searcheth " all things, yea, the deep things of God." And again ; " Now we " have received, not the spirit of the world, but the Spirit which is " of God ; that we might know the things that are freely given to

" us of God." [1 Cor. 2. 9, 10, 12.] Peter also bore testimony to the same things, when speaking of the salvation of Christ; " Of " which salvation the prophets have enquired, and searched diligently, " who prophesied of the grace that should come to you; searching " what, and what manner of time the Spirit of Christ which was in " them did signify, when it testified beforehand the sufferings of " Christ, and the glory that should follow. To whom it was revealed, " that not to themselves, but to us, they did minister the things which " are now reported to you by them that have preached the gospel to " you with the Holy Ghost sent down from heaven; which things the " angels desire to look into. (1 Pet. 1. 10, 11, 12.)

In like manner, the apostles knew not what should be in the day of Christ in his second appearing; all these things being shown to them in symbols, mataphors, allegories, and the like. Thus saith Paul; " For we know in part and we prophesy in part. (Of things " yet unknown.) But when that which is perfect is come, then that " which is in part shall be done away. When I was a child, I spake " as a child, I understood as a child, I thought as a child: but when I " became a man, I put away childish things. For now we see through " a glass, darkly; but then face to face: now we know in part; but " then shall I know even as also I am known." (1 Cor. 13. 9 to 12.) These reflections teach us, irresistibly, that they considered themselves only in their infancy, or childish state, compared with that perfect day, which they believed would come, and of which they prophesied, but did not fully know what it should be. This much they knew by faith, and not by sight, that it would be perfect. So saith John; " Beloved, now are we the sons of God; and it doth not yet " appear what we shall be: but we know that when he shall appear, " we shall be like him, for we shall see him as he is." Accordingly, to that same John were shown many things which were to come to pass afterwards, which neither he, nor those who have consulted his writings, have ever been able to understand, nor ever will, otherwise than by the opening of the day in which they will have their final accomplishment. It is therefore impracticable for any man to know what is the order, or manner of the work of the last day, or day of judgment, until taught by the light and revelation of that day. " But " of [or περι, concerning] that day and hour knoweth no man, (until it commence,) no, not the angels who are in heaven, neither the Son, " but the Father." (Mark 13. 32.) As the prophets inquired and searched, *what time and what manner of time*, the Spirit of Christ in them did signify; so the people have sought in vain, to find *what time*, or when, and *what manner of time*, or what should be the work of the day, when the Son of man should appear, but could never know these things, and never will, only as the day declareth them. Yet these searchings have not been altogether in vain; for it is expedient after the example of the prophets, the example and exhortations of the apostles, and the commandments of Jesus Christ, to be on the alert, watching, and " Looking for and hasting to the coming " of the day of God, wherein the heavens (as well as the earth,) be-

JUDGMENT.   425

"ing on fire, shall be dissolved, and the elements (the rudiments of the world) shall melt with fervent heat." (2 Pet. 3. 12.)

But the evidence is too strong and clear to be overturned, that the last day, or day of judgment, is a time of preaching the gospel of the Son of God, for the final destruction of the man of sin, and finished redemption of all God's people—the day of the fall of Babylon and final victory and triumph of the church. The day of judgment therefore is, in plain terms, a new and last dispensation of the gospel of the same Christ in his second appearing, in which all mankind are to be called into a deeper work, and a more consummate trial of their true state and character, than in any other work which hath ever appeared on the earth before, and their final character and condition to be unalterably decided according to their works. It is therefore justly esteemed, the day of the judgment and perdition of ungodly men, and the day of redemption to the just. There can therefore be no impropriety in employing an exhortation of the apostle in the first dispensation, as expressing the leading parts of the duty and work of the day in the second, although much hath yet to be learned in addition thereto in its own order. "Awake thou that sleepest, and arise from the dead, and Christ shall give thee light."

This is a just epitome of the last trumpet, although it containeth no explicit account of the judgment; for that the resurrection and the judgment are too intimately connected together, for the one to be effectuated without the other, will not be denied; they are expected and believed to be executed in the same great day. And as the representations of the coming of Christ to the judgment and overthrow of Babylon, and the setting up of his kingdom, or Millennial reign, and the representations of his coming in the last day, to execute final judgment on the wicked, and finish the redemption of his people, are the same in substance, and agree to one another so well, that none can draw any real line of distinction, or show what particulars belong to the one, not compatible with the other; and whereas we read of seven trumpets in succession, the seventh of which is necessarily the last, and we have no account of the eighth, or any one after the seven, the last of which proclaims the resurrection of the dead, the judgment of the wicked and the reward of the righteous, the argument is fair and conclusive, that these appearings, or comings of Christ are not two, but one, and that when the Millennial reign of Christ commenceth, the last judgment commenceth also; and according to what has been already stated, that day is acknowledged to have already commenced.

From this view of the subject, it is evidently a progressive, and not an instantaneous work. And in no other view, than that of a progressive work, having a succession of events, can it agree with the representation given by Paul, in as explicit language as can be expected in prophecy. "Christ the first fruits; afterwards they that are Christ's at his coming. Then [ειτα afterʔ] cometh the end, when he shall have delivered up the kingdom to God, even the Father, when he shall have put down all rule, and all authority;

"and power." This is the work to be executed between his coming and his delivering up the kingdom to the Father, as the judicious reader may easily perceive. "For he must reign till he hath put all "enemies under his feet." A few more examples will be of benefit, to elucidate the position that the work of the resurrection and judgment is a work of orderly progress, and not instantaneous. [Matt. 13. 4 to 43.] "As therefore the tares are gathered and burned in the "fire; so shall it be in the end of the world. The Son of man shall "send forth his angels, and they shall gather out of his kingdom all "things that offend, and them who do iniquity; and shall cast them "into a furnace of fire: there shall be wailing and gnashing of teeth. "Then shall the righteous shine forth as the sun in the kingdom of "their Father." This then is the procedure which is to obtain at the end of the world; all things which offend and those who do iniquity, are to be gathered and cleared off, before the kingdom is in readiness to be delivered up to the Father; and these things cannot be executed without a fair trial. "Again, (47 to 50.) the king- "dom of heaven is like unto a net that was cast into the sea, and "gathered of every kind: which, when it was full they drew to "shore, and sat down, and gathered the good into vessels, but cast "the bad away, so shall it be in the end of the world: the angels "shall come forth, and sever the wicked from among the just, and "shall cast them into the furnace of fire; there shall be wailing and "gnashing of teeth." Thus the gospel net, *at the end of the world*, gathers of every kind good and bad, and the result of a fair trial and impartial examination, is, that the good are preserved, and the bad are cast away. Once more, [Matt. 25. 31 to 33.] "When the Son "of man shall come in his glory, and all the holy angels with him, "then shall he sit upon the throne of his glory: and before him shall "be gathered all nations; and he shall separate them one from "another, as a shepherd divideth his sheep from the goats: and he "shall set the sheep on his right hand, but the goats on the left." This separation irresistibly carrieth with it, according to the similitude which is employed to set it forth, the idea of a progressive work, as well as the remaining part of the process of that day, which the reader may peruse at discretion.

All these statements show the necessity of a sufficient length of time to give every one a fair trial in all his character. The narratives of the tares as being selected from the wheat, which requires careful and particular work, and of the good fish being severed from the bad, so that none of them may be cast away, and none of the bad left to defile or corrupt the good, and of the gathering of all nations before the Son of man and then dividing them, so that each one shall belong to his proper class, irresistibly fix the impression, according to the nature of the figures, of a serious and careful work of time. The work is also to be executed by the ministry of the angels of him who maketh his angels' ministers; which rendereth the whole matter entirely consistent with these angels' being the ministers who preach the everlasting gospel to those who dwell on the earth, in the hour, or time of judgment.

But it may be objected here, that neither of these representations showeth any change from an evil subject or being to the good; no tares are converted into wheat, no bad fish into good, no goats into sheep; consequently, according to these representations, no wicked men are converted into righteous men, in that day of which these things are spoken, called *the end of the world*, or *day of judgment*. To obviate this reasoning, let it be remembered, that the natural creation, according to its own laws doth not admit of such conversions. And it is not the order or law of parables or metaphors to subvert the regular laws of nature. It is therefore not strange, neither is it inconsistent with the doctrine here contended for, that there is no mention of any such conversions in any of these figurative representations. These remarks will apply to the parable of the wise and foolish virgins, and many others by which the procedure of the day of God is represented: they are counted foolish virgins, and neglecters of the gospel invitation, who remain such until their day is done. But other scriptures of which we have had a view, afford satisfactory and conclusive reasons to believe that repentance and the remission of sins will be found in the hour of judgment.

The above objection would equally militate against the efficacy of the gospel to convert men from wicked to righteous, at any time, or against its opening such a privilege, if it must be tried according to some of the parables or sayings which he delivered, and which appeared to confine his mission to those who were beforehand in possession of the appropriate character of his people or property. " I " am not sent but to the lost sheep of the house of Israel." [Matt. 15. 24.] " And other sheep I have, which are not of this fold: them " also I must bring, and they shall hear my voice; and there shall " be one fold and one shepherd." [Jno. 10. 16.] So that saying of Peter, " For ye were as sheep going astray; but are now returned " to the shepherd and bishop of your souls." [1 Pet. 2. 25.] In all these cases and more which might be adduced the people called sheep were previously to their calling by the gospel, of the wicked, and therefore as properly goats, or dogs, as others are before they have a trial by the gospel. But it is not to be expected, that the nature and design of the second appearing of Christ would be as clearly developed, so long beforehand, as in the opening of the day.

Before I dismiss this part of the subject, it will be proper to instance one other scripture relating to the second coming of Christ, and the rather because it is alledged by some as a proof of an instantaneous work. " For as the lightning cometh out of the east, and " shineth even unto the west; so shall also the coming of the Son " of man be." [Matt. 24. 27.] The argument for the instantaneous appearing of Christ, and at the same time universal, and for the sudden accomplishment of the whole work, seems to be grounded on the term, *lightning*, which is used in the common English reading, and is supposed to denote those streams of elemental fire, or electrical fluid, which appear in our atmosphere commonly attended with thunder, and called *lightning* But a few remarks on the passage will be sufficient to resolve all doubts with the candid. The original word here translated, *lightning*, signifies any glittering brightness, or shining light, and would well express the fulgor of the bright luminaries in the visible heavens, as of the stars, not being unlike a derivative of the Greek term, αϛηρ [aster]which signifies a star, and ιαπτω [iapto] to send forth. And although it is not improperly translated, *lightning*, in different parts of the new testament, the attending circumstances sufficiently show, that the prediction will by no means agree to that acceptation of it here, as we commonly understand the term *lightning*. That lightning, or light, to which the coming of the Son of man is compared, " Cometh out of the east, and shineth " even to the west," so as to include the whole circuit of the earth. Or as Luke hath it ; " For as the lightning, that lightneth out of " one part under heaven shineth to the other part under heaven ; so " shall the Son of man be in his day." (Luke 17. 24.) He will continue to shine until all and every part under heaven be illuminated. But what is commonly called lightning, hath no peculiar direction from east to west ; neither when it bursteth from one part under heaven doth it shine to another part under heaven, so as to become at all universally visible, but it might shine for hours, days or years, if the elemantary laws would continue it, and the inhabitants only a few miles distant see nothing of it. Besides, it hath its direction, either immediately to the earth, or to some conducting or attracting body, or where the heaviest train is laid, according to its own laws, perhaps the least understood of any other on earth, and hath no part in the common illumination of the world.

But all that lightning, or glittering light, which, according to common language and conception, cometh out of the east and without intermission or interruption, moveth forward until it shineth even to the west in every part of the earth, so that all behold the same light in its course, as the light of the sun and other heavenly luminaries, is a proper emblem of the Son of man in his day, whom every eye shall see. But as this light moveth gradually according to the laws of nature, so that every one may improve the light to his comfort and advantage, while it shineth ; so the Son of man according to the law of his grace, will give to every one an opportunity to gather fruit and lay it up for eternal life. But as the sluggard shall beg in harvest and have nothing ; so they who stumble at the cross, being disobedient will not find salvation, in the midst of all this grace.

As an equitable and just prince, who hath conquered, or is fully able to conquer, a country of rebels, having made good an entrance, setteth up his standard, and erecteth his throne of judgment, proclaiming universal amnesty, to all who will confess their rebellion, lay down their opposition, and become hearty subjects of his government, learning to do his will in all things, so Christ in his last coming, and the setting up of his everlasting kingdom, issueth forth the benevolent proclamation of pardon and peace to all who are truly willing to confess their sins, nail their rebellious nature to the same cross which Jesus bore, renounce their own will and become heartily subject in all things to the will of God. And this proclamation is made without any respect of persons, or any other condition than *whosoever will* ; and to men of all ranks, the various pursuits and prospects of the world notwithstanding, to call in a willing people out of all nations to the standard of the prince of peace. "For " in the last days it shall come to pass, that the mountain of the house " of the Lord shall be established in the top of the mountains, and " it shall be exalted above the hills ; and people shall flow unto it. " And many nations shall come and say, Come, and let us go up to " the mountain of the Lord, and to the house of the God of Jacob ; " and he shall teach us of his ways, and we will walk in his paths : " for the law shall go forth of Zion, and the word of the Lord from " Jerusalem. And he shall judge among many people, and rebuke " strong nations' afar off ; and they shall beat their swords into " plough-shares, and their spears into pruning-hooks : nation shall " not lift up sword against nation, neither shall they learn war any " more." (This shall be the result of the law and government of the prince of peace.) " But they sit every man under his vine " and under his fig-tree ; and none shall make them afraid ; for the " mouth of the LORD of hosts hath spoken it. For all people will " walk every one in the name of his God, and we will walk in the " name of the LORD our God for ever and ever. In that day, saith " the LORD, I will assemble her that halteth, and I will gather her " that is driven out, and her that I have afflicted ; and I will make " her that halteth a remnant, and her that was cast far off a strong " nation ; and the LORD shall reign over them in mount Zion from " hence forth, *even for ever.*" (Mic. 4. 1 to 7.)

Thus while he shall dwell in Zion and issue forth his law, he shall judge among many people ; and the result thereof shall be peace among all nations ; to the once halting church of God, and to all who join themselves to her, and the Lord shall reign over them *in mount Zion, for ever.* That the effectuation of all these things is not an instantaneous work but requireth a series of time, needeth not be denied. The notion of an instantaneous establishment of universal happiness and peace, is indeed sufficiently preposterous, as some seem to have it, who reject the testimony of that happy period as having commenced, because the nations are yet learning war, not considering that peace is to be *the result of that day*, which is to be ushered in with *great trouble and distress.* " And there shall be a " time of trouble, such as never was since there was a nation even " to that same time : and at that time thy people shall be delivered, " every one that shall be found written in the book." [Dan. 12. 1.] " Better is the end of a thing than the beginning thereof." (Eccl. 7. 8.)

Now with respect to the commencement of the everlasting kingdom, or the judgment of the world ; many have labored abundantly to find what and what manner of time that should be. But the words which have prophesied of that time, have been closed up and sealed till the time of the end. We have paid some attention to a late writer who hath acknowledged with caution, that the morning had dawned, and who also stated that this sentiment is extensively embraced. But others fix the time to a period yet to come. In a pamphlet written a few years ago, in Carolina, by William C. Davis, the commencement of the Millennium, or reign of Christ on earth, is with much confidence, fixed in the year eighteen hundred and forty-seven, or eight. Davis's method of calculation is ingenious, and indicative of wisdom. But as the words are closed up and sealed until the time of the end, and that can be known by its own light only, it is not strange that they who are not in the light should be always found in more or less mistake, both with respect to what time and what manner of time that day is.

The calculation made by Davis, is grounded on two prophetic scriptures, the periods of which he hath considered as commencing at the same time ; so that they serve as two parts of a clue or key to the prophecies which designate the time of commencement. The first part of the clue is this ; (Dan. 8. 13. 14.) " Then I heard " one saint speaking, and another saint said unto that certain saint who " spake, How long shall be the vision concerning the daily sacrifice, " and the transgression of desolation, to give both the sanctuary and " the host to be trodden under foot ? And he said unto me, Unto " two thousand and three hundred days; then shall the sanctuary be " cleansed :" or as the marginal reading and the Hebrew text say ; " Then shall the sanctuary be justified ;" the living temple, or church of God. The aforesaid William Davis hath very justly stated that the end of these 2300 days is the restoration, or as we may say, commencement of the true worship of God in the church, or the beginning of the Millennium.

The second part of the clue is this, (Dan. 9. 24, &c.) " Seventy " weeks are determined upon thy people, and upon thy holy city, " to finish the transgression, and to make an end of sins, and to make " reconciliation for iniquity, and to bring in everlasting righteousness, " [or the righteousness of the everlasting ones, or saints,] and to seal " up the vision and the prophecy, and to anoint the Most Holy [the " holy of holies, that is, the habitation of God.] Know, therefore, " and understand, that from the going forth of the commandment to " restore and to build Jerusalem unto Messiah the Prince, shall be " seven weeks, and three-score and two weeks ; the street shall be " built again, and the wall, even in troublous times. And after " three-score and two weeks shall Messiah be cut off, but not for " himself :—And he shall confirm the covenant with many for one " week ; and in the midst of the week he shall cause the sacrifice " and the oblation to cease." This prophecy is supposed to include, in clear terms, the grand criterion by which the times are to be known. I shall not transcribe his words, they are too many, and mingled with unnecessary remarks as to the present inquiry. The reader may consult his pamphlet, called THE MILLENNIUM. But his reasonings are to the following amount. That after seven weeks and three-score and two weeks ; which make 69 weeks, and in the midst of the last or seventieth week, from the going forth of the commandment to restore and to build Jerusalem, the Messiah was

JUDGMENT.   431

cut off, or crucified. Now 70 weeks are 490 days, or years, counting a day for a year in prophetic language. And to place the crucifixion in the midst of the last week, showeth that Christ was crucified in the four hundred and eigthty-sixth year after the going forth of the commandment, and in the thirty-fourth year of his own age. The other part of the clue, the 2300 days, or years, our author argues, commenced with the 70 weeks; (here, it will be found, he is in an error,) and that by subtracting 37 years (the age of Christ when crucified being thirty three and a half, and allowing three and a half, the last half of the seventieth week, to the Jews, before the gospel was sent to the Gentiles,) from the 2300, there remain 453 before the christian Era; which being subtracted from the 2300, leave 1847 to come out of the christian Era, before the commencement of the Millennium: that in that year therefore, or the next, (admitting one year of an error in our calculation of the christian Era,) the Millennium will surely commence.

Or the calculation may be made thus. The christian Era being counted from the birth of Christ; he is said by Luke to have been about thirty years of age when he was baptized of John, and received the gift of the Holy Ghost, and was thus inaugurated according to the correct order of God, into the ministry and work which the Father had sent him to perform. He ministered three years and a half, and was cut off, or crucified, in the midst of the week, or last seven years, of the 70 weeks, or 490 years, from the going forth of the commandment. Thirty-seven years therefore are to be substracted from the 490; which leave 453, from the going forth of the commandment, to the birth of Christ, or first of the Christian Era; which being substracted from 2300, leave 1847.

The calculation of the 70 weeks appears to be not only ingenious but correct. But to fix the commencement of the 2300 days at the going forth of the commandment is erroneous. For in the first place divine revelation hath given no authority; it hath not made any mention of such a point of time for the commencement of those days. And should any man ask me how long shall it be until the restoration of the captives, and I answer until 1500 days; would any one, who heard our communications, fix the commencement of those days to some after period, and not rather count from the time of the conversation, or from the beginning of the captivity? The captivity of the Jews had been going on for more than fifty years, when the prophecy of the 2300 days was given to Daniel; and the commencement of the 70 weeks was long enough after, to fulfil 70 years of captivity; if we count the decree of Cyrus the matter designated in the vision. But not a word in the scriptures to intimate that the two periods commenced together. As to our author's arguing that the latter vision was an explanation of the former; it is all conjecture and hypothesis, with respect at least, to its unfolding, or showing its commencement; for not one expression is in the second to indicate such a matter.

But to the 453 years, which remain from the 490, or 70 weeks, after the 37 of the christian Era are left out, add the 70 years of the Jews' captivity, and they make 523, which substracted from 2300, leave 1777, of the christian Era, and so mark that year, 1777, as the time for the sanctuary to be cleansed; about 30 years after the true light first dawned in England, to effect that object. About this time, or early in the year 80, the testimony of the everlasting gospel began to be publicly opened in America, and mankind were invited into the sanctuary; but the sanctuary, or church, was not established in full order until in the year 1792; 45 years after the first dawn of the true light; according to the words of Daniel; " And from the " time that the daily sacrifice shall be taken away, and the abomina- " tion that maketh desolate set up, there shall be a thousand two hun- " dred and ninety days. Blessed is he that waiteth, and cometh to " the thousand three hundred and five and thirty days." [Dan. 12. 11, 12.] Until that year the true order of the new creation in Christ was not fully known. But it then began to be known; and hath continued ever since. The church had been measurably gathered before, and there was a sharp ministration, preparing the way for perfect order; but there were no regular orderly gifts or lots of continual standing, as Elders, Deacons, or Elder brethren and sisters. But at that time; the lots, gifts and privileges of the members of the body were found, both in the male and female. Elders were found in the line of the one and of the other. Deacons and Deaconnesses; Elder brethren and sisters; each in their proper line, found their places and their duty in the proper order of the new creation in Christ, and the perfection and blessedness of the church began to appear. The spiritual union between the two, who are the first parents of the new creation, was never openly exhibited on earth, in their proper persons; but it now began to appear in their faithful seed, as the true order of the kingdom of God on earth, that kingdom of heaven which is to abide for ever and ever.

It is remarkable that the prophecy of the 2300 days, is dated in the chronological notes in the large bibles, in the year 553 before Christ; and by counting those days to commence then, they end in the year 1747 of the christian Era; the very year when the true light sprung up. So that by these different calculations, or by either of them, the time hath come. But as these chronologies are at best uncertain, or rather certainly incorrect, most of them by many years, as the light of the kingdom increaseth, the truth will be known without them. For the light of that day, is that which alone will fully reveal to men, especially to those who are in it, *for none of the wicked shall understand; but the wise shall understand*, when and what manner of time that day is. And as fast as it is made known, it will be found to answer to the prophecies of the scriptures, which cannot be broken.

But in vain doth any man attempt to tell the commencement of that time and day, by the letter of the prophecies. Although there is a propriety in studying them and may be often an advantage; and so much the more as we see the day approaching; that men may be in readiness to receive the kingdom as it appeareth to them. But it is evident that prophecies were not intended to be understood, neither in their numbers, times and seasons, which generally were designedly delivered in obscurity, nor the things themselves which were predicted, they being generally delivered, in symbols and metaphors, and the like, until the times of their accomplishment. "We have "also a more sure [βεβαιοτερον, more permanent or steady,] word of "prophecy; whereunto ye do well to take heed, as unto a light that "shineth in a dark place, *until the day dawn and the day-star arise* "*in your hearts;* knowing this first," (that ye may have a right understanding of the subject,) " that no prophecy of scripture is of any "private interpretation. For the prophecy came not in old time by "the will of man;" (else men might understand and interpret it. " For what man knoweth the things of a man save the spirit of man " which is in him?") " but holy men of God spake as they were " moved by the Holy Ghost." The same Holy Ghost, therefore, must interpret these prophecies; for " Even so knoweth no man the " things of God, but the Spirit of God." [2 Pet. 1. 19, 20, 21. 1 Cor. 2. 11.

Now it is evident enough the aforesaid William Davis is wrong in his calculation of the time for the commencement of the Millennium, or day of Christ's setting up his everlasting kingdom. For according to him it is not yet come; and until then the time cannot be known; which is yet farther evident from the following considerations. " Of that day and hour knoweth no man;" until it come: " For the words are closed up and sealed till the time of the end." If therefore the time of the end of the desolation be not come; if the everlasting kingdom be not begun, our author is wrong in his calculation, being ignorant of the whole matter; for the words are yet closed up and sealed, and neither he nor any other man knoweth *what* or *what manner* of time that shall be. But if the time is come, and the everlasting kingdom begun, which is the existing truth, he is wrong; for he hath fixed it to about thirty years yet to come. " And none of the wicked shall understand; but the wise shall un-
" derstand."

Nevertheless, his calculation is so important, and so correct in some part, as it proves with great propriety that the commencement of the Millennium, or everlasting kingdom cannot be later than his calculation, that it is not an undesirable thing that people should become acquainted with it and understand it correctly; so that they who cannot, or rather will not, be convinced of the day in which they live, may at the end of that calculation, be so far overcome, as to consent to receive the work of God in his own order, when they see nothing come forth to answer their own sense or to fill their expectations. In the mean time, much credit is due to the light and wisdom which appeareth in that calculation; and the author is not unjustly esteemed as an instance of the fulfilment of that prophecy of Daniel; " Many shall run to and fro, (while they know not where to "fix,) and knowledge shall be increased." Let every man have his due; and God the glory.

This is that day of the LORD, which hath already begun to shine forth on the earth, to which the Spirit of Christ which was in the prophets directed their prophetic language; and the day to which the same Spirit directed Peter and the rest of the apostles on the day of Pentecost; and to which he directed the people after he, with John, had healed the lame man. " Repent ye, therefore, and be " converted, [επιςρε+ατε, convert,] that your sins may be blotted out, " when the times of refreshing shall come from the presence of the " Lord, and he shall send Jesus Christ who before was preached " unto you; whom the heaven must receive until the times of res- " titution of all things, which God hath spoken by the mouth of all " his holy prophets since the world began." I am indeed aware that the translation of this scripture is disputed; and it is argued that in its correct design and acceptation, it is no proof of an after dispensation. But in the common translation, it contains nothing more than the same apostle hath taught, speaking of those who be- lieved in that day; " Who are kept by the power of God through " faith unto salvation *ready to be revealed in the last time.*" There- fore not yet known; for they were not yet in possession, but [κομιζο- μενοι] " Carefully pursuing the end of their faith—the salvation of " their souls." And a little after he saith; " Wherefore gird up the " loins of your mind, be sober, and hope to the end for the grace " *that is to be brought to you at the revelation of Jesus Christ.*" (1 Pet. 1. 5, 9, 13.) Thus he directed the believers to look for- ward to the second or last revelation of Christ, for finished salva- tion; because the first revelation had already come.

I grant the words are not as literally translated as they might be ; for I know no reason for translating a past tense of the subjunctive mood by the future indicative. But all that can be gained by an exact translation will not prevent the relation which that text hath to the appearing or sending of Jesus Christ in a future day. For [οπως αν] the phrase rendered *when*, is never used by the apostles, except in connection with the subjunctive mood, and with respect to futurity. " Repent therefore, and be converted [or convert,] for " the blotting out of your sins; that the times of refreshing may come " from the presence of the Lord, and he may send [αποςειλη] Jesus " Christ, who hath been preached to you before hand, whom heaven " must have received until the times of the restitution of all things, of " which God hath spoken by the mouth of all his prophets in the " time past. For Moses truly said unto the fathers, A prophet " shall the Lord your God raise up unto you, of your brethren, like " unto me; him shall ye hear in all things whatsoever he shall say " unto you. And it shall come to pass, that every soul who will " not hear that prophet, shall be destroyed from among the people. " Yea, and all the prophets from Samuel, and those that follow after, " as many as have spoken, have likewise foretold of these days." (Acts 3, 19, to 24.)

JUDGMENT. 435

Now it is evident that the times of the restitution of all things of which God had spoken by the prophets had not then come; for the falling away had not yet come, which was to precede those times. But the Spirit of prophecy looked forward with such earnestness to the latter days, as the time of accomplishing the glorious and mighty works of God in his church, that the lesser changes which were to intervene, were sometimes passed over without notice. Thus the two thousand and three hundred days, predicted by Daniel, seem to have included all the time from the captivity of the Jews by the king of Babylon to the commencement of the final purification of the church and the setting up of the everlasting kingdom in the second coming of Christ; without so much as noticing the partial restoration of the Jews, before the coming of Christ; the introduction of the gospel in his first appearing; or the rise and reign of the beast, or anti-christ. In like manner the Spirit in Peter pointed directly to the latter days, or times of the restitution of all things, when the kingdoms of this world should become the kingdom of our Lord and of his Christ, and there should be one Lord and his name one: for all this was included in the things of which God had spoken by his prophets. But these times were not to come until the seventh angel should sound. Thus these sayings of Peter agree with what he wrote afterwards, giving counsel to believers how they ought to live; " Looking for and hasting unto the " coming of the day of God;" as though it had been close at hand. And on this principle, that the Spirit of prophecy looked so intensely towards the latter day, or times of restitution and glory, we may account for the trouble and uneasiness, among the believers in Thessalonica, as though the day of the Lord were at hand; which occasioned Paul to write to them to not be soon shaken in mind or troubled, for that day should not come except there come a falling away first and that lawless, or man of sin be revealed whom the Lord would consume with the spirit of his mouth and destroy with the brightness of his appearing. But the day is now come; and is as a snare on all the earth.

But the length of time necessary for the accomplishment of the work, is no argument against the suddenness of its introduction, or the sudden awaking of those who are asleep, when the voice of the trumpet reacheth them. So that the awaking of those who are asleep, and the equivalent change in those who are not asleep, at least in the same sense, when compared with the same length of time which the prophets and martyrs have been waiting for the kingdom of God, may in prophetic style be said to take place, in a moment, in the twinkling of an eye. But it doth not appear fair arguing, in those who understand the nature of language, to insist that the apostle, by that phraseology, teacheth that the dead shall be raised incorruptible and the living experience an equivalent change, literally in the period of time there marked. The words, *In a moment, in the twinkling of an eye, at the last trump*, are detached from those which follow, *For the trumpet shall sound, and the dead shall be raised incorruptible, and we shall be changed*, by that state, or structure of language, called a parenthesis, and properly relate to that change which is equivalent to the waking of those who are asleep.

"Awake thou that sleepest, and arise from the dead." It is quite a natural thing for those who are asleep to awake, and for those who are not asleep, in the same sense or degree, to undergo a sudden change of state by the blast of a loud trumpet, which cometh after being expected, with the most momentous news. This may be in the things of nature; and it will be granted by all judicious and considerate people, that the apostle here useth metaphorical language, representing spiritual things by natural; some general resemblance therefore is to be expected. After waking, which is readily effected by the sound of the trumpet alone, follows arising from the dead, which is the duty of the awakened subject, and on which the promise of light from Christ depends. "Wherefore come out from among them, and be ye separate, saith the Lord, and touch not the unclean thing; and I will receive you." (2 Cor. 6. 17.) After receiving the light, the next thing in course is to enter on the duties of the day. It is an egregious error, however common, to suppose that the works pertaining to the coming of Christ to judgment are all done in an instant. It is common to all God's dealings with men to proceed by successive steps, and there is no unambiguous authority that he ever intends to depart from that method. The apprehension of a momentary or instantaneous effectuation of the resurrection and judgment hath unquestionably arisen from considering metaphorical language in its appropriate meaning, while the subject in the true spirit of it was misunderstood. That apprehension is also contrary to, by far, the greatest part even of that kind of language, used in the scriptures on that subject.

Shall not the judge of all the earth do right? Shall God consign the immensurable majority of mankind to eternal damnation, hopelessly excluded from the peaceful society of the just, who have hitherto remained in invincible ignorance of the way of salvation? Ignorance invincible without farther light and revelation from God! For it is found by painful experience, that with all the knowledge which men can obtain by the letter, multitudes remain in total ignorance of salvation. They cannot gain power over sin; they are overcome by it, and are therefore in bondage to it, and consequently, by the authority of that same word, excluded from the society of the blest. Some, whether to alleviate the allegation of injustice against God, and to dissipate the clouds of horror, or from whatever cause, have palmed on God a contrivance, that all have light enough to leave them without excuse, but not sufficient for their salvation. An allegation this, which could not comport with the honest reputation of the weakest man on earth; and how shall it apply to the infinitely wise and just God? Who cannot, in one moment, see the fallacy and iniquity of supposing a man inexcusable, by having any degree of light, or any privilege, if it may be so called, which can show him that he is wrong, and ought to do better, but doth not supply him with means competent to the end? Some times on the other hand, it is stated, that whosoever will follow the dictates of his own judgment will end safely. But this is the ground work of infidelity, the pivot on which it turns, and disannuls or supersedes the gospel altogether. It is indeed a reasonable and just position, that those who honestly obey the light which is in their reach, and lie open to conviction, ready to receive an increase, and do not reject it when offered, but persevere in their honesty, will in the event find salvation, For to him who hath shall be given, and he shall have abundance. But from him who hath not, or doth not make his own by right improvement, shall be taken away even that which he hath. And in this view, it may be said that men are inexcusable, if they are not saved. And this is precisely the principle on which the apostle states that men are without excuse, their not improving of the degree of light which they have. " So that they are without excuse: " because, that when they knew God, they glorified him not as God, " neither were they thankful." (Ro. 2. 20, 21.) Herein also men are justly criminated, and die with a double, or tenfold damnation, who reject and disobey, in the blaze of gospel day—emphatically the day of judgment and perdition of ungodly men.

THE

MANIFESTO.

PART IV.

Comprised in the substance of a Letter to

BARTON W. STONE.

SECTION I.

Of Freedom in religious conversation.

BARTON; I have inscribed this letter to you as being the most proper person to whom I could direct it, to answer the proposed ends. Your situation in religious life, and the active part which you take, the liberality of your sentiments, formerly, and your professedly retasning the same to this day, according to the contents of your Address *to the christian churches*, and the freedom which you have therein used, on different subjects, together with the impression that the truth ought to be fairly investigated and correctly known by all its friends, have induced me to use this freedom with you.

Nothing on this earth is of such importance as christianity; and no correspondence of the most intimate friendship can be of such utility to mankind, as that which promotes the increase of gospel light and knowledge, and thereby leads to the salvation of souls. However useful other employments may be in their proper place, and however expedient an open and free correspondence on other topics, all must yield to christianity, in point of utility. " For bodily exercise profit-" eth little, but godliness is profitable to all things, having promise of " the life that now is, and of that which is to come." Such considerations as these evince the necessity of openness and freedom among those who believe the truth of christianity, with a readiness to give and receive every aid to the work. Nothing is more calculated to impede the progress of genuine christianity, which is itself most liberal, than a spirit of censorious illiberality, or an unwillingness to communicate where opportunity is offered, or to receive instructions where they can be had.: no man is so wise as to be out of the reach of more useful knowledge. But a peremptoriness to reject and condemn those doctrines and practices with which we are unacquainted, without a fair examination, is too prevalent among those who profess the christian religion: and especially when contrary to our prepossessions, or against our inclinations; insomuch that many boldly step into the rank with those whom the apostle describes in this emphatical language; "But these speak evil of the things which they know not; but what they know naturally, as brute beasts, [irrational animals,] in those things they corrupt themselves." And these also presumed to name the name of Christ and unite themselves, by profession, to the faithful, as appears from his words a little after. "These are spots in your feasts of charity, when they feast with you, feeding themsives without fear." (Jude 10, 12.)

Contracted views, and a contractedness of spirit, being most effectual barriers to improvement, appear likely to prove the ruin of many; and these too of the zealous, who make to themselves no other proposals than to make the best improvement of what they have, but at the same time scrupulously reject every idea of changing grounds for the better, or of giving up a single article of that faith into which they have been initiated from the beginning. The alarming allegation of changing religion, which with some appears to be an enormous crime, threatens to preclude all prospect of advancement in the knowledge of God and his work of salvation, unless it can be obtained where they stand, whether on the right foundation or not. And the proposals or prospect of any such change, is rebutted by such arguments as these. "He that shall endure to the end the same shall be saved." "Whose house are we, if we hold fast the confidence and the rejoicing of the hope firm to the end." "Let us hold fast the profession of our faith without wavering." "Cast not away therefore your confidence which hath great recompense of reward." "Be not carried about with divers and strange doctrines." "That we be no more children tossed to and fro, and carried about with every wind of doctrine, by the slight of men, and cunning craftiness, whereby they lie in wait to deceive." (Matt. 24. 13. Heb. 3. 6. and 10. 23, 35. and 13. 9. Eph. 4. 14.) While those who proffer such arguments, do not correctly consider that they are applicable to those only who have infallible testimony that they are already built on the only foundation which God hath laid in Zion, not in name but in works. "Not every one who saith to me Lord, Lord, shall enter into the kingdom of heaven but he that doeth the will of my Father who is in heaven." "And, Let every one that nameth the name of Christ depart from iniquity." (Matt. 7. 21. 2 Tim. 2. 19.) The application of such scriptures as those noticed above, by one and another among the mass of professors, with all the incoherent sentiments which abound, bears a very different aspect from their original application to believers in the one faith and the one Christ, all belonging to one body, and known to belong to that faith which was exclusively the faith of Christ, and when all that was necessary to be done, was to confirm them and build them up in that one faith. But that kind of spirit which the apostle reproved as being antichristian, telling those who said, I am of Paul, and I of Apolos, that they were carnal and not spiritual, hath so far prevailed, that there are as many faiths as we find different denominations of professors, and each of these, in terms either stronger or weaker, announces itself the true faith of Christ.

Now when a man hath honestly proved the faith and practice of one society, and hath not found that which can fill his soul and satisfy his conscience, to remove where the evidence of the light and truth of God is satisfying, is no more a violation of the faith of Christ or a wresting of the scriptures, than for Paul to renounce the religion of the Jews and become a christian, or for Martin Luther to renounce popery and go in the pursuit of a better religion, or for any other man to forsake that church which hath the form of godliness but denieth the power, and unite with the living body : this needs no proof but the statement. Should a man change his profession thus, ten times, as one emptied from vessel to vessel, or tossed on the tempestous waves, until he at last find the true body of Christ, (for there is one body and one Spirit,) which can fill his soul, and satisfy his conscience in the peace of God, he is, in so doing, as innocent as the Lamb. For no church can have any just claim to the character of the church of Christ, unless it hath, resident in it at all times, that gospel, known to all its members, which can thus fill their souls, enabling them to crucify the flesh with its affections and lusts, and efficaciously teaching them that denying ungodliness and worldly lusts, they should live soberly, righteously and godly in this present world, and enabling them to die to sin and live to God in the Spirit, after the example of Jesus Christ. These things are too expressly scriptural, as pertaining to the true gospel of Christ, to need logical argumentation with those who believe revelation.

While using this plainness of speech, I desire to notice one thing which is, as I apprehend, gaining ground among professors, though strictly a branch of infidelity. Interrogate a professor closely on the ground of his faith and its fruits, or the whole of his evidence for eternal life, and he will often ward off the conversation with this ; " I am willing to let every one alone to take the way which he " chooses, or which he thinks is right." This seems to be esteemed an eminent degree of christian charity, to let others alone ; and though you are ever so sure they are going in the broad way to destruction, (and especially if they are professed christians, for many such are confessedly in the broad way,) put the matter off with, It is the way they choose : for every christian church knoweth who are in the way of destruction and who are in the way of life.

Now the question is, Can this be christian charity or duty, to let men sleep on, under fatal deception, when there is access to them ? Or how doth such a temper comport with the instructions and example of the apostles of Christ ? " Whom (saith Paul,) we preach, " warning every man in all wisdom : that we may present every " man perfect in Christ Jesus." " And (saith Jude,) of some have " compassion, making a difference ; and others save with fear, pull- " ing them out of the fire ; hating even the garment spotted by the " flesh." [Col. 1. 28. v. 22, 23.] God loveth a cheerful giver ; and there is no doubt but all christians having the true Spirit of Christ, (For if any man have not the Spirit of Christ he is none of his,) are free to impart, on any suitable occasion, what they have freely re-

ceived, according to their ability and calling. "For the love of
"Christ constraineth us; because we thus judge, that if one died
"for all, then were all dead; and that he died for all, that they who
"live, should not henceforth live to themselves, but to him who died
for them, and rose again." [2 Cor. 5. 14, 15.]

Another question occurs; Can they be christians who refuse access to themselves, by those who propose free conversation on this important point, to bring the matter to a fair trial, for edification, or with that professed and apparent reason? Let the words of Peter be considered in this place. "But sanctify the Lord God in your
"hearts; and be ready always to give an answer to every man that
"asketh you a reason of the hope that is in you with meekness and
"fear; having a good conscience; that whereas they speak evil of
"you as of evil doers, they may be ashamed that falsely accuse your
"good conversation in Christ." [1 Pet. 3. 15, 16.] When a man can evade a free conversation on the ground work of the gospel—faith, hope and charity, with the correspondent works, by saying that he is willing to let every one take the way which he thinks is best, he exhibits to me the strongest evidence, that he is conscious to himself of not having a good conscience, of not sanctifying the Lord God in his heart, and that he has not become willing to part with all things for Christ, but hugs in his bosom a beloved idol, which he is afraid the truth would discover and wrest from him, and is also jealous or apprized that he who proposes the conversation is possessed of that truth of God, which can strip him, would he come fairly to trial: for he who has parted with all can lose no more; but he who hath kept a reserve may be in danger. Honesty and truth are not afraid of the light, or of examination, but dishonesty and wickedness love the dark. "For every one that doeth evil hateth the light, nei-
"ther cometh to the light, lest his deeds should be reproved. [Gr.
"convicted.] But he that doeth truth cometh to the light, that his
"deeds may be made manifest that they are wrought in God."

Some may plead that it is of little consequence to bring a man's religion to trial before other men, for the judgment of man is an uncertain matter at best. True enough; the judgment of man is an uncertain matter. But when a man is not able to support his religion in the judgment of men who soberly appeal to revelation, it is poor religion indeed. And when a man cannot maintain the safety of the foundation on which he is building, by good and rational evidence, in the judgment of men who soberly appeal to revelation, it is a poor foundation. But the truth is, that the people of God have the discernment, or judgment of God in them, and hypocrites and those who are not in possession of the truth of God, can feel it in them, (and can also feel the light in some who have a good degree of light from God, and yet have not experienced the work and travail of regeneration,) a light and a judgment able to comprehend them. "For he that is spiritual judgeth [or discerneth,] all things,
"yet he himself is judged, or discerned of no man."

OF CONVERSATION.

The unlimited bounds ascribed to charity, by some, is another source of excuse on this subject. It is not enough to let every one choose his own way, but it must be hoped in charity that all are right, or at least some amongst all, so that it is no matter what people's sentiments are, provided they only practise what they think is right. Thus the noble man-made charity becomes a covert for errors in faith and practice; and what is more, demands of God the approbation of every man's ways, various as they may be, provided they can find acceptance in his own mind, whether according to the will of God or not; and thus subjects God and his worship to every man's judgment: for except God approve there can be no justification or salvation. It is esteemed quite an uncharitable thing to suppose that any denomination of professors have not the true faith of Christ and power of salvation; or that their tenets are such that if put into practice, (and they are useless without practice, for faith without works is dead,) they will exclude them from a participation in the kingdom of heaven, or fail of connecting them with the followers of the Lamb. But it is not uncharitable nor unchristian to believe the truth. Charity believeth all things; but it is not required to believe things which have no existence, or to believe a lie. Charity doth not require me to believe a man is right when he is doing wrong; neither to believe he has the faith of Christ, or that faith, in the possession and exercise of which he can be saved, unless his fruits are in all things according to Christ. For by their fruits ye shall know them, and a good tree cannot bring forth evil fruit. Charity doth not require me to believe that any man or people have the faith of Christ, who openly acknowledge and avow that faith which admits the possibility of sin, the work of the flesh, or any thing contrary to the order and life of Christ, in a christian. If all denominations produce the genuine fruits of christianity—if all keep that unity of the Spirit in the bond of peace, which belongs to that *one* body of Christ, having *one* faith and *one* Spirit—if all have that inimitable love and union which no hypocrite can counterfeit, and by which all men shall know, that they are the disciples of Christ, and the world shall believe and know that the Father hath sent him, and hath loved them as he hath loved him, or by which the truth of christianity is established and confirmed—if all have that faith which influenceth them to walk even as he walked, who left us an example that we should follow his steps, then all are right; but all who fall short in these things are wrong, and must, while in their present standing, come short of salvation. I presume the scriptures to which these things relate, are too familiar to you, to require a particular citation. But if all are right, or if any are right, having the faith of Christ and power of salvation, (for without these none can be right,) I see no reason why those who are right, should not exhibit the righteousness of their faith and practice on all proper occasions, with freedom and humility, or why they are not in the number of those whose hearts condemn them, who can cover their light under a bushel, and avoid the scrutiny of the light under such subterfuges as have been common. I do not mean that christians ought to vociferate like public criers; humility and modesty become them. I only plead for that openness of heart, which will prove that their souls are not in bondage; and that they are not ashamed of the gospel of Christ, or the views and practice which they maintain, while in them it proves itself to be the power of God to salvation.

With some it would appear, that an effectual hindrance to freedom of communication, is the fear of giving offence, especially where there are different sentiments on some leading points. I am not pleading for any improper or ill-placed communications. We are not required to cast pearls before swine. Where the gospel is not acceptable, and there appears no prospect or place for any benefit, officious urging would be imprudent. But I see no need of these difficulties among christians, or professors, who aim to be honest. If they possess the faith of the common salvation, why not unbosom one to another, at least so far, that their unity of faith and spirit might appear. " Then they that feared the Lord spake often one to ano-" ther; and the Lord hearkened and heard it; and a book of remem-" brance was written before him for them that feared the Lord, and " that thought upon his name. And they shall be mine, saith the " Lord of hosts, in that day when I make up my jewels; and I will " spare them as a man spareth his own son that serveth him." (Mal. 3. 16, 17.) It is not justifiable to omit duty, or cover the truth, with fear of offending. There is indeed no impropriety in addressing mankind in the most inviting and inoffensive terms which the nature of the case will admit in honesty. The haughty spirit of man is apt enough to rebel; and the gospel is offensive enough to him without adding to it, any thing disgusting. But the truth of the gospel must not be corrupted by those who publish and possess it. Although Paul availed himself of every justifiable method to escape censure and persecution, being wise as a serpent and harmless as a dove, he could not preach to please his brethren, the Jews, although by that he might have escaped all persecution for Christ. But thus he must have fallen from grace, and have been separated from Christ. He therefore adhered to the gospel by the cross. " And I, brethren, if " I yet preach circumcision, why do I yet suffer persecution? then " is the offence of the cross ceased." " But God forbid that I should " glory, save in the cross of our Lord Jesus Christ, by whom the " world is crucified to me and I to the world." (Gal. 5. 11. and 6. 14.) Could Paul have discharged the duty of his calling, and have preached salvation by circumcision and other Jewish rituals, leaving out the cross of Christ, there had been no offence. For those outward signs were they to which circumcision related; because he did preach circumcission; not the outward sign in the flesh, but that which is made without hands, in putting off the body of the sins of the flesh by the circumcission of Christ; that which is of the heart, in the Spirit, not in the letter; whose praise is not of men but of God. (Col. 2. 11. Ro. 2. 29.) This circumcission of the heart and in the spirit was the great stumbling stone, against which all the persecution was raised. Just so; could believers in this day, fulfil the duties of their calling, and omit the cross; or could they be justified in preaching salvation by outward forms and ceremonies, without the necessity of walking in the footsteps of Christ and bearing his cross; such a gospel (though indeed no gospel at all,) would be welcomed by the inhabitants of the land, professors not excepted. But the cross of Christ hath always been offensive to the world, and always will, while such a world is in being.

But may I not add, that some are prevented from using that freedom with others of different sentiments, and conversing freely as they might otherwise do, especially with those who are counted great deceivers, lest their fellow professors should be offended. And the charity of some is so exquisitely favorable, that it will not allow them to offend others, if by this tenderness they should neglect a duty to God and their own souls. And they can avail themselves of the impropriety of offending a brother, or one of Christ's little ones, and the sin and woe of those who cause offences to come. Not considering that those offences which the scriptures condemn, were committed against the faith of Christ, and not against the selfish feelings of partisans. But I am thankful that all are not so weak and ignorant. It needs no proof that those warnings against offences, are no impediment in the way of honest people examining into the grounds of their faith and practice, and obtaining every degree of light and help in their reach, but that they who are opposed to such freedom, are offenders in the true meaning. " Prove all things and hold fast " that which is good." (1 Thes. 5. 21.) The word of God is not bound; and where the Spirit of the Lord is there is liberty. The people of God have not received the spirit of bondage again to fear; but the Spirit of adoption whereby they cry Abba, Father. They are Christ's free men, and are under no restraint from acquiring all that knowledge which is necessary to fill the soul with good things to their own satisfaction.

But I must use the freedom to mention another avowed reason with many, for their refusing to converse freely and openly on the foundation of their hope, especially with those who believe that Christ hath made his second appearance, and are by many esteemed the greatest deceivers—the danger of being deceived. They are, or affect to be, much afraid of deception. Yet of those whose ostensible reason is fear, many will say they are not afraid on their own account, but on the account of others who are weak. Thus will carnal professors endeavor to exculpate themselves from all unsoundness or weakness in their own standing, while they stand as sentinels to keep the truth of God from their house and neighborborhood. The danger also of giving heed to seducing spirits, has been alledged; as if to inquire soundly into the foundation of a man's faith, were the same thing as to submit to the dictates of manifest seduction.

Other particulars might be mentioned, (and perhaps some may in the sequel,) as causes of fear, real or pretended, all which to an honest man, appear at the first view, to be mere bugbears, while the true source of fear is an inward conviction that all is not right towards God, and that the truth requires them to give up more for Christ than they are willing to lose. It is no part of christianity to be afraid of being deceived; for christians know who are of the truth and who are not, by the spirit which they possess and the doctrines which they bring. "We are of God: he that knoweth God heareth us; he that is not of God heareth not us. Hereby know we the Spirit of truth and the spirit of error." [1 Jno. 4. 6.] Proper as it is, and justifiable, to avoid closing in with error, or countenancing it; that faith, or foundation, which can be shaken by error, is not the faith of Christ, or the foundation which God hath laid in Zion; and little matter how soon it be dissolved. The promise of God is faithful and good; "Surely there is no enchantment against Jacob, neither is there any divination against Israel." [Numb. 23. 23.] Honest souls have no cause of fear; deception belongs to those who choose it; neither need any people, or any man, exhibit a better proof of living in deception and hypocrisy, than fear of being deceived. Christianity includes too much light for those who possess it, or even know where it is, to be afraid of being deceived against their own choice. "I am," said Jesus, "the light of the world; he that followeth me shall not walk in darkness, but shall have the light of life." [Jno. 8. 12.] And again he said to his disciples, "Ye are the light of the world. A city that is set on an hill cannot be hid." [Matt. 5. 14.]

After all the incoherent notions and various persuasions in the profession of christianity, and all the uncertainty with which people have suffered the most exquisite distress, and all the reproaches with which the name of Christ hath been blasphemed, by the ungodly and unmortified lives of professors, until it is true of them, as of the Jews of old, that the name of God through them is blasphemed among the Gentiles, and all the support which has been ministered to infidelity, by the inconsistent, jarring and irregular course of those who have named the name of Christ, and have not departed from iniquity, the foundation of God standeth sure, and his church must eventually emerge from those clouds of superstition and error, which have so long obstructed and prevented his goings forth as the morning, with that distinguished light and evidence which cannot admit of deception. And it is fully time that such a work should be seen on the earth, the true church of God, and that the people should begin to flow together into it, that the honest sufferers may find relief, and the weary of sin may be at rest in Christ. Accordingly the day has dawned, the testimony has gone forth, and the Sun of righteousness has arisen with healing in his wings.

About the time when that society to which you are still attached began to be distinguished from the common mass of professors, out of which it sprung. I felt more confirmed that I was doing the will of God, and under the direction of his special providence, than I had ever been before. Neither do I at all scruple at this day, to acknow-

OF CONVERSATION.

ledge the special hand of God, in selecting that society from among others, in conjunction with whom, its members could not have enjoyed the free exercise of that light and power, which they had received in that mighty work of God, called the Kentucky revival. And I always feel willing to acknowledge the good hand of God in the various ministrations of clear light, which were received from him during the work of that day. And though I now stand where I do; I say the truth in Christ, I lie not, my conscience also bearing me witness in the Holy Spirit, when I attest that I have no less esteem for the work of that day, than I had then; although to the best of my remembrance, I then esteemed it as by far the greatest which I had ever witnessed. I may add farther, that I now esteem it inexpressibly more than I did then, as being much better acquainted with its tendency. " Better is the end of a thing than the beginning " thereof." [Eccl. 7. 8.] I can also bear witness, that my regard for the subjects of that revival, who have honestly retained the life and spirit of it to the best of their understanding, is by no means abated. And even those, who have ceded their power and privilege to the spirit of fear and unbelief, or to the corrupt influence of prejudicial gainsaying, are not out of the reach of my good will, nor the embraces of my desires and longings for their recovery. Of whom, if accessible, I am ever willing, and would count it my joy, to travail in birth again until Christ be formed in them.

It was not from any unkind feelings towards that revival or its subjects, that I stand where I do, or that I have not had an uninterrupted intercourse with you all to this day. I had no intention, God is my witness, of withdrawing my friendship from them, until they, to the pain of my heart, refused me access. I remained in the exercise of all the freedom which I could obtain among them, until constrained by the call of God, by the clear testimony of the truth of God in my own conscience, that a deeper work than could be had there, was necessary to my salvation, and by the all-prevailing love to truth, to step forward in the increasing manifestation of the light and knowledge of God, and leave my former brethren, who were not far from the kingdom of heaven, to give over their pursuit, and making vigorous efforts to retain and content themselves with what they had. Nay more; many of them have receded from that, and taken refuge under the rudiments of the world, those beggarly elements in which they desire again to be in bondage.

Neither was it any thing in the testimony of the gospel which I received, and wherein I stand, which was so agreeable to my nature as to invite me in. Every man who has but a little understanding of the self-denial and cross which we bear after Christ, has an invincible testimony in himself to the contrary—that the gospel is not inviting to man's nature, but to the spirit that feels the need of salvation. And the clear testimony of God corresponded with my understanding and faith, and with the light of God which I had received in the late revival, so that I must now of necessity, by the call of God, make my choice to go forward into the opening of the kingdom of Christ, or renounce what I had received. I therefore began to deny myself, to take up my cross and follow Christ in the regeneration; and have thenceforth been learning by a solid experience, that it is better to obey God than man. The same testimony agrees also to the understanding and light of every man and every woman, who were real subjects, and had a real understanding of the work of the revival: of the truth of which there are many witnesses who do not obey the gospel.

Some years ago, the piercing cries of many were, *What shall we do to be saved?* And nothing then would satisfy short of that substance which could not be shaken or disputed. But when the safe and only way appeared by the cross, they stumbled at it, being disobedient; and many of those who were piercing the heavens with their cries, have settled back into the rudiments of the world. While it remains true, that the cross which we bear, and at which they stumble, and the self-denial which we practise, who are called by the everlasting gospel, are sanctioned by the example of Christ, with such certainty that no man can with any plausibility deny it. The current argument is, that such a cross is not required of the followers of Christ; that is, that Christ doth not require his people to take him as an example in ceasing from the first Adam's works in the radical distinction of their several orders. This kind of reasoning, in those who expect to be justified by the righteousness of Christ imputed to them, is quite consistent with the rest of their views. But for those who have rejected the doctrine of vicarious sufferings and obedience, or imputed righteousness, to argue in that manner is not so consistent.

SECTION II.

Free and friendly observations on the sentiments and practice of the Superscribed, and the subjects of the revival.

BARTON;
    WHEREAS in your Address you have expressed a warm disapprobation of the insinuation that your doctrines lead to Shakerism, to be consistent you will heartily consent that Shakers should object to your views. And whereas you so earnestly plead for freedom among christians, or professors, and insist on the propriety of scriptural and rational arguments, you cannot with propriety feel any chagrine, if I should examine your writings, and state my objections in a few particulars. And as the first LETTERS ON ATONEMENT, the REPLY to Campbell, and your late ADDRESS, are mainly on the same subjects, I shall consider them as containing your full faith on those points, and as showing the substance of the difference between the society with which you are connected, and professors in common. I

intend not to be at the pains to make remarks on every particular, but only to attend to some leading points.

These doctrines have thoroughly undermined the doctrine of imputed righteousness, and surety payment. At the same time you must allow me the liberty to remark; That they have not removed all difficulties, nor carried the matter clearly through to full satisfaction, although they have effectually refuted the doctrine itself. Some talk of the righteousness of Christ imputed, and some, of the same righteousness applied, or imparted, to believers for their justification. But as there is no account nor authority for such doctrines, in the revelation of God to men, you have justly rejected the whole plan. But in the accomplishment of this object there is something lacking, which is of no small consequence.

You appear to have left the people without any clear ground of justification. Having taken away the righteousness of Christ imputed and received by faith, and yet left the righteousness of God to be received by faith, you have laid open no safe and unequivocal ground on which for the believer to make use of Christ. " But " how do we get this righteousness? By faith. Hence it is called, " the righteousness of faith; the righteousness which is by or " through faith." (Atonement, P. 13.) Now the Calvinist who maintains the doctrine of vicarious sufferings and obedience, and imputed righteousness, will not hesitate to acknowledge, that the righteousness of God is received by faith. The same will be granted by those who teach that justification is by the righteousness of Christ *applied* or *imparted*. In a word; faith is acknowledged by all professed christians, with whom I have been acquainted, as the *sine qua non* of the christian religion, without which it is impossible to please God. So that the Letters thus far afford no definitive information on which the mind can rest. If I believe in Christ and receive his righteousness, or the righteousness of God in him, one calls this receiving, *imputation;* another, to avoid that term and its offensive consequences, calls it, *application* or *impartation;* and what shall I call it? To avoid the terms and consequences of them both, as I intend it, I say, By or through faith, and leave them to apply their peculiar terms: but the subject matter is the same without farther explanation.

But the Letters have carried the subject some farther. " How do " we get the righteousness of God by or through faith? Because " by faith we are ingrafted into, or in Christ: and by this union with " him we become partakers of his nature, which is righteousness or " holiness. Therefore we are justified, *made* just and *declared* just, " or righteous by faith, without the deeds of the law." (Ibid.) And again; " How is he made unto us righteousness? By making us " righteous; for, as I have already shown, the branch ingrafted par- " takes of the nature of the vine; so they, who are in Christ Jesus, " are partakers of his divine nature, which is righteousness. This " is called " the righteousness of God—the righteousness of faith— " the righteousness which is of God by faith of Jesus Christ." (P. 9.) According to these statements then, justification is the fruit of holiness or righteousness; " that is (we are) made just and righteous, " even as he is righteous, and then declared so of God because we " are so." [P. 17.] This effect you have every where attributed to faith alone, or without carrying the matter any farther. But we may remember, that in all which the apostle hath said of justification by faith and without the deeds of the law, he hath never said *by faith alone*, nor ever excluded obedience to God according to the gospel, but ever enjoined it. " For in Jesus Christ neither circumcission " availeth any thing, nor uncircumcission; but faith which worketh " by love." And again; " Circumcission is nothing, and uncircum- " cission is nothing, but the keeping of the commandments of God." Now christians, though free from the Mosaic or ceremonial law are " not without law to God but under the law to Christ." (1 Cor. 9. 21.) Obedience therefore is the end of faith, the point to which it leads the man for justification and final salvation; " According to the " revelation of the mystery, which was kept secret since the world " began, but now is made manifest, and by the scriptures of the pro- " phets, according to the commandment of the everlasting God, " made known to all nations for the obedience of faith."

And the apostle John proposes a very different method for a man to be righteous and so called, from that by faith and there stopping— that of doing righteousness; " He that doeth righteousness is righ- " teous." Yet none were more swallowed up in faith than John. And this is quite consistent with what you have stated in your Letters, (P. 9.) " Therefore he is the end of the law; and answers it " completely to all believers; for " the righteousness of the law is " fulfilled in us (not for us) who walk not after the flesh but after the " Spirit." Thus these Letters lead to the very brink of the river of life, but, as if alarmed at its depth, would not come in; a river of waters which no man can pass, waters to swim in. You were then not far from the kingdom.

But is it not remarkable if at that day, when you stood in the blazing light of the revival, the apostolic light revived, you never conceived that Jesus Christ is our example, whom we are to follow in all things; seeing he so expressly taught, saying, " If any man will come after " me, let him deny himself, and take up his cross and follow me."

People talk of following Christ, and if they are admonished that certain things which they practise, are not after Christ, they immediately appeal to the law given to Adam, or to Moses, or to some other before Christ appeared, as if these laws or commandments were the rule of the life of Christians. But let us remember, that Jesus never taught the people to follow Adam, or Moses, or David, or Solomon, or any other who had been before him. So far from it that he said, " All that ever came before me are thieves and rob- " bers." (Jno. 10. 8.) It is commonly insisted that he meant false christs, or those who presumed to be the true Christ. But this is mere supposition; for we read of no false christs until the true Christ appeared. Men may mimic the works of God in some part, after they have appeared, but the counterfeit implies the pre-existence of the true. But all who ever came before him fell short of the mark, the doing of the will of God in all things; so that when he came he stood alone, and of the people there was none with him. Until he taught it, no man ever knew that it was necessary for him to take up his cross and deny himself, or that he must lose his life to save it: therefore saith he, Follow me. And as none before him knew the perfect way, the effect was accordingly; for saith he, on another occasion, " And no man hath ascended to heaven but he that " came down from heaven, even the Son of man who is in heaven." (Jno. 3. 13.) It is here alledged that he meant, no man in the flesh. But that is mere evasion, for a spiritual man, is a man, as well as a man in the flesh: besides he made no such reserve—He is the way.

Now when people profess to be christians, or followers of Christ, and use no more self-denial, and bear no cross beyond what was contained in the law of Moses, or in any law before Christ, they necessarily impose this as their belief, that Christ has done no more, by either example or precept, towards the extirpation of sin, than Moses, and that to follow Christ is no more than to follow Moses, nor indeed half so much, for he is the end of that expensive and burdensome yoke. So that all he seems to have done against the nature of sin, on that plan, is to have taken off those burdensome restraints from the flesh, and left it full indulgence in its own circle.

But if the righteousness of the law is fulfilled in us who walk not after the flesh but after the Spirit, it must be fulfilled by us, as those who take him for our example. For believers are not without law to God, but under the law to Christ. And thus the scripture is fulfilled; " He that saith he abideth in him, ought himself also so to walk even " as he walked " (1 Jno. 2. 6.) If then believers ought so to walk, those who do not, transgress the law of Christ, and are no more in him. Thus, if we pursue the doctrine of Christ and his apostles, we shall find, that while he disannulled the outward rituals of the law, which were only a shadow of things to come, and which were a yoke too grievous to be borne, he brought in the substance, and imposed a more grievous burden and death on the flesh, than it had ever felt before. No less than the death and destruction of the flesh, that the spirit might be saved. " And (accordingly) they that are Christ's have crucified the flesh with the affections and lusts." [Gal. 5. 24.]

The flesh had many indulgences in the law, which it cannot have in Christ: many things were lawful which are not christian. This shows that the law, or faith of Christ, makes the way much narrower and straiter than the law of Moses. Thus it was lawful to swear, but not christian: the words of Christ forbid it. It was lawful to resist evil, but not christian: [Matt. 5. 38, &c.] It was not lawful to commit adultery, or to covet another man's wife; yet it was lawful for a man to look on a woman to lust after her, even though she was of a strange nation, taken captive, and it was tolerable though the man had another wife before. But these things are all contrary to the faith or law of Christ: they are not christian. [Deut. 21. 10, to 17. Matt. 5. 27, 28.] These are a few particulars selected from many more, which I omit to avoid prolixity, which show that the law of Moses, though the greatest dispensation before Christ or his immediate forerunner John, fell far short of that strait and narrow way, which Christ taught in his example as well as in word: for he left us an example that we should follow his steps. Although many Jews might have lost their natural lives in defence of their law and religion, it was never known to them that whosoever would seek to save his life should lose it, and whosoever should lose his life for Christ's sake and the gospel's should preserve it. The great work of dying with Christ could not possibly be known, until he appeared and set the example.

By the law was the knowledge of sin to a certain length, and that far it was condemned; but in the root of sin, the flesh, which lusteth against the Spirit, and is contrary to it, and to which is justly ascribed the production of all sins, it never was condemned by any law, first or last, until Christ came. This is expressly that which the law could not do; and which remained for God to do in the mission of his own Son. " For God, sending his own Son in the likeness of sin-
" ful flesh, and on account of sin, condemned sin in the flesh; that
" which the law could not do, in that it was weak through the flesh;
" that the righteousness of the law might be fulfilled in us, who
" walk not after the flesh but after the Spirit."

It is commonly argued, that to live in the generation, with a lawfully married wife, is not to live after the flesh, and therefore, that to condemn the flesh, or sin in the flesh, it is not necessary to fix condemnation on that work or those propensities which lead that way. But let me ask, What other work or nature in the flesh could it be, which the law could not condemn? For if the law admitted to lust after a woman, it was only as preparatory to taking her to wife; and it was not possible for a man to forsake his father and mother and cleave to his wife, without it, in that day, neither is it in this. So that if the work of natural generation, lawfully or unlawfully, be consistent with the faith of Christ, he hath done nothing on that score more than the law could do and actually did. And should it be argued that the law admitted polygamy, but the faith of Christ condemns it; there appears no reason why the law *could not* have condemned that also, unless the same for which it could not condemn sin in the flesh in a single marriage. For polygamy was not the spirit of the law, it was only suffered so to be; but from the beginning it was not so. " And did not he make one? yet had he the re-
" sidue of the Spirit. And wherefore one? That he might seek a
" godly seed." [Mal. 2. 15.] But Christ did that which the law *could not* do, in that it was weak through the flesh. And why was it weak through the flesh? Because there was nothing in it but what was consistent with the life of the flesh. It had not a single precept to crucify the flesh; but it justified it; consisting only in meats and drinks and divers washings and *carnal ordinances* or *justifications of the flesh*. [See Address, P. 29.] The law, therefore, justifying the flesh could have no power to condemn it; or sin in it;

for while the flesh was protected, the sin in it would find an harbor. But Christ did that which the law could not do, or the impossibility of the law, [το αδυνατον του νομου]: he condemned sin in the flesh. And how did he condemn it? He gave it no patronage, no license, neither married nor participated in marriage or its works: he lived in the flesh, a life of perfect virgin purity, not stained with its lusts. And why did he condemn it? That the righteousness of the law, which it could not fulfil in the Mosaic dispensation might be fulfilled in us, who walk as he did, not after the flesh but after the Spirit—a life in the flesh, unstained by its lusts. "For whosoever looketh on "a woman to lust after [desire] her, hath committed adultery with "her already in his heart." And now let me ask again; In what other work or way *could not* the law have condemned sin in the flesh?

Observe; The righteousness of the law is fulfilled in those who walk after, or according to the Spirit, but not in those who walk after, or according to the flesh. Now the Lord Jesus Christ is that Spirit. [2 Cor. 3. 17.] For "The first man Adam was made a liv- "ing soul, [a rational animal] the last Adam a quickening Spirit. The "first man is of the earth, earthy; the second man is the Lord from "heaven, as is the earthy, such are they also that are earthy; and as "is the heavenly, such are they also that are heavenly." Those therefore who walk in the ways, or do the works of the first Adam, or which are peculiar to him and his order, walk after the flesh. For this is the order of the first Adam; "A man shall leave his father "and his mother, and be joined to his wife, and they shall be one "flesh; therefore," said Jesus, "they are no more twain but one "flesh." But those who walk in the ways of Christ, walk after the Spirit, and leave the order of the first Adam; for the law, or order of Christ is, That except a man forsake all that he hath, and hate his father and his mother, and his wife and his children, and his brethren and his sisters, yea, and his own life also, or the flesh and all its relations, he cannot be his disciple. So again, "He that is joined to an "harlot is one body: for two (saith he) shall be one flesh." This therefore is according to the order of the first Adam, and they are as certainly one as the man and his wife. But according to the second Adam there is no one flesh in the case, "But he that is joined "to the Lord is one Spirit."

On the whole; it is evident that Christ hath left us an example, and requireth us to follow him, in preference to all, and separately from all who walk in a different order. It may with propriety be asked; If we by faith receive the righteousness of God, or divine nature, according to your writings, what doth it avail us, or rather, What evidence can we have that we have received it, unless we live as he lived and walk even as he walked? "For as many as are *led* "*by the Spirit of God they are the sons of God*," and none else. But it remains invincibly true, that as many as do the works of the first Adam, are led by his spirit, and therefore serve the flesh.

An unhappy cause will produce an unhappy effect. With all the superior discoveries of truth, during the Kentucky revival, which

indeed were not inconsiderable, and concentrated for a time, mainly among the people of that society to which you are attached, I must use the freedom to remark, that they have made shipwreck of faith and a good conscience, on the same rock with others; that of undertaking to serve two masters, Christ and Adam, or the Spirit and the flesh. Hence it is, that the work of salvation cannot be completed, nor advanced beyond certain limits. Neither can the people retain what they gain; for as new wine put into old bottles will burst the bottles, and the wine will run out, so the power and gift of God are wasted, being consumed on their lusts. " For the flesh lusteth a-
" gainst the Spirit, and the Spirit against the flesh; and these are con-
" trary the one to the other; so that ye cannot do the things that ye
" would." (Gal. 5. 17.)

It is a plausible argument with some, that Jesus Christ did not forbid to marry. But however plausible, it shows great weakness in the faith of Christ and ignorance of his Spirit. The Spirit of the gospel is not ministered by commandments and prohibitions only, but by evidence, faith and choice, telling what is the way and leaving the people to make their choice, after hearing the consequences on each side. " If any man will come after me, let him deny himself, and
" take up his cross, and follow me. For whosoever will save his life
" shall lose it: and whosoever will lose his life for my sake, shall
" find it." (Matt. 16. 24, 25.) Jesus never, that we know of, forbade the people to circumcise; but his apostle taught that it was one side of the faith of Christ. " Behold, I Paul say unto you, that if ye be
" circumcised Christ shall profit you nothing." (Gal. 5. 2.) So neither did Jesus ever, that we know of, expressly forbid to marry; but he taught that marriage belonged to another order than his, that is, to the world; but of his disciples he said expressly, that they are no more of the world than he; " They are not of the world, even as I
" am not of the world." (Jno. 17. 16.) The disciples of Christ therefore do not marry, because they are not of the world but of Christ. " The children of this world marry, and are given in mar-
" riage; but they who shall be [Greek, are] accounted worthy to ob-
" tain that world, and the resurrection from the dead, neither mar-
" ry nor are given in marriage." If therefore God's children are accounted worthy to obtain that world and the resurrection *from* the dead, it is conclusively proved, that they neither marry nor are given in marriage. And they are no losers by it. Paul hath showed what is the good way, that " It is good for a man not to touch a woman." (1 Cor. 7. 1.) And, notwithstanding all the permissions or forbearances, which he exercised towards those carnal people, who were not able to bear sound and naked truth, (3. 23.) because they were yet carnal and walked as men, and also had the grossest of fornication among them, (5. 1.) he maintains this proposition, as that to which he would have all men come; " For I would that all men were even as I myself," (7. 7.) and as most conformable to the Lord. " And this
" I speak [V. 35.] for your own profit; not that I may cast a snare
" upon you, but for that which is comely, [suitable to the christian

OBSERVATIONS. 453

" profession,] and happily corresponding with the Lord, without vio-
" lence:" the common reading, "That ye may attend upon the Lord
without distraction," being a forced translation and unnatural. But
he maintains his proposition; for when he hath considered the case
through, he saith; " So then, he that giveth in marriage doeth well;
" but he that giveth not in marriage doeth better". " But she [the
" widow] is happier if she so abide, after my judgment: and I think
" also that I have the Spirit of God." Thus he neither commands
nor forbids, but shows what is the best way, and leaves them to make
their own choice according to their own faith, for the time being.

Some acknowledge that the best way is to not marry; that such
have the advantage over the married, in living a life of devotion to
God in the Spirit, and yet persist in the married life; by which they
prove to all men, that they esteem the flesh more than the Spirit—
the pleasures of sense more than Christ. For no matter what the
advantages of the unmarried life are, whether convenience or holiness,
or both, the benefit is to the spirit; those therefore who forego that
benefit for the married life, are practically of those who love pleasures more than God, and are unworthy of Christ. But once more;

The introduction of the gospel of Christ was undeniably a new
dispensation, on different principles from any before, and more into
the Spirit. Nothing therefore can claim any place or part in this because of its having a place in the former: the express authority of
revelation is necessary for the introduction of every thing. Consequently, instead of demanding proof that Christ excluded the fleshly
rite of marriage, or the work of natural generation, from any place
in the christian church, it belongs to those who believe that manner
of life to comport with the spiritual kingdom of Christ, or the life
of a spiritual man in Christ, who hath crucified the flesh with its affections and lusts, to furnish proof by the authority of Christ, that he
hath introduced marriage, which is a civil right of the world, into his
kingdom, which is not of the world. The demand for proof is en
the other side; especially considering his own example set for all
christians, and the many things spoken to the contrary of christians'
marrying.

But it is not my intention to dwell largely on this subject in this
place. Those who are led more forcibly, by the determination of
their own will and their own inclinations, than by the will of God,
will not likely be easy to satisfy with arguments that they are wrong;
while on the other hand, those who seek to serve God more than to
please the flesh, or who practically esteem salvation above all other
things, are easily convicted. Every honest and reflecting man will
acknowledge, that his strongest inducements to marry, have ever
been his own propensities. In this therefore he does his own will
more than the will of God; consequently, in that matter at least,
is contrary to Christ, who came down from heaven not to do his own
will, but the will of him who sent him.

But on this ground have all the churches stumbled, to whom the
mystery of iniquity has not been revealed sitting in the temple of

God, or the abomination of desolation standing where it ought not. The fleshly work of generation is kept among those who profess to be of the regeneration. And with them the work of salvation can never rise beyond a certain limit ; it cannot be completed, neither can it continue whereunto it has often attained. Neither will it ever be better with any people, until they receive and obey the faith of Christ in his second appearing, consuming the man of sin with the Spirit of his mouth, and destroying him with the brightness of his coming. How cometh it to pass that revivals cease so soon, among those too who make the most vigorous efforts to promote and continue them ? Is God unwilling to save souls ? Or is the death, the bane of godliness in the people, an idol, a lust which they have no feelings to renounce.? People may plead their own disobedience and backwardness in other respects as the cause of the declensions of revivals. If the cause lies any where else, would to God ye would agree, who are friendly to Christ, and remove it out of the way, that the gospel might have free course and be glorified. But ye will object that ye cannot come to this agreement. What ? not two or three in all the land to agree in so important a matter? Then it is time to cease talking of being christians, and to acknowledge ye are not built on the true foundation stone ; for they who are, agree in all such matters, having one faith and one spirit, and the work of salvation increases all the time, and all who are willing to have salvation by the way of the cross, find it. But I proceed to a somewhat different subject.

For the want of taking the proper grounds of justification, the obedience of faith, and Christ whom to believe and obey as an example as well as a teacher, in all things, not excepting the rejection of the flesh, or natural generation, from the life of a christian, you are unable to come out clearly in the apostolic language and confidence. " We are of God: he that knoweth God heareth us ; he that " is not of God heareth not us. Hereby know we the Spirit of truth " and the Spirit of error." " And we know that we are of God, and " the whole world lieth in wickedness ;" or in the wicked one ; [εν τω πονηρω ;] that is, in the devil. But this you can never do, neither the people in your faith, nor in any other, until they receive and obey the faith of Christ in his second appearing, for reasons which you will find in the sequel.

The testimony is gone out, that Christ has made, and is now making to those who look for him, his second appearing without sin to salvation. This you know, is the faith, and consequently the testimony, of the people with whom I stand connected. And we are always willing to have the matter thoroughly investigated ; and if on a fair trial we cannot offer better evidence for our faith than any other people for theirs, we are willing to fall to the ground with the rest. For ;

Connected with the foregoing is this, That all those churches which have not received and obeyed the faith of Christ in his second appearing, are essentially wanting in respect to that gospel which is the power of God to salvation. And it is fair reasoning, that a former dispensation cannot have the light and power of the succeeding one. Thus the Jews with all their prophets and their writings, could not attain to the knowledge of salvation, or that light and power which was in the christian dispensation, nor even to the light of the short intermediate dispensation of John the baptist, until it was opened in its own day. It is conclusively true, that after the introduction and promulgation of a new dispensation, no people who have the knowledge of it, can retain that degree of light and power, or that measure of the work of salvation which they had, if any, unless they unite with the new and increasing work. Accordingly, the Jews could no longer keep their justification by the observation of their law, after Christ had made known his mission, even though they did not believe in him, nor know who he was. For if they had known him, or the wisdom of God, they would not have crucified the Lord of glory. (1 Cor. 2. 8.) " And now, brethren," said Peter, " I wot that through ignorance ye did it, as did also your rulers." (Acts 3. 17.) " But all these things," said Jesus, " will they do unto " you for my name's sake, because they know not him that sent me. " If I had not come and spoken to them they had not had sin; but " now they have no cloak for their sin. He that hateth me, hateth " my Father also. If I had not done among them the works which " none other man did, they had not had sin; but now they have both " seen and hated both me and my Father." " And this is the con- " demnation that light is come into the world, and men loved dark- " ness rather than light, because their deeds were evil."

Accordingly, we have uniformly found, that wherever the testimony which we have received is made known, those who reject it are not able to retain that measure of the work of salvation which they had, where they had any, although in many cases they did not really believe that it was in truth the testimony of God. But people may reject the gospel to their condemnation, when their faith is not unwavering. Many see so far into the gospel, as to discover the sure means of death to their nature and their carnal delights, by the cross of Christ, and evade farther conviction, if possible, and often by the most disingenuous subterfuges, refusing to give testimony its proper weight. " The publicans and the harlots," said Jesus, " go into the " kingdom of God before you. For John came to you in the way " of righteousness, and ye believed him not; but the publicans and " the harlots believed him; and ye, when ye had seen it, repented " not afterward that ye might believe." (Matt. 21. 31, 32.) Many acknowledge that the testimony is rational and fair; but they cannot feel reconciled to the death of the old man which it contains, and so stumble at the cross being disobedient. Thus after the cure of the lame man, by Peter and John, the Jews evaded conviction by a very unwarrantable method, " Saying, What shall we do to these " men? for that indeed a notable miracle hath been done by them is " manifest to all them that dwell in Jerusalem; and we cannot deny " it. But that it spread no farther among the people, let us straitly "threaten them that they speak henceforth to no man in this name. "And they called them, and commanded them not to speak at all, "nor teach in the name of Jesus." (Acts 4. 16 to 18.

But to open this subject more fully. It is acknowledged that Jesus and his apostles foretold an apostacy in the church; that false christs and false prophets should arise; or, that anti-christ should come. When the testimony of Christ in his second appearing was opened in this country, by its first witnesses to us, the cry was raised, that these are the deceivers, that these are the anti-christ who was to come. But without taking the time in this place, to delineate the character of anti-christ in full, and show the contrast, a few observations will be sufficient to show the fallacy of such clamors.

In the first place, Anti-christ was to deny the true Christ, or to deny that he had come in the flesh. [1 Jno. 2. 22.] "Who is a liar, "but he that denieth that Jesus is the Christ? He is anti-christ that "denieth the Father and the Son." And [4. 2, 3.] "Hereby know "ye the Spirit of God; Every spirit that confesseth that Jesus Christ "is come in the flesh is of God; and every spirit that confesseth not "that Jesus Christ is come in the flesh is not of God; and this is "that spirit of anti-christ whereof ye have heard that it should "come." But these people do not deny that Jesus Christ has come in the flesh; so far from it, that this was then, and remains to be, the very ground of opposition; because Christ having come in the flesh, first or last, makes it necessary that the flesh, or body, be devoted as a sacred temple to his use in all who name his name, and that the affections and desires of the flesh should be denied and crucified. This presented the cross. And short of such a testimony and such a cross, no spirit or people can have any claim to their being of God, or being those people who confess that Jesus Christ has come in the flesh." "What? know ye not that your body is the temple of the "Holy Ghost which is in you, which ye have of God, and ye are not "your own? for ye are bought with a price: therefore glorify God "in your body and in your spirit which are God's." "I beseech "you, therefore, brethren, by the mercies of God, that ye present "your bodies a living sacrifice, holy, acceptable to God, which is "your reasonable service. And be not conformed to this world." (Ro. 12. 1, 2.) "And if Christ be in you, the body is dead because "of sin; but the spirit is life because of righteousness. But if the "Spirit of him that raised up Jesus from the dead dwell in you, he "that raised up Christ from the dead shall also quicken your mortal "bodies by his Spirit that dwelleth in you. Therefore, brethren, "we are debtors, not to the flesh, to live after the flesh. For if ye "live after the flesh ye shall die; but if ye through the Spirit do "mortify the deeds of the body ye shall live. For as many as are "led by the Spirit of God, they are the sons of God." "And they "that are Christ's have crucified the flesh, with its affections and "lusts." And much more to the same purpose. It is manifest that the verbal acknowledgment of Jesus Christ, or of his having come in the flesh, is not proportionate to the apostle's design; for multi-

tudes do that, and the subjects and ministers of anti-christ as freely as any, who fall into the rank of those, " Who profess that they know " God, but in works deny him, being abominable and disobedient, " and to every good work reprobate." (Tit. 1. 19.) Again;
Anti-christ was to be held in great admiration and esteem by all the world. " And all the world wondered after the beast. And they " worshipped the beast, saying, Who is like unto the beast? who " is able to make war with him? And all that dwell upon the " earth shall worship him, whose names are not written in the " book of life of the Lamb slain from the foundation of the world." (Rev. 13. 3, 4, 8.) But the testimony of Christ's second appearing and the witnesses of it, are rejected with the most cordial and universal disapprobation of any thing ever known on earth by the name of christianity, except the first ministration of the same Holy Spirit. The character of anti-christ, therefore, will not apply to the present testimony. Farther;

The spirit of anti-christ, or man of sin, the son of perdition, which is confessedly the same, is described as one " Who opposeth and " exalteth himself above all that is called God, or that is worshipped; " so that he, as God, sitteth in the temple of God, shewing himself " that he is God." (2 Thes. 2. 4.) But the people of whom I speak, acknowledge and practise the worship of one God, who is the Father of our Lord Jesus Christ; and the deficiency which they discover in all others is, that they fall short of the true and perfect worship of the one true God, in the faith of his Son Jesus Christ. But say some, that is a true mark; ye prove yourselves to be anti-christ, and that ye presume to be God, by saying that none else are right, for ye exalt yourselves above all. But the apostle John did not reason so when he said, " We know that we are of God and the whole " world lieth in wickedness, or in the wicked one." And again, " We are of God: he that knoweth God heareth us; he that is not " of God heareth not us. Hereby know we the Spirit of truth and " the spirit of error." It is preposterous reasoning indeed, that I must call myself God, because I maintain that I have found the only perfect way to the Father. By parity of reason, all who profess to have found the only way to the Father, which is Christ, (and there is but one,) thereby presume to be God.

But the witnesses of the testimony of which I speak, do not sit in the temple of God, according to the understanding of the people in common, the people themselves being judges; for they are not acknowledged by the denominations as being of the church of Christ at all. And if the testimony which they bear, or the spirit which is in them, be the spirit of anti-christ, these witnesses and people are the only temple or church of God, remaining on earth. Thus the above objection destroys itself by its absurdity. Once more;

The time of anti-christ's appearing was in the apostles' days and the time immediately succeeding. " For the mystery of iniquity," saith Paul, " doth already work." (2 Thes. 2. 7.) And John hath announced that " Even now already is it in the world." And again;

"Little children, it is the last time: and as ye have heard that anti christ shall come, even now are there many anti-christs; whereby we know that it is the last time." (1 Jno. 4. 3. and 2. 18.) But the present testimony had its rise, more than twelve hundred and sixty years afterwards, at the time when the reign of anti-christ began to be diminished and destroyed. The period of his reign was twelve hundred and sixty; accordingly the sentiment is extensively embraced, and that for many years back, and with good reason too, according to the prophecies, that the seventh angel hath begun to sound his trumpet, and consequently, that the dominion of the beast hath begun to decline. On the whole therefore, the charge of anti-christ and apostacy, against the people who testify that Christ hath made his second appearance, is groundless and unjust.

But to discuss this subject profitably, one thing more is worthy to be noticed; which is to inquire into the extent and degree of the apostacy under anti-christ—whether it was total or partial. This is an important question, attended with the most momentous consequences. For professors in common, believing the apostacy only partial, and that Christ has always had a true church on earth, endued with the power of salvation; (for without that it is not the church of Christ; as it is written; " I will place salvation in Zion " for Israel my glory;" and again; " It shall come to pass that " whosoever shall call on the name of the Lord shall be delivered: " for in Mount Zion and in Jerusalem shall be deliverance, as the " Lord hath said, and in the remnant whom the Lord shall call." And where the true church is, which is the ground and pillar of the truth, there is the true gospel which is the power of God to salvation;) I say, people believing the apostacy to have been only partial, have hitherto applied all their wisdom and strength to build on the old dispensation; whereas if the apostacy was total, and the corruption and spirit of anti-christ universal, so that there was a time when there was not a church on earth, in the order of Christ, and possessing the power of salvation, their labors will prove to be abortive, until Christ the true foundation be again revealed from heaven, and they come to the knowledge of it, and build on him in that last revelation. For it is evident that that which God only can give, or make known, if once lost, can never be recovered again, unless by another revelation of God, or a manifestation of the same power and gift of revelation. A man can receive nothing of that kind except it be given him from heaven. And to build on that which is lost, or which hath passed away, must, to the understanding of all men, be insufficient.

The belief of the people with whom I stand connected is, that the apostacy was total and universal; insomuch that in that period, although many honestly sought the way, whom God noticed accordingly, and kept in reserve until the opening of full redemption, yet there was no true church or body of Christ in order, and possessing the power of salvation; the true way of God being unknown for a time. This being admitted, the necessary consequence is, that all churches not built on Christ in his second appearing, or revelation, are either in the full government of anti-christ, or, to say the best, under the influence of some degree of preparatory work, leading them out by degrees, that they may be in readiness for salvation when the way is opened to them. Let us now inquire a little into the evidence of this faith.

The very description of anti-christ, or the man of sin, as sitting in the temple of God, showing himself that he is God, and of his there continuing until the Lord shall consume him with the Spirit of his mouth and destroy him with the brightness of his coming, argues strongly, or rather conclusively, in defence of what is stated on this subject. For, in the first place; While the man of sin was there Christ had no place, unless he should divide the government with the beast. But this could not be; " For what fellowship hath right-
" eousness with unrighteousness? and what communion hath light
" with darkness? And what concord hath Christ with belial? or
" what part hath he that believeth with an infidel? or what agree-
" ment hath the temple of God with idols? for ye are the temple of
" the living God; as God hath said, I will dwell in them, and walk
" in them; and I will be their God, and they shall be my people.
" Wherefore come out from among them, and be ye separate, saith
" the Lord, and touch not the unclean thing; and I will receive you,
" and will be a Father to you, and ye shall be my sons and daughters,
" saith the Lord Almighty." [2 Cor. 6. 14, to 18.] These then are the conditions on which God will accept a people—to come out from them that do evil—to be separated to God—to touch no unclean thing: and these things are inconsistent with anti-christ's having any place in them.

This sitting in the temple of God was also universal; for had there been any part on earth where Christ had abode, and consequently anti-christ had been excluded, that would have been the temple, and the man of sin would not have sat in the temple and there exalted himself above all; for he would have felt, and the people would have felt it, that one in the temple had power over him—Devils know the holy One of God, who he is. Besides, that part where anti-christ reigned would have been the world in distinction from the temple. For the *world* worshipped the beast; and in this case the temple is included, because when the church had lost the power of salvation, or Spirit of Christ, and the man of sin reigned, the power of the holy people was scattered, and the truth trodden to the earth, and all were world together in the governing principle. Besides; His sitting there until the coming of the Lord, proves that after he fairly had got possession, there could be no more a true church, in the order and power of Christ, until his second appearing. And this agrees with that saying of Christ; " Nevertheless when the son of man " cometh shall he find faith on the earth?" A question proposed not to receive an answer, as all may see, but to show the extent and depth of the apostacy, and fix truth on the mind with more weight than could be done by simple assertion, as well as to leave the subject under that prophetic vail which was often expedient.

Jesus also describes the apostacy in such language as plainly to show, that all were totally corrupted, and none knew the true Christ. "Then if *any man* shall say unto you, Lo, here is Christ, or there ; "believe it not. For there shall arise false christs, and false pro- "phets, and shall show great signs and wonders; insomuch that if "possible, they shall deceive the very elect." [Matt. 24. 23, 24.] This was the time of anti-christ; and it is evident that none really knew the true Christ; for had not that been the case, Jesus could not have told them not to believe or follow any of them ; for they who know the true Christ are of the truth, and are therefore to be believed and followed; as said Paul, Be ye followers of me. But no one knowing him, they said, in the rage of their ignorance and uncertainty, *Lo, here*, and *lo there ; he is in the desert*, and *he is in the secret chamber.* And so do the false prophets to this day, in their ignorance and uncertainty about the safe path ; sending the people who come to inquire of them, (expecting them to be ministers of Christ,) what they shall do to be saved, to seek him in secret, instead of ministering Christ to them. Those were the days of which Jesus said expressly ; " Ye shall desire to see one of the days of the "Son of man and ye shall not see it ;" [Luk. 17. 22.] and without a day of the Son of man there could be no true church or gospel.

But, said Jesus, " Jerusalem shall be trodden down of the Gen- "tiles, until the times of the Gentiles be fulfilled." [Luk. 21. 24.] This could not have related merely to the Jerusalem of the Jews ; but must have related mainly to the spiritual Jerusalem, or church, of which the first was a figure ; for immediately after the tribulation of those days the Son of man is seen, and christians are called upon to lift up their heads expecting speedy redemption. " And "then shall they see the Son of man coming in a cloud with power "and great glory. And when these things begin to come to pass, "then look up, and lift up your heads; for your redemption draweth "nigh." [v. 27, 28.] But the time of the redemption of christians is in his second appearing. " And if I go and prepare a place for "you, I will come again, and receive you to myself; that where I "am there ye may be also," " And to them that look for him shall "he appear the second time without sin to salvation."

Parallel with this prophecy is that in the Apocalypse, [11. 1, &c.] " And the angel stood saying, Rise, and measure the temple of God, "and the altar, and them that worship therein, But the court which "is without the temple leave out, and measure it not; for it is given "to the Gentiles ; and the holy city shall be trodden under foot forty "and two months. And I will give power to my two witnesses, and "they shall prophesy a thousand two hundred and three-score days, "clothed in sackcloth. These are the two olive trees, and the two "candlesticks, standing before the God of all the earth." It has been argued that only the outer court was given to the Gentiles. But what then ? The holy city was trodden under foot without exception. And, to follow the metaphor, it is manifest, that while the Gentiles had the outer court in full possession, (for it was given to them,) there was no access to the inner. Those who were safe in might stay, but could take in no more. They who had received and kept the true faith were preserved from the corruption which crept in, and kept by the power of God through faith to the final salvation, ready to be revealed in the last time, or second appearing of Christ; but none more could attain to that same faith until it was again revealed. Accordingly, the temple of God was no more opened in heaven, until after the sounding of the seventh angel, bringing on the judgment. " And the temple of God was opened in heaven, and there was seen in his temple the ark of his testament."

But it has also been argued, that the two witnesses were the true church, and that as they continued to prophesy during the 1260 days, the church therefore did exist. That these two witnesses were the Spirit of God, who also dwelleth in the church when in its order and power, will not be contested, being the two olive trees and the two candlesticks which stand before the God of the whole earth, the two having respect to the revelation of God to men in the first appearance of Christ in the male, and the second in the female. But the propriety of representing the church in order and having the power of salvation, as being clothed in sackcloth, remains to be shown, or rather to be rejected as absurd; the church being always in a prosperous state when it hath Christ in it. Accordingly, through the long period of darkness, many witnesses arose, influenced, no doubt, by the true Spirit, who testified against the errors and corruptions of the times, but could not show the substance otherwise than in prophecy, and the more pure their testimony was, to the greater distance they were secluded from the only remaining church on earth— that which had the form but denied the power. These two witnesses therefore, so far from being the true church, or even having any access to the true church on earth, were turned out of doors to go in slackcloth during that period, while they made war on the usurpers of the temple to regain it in the end.

But admitting that those two witnesses were the true church they also had to be killed. " And when they shall have finished their tes-
" timony, the beast that ascendeth out of the bottomless pit shall make
" war against them, and shall overcome them and kill them. And their
" dead bodies shall lie in the street of the great city which spiritually
" is called Sodom and Egypt, where also our Lord was crucified.
" And they of the people, and kindreds, and nations, shall see their
" dead bodies three days and an half, and shall not suffer their dead
" bodies to be put in graves." Where then was the church when the only remaining witnesses were killed? It could have no existence even on that plan, until the Spirit of life from God entered into them again, or until the revelation of God began again to be restored, which was introductory to the sounding of the seventh trumpet in the coming of Christ to judgment. Thus as the Christ of God was killed, or put to death in the flesh and revived in the Spirit, previ-

ously to the giving of the Holy Spirit for the building and forming of the gospel church in his first appearing, so in his second appearing the same Christ, or two witnesses, as aforesaid, were killed, being put to death in the people who bore the testimony, and after three days and an half revived again, the testimony of God having then revived with a deeper work than ever, preparatory to the giving of the Holy Spirit, or the coming of Christ in his spiritual kingdom, to be built up for ever. But it is no doubt correct to consider the three days and a half, the same time, as the forty and two months, during which these witnesses prophesied clothed in sackcloth. But they were killed ; and had no continuance to build the church in the order and power of salvation. All they could do in that time was to bear testimony ; and as they finished their testimony from time to time, they were killed. And the representation is sufficiently strong to confirm the fact, that no church existed in order, or having the power of salvation, during those 42 months, or 1260 years.

The result then, of our inquiry must be, according to the few things here stated, to which more might be added if consistent with the present design, that the apostacy and corruption, during the reign of anti-christ, were universal and total; so that although many rose up from time to time, and testified against the prevailing errors, none were able to stand, or to support the unity of the Spirit in one body, at all on the earth; for the beast made war with the saints and overcame them. It must therefore necessarily follow, as before stated, that all those churches which are not built on the second revelation of Christ, are one side of the foundation, and are lacking in all respects to that gospel which is the power of God to salvation ; although among many of them there may often be a good degree of the power of God, as the voice of the Spirit of life from God, which has again entered into the witnesses, which serves as a preparatory work like the ministry of John, to prepare the way for Christ in his kingdom : for this is God's manner of working.

And that this is the true state of the churches, is proved by painful experience, not only in their not being able to keep their revivals, and the degree of power which they once had, but by another concomitant and universal inability to minister necessary and competent relief to souls who come inquiring what they must do to be saved. This is the case with them all, without the exception of a solitary case. Some acknowledge it openly, and plead that it is the prerogative of God only, in, as they say, his own time : as if his time were not now. " Behold now is the accepted time ; behold, now is the " day of salvation ;" and again ; " To day, if ye will hear his voice " harden not your hearts." Others say, They are able by the help of God, as they speak, to give sufficient instructions, but God must accompany the word with his power, or it will be of no force. Because, say they, Paul may plant and Apolos may water, but God giveth the increase. As if the gospel itself were not the power of God to salvation, or the very word of power from God ; or as if the increase were any the less ascribed to God by its being the genuine fruit of the true gospel, ministered, received and obeyed: the gospel is of God.

But others maintain that the fault rests with the people, who, though some of them inquire, are not willing to be saved on God's terms. No doubt resisting the Holy Spirit, or the truth, will prevent the most genuine gospel from producing its desirable effects. But this is not the case of which I speak; there are many swift witnesses against the societies of people who are called christian, and have not received the faith of Christ in his second appearing, that none of their best preachers or brightest christians, are able to direct souls in the way to God, or in other words, to preach to them Christ, to the satisfying of their judgment and conscience, let their inquiries be ever so sincere, or their efforts ever so violent. But the best they can do, and farthest they can go, is, when they have given all their counsel, and used all their endeavors, to leave the matter, as they say, with God; as if the ministers of Christ had not Christ to minister, or were not sent to do his work, notwithstanding that God hath made them able ministers of the new testament, or covenant, not of the letter but of the Spirit, that is, of Christ, for " the Lord is that Spi-" rit. And where the Spirit of the Lord is there is liberty." [2 Cor. 3. 6, 17.] This sentence; *Now the Lord is that Spirit*, hath direct relation to the words, *Not of the letter but of the Spirit;* the intermediate verses being a parenthetical digression, as was common with Paul. I say; sometimes they charge it on the inquirers who cannot get salvation, who are also ignorant enough to take the blame, and clear God, as they speak; as if that were any exculpation of the character, or name of God, after all the fair and unreserved promises in the gospel to those who seek, to leave souls under condemnation, and finally in damnation, because they cannot get salvation, neither are able by any means to find in themselves the cause which prevents them, nor to put it away if found. But had they true ministers of Christ to preach to them, they could find the cause, and if they chose, an adequate method to remove it.

All these pleas, and all others, which any people can use, for their own exculpation, who call themselves christians, and are at any loss, to tell honest inquirers, at any time, to the satisfying of their judgment and conscience, the way of eternal life, without any insurmountable difficulty attending it, unavoidably accuse those who make them, of the belief, that the power of God to salvation is a power one side of the gospel and distinct from it, thus making the gospel a lie and God a liar; for according to his authority, it is the power of God to salvation. Such also, to be consistent, must believe in absolute and particular election: because there is no other principle according to which any man may not find salvation where the gospel is preached.

All these professors, however, can borrow the words of holy men out of the scriptures, (or oftener steal them, conscious that they do not fill up the character, nor possess the same power of the gospel which dictated those words,) and say; " Believe in the Lord Jesus

"Christ, and thou shalt be saved and thy house;" and "He that believeth and is baptized shall be saved;" and the like. But these sayings have not the desired effect. For though they can borrow the words of those holy men at their pleasure, they cannot communicate the same in power, so as to beget faith in the people and set them in order for eternal life when they believe. And even when one among them has received, or experienced what they call religion, he cannot tell another how to get it: I speak of these, you may know, who believe that religion is a living principle.

But it will be argued that this statement is not correct; for this is not always the case with those professed christians; often their ministers preach, and the people believe, and receive the very same powerful religion which is preached. A man can without doubt minister that which he hath in his heart. Therefore in times of revivals there are many instances of this kind, which are a good pattern of the true gospel. But as before stated, this power they are not able to keep; which proves, that it is at best, only as new wine in old bottles, therefore it runneth out and the bottles perish. After a time they become dry and formal, and can help no soul. And not only so; but in the best times, and warmest revivals, when the power is flying from soul to soul, and from faith to faith with great success, many inquire the way who cannot find it, and none can tell them; which shows in their best times, that they are lacking in respect to that treasure of gospel knowledge and power, necessary to that perfect gospel, which is the power of God to salvation to *every one* who believeth, and hath also in it, the power of begetting faith in the hearers. Hence it comes to pass in such times, that some of those who believe as clearly and firmly as any others, in the ministrations of those times, can neither give nor receive any satisfactory evidence of eternal life. This could not be where the true gospel is preached, unless by known and wilful disobedience. But farther yet, censorious as it may appear, it is true, that in the best of times among those professors, none of them experience that work of grace which abidingly maintains its ground with unshaken confidence that they are the children of God and in the way of eternal life They have their doubts and fears, and do not hold fast the beginning of their confidence stedfast to the end, as those who are partakers with Christ. (Heb. 3. 14.) Generally the most dishonest and least enlightened have the least trouble about their condition; and when the power is greatly abated many can become professors, who could make no stand in the heat of a revival. And the confidence of many, not to say the major part, is built on the bare assertions of another. Their preachers and others tell them that to experience certain exercises, is conversion; and on these they build; and that is about all they know. "But they, measuring themselves by themselves, and "comparing themselves among themselves, are not wise." (2 Cor. 10. 12.)

In this situation I found the churches before I found the everlasting gospel. There had been a very great and general revival. The

OBSERVATIONS.

people of different denominations were more or less under its influence. Converts had been numerous and their exercises extraordinary; convincing and alarming to the beholders, and marvellous in their nature and appearances; with which you are not unacquainted. Those amongst us who followed the light of God, ministered in that revival, and were not held in bondage by the traditions of men, or the comments of human wisdom, received from time to time, renewed and increasing light from God, opening their understanding, to understand the scriptures on one subject or another. Agreement in sentiments became great, though far from perfection; as that was not the perfecting work, but sent before to break in pieces the old and prepare the way for the new. Yet forbearance and fellowship, among those of different tenets, abounded to an admiration. And the testimony, or prophecy was, That the day of the Lord, or Millennium, was at hand, and that that revival would never cease until that day should commence.

We began to learn, in contradistinction from all the received traditions, that it is the privilege and the character of a christian, to live free from sin; and many aimed to put it into practice, but power was wanting; although some got so far as to be almost persuaded, and on occasions to assert with great boldness, that they had attained to it. But in a short time, by painful experience, they would find to the contrary, and in a few days, or perhaps hours, be (I knew for one) almost in black despair of ever being saved. We also began to learn, that the work of God in Christ is an increasing work to the perfect day; and that by the true gospel of Christ and in him, there is access to the Holy of Holies, and that this access is the privilege of all true believers. In preaching publicly on these topics, which I saw as it were through a vail, I have seemed to myself as it were on the threshold. But as yet there was no entrance, though I scarcely knew why; for though I believed, or rather knew the lack was in me, I found no way to get it removed. And O to be enlarged was my cry; and to be delivered from the spirit of bondage again to fear, and to be freed from all the fetters of sin and darkness which surrounded me—But no escape yet. My distress and pain increased; though sometimes I seemed to myself almost ready to be delivered. We had begun to believe (I can say for one,) that in a true mission of a minister of Christ, the gospel would be so clear and intelligible, that all could understand it, and a minister could teach it as correctly and as readily as a teacher of letters could teach his pupil to say his lesson. And it was my understanding that I never could be a true minister of the gospel, until I could stand in such near relation and communion with Christ, that I could minister the gospel in that direct and intelligible clearness, that any one could receive it who would. In connection with this we also began to believe, that where the gospel does not flourish, the defect lies primarily and principally in the ministry. Thus when Jesus had any thing against any of the churches in Asia, it was primarily charged against the angel, or minister.

These, with many other serious truths, we began to learn in that day. And we labored in sore travail of spirit to get forward. But many began to find themselves at the end of their journey, until something farther should be made known. Some traveled from place to place, wherever they could hear of, or hope to see, a greater or deeper work of God than they had yet found. Some beginning to despair of ever finding salvation, and some using the most vigorous efforts, in a firm and full faith that God would increase his work and bring on the latter day of glory. The parts where I lived were visited from a great distance in quest of clearer light; while during the time I was in great anxiety to see some of my brethren in the ministry, who lived at a distance, to know if they could help me any farther in the way of God. In this situation I spent many doleful nights and sorrowful days; yet not without some cheering support from God. Generally, when ministering in the public, I was measurably comfortable, in the bold hope of eternal life, firmly believing in the truth of the gospel. But in the intermediate times, I commonly suffered sore travail, frequently on the borders of despair; by which I no doubt gained more real substance eventually, than if I had enjoyed more ease and comfort. But the nature of sin I could not get removed out of my heart and breast; it would show itself, or rather, it was shown to me, as a separating wall between God and my soul: That was my plague; it kept condemnation in sight.

In the mean time some were sinking deeper into the flesh, and settling back into the beggarly elements of the world; while others were growing bold in their testimony against the flesh and all sin, ready to take the kingdom of heaven by violence. But the day drew near; and God would not let the people rest, until he had given them a fair trial for eternal life, and an opportunity to show themselves. Who were honestly in pursuit of salvation to the spirit, and who loved the flesh and their own pleasures more than God and salvation. And thus it is written; (Mal. 3. 18.) " Then shall " ye return, and discern between the righteous and the wicked ; be- " tween him that serveth God and him that serveth him not."

In this situation of things, of which I have given a very short and general sketch, the everlasting gospel reached us, and soon began to sever the precious from the vile. The spirit, which is for salvation, began to be clearly distinguished and separated from the flesh, which is to be destroyed. And honest souls, who did really hunger and thirst after righteousness, found a safe refuge in the blood and cross of Christ, while those who preferred the flesh had a fair and open opportunity to retreat. And so it is to this day. Men will stumble at the cross being disobedient. But the fair and equitable privilege of the gospel will never fail, until all souls have had a fair trial, and made their final choice, each one for one. For this reason it is justly called the everlasting gospel : it makes finishing work.

This is the gospel which the people called Shakers have received, and in which they stand; and this is the radical difference, between them and all other people, that they believe in Christ as having made his appearance the second time on earth, and having again found to himself a body, the church. Their faith and testimony on this point, are eagerly contested in the world, while on their part they are willing and desirous to have the matter investigated with all diligence and honesty, and to let their works be the final test. The testimony is either true or false; and the trial of it stands thus, That in it we are able to keep the power of salvation, in the experience of all who will receive it. If therefore the testimony be not true, a falsehood is capable of producing better effects than all the truth on the earth, and of being the power of God to salvation. For this is the testimony on which the work stands; it is therefore true. With respect to the visible fruits, they are open to the inspection of all men, as it is written; "He shall set up an ensign for the nation." And again; "Go through, go through the gates; prepare the way of the people; cast up, cast up the high way; gather out the stones: lift up a standard for the people." (Isa. 11. 12. and 62. 16.)

When this gospel appeared to me, and I became acquainted with it, I found it answered my faith and filled my soul in all things. But with it appeared the cross. In it, and in those who bore it, appeared the holiness of God in a degree beyond any thing which I had ever seen or heard. And in this I was not alone; others also said the same; and I heared the report of it among those who eventually rejected all for the pleasures of the flesh. My nature also rebelled against the cross; being the same with that of all other men; Enmity against God; because not subject to the law of God, neither indeed can be. If therefore any possible way could have been devised, or could have existed, one side of the cross, that way would have been chosen. My nature did not love the sword a whit better than the same in others; but God had in righteous judgment appointed it to death, or no soul could inherit life. "For whosoever will save his life shall lose it; but whosoever shall lose his life for my sake and the gospel's, the same shall save it." [Mark 8. 25.] The cry of *antichrist, delusion, deceivers*, and the like, was clamored all about; but with me the matter was serious in the fear of God. I had read in the scriptures, concerning the work of God in the last days, that, "None of the wicked shall understand; but the wise shall understand;" [Dan. 12. 10.] and I weighed the matter soberly, fearing lest, if I hastily rejected the testimony of the last and finishing work of God, as that was said to be, I should lose my soul, being found among those who are wicked and understand not. Dost thou not remember, that I told thee of these things while I was yet with thee on the road from Flemingsburg, on the last day we ever rode together? Another scripture which took hold on my soul was, that " Satan is not divided against satan." This testimony was, and is now, the swiftest witness against satan of any thing which I had ever heard.

And now the question is; Didst thou deal thus honestly and carefully in the fear of God, with thy own soul, always keeping that side where truth and the example of Christ had the lead, without being swayed by the desires and enjoyments of the flesh? I trow not; else thou also hadst been as I am. Dost thou not remember telling me, on that same day, that thou wast never so completely swallowed up with any man as with Issachar Bates, while he opened the testimony? And that thou hadst never heard any thing with which thou wast so well pleased, or which so perfectly filled thy soul, as the testimony of the Shakers, until they came on marriage? that that was the first thing on which thou didst think them lame? But that thou didst not object to that first, but to the doctrine of the resurrection? I say, dost thou not remember these things? Concealment before the world may stand a while; but concealment before God will not avail.

But with me the point to be settled was, whether I could not, on the evidence which I had found, venture my soul in the same faith with those people, were it not for the cross. The answer was unavoidably in the affirmative; as it also is with all those who honestly propound it to their own consciences, after making themselves acquainted with the faith. Of course, the next question to be settled was, Shall I take up my cross, and deny myself and follow Christ, suffering all the privations against the flesh, which the gospel requires, that I may obtain salvation by the cross, or shall I refuse and lose my soul and all my labors? But this question I confess I never spent the labor to form, as I remember. Salvation was at that time the uppermost matter in my mind, as it had long been. All my efforts, all means, and every thing called gospel heretofore, had failed of producing this effect, and of affording genuine satisfaction that it would be gained. I therefore had not found that peaceable satisfaction without wavering; neither had I ever found or conversed with any one who had it, except partially and with inconstancy, until the present faith was opened, with the testimony that Christ had appeared the second time, to make a last and finishing work with men. This testimony in its opening gave a good and favorable prospect, which continued to increase on farther trial. I therefore, after mature deliberation, closed in with it, and I do not repent; being always able to appeal to God and my own conscience, that what I have done, I have done in the honesty and integrity of my heart before God; and the fruits have been accordingly. "The work of "righteousness is peace, and the effect of righteousness, quietness "and assurance for ever." This is an effect, which nothing but righteousness, even the righteousness of God can produce, and which every man inherits according to his progress in the work.

No doubt you still hear more or less of the cry of deception and wickedness, against this work and this people; and for ought I know, may be an active propagator; (See Reply P. 76, and Address P. 106, 107.) "For as concerning this sect, we know that every where "it is spoken against." But with every judiciously informed and candid man, these clamors are idle tales, however they may influence dupes and bigots. (See Letters P. 1.) It is a conclusive fact that no combination in wickedness, or for wicked works, or deceptions works, can stand together in the open light, and for the inspection of all civil characters, with a bold and open testimony against all evil, and contrary to the torrent of corruption naturally prevalent in the world, without any other bond than faith and love. The combination therefore, or union more properly which obtains with us, and which is often objected as an allegation of evil, is an irresistible argument to the contrary, so long as the rule of Christ is good and safe, that " By this shall all men know that ye are my disciples, if ye have love " one to another." If this rule could be imitated it could prove nothing ; for how should it be known who had the true love and who the counterfeit ? This union is more than can be produced and practised by any people of a different faith. I suppose thou art not unmindful that ye tried it in Caneridge and Concord, and could not affect it. This union which is the effect of that faith which is of Christ, and that love which is the bond of perfectness, the unity of the Spirit in the bond of peace, is an ensign visible to all who have eyes to see. In this can be seen that love which is not in word and in tongue, but in work and in truth. And as for the secret iniquities and impositions of which some talk, who love the world more than the Father, the refutation is easy, if a serious reply be eligible ; If two cannot walk together except they be agreed, how much more impracticable for a numerous society to remain together, unless all agree in a firm faith of the truth and honesty of the work? For who will devote their all, for that which they do not believe is worth all ? By what law can men be compelled to continue in such a society against their own faith and choice? Or who is ignorant enough not to know, that where wicked deeds are practised, in violation of what is testified, the whole scheme is evil ? The argument therefore is conclusive, that the union which obtains with us, and though small in the beginning increases in the progress of the work, is the unity of the Spirit in the bond of peace. It therefore remains true, as before stated, that if this testimony be false, unrighteousness, or a lie, can produce better fruits than all the righteousness, or truth, on the earth : it is therefore true and no lie. As for disaffected persons, those who stumble at the cross, they go away, as it is known, and carry such reports as their own consciences and other influences will permit. But such cannot stop the progress of the truth ; few of them have the hardihood to attach any criminality or error to the faith or practice of the people, except this be criminal, that it is all against the carnal mind Yea, where is the man of upright deportment, who has made himself acquainted with the people, and will say any evil of them ?

Some indeed have raised heavy objections against the faith in which we stand, because of the confidence which it inspires ; they cannot endure such assurance and boldness in the faith. I was told by a bold professor in my last discourse with him, that confidence is the very mark of superstition. I confess however such assertions have little weight with me, as I have never read, nor received any such instructions through the medium of revelation, and while I can read on the contrary in the scriptures, that we are God's house if we hold fast the confidence and the rejoicing of the hope firm unto the end: and that we are made partakers with Christ if we hold the beginning of our confidence stedfast to the end; and again, "Let us hold fast "the profession of our faith without wavering; for he is faithful that "promised." (Heb. 3. 6, 14. and 10. 23.) If the effect of righteousness be quietness and assurance for ever, it is strange if the effect of error and superstition be the same, which has always been marked with mobility and change, because a wrong foundation cannot support a building. But if this be the promised effect of righteousness in the latter days, or time of the gospel, is it not strange that any can call themselves christians without it?

In the beginning I was warned by my former brethren, against hearing the Shakers; as you complain, the people are warned of you, and fly from you as from the face of a serpent. But I determined to be honest; and told my hearers boldly, that I would follow the light and the truth where I could find it, and that if these led me to the Shakers, to the Shakers I would go; and said also, that if the Shakers would show me evidence according to the scriptures that they were right, I would submit; although I, that is my flesh, was in opposition all the time. By approaching so near and looking into their testimony, I was taken, by that which cometh as a snare upon all the earth. On this account I have suffered reproach and rejection by my former brethren and connections, even to the violation of the bonds of natural friendship. (See Address, P. 5.) But as I esteem it better to retain the truth, with openness of heart, and in the light, than to be governed by my own fleshly mind in concealment from the light, I am not sorry that I made as free with the Shakers as I did. And notwithstanding that I have been rejected as an heretic by the majority of those with whom I formerly had fellowship, as Paul once was, and on that account have suffered many inconveniences, and the privation of much satisfaction which I would have found, in seeing them heartily enter the way of life and peace, when many of them were at the door, I am not yet overcome, nor in despair of yet seeing God gather a people to his name out of those societies. Although the present prospect is poor towards the majority of those who have seen the light of the day, and have closed their eyes against it, some may yet be found, who being relieved from the fetters of prejudicial opposition, will more deliberately and candidly prove all things, and finding the work imperfect where they are, will eventually submit, to take up their cross, and suffer shame for the name of Christ. Besides; The rising generation must have their day and offer of the gospel. Nothing of the same nature and extent could be more grateful to my spirit, than to find those people sensibly and tenderly feeling the ground on which they stand. For I am still persuaded, that many among them would yet be willing to follow Christ bearing his reproach, were the hindrances taken out of the way. When! O when will men be wise, and cease to condemn without a fair hearing, and to reject at a distance what is unproved?

Or when will they cease to use their strongest efforts to prevent others from examining what they have disapproved, *without a fair trial?*

The very unfavorable and ungenerous reception which the gospel found among many at first, prevented many others from a fair hearing. The leaders of my people, said God, have caused them to err. The preachers who had, some of them, promoted the revival with great industry and zeal, and had looked with earnestness for the commencement of the latter day of glory, were foremost in the opposition when it appeared. Many first shall be last. As soon as it was found that the testimony of Christ ran counter to the core of carnal delights and fleshly lusts, the HUE AND CRY of *deceivers*, was raised against his witnesses; and all were warned to keep at a safe distance from them. Preachers soon began to give back from the light which they themselves had received and propagated. I presume thou art not unmindful of the sermon which one of them preached at Cabincreek; and afterwards, by my request, at Bethel; after reading these words; " Ask ye of the Lord rain in the time of the latter rain; so " the Lord shall make bright clouds, and give them showers of rain, " to every one grass in the field." (Zech. 10. 1.) In which he stated, that Christ would come to judgment in his people, and would never be seen coming in any other manner—that these were the clouds in which he would be seen coming—that these were the white horses— and that Christ would judge the world by the preaching of the gospel and by the power of his Spirit in the gospel, and no other way— and that the day was at hand and the work then commencing. I presume thou canst also remember, when the same preacher, after he had heard the testimony of the kingdom of God, that Christ cometh to judge the world in his saints, and that in the kingdom they do not marry, went back and in my presence again, preached the old traditionary system which he had exploded! One who had preached in the blazing light and power of God in the revival, determinately announced in a general conversation, that he would renounce all the preaching which he had preached for an indefinitely limited time, perhaps a year or more, time enough to include both those sermons, For, said he, it has just been preparing the way for the Shakers. And what was the matter, which put the preachers into such commotion? Why, they that have turned the world upside down have come hither also. True enough, it was a real preparatory work in the light and power of God, for the entrance of his eternal kingdom.

Two more preachers, after a time, (who were present and consented to the aforesaid renunciation,) who had never given the subject a fair hearing, having been early in the opposition, and having found sure enough, that the light of the revival opened the way for the Shakers, and that many were closing in with the faith, have given these an eminent place among their reasons for retreating to their former ground, as the event showed. " In a few months more he, " (Richard M'Nemar,) John Dunlavy and a great many of the peo- " ple were caught in the net of Shakerism"—(For as a snare shall it come on all them that dwell on the face of the whole earth. Luk. 21. 35.) " In one year more Matthew Houston, who had been con-" verted to our church by the Letters on Atonement, became a Sha-" ker also. Are these things not worthy of notice? Who can keep " their eyes from the light, however mortifying it may be? On the " review of all these things, and more which might be mentioned " we were obliged to change our minds." (See R. Marshall and J. Thompson, P. 23.) Yea, and it will be more mortifying yet, when they have to repent and change their minds once more, and avow, that this wild enthusiasm by which they allout confess they were obliged to change, is of God, to which they have to come or never see salvation, and that their enmity against the cross and self-denial of Christ constituted the real cause of their renunciation of, at least some of those doctrines which they now term errors. But who cannot see the disingenuousness of such reasoning? And what is the result? They have renounced the sentiments which sprung up in the revival, out of the light and power of God, which the people received therein; they would not be counted enemies to the revival; but having lopped off the tender fruit they have lost the substance—the revival with them all is no more. It has been on the decline for the most part, since about the time they and others began to indulge in their opposition to the Shakers; or rather declined faster then; for with many it had about done its work before. Such revivals cannot go beyond a limited extent, in that they are weak through the flesh. It is now with them, reduced to a shadow or less.

One preacher in a conversation said, he was more afraid of those three men, meaning three Shakers, than of all the other opposers to the revival. But if the Shakers be enemies to the revival, and their testimony not true, how cometh it to pass that the people who know these things, and also know where the truth is, do not keep the revival? Or is the devil stronger than God? Or did God send in enemies to destroy his own work? How preposterous is the mind of man! of man, while unwilling to submit to the self-denying teachings of the Spirit, and the cross of Christ! Are all or any of these people who dread the Shakers, christians? I trow not. Shakers are not built on so flimsy a foundation as to change their sentiments, or be afraid of the doctrines, or of the light of any people. Having renounced the things which may be shaken, to hold fast those which cannot, they receive a kingdom which cannot be moved.

Had I, with the rest, determined to serve the flesh at all adventures, I suppose I could have fabricated an objection to some article of my former faith, affected a conviction, and returned to the *dead sea* of calvinism in whole or in part. But what would I have gained? I should have been enveloped in darkness and death—Beset with the distressing apprehensions of eternal death; or sunk into insensibility. I might have had the approbation of the world and of carnal professors; unless the judgment of God had pursued me so closely as to deprive me of that also. For if the light which was in me had become darkness, how great would that darkness have been!

But I could not have enjoyed the cheering approbation of a good conscience. I could not have said, *what I have done, I have done for the sake of Christ*, or in simple obedience to God—It would have been to subserve the purposes and desires of the flesh. I have made thorough proof of what is called religion, or gospel, in the world, and salvation is not known one side of the faith of Christ in his second appearing.

Besides; as God deals with people according to their privilege and the use which they make of it, before the true light was restored, many had more justification and peace than can be experienced now, where the true gospel is known and not obeyed. " The times " of this ignorance God winked at." " And this is the condemnation, " that light is come into the world, and men loved darkness rather " than light because their deeds were evil."

SECTION III.

The subject continued, with farther remarks on the writings of the Superscribed.

BARTON;
 I DISPUTE not but that you have received more light, and a better understanding of the gospel and its provisions, than people have generally had. You acknowledge the unquestionable privilege of all who hear the gospel of Christ to believe in him, on the evidence and authority of the gospel, without any previous renovating work of the Spirit to enable them, and so to receive of his fulness and grace for grace. But all this liberality true as it is, cannot show the way of life. You attribute the whole to faith *alone*, as its immediate effect; so do they generally who oppose you. They say by imputation, impartation, or application. These terms and their connections you justly reject. You have also undertaken to show what that faith is by which a man becomes a christian; and when it is all said, it is a mere moralizing theory, by which some would be affected, if well narrated, and some not, like the other systems. Accordingly, with but a little discernment, you may find numbers who believe these statements as firmly and heartily as you, and yet feel no life of Christ, because the real grounds of christianity are wanting. " By faith," you say, " in the blood of Jesus, is not merely to be- " lieve that he died on Calvary—We must know the designs of the " death of Jesus, before we can be rightly affected by it. To be- " lieve therefore in the blood of Jesus, is, to believe in the designs of " it as well as that it was shed—That the law is abolished—the new " testament, with all its fulness, introduced and confirmed to every " creature—the resurrection procured—the dark veil between earth " and heaven torn away—Heaven opened—life and immortality

"brought to light—and the love of God to sinners displayed." (Address, P. 53, 57.) And what is there in all this, different from calvinism, except as to the extent of the new testament? Thus men have been for centuries, fabricating systems, to get the hearts of mankind affected, that they may be saved without living the life of Christ, who left us an example and said, *Follow me.*

But you add a little after; (P. 58.) " From this we see the natural " connection between faith in the blood of Jesus Christ and sanctifi- " cation, redemption, &c." Perhaps you see the connection, as plainly as calvinists see it between the imputed righteousness of Christ and the justification of the elect. But I confess I see no perfect connection in either plan; In the calvinistic, because there is neither scripture nor reason to support it; In yours, because you have left out a main link in the chain which is taught in the scriptures, that of *doing the will of God*, or following Christ who hath left us an example that we should follow his steps. I know that souls are justified, sanctified, and finally saved by or through faith, and never without it; but not as the proximate cause; the immediate, procuring cause of justification, sanctification, and whole salvation, is obedience. " Ye have purified your souls in obeying the truth." " And being " made perfect he became the author of eternal salvation to all them " that obey him." And this view of the subject by no means weakens the efficacy of faith, or derogates from its honor. It is the spring to that obedience by which men please God. " But without faith it " is impossible to please him ; for he that cometh to God must be- " lieve that he is, and that he is a rewarder of them that diligently seek " him." But without obedience faith can justify none. " But wilt " thou know, O vain man, that faith without works is dead?—Ye see " then how that by works a man is justified and not by faith only," or without works. " For as the body without the Spirit is dead, so " faith without works is dead also." (Jam. 2. 20, 24, 26.) This witness is true ; so that faith can no more justify, or sanctify, without its soul, that is, works, than a dead body can live, and perform the actions of life, without its spirit.

But you have added ; (Ibid.) " I am far from thinking that every " one must have a view of all these designs of his blood, before they can be christians. Some, in the death of Jesus, may only discover the love of God to sinners, and by this be encouraged to trust in him." But how do they discover this ? Simply by believing the report of it in the word, or by preaching ? for faith cometh by hearing. Then what is the reason that all those who unhesitatingly believe this report, " That God hath commended his love toward us in " that while we were yet sinners Christ died for us," are not christians, justified and sanctified ? But many of these, I conclude thou knowest, have no more living christianity than the devils who believe and tremble. You will perhaps say they do not believe aright, or in the spirit, or with all the heart. But they believe according to the testimony, or they believe what they have heard, and on your own avowed plan, this is all you can ask ; but yet many of them know their souls are not safe. Now resolve the doubt. But I presume you are not unaware, that something more than faith is necessary; though you are not able to tell what, more than I was before I found the everlasting gospel, unless you would approach still nearer to the Shakers. These things are written in great freedom but in real friendship.

But you have introduced a comparison; (Ibid.) "A father pro-" vides plentifully for a large family of children. Some of them "may know the means by which the father got the provisions—" others may not so well know, and the youngest may scarcely know "any thing more than that the father's love provided these things. Yet they all eat and thrive without quarreling about the means by " which the provisions were obtained." And you might have added, that they eat and thrive just as well, without knowing, at least when young, whether the father's love provided these things, or whether the earth produced them spontaneously, or whether they came some other way. Thus by your own simile, if a good one, your plan of faith has tapered out to a POINT NO POINT. And let me honestly admonish you to look out, that all your labors in religion do not end there.

In all your writings you have not once opened, if named at all, the real ground of justification, or that in which the life of christianity consists, clearly to the understanding. For the gospel is preached to natural men, to sinners, and they are to believe before they can be justified: this is your avowed plan, and it is a true one. It is therefore necessary that the proper and immediate ground of justification be made plain to the physical man. In plain terms; you have never shown the cross of Christ. I do not mean that wooden, Roman cross, on which his animal body was crucified by wicked and cruel men. But you have not shown how he died to sin; for that was his death, according to Paul; and what is that cross which believers in him have to bear daily, (not if perchance they meet with it,) else cannot be his disciples—a cross daily: "If any man will "come after me, let him deny himself, and take up his cross *daily*, "and follow me." "And whosoever doth not *bear his cross and* "*come after me,* cannot be my disciple." [Luke 9. 23, and 14. 27.] What is that self-denial? Is it practical, or merely sentimental? Now these words of Christ have a meaning, and no doubt an important one. If therefore the Shakers put a wrong construction on these and such like sayings, they who have the truth ought to open to the understanding of the people, what is that daily cross, and what that self-denial in which believers follow Christ, and by which they are distinguished from all the world: for it is irresistibly true, according to the above, and such like sayings, that they who deny themselves and follow Christ, bearing his cross, are exclusively his disciples.

You will perhaps say, that your writings are not on this subject, they ought not therefore to be expected to open it. But in treating on the doctrine of justification, or atonement, it is as preposterous to leave out this, which Christ makes the very essence of religion, as for the scriptures to never once have named the imputation of the righteousness of Christ to believers, if that were the efficient cause or grounds of their justification. But,

As you have never taken the true ground of justification; consequently, you have no where exhibited in your writings, the character of a real christian. "Whosoever is born of God doth not commit "sin ; for his seed remaineth in him: and he cannot sin because he "is born of God. In this the children of God are manifest and the "children of the devil." Dost thou not remember, that ten or twelve years ago, a number of you acknowledged, on that very principle, that ye were not christians? What has become of that matter now? Would such an open acknowledgment of the simple truth of the holy scriptures, approach too near to the Shakers? But let truth, be truth, lead where it may—it will not lead from God.

It is indeed not to be expected of one who hath not traveled on that ground, to describe in clear colors, without a scruple, the genuine character of a christian, or to lay open the way to come to that mark. None, abstractedly from the faith of Christ in his second appearing, can direct inquiring souls in the way of eternal life. Neither can they find out the reason of their incapability, else it could be alleviated. The instances, occasional or numerous, of some who meet with what is called conversion, under such ministrations, are no proof of their having the true gospel, but the contrary, for if they had it they could teach it to others with such clearness that no soul, who heard them, would fail through ignorance or inability, to find the treasure of salvation. For what a man hath he can minister to others. "Freely ye have received freely give." And the way which a man knoweth, he can tell to another. If therefore those people or churches had the true gospel, or had they come in by Christ the door, they could open the door and show it to others, so fully that there would be no difficulty on that ground : all could get in who would, on the terms of forsaking all for Christ. For all true ministers of Christ have entered in at the door, and have the key of the kingdom of heaven, and can readily open to those who come. The key of the kingdom is not gold nor silver, but the knowledge of Christ and the way of salvation through him. To have the key of the kingdom therefore, is to have the understanding of the gospel. If Christ is the door, according to the scriptures, and the church the house, every member of the church must know how to get in; and those members who cannot inform those who would come, with such clearness, that they can enter without uncertainty or doubt, neither know what Christ is nor where he dwells. This however is not intended to deny, that many people, who have not received this faith, have had a degree of the power of God, more or less, and have kept it as long and as honestly as they knew how, and have therein been accepted of God, and kept until the day of the perfect gospel—"Kept by "the power of God through faith unto salvation ready to be reveal-"ed in the last time." And with these it has often occurred that the same degree of faith and honesty has been communicated from one to another, and improved with great zeal and fervent labor, to great extent, and according to their devotion to God in obedience, accordingly has been their prosperity and blessedness. Here is something more than faith alone; and yet for the want of receiving and cultivating the perfect gospel, it cannot extend beyond a very limited boundary, nor keep whereto it hath obtained. Thus all such revivals run through.

It would appear from some parts of your Address, that you utterly discard the idea of christians' being unwaveringly established in the correctness of their sentiments, or the rectitude of their faith. But if you would look for a moment where the charge falls, you would probably reflect seriously on renouncing your present views on that subject. The charge of uncertainty must fall, not on human imperfection, or fallibility, which is exhibited to the view of the public as unavoidable, and thus becomes the protector and fosterer of uncertainty and unrighteousness, divisions and heresies—but on the gospel—but on Christ the author of it—but on God who sent him. Accordingly you have said; " Upon the rectitude of my faith and prac- " tice my eternal interests depend." (Address, P. 5.) And doth God require rectitude of you with such exactness that your eternal interests depend on it, in matters of which you have no way to be certain? Doth it surpass the power and promise of the Father and of the Son, who both dwell with the true believer, to make him certain, infallibly certain of the rectitude of his faith and practice? Or shall I reverse the question and ask, Is it consistent with the truth and other perfections of Deity, to leave a faithful honest believer (and none else deserve the name of christian,) in any uncertainty about the rectitude of the way in which he walks, or his faith and practice, after the unreserved promises which he hath made? " This " then is the message which we have heard of him, and declare to " you, that God is light, and in him is no darkness at all. If we say " that we have fellowship with him, and walk in darkness, we lie, and " do not the truth: but if we walk in the light, as he is in the light, " we have fellowship one with another, and the blood of Jesus Christ " his Son cleanseth us from all sin." (1 Jno. I. 5, 6, 7.) They then are christians, and none else, who walk in the light as he is in the light. " I am the light of the world; he that followeth me shall not " walk in darkness, but shall have the light of life." (Jno. 8. 12.) So that the confidence of a christian, as to the rectitude of his sentiments, or more properly of his faith and practice, is the fruit of the light, the truth and the infallibility of God and of Christ, and not of any perfection, fallibility, or infallibility, of the creature. But to all who follow Christ, his Spirit and his promise confirm them in infallible certainty. Every man therefore, who is uncertain whether his faith and practice are of the true faith of Christ, is in possession of full proof that they are not—that he is not a christian.

Indeed it is no far-fetched inference from your writings, that practical christianity, or union with Christ, hath no effect or influence towards establishing the heart in a good thing; " Being well convinc-

" ed," you say, " of the fallibility of mortals—seeing the fluctua
" tions of great and good men amongst us from system to system,
" and then reverting to the relinquished system—viewing the
" confidence of every sect in the rectitude of their doctrines, and all
" believing and declaring they are honest—hearing every party pro
" nouncing us wrong, and joining their general voice against us—
" seeing these things I determined to re-examine my views of the
" gospel." (Address, P. 4, 5.) I have nothing to object against repeated examinations and searchings after truth, until it is found to
full satisfaction, proving all things and holding fast that which is good.
But surely in these statements you make no account of the infallible
truth of the gospel, (but measure all by the fallibility of mortals,)
nor of the promise of Christ to his people, that the Holy Spirit
should abide with them for ever, and guide them into all truth.
" And I will pray the Father, and he shall give you another com
" forter that he may abide with you FOR EVER." " Howbeit when
" he, the Spirit of truth is come, he shall *guide you into all truth*—
" He shall teach you all things." (Jno. 14. 16, 26, and 16. 13.) You
might think it disingenuous (and I do not desire to say any thing disingenuous or unkind,) to compare you and your *great and good* men
to the heathen philosophers and other moralists, ever revolving and
never able to come to a permanent standard, or to those silly women
and those who lead them captive, all laden with sins, and led away
of divers lusts, ever learning and never able to come to the knowledge of the truth. (2 Tim. 3. 6, 7.) But wherein do ye differ from
them? But let the truth appear. You have not shifted your ground
so overtly as some others; you have affected a more steady perseverance; but you acknowledge those fluctuating, unstable spirits as
brethren and as christians, as *great and good* men, and more than
implicitly patronise instability in the gospel.

" But," you say, " great and good men have differed." (Ibid.)
And how shall we prove that great and good men have differed in the
faith and practice of the gospel? By the same rule by which we
can prove that the scriptures are a lie, which inform us, that with
great and good men, (if such are christians,) at least in the true
church of Christ, There is one body, (not two differing,) and one
Spirit, (not two differing,) even as they are called in one hope of
their calling; one Lord, (not two competitors,) one faith, (not two in
opposition,) one baptism, (not two,) being all baptized by that one Spirit into one body, one God and Father of all, who is above all, and
through all, and in them all. [Eph. 4. 4, 5, 6. 1 Cor. 12. 13.] But
not many wise men after the flesh, not many mighty, not many noble
are called. [1 Cor. 1. 26.] But you add, " Therefore from the Bi
" ble I wish to draw my sentiments, and by the Bible to have them
" judged." [Ibid.] The same source from which these *great and
good* men who differ, say they draw theirs, and to which they appeal
as the judge or test of their sentiments. Therefore the Bible is either not the proper guide of christians, (not denying its usefulness in
the hands of the men of God, in subordination to the true guide, as

being written by the influence of the same Spirit,) or none of you, who thus differ among yourselves, are christians indeed. And indeed it must be a poor guide, when great and good men cannot agree in the purport of its instructions.

It may be asked if these things are so, how are we to know who are right, seeing all are so confident? I answer; Find what the true church is, and you will be at no loss to know where it is, and of whom it is constituted. The knowledge of the truth is not to be obtained unless in that church, or issuing from it, which is the house of God, the ground and pillar of the truth. The law goeth forth of Zion and the word of the Lord from Jerusalem. But to bring the matter nearer to the popular understanding; The rule of Christ is always good; By their fruits ye shall know them. But it is a mistake to suppose that professors are all confident of the rectitude of their faith and practice; although it would be imputing wilful error to any people, to suppose they do not believe their systematic tenets to be the best they know. Yet few, very few, have I found put to the trial, in thirty years, (for about that long I have been observing professors,) who without a scruple, will assert their certainty of eternal life from day to day. I am not sure that I ever found one out of the present faith, (and these have seldom an occasion, their faith and works are their witness,) except those who do it through ambition. Some say the Roman Catholics are confident; and they are alledged as a proof, that clear confidence is not the attendant of the true church, or at least no evidence. I doubt not but they assert that salvation is not known out of the Catholic church. But I have not found one, nor heard of one in late days, asserting that he or the other members are christians in the present tense. And were it not that their fruits testify too plainly, that they are, at least in part, the people who have the form and deny the power, they have in many respects, a better claim to being the true church than any who have separated from them. But what is form and correct sentiments without fruit to holiness? Such people are no stumble to an honest man, after hearing what the truth is.

This is a convenient place to introduce the notice of another error, which is eminently marked, not only throughout your writings, but in most, if not all the denominations of the christian world. It is this; That they who heard the apostles preach, and believed, were then born of God, and christians in the full sense of the word. This opinion is the source of much mischief. For men read in the scriptures, of those people who were called by the gospel, among whom were yet many evil things; and concluding that these were christians, it is an easy inference, that people in these days may be christians also, although corrupted in the same manner. Whereas with a moderate attention to the scriptures, and a just conception of the gospel, it is not difficult to learn, that when they believed they were only entering into the work of being born again, to the effectuation of which they had to attain by denying self, bearing the cross and following Christ in the regeneration. They then took on them the yoke or cross of

Christ, and began to learn of him, and in proportion, to find rest for their souls; and were supported by the power and gifts of the Holy Spirit, as many as were found faithful, which protected them, and elevated them above all opposition, that they might not be overcome, but according to promise, have strength equal to their day, in that time of heavy and bloody persecution. As many therefore as were simply honest and faithful, although they had not arrived to that stage which is called the being born of God, in which there is complete and perpetual power over all sin in nature and works, were owned of Christ as his disciples, and were properly in him thus far. And notwithstanding that many wrongs and improprieties might be found with them, while as yet their corruptions were not purged out in a perfect obedience to the truth, they were treated in forbearance, with suitable admonitions and reproofs, until by time and experience they ceased to do evil, and learned to do well; until they were capable of becoming, in full order, living members of the one living body.

But that they were not all born of God who had believed and were gathered into churches, is evident from many considerations. The apostle James hath written the main part of his epistle, to prove to his hearers that they were not justified christians, with all their faith, because they had not works. The Galatians to whom Paul wrote, with all their zeal and swift running in the beginning of their faith, were in danger of returning to Judaism, or to the beggarly elements of the world. And he tells the Corinthians in plain terms that they were yet carnal, and that he could not speak to them as to spiritual, but as to carnal. Now they who are carnal and not spiritual, are not born of the Spirit—they are not in Christ in the full sense of the word—they are not new creatures, old things having passed away and all things having become new, and all things of God, as he tells those same Corinthians is the case with those who are in Christ; for carnality is not of God—they are under the power of death, For, to be carnally minded is death. [Ro. 8. 6.] It is not however to be understood, that they were called carnal who bore a faithful cross against all carnality from the beginning, or who came to it in honest simplicity. But these Corinthians had not yet arrived to that simplicity. They were therefore carnal and walked as men, not as christians. [1 Cor. 3. 1, 2, 3.]

It is indeed preposterous enough to imagine that they were born of God, who lived in such divisions and other disorders, and fell so far short of that order and power of the true church, which he taught to them and others; and who also had fornication among them of the most aggravated kind, That one should have his father's wife, and that publicly known, and there was not as much christianity among them all, as could exterminate that evil, and with it all, they were not humbled, but puffed up. And yet in our days, these are accounted a church of the true saints of God, born of the Spirit, and esteemed as patterns for believers. Notwithstanding there were many, and perhaps some even at Corinth, who bore a full and faithful cross against the flesh and all evil, walking in the simple Spirit of the gospel, who were the church in the true sense of the word in that day; with whom they who were carnal and walked as men could not keep full fellowship, but were the outer court, or worldly sanctuary, to whom the enemy had access, to keep up divisions and promote the practice of living after the flesh, as most acceptable to human nature, to the utter overthrow of genuine christianity in that day. Accordingly, anti-christ is of the world, but went out from the church, that is, from among the faithful. " Little children, it is the " last time : and as ye have heard that anti-christ shall come, even " now are there many anti-christs; whereby we know that it is the " last time. They went out from us, but they were not of us; for " if they had been of us, they would no doubt have continued with " us : but they went out that they might be made manifest that they " were not all of us." " They are of the world, therefore speak they " of the world, and the world heareth them." [1 Jno. 2. 18, 19, and 4. 5.]

This view of the subject shows why the apostles dealt with the people as they did, in all long suffering and forbearance; Warning every man, and teaching every man in all wisdom, that they might present every man perfect in Christ Jesus—that if by any means they might hold all those who believed, or as many as possible, to the simplicity of the gospel, until they should gain the point of salvation, or power over all sin, and not be carried away with the spirit of the world, which is anti-christ, as it exists in professors. Accordingly, they were reminded of that to which they were called by the gospel; " To put off, concerning the former conversation, the old " man which is corrupt according to the deceitful lusts; and to be renewed in the spirit of their minds; and to put on the new man who is created in righteousness and true holiness, and thus to become new in all respects.

One other subject I must notice in this place. It becomes necessary, according to the testimony of the denominations, who have not the faith that Christ has come the second time, to leave their present standing and receive a different faith. Their testimony is that the day of the Lord is to come ; and with many of them it is, or has been, that it is at hand ; consequently, they are not in it, but, on the contrary, if they desire to see one of the days of the Son of man, they cannot see it without a change. For the introduction of the day of the Lord must produce a change in all who receive him ; because if they had the same faith and the same understanding of things before as after, they would have already, all things pertaining to that day, but the practice, which they might at any time commence. But this they know is not the case ; they know not what the work of that day is ; for of that day and hour knoweth no man before its commencement, and how should he perform its duties ? The people of each denomination have the perfect gospel and power of salvation, or they have not. Those who have, bring forth the fruits heretofore stated in different places ; and may increase on the same ground; and those who have not, are subjected to the indispensable necessity of moving forward to perfection, or of perishing without. For God will finally accept of nothing short of perfection; Be ye therefore perfect even as your Father in heaven is perfect.

The alarming apprehension, therefore, of innovation, which systematics and formalists so much dread, and against which they watch with so much assiduity, is an insidious usurper of the throne of God, and an enemy to the coming of the Lord. Without such innovation how should there ever be any recovery from the darkness of any formal or anti-christian religion? But it is conclusively evident, that they who testify that the day of the Lord, or latter day of glory is at hand, are conscious, that it hath not yet come, at least to them. Yet this is no proof that they are not moved by the Spirit of God in their testimony. God sent John to baptize and to preach, saying, Repent for the kingdom of heaven is at hand. Yet John was not then in it; for the least in the kingdom, or gospel church, was greater than he. But such a testimony proves that those who bear it have not the thing in possession; according therefore to their own testimony, the work in which they stand must cease and give place to that which is greater. Thus John honestly confessed the ground on which he stood and the nature of his mission. "And he confessed, and denied not; but confessed, I am not the Christ." "He must increase but I must decrease." [Jno. 1. 20. and 3. 30.] Dost thou not remember the time, when on a certain morning, at the time of writing *The last will and testament* of the Springfield presbytery, one of the brethren, being in a peculiar operation of the Spirit, exclaimed, in thy house, Ho! this is not the Christ! It is only John the baptist! relating to a greater work to come. For though Christ was then amongst us, we knew him not in the work of full redemption.

But as well might John and his disciples have rejected the testimony of Jesus, and have said, We have the truth, and stand in the true testimony of God, (and so they did, for it was true as far as it went,) as they who have received a measure of light from God, to let them know that the day of the Lord is at hand, and that God is about to restore the pure work of the gospel on the earth, can maintain that they are in the true and perfect way. They may plead that they have evidently had the power of God among them: but that is no proof, as already shown, that they are in the perfect way, or have that work which is competent to salvation. For John had the power of God with him; he was a burning and shining light, but he was not the true light: he was sent to bear witness of that light. Thus after the apostacy had had its day, and had begun to verge towards a close, God raised up many witnesses in the Spirit of the apostles, as John had once come in the Spirit of Elias, all testifying that the kingdom is at hand. And in the midst of this testimony the kingdom appeared. But as John said, He must increase, but I must decrease, so has it been with them in part, and still continues to be.

But as the first appearing of Christ was to be made among the Jews only, the Gentiles having not yet been invited to salvation, one principal forerunner was sufficient; whereas the second, or last, appearing to those who look for him, being to include the face of the whole earth, it becomes necessary that a testimony of the same kind, be sent forward from time to time, and in divers places, to prepare the way of the Lord—to wake the people up to some care and feeling after salvation, that they may be in expectation of the coming of the Lord. But as with the testimony of John, so with that of all the rest. It accomplished the work which it was sent to do, and, in a while, ceased; and those who would not receive the testimony of Jesus perished, their standing for a time in the light and truth of God, sent by John, notwithstanding. So it is with all the subjects of the preparatory work of God in this day of Christ which has now opened; all those who reject the testimony of Christ in his second appearing, soon lose their power, and become formal and earthly, scatter and divide, and show in all respects, that notwithstanding they have had a day of the mighty power of God, they have finished their work and done all they can do on that gound; and that if ever the subjects of that day of power would find salvation, it behooves them to leave the ground whereon they stand, and advance into the perfect work; like John to decrease, and be superseded by that kingdom which is superior, perfect and everlasting.

An urgent argument among the people some years ago was, Stay where you are and get more—stay where you are and get more; as if more could be had without advancing. I stayed there until I had gotten all I could get, or saw any prospect of getting, and have never seen any one gain any thing by staying there past the time. Such was the language of the Jews as if they had said; Stay where you are; Go not after this innovator. We know that God spake to Moses; but as for this fellow, we know not whence he is. True enough; God spake to Moses; and by Moses taught that another should supersede him. "A prophet shall the Lord your God raise up unto "you of your brethren, like unto me; him shall ye hear." [Acts 7. 37.] So might the disciples of John have said; We know that God sent John, let us hold fast to him. True, God sent John, and by him taught that a greater than he should come after him, to whom he must yield. So may the society of the Friends say, Let us stay where we are. We know that God spake by Fox, but as for this Anna Lee, or her followers we know not whence they are. True enough; God spake by Fox, and by Fox taught that the kingdom was at hand; of course that he had it not, and therefore must be superseded. Accordingly this testimony of Fox, having done its work, ceased—the Friends have not their former power. So may the Methodists say; Let us stay where we are. We know that God spake by John Wesley; but as for these Shakers, we know not whence they are. True; God spake by Wesley, and by Wesley foretold, or signified, a greater and deeper work than was in his days, or ever had been; for which he was no doubt sent to prepare the way, but not to build it up. It therefore behooves them also, if they would be saved, to be superseded. For it is manifest they have not the kingdom; their day of power is too unstable and fleeting. So may the people of the late revival say, Let us stay where we are, and get more. We know that God spake by his Spirit in the revival, and is not that enough? but as for those who tell us that Christ has come the second time, we know not what to make of them, we do not see him. True; God spake by his Spirit in the revival, and by that Spirit he said, That his everlasting kingdom was at hand; and also, That that revival would never cease until the latter day of glory should commence. But the revival is gone. The people who were the subjects of it, have no more the spirit and power which they once had, as many as have rejected the testimony of Christ in his second appearing: little if any, is among them all. Now that revival was either false and no work of God, (for it could not be a true work and its testimony false, because a good tree cannot bring forth evil fruit,) or the work which entered at the latter part of it, and which claims the character of the everlasting kingdom, is true. But the revival carried such convincing marks of the work of God, that almost all who believe in christianity as being a living work of God, claim the honor of acknowledging the revival; even those who have turned away from it, to escape the cross which was found in the fulfilment of its testimony. Its testimony therefore, that the latter day of glory would be introduced before it closed, is also true.

This work differs from all those which have preceded as forerunners, in this amongst other things; that whereas they have testified that the kingdom is to come, and therefore, according to their own testimony, must cease, and give place to it, on its appearing; the present work testifies, that the kingdom has commenced, and that this is it; and therefore according to its own testimony, seconded by others, ought to stand for ever. Accordingly it has outlived all those revivals and testimonies which have preceded and testified of it; for though they keep some form, or shadow, they lose the power. And this is not all; God will yet send the same Spirit of Elias, or rather of the apostles, to wake up the people, and make farther preparation for the work and testimony of the everlasting kingdom, which has entered on the earth for the salvation of souls. " But now he hath " promised saying, Yet once more I shake not the earth only, but " also heaven. And this word, Yet once more, signifieth the remov- " ing of those things that are shaken, as of things that are made, that " those things which cannot be shaken may remain." The day is come; and God hath begun to remove the things which may be shaken, as things which are made by the contrivance and wisdom of men, that the work of the kingdom, which shaketh all things and cannot itself be shaken, may remain. " Wherefore, we receiving a " kingdom which cannot be moved, let us have grace, whereby we " may serve God acceptably, with reverence and godly fear: for our " God is a consuming fire." [Heb. 12. 26, to 29.]

SECTION IV.

Farther observations and corrections; together with sundry matters pertaining to the revelation of Christ in his everlasting kingdom.

BARTON;

I NOW come to consider those parts of your writings, which immediately respect the faith of Christ in his second appearing, or the faith of the people called Shakers. And on your own principles, you cannot count it ungenerous, if I point out some of the same evils in you, of which you so heavily complain in others, and require you to prove by the scriptures, that our tenets are wrong, before you condemn them and reproach us as the degenerate sons of the pope of Rome. We are, it is true, charged with claiming infallibility, because we maintain, (as the only pretext for such allegation with which I am acquainted,) that God hath opened and confirmed in Christ, the everlasting gospel, which is his perfect work, and infallibly saves from sin and ruin, all who keep it, and that in keeping this gospel we are saved from sin and all criminal or dangerous error, and that God hath made this gospel known to us, for the use of all men who are willing to be saved. If maintaining this gospel be to claim infallibility, we shall not repel the charge. We will bear the censures of men, rather than deny the work of God.

You complain of a flood of opposition poured forth against you, and yet pouring. And if you bore it in the simple defence of the truth, without endeavoring to choak it in yourself, or to disguise and pervert it in others, I would compassionate your distress; but as you do the same things of which you complain, your calamity is not so pitiable. I intend therefore to deal freely with your publications, on those points which I shall notice in them, and with yourself, as a professed christian, even as freely as you did with another, not without reason, when you said, "Heaven knows you are wrong." I deal thus freely, purely for the sake of uncovering the truth, in those matters which ought to be known, for the information of those who seek the truth, and not instigated from the beginning, with any sanguine expectations that it would be of any benefit to you, or to many of your present adherents. For as it is written; "Israel hath not "obtained that which he seeketh for; but the election hath obtained "it, and the rest were blinded to this day;" so the people in the revival have not obtained that kingdom which they expected, but the election hath obtained it, and the rest were blinded to this day. Yet it is not wrong to provoke them to jealousy; that if by any means we might save some of them.

You say you have no interest in being wrong, (Address P. 5.) But if you have no interest in being wrong, we more so. We know godliness hath promise of this life, as well as that which is to come; but we do not know, that it indulges in fleshly lusts and gratifications, lawful or unlawful, the rejecting of which is the cause of our heaviest oppositions, and the central barrier in the way of general approbation. But if we are right, you have an interest in being wrong—an interest, for which many have labored hard, at the expense of being wrong and missing the point on which their eternal interests depend—an interest, for which every man and woman on earth would forego every other inheritance, until eternal things become the most important with them—an interest, which is the life of every man in nature—this interest is, to escape the cross of Christ and save the life; "For whosoever will save his life shall " lose it, and he that will lose his life shall find it." If you have no interest in being wrong, you must reasonably conclude, that others have as little, especially those who sacrifice more than you, for the sake of being right. You have not sacrificed all for Christ. You have reserved the most precious of your idols. Ananias like you held back part of the price with this pretext, that Christ doth not require that part—that which is more dear to you than life—more precious than Christ. Was it not in opposition to the testimony of God borne to you by his witnesses, that you told with your own mouth, that you felt a disposition to blaspheme God? It wrought in me, said one, all manner of concupiscence. Was it not through opposition to the same testimony, and your grief at finding some of the people likely to bear their cross, that you spat blood a considerable part of one night, or perhaps more? And thus, while some are called, and obey the call, to resist to blood striving against sin, did you not resist to blood striving for the life of an idol? And have you no interest in being wrong? If we are right, we presume you have. And none have yet been able to show us that we are wrong, in not reserving that most precious jewel, when we make our surrender to Christ. For it is poor reasoning to us, *that you believe* we are the people, " Who creep into houses and lead captive silly women laden with " sins, led away of divers lusts : ever learning and never able to " come to the knowledge of the truth," because we reject in word and works, every sin, and every fleshly lust, lawful and unlawful, and remain abidingly established in the knowledge of the truth. Our logic tells us, that such scriptures better apply to those who live after the course of the world, and are always more or less in uncertainty ; or changing from system to system and then reverting to the relinquished system.

After complaining of the flood of opposition which you have had to meet, you add, " We are not to be driven from our sentiments " by bare assertions or ill natured scurrility—heretical names, or pa- " thetic lamentations. These substitutes for argument have been " frequently tried ; but to me and many others in vain." (Addr. P. 1.) In the last of your reply to Campbell you say ; " Let us, after this, " ever keep in mind that memorable description of a citizen of Zion. [Psm. 15.] " He backbiteth not with his tongue, nor doth evil to his " neighbor, nor taketh up a reproach against his neighbor." Peo- " ple," you continue, " in these days are as they were in the days of " Jeremiah. They hated Jeremiah, and wanted to blast his reputa-

"tion. " Report, say they, and we will report." Let us not take up ungrounded reports any longer." *After this*, and *any longer*— After the preceeding paragraph, in which the most ungrounded reports which heaven ever witnessed from a malignant heart are liberally poured forth against an innocent people who have forsaken all for Christ—who have given up more than you have done to be right, and therefore if possible have less interest in being wrong—a people who never interrupted you, or any of your adherents, or any other people, in any sense, except by urging on them the necessity of salvation, and claiming the privilege to freely minister the gospel, publicly and from house to house, to all who would hear it—a people against whom all manner of evil is spoken falsely for *his* name's sake whose reproach they bear, and who once bore for us the reproaches with which they reproached God—a people against whom you can support no charge, except what is included in pursuing the light of the revival to the end, that is, to the introduction of the everlasting kingdom; as things appeared according to our understanding as well as that of many who are not willing to lose all for Christ, and which could not be very far from your own understanding, if you spoke the sentiments of your heart, of which I have no doubt, when you said your preaching had just prepared the way for the Shakers: and in that you were not alone.

But you state, that there has been a "Lamentable departure of " two of our preachers, and a few of their hearers, from the true " gospel into wild enthusiasm. They have," say you, " made ship-" wreck of faith, and turned aside to an old woman's fables, who " broached them in New-England about twenty-five years ago. " While we weep for them many rejoice, and hope and expect this " will be the end of us all." But what is this wild enthusiasm? That with which you were more completely swallowed up than any thing you ever heard, until you found the people in the kingdom did not marry? That kingdom for which you were then looking and which you said had already begun? That Millennium which, when one of your brethren asked you to help him out, that he saw there was some devil about marriage, you said was just at hand, and then there would be none of these things? For did you not preach boldly that Christ had already come and was in his people? And did you not say once and again, that if any man wants to see Christ, let him look at a christian, and he will see him? and that Christ would never be seen any other way in the judgment of this world? But what are these old woman's fables? These; That no unclean thing can enter into the kingdom of heaven—that if any man will be a disciple of Christ indeed, he must deny himself, and bear his cross daily, and come after Christ—that the true gospel teacheth us, that denying ungodliness and worldly lusts we should live soberly, righteously and godly in this present world—that if we confess our sins, he is faithful and just to forgive us our sins, and to cleanse us from all unrighteousness. These and such like being the fables of that woman, young or old, bear witness that she was a heavenly minded woman, that she was indeed a lovely Mother in Israel, and an heiress of glory—quite likely to be the one who the people with her say she was, —the woman whom God hath chosen to reveal Christ the second time to those who were looking for him.

"But," you continue, "we find that nothing new has happened "under the sun *** Of the twelve who followed Christ, one proved "a devil, and another denied him, and all the rest forsook him; but "all repented, except Judas. This may yet be the case with our "deluded brethren—In Paul's day, Hymeneus and Alexander, Her- "mogenes and Philetus, and *all them of Asia*, made shipwreck of "faith. If it is an argument that we are wrong, because two of our "preachers have revolted from the truth—the argument is equally "strong against the truth of the christian religion, because many of its "professors in every age have done the same. ** It is rather in our "favor that we are right, because wolves always go among the sheep "for prey. These wolves, in sheep's clothing, have smelt us from "far, and have come to tear, rend and devour." Thus you have condemned without hearing and knowing what we do, and hated without cause, as the enemies of Christ always do; have used *bare assertions*, *scurrility*, and *heretical names*, without argument, just as preposterously as you complain that others do with you. Have you ever shown to us or to the world, in this public manner, what proof we carry of being wolves in sheeps clothing? Have you told them or us, what is the sheep's clothing, whether a fair profession or a righteous life? O Barton—O Barton—when will you be as liberal to others as you ask them to be to you? Whether is this paragraph of yours, reasoning or scurrility? If we as a people are wolves in sheep's clothing, why do you not show us and the world wherein, and not be daubing about your *heretical names, and pathetic lamentations*, without offering the shadow or pretence of a reason? All which you have yet to lift at your own expense. But what do these tear rend and devour? Have they, now in ten years, spoken a word against any thing but the flesh and its lusts, or all sin? Or have they ever usurped or asked any power, except the power of the gospel and the person's own faith, to persuade any man or woman to believe as they do? And do not you publish your faith in the most forcible and engaging manner you can? But these Shakers have disturbed and even broken up some congregations, they must therefore be wolves. And have not you and your brethren disturbed or even broken up some congregations of other professors, often divided them, and swept, not a few, but many of the people, and caused them to be rejected as heretics, as you reject us? Are ye not therefore wolves in sheep's clothing? But these Shakers, according to some, are the best calculated to deceive of all people—they make the fairest appearance and look the most like christians—they can tell a man all his experience in religion, and a great deal more, (didst thou not talk this way?) they must therefore be deceivers, or wolves. But if the best appearance, the most righteous life and deepest knowledge in religion, be the sure marks of wolves, what are the true marks of the sheep? Are they in ignorance of God, a carnal life and ungodly deportment, or wearing a wolf skin and appearing just like the rest of the world, without knowing who is a christian and who is not? Let reasonable men consider. But these Shakers, according to some, have devoured and broken up many families. Yea, true enough; by preaching and propagating the spirit of faith and unity, in Christ, many families have united together for the salvation of all, in the joint work of the Lord, as it is written; "They shall "flow together to the goodness of the Lord;" and again; "And "the multitude of them that believed were of one heart and one "soul: neither said any of them that ought of the things which he "possessed was his own; but they had all things common;" (Acts 4. 32.) where the rich and the poor feed in common bounty and good will, and all other families, or as many as choose, are invited to partake of the same bounty on the same principles—just to confess and forsake all sin. Perhaps you may remember your reply to an opposer of the work of God, in the revival, when he said it was of the devil. "*A good devil; I should love to have fellowship with* "*him.*" These are good wolves; I should love to be devoured by them.

But I look on this last page of your reply, and wonder, If you were so far lost to all sensibility and reason, as to suppose that the treachery of Judas for money, the forsaking of the disciples and the denial of Peter through fear, and departure of Hymeneus and Alexander, of Hermogenes and Philetus and them of Asia, who forsook Paul to escape the persecution and the cross, and thus made shipwreck of the faith, bore any resemblance to our case, who received and kept the faith of Christ, which involves tenfold more opposition than we had to meet before, as well as an infinitely greater cross to human nature. It is true, similes prove nothing. But a man who uses them to gain illustration or energy to his statements, ought to see that they are apt. The introduction of the above characters proves nothing; universal logic forbids it. It gives no illustration; because there is not the smallest likeness between the two cases. It can only therefore be a disingenuous burlesque—mere scurrility. It is a pity a man of your light and reason should descend to such measures. But you had no better weapons. But perhaps you thought you saw great likeness to us in Hymeneus the friend of marriage and Philetus the carnal lover, because they taught that the resurrection was already past, or perfected; consequently, that there needed be no difficulty in using the bodies they then had in marriage and the indulgence of sexual love; while we teach, near two thousand years afterwards, that the resurrection is not past yet; that it is a fountain of deep waters through which no man can pass, and that in the resurrection they neither marry, nor are given in marriage, and therefore, that all who come into it give up with marriage and carnal love for ever. The judicious may discern how much resemblance there is in the two cases.

" But God," say you, " has lifted up a standard against them," (Ibid.) that is, against the Shakers. And what is it? This kind of opposition which you justly reprobate, as being ineffectual with you and others? Or is it the preaching of you and your brethren? one of whom would not thoroughly perform a candid, open conversation with one of our preachers, on the faith of Christ, for all his religion, because it would surely cost that and more, in the end. Therefore, as in your words, *they fly from us as from the face of a serpent.* But why should any man who knows the truth and walks in it, be afraid of being charmed by the serpent? It is a proof that such people are not right. But what hath this standard done, which God hath lifted up? The people of the revival have not been able to stand by its protection; they are scattered like the Jews to the four winds of heaven, and have no more the power which they once had; whilst the Shakers, in possession of that gospel which shaketh all and can be shaken of none, are abundantly more numerous than when those things were written, as well as much more like the Jerusalem of God, *compactly built together*. But;

No doubt you have also increased in numbers; and would to God ye were tenfold as many as ye are, and all in the genuine spirit of the revival. I am not going to count on numbers to confirm the faith, or on any thing else which is according to the honor and glory of this world. But I mention these things as a visible sign that God hath not lifted up a standard against us. I desire that they who are willing to see, may see things as they are, and know, as the people are learning more and more, that no religion which cometh in opposition, is able to stand against the sharp two-edged sword, which is put into our hand and goeth out of our mouth; that is, the gospel. There are two methods now in practice to keep from visibly falling before it; the one is not to come into contact, or to avoid all free conversation, and the other to determine not to submit, true or false: and the way of God—the nature of the gospel, is not to force but to invite. But I have no feeling to contest the ground with you in respect of credit in the world. I should there have no prospect in respect to faith. For though it will be found true, that the present work of God will carry the palm in every thing which is truly worthy of a rational man, so that it will be true as it is written; " When a man's ways " please the Lord, he maketh even his enemies to be at peace with " him;" (Prov. 16. 7.) Yet the faith and cross of Christ will always be hateful to the world, while such a world exists. For our faith is not of the world, therefore the world hateth it. But your faith it cannot hate, farther than as it coincides with ours. As far as it is different from our faith, people will generally bear with you; for in it you have no death, no cross against the old man. It is true, you have spoken of self-denial in a christian. (Reply, P. 66.) But what do ye deny? Not self; not the old man with his deeds; for ye live after the course of the world, marrying and giving in marriage, as the rest of the world; your bodies are not dead because of sin; they do the appropriate works of the first Adam, and bring forth the appropriate fruits of the world; ye partake of the honors and friendship of the world like the rest. Your people fill posts of honor and profit, civil and military, and are therefore of the very members of the world. Your Brother, Elder David Purviance, seems to have had no scruple of conscience for years, against filling a place in the state legislature, since he has lived in a state whose constitution admits preachers to the house of Assembly; although some years ago, when in the spirit of the revival, he rejected that seat, if I am not misinformed, as not being the place of a christian. He must therefore of the world, and the world love him, or they would not appoint him to make their laws. Where then is your cross against the old man. Your religion is accommodated just to his wishes. You may be Calvinist like, of Christ bearing the cross for you. But without speaking Calvinist or anti-calvinist, Jesus talks of every one bearing his own cross, and that daily, and coming after him, otherwise he cannot be his disciple. You may talk of the cross of Christ, or self-denial, in the spirit. But who will believe that a man denies himself, or follows Christ in the spirit, and the world in his works? Not one who knows the gospel. On the whole it is evident, that they who participate in these things which are of the world, bear no real cross against the old man.

Those things which have been written so long ago, I suppose I should not have noticed now, had it not been, that in your last publication you have shown the same ungenerous opposition and the most disingenuous misrepresentation, by which you show that your former enmity, against the faith of Christ in his second appearing, remains intire. And it is not necessary that your unprovoked slanders should remain unnoticed. You have misrepresented us with the pretext of defending yourself—This is uncandid, and to the prejudice of truth, be that found where it may. An ingenuous man will let all other people's sentiments alone; or represent them as they are, according to their own statements of them, or the best information, if their own cannot be obtained. And if, on their own statement, he can confute them, he is justifiable in so doing. But loathsome as our faith is to this world, it is certainly to your disadvantage as a man of sense and piety to misrepresent us, for your own extrication. If you are conscious of having a correct understanding of the perfect gospel, what need you care where the people say it leads, or to whom it is akin? To have some likeness is not to be the same thing. Some people argue that our faith has a resemblance to the Roman Catholic, which to many would appear a strong argument, if not conclusive, that we are wrong. And what of it? That insinuation will not prove us wrong, neither will it prove that our faith leads to the Romans. We have no need to misrepresent them. I am not to reject a truth because the Roman Catholics believe it. It is my joy to find truth believed and error rejected by any people.

You have said, (Address, P. 106.) " I do not design to investigate " the doctrines of the Shakers; but to remove a frequent insinuation " against us, which is, that our doctrines lead to Shakerism. By

Shakerism I understand the peculiar doctrines of that denomination." After stating some, in your manner, of which I shall take notice, you say, " Now to which of these doctrines or to any other peculiar doc- " trine of the Shakers, does one doctrine we hold lead ? Did we " profess to receive immediate inspirations and illuminations before " we could believe the gospel, the objection would be weighty." Now Barton, candor ; O for that candor which you so highly recommend to others. Duplicity in the statement of other people's doctrines—bold insinuations of peremptory falsehoods, which cannot be stated in the affirmative for the want of authority, are poor means for a man's own exculpation at the expense of others. May I have the liberty to put a construction on this last sentence, at least thus favorable, that possibly, through the determined opposition to the testimony, so early imbibed, and giving full credit to the envious reports, you might have come to believe, at least partly, that Shakers hold to immediate inspirations and illuminations before believing. If this be the case, for your credit's sake and for the truth's sake, inform yourself better, before you say any more about the doctrines of the Shakers; and wherein they agree with you, acknowledge the truth, and let it have its own weight and stear its own course. But if you believed it true, that Shakers profess such illuminations before believing, why did you not state it among their peculiar doctrines ? Or did you suppose it *not peculiar* to us, and place it where you did, to return a well played sarcasm on the Calvinists, by insinuating that their doctrines lead to Shakerism, because they hold to the illumination, or a renovating work of the Spirit before believing ? But even in that case, you had no right to misrepresent our faith. Shakers believe in the illuminations or inspirations of the Spirit in the present day, as far as may be necessary, whether mediate or immediate, to build up the church of Christ and to promote the gospel in the world, and to understand the scriptures sufficiently for their proper use ; but they are so far from believing as you have stated above, that they do not believe immediate inspirations or illuminations necessary to the salvation of individuals, (otherwise than as the Spirit dwells in each faithful believer with proper gifts and graces,) either before believing the gospel or after. Shakers believe, that it is the undeniable privilege of every one who heareth the gospel to believe on the authority of God therein ministered, without waiting or looking for any other work or power. But the public will soon have in their hands information enough on that subject.

If I reverse your sentences in my remarks on them, it will not be to avoid their force, but to get those last on which I design to treat to the greatest extent. And when I have done, you may reflect whether the wise, or less informed, are most likely to conclude your doctrines lead to Shakerism. I cannot deny but there is some ingenuity in your statements, as well as duplicity handsomely covered, and calculated to conceal the true state of things from the weak and less informed. You undertake to clear yourself of the " *insinuation*" that your doctrines lead to Shakerism. To effect this, you state

what you understand by Shakerism—" *The peculiar doctrines of that
" denomination;"* as if because you do not believe the doctrines
which none believe but Shakers, therefore your doctrines do not lead
that way. But you ought to know that to be in the doctrines of the
Shakers, and to hold doctrines leading that way, are two things. But
that the doctrines which you hold, are quite favorable to the Shakers,
when compared with those of Calvinists and some others, cannot be
denied by any man of candor and discernment. For instance;

Calvinists believe that God, by unchangeable decree, hath ordained all things to be just as they come to pass, and that the eternal condition of every man is unalterably fixed without respect to his character or works. This doctrine you deny—So do the Shakers. Calvinists and some others hold the doctrine of surety righteousness, and
surety payment, and that the righteousness of Christ is transferred,
or imputed to the elect, or to believers, for their justification. But
this doctrine of suretiship on which all these things depend, you reject with all its consequences—So do the Shakers. Calvinists believe that the regenerating work of the Spirit is necessary in every
one to enable him to believe the gospel. This you deny, and maintain that a sinner is capable of faith in Christ previously to regeneration, or the gifts of the Spirit, because the Spirit is received through
faith—So do the Shakers. Calvinists and others also hold, that there
are three distinct persons in Deity. This you deny—And so do the
Shakers. Those also hold that Jesus Christ, the Son of God, is true
and very God, the same in substance with the Father. This you
deny, and believe that he is a creature, and that his divinity consists
in the principle that the fulness of the Godhead, or Deity, dwelt in
him bodily—So do the Shakers. Calvinists, generally, and with abhorrence, reject dancing from the worship of God; which ye approve and practise—So do the Shakers. In these and other things
there is no just ground of contention between us. And it is strange
if your doctrines do not lead towards Shakerism, when Shakers and
you agree in so many points which are rejected by others, more than
those in which others and you agree, and which the Shakers reject.
I know you are not a Shaker. I suppose the Shakers' full illustration of some of these points might be too hot for you to swallow.
Besides; Shakers believe matters which you disbelieve. I know
also, that you are not disentangled from Calvinism, although you discard the greater part of it in words, and have in the Letters effectually refuted it past recovery. But to be completely unfettered, you
never will, until you be a partaker of the faith of Christ in his second
appearing. For it is true, as Calvinists say, that there is no place to
stand between them and us. After rejecting the Calvinist doctrines
which you have rejected, particularly that of *surety righteousness
imputed*, you only need an open and hearty acknowledgment of those
practical words of Christ, " If any man will come after me, let him
" deny himself and take up his cross, and follow me," to preponde-
rate swiftly towards the Shakers. And is it not highly probable that
you had been with them before now, had you not rejected your own

light, which you had received of God in the revival, which had been just preparing the way for the Shakers, especially such as that which you ministered in that sermon, in which you taught that Christ would come to judgment in the people, and in no other way? Was not that doctrine leading towards Shakerism? And did it spring from the commonly received doctrines, or from the same source whence also sprung your other doctrines which formal professors oppose? And from what source did it spring; from the commonly received doctrines, or from the same source of your other offensive doctrines, that you maintained the proriety of a community of interests and of living, in the christian church? and that to your shame the Shakers had the lead of you in that respect? Did you not preach it boldly, and argue that you could then send out preachers free from the incumbrance of a family? And did you not persist in those views until some began to insinuate that that plan led to Shakerism? and did you not then turn back and oppose what you had maintained as truth? And has not this been your continued method of evading the truth, to preserve the flesh, since ever the cross of Christ presented itself for your crucifixion? As " I cannot dig, (can get no deeper into the " revival to be supported in spirit there,) to beg I am ashamed. (to " go back to Calvinism, after such a mortal wound as you have given, " and beg for quarters,) I have resolved what to do, that when I am " put out of the stewardship, they may receive me into their houses." Accommodate matters by degrees.

But before I examine all your statements of our doctrines, I feel inclined to help you to an eclaircissement of a proposition which seems to be used to confirm the insinuation, that your doctrines lead to Shakerism. " But it is said, that the most of those who joined " the Shakers were of our communion. * * * But I would ask, " who were the people who joined them in such multitudes in the " eastern states some years ago?—We did not then exist as a peo- " ple." (Ibid.) Yea, but a people much in your situation did; that is, in the situation in which you were when the first witnesses came to this country—a people who had been the subjects of a noted revival, and were waiting for the kingdom of God, in full expectation that it was at hand—a people who were led by the power of God in that revival, forward of the denominations, to be in a waiting posture for the Bridegroom. And should you ever see another revival, equal to the former, in this or any other country, you will find that the subjects of it will again join the Shakers, or in other words, take up their cross and follow Christ in the path of self-denial, and then the world will hate them and call them Shakers. And should you never see another general revival ; yet it will be true, and if you will be liberal enough to inquire into the reason of things, you may see it with your eyes, and understand it with your heart, that all souls who become heartily willing to have Christ and his salvation, at the expense of all carnal things, as soon as they get opportunity, will unite with the Shakers and follow Christ bearing their cross, that is, his yoke.

But to return to what you say are the peculiar doctrines of the Shakers. "They deny," say you, "the resurrection of the body "from the dead, or from the grave—they hold to auricular confes-"sion of sins." On these points I shall not contest your statement. The public have been furnished with some information respecting our reasons, and the nature of our faith on those points, and will be with more—Perhaps you have forgotten the spirit of open confession which appeared in the revival, in several instances.

You say, "They forbid to marry." This assertion is not correct. Shakers do not marry; that they may follow Christ; and that they have his example; and that he taught his people to follow him, as well as that he left us an example, that we should follow his steps, you cannot deny. You and your people marry after the course of this world, or the first Adam, and yet presume to be followers of Christ. Shakers teach that marriage is a civil right of the world, and not a christian institution, and that according to the faith and example of Christ as well as his doctrine, it is not the part of a follower of Christ to marry, yet leave it with all men to do that by which they can live most acceptably to God and their own consciences. But we are satisfied, and no man hath yet been able to show us that we are mistaken, when we say, that neither we, nor any other people, can walk in the Spirit, and live at the same time, after the course of this world. May I once more refer you to your own words, and pray you to be consistent with yourself. (Address, P. 5, 6.) "Should "any say we deny their explanation of such doctrines, they would "speak correctly." Had you said the Shakers deny that marriage is according to the example or faith of Christ, and believe it has no place in the kingdom of God, or gospel church, you would have been correct. But this would have been acknowledging too much truth with the Shakers. It is a pity that a man who has assumed the name of a christian, should not exercise the same candor towards others, which he claims of others towards himself.

But another doctrine, you say, is, "That the final judgment is "come and going on by the Shakers." This statement is lame, and calculated to make false impressions, for the want of something explanatory. That the judgment hath commenced, and that we have found and obeyed the gospel by which God is judging, and eventually will judge, not only us who have now believed, but all other men, we will not deny—this is our faith. But human nature is as it has been, enmity against God. No message has ever been sent from God to increase the knowledge of his name or worship, but there were some to oppose and misrepresent it. "Report, say they, and "we will report." "But the disciple is not above his master, nor "the servant above his Lord. It is enough for the disciple that he "be as his master; and the servant as his Lord." We need not therefore expect to escape misrepresentation. And again said Jesus; "I am come in my Father's name, and ye receive me not; if "another shall come in his own name, him ye will receive." (Jno. 5. 43.) If the testimony were according to the desires of men, it would be received. It has perpetually been represented as though the Shakers want to claim the work as being their own—that they run before God and aim to take the work out of his hands notwithstanding that their testimony uniformly is, That God is the judge of all, and they are his witnesses—that Christ is come to judge the world according to the gospel, or that Word which he said would judge them in the last day; and they are his witnesses to the people —that the time is come that judgment must begin at the house of God—and that now is the judgment of this world, and now shall the prince of this world be cast out; and that in all these things they are witnesses to the people.

Now in these things we may discover, that the judgment is not to destroy the lives or souls of men, but to judge and cast out the prince of this world, that is the devil, and that all souls who will submit to the judgment and freely cast out the prince, or spirit of this world, that spirit that now worketh in the children of disobedience; may be saved, and become also witnesses of God and of his righteous judgment, and helpers of the Lord against the mighty, and thus all join issue with God against the nature of evil: none being finally condemned only those who refuse to submit. And farther, it is evident according to this doctrine, that the work of the judgment, and the privilege of being witnesses for God in the judgment of the wicked, is not arrogated by a few, or by any number whatever, as though they thought themselves any better than other people, or in any peculiar sense the favorites of heaven, to the disadvantage or degradation of others, but the testimony of God which they have received, is equally held out to all, and with equal privilege. The true statement therefore is, that God hath begun to call the world to a final settlement, or to judgment, and that as fast as the people come to a settlement of their accounts, they are called Shakers. You and the rest of the world may exclaim, that we are deceived and have a devil; but we can reply, in the words and Spirit of our meek and patient Master, We have not a devil; but we honor our Father and our Master. Satan is not divided against satan, and Which of you convinceth us of sin, in the faith which we have against it? " They " never yet have done it; and if we may guess their future success " by their former efforts, I almost conclude they never can. It is " easier to declaim against some doctrines than to refute them. " Many have chosen the former, and have gained their point with the " unthinking and prejudiced." (Address, P. 61.) But the truth will stand.

You say Shakers teach, " That Christ has come the second time " in Ann Lees, without sin unto salvation—that we are now to obtain " salvation by Ann Lees and not by Jesus of Nazareth." I take these sentences together, as being intimately connected, that I may consider them with the less labor. There is enough written, and in the hands of the public, to have informed you better than you have here stated. But perhaps your prejudice ran too high to let you read. It is more agreeable to the carnal mind to live on the vague reports of the enemy, than to come to the knowledge of the truth.

According to your statement, the faith of the Shakers is to set Jesus Christ aside from being the author of salvation, and the salvation of God to the ends of the earth. On that principle they must be fools in the extreme, to suffer as much opposition as they do, or have done, for the sake of keeping the faith of Jesus of Nazareth; to stripes often; to bonds and imprisonment in some cases; to the destruction of much property by the burning of barns and the like; and all because they keep the faith of Christ, from whom, according to you, they expect no salvation, consequently no reward. Besides the daily cross which they bear, and the self-denial, which to you are more than death, together with the universal torrent of opposition from the corruption of the whole world; and all for Christ whom they esteem as nothing—no Savior. That woman also, of whom you speak, as the supplanter, or substitute of Jesus, must have been a most tremendous fool indeed, to have suffered such things, and much more than any, to support the character, cross and faith of Christ, if she counted herself able to save without him. I wonder how such a woman as you say she was, could gather so many people to receive her testimony which is so offensive to human nature, thou thyself being witness; people too who have been waiting for the salvation of God for years, and have undergone more pain and distress about that one thing than all others—a people, many of whom were led forth to where her testimony found them, by that revival and that manner of preaching in which you were once a bold laborer. And I wonder how such dupes as could be led by such a woman, are able to live together in a society, (for great wisdom, either human or divine, is necessary to govern mankind in close connection; something more than common fools possess;) and not only in society, but in the best order and under the best regulations of any people on earth; to the admiration of the beholders, and confounding of the wisest men on earth; (hath not God made foolish the wisdom of this world? " For it is written, I will destroy the wisdom of the wise, " and will bring to nothing the understanding of the prudent;") to the terror also of anti-christians whose consciences are awake, because they feel that these foolish people have the fear, knowledge and powerful presence of God, in a manner or degree which they never experienced. As thou also knowest, that the only way for thee to escape the terror of death, is to keep well out of the Shakers' reach; because to be familiar or accessible with them on the affairs of the gospel of Christ, the sharp two-edged sword which goeth out of their mouth, would goad thy religion out of thy soul. That which cannot be shaken, shaketh all. The foolishness of God is wiser than men.

But how did you find out that the Shakers expect salvation by Anna Lee *and not by Jesus of Nazareth?* By the same rule which a man would take to find out that Paul expected salvation by Ananias *and not by* Jesus of Nazareth. For Paul was not afraid nor ashamed to acknowledge before the world, that Ananias ministered to him Christ, and told him what was appointed for him to do; so neither do the Shakers fear or refuse to acknowledge, as they have published to the world, that Anna Lee did minister to them Christ, and teach them the way of God in all things, in subjection and subordination to Jesus Christ her LORD and MASTER, whom she ever acknowledged, and for whom she suffered the loss of all things, and endured the reproaches, the hatred and the persecution of this evil world, as her children also do to this day, for his name's sake. But can you produce any writings of theirs, any authentic documents to show that they ever bore such a testimony, or intimated such a thought, as salvation by Anna Lee without Jesus Christ? whom you and Pilate have called Jesus of Nazareth; which name you seem to have adopted, (not that there is any real evil in the term. See Acts 3. 6, and 10. 3, 8.) for the sole purpose of keeping the anointing Spirit, which constituted him the Christ, as far out of sight and as deeply vailed in humanity as practicable, that you might exclude the possibility of his being revealed according to the order of God in the present day. But all such attempts will prove abortive. Must I once more refer you to your own lessons, that you may study them, and learn to state other people's doctrines as they state them, and to look into all their reasons? and then if you can refute them do so.

But it is easier to declaim than to refute. (Addres, P. 61.) Perhaps that was the reason that one of your brethren exclaimed as it is said he did, and with Paul, I at least partly believe it. "*That* "*woman God my soul abhors.*" And what would ye think of a man God? Or do ye suppose that God is any more in the shape of a man than of a woman? Or that there is any more inconsistency in the revelation of the Spirit or Word of God in a woman than a man? Or do ye account a woman too inferior a being for God to take any notice of her, or give her any part in the work of redemption, being fit for nothing but the gratification of the lust of concupiscence in carnal men? You may esteem the foregoing intolerably satirical; but whether it be more so than your own language calls for, or whether it be not the most eligible kind of reply, they who see both may determine. What is more unpardonable in a writer, than thus barefacedly to misrepresent the faith of others? It is a pity, Barton, that you should act the same part against us, which he acted against you, to whom you justly replied, "*Heaven knows you* "*are wrong.*" You are a man whom I have greatly esteemed, and am still ready, as soon as your opposition to the cross of Christ shall be so far abated as to invite me, to esteem and treat as a man of real worth. But I must proceed. You and others are welcome to the knowledge of the truth, as fast as ye will obey it.

That Christ has come the second time without sin to salvation, and that he dwelt in Anna Lee, and was by and in her revealed to those who were looking for him, as the chosen vessel appointed of God to that work, Shakers do not deny, else they had never made such clear and explicit publications to the world as they have. But with all

OF CHRIST.

this, they do not expect to obtain salvation by Anna Lee *and not by Jesus Christ*, any more than the apostles and other christians, because Jesus revealed the Father to them, expected to obtain salvation by the man Jesus *and not by God the Lord*, the Savior of Israel, whom Jesus ever acknowledged as the doer of the work. They also acknowledge her as their spiritual parent; and that she is the first Mother in the new creation, of all who are saved, as really as Jesus the Lord, hers and ours, is the first Father; and that she is coheiress with him, in the honor and glory of our redemption. But the man is the head of the woman; nevertheless, neither is the man without the woman, neither the woman without the man, in the Lord, more than in Adam. For as the woman is of the man, even so is the man also by the woman; but all things of God. And we have a right to represent our own faith as we understand it, and no man nor angel hath any right to subvert, or misrepresent it. And we are able, as a people, to exhibit to honest inquirers, better evidence of the correctness of our faith in Christ, than any people on earth, who do not know Christ as revealed in our Mother. But of the nature and consistency of such a revelation of Christ we will state a few things, the plain publication already made notwithstanding.

The coming of Christ is a matter unknown to all men, until learned in the event; notwithstanding that so many are weak enough to imagine they can understand it by the language of the scriptures. And although all the scripture language on this subject is necessarily prophetic; and is also full of symbols and metaphors; the people intensely look for a literal fulfilment. But of the different descriptions of his coming, if literal, which one would apply to the event, no man could tell. It is written; " This same Jesus which " is taken up from you into heaven, shall so come in like manner as " ye have seen him go into heaven." Hence men conclude, that Christ will come in a visible cloud, or sitting on it, visible to the physical man. But they forget two things. The first is; That he was not visible to the physical man or natural sight when he ascended, nor at any time after he came forth from the grave, or place of the dead. Therefore his disciples, being yet natural, could never see him only when there was a special gift of God for that purpose; and none but disciples ever saw him all the time he abode with them or when he ascended. And in the second place; *Shall so come in like manner*, cannot be a full description of his coming. For if the description and the language be figurative, as they no doubt are, with all the rest, we are left to learn the manner by the event. But if any consider the description and coming to be literal; many important matters which are predicated of his coming are lacking. He was to come *In flaming fire;* but we find no such account in his ascent. He was to come with the sound of a trumpet, with a shout, with the voice of the archangel and the trump of God; but no account of any such matter in the ascent. But if he went into heaven *in flaming fire*, it was in the power and Spirit of God, who is a flaming and consuming fire; but unknown and unseen by any but those in the Spirit; and thus he cometh. If he ascended with a shout; as it is written; "God is gone up with a shout, the LORD with the sound of "a trumpet;" it was only heard and understood by those in the Spirit and not by those in nature. And so is his coming *in like manner*, known only to those in the Spirit, and by those who have the Spirit in them. And if a cloud received him out of their sight, in a cloud shall he return, *in like manner, in myriads of his saints*, in a cloud composed of all the saints who had waited for his ascension from the beginning. And the shout of a King was among them. Thus his coming is *in like manner* as his ascension; In the Spirit, known and understood only by those in the Spirit; and in the presence of witnesses, who are to bear witness to the people.

A few words to show what Christ is, may help to illustrate this subject. The term Christ, you know, is from the Greek, and signifies *the Anointed*. The Christ therefore, is one anointed of God and set apart to a certain office or lot, or the performance of an appointed work. Thus Jesus, the Son of God, was anointed and consecrated by the gift of the Spirit to open the new and living way, and to do all things necessary to the bringing in of the better hope, the gospel of perfect salvation, and thus to be the Redeemer, the Captain of all who are saved, and the Head of the body. And when Jesus ascended the Same Spirit was given to the apostles and other disciples to carry on and perfect the work of salvation. "As my Father hath "sent me, even so send I you." "It is expedient for you that I go "away: for if I go not away, the Comforter will not come unto you; "but if I depart I will send him unto you. And when he is come "(to you, and abideth in you for that purpose,) he will convince the "world of sin, of righteousness, and of judgment." Accordingly, the disciples and other members of the body, Jesus Christ being the head, are one body; and it is called Christ. "For as the body is one, "and hath many members, and all the members of that one body, "being many or one body; so also is Christ;" that is the body, or church. This is correctly according to your own statement. (Reply, P. 19.) Therefore, wherever the anointing of the Spirit is, with the power of salvation, there is the true Christ of God—there is Jesus the Savior. "For where two or three are gathered together in my "name, there am I in the midst of them:" not the man, as a distinct personality; but the anointed Savior; the Christ.

Consistently with these things, the anointed ministers of God under the law, before the gospel or the true Christ was known, were called christs. The ministering priest under the law of Moses was the christ [:המשיח] of that day, a mediator between God and the people. And the priests of the whole congregation of Israel, as set apart to the work and worship of God, each in his proper office, were his christs; as it is written; "Touch not mine anointed, [:משיחי my "christs] and do my prophets no harm." (Psm. 105. 15.) Cyrus also, the king of Babylon, being set apart by God's appointment, to bring about the deliverance of his people, was called his *christ*. "Thus saith the LORD to his anointed, [:למשיחו to his christ."]

(Isa. 45. 1.) From these examples it is plain, that the anointed of God is the Christ. And when Jesus was anointed to the work of redemption, as the high priest of our profession, he became pre-eminently the Christ; and the same anointing in the church, his body, constitutes that body, the Christ of God. After the falling away therefore, when the power of the holy people was scattered, when once the same anointing is found in the church on earth, in the power of salvation, there is Christ in his second appearing—there is the anointing—there is the Spirit; and that Spirit is the Lord: he is a quickening Spirit. And, if men argue, that it is said, *This same Jesus*, shall so come; that argument will not overturn or weaken what is here stated; for *this same Jesus* is not a body of flesh and bones, but a quickening Spirit—Christ in his people.

And that Christ may be revealed to those who look for him to their understanding and salvation, without any advent or vision of that human body, or visible personality, in which he once appeared, is proved as follows. In the first place; He is a Spirit; as it is written, " Now the Lord is that Spirit; and where the Spirit of the " Lord is there is liberty." Thus the Lord, or the true Christ is the Spirit of the Lord; that very Spirit which his apostles, or ministers, minister to the people. This is still farther evident by observing that the words, " *The Lord is that Spirit*," are in direct relation to the words before written, " Who hath made us able minis- " ters of the new testament; not of the letter, *but of the Spirit*. (v. 6.) Now the true Christ being the Spirit of the Lord, as here proved, can be revealed to men and they can know him, without the vision or presence of any material personality. For Christ is in all his saints, as it is again written; " Christ in you the hope of glory." [Col. 1. 27.] This was not any visible body, or personality, but that Holy Spirit of promise, or promised Spirit, which is the earnest of our inheritance, or hope of glory. [Compare Eph. 1 13, 14.] In the same manner the Father dwelt in Jesus the Son; and the Father and the Son dwell with those whom the Father loveth, because they love the Son and keep his words. " If any man love me, he will keep " my words; and my Father will love him, and we will come to him, " and make our abode with him." " At that day ye shall know that " I am in my Father, and ye in me, and I in you." "But if the Spirit " of him that raised up Jesus from the dead dwell in you, he that " raised up Christ from the dead shall also quicken your mortal " bodies by his Spirit that dwelleth in you."

This then is the order in which Christ is revealed in his people, and by or in them to the world who cannot otherwise come to know him, as he said again. " That they all may be one; as thou, Father, " art in me, and I in thee; that they also may be one in us; that the " world may believe that thou hast sent me—I in them and thou in " me." (Jno. 17. 21, 23.) And in this manner he was to be revealed in the final judgment. " Behold the Lord cometh with ten " thousands [Greek, in myriads,] of his saints, to execute judgment " upon all and to convince all that are ungodly among them." (Jude

14, 15.) "When he shall come to be glorified in his saints and to "be admired in all them that believe in that day."

Now there is no more inconsistency, or impropriety, in saying that Christ hath come the second time without sin to salvation, when the same anointing which gives power over all sin, is again restored to those who have been looking for him, than in the saying of Jesus, that *Elias is already come*, meaning John the Baptist, in the Spirit of Elias, that is, of the prophets in him. For according to those sayings which are used concerning John, it is evident, that the advent, or presence of the visible personality, is not necessary to the fulfilling of a prophecy that one should come again. For thus it is written; "And if ye will receive it, this is Elias who was to come," and again, "He shall go in the spirit and power of Elias." (Matt 11. 14. Luke 1. 17.) And this was the fulfilment of that prophecy; "Behold, I will send you Elijah the prophet." (Mala. 4. 5.) In like manner was this prophecy fulfilled in John. "The voice of him "that crieth in the wilderness, Prepare ye the way of the Lord, "make strait in the desert a high way for our God;" for "He said, "I am the voice of one crying in the wilderness Make straight the "way of the Lord, as said the prophet Esaias." [Jno. 1. 23. Isai. 4. 3.] Now he was not literally that voice; but that voice or spirit was in him, and he uttered it. When therefore Mother said, "I am ANN the WORD," meaning that the WORD dwelt in her; the expression was correct; no objection can be supported against her on that score. Thus, "The Word was made flesh and dwelt amongst us," is true language, though figurative; for that flesh was not God, but the Word was God; the meaning therefore is, that the Word dwelt in flesh. I have also proved that Christ was thus to come in his people; and that the revelation, or manifestation, of that Spirit, or Word, which is Christ, is the revelation, or appearing of Christ. No argument therefore can be supported against the consistency of this doctrine, that Christ is revealed in Mother, whose name according to the flesh, is originally Anna Lee, and by her to the people.

As to what may be objected, that according to this view he is revealed only in one, whereas according to the scriptures he was to come with or in many; Let it be remembered that every dispensation of God had its beginning in one, as in Adam, in Abraham, in Moses, in John, in Jesus and in Mother. And as the Word was first revealed in one, who was the man Jesus, so last of all it is revealed the second time in the one woman, who is called Mother. But this will be farther opened in the sequel.

But the egregious reproach and stumbling block are, that Christ should be revealed in a woman. No doubt this is degrading and mortifying to proud human nature, to the carnal mind which exalteth itself above all that is called God or that is worshipped, to yield to the gift and revelation of God in a woman, for its own destruction. But thus God works, "To stain the pride of all glory, and to bring "into contempt all the honorable of the earth, whether male or fe-"male; and that no flesh should glory in his presence." Thus God laid a brand of contempt and reproach on the seat of the pride and glory of man, which was the outward sign of circumcision in the flesh, and was committed to Abraham the typical father of the faithful. This seems to have been a cause of reproach to the Jews; hence the Roman poet; "Credat Judæus apella, non ego;" *A circumcised Jew may believe it; I cannot.* This stigma was of such a nature as to be exclusively fixed on the male.

But when Christ appeared in the true circumcission in the Spirit, making no exception of male or female, which was so deep that the flesh could not carry it and live, because it extended to the putting off of the whole body of the sins and lusts of the flesh, (for they that are Christ's have crucified the flesh with its affections and lusts,) this offended the whole world, both Jews and Gentiles. " The world " cannot hate you ; but me it hateth, because I testify to it, that the " works thereof are evil." " Whose God is their belly, and whose " glory is in their shame, who mind, or savor, earthly things." " For " it is a shame even to speak of those things which are done of them " in secret." (Jno. 7. 7. Phil. 3. 19. Eph. 5. 12.) During the Mosaic dispensation, the works of the flesh could be performed, and it could live and glory, notwithstanding the stigma fixed on the seat of the beast. But in Christ the circumcission is real and not a sign; in the Spirit, and cuts off the whole body, through faith and not with the hands; not only in the man Jesus, but also in all those who are in Christ, and who walk not after the flesh but after the Spirit; for in such the righteousness of the law is fulfilled, as it is written; " For " God sending his own Son in the likeness of sinful flesh, and on ac- " count of sin, condemned sin in the flesh; that which the law could " not do in that it was weak through the flesh; that the righteous- " ness of the law might be fulfilled in us, who walk not after the " flesh, but after the Spirit." " And ye are complete in him, who " is the head of all principality and power; in whom also ye are cir- " cumcised with the circumcission made without hands, *in putting* " *off the body* of the sins of the flesh, by the circumcission of " Christ:" not imputed to them; but being themselves circumcised. [Ro. 8. 3, 4. Col. 2. 10, 11.]

Yet in the first appearing of Christ it was not unexceptionably required of all who believed, to cease from all the works of the flesh, or to receive this saying, that "It is not good to marry ; But he that " is able to receive it let him receive it." All that was in that day absolutely required, was, that all should live up to that which they professed, and not pretend to bear a full cross, and afterwards incline to marry ; for by so doing they fell under guilt, and gave an advantage to the enemy to reproach the profession, lost their power and proceeded to greater lengths in wickedness, than if they had never made such a profession. Hence Paul advised Timothy to receive into the number none but the best characters, and those who were also supposed to be past the age of marrying, and preferred that the younger widows should marry, and only profess that order which they were able to keep. " Let not a widow be taken into the num-

"ber under three score years old having been the wife of one man,
"well reported of for good works: if she have brought up children, if
"she have lodged strangers, if she have washed the saints' feet, if she
"have relieved the afflicted, if she have diligently followed every good
"work. But the younger widows refuse, for when they have begun
"to wax *wanton against Christ*, they are willing to marry; having
"damnation, because they have cast off their first faith. And withal
"they learn to be idle, wondering about from house to house, and
"not only idle, but tattlers also, and busy bodies, speaking things
"which they ought not. I will therefore that the younger widows
"marry, bear children, guide the house, give none occasion to the
"adversary to speak reproachfully. For some have already turn-
"ed aside after satan." (1 Tim. 5. 9. &c.) Considering your
acquaintance with the Greek language, it might be thought imperti-
nent in me to apologize to you for the variations which I have made
from the common translation. It was a bold blunder, to use the
mildest term, in the translators, to supply the above elipsis with the
word *women*, when it is so evident to every scholar, that *widows*, is
the only admissible word. Now it is impossible that this number
should be merely that of the widows to be maintained; for it would
be cruel in the extreme, not only unchristian, but inhuman, to refuse
a widow who had no living, because she was not sixty years old; and
for a young widow to marry, would be no reproach but a credit, as
well as to releave the church of that much expense, if marrying had
been according to Christ, or her first faith had not been to the contrary; by the casting off of which she received damnation; which
also could not have been if that first faith had been unnecessary or
improper: for who can be condemned for doing what is proper?
Besides; When they wax wanton *against Christ* they are willing to
marry, and not before. That number therefore could be none else
than those who undertook to bear a full cross after the example of
Christ, who were in truth the church, and willing to maintain all
widows who were widows indeed. (v. 16, and 5, 6.)

In that dispensation there was still some indulgence; many things
pertaining to the flesh, that source of mischief, were borne with in
those who could come no nearer. But the second appearing of
Christ is completely without sin to salvation; no sin, no fleshly thing
can be endured in those who keep relation to the church of Christ.
Accordingly, the apostle, writing to those carnal Corinthians, who
could not endure strong meat, among many other instructions, in all
which he counsels them not to marry, if they can contain, but doth
not enjoin it, hath these words; "But and if thou marry thou hast
"not sinned; and if a virgin marry she hath not sinned: neverthe-
"less, such shall have tribulation by the flesh: but I spare you.
"But this I say, brethren, the time is short: it remaineth that both
"they that have wives be as though they had none; and they that
"weep, as though they wept not; and they that rejoice, as though
"they rejoiced not; and they that buy, as though they possessed not;
"and they that use this world, as not abusing it: for the fashion of

"this world passeth away." It therefore remained for all those worldly customs to cease from the church.

And to complete the mortification and destruction of the pride of the human heart, the last appearing of Christ, to make an end of sin, is in a woman, from whom the world never expected any thing, except what would be consistent with the low grade in which they had placed her for the lust of concupiscence. But the Lord hath looked on her in her low estate, and hath remembered his covenant and his promise; " For thy Maker is thine husband; the Lord of hosts is " his name; and thy Redeemer the holy One of Israel: The God " of the whole earth shall he be called. For the Lord hath called " thee as a woman forsaken, and grieved in spirit, and a wife of " youth, when thou wast refused saith thy God. For a small moment " have I forsaken thee; but with great mercies will I gather thee. " In a little wrath I hid my face from thee for a moment; but with " everlasting kindness will I have mercy on thee, saith the Lord thy " Redeemer"—" For more are the children of the desolate than the " children of the married wife, saith the Lord." (Isa. 54. 5, to 8, 1.) And again; "How long wilt thou go about, O thou backsliding " daughter?" (as in the days of the church's apostacy; the result of which was to deprive the woman of what little she had gained by obedience in the first dispensation, and sink her again to that inferior stage of slavery, to which the world have degraded her, while they adore her as a god, because of her willing subjection to which she is reduced, for the purposes of the flesh, and for no other reason,) " for " the Lord hath created a new thing in the earth, A woman shall " compass a man."

This prophecy was fulfilled in Mother with great exactness; who was enabled by the gift of God which was in her to compass the whole of man's nature, and to show him his fall and all his works wherein he had gone away from the true gospel of Christ. This was a new thing which the world had never seen and never expected. And I cannot feel reconciled to pass over this opportunity without obviating a deceptious construction, now an evasive turn given to this phrase, *A woman shall compass a man.* It is commonly understood, and no doubt justly, as a prophecy of the coming of Christ; and being ignorant of the order of Christ in his second appearing, men have applied it to the extraordinary conception by Mary, as of the same import with, *A virgin shall be with child,* understanding *compass* as tantamount with *avoid* or *not use.* But that acceptation is evidently contrary to the universal use of that word, and subverts the natural force of that prophecy. The word compass means to *surround, encircle* or *enclose,* either for good or evil, and includes the comprehending or possessing of the thing compassed. Thus the Psalmist; " For " thou, LORD, wilt bless the righteous: with favor wilt thou compass " him as with a shield." (Psm. 5. 12.) And the prophet; " For " the wicked doth compass about the righteous; therefore wrong " judgment proceedeth." (Heb. 1. 4.) So said Jesus; " And when " ye shall see Jerusalem compassed ['environed or besieged] with "armies, then know that the destruction thereof is nigh." [Luk. 21. 20.] So; *A* woman shall compass, *envi on* or *comprehend*, a man, and take him by the gift of God: for *the Lord hath created it*. Hath not God chosen the foolish of the world to confound the wise, and the weak to confound the mighty.

Now that it is perfectly consistent with the character and order of Christ, to be first revealed in the male and then in the female, and that both these revelations are of one Christ, is farther evinced as follows. " Neither is the man without the woman, neither the wo- " man without the man, in the Lord." Thus it was in Adam who was the figure of him who was to come, that is confessedly, of Christ. And as Adam was created male and female, they were both one, " In the image of God created he him; Male and female created he " them; and called their name Adam, in the day when they were " created." But the woman did not exist separately, and was not known in her order for some time. And even after she stood in her separate order, they were one, particularly as they, or he, was the figure of him who was to come, which is admirably adapted to the present inquiry. For it is not disputed that the woman was first in the transgression, and therefore by her sin first had its entrance into the human race. " And Adam was not deceived; but the woman, " being deceived, was in the transgression." " She took of the fruit " thereof, and did eat; and gave also to her husband, with her, and " he did eat." [1 Tim. 2. 14. Gen. 3. 6.] But when the similitude is drawn by the apostle, between Christ and Adam, the introduction of sin is imputed to one man, even to Adam, as explicitly as the introduction of righteousness, to one man, Jesus Christ. " Wherefore " as by one man sin entered into the world, and death by sin; and so " death passed upon all men, for that all have sinned; (For if through " the offence of one many be dead; much more the grace of God " and the gift by grace, by one man, Jesus Christ, hath abounded to " many.) Therefore as by the offence of one judgment came upon " all men to condemnation; even so by the righteousness of one the " free gift came upon all men to justification of life." [Ro. 5. 12, 15, 18.] If then Adam was the figure, or type, of Christ, it comes out straight, that the man is not without the woman, neither the woman without the man in the Lord Christ, notwithstanding that Christ is one. For it cannot be that the figure should be more perfect than the substance, the type than the antitype, or the order of nature than the order of grace; but the antitype must fill the type in all its material parts, to be perfect, however superior in quality and real worth, as it is always expected of the antitype to be superior in point of value. " For this cause shall a man leave his father and mother, and " shall be joined to his wife, and they two shall be one flesh. This " is a great mystery: but I speak concerning [in or towards] Christ " and concerning the church." [Eph. 5. 31, 32.] This then, of the two being one, is properly a figure of Christ and the church. " I " speak concerning Christ and concerning the church." As therefore Christ is two in one, or one revealed in two, the male and the female, which two become one in him, even one Spirit, so are the two, the male and the female, united in the church into one Spirit. Accordingly the man Jesus forsook his father and his mother according to the flesh, and immediately clave to his spiritual relation, and correspondent Spirit in the church. " Wist ye not that I must be " about my Father's business, or at my Father's" ? [Luk. 2. 49. See Doddridge on the text.] And who is my mother and who are my brethren ? Whosoever shall do the will of my Father who is in heaven, the same is my brother and sister and mother. [Matt. 12. 49.] And we have no account that he ever called those earthly *reputed* parents either father or mother, but showed in all things that all his kindred were of another order. And as in the natural creation, the man should leave his father and mother and be joined to his wife, the same also applies to the woman. So likewise in the spiritual family. Accordingly, Mother forsook her father and her mother and was joined to Jesus Christ in the Spirit ; for whom she forsook all, and suffered the loss of all things, as it is written of her ; " Hearken, O daughter, " and consider, and incline thine ear ; forget also thine own people, " and thy father's house ; so shall the king greatly desire thy beauty ; " for he is thy Lord ; and worship thou him."

Thus it is evident and intelligible that " Neither is the man with- " out the woman, neither the woman without the man, in the Lord. " For as the woman is of the man, even so is the man also by the " woman ; but all things of God." Adam indeed was not by the woman, but Jesus was; for he was born of a woman into the world. But as the woman was of the man, according to the work of God in the natural creation, for he had been alive for some time, and had fallen into a deep sleep, which put him past the order and power of sensation, and the performance of the actions of life for a time ; so was the spiritual woman, called the Queen, or the Bride the Lamb's wife, of the man Christ Jesus, after he had been alive in the power of his Spirit, and had fallen into a deep sleep, that is, the Spirit, as to the proper order and power of spiritual life and salvation, had been removed from his body the church. Out of that body was this woman taken ; and endued with that same spiritual life which had been in that body before, even Christ, and thus became one with him, as the first woman was endued with the same animal life and rationality of soul which existed in the first Adam, and was one with him as already shown.

It hath been commonly understood that the Church is called the Bride the Lamb's wife, and that the term or relation consists in the union which subsists between Christ and the church, as he is her Savior, and she is a partaker of his Spirit. This union or relation is not to be denied; but this alone by no means fills up the prophecies on that subject. If the church is called the Bride, the same church is also called Christ, and also his body. " And all the members of " that one body, being many, are one body ; so also is Christ." [1 Cor. 12. 12. See also Reply, P. 19.] And every body has its head ; Jesus Christ therefore is the head of that body which is the church,

and is called Christ; as saith the apostle; "And he is the head of the body, the church." [Col. 1. 18.] And if we view the church in the line of the female or Bride, it is still necessary that this Bride or body have a head. Accordingly, it is recorded in scripture of the King and Queen, as being united in one. "Thy throne, O God, is
" for ever and ever : the sceptre of thy kingdom is a right sceptre.
" Thou lovest righteousness, and hatest wickedness : therefore God,
" even thy God, hath anointed thee with the oil of gladness above
" thy fellows. Upon thy right hand did stand the Queen [in the He-
" brew, Bride, or wife,] in gold of Ophir. The King's daughter is
" all glorious within : her clothing is of wrought gold. She shall be
" brought to the King in raiment of needle work : the virgins her
" companions that follow her shall be brought to thee. With glad-
" ness and rejoicing shall they be brought : they shall enter into the
" King's palace. Instead of thy fathers shall be thy children, whom
" thou mayest make princes in all the earth." [Psm. 45. 6, &c.]
Now it will readily be granted that the King's Son who is anointed King, is Jesus Christ, the Son of God; for the apostle expressly applies this prophecy to him, saying, "But to the Son he saith, Thy
" throne, O God, is for ever and ever : a sceptre of righteousness is
" the sceptre of thy kingdom." [Heb. 1. 8.] But who is the King's daughter, called to be the Queen, or King's Bride? If it be said, she is the church; It may be asked; Doth the church mean all the members, or only a part? Unquestionably the whole. Then who are the virgins the companions of the Queen, who are with her brought safe into the palace of the King? From these things it is plain that there is a female head, a Bride, or Queen, in the church, as well as a male, and that these virgins, who follow that female head, are brought safe to the King and into the kingdom. And who are these virgins but believers, the spiritual children of these spiritual parents? Thus far then, I have shown the way clearly, that Mother is the chosen of God to reveal Christ to the world the second time ; and that there is safety in following her and obeying her testimony, for all are brought safe to Christ; and because he is her Lord and theirs, they all worship him with gladness and rejoicing. Thus Christ came in his glory, according to his promise ; for the woman is the glory of the man, and showeth forth his glory and power, even as the man, especially the man Christ Jesus, is the image and glory of God. And being revealed in the woman, he immediately fills his parental order with her, and becometh a Father, and hath children, whom he may make princes in all the earth ; as again written ;
" And (thou) hast made us to our God, kings and priests ;" and we
" shall reign on the earth." •And in this order his name becomes universally known and honored, as it is added ; " I will make thy
" name to be remembered in all generations ; therefore shall the
" people praise thee [or as in the Hebrew, confess to thee,] for ever
" and ever." (Rev. 5. 10, 17.)

But it hath been asked by way of objection ; If Jesus Christ is revealed the second time in a woman, as coheiress with him in the kingdom, why did he not take one who had never sinned, or lived according to the corruption of fallen nature? Or why did she have to confess her sins when she first united herself to the people who were looking for him? But the ways of God are not as man's ways. It is the way of God and of Christ to stoop to the lost and to those who need redemption. And the confessing of her sins in the order and gift of God, which had been established among the people of God before she came, only shows the greater likeness to her Lord, when he first entered on the ministry; who having no sin to confess, nor any thing of which to repent, (because it was necessary that the first foundation pillar, who was to connect the church to be redeemed, with God the head of all and the fountain of purity, should keep that union unsullied,) went to John and was baptized of him, in the baptism of repentance and the confession of sins, saying, Thus it becometh us to fulfil all righteousness, and was thus set apart by John, according to the appointment of God and the gift of the Holy Spirit, for the work which he came to fulfil. But he had his Bride to redeem out of the fallen nature and works of the common mass, and to call away from her father's house and the people of her kindred, as stated above, by that same arm, or power, which brought salvation to him, and kept him pure from that fallen nature of the flesh and blood of the common mass, of which he partook and in which he was tempted. When he stood alone; and trode the wine presses alone, and of the people there was none with him. And he gained access to the throne of God, or to the mercy-seat, in his own person, when there was no intercessor, no Mediator before him: none to help him. Thus he overcame the world and all evil and sat down with God, as the first foundation pillar in the new creation, the first medium of access for all others; the first leader and perfecter of faith. "And he saw that there was no man, and "wondered that there was no intercessor; therefore his arm brought "salvation to him, and his righteousness it sustained him." "Though "he was a Son, yet learned he obedience by the things which he "suffered; and being made perfect, he became the author of eter- "nal salvation to all them that obey him." Therefore she who was called of God to be first in the line of the female, having the works of the fallen nature, actually confessed her sins, and took up her cross against all sin in nature as well as works, according to the gift and appointment of God in this last day, and thus in the fulfilling of all righteousness, received the same Spirit and became united with him who lived in human nature without sin, and was thus set apart to the work of the everlasting gospel of Christ's second appearing.

This is the WOMAN, to whom the promise is fulfilled, with good witness; "I will put enmity between thee and the woman, and be- "tween thy seed and her seed: It shall bruise thy head, and thou "shalt bruise his heel." The first woman was not the one; for she was the first transgressor; and her seed are the seed of the serpent whom she obeyed. "Ye are of your father, the devil, and his lusts "ye will do." Some may count Mary, the reputed mother of

Christ, the woman. But, according to what she said, that all nations should call her blessed, so it came to pass: there is no special enmity of the serpent against her: she did not bring forth the promised seed, but only the tabernacle in which he dwelt for a time, in the line of the male. For the MAN, who is the head of the WOMAN and of the whole body, must of necessity be first, that the woman, coming after, may be subject in her own lot. The seed of the woman is very correctly granted to be Christ; and thus it comes to pass, that as she led the way into sin, she is called of God to lead the way, and bear the burden and suffer the persecution of the serpent, in making a final end of sin in the church of God.

Now while the enmity between the serpent and the woman, and between his seed and her seed, remains, it is unavoidable, that the nearer any people come to the footsteps of the true seed, which is Christ, the more the enmity will be raised against them; and when any come to walk correctly in his steps, the enmity of the serpent and his seed, will come to the highest pitch. And herein the wicked world, but especial the professors, are our witnesses, however much against their intentions, that we are the true seed, the real body, the church, of which Christ is the head, and our Mother, the woman of the promise. This is THE WOMAN, against whom the enmity of all men, under the influence of nature, is most deeply rooted; not as *a woman*, but as *a woman devoted* to the life of Christ; because, by the living testimony of the Spirit of Christ through her, their worldly glory and honor, their pride, and their fleshly lusts are cut off: and this they count ruin. As a young man not long ago, said; (as I was told by his father, and with Paul, I at least partly believe it; for it was a very natural and probable saying, and represents the spirit of the world to an exactness;) " If there are a people of God on the " earth, these are the people; and they will ruin our family. My " father is sure to go with them, and my sister is sure to go with " them; and they will ruin our family." This is THE WOMAN of whom your brother in the ministry is reported to have exclaimed; " That woman God my soul abhors." This he pretended was because she was owned and worshipped as God; but that was a lying affectation. A woman-god is his soul's delight; a woman, devoted to the sacrifices of the flesh and addicted to receive them. According to the words of the old ceremony; " With my body I thee wor- " ship." But the true source of his abhorrence of *that woman*, is the same in him as in all other men in nature; (though many are more modest and gentlemanly than to give it full vent,) because she was a worshipper of the living God and his Christ, a follower and helper with Christ in the work of the regeneration, and the woman, who is the head, in the female line, of his body the church; being the Bride the Lamb's wife, and by whom, in that relation, the man-child is brought forth, " Who was to rule the nations with a rod of " iron," " Thou shalt break them with a rod of iron; thou shalt " dash them in pieces like a potter's vessel." Not by tyranny or cruelty; but with the power and edge of truth. No usurpation in

Christ or in his church. You have called the man-child, *truth:* I feel no disposition to contradict you—Christ is the truth.

This is THE WOMAN, against whom the enmity of all women in nature, and living after the course of the world, is strained to the highest pitch; because by the living testimony of Christ, through her and her seed, their earthly consequence, glory and honor, the carnal worship paid to them; the sensual pleasures and glory of this world and the kingdoms of it, are all cut off. They frequently cry out; that they will be ruined, and that their children will be ruined, and their souls be lost. But this is an artful pretext to preserve the flesh—a deceptious affectation. For as soon as the sacrifices of the flesh are restored or secured, their great concern for the salvation of their children, or themselves either, is of little force—it soon abates. No great lamentation for the want of salvation to their own souls or those of their children; no great labor to obtain it, is found among women more than men, where none of them are likely to confess and forsake their sins, and follow Christ in the faith of his second appearing. Not much matter how ungodly they are, provided they are prosperous in the glory, the honors and pleasures of this world. But the true cause of the enmity and offence of women in nature, against the testimony of Christ in his second appearing, is, that if they and their children receive it, *Christ will get them;* and then they must follow him and not Adam; For in Christ they neither marry nor are given in marriage. And this being the case, the glory of this world and of the kingdoms thereof, is cut down and withereth. *Woe to them that are with child, and to them that give suck in these days;* and they that beget are not exempt. Finally here; Women who are difficulted and in trouble, from a sense of duty and therefore not so chargeable as others with the ungodly temper above described, are moderate and teachable; and never afraid to converse freely with the believers in Christ's second appearing, who are called Shakers; never boisterous, never commanding or authoritative over their husbands. For the man or the woman who is afraid to converse with these believers, or is boisterous and unruly, is governed by the enmity of the serpent against the woman and her seed. But again;

This revelation of Christ the second time, in the line of the female, is also by believers considered as the revelation of the Holy Ghost in her proper order and character, as the Mother of Jesus the Son of God, and of his Bride, and through them, of all believers; as well as of the whole creation, both old and new. As God in the relation of Father, is the fountain and spring of all power, and the original source of all being, and from whom is the Word, or seed, by which all things are made, or generated, so may the Holy Ghost be considered as the corresponding relation or power in God, through whom the Word, which is the united operation or going forth, of the two, hath its effect, to the orderly production of all things. Thus, " In " the beginning God created [or procreated] the heaven and the " earth. And the earth was without form and void; and darkness "was upon the face of the deep: and the Spirit of God moved [in the Hebrew, sat, or brooded] upon the face of the waters." (Gen. 1. 1, 2.) After which the various parts of creation were distinctly brought forth in order as the power and Word of God called them out. "And God said, Let there be light: and there was light." Farther; "And God said, Let us make man in our own image, after our likeness," doth not necessarily imply three, two being equal to that manner of language. And when the work came forth according to the proposal, it consisted in two, not in three: and these two were one. "So God created [or procreated]* man in his image: in the image of God created he him; male and female created he them; and blessed them, and called their name Adam, in the day when they were created." And with respect to the new creation, of whom Christ Jesus is the beginning, it is written; "The Holy Ghost shall come upon thee (to enable thee to conceive,) and the power of the highest shall overshadow thee; (by which power thou shalt conceive;) therefore also, that holy One, when born, shall be called the Son of God," as being begotten of the Father, and conceived by the Holy Spirit; as is evident afterwards, (Matt. 1. 20.) "That which is conceived in (not by) her is of the Holy Ghost," by whom it was conceived, and deposited with Mary, to be endowed with a body of the same flesh and blood with those who were to be saved, and that he who sanctifieth and they who are sanctified might be all of one. And there were evidently two co-operating in the generation of Jesus the Son of God, without considering Mary as having any part in it; as she evidently had not, the whole matter being entirely beyond the sphere and power of natural generation; although the material body which he inhabited was formed of her substance, in the ordinary line of physical production.

On this subject I shall be as concise as I can to comport with plainness, as it is mainly known and understood by the revelation in the present dispensation, and because there is already such a clear and explicit publication made. The knowledge and understanding of this particular, depending on the revelation of the present day, are not so likely to be received, except by those who have faith in the existing testimony, or are possessed of more than ordinary candor and simple intelligency. But to such it will appear plain, according to the scriptures, that there was yet something material to be revealed in the character of God, which Jesus Did not make known. For though he revealed God in the relation of Father, he did not show

---

* *It may be expedient to advertise the unlearned reader, the learned I need not, that* [ברא] *the word here used, is not that which is commonly used to express the direct procreation of men,* [*that word is* ילד *iled*] *but is handed down as having the above acceptation in ancient days; and it aptly expresses the work of God in producing the whole creation by his own power and energy, without the aid of any other. It is also an acceptation well adapted to express the coming forth of the creation in order, and of men in the image of God.*

him out fully in that relation: Therefore he saith, "These things have I spoken to you in proverbs: but the time cometh when I will no more speak to you in proverbs, but I shall show you plainly of the Father;" and again; "But in the days of the voice of the seventh angel, when he shall begin to sound, and the mystery of God shall be finished." (Jno. 16. 25. and Rev. 10. 7.) Thus the mystery of God, and of the Father and of Christ, which began to be opened in the first appearing of Christ, remained to be finished when the seventh angel should begin to sound, so that it might be understood in the progress of the work from the beginning, and believers be built up in that knowledge. And nothing can be more consistent and according to order, than the idea of a twofold corresponding relation in God, as exhibited in his creation, called Father and Holy Ghost, or Mother, as the source from whence Christ in his first and second appearance, or the Son and the Daughter, should spring and come forth, to be in their proper lot, and corresponding relation, the joint visible parentage of the faithful family of God. Nothing can be better in order than that the King's Son, who is anointed King, and the Queen, or Bride, who stood on his right hand, who forsook all for him whom she worshippeth, and who is brought into his palace with the virgins who abide there for ever, as on the day of his marriage, according to what is again written, "The marriage of the Lamb is come and his Bride hath made herself ready;" I say, nothing can be better in order than that these should be the Son and Daughter of the Father and of the Holy Spirit, one God, and these the one joint parentage of the church of God, in which there is but one Spirit.

But was not the Holy Ghost revealed in the first appearing of Christ? As God was revealed to men before the coming of Christ at all, but was never known in the relation of a Father in that Spiritual manner in which he is revealed in Christ Jesus; so the Holy Ghost was made known in the first appearing, as the Spirit of truth, and the Spirit of promise, by which Christ dwelt in his church. But in her corresponding relation to the Father, as a Mother having children, she was never fully revealed until the present day. In this day the mystery of God is finished.

An argument hath been urged against this doctrine, That the phrase, HOLY GHOST, in the scripture is always used in the masculine gender. And what then? Because the terms *Father* and *he* are applied to God as being masculine, are we therefore to suppose that there is in God any thing properly and essentially masculine, or of the male, as in mankind? But as the male is the head, and has always been accounted the most honorable in creation, and God is the most honorable of all beings, and the head over all, and finally as he is called the Father, his name is used in the masculine. And when the Holy Ghost is named as being the Spirit of the Father and the Son, especially when personified, the male epithet is sometimes used. But what is in this to make the feminine improper, when the Spirit is made known in her proper relation, in the second revelation of Christ in the female, even by that woman who said, "I am Ann the Word." Is this to signify that in God there are two parts, or essentially distinct persons, the male and the female? By no means; these are all relative titles. But these various and corroborating considerations show, that in God, there is that which answers to these relations, that is, union as between two, and correspondent operations, as being of the Father, the fountain of power, whence all things originate, and the Spirit as the Mother of all creatures, who produceth all by the same Word of power as the co-operating energy of the two. Accordingly, the Spirit of God speaks in the feminine, by the title of Wisdom, as a copartner and companion with him, and of co-eternal existance—saying; "The LORD possessed me in the beginning of "his way, before his works of old. I was set up from everlasting." Of which hereafter. But you are not unacquainted that in the Greek language the term, *Holy Ghost*, is neuter gender, and therefore equally applicable to male or female, although its relative or concordant words are sometimes masculine. These are also different times translated in the masculine, in English, when they are neuter in Greek. It is furthermore worthy of notice, that in the Hebrew the term SPIRIT of God is used in the common gender, which, you know, includes both male and female. If therefore the male epithet hath been commonly used in former dispensations, the adoption of the female in this, is by no means improper, when her appropriate relation and works are made known. Besides; In the work of creation, the term, SPIRIT of God, is in agreement with a feminine participle, by which it becomes definitively feminine, and the Spirit is represented as a Mother producing all things. "And the Spirit "of God was brooding on the face of the waters. And God said, "Let there be light and there was light." This agrees with the order of the generation of Jesus Christ as the beginning of the new and superior creation. These things show that these epithets greatly depend on the idiom of languages, and the conceptions which men have of the relation in which God stands towards them. At the same time that the scriptures and the works of God in both the old and new creations manifestly teach, that the male and the female are the nearest that any thing can come to that incomprehensible nature of two in one, which is in God, and to which these answer.

So much being said of the two, the Father and the Holy Ghost, may lead to an inquiry respecting *the three*, who are said to be one. "For there are three that bear record in heaven, the Father, the "Word, and the Holy Ghost: and these three are one." We also read of the Word, in the beginning of John's record of the gospel; "In the beginning was the Word, and the Word was with God, and "the Word was God: the same was in the beginning with God. "All things were made by him; and without him was not any thing "made which was made. And the Word was made flesh and dwelt "among us (and we beheld his glory, the glory as of the only be"gotten of [from or by] the Father,) full of grace and truth." This being the Word who is God, by whom all things were made, and who was made flesh, or clothed with it, in the person of the Son of God, is God, the same who was revealed in him in whom dwelt the fulness of the Deity bodily, who is Jesus Christ. This Word then is the revelation of God, the Father and the Holy Ghost; or it is God revealed, the Word of revelation—the manifestation or exhibition of the power and energy of God, the Father and the Holy Ghost, as when God said, Let it be, and it was, and again, Let us make man in our image and after our likeness—or it is God operating; for by him all things were made. As therefore the Father and the Holy Ghost are one, the Father and the Word and the Holy Ghost are also one. This Word is Christ, or it is God dwelling in the Son by the gift and power of the Holy Ghost; accordingly the term Son, is used in the same order as Word; " Go ye, therefore, and teach all " nations, baptizing them in the name of the Father, and of the Son, " and of the Holy Ghost." The Holy Ghost being named last in order, because the Father and the Word, and the Son, were more fully revealed in that day, than the Holy Ghost; of whom nothing was then known and understood, only as the Spirit of promise, and as the Spirit of God in general terms, the Spirit of the Father and of the Son, the Spirit of truth, and the like; but nothing correctly to her correspondent relation to the Father in the works of creation both old and new; and because the Father and the Son are in the line of the male, the Father being revealed, or declared by the Son, they are named first in order, and the Holy Ghost and the Daughter, are named next in order. In the mean time; as Son implies Father, the same also implies Mother; and as Daughter implies Mother, the same also implies Father; these, therefore, have revealed or declared the Father and the Mother, who are God, the Father and the Holy Ghost, and the same Word, being one with the Father and the Holy Ghost, is revealed in them both; this Word is Christ in his first and second appearing: God and Christ are one.

Little as was understood of the Holy Ghost in her correspondent relation to the Father, in Christ's first appearing, some scriptures, a part of which I have already noticed, are properly applicable to this subject. It will be expedient to notice a few more. In the book of the Proverbs, (8. 22, &c.) the Spirit speaks by the name of Wisdom, saying, " The Lord possessed me in the beginning of his way, before " his works of old. I was set up from everlasting, from the begin- " ning, or ever the earth was. When there were no depths I was " brought forth." This scripture, tradition has applied to the Son, as being one of its three persons in Deity, and co-eternal with the Father; but as co-eternal and co-essential with the Father, are epithets never applied to the Son, by the authority of revelation, neither any thing tantamount, there is no reason for such an acceptation of this scripture. You have applied it to the Son as a created being. But such an acceptation appears rather forced, and the language too strong to apply to one who is in any sense a created being, no doubt as strong as the author could find to express that which had no beginning. " The Lord possessed (not created) me in the beginning of his way, (before he had made any thing,) before his works of old," and " Then I was by him, as one brought up with him :" (as though I were his fellow or equal: אמון a nurse or parent of the same power and age. See Numb. 11. 12. Isa. 49. 23. and therefore as completely everlasting as he.) This same word, which is translated *a nursing-father*, in the book of Moses, " As a nursing-father beareth a sucking child," ought rather to be rendered *a nursing-mother*, as it is the appropriate work of the mother to nurse the sucking child; " Thy kings shall be nursing-fathers and thy queens nursing-mothers." Accordingly, the Seventy have translated the word in both the above passages by a word [τιθηνος] which is definitively feminine; and this helps to illustrate the idea of Wisdom in the feminine, as the co-essential and co-eternal One with the Father, and therefore as being the same with the Holy Ghost. " And I was daily his delight, rejoicing always " before him ; rejoicing in the habitable part of the earth; and my " delights were with the sons of men." And said Jesus, " Wisdom " is justified of all her children." Wisdom therefore is a Mother and hath children, of whom Jesus is the first born, and all the rest who are younger approve her work and justify her in him. I do not intend to insist on the female epithet in these scriptures, the term *Wisdom*, being femanine in those languages. But those who apply that passage in the proverbs to Christ, and make any account of the masculine as applied to the Holy Ghost, ought at least to remember, that if Wisdom in that place means Christ, it is Christ in the feminine gender, and therefore the idea is not unfavorable to his being revealed the second time in the female, and that the revelation of the Holy Ghost in the same, is a perfectly consistent matter. But the words of Jesus Christ have fixed the matter, that Wisdom as being in the female line, is a Mother having children ; which perfectly agrees with her being the Holy Spirit, the Mother of the Son of God, who after having brought him forth preserved him as a mother doth her son, and laid special claim to him after his baptism. " And " the Holy Ghost descended in a bodily shape, like a dove, upon " him, and a voice came from heaven, which said, Thou art my be-" loved Son; in thee I am well pleased. And Jesus being full of the " Holy Ghost returned from Jordan, and was led by the Spirit into " the wilderness, being forty days tempted by the devil;" but was safely kept until he returned in the power of the Spirit into Galilee, and there the Spirit of the Lord was upon him, and so remained.

And thus the whole subject eventuates according to the words of the Lord by the prophet Jeremiah ; " Behold the days come saith " the Lord, that I will raise unto David a righteous Branch, and a " King shall reign and prosper, and shall execute justice and judg-" ment in the earth, In his days Judah shall be saved and Israel shall " dwell safely ; and this is the name whereby he shall be called, THE " LORD OUR RIGHTEOUSNESS." (Jer. 23. 5, 6.) But in a little time the whole land is corrupted and desolate ; " For the land is full of " adulteries ; for because of swearing the land mourneth, the plea-" sant plains of the wilderness are dried up ; and their course is evil, "and their force is not right. For both prophet and priest are pro-"fane; yea, in my house have I found their wickedness, saith the "Lord. The abomination that maketh desolate, in the holy place, where it ought not to be—the lawless sitting in the temple of God. But in the next place, as of the second appearing of Christ in the female in union with the male, both being expressed in the prophecy, the promised blessing was never to come to an end. "Behold the "days come, saith the Lord, that I will perform that good thing "which I have promised to the house of Israel, and to the house of "Judah. In those days, and at that time, will I cause the Branch of "righteousness to grow up unto David; and he shall execute justice "and righteousness in the land. In those days shall Judah be saved, "and Jerusalem shall dwell safely; and this is the name wherewith "she shall be called, The Lord our righteousness;" and this is followed by a bold account of the everlasting prosperity of the church of God. (Jer. 33. 14, &c.) Should any suppose that the church, or Jerusalem, is the *she*, who is called THE LORD OUR RIGHTEOUSNESS, Let such consider, that by parity of reason Judah or Israel, is the *he*, who is so called in the former prophecy as quoted above; and thus by excluding the Christ or Word, from the character or name of *The Lord our Righteousness*, in the female, he is also excluded from that honor in the male. For, as before shown, the church hath a head; and if in the first instance, the term HE, be used in relation to that head, who is the male, it is as natural and fair a construction to understand the term SHE, as relating to that head who is female, in the second, and in union with the first. Besides; for the church to call herself The Lord our righteousness, is too absurd to be admitted by people of liberal information. Nothing therefore is more natural and easy, according to the plain language of those prophecies, as well as the revelation of the present day than to understand the first as relating to the first appearing of Christ in the male only, and the second, to the revelation of the same eternal Word, or Anointing Spirit, in the female, in union and corresponding relation to the male. And thus it is finished; that as the woman is of the man, and Mother sprang up of the same body, in the same faith and Spirit of Christ, God causing the Branch of righteousness which had once been raised, to grow up, so the man is by the woman, Christ the same eternal Word, or Anointing, being again revealed in her, while she acknowledged him, as her Lord and head—the head of the woman is the man.

Thus I have stated concisely, according to the scriptures—that Christ is a Spirit—that his being revealed or coming again doth not require the vision, or appearance of that material body, or personality, which was once seen among the people—that he was to come in his people, or church—that the church hath a head, or beginning— and that it is according to the scriptures, that this beginning, in which the second revelation should commence, should be a woman—consequently all reasonable objections against Mother, as the Anointed of God for that purpose, are obviated. This being done, every reasonable man is satisfied of the truth of the testimony as it stands. And I now bring my long epistle to a close; in which I have used freedom with a few parts of your publications, and only a few, as I had no intention of noticing the whole. And although I have passed over several sentences and some sentiments which I could not adopt, which would have led into discussions more extensive than convenient, many other parts I should have no feeling to oppose, as being written to good purpose, and containing sentiments which I most cordially approve, and which are well supported by divine revelation.

With due esteem I am your friend,
JOHN DUNLAVY.

Pleasant Hill, November 4, 1815.

POSTSCRIPT.

BARTON;
SEND me a copy in your handwriting, of the sermon which you preached on the coming of Christ in the clouds to judge the world, Zech. 10. 1.; and let it contain all the doctrines and ideas in explicit terms, which you delivered on that subject in the summer and fall of 1804, and then I will be better prepared to inquire of you, Why it is more inconsistent for the Shakers to say Christ has come in his people and is calling men to judgment by the gospel, than for you to preach that the judgment had then begun, and would be carried on in the people; that these were the white clouds, white horses, &c. When you send me this sermon to my satisfaction; you may demand of me twenty dollars which I hereby agree to pay.

J. DUNLAVY.